Soviet Russian Literature
1917–50

SOVIET RUSSIAN LITERATURE

1917-50

By GLEB STRUVE

UNIVERSITY OF OKLAHOMA PRESS

NORMAN

By GLEB STRUVE

I. Bunin, *The Well of Days* (translation with H. Miles), London, 1933

Twenty-five Years of Soviet Russian Literature, London, 1944

Histoire de la littérature soviétique, Paris, 1946

Practical Russian (with E. A. Moore), London, 1946

Russky Evropeets: Materialy dlya biografii i kharakteristiki knyazya P. B. Kozlovskogo (A Russian European: Materials towards a Biography of Prince P. B. Kozlovsky), San Francisco, 1950

I dedicate this book to
Osip Mandelstam
Isaac Babel
Boris Pilnyak
and other victims of Soviet thought control
whether alive or dead

Foreword

THE BOOK which is now being offered to the reader is based on my *Soviet Russian Literature,* first published in Great Britain in 1935. A new edition of it, with a postscript covering the years 1935-43, appeared in 1944 under the title 25 *Years of Soviet Russian Literature.* In the present version the story of post-Revolutionary literature in Russia has been brought up to the year 1950. Large portions of the earlier text have been revised, both stylistically and through the inclusion of a great deal of new material in the part dealing with the first decade of Soviet literature. The arrangement of the book has been considerably altered, new sections have been added, and some material has been suppressed. When I first wrote my book on Soviet literature it was meant to be a sequel to D. S. Mirsky's *Contemporary Russian Literature,* where the story ends with 1925. I therefore left out of my account some important aspects of the early period, or referred to them very briefly. Since then Mirsky's book has gone out of print, and in the new one-volume edition of his survey of Russian literature the chapters dealing with the beginnings of Soviet literature have been omitted. While enlarging my early material to fill in that gap I thought it also best to adopt a more strictly chronological order of narrative. To adhere to this throughout was not an easy task, and in the case of some authors whose work offers a certain unity I preferred to break beyond the strictly chronological bounds of the respective chapters, in order to avoid too scrappy a presentation. A certain amount of overlapping and of cross references proved inevitable. But in general the chronological trend is followed, and it is suggested that the reader should also approach the book chronologically. This will give him a clearer picture of the successive phases in the evolution of Soviet literature, of its "rise and decline," as well as of the interdependence of literature and politics in the Soviet state and of the effect of this interdependence on individual authors.

In revising the book I also took the opportunity of correcting, with the aid of the new sources available to me in the libraries of the United

States—and above all in the library of the University of California where most of my work was done—various factual inaccuracies that had crept into the earlier editions, especially in dates. The problem of dating Soviet fiction involves many difficulties, some of them insoluble outside the Soviet Union. Numerous editions of Soviet authors never mention the year of the first publication. Besides, most Soviet novels were first serialized in the principal literary magazines, and since sometimes it seemed to me important to give the date of the preoriginal edition I must confess to a certain inconsistency in this respect. Nor can I vouch for the absolute accuracy of all the dates, though I did my best to check various sources. Experts in Soviet literature will no doubt find gaps and disproportions in my work. Some authors, originally included by me, I had to leave out reluctantly, for reasons of space. For the same reason I could not discuss certain side aspects of Soviet literature, such as literature for children, or various national literatures of the Soviet Union, of which I, moreover, do not feel competent to speak. Nor am I concerned here with Russian literature outside Russia, the so-called *émigré* literature. It would deserve a special study. One day, it is to be hoped, such a study will be forthcoming—it will form an interesting pendant to the story of Soviet literature.

The reader will easily perceive that I am not in sympathy with the present-day totalitarian regime in Russia. I see no reason for concealing this fact, for I think that lack of sympathy with Marshal Stalin and his police-state no more disqualifies me from appraising Soviet literature than, in itself, lack of sympathy with President Truman and the American democracy disqualifies a Soviet scholar (let us say, Mr. Mendelson or Mr. Startsev) from judging American literature. I reject therefore in advance all criticism of my book based on this assumed "lack of sympathy." In speaking of literature in the Soviet Union it is, of course, impossible to divorce it from political, social, and economic problems. Without being a Marxist, one is willy-nilly obliged to adopt to some extent the Marxian approach to literature. Communist critics in the U. S. S. R. should be the very last to object to such an approach. However, I have done my best to consider Soviet literature as objectively as possible, and to consider it, above all, as literature. As I said in the Introduction to the first British edition of my book, in referring to Mr. Max Eastman's *Artists in Uniform* which appeared when my book was in the press:

> I was writing an objective history (inasmuch as one can do so with regard to what is contemporary) of the last ten years of Soviet Russian literature, and I wanted to show, not what literature in Soviet Russia was *unable* to accomplish *because* of being stifled and

"bureaucratized" (which it, no doubt, is), but rather what it *has* achieved *in spite of* all the efforts at bureaucratization.

This was written in February of 1935. Unfortunately for Soviet literature, the conditions under which it has to work have since become infinitely worse, and consequently the stress in the latter part of my account had to be considerably shifted from "what has been done" to "what cannot be done," or "what must be done." On the other hand, the picture which Soviet literature offers today places its output of the earlier period in a much more favorable light and gives it an added significance and value. Hence the disproportionately large amount of space I give in my book to the first ten years of Soviet literature. I may add to this that no truly complete and objective history of Soviet literature can be written at present. Why it is impossible in the Soviet Union must become plain to anyone who reads this book without prejudice. Outside the Soviet Union we are, in many respects, better equipped for this task—from conversations with recent Soviet citizens I can see, for instance, that many writers who played an important part in the earlier stages of Soviet literature are no more than names to them, and where the younger generation is concerned, sometimes not even that. But we on the outside, too, have to overcome great handicaps such as the deliberate suppression of facts and the equally deliberate creation of myths. And we can only presume, for instance, the existence of a considerable body of unprinted literature—the fact that many Soviet authors must be writing for their own inner satisfaction, without any hope of seeing their works in print, was hinted at recently (in an article in *The Nation*) by such a staunch apologist of Stalin's regime as Alexander Werth, who spent the years 1941–48 in the Soviet Union and met in person many Soviet writers.

In conclusion, I should like to quote here the following passage from the Introduction to the 1944 edition of my book:

With a literature abounding in works written—to use a phrase of Ilya Ehrenburg—"for the one second," it is not easy to pass final judgments, to assess the enduring, permanent value of a literary work. Some of my readers may be struck by the apparent paucity of such enduring works. This is inevitable. Literature of the Revolution has produced many works of human and documentary interest, but hardly a single great work of art. Perhaps the Revolution has been too insistent a background for literature. What Soviet literature reflects, is either this everpresent background or the bright but fragmentary flashes. It has so far failed to encompass, in fearless detachment, the whole of the Revolution. It has also been too much governed by external impulses. . . . What the future holds in store for Russian literature is not for me to surmise. It depends, after all, on what lies in store for Russia after her many and terrible ordeals crowned by the horrors of the present war. It is an ordeal by fire, and every true Russian hopes to see his country emerge from it purified, freer and happier.

It has to be admitted that the pious hope voiced in these lines, written in April of 1943, in wartime England, soon after the victory of Stalingrad, has not come true. Russia's terrible ordeals are not over. As for Soviet literature, it has been subjected to new and worse trials.

GLEB STRUVE

Berkeley, January, 1951

Contents

Contents

Contents

Soviet Russian Literature
1917–50

I. Literature in Transition
1917—21

1. *Literature on the Eve of the Revolution*

THE Bolshevik Revolution of October 25, 1917, found Russian literature in a state of disintegration—its outward shock accelerated and intensified the inner processes that had been going on for some time. The Revolution, contrary to the expectations of many of its opponents, but also of some of its leaders, was to weather all the storms and to inaugurate a new period of Russian history—the Soviet period.

It is usual to speak of two principal movements in pre-Revolutionary Russian literature of the twentieth century: Realism and Symbolism. Realism was a survival, and a continuation, of the great age of the Russian novel which, with Dostoyevsky and Tolstoy, had reached its point of saturation and then gradually degenerated, until it took a new lease on life—in a different form—in the subtle and peculiar art of Chekhov as a short-story writer, from whom nearly all the twentieth-century realists stemmed. Its greatest modern exponents were Maxim Gorky and Ivan Bunin. Symbolism, on the other hand, whose origins in Russia can be traced back to the last decade of the nineteenth century, was a product of the general modernist movement in European art and literature, while at the same time it was closely bound up with, and affected by, important processes and changes in Russian cultural life at the turn of the century. Of the two, it played undoubtedly by far the more important and vital part in the period preceding World War I. Taken in a wide sense, Symbolism pervaded nearly everything that was talented and alive in modern Russian literature. It had renovated the very spirit of literature and raised the standards of literary technique—especially in poetry, which was its principal medium; it had opened new vistas before literature and freed it from the deadening influence of social and political tendentiousness, and from the narrow tenets of naturalism. The period between 1900 and 1912 can be rightly described as the period of Symbolism.

The important point about Russian Symbolism is that it was something more than a literary school: it implied a reversal, not only of the literary technique, but of the whole aesthetic and spiritual outlook; it

3

was connected with the rise of individualism and of religious idealism; it was part of a general revaluation of the traditional values of the Russian intelligentsia, with its agnosticism, or even atheism, its cult of civic duty, and its stress on the social significance of art. Symbolism itself was a complex phenomenon. Some of its exponents, like Valery Bryusov, wanted to remain within the narrower limits of art, stressing the aesthetic aspects of the changes effected by the Symbolists in Russian literature. Others, like Andrey Bely and Vyacheslav Ivanov, spoke of the "new consciousness," of "mythmaking," of a new religion. At the same time, within the Symbolist school itself, a reaction was born against both these tendencies—the cold aloofness and exclusiveness of the esoteric aestheticism of Bryusov and the metaphysical nebulousness of Ivanov. It was a reaction in the direction of realism, and its slogans were: "Down to earth" and "Closer to man." It was represented by Alexander Blok, the greatest of all the Symbolist poets. By 1910, the conflict between these warring trends came to a head and found its expression in a heated controversy on the "crisis of Symbolism," in which Blok, Bely, Ivanov, and Bryusov took a lively part. Moreover, two movements came to attack Symbolism and its philosophy from the outside. One of them was an offspring of Symbolism. It took the name of Acmeism and, as far as labels are of any use, may be conveniently characterized as modern Neoclassicism, since Symbolism, *mutatis mutandis*, was a modern variant of Romanticism. Its principal representatives were Nikolay Gumilyov, Anna Akhmatova, and Osip Mandelstam, with Gumilyov, an earlier disciple of Bryusov, acting as the main theoretician and *maître d'école*. Acmeism adopted and developed the slogan of "beautiful clarity," which had been advocated by Mikhail Kuzmin in an earlier controversy with the Symbolists. Gumilyov was also very fond of quoting Coleridge's description of poetry as "the best words in their best order." The Symbolists had emphasized the hidden, associative, musical elements in poetry; the Acmeists in reply asserted the elements of sense and logic in the art of words. The Symbolists had tended to disembody words as a medium of poetry; the Acmeists tried to clothe them with a new flesh. Their ideal was Adam, the first namegiver, and at one time this new movement even thought of calling itself "Adamism." To the growing tendency of Symbolism to regard the poet as a prophet, a mythmaker, or to stress his passive, mediumistic nature, the Acmeists opposed the conception of the poet as a craftsman: their principal literary organization significantly bore the name of "Poets' Guild." Though romantic in some of its manifestations, Acmeism on the whole strove toward greater realism and simplicity. It made no attempt to revolutionize the poetic technique. Availing itself of the technical achievements and innovations of its predecessors, it developed the

4

poetic diction in a different direction, by bringing it closer to the accents and intonations of everyday speech: this is particularly true of the poetry of Anna Akhmatova.

The other movement which declared war on Symbolism and contributed to its ultimate disintegration was Futurism. Though in its origins it was allied to the Italian Futurism of Marinetti and its other European products, Russian Futurism was a peculiar growth. It was essentially a negative, destructive, revolutionary movement. It waged war on bourgeois culture, on all conventions, on the art of the past, all in the name of the vaguely formulated art of the future.

Some of the Futurists combined revolutionary ideas about art with revolutionary ideology in politics, though this was by no means true of the movement as a whole at its inception. It was, however, true of one of the early spokesmen of the Futurist movement, Vladimir Mayakovsky, who was to become the acknowledged leader of post-Revolutionary Futurism when this school for a time attained literary supremacy.

When the Bolshevik *coup d'état* took place at the end of October, 1917, the great majority of the established writers, in common with the bulk of the Russian intelligentsia, took an uncompromisingly hostile attitude toward the new regime. In the course of the next few years, while the Civil War raged in Russia and immediately upon its conclusion, many of the writers found themselves on the other side of the fence, and eventually became political exiles. At various times between 1918 and 1922, the following well-known writers left Russia: Ivan Bunin, Alexander Kuprin, Mikhail Artsybashev, Ivan Shmelyov, Boris Zaytsev, Leonid Andreyev, Dmitry Merezhkovsky, Alexey Remizov, Alexey N. Tolstoy, V. Ropshin (Boris Savinkov), and M. Aldanov, of the prose writers; Konstantin Balmont, Zinaida Hippius, Vladislav Khodasevich, Ilya Ehrenburg, Marina Tsvetayeva, Georgy Ivanov, and Georgy Adamovich, of the poets.[1] Of these, Ehrenburg and Alexey Tolstoy returned in 1923 to Russia and won for themselves a place of honor in Soviet literature. Alexander Kuprin and Marina Tsvetayeva made their way back much later, in the mid-thirties, the former dying in 1938, and the latter committing suicide in 1941; neither made any important contribution to literature after this voluntary repatriation.[2] On the other hand, to the ranks of the exiles was added, in 1924, one of

[1] For an evaluation of their respective places and roles in pre-Revolutionary literature, see D. S. Mirsky, *Contemporary Russian Literature.*

[2] Much of Kuprin's pre-Revolutionary work was reissued in the Soviet Union after his return, but he wrote practically nothing new. As for Tsvetayeva, even her earlier poetry, too romantic or too "formalistic" for the prevalent taste, was not republished, and I have been able to find only one new poem of hers printed in a Soviet magazine—*30 dney* (*30 Days*), No. 3 (1941).

the leaders of the Symbolist movement, Vyacheslav Ivanov, who settled in Italy, became a convert to the Roman Catholic church, and died in Rome in 1949.

Of those who stayed behind, only a few welcomed the Revolution and openly took sides with the new order of things; the others submitted passively, continued writing and publishing, but often were latently hostile to the Soviet regime. The former included Gorky and Serafimovich, of the Realist group of writers; and Bryusov, Blok, and Bely, of the Symbolist poets, not to speak of some younger poets like Mayakovsky and Esenin. Among those who remained in Russia but did not "accept" the Revolution were the poets Fyodor Sologub, Nikolay Gumilyov, Anna Akhmatova, and Osip Mandelstam. Their work published in the very early years of the Revolution belongs fundamentally with their pre-Revolutionary output and cannot be regarded as part of Soviet literature. Gumilyov was shot in 1921 on a charge of participating in a counterrevolutionary conspiracy. Sologub died in 1927, a broken and disillusioned man, unable to recover from the personal tragedy of his wife's suicide, which was a direct result of revolutionary conditions. Akhmatova's and Mandelstam's subsequent fate will be referred to later. Somewhat apart from the rest stood Maximilian Voloshin (1877–1932), who after 1917 wrote a great deal of poetry which had the Revolution for its subject. He stressed its national, anarchistic aspect and at the same time denounced its terroristic excesses. During the Civil War he lived under the Whites in the Crimea, where he remained even when the Reds came there. Regarded as a counterrevolutionary, he published nothing after 1925, but his villa at Koktebel was a popular meeting place of the literary and artistic intelligentsia. His poems about the Revolution enjoyed a great success with *émigré* readers.[3]

Some of the pre-Revolutionary prose writers who went into a temporary silence but re-emerged later and gradually adjusted themselves to the new conditions will be discussed briefly in Chapter III.

The adherence of Bryusov, Blok, and Bely to the Revolution was of some importance. All three had stood in the forefront of the Symbolist movement. Many of their friends and literary allies regarded their acceptance of the Bolshevik Revolution as an act of treachery, a

[3] For the early post-Revolutionary work of Sologub (1863–1927), Gumilyov (1886–1921), Akhmatova (b. 1888), and Mandelstam, I again refer the reader to Mirsky. Much of Sologub's work of the last years remains unpublished; as does Gumilyov's tragedy in verse, *Otravlennaya tunika* (*The Poisoned Tunic*), written in 1917–18—see Mary Kriger, "An Unpublished Tragedy of Nikolaj Gumilëv," in *The American Slavic and East European Review*, Vol. VIII (October, 1949), 175–84. Mandelstam's work after 1922, as well as Akhmatova's poetry published between 1940 and 1946, will be discussed in their proper place. For Voloshin, see also Mirsky.

betrayal of their ideals and of Russia. Blok especially, many of his friends found it difficult to forgive. Bely had always been too irresponsible, morally and politically, to be taken seriously. In Bryusov's adherence to the Revolution the element of calculation and timeserving played a large part: quickly forgetting the patriotic poems in which he had extolled Russian victories in the war, he now hastened to join the Communist party (of all three he alone took this step) and received an appointment under the new Commissariat of Education.[4]

2. *Alexander Blok* (1880-1921)

BLOK'S welcome to the Revolution was a different proposition: there was in it a note of deep and anguished sincerity. The Revolution to him was much more than just a political, economic, and social change; it was the crumbling of a whole world, of the old bourgeois, humanistic culture, the hatred for which is sounded so strongly in his pre-Revolutionary diaries and letters. As early as 1909, he wrote in a letter from Italy to his mother:

> More than ever I see that to my dying day I shall not accept anything of contemporary life, nor submit to anything. Its disgraceful order makes me feel nothing but revulsion. No longer can anything be changed—no revolution will change it . . . .

But when the revolution did come at last Blok saw it as a beneficial spiritual storm, the beginning of a great transformation. And he responded to it, early in 1918, with his two famous poems *Dvenadtsat* (*The Twelve*) and "Skify" ("The Scythians") which can be regarded as the starting point of post-Revolutionary literature. Both were first published in the newspaper *Znamya Truda* (*The Banner of Labor*), the organ of the Social-Revolutionaries of the left, at that time the only party, outside the Bolsheviks, adhering to the new regime. Both poems soon won great popularity and came to be recited at various literary meetings. Two years later, in April of 1920, Blok wrote an explanatory note about the genesis of *The Twelve,* in which he said:

> In January 1918, for the last time I yielded to the elements no less blindly than in January 1907 or in March 1914. If I do not

[4] Valery Bryusov (1873–1924) wrote a great deal of poetry after 1917, and was also active as a critic. Although there were in his post-Revolutionary poetry new notes (he was the only one among the older Symbolist poets to be influenced by the Futurists), this later work adds nothing to the essential Bryusov whose best poetry was produced before 1912. Apart from Blok, Bryusov was the only Symbolist poet to receive special attention from Soviet scholars and critics: there are two comprehensive studies of his work, one by G. Lelevich (1926), the other by D. Maksimov (1940).

7

recant what I wrote then, it is because it was written in accord with the elements: for example, at the time of writing *The Twelve* and after finishing it, for several days I felt physically, with my ears, a great noise around, a continuous noise (probably the noise of the crumbling of the old world). Therefore, those who see in *The Twelve* a political poem are either very blind to art, or are immersed ear-deep in political mud, or are possessed by great wrath, whether they be enemies or friends of my poem.

The poem is now generally recognized as one of Blok's masterpieces and one of the greatest works produced by the Revolution. It is a vision of the streets of Petrograd in the early days of the Revolution, when murder, looting, and drunkenness were rampant. A patrol of Red Guards, twelve soldiers of the Revolution, is marching along the streets. The only "incident" in the poem is the killing of Katka, a prostitute, the faithless friend of one of them. The rest of the poem consists of short, fragmentary scenes of the Revolution in Petrograd, scenes imbued with irony and pathos. Blok's familiar motif of the blizzard, here symbolizing also the Revolution, runs through the poem. The combination of realism and symbolism, the rich polyphonic quality of the poem, full of sudden rhythmical breaks and transitions, the skillful use of the rhythms and language of factory songs, creates a powerful and striking effect. This effect, however, does not depend on any message. Did Blok intend any message? The poem ends with a *pointe* which to many appeared as its real intended message. Here we see the Twelve marching along, followed by the mangy dog which throughout the poem symbolizes the old defeated world, and preceded by Christ:

> *So they march with sovereign tread:*
> *Behind them a hungry dog,*
> *Before them, with a bloodstained banner,*
> *Unseen through the blizzard,*
> *Unscathed by the bullets,*
> *With soft step above the storms,*
> *In a pearly whirl of snow,*
> *With a white halo of roses,*
> *Before them—Jesus Christ.*[5]

[5] I give here this passage in my own translation, aiming at the greatest possible accuracy and disregarding the subtle beauty and music of the original. All the existing English verse translations take some liberties with Blok's text. That of Babette Deutsch and Avrahm Yarmolinsky, otherwise perhaps the best, destroys the effect of Blok's vagueness by making his Christ lead the Twelve.

The wording is ambiguous: Is Christ leading the Twelve (their number seems symbolically significant)? Or are they shooting at Him, suspecting in Him an enemy lurking round the corner in the winter darkness? The former interpretation is the more usual, and was probably the one intended by Blok. When Gumilyov, in a lecture he gave about Blok in June of 1919, reproached Blok for bringing in Christ and said that this seemed to him artificial, aimed at a purely literary effect, Blok replied: "I don't like the ending of *The Twelve* either. I wish it were a different one. When I finished it I was myself surprised: 'Why Christ?' But the more I looked at it, the clearer did I see Christ. And I wrote down then and there: 'Unfortunately, Christ.' "[6] Actually what Blok wrote in his *Notebooks* was: "That Christ is marching before them is beyond doubt. The point is not whether 'they are worthy of Him': what is terrible is that He again is with them, and there is no other so far. But must there be the Other—?" These cryptic words still do not make the meaning of the poem's ending quite clear: Is Christ leading the Twelve? Are they marching toward Him? If so, who is "the Other"? Antichrist? But the value of the poem, I repeat, is not in its message.

"The Scythians" is not one of Blok's great poems, though its popular appeal was—and in some circles still is—greater than that of *The Twelve*. It is an effective piece of rhetorical poetry, an impassioned appeal to the West, on behalf of the new revolutionary Russia, to come and join the cause of peace and revolution. In form it bears a resemblance to Pushkin's famous poem "To the Slanderers of Russia," written after the suppression of the Polish insurrection in 1831. It exploits also the Dostoyevskian motif of the receptivity of the Russian genius, open to all outside influences and stimuli, as well as the motif of the "yellow menace" found in Vladimir Solovyov's poem "Pan-Mongolism." It strikes a Slavophile, and at the same time a pacifist, note. Those who believe in Russia's apartness from the West are fond of quoting it. It has some powerful lines, and lends itself well to declamation: it is a modern revolutionary ode.

With those two poems Blok seems to have spent both his poetic power and his revolutionary ardor and enthusiasm. The last two years of his life were marked by silence and by growing disillusionment, bordering on despair and accompanied by a rapid weakening of his physical forces. He died on August 7, 1921, in hungry, blockade-bound Petrograd, after all attempts on the part of his wife and friends to obtain for him permission to go abroad to recuperate had failed. One of his last appearances before the public was some six months before his death, in February of 1921, when at the celebration of the anniversary of Push-

[6] K. Chukovsky, *Blok kak chelovek i poet* (*Blok as Man and Poet*).

kin's birth he delivered an address that, in the history of Russian literature, will be remembered alongside Dostoyevsky's famous address of 1880. Blok spoke of the "mission of the poet," and his speech, in which he enjoined his audience to remember a few truths and swear to them "in the gay name of Pushkin," was an almost deathbed profession of an ineradicable belief in the freedom and independence of art. Quoting Pushkin's line, "There is no happiness in the world, but there is peace and freedom," Blok said: *"Peace and freedom.* The poet needs them to release harmony. But peace and freedom are also taken away. Not the outward peace but the creative. Not the childish freedom, the freedom of being a liberal, but the freedom of creation, the secret freedom. And the poet dies because he can no longer breathe: life has lost its meaning." The same day he wrote his last poem, a wonderful short poem inscribed in the album of the Pushkin House of the Academy of Sciences and dated "February 11 (January 29), 1921." Here, just as in his Pushkin address, he referred to that "secret freedom" which Pushkin had sung.

Six months later Blok died because he, too, could no longer breathe, and life had lost for him its meaning. His diaries and notebooks for the last two years are full of tragic references to the deafness which had suddenly submerged him who had been endowed with such a hypersensitive ear. Music was gone, not only out of the Revolution, but out of life.

3. *Andrey Bely* (1880-1934)

OF all the great figures of the period of Symbolism, Andrey Bely (pseudonym of Boris Nikolayevich Bugayev) continued longest in post-Revolutionary Russia, and, although he failed to integrate himself in the new Soviet literature, some account of his post-Revolutionary work is necessary.

A revolutionary by temperament, and extremely sensitive to the flavor of the epoch, Bely was one of the few older writers who "accepted" the October Revolution. But, like Blok, he saw in it what he chose to see, and not what it really was. He welcomed it not as a political, economic, and social revolution, but as a great religious and cultural transformation; as an end of the old world, which fulfilled the Symbolists' eschatological expectations; as that catastrophe which he and his like never tired of predicting; as a national upheaval which would enable Russia to assume world leadership and fulfill her universal mission. A disciple of Rudolf Steiner, he visualized that mission through the prism of anthroposophy. But, unlike Blok, his acceptance of the Revolution did not receive an adequate poetic expression. Its only direct outcome was his grandiloquent poem *Khristos Voskrese*

(*Christ Is Risen*), which can bear no comparison with Blok's *The Twelve*. During the years of War Communism, Bely, like many other writers who stayed behind in Russia, was active, teaching in various literary studios and giving public lectures. He founded the Free Academy of Philosophy (known under its abbreviated name of *Volfila*), and was the leading spirit behind the publishing enterprise called "The Scythians." His long poem *Pervoye svidanie* (*The First Meeting*, 1921), of frankly retrospective nature, recalling the atmosphere of his youth and giving a picture of life of the Moscow intellectual elite in the first years of the present century, is a work of great charm, combining effectively the two important elements of Bely's art: his irrepressible verbal inventiveness and his puckish, realistic humor. It is Bely at his very best. On the other hand, the volume of lyrical poems, published in 1922 under the title *Posle razluki* (*After the Parting*), adds nothing to his stature as a poet.

More important is Bely's post-Revolutionary prose work. This can be divided into works of fiction and memoirs. Among the former by far the most original and significant is a short "autobiographical" novel *Kotik Letayev,* published in 1922 but written considerably earlier. This work inevitably calls to mind James Joyce, although there can be no question of mutual influence. Its subject is the formation of a child's consciousness. It begins with prenatal experiences and shows the gradual process of the formation of the child's perception of and reaction to the external world. Written in Bely's customary rhythmical prose, full of musical associations, with more than his usual amount of daring word-creation (and in this case more than ever justified), it has been rightly described as a work of genius,[7] though it can hardly be to the taste of many readers and many of its anthroposophic implications will be understandable to the initiated only. Its sequel, *Prestuplenie Nikolaya Letayeva* (*The Crime of Nikolay Letayev*, 1921), later revised and renamed *Kreshchony kitaets* (*A Baptized Chinaman*), though full of typical "Belyisms," is much less abstruse and is set on a realistic plane. These two works were meant as part of a larger autobiographical whole with which Bely did not proceed. Instead he wrote, after 1923, three other novels, forming a sequence and also incomplete—*Moskovsky chudak* (*A Moscow Crank*), *Moskva pod udarom* (*Moscow Exposed*), and *Maski* (*Masks*). These have a highly improbable, melodramatic plot, involving scientific secrets, German spies, and Communists, and the typical Bely mixture of realism and fantastic delirium. There are, however, some extremely effective nightmarish scenes. The plot, for all its improbability, is handled very skillfully; but some of Bely's usual defects—the monotonousness of his rhythmical prose; the unreal ab-

[7] Mirsky, *Contemporary Russian Literature*, 234.

11

stractness of his psychological presentation; the rather tiresome puns and neologisms—are more conspicuous than in his earlier novels. The essential and irreconcilable dualism of Bely's nature—Bely the irrational dreamer and Bely the admirer of abstract and rational schemes—is apparent in them. Unlike *Kotik Letayev,* which, even if a failure, was a brilliant failure, and an anticipation of Joyce's most daring experiments in technique, these last novels of Bely did not constitute a step forward or open new vistas to literature.

In 1922 Bely went, as did several other Soviet writers, to live in Berlin. Here he edited the literary magazine *Epopeia,* took part in the *émigré* literary life, and at one time apparently contemplated staying abroad. However, he went back to Russia in 1923. While in Berlin, he continued working on his *Recollections of Alexander Blok,* parts of which had appeared before, and which were now printed in *Epopeia.* This is one of Bely's most interesting works; for a student of Blok and of Russian Symbolism it is invaluable. On his return to Russia, Bely did his best to harness himself to the cart of the Revolution, but his efforts ended in a pathetic fiasco. His attitude toward the Revolution lacked consistency. Its political aspect was quite alien to him, and he could not possibly feel congenial to it. Despite his essential dualism and all his intellectual and spiritual vagaries, his outlook on the world was fundamentally religious and idealistic, and he could have no sympathy with dialectical materialism. All his professions to the contrary were insincere.

During the last years of his life Bely was engaged on his *Memoirs,* three volumes of which appeared between 1929 and 1933: *Na rubezhe dvukh stoletiy (On the Border of Two Centuries), Nachalo veka (The Beginning of a Century),* and *Mezhdu dvukh revolyutsiy (Between Two Revolutions).* In one of them he incorporated his *Recollections of Blok* in a thoroughly revised form. For a historian of Russian Symbolism these memoirs are a source of valuable information. For an understanding of Bely himself they are indispensable. As literature, they are a brilliant piece of work: all the best and all the most annoying of Bely is to be found in them. But their value as memoirs is more than doubtful. Veracity was never Bely's strong point: all who knew him well agree on this. In his account of the events of the past Bely is as elusive, as unaccountable, as subjective, and, ultimately, as untruthful as he was in life. The element of personal rancor is quite obvious (the way in which he revised the account of his relations with Blok is only the most glaring example among many). Throughout, one feels a tendency —often undoubtedly dictated by political considerations—to read a new meaning, in the light of subsequent happenings, not only into the events of the past, but even into the author's inward experience. Much of what he tells us in his memoirs has to be taken with more than a pinch of salt; his omissions and evasions are numerous; and even his factual statements have to be checked with other sources. Nevertheless, these three volumes remain a valuable and interesting document of one of the most brilliant and exciting periods in the history of Russian literature, in which Bely himself played one of the leading roles. Some of Bely's portraits of his contemporaries, bad history though they may be, are certainly brilliant literature.

Bely's place in modern Russian literature is extremely important, not only on account of his personal contribution to it, but also because of the influence which he, especially through his prose fiction, exercised on the young generation of post-Revolutionary writers. The musical, contrapuntal prose of his *Symphonies;* the system of shifting, dislocated planes in his novels; his experiments with the Russian language, both in vocabulary and in syntax, have all left their traces in the work of Zamyatin, of Boris Pilnyak and his school, in Fedin's *Cities and Years,* in some of the early work of the young proletarian writers, in the historical novels of Yury Tynyanov, and so on. Bely's poetry had a great influence on Russian Futurists and Imaginists and on the so-called Cosmists, while his studies of Russian prosody largely determined the work of the Formalist school in literary science and criticism. In fiction, however, none of his disciples have produced anything equal to their master's best work. In the long run Bely's tradition in Russian prose fiction did not prove enduring; the influence of Leskov and Remizov, which went parallel with it, was more fruitful and lasting. Of late, as will be seen, there has been a definite reaction against all experimentation *à la* Bely. Whatever may lie in store for Russian literature, Bely will never be regarded as a typical figure of its "Soviet" period: his place, including his post-Revolutionary work, is in the age of Symbolism.

4. *Mayakovsky and Futurism*

THE most outstanding figure among the Russian Futurists was Vladimir Vladimirovich Mayakovsky (1893–1930), and it was his personal ascendancy that made the close alliance between Futurism and the post-Revolutionary regime such an important fact in the history of the first decade of Soviet literature.

Russian Futurism developed as a movement parallel to, but ideologically independent from, the Italian Futurism of Marinetti. Its beginnings go back to 1910, when appeared the famous poem of Viktor (Velemir) Khlebnikov (1885–1922) about laughter. It consisted entirely of ingenious variations on the root *smekh* ("laugh"), most of them words coined by Khlebnikov, but with considerable regard for, and understanding of, the spirit of the Russian language. With two other early Futurists, David Burlyuk (b. 1882) and Alexey Kruchonykh (b. 1886), Khlebnikov represented one of the main tendencies of Futurism, a movement that almost from the very first lacked homogeneity and split into a number of factions, such as Cubo-Futurists, Ego-Futurists, and others. This was a tendency toward innovation at all costs. The Futurists (or *"budetlyane"* as some of them preferred to call themselves in Russian) rejected uncompromisingly all art of the past and looked toward an art of the future. They spoke of throwing Pushkin and Dostoyevsky, Raphael and Michelangelo "overboard the ship of modernity." The movement was essentially revolutionary and, in ideal at least, cosmopolitan, though in practice there was in some of the leading Futurists, and in Khlebnikov especially, a strong nationalist, "Slavophile" strain. It was a reaction against both the leading currents of contemporary Russian literature: against Realism with its "photographic" reflection of reality, and against Symbolism with its transformation of reality in the name of some higher reality. The object of art, said Burlyuk, was neither to reflect nature nor to transform it, but "to *deform* it such as it is fixed in individual consciousness." Art was autonomous, it had no object outside itself, it was not in any way "co-ordinated" with the world. Fundamentally, this anticivic aesthetic credo was, of course, much closer to Symbolism than to Realism, and it is possible therefore to say that Futurism was a continuation of Symbolism with which it had some sources in common (the poetry of Rimbaud and Mallarmé, for example). However, since Symbolism at the time dominated the literary stage in Russia, it was also a revolt against some of its practices, and especially against all attempts to invest poetry with philosophical or religious meaning. Some of the extreme Futurists went very far in their attempt to revolutionize the very medium of art; in poetry, this meant the language (there were parallel movements in painting and in music, and some of the Futurists, like the brothers Burlyuk, were active in more than one field). In one of their publications (*Troye,* Moscow, 1913) they proclaimed that words "hitherto fettered to the meaning" had to be freed from this dependence, and a new "trans-sense language" (*"zaumny yazyk,"* or *"zaum"*) was to replace the ordinary human speech. Khlebnikov—held by some to be a linguistic and poetic genius; by others, a madman; and by still others, a combination of the two—and Kruchonykh gave in their poetry many examples of this trans-sense language.

Mayakovsky did not adhere at once to the Futurist movement with its distinctly asocial tendency. At an early age he had manifested an interest in political and social questions and, when still at school, joined the Bolshevik faction of the Social-Democratic party. This resulted in his being expelled from school. Later, he studied in the Moscow School of Painting and Sculpture, showing a considerable talent as an artist. By 1911 he became associated with Burlyuk and was drawn by the latter into the Futurist movement. In 1912 he was one of the signatories of the Futurist manifesto entitled *Poshchochina obshchestvennomu vkusu* (*A Slap in the Face of Public Taste*), and after that for some years he played the leading part in various activities of the Futurists intended to scandalize the philistine public: the bright yellow blazer he wore became the symbol of the Futurist challenge to all bourgeois conventions. He traveled about Russia, lecturing and giving recitals of his poetry. His work written during 1912–13 came closest to the theoretical demands of Futurism, but although it lacks the simplicity and mass appeal of his later work, he never composed trans-sense poetry or acceded to the other excesses of Khlebnikov and Kruchonykh. He shared, however, the Futurists' general aversion to realism and to any "message" in art and spoke slightingly of the writers who were being made into "harbingers of truth and posters of virtue and justice." All a writer does, he said, is "to mold a skillful vase, and it is of no account whether wine or slops is poured into it." This glorification of form and indifference to content were, in Mayakovsky's case, purely superficial—mere lip service to the tenets of the Futurist credo. Soviet students of Mayakovsky are probably right when they say that what attracted him to Futurism was its apparent revolutionary spirit ("Down with all accepted, traditional values!") and its universalism. Even in his most individualistic early works his great concern with the surrounding realities, his deeply-rooted revolt against them, is easily discernible. This is particularly true of his first important long work, the tragedy *Vladimir Mayakovsky* (according to Korney Chukovsky, Mayakovsky changed its title from *I* to *Vladimir Mayakovsky* after reading Chukovsky's translation of Whitman's *Walt Whitman*),[8] and still more so, of such poems as "Man" (1917), "A Cloud in Pants" (1915), and "War and Peace" (1916). The last-named was a protest against the war (parts of it were banned by censorship), although at first the war had inspired some exhilara-

[8] See K. Chukovsky's Introduction to his translation of Whitman's *Leaves of Grass*, 6–7, and A. V. Fyodorov's very interesting essay "Mayakovsky i literatura Zapada" ("Mayakovsky and the Literature of the West"), in *Vladimir Mayakovsky* (edited by A. L. Dymshits and O. V. Tsekhnovitser), 113. Both Chukovsky and Fyodorov make much of Whitman's influence on the pre-Revolutionary Mayakovsky. On the other hand, David Burlyuk, who introduced Mayakovsky to foreign poets (Mayakovsky's linguistic equipment was very poor), denied later any influence of Whitman on Mayakovsky. See A. Kaun, *Soviet Poets and Poetry*, 51–52. It is possible that Mayakovsky's attitude toward Whitman was ambivalent; in his poetry there is at least one derogatory reference to Whitman, where Whitman is bracketed together with Longfellow. However, Chukovsky's testimony to Mayakovsky's interest in Whitman's "eccentricities" is sufficiently authoritative and convincing.

tion in Mayakovsky, as may be seen in some of his 1914–15 articles. Together with other Futurists he saw in the war an opportunity for the Futurists to assert their supremacy in literature, just as later he was to see—and seize!—such an opportunity in the Revolution. He even sounded some Slavophile, anti-Western notes *à la* Khlebnikov.

With all the differences between the early and the post-Revolutionary Mayakovsky, some of the essential characteristics of his poetry are to be found already in this earlier period. Without going into the excesses of the "trans-sense" poets, he made a more lasting contribution to the deformation of the Russian poetic language than any other Futurist. He deformed the syntax, both by use of archaic inversions and of elliptical locutions. He took up and systematically developed some of the prosodic innovations of the Symbolists and Acmeists, discarding the traditional tonicosyllabic versification and substituting for it a verse based solely on the count of stresses in a line, with complete disregard of the intervening unstressed syllables. Thus he succeeded in creating an instrument that was both unmistakably his and eminently suited to his purpose of "depoetizing" the language of poetry, of approximating it to the language of the street and of the tribune: it is the effective combination of the conversational, verging on the slang, with the rhetorical and the declamatory that is characteristic of Mayakovsky's diction. His verses are made to be declaimed. In his hands Russian verse lost the melodiousness which the Symbolists had endeavored to give it, but it gained in virility and in rhythmical power. Mayakovsky's rhythms are his forte. This process of "depoetization" was further enhanced by the deliberate use of a coarse, vulgar vocabulary, and of unpoetic imagery, especially where nature was concerned. This was a general tendency among the Futurists, but no one showed it more thoroughly and consistently than Mayakovsky. A title like "A Cloud in Pants," or a comparison of stars with spittle, is a typical example of this unpoetic treatment of nature. There is much in the early Mayakovsky that resembles E. E. Cummings.

Another characteristic feature of Mayakovsky is his inordinate love of hyperbole: himself an outsize man, measuring well over six feet and endowed with a stentorian voice, he always dealt in outsize images, and many of his effects were achieved through a combination of the grandiose with the grotesque.

Mayakovsky's favorite device is a long and elaborate metaphor—what the Futurists called "a realized metaphor"—and more often than not his metaphors were blatantly coarse, stripped of all conventional poetic veneer. He would compare himself to a sun-scorched July pavement on which a woman throws cigarette stubs of kisses; or speak of the unwanted, flabby moon wobbling beyond the suns of the streets;

or of the street being fallen in like the nose of a syphilitic; or compare a crowd to a hundred-headed louse bristling its legs and rubbing them against the butterfly of the poet's heart.

In the Bolshevik Revolution Mayakovsky saw the opportunity he had been looking forward to—of placing his art in the service of the people. Although not an orthodox Futurist in the earlier sense of the word, he had come to be looked upon as the acknowledged leader and mouthpiece of Futurism, which in its turn came to be regarded as the extreme left in art. The primary task of the Bolsheviks, when they won power in October, 1917, was to do away with the bourgeois institutions and the bourgeois mentality. The Futurists had always professed hatred for the bourgeoisie and all it stood for. Hence the natural tendency of Futurism not only to ally itself with the new regime but also to identify itself with the Revolution. Many of the Futurists cared little for the political or social revolution per se, but they saw in it a wonderful chance for carrying out under its cover their own revolution in the field of art. So they made a bold bid to secure a virtual monopoly in that field. Their official organ, *Iskusstvo Kommuny* (*Art of the Commune*), openly spoke of a Futurist dictatorship in the realm of art, parallel to the dictatorship of the proletariat on the political and economic plane. In its first number this magazine printed an article by Osip Brik, a friend of Mayakovsky and one of the principal theoreticians of Futurism, entitled "The Draining of Art." New art, wrote Brik, must break completely with the bourgeois art of the past. The object of art was to create new and unprecedented things. Artists must go to factories and plants to learn new ways. Futurism and proletarian art were synonymous. In another article Brik wrote: "Art shall be proletarian, or there will be no art at all." This bid for supremacy was, in the early phases of the Revolution, encouraged by the first Soviet Commissar for Education, Anatoly Vasilievich Lunacharsky (1875–1933). Prominent Futurists like Brik, Punin, and others were appointed to leading posts in the Commissariat of Education and placed in charge of literary, artistic, and theatrical policy. It was all the easier for the Futurists to conquer these key positions as most of the other writers kept aloof from the new regime or hastened to emigrate. Among the exceptions was Valery Bryusov, who joined the Communist party and also received an appointment under the Commissariat of Education. But the Futurists were already so powerful that even Bryusov was forced to play up to them. The abnormal conditions of life which prevailed during this period—with Russia torn by the Civil War and cut off from the outside world—made the publication of books very difficult, if not impossible, and literature continued mostly in the oral form: poets gathered in various cafés and taverns, especially in Moscow, and recited their new

works. These cafés were for the most part monopolized by the Futurists
and their principal rivals, the Imaginists (of whom more below). The
whole period is therefore often spoken of as the "café period" of Russian literature.

Mayakovsky threw himself heart and soul into the Revolution.
He described himself as its "drummer," and was accepted as such.
Whether his revolutionary ardor had anything to do with a real sympathy with the "toiling masses" is very doubtful. The more perspicacious
among the Communist critics were fully aware of the fundamental loneliness of Mayakovsky and of his immeasurable egocentrism. It is perhaps this ineradicable sense of loneliness, of utter isolation from the
people, that gives such truly tragic accents to the best poems of this
self-styled bard of the Revolution, whose "Left March" became for a
time its anthem. They are all about himself. Mayakovsky's only real,
live hero is Vladimir Vladimirovich Mayakovsky, a man of flesh and
blood, with raw skin. His other characters are just puppets. And the
Revolution, as we see it in his poetry, is, after all, a gigantic puppet
show played out among the gaudy cardboard *décors and Rosta*[9] posters
of his own designing. The Revolution was for him a means of escaping
from himself, though in the end it was he who escaped from the Revolution. Nevertheless, he welcomed the opportunity of placing his art in
the service of the masses and began writing feverishly propaganda
verses, issuing "Orders of the Day" to "the Army of Art," giving pep
talks to fellow artists and writers, and designing posters for the Russian
Telegraphic News Agency: these were displayed for the public in its
windows and accompanied by terse epigrammatic lines on topical subjects in the style of popular factory ditties. This "agit-poetry," as it was
called, enjoyed a great success during the Civil War. In it Mayakovsky
retained certain characteristic features, but discarded some of his earlier
sophistication: simplicity and directness of appeal became his primary
aims. Theater being regarded by the new regime as one of the most
effective means of mass propaganda, and therefore particularly encouraged, Mayakovsky wrote for it his "dramatic poem," called *Mis-
teriya-Buff* (*Mystery-Bouffe*), a glorification of the Bolshevik Revolution and a vision of the coming millenium, a sort of a cross between a
grandiose parody of medieval mysteries and a Russian popular play,
with a multitude of characters and an elaborate stage machinery, designed for open-air production: its first public performance, directed
by Vsevolod Meyerhold, took place in front of the Petersburg Stock
Exchange.

In 1920 Mayakovsky published his long poem *150,000,000*. Full of
bombastic Soviet patriotism and revolutionary spirit, it was primarily

[9] *Rosta*—Russian Telegraphic News Agency.

an invective of the capitalist West which was personified in Woodrow Wilson, president of the United States. Soviet Russia, with her one hundred and fifty million inhabitants, was personified in the hyperbolically heroic and unlifelike figure of the peasant Ivan. Here the satirical note which had always been prominent in Mayakovsky is very strong. Later, Mayakovsky's satire was to be directed at some of the aspects of the new regime: Lenin, although on the whole he disliked Mayakovsky's poetry and preferred to him such old poets as Pushkin and Nekrasov, is said to have particularly admired one of Mayakovsky's satirical poems in which he ridiculed the early Soviet mania for official meetings and portrayed Soviet officials who had to take part in so many meetings that they attended them in halves—one half of the body, down to the waist, at one meeting, and the lower half, at another. The poem ended with a pious wish for "a meeting to abolish all meetings." Mayakovsky's humor is somewhat on the heavy side, but his use of the hyperbolic and the grotesque for satirical purposes is very effective. Foreign themes were also treated by Mayakovsky in this satirical vein, especially after he had traveled abroad and visited the United States and Mexico as well as Germany, France, and other European countries. He lectured all over Russia on his travels, accompanying his lectures with the recital of his newly-written poems. His personal popularity was very great, his manner of reciting very effective, and his lecture-recitals drew large crowds.

Of the later fortunes of Mayakovsky and of Futurism more will be said in Chapters II, III, and IV.

5. *Esenin and Klyuev*

IN 1918–21 Mayakovsky's popularity was equalled, and later even surpassed, by that of Esenin. One can say that the two shared between them the literary stage in the early, "heroic" period of the Revolution.

Sergey Alexandrovich Esenin (1895–1925) came of a true peasant stock. He grew up in his native village in the Ryazan province, in Central Russia, in the family of his grandparents who were "Old Believers," in an atmosphere of strong religious traditions. This early religious background is clearly reflected in Esenin's poetry, even though much of it is not only profane but frankly blasphemous. After graduating from the local parish school, Esenin went to Moscow and enrolled in the Shanyavsky Free University, working at the same time as a proofreader in a printing office. In 1915, on the way to his grandfather in Riga, he stopped in Petrograd. A meeting with Blok, to whom he read some of his poetry, decided his fate: he remained in Petrograd and devoted himself to literature. Blok introduced him to the leading poets of the time, and he became a regular visitor of the Symbolist salons and literary gatherings. The Symbolists were attracted by the fresh accents they discerned in the poetry of this good-looking, blue-eyed, golden-haired peasant youth. The rustic sources of Esenin's early poetry, published before the Revolution, full of colorful imagery and religious symbols and showing an inborn gift of song, are indubitable. He was hailed as a peasant poet, and fame came to him rapidly. But he himself acknowledged the debt he owed to his Symbolist masters, especially to Blok and Bely. In a short autobiographical note, which Esenin wrote in 1925, he said: "Bely gave me a great deal from the point of view of form, while Blok and Klyuev taught me lyricism."

When the Revolution broke out, Esenin welcomed it enthusiastically. Like Blok and Bely, he saw in it a spiritual upheaval, a renewal, and more particularly a victory of the peasant, "wooden" Russia. His acceptance of the Revolution was tinged with messianic expectations. The political and social aims of the Communist party were alien to him; he was more in sympathy with the Social-Revolutionaries who claimed to represent the peasantry and its aspirations. It was the anti-urban, anti-Western aspect of the Revolution as he saw it, that appealed to Esenin, and he voiced these sentiments in the picturesque, blasphemous imagery of his poem *Inonia,* a vision of the coming "peasant paradise."

In 1919 Esenin moved to Moscow and joined the literary group which called itself "the Imaginists," signing on its behalf a manifesto in which the new group claimed the legacy of Futurism which it pronounced "defunct."

During the years of War Communism the Imaginists were, besides the Futurists, the only organized literary group. Their attitude to the new regime was much more independent—at times even defiant. They had their own cafés in Moscow (one of them was called "Pegasus' Manger"), and their noisy and truculent behavior was one of the features of the literary life of this period. Next to Esenin, whose connection with the group was somewhat loose, although he was regarded as its leader, its principal representatives were Vadim Shershenevich (a former Ego-Futurist), Anatoly Marienhof, and Alexander Kusikov. The theory of Imaginism, with its stress on striking and daring images as the principal element of poetry, had nothing original in it, while in their practice the Imaginists followed in the wake of the Symbolists and the Futurists. What they had in common with the latter was their utter disregard of all taboos, the use of the coarsest language and the crudest imagery. But, unlike Mayakovsky and his followers, they lacked even the semblance of any healthy or vigorous optimism. Their attitude toward life was thoroughly pessimistic. They reveled in morbidity and perversions. Both their poetry and their actual behavior were full of bohemian rowdiness, and they were often involved in all sorts of drunken rows and scandals. Works like Esenin's "Ispoved khuligana" ("Confession of a Rowdy") and "Moskva kabatskaya" ("Tavern Moscow"), or Marienhof's obscene and blasphemous poems, were typical of this aspect of Imaginism. In outspokenness of language the Imaginists left Mayakovsky and the Futurists far behind: beside Marienhof, Kusikov, and Shershenevich, Mayakovsky looks almost respectable. With some of them this was merely a literary pose, an affectation dictated by the desire to *épater les bourgeois,* just as had been the yellow blazers, painted faces, and carrots for buttonholes of the earlier Futurists and Cubists. But in Esenin's case this mood of rowdy despair and nihilistic defiance had deeper roots. The Revolution had deceived his expectations ("The stern October has deceived me," he wrote in one of his poems); the dream of a peasant paradise had failed to materialize. When the anti-peasant, industrial, urban and proletarian aspects of the Revolution came to the fore, he felt a bitter disillusionment, which gave his poems a note of tragic despair. His "tavern" poetry sounds poignantly sincere. His ill-starred and short-lived marriage to Isadora Duncan in 1922, and the subsequent world tour marked the culminating points of this period of drunken rowdiness and reckless abandon. When he sobered down, repentance came, followed by desperate attempts to adjust himself to the new conditions of life, and to recapture something of the old closeness to the native soil from which he had forcibly uprooted himself. This mood found its expression in a number of poems about "Russia of the Soviets." He revisited his native village, but the experience was rather bitter.

While some of his later poems reflect the renewed spell of "wooden" Russia and are full of fresh and charming imagery, there is also in them the sad awareness that this new and unfamiliar rural Russia has no use for him or his poetry. In some poems of this period we see Esenin trying to reconcile himself with the new Russia in the process of industrialization and proletarianization, the symbol of which he saw in the "iron steed" (the railways).[10] This attempt at adjustment to something to which he was instinctively hostile proved a complete failure, and Esenin's suicide on December 25, 1925, came as a natural denouement, as the only possible way out of hopeless contradictions and entanglements.

10 In his reminiscences of Esenin the Soviet critic Voronsky quoted the following words of Esenin: "Mind, I know you're a Communist. I am also for the Soviet power. But I love Russia. I shall not allow myself to be muzzled, nor am I going to dance to anybody's tune. This won't do." These words were said when Esenin visited Voronsky at his editorial office soon after returning from his trip abroad. *Literaturnye portrety (Literary Portraits)*, I, 247.

Esenin will be remembered for his earliest and his latest poems, with their simple, wistful and melodious evocations of the Russian countryside. He had a true gift of song, and in his poems the spirit of Russian folk-poetry was revived, even though he made no conscious attempt to reproduce its meters. His diction was closer to Nekrasov, Blok, and Bely, and later to Pushkin, to whom he felt irresistibly drawn in the last two years of his life; some of his latest poems have the Pushkinian limpidity. But the personal Esenin ring in them is unmistakable.[11] The texture of his verse, simple and musical, is the very opposite of Mayakovsky's. Esenin was essentially a lyric poet, and his attempt to write a large-scale work (*Pugachov*) ended in a failure: this would-be "tragedy in verse" remained a series of disjointed lyrical fragments of uneven value.

Esenin enjoyed an enormous popularity during his lifetime, and his sensational suicide in a room in the Hotel Angleterre in Leningrad (he cut his wrists, wrote his farewell poem with his own blood, and then hanged himself) enhanced it still further. It came at the height of widespread disillusionment engendered by the New Economic Policy, when suicides were becoming a frequent phenomenon. People were reminded of the suicide, only a year before, of the twenty-year-old proletarian poet Nikolay Kuznetsov, which had been widely talked about. The death of the popular poet recalled also the tragically early end of Russia's two greatest poets, Pushkin and Lermontov. Esenin's popularity was very great among all the classes of the population, but he was particularly popular with the younger generation, including the young Communists, members of the *Komsomol* (League of Communist Youth). This popularity rested partly on his "hooligan" poetry, which impressed by the sincerity of its boundless despair and self-castigation; but it was mostly due to his slightly sentimental, wistful, and melancholy pictures of rural Russia, full of genuine and peaceful love for his native land. At one time this popularity caused considerable misgivings in the official circles: "Eseninism" came to be spoken of as a dangerous disease undermining the Soviet body politic, as a sign of degenerate and debile individualism, incompatible with the prescribed optimistic attitude toward life.[12]

Esenin was only one of a number of poets who were prominent in the early years of the Revolution and who voiced the sentiments and

[11] Mirsky, in his short chapter on Esenin in *Contemporary Russian Literature*, appears to deny all religious inspiration in Esenin's poetry. However, for all his blasphemies there seems to be some genuine religious feeling in Esenin. Characteristic of Esenin's contradictory attitude are the lines where he says that he feels ashamed of having believed in God and bitter about not believing in Him now.

[12] Georgy Gorbachov, *Sovremennaya russkaya literatura* (*Contemporary Russian Literature*), 61.

aspirations of the Russian peasantry. This class, despite the supremacy attained by the Bolsheviks, regarded the Revolution—not without some justification—as its own achievement.

Among the peasant poets the most interesting and original was Nikolay Alexeyevich Klyuev (1885–1937). His first book, published in 1912, attracted attention in the Symbolist camp. The Symbolists saw in Klyuev a disciple of theirs, but at the same time he was genuinely of the people, steeped in the folklore and religious "dissenter" tradition of northern Russia and full of mystical revolutionary "Populism," which appealed particularly to Alexander Blok. Later, Klyuev was to guide the first steps of Esenin. Like Esenin, Klyuev welcomed the Revolution as a kind of mystical revelation of the "peasant paradise." It was the national Russian, or "Scythian," aspect of the Revolution that fascinated him. He wrote a great deal of revolutionary poetry, and in his *Lenin* portrayed a legendary figure of the Bolshevik leader from the standpoint of religious revolutionism, likening Lenin to Archpriest Avvakum, the leader of the seventeenth-century dissenters.

Unlike Esenin's, Klyuev's poetry is heavy and ornate, with a strong bookish and traditional background, full of exotic imagery, of North Russian local color, and of symbols of religious ritual, which in his case have a deep significance and are not used for mere outward effects as they often are in Esenin's. It is somewhat monotonous in its single-mindedness, but at his best Klyuev is a genuine and powerful poet. His disillusionment with the Revolution, which did not fulfill his dream of a peasant paradise on earth, was inevitable. Also unlike Esenin, he was not a *déclassé* peasant, but was deeply rooted in the traditional soil. He therefore viewed Esenin's attempts to integrate himself with city life, and especially his "rowdiness," as a betrayal. But Klyuev was regarded by the orthodox Communist critics as a true embodiment of the "kulak" spirit among the peasants, and he soon fell out of favor and was reduced to silence. There are reasons to believe that at some point he was arrested and exiled. He apparently died in a concentration camp.

Many other peasant poets who were active during those early years of the Revolution—Pyotr Oreshin (b. 1887), Rodion Akulshin (b. 1896), Sergey Klychkov, and others—disappeared later from the literary stage. The names of Oreshin and Klychkov, for instance, which had appeared in the *Little Soviet Encyclopaedia,* were not included in the later *Great Soviet Encyclopaedia,* for by that time they came to be regarded as "enemies of the people." Their fate is unknown. However, a few of these poets succeeded in ridding themselves of their specific peasant ideology and adapting themselves to new conditions.[13]

[13] Numerous specimens of this peasant poetry—of very uneven quality—will be

6. *The Proletkult. The Cosmists*

PARALLEL with the encouragement which the new regime gave to the Futurists as the only organized literary force that was willing and ready to support it unconditionally, attempts were also made, from 1918 on, to foster a specific proletarian literature and to train budding writers belonging to the new ruling class of industrial proletariat. This task fell to the lot of the so-called *"Proletkult"* (an abbreviation of "Proletarian Culture"). Its leading spirit was Bogdanov (pseudonym of Alexander Alexandrovich Malinovsky, 1873–1928), one of the early theoreticians of Russian Marxism, whom Lenin had earlier charged with Machian heresy.[14] Bogdanov's conception of the *Proletkult* was based on the assumption that the working class should advance toward Socialism along three parallel and independent roads: next to the political and economic action which belonged to the competence of the Communist party and the trade-unions respectively, Bogdanov placed the cultural action which was to be exempted from the control of the political mechanism of the Communist party. The *Proletkult* was to be a separate, autonomous organization, using its own methods. In 1918–20 the *Proletkult* displayed a great activity: it published its own magazine, *Proletarskaya Kultura* (*Proletarian Culture*); it convened an all-Russian conference to discuss the issue of proletarian culture; it organized, all over Russia, a great number of literary and artistic studios or training centers for workers, where the latter were taught by bourgeois literary specialists how to write verse and prose. Among those who taught in these studios were some of the leading pre-Revolutionary writers: Bryusov, Bely, Gumilyov, Zamyatin, and others. The *Proletkult* succeeded in drawing into its sphere of influence a number of writers from among factory workers, soldiers and sailors, as well as some peasants. In 1920 several proletarian writers who had seceded from the *Proletkult* formed in Moscow a literary group called *Kuznitsa* ("The Smithy"). Their counterpart in Petrograd was called *Kosmist* ("The Cosmist"). Most of them were poets: Vasily Alexandrovsky (b. 1897), Alexey Gastev (b. 1882), Mikhail Gerasimov (b. 1889), Vasily Kazin (b. 1898), Vladimir Kirilov (b. 1889), and Sergey Obradovich (b. 1892). Some of them had begun writing and publishing before the Revolution. Several of them were industrial workers and could boast of proletarian "blue blood." It was, however, not so much the proletarian origin as the acceptance of Communist ideology that qualified one as

---

found in G. Z. Patrick, *Popular Poetry in Soviet Russia,* which deals also with "proletarian" poets.

14 Bogdanov was strongly influenced in his views by Ernst Mach's philosophy of empiriocriticism.

a proletarian writer. The ideological content of the work produced by
these poets satisfied this demand: it was full of revolutionary fervor, it
extolled collectivism, and factory labor was its principal theme. But
there was little that was specifically proletarian in their poetry. Their
form, their technique, their methods, and often their vocabulary were
largely derived from Symbolism, with a slight admixture of Futurism
and Imaginism. The revolutionary message of their poetry was strongly
tinged with romantic heroism. Factory themes were treated by most of
them, not in terms of everyday factory life, but on a cosmic, planetary
plane. Cosmic terminology, grandiloquent, hyperbolic images characterized the majority of these poets; they were guilty of some of the
worst sins of Symbolism, the only difference being that the old Symbolist dishes *à la* Balmont were now being served up with industrial
and revolutionary seasoning. Compared with what was being offered
by Mayakovsky and his disciples, or even the Imaginists, there was
little that was fresh and novel in these proletarian poets. One exception among the "Smithy" poets was Vasily Kazin who, besides the usual
"cosmic" stuff, wrote also simple down-to-earth poems about workers
and artisans, in which he struck a fresh note.[15]

The "Cosmists," as they were often called in those days, followed
at first the Futurists in their wholesale rejection of the art of the past.
One of the most talented among them, Kirilov, in a poem called "My"
("We") summoned his fellow proletarians to destroy museums and
burn Raphaels "in the name of our Tomorrow." But this was only a
temporary phase, and two years later the same Kirilov wrote a poem
in which he spoke of "radiant Pushkin" and other Russian classics as
friends and allies of proletarian poets.

The problem of the cultural heritage of the past—of the attitude to
be taken toward it in the new proletarian state—occupied at this time
the leaders of Communism. It was this problem that revealed the first
serious rift between the new regime and its Futurist allies. As early as
December of 1918, Lunacharsky gave a warning to the Futurists when
he wrote in *Art of the Commune*: "It would be a nuisance if the vanguard artists were definitely to imagine themselves as a state-spon-
sored school of art, representing official art, which, albeit revolutionary,
is dictated from above." And he went on to say that one of the alarm-
ing features of the extreme left in art was its purely negative and destructive attitude toward the art of the past. Equally dangerous was its
claim to speak in the name of the government while representing a
specific school. Lunacharsky himself, while flirting with Futurism and

15 Many examples of the work of the proletarian poets belonging to the Smithy
and other groups, and of their theoretical pronouncements, will be found in Kaun,
Soviet Poets and Poetry.

25

other advanced movements, advocated a reverent attitude toward the artistic heritage of the past, insisted on the necessity of preserving its monuments, which the Futurists and the Cosmists were anxious to destroy, and enjoined proletarian artists to learn from the old masters. He disapproved of a similar tendency manifested at first by the extreme wing of the *Proletkult* (although not by Bogdanov himself), but on the whole the latter also enjoyed his protection. In this he was at variance with the top leaders of Communism, for both Lenin and Trotsky looked with disfavor upon the attempts of Bogdanov and the *Proletkult* to assert their independence and to carry out an isolated cultural action.

For the time being, however, the leadership of the Communist party was beset with other and more urgent problems arising out of the Civil War and foreign intervention, and did not interfere with the *Proletkult,* which was allowed to proceed with its plans for building up proletarian culture. It was at the end of 1920, when the Civil War was over, that Lenin put his foot down, and a decree was promulgated placing the *Proletkult* under the direct control of the Commissariat of Education. Three years later an end was put to it, and "Bogdanovism" was denounced as a dangerous deviation from the Party line. But in summing up the achievements of Soviet literature during the first post-Revolutionary decade most Soviet critics admitted the beneficial role of the *Proletkult* in initiating workers and peasants into the artistic and cultural life, even though they continued to regard it on the whole as a failure. However, before the days of the *Proletkult* were over, other methods of fostering proletarian literature and art were proposed, and the whole subject of a specific class culture, and of its role in the new society, gave rise to a violent controversy which will be discussed in the next chapters.

7. *Demyan Bedny* (1883-1945)

NO history of Soviet literature can be complete without at least a brief mention of Demyan Bedny (pseudonym, meaning "Damian the Poor," of Efim Alexandrovich Pridvorov). A Bolshevik of old standing, a regular contributor to *Pravda* and other Bolshevik papers before the Revolution, he held during the first years of the Revolution the position of unofficial poet laureate of the new regime. His poetry is simple, even primitive, entirely "civic-minded," and devoid of all personal motifs. It is not so much poetry as rhymed journalism on topical subjects. Before the Revolution he excelled in political fables, a form that was particularly suited for dodging the vigilance of censorship. Many of his fables were frank, but skillful, imitations of the great Russian

fabulist Krylov. There is also in his poetry a strong influence of Nekrasov's civic verse. After the Revolution he wrote more topical fables, as
well as songs, ditties, and satirical poems.

A peasant himself by origin, he regarded the alliance between the
proletariat and the peasants as essential for the success of the Revolution, and much of what he wrote was meant for the peasant audience
and clothed in simple, easily accessible language. Esenin, in one of his
poems, refers, not without some contempt, to the popularity of Demyan
in the post-Revolutionary village. One Soviet critic described Bedny as
"the trumpeter" of the Revolution's battles and victories. His verses
breathe a violent, unquenchable hatred of the upper classes. There is
also in them a strong antireligious bias, and at the height of the Communist party's campaign against religion Bedny was one of its principal spokesmen and a regular contributor to *Bezbozhnik* (*The Godless One*). Regarded as the quintessence of proletarian "agit-poetry,"
Bedny's work was equally removed from Mayakovsky's and the Futurists', with their "decadent" tendency to innovations, and from the
Cosmists', with their "industrial romanticism." Taken as a whole, his
output is monotonous, repetitious, and crude. As propaganda poetry
it served its purpose well, and Bedny's official reputation stood very
high until 1936, when he was snubbed for his play *Bogatyri* (*Epic
Heroes*), to which reference will be made later. Although the war
against Germany gave him a chance to write more propaganda poetry,
he somehow never recaptured his erstwhile popularity.

II. Revolutionary Romanticism
1921–24

1. *From War Communism to the New Economic Policy*

THAT literature continued to exist, even in an embryonic form, during the terrible years of War Communism, was something of a miracle. In the country torn by Civil War, ravaged by hunger, suffering from lack of fuel, the intelligentsia—writers, artists, journalists— was hit perhaps more severely than any other single group. Victor Shklovsky has left a grim picture of the conditions prevailing in Petrograd in the winter of 1920, when "all was ruin and hopelessness," and "to live at all was a battle," when people "stood in a queue to get one degree of heat," or chafed their hands with ashes to cleanse themselves. The cold was even a greater scourge than the hunger:

> What did we use for heating? A few of the surviving bourgeoisie, having turned traders in saccharine and other imponderable stuff, burned wood. As for us others, we burned everything. I burned my furniture, my sculptor's stand, bookshelves and books, books beyond count or computation. If I had owned wooden arms or legs I should have burned them and found myself limbless in the spring.
>
> One of my friends burned nothing but books. His wife sat by the little smoky iron stove and stoked and stoked it with journal after journal. Elsewhere doors were burning and furniture from others people's dwellings. It was a festival of universal destruction by fire. . . . People slept in their overcoats and very nearly in their galoshes.
>
> Everyone gathered in the kitchen; in the abandoned rooms stalactites grew. People drew close to one another and in the half-empty town they squeezed together as tight as toys in a playbox. Priests in churches conducted the services in gloves with the surplices put on over their fur coats. Sick school-children froze to death. The Arctic Circle had become a reality and its line passed through the region of the Nevsky Avenue.[1]

[1] V. Shklovsky, "St. Petersburg in 1920," in *Bonfire: Stories out of Soviet Russia. An Anthology of Contemporary Russian Literature* (edited by S. Konovalov). This passage is taken from Shklovsky's *Khod konya* (*Knight's Move*).

After reading this realistic, matter-of-fact description of Shklovsky's, one can feel better the full force of Zamyatin's surrealistic vision of Petrograd and its "cave-dwellers" in "The Cave," one of his most effective stories and one of the best "documents" of this period:

> Glaciers, mammoths, wildernesses. Pitch-dark, black rocks, somehow reminding one of houses; in the rocks—caves. And one cannot tell who trumpets of a night along the stony path amid the rocks and, sniffing his way, drives the white snow dust before him. It may be the grey-trunked mammoth; it may be the wind; and it may be that the wind is only the icy roar of some super-mammothish mammoth. One thing is clear: it is winter. And one must clench one's teeth as tight as possible, to prevent them from chattering; and cut wood with a stone axe; and each night move one's fire from cave to cave, always deeper; and muffle oneself up in an always increasing number of shaggy hides.

The story is of a couple of such cave-dwellers over whose life presides an insatiable god—the iron stove:

> In this cave-bedroom of Petersburg, things were like in Noah's ark: clean and unclean creatures in ark-like promiscuity. Martyn Martynych's writing-desk; books; cakes of the stone-age looking like pottery; Skryabin, op. 74; a flat-iron; five potatoes lovingly washed white; nickelled bed-frames; an axe; a chest of drawers; a stack of wood. And in the middle of all this universe was its god: a short-legged, rusty-red, squatting, greedy cave-god: the iron stove.[2]

These horrors of everyday life reached their apogee in the winters of 1919–20 and 1920–21. The spring of 1921 brought with it some relief. The Civil War was practically over by November, 1920; sporadic hostilities still went on in the Far East, but the organized and centralized resistance to the new order was at an end. However, soon after this military victory, the Soviet government, under the growing pressure of economic necessities and faced with the specter of peasant discontent, had to beat a retreat on the home front: in February, 1921, Lenin promulgated his famous decree inaugurating the New Economic Policy, which came to be commonly known as the "NEP." This meant a partial restoration of a bourgeois economy, a loosening of the taxation screw as applied to the peasants, and a resumption of private trade; in other words, the end of War Communism.

This year inaugurated also a new period in Soviet literature. The main factors which determined the change were: the reappearance of

[2] E. Zamyatin, "The Cave" (translated by D. S. Mirsky), in *The Slavonic Review* (London), Vol. II, No. 4 (June, 1923).

private publishing enterprises;[3] the growth of book-printing and book-selling facilities; the resumption of cultural intercourse with the outside world; and the entry into literature of a number of new writers. Some of them had been fighting in the Red Army, and were now demobilized; others were civilians whom the conditions of War Communism had deprived of a chance of exercising their vocation.

By 1922 the literary scene had undergone a number of changes. Publishing enterprises grew like mushrooms. Many of them, it is true, were of an ephemeral nature. But there were some that flourished and gradually extended their activities even beyond the borders of the Soviet Union, organizing branches in Berlin where the postwar inflation proved highly propitious for this kind of activity, and where a number of Soviet writers (Gorky, Bely, Shklovsky) were living at the time. Many books by Soviet authors published during 1922–23 bear the double imprint "Moscow-Berlin" or "Petersburg-Berlin." Some publishing firms even published Soviet and *émigré* authors indiscriminately. At no other time was the intercourse so easy between Soviet writers, *émigré* writers, and "borderline" writers (that is, either those who, escaping to Berlin, lived there as Soviet citizens, but later chose not to return; or those who, while still officially *émigrés*, were contemplating a return to Russia). In Russia itself, several new magazines were launched. Privately sponsored—although in 1922 still subject to censorship and bearing its official imprimatur—they strike one today by the variety and freedom of the opinions expressed in them, and by their quick and ready response to cultural developments outside Russia. One of the most typical, and also one of the best, was *Literaturnye Zapiski* (*Literary Notes*), published by the *Dom literatorov* (*House of Writers*) in Petrograd. An institution organized earlier, chiefly for the purpose of relieving the material hardships of writers' life, it was the meeting-point of the old intelligentsia, mostly liberal and radical writers and journalists whom the suppression of the independent press had thrown out of work. Every number of this magazine contained a chronicle of literature abroad and reviews of foreign books, in original and in translation. *Émigré* literature was often discussed in a detached, impartial manner, and in one article the well-known pre-Revolutionary critic A. Gornfeld went so far as to compare it favorably with what was being produced in Russia. The literary policy of the new government came in for a share of outspoken criticism, and the general tone was one of dignified independence. The Futurists and other literary hangers-on

3 Not all private publishers closed down during 1918–20. But the State Publishing Company (*Gosizdat*) wielded a virtual monopoly, and writers who like Alexander Blok refused to work for it were placed under a handicap. See the lead article in *Literaturnye Zapiski* (*Literary Notes*) (*Petersburg*), No. 2 (June 23, 1922).

of the new regime were often attacked. This was another sign of the change that had set in; and although the Futurists, their rivals the Imaginists, and the Cosmists continued to be as vociferous as before—each group claiming to be the only one truly representative of revolutionary art—they no longer held the floor alone. Other forces came into play. With new facilities for publication of books, the predominance of the poets ended.[4] Prose writers appeared on the scene and soon captured the attention of the public. A list of the "most interesting" prose works published in 1921–22 contains over thirty titles.[5] Many of the authors whose works, both in prose and in verse, appeared during these first years of the NEP were newcomers to literature, but there were also among them older writers, most of whom were soon either to emigrate (Shmelyov, Zaytsev, Muratov, Georgy Ivanov) or to go silent (Sologub, Akhmatova, Kuzmin). Two books of Gumilyov's poems and a book of his stories appeared posthumously in 1922. There were also numerous ephemeral magazines and almanacs which printed both prose and verse. A "fat" monthly review—this indispensable feature of the Russian literary scene before the Revolution—was launched in 1921. Called *Krasnaya Nov* (*Red Virgin Soil*), it was edited by A. Voronsky, one of the most broad-minded of the Marxist critics. This review and its editor were to play a prominent part in Soviet literary life during its most flourishing period. Another important review to be founded soon, under the editorship of Vyacheslav Polonsky, was *Pechat i Revolyutsiya* (*Press and Revolution*).

2. *The Revolutionary Romantics*

THE period of Soviet literature between 1921 and 1924 is sometimes described as the period of Civil War literature. This is true in the sense that the Civil War—and, in general, the period of War Communism—became one of the main themes of literature during this period. For many young writers it was a great and harrowing experience which they sought to transmute creatively. More generally, one can say that from this moment on the Revolution became the principal theme of Soviet literature. The new prose writers desired, in the first place, to describe the Revolution, to put on record their experiences and the impressions gathered during those fantastic years. Their interest was centered on the elemental and romantic aspects of the Revolu-

---

[4] One critic said significantly at this time that "the death agony of poetry" had begun with the death of Blok and Gumilyov in the autumn of 1921. I. N. Rozanov, "Khudozhestvennaya literatura za dva goda" ("Imaginative Literature During the Two Years"), in *Literaturnye otkliki* (*Literary Echoes*) (Moscow, 1923), 72.

[5] *Ibid.*, 79.

tion, and the main trend of this period can be described as revolutionary romanticism. The Civil War; the partisan activities on the fringes of Russia, in the South and in the Far East; the terrible famine which befell Eastern Russia and the Volga region in 1921; violent conflicts between the old and the new as the Revolution ate deeper and deeper into the traditional mode of life; the gigantic reshuffle of the population, resulting in thrilling adventures—such were the staple themes of this early post-Revolutionary prose fiction. Its form, its manner, and its style were in harmony with the quick, staccato tempo of life. These young Soviet writers, bent on hurriedly recording their rich stock of experiences, cared little for long, elaborate, slow-moving novels in the old manner, or for large canvases. A short story, an anecdote—told in a hurry, brimful with incident, devoid of all psychological probing or detailed analysis—became the favorite form. Often these stories were written in a high-pitched emotional tone.

In the case of longer works, such as some of the "novels" of Pilnyak, Nikitin, and Vsevolod Ivanov, there was no unity of plot, the narrative being conducted simultaneously on several planes and constructed according to the laws of a musical theme with refrains and variations. From the formal point of view these newcomers to literature were greatly influenced by two prose writers of the age of Symbolism, Andrey Bely and Alexey Remizov. To Bely can be traced their tendency to rhythmical prose, with recurring leitmotifs; their broken, disjointed composition, with constant shifting and intersection of the narrative planes; and their feverish, strained, hyperbolical diction. Through Bely these writers go back to Gogol more than to any other of the older Russian writers. Remizov's influence, on the other hand, is felt in their predilection for pure anecdote, for ornamental speech, for *skaz*—that is, an exact rendering of the peculiarities, local and individual, of the spoken language—and for folklore stylizations. Through Remizov these young prose writers looked back to Leskov, the great nineteenth-century master of *skaz*. Thus, somewhat paradoxically, Gogol and Leskov became the most powerful and vital factors of influence in the shaping of post-Revolutionary Russian literature.

The grim experience of the Civil War, when the price of human life had slumped so visibly, taught writers to face with fearless indifference the most horrible sights and to speak with cool detachment of gruesome and terrible things. Stark realism, bordering on naturalism, and outspoken cynicism characterize many of the works of this period. But their realism is often frankly fantastic. So fantastic, so gruesomely unreal had life become in those days, such unexpected adventures did it hold in store, that the border line between the real and the unreal seemed to be obliterated. In setting out to be matter-of-fact and realistic, these poets of the Revolution often achieved their most fantastic effects: life had indeed become "stranger than fiction."

It was only gradually that out of this welter of what came to be described as "dynamic" or "ornamental" prose there emerged, toward 1924, definite literary genres—first, the short, pointed *nouvelles* of Babel, and then later the novel.

3. *Boris Pilnyak*

THE dominant figure in Soviet literature, during the years 1921–23, was Boris Pilnyak (pseudonym of Boris Andreyevich Wogau). Born in 1894 at Mozhaysk, he was the son of a veterinary surgeon and was descended, on his father's side, from the Volga-German colonists. His first story appeared in print when he was only seventeen, but his real literary debut was a short story published in 1915 in the magazine *Russkaya Mysl*. This story, called "Tselaya Zhizn" ("A Whole Life"), had no human characters in it: it was about an owl couple and their life in the woods. It revealed one of the characteristics which later came very much to the fore in Pilnyak's work: his interest in biological, and even animal, manifestations of life. Several stories of Pilnyak's were published in various reviews and magazines between 1917 and 1921. But it was the publication, in 1922, of his "novel" *Goly God* (*The Bare Year*) that brought Pilnyak fame, placed him at the head of a whole school, or movement, in Soviet literature, and made Soviet critics speak of "Pilnyakism." Until the early thirties Soviet critics and historians of literature gave Pilnyak the credit for being the first young writer who chose the Revolution and its impact on Russian life as his main subject.

A future student of Pilnyak who undertakes to write a monograph about him will have to face great difficulties. Not only is Pilnyak an intrinsically difficult, complex, and chaotic writer, but there is also the additional, purely external, difficulty of disentangling the intricate chronology and interrelation of Pilnyak's writings. Many of his stories were published under different titles in different collections and combinations, while many others were subsequently incorporated bodily into his "novels." He also made a considerable revision of earlier versions of his stories for the uniform edition of his *Collected Works*, which began to appear in 1929 and was then planned for eight volumes.

The Bare Year is, in a way, the most typical of Pilnyak's works. Although it set the pattern for his later novels, it is no novel in the traditional acceptance of the word, but a loose collection of stories, or rather episodes, of which many were actually included as complete, separate stories in the volume *Bylyo* (*The Bygones*). This incompleteness, this lack of any unifying plot, is one of Pilnyak's primary characteristics, both in his short stories and in his longer works which he arbitrarily designates as "novels": *Mashiny i volki* (*Machines and Wolves*), *Tretya stolitsa* (*The Third Metropolis*), *Chertopolokh* (*Thistles*), and *Rossiya v polyote* (*Russia in Flight*). As a writer Pilnyak is a direct descendant of Andrey Bely and Alexey Remizov, though other, and often contradictory, literary influences, both formal and ideological, are readily discernible in his work: above all, those of Gogol, Dostoyevsky, Turgenev, Leskov, Chekhov, Bunin, and Zamyatin. The influence of Bely and Remizov on Pilnyak is very strong, and it is largely through Pilnyak that these modern Russian prose writers exercised such a powerful sway over early post-Revolutionary literature. From Bely comes Pilnyak's predilection for "musical," rhythmical, contrapuntal prose, for persistent repetition of verbal refrains (in *The Bare Year* whole pages recur verbatim in different parts of the book); for lyrical and historico-philosophical digressions; for rhetorical questions and exclamations; as well as for the highly involved syntax with a complex agglomeration of parenthetical clauses, of broken, unfinished sentences full of hints and allusions. It was Bely who cultivated this difficult manner, requiring a creative effort on the part of the reader; and Pilnyak is one of those writers whose subtle allusive method, abounding in hidden clues and "signs," usually necessitates a second reading for the complete understanding of much that at first reading appears obscure or even unintelligible. Back to Bely goes also the involved chronology in Pilnyak's novels, the constant shifting and interlocking of temporal planes. Another point which Pilnyak has in common with Bely is his interest in the problem of Russia's historical destinies—of the East and West in Russian history and psychological make-up. Such a story of Pilnyak's as "Sankt-Pieter-Burgh" is really a variation on the theme of Bely's famous novel *Petersburg,* while in *The Bare Year* there are indubitable echoes both of *Petersburg* and of *The Silver Dove.*

From Remizov, on the other hand, comes Pilnyak's use of the *skaz* manner, which consists in substituting for the author's narrative the individual manner and intonation of his fictitious characters. With Pilnyak, however, this *skaz* manner is never simple and straightforward: not content with one fictitious narrator and a faithful rendering of the peculiarities of his speech, Pilnyak continually keeps changing his manner and style and adapting it to various characters. To Remizov can also be traced Pilnyak's attraction for the old, pre-Petrine Russia and his use of old language and quotations from old documents. Quotations are one of Pilnyak's favorite devices: his narrative is interspersed with them, and he draws them from both old and modern sources, often without any acknowledgement. He likes also to introduce fictitious quotations from the writings of his own characters (the work on Russia and the Revolution, written in imitation of the Old Russian Chronicles, by Archbishop Sylvester in *The Bare Year;* the "statistical" treatise about the Revolution of Ivan Alexandrovich Nepomnyashchy, the "hero" of *Machines and Wolves,* for example). There is in Pilnyak something of the old Russian scribe or of the compilers of miscellaneous collections of stories and aphorisms known in Byzantine literature as the *Bees*: Pilnyak himself said that he was fond of "gathering trifles like honey." But some of his stories are so overweighted with such trifles that their balance is completely upset. In some, too, he lets his predilection for outlandish, obsolete, or dialect words run away with him: this is particularly true of his stories about Peter the Great.

To tell the story of *The Bare Year* is a hopeless task: it is fragmentary and disjointed, without a unified plot or a central character. Its separate parts have no organic connection, and the novel can be easily broken back into the separate stories which went into its making. Its subject is the early phase of the Revolution (1918–19) and its impact on Russian life, but apropos of it Pilnyak ventures in his digressions into a great variety of subjects. There is in it a little of everything—a picture of the decay and fall of the house of the Ordynins, an old degenerating princely family; a description of the life of an anarchist commune on one of the Ordynin estates; a terrifying, highly impressionistic vision of an overcrowded goods-train in which starving people from the north of Russia travel southeast in search of bread; an equally impressionistic picture of true Bolsheviks—"leathern men in leather jackets"—feverishly rebuilding one of the plants in northeastern Russia laid waste by the Civil War; and so on, and so on. There is a multitude of characters who are purely episodic: often the author does not even bother to introduce them to the reader and they flit in and out of Pilnyak's pages without the reader's being able to identify them. This is not to say, however, that beneath this chaos there is no central, unifying idea. Pilnyak is never content, as some of his contemporaries and followers were, with merely putting on record his experiences and impressions. He always philosophises about them, for he has, or thinks he has, his own "philosophy" of the Russian Revolution. This philosophy may appear confused, contradictory, shallow, and unoriginal, but it gives unity and meaning to Pilnyak's chaotic productions.

Orthodox Soviet critics described Pilnyak's attitude toward the Revolution as purely aesthetic and emotional. That Pilnyak is an emotional writer, that his vision of the Revolution is always highly emotionalized and subjective, there can be no doubt. But his emotionalism is of a special kind, which distinguishes him from some of his closest followers in Soviet literature and allies him to Andrey Bely: it is intellectual emotionalism. One orthodox Communist critic characterized

Pilnyak's attitude to the Revolution as "a synthesis of Slavophilism and of *'kulak'* neo-Anarchism and neo-Populism."[6] Pilnyak had no hesitation in "accepting" the Revolution. But he accepted it much as did Blok, Bely, and Esenin—as a salutary destructive movement, as a blizzard which was to sweep away the rotten fabric of the old bourgeois world, as that "Russian revolt, senseless and ruthless"—to use the famous words of Pushkin—the roots of which are to be sought in such popular movements as the revolts of Razin in the seventeenth century and of Pugachov in the eighteenth. References to both are constant in Pilnyak's stories. Equally persistent is the theme of Russia's dual face. In *The Bare Year,* just as in the stories about Peter and about Petersburg, one of the recurrent symbolical motifs is the symbol of *Kitay-Gorod* (Chinatown) in Moscow and other Russian cities, and the contrast between its truly Russian nocturnal life and its diurnal aspects dominated by Europeanized individuals in bowler hats. Echoing the Slavophiles and Merezhkovsky, Pilnyak speaks also of Peter the Great as antichrist who enticed Russia away to Petersburg—the Revolution made her return to Moscow, her veritable cradle, possible.

Judged by absolute standards, the work of Pilnyak has much in it that is unsatisfactory: he has little sense of form; his confused composition is still further obscured by his shallow "philosophy of history" to which everything in the narrative is subordinated; his efforts at psychological analysis, especially in the erotic genre, smack of a cheap imitation of Dostoyevsky; much of his art is of bookish derivation and has a secondhand flavor, certain ready-made patterns being merely cut to post-Revolutionary measure;[7] and his monotonous, shrill diction soon palls on the reader. But, judged in the general context of Soviet literature, there are in Pilnyak many valuable elements: his keen sense of the Russian language and of words in general; his interest in ideas, whatever may be their intrinsic worth; his deep-seated humanism and sympathy with the suffering, which goes back to the best traditions of Russian literature. His courage and independence were also conspicuous among his contemporaries. Whatever his later concessions to the demands of those in authority, and his efforts to adjust himself to the new conditions, he was obviously sincere in welcoming the Revolution at first. As he put it himself, he saw the artist's "bitter duty" in being honest with himself and with Russia. Almost from the outset this attempt at being honest involved him in troubles with the powers that

6 Gorbachov, *Contemporary Russian Literature,* 142.

7 Several Soviet critics have pointed out the close parallels between Pilnyak's picture of the decaying Ordynin family in *The Bare Year* and the Karamazovs of Dostoyevsky on the one hand, and the Golovlyovs of Saltykov-Shchedrin on the other; there is also much that goes back to Bunin, especially to that great masterpiece, *Sukhodol.*

be. In the twenties he incurred displeasure by his story "Povest o nepogashennoy lune" ("The Tale of the Unextinguished Moon," 1927), the subject of which was the death, on the operating table, of one of the outstanding Communist leaders in the Civil War, Frunze. Pilnyak's later scrapes and his final undoing will be told in due place.

4. *Zamyatin* (1884-1937)

ANOTHER writer whose influence during this period was of paramount importance was Evgeny Ivanovich Zamyatin. Although his literary career had begun long before the Revolution, it is his work published between 1922 and 1928 that will secure him a place in the history of Russian literature.

Born in Central Russia in the town of Lebedyan, Zamyatin studied in the Department of Naval Construction at the Polytechnic Institute in St. Petersburg and became a naval engineer by profession. As a student he belonged to the Social-Democratic party and took an active part in political activities. In an autobiographical note, published in 1928, he wrote: "I was then a Bolshevik (now I am not)."

Zamyatin's first story appeared in print in 1908, but he did not take seriously to writing until 1911 when his "Uezdnoye" ("A Tale of Provincial Life") was published: a grotesquely realistic picture of life, it was strongly influenced by Gogol and Remizov. His next story, "Na kulichkakh" ("At the Back of Beyond," 1914), led to judicial proceedings against him, and for several years he published nothing. In 1916 he was sent to England to supervise the construction of ice-breakers for the Russian government. In two stories, written and published after his return to Russia in 1917—"Ostrovityane" ("The Islanders") and "Lovets chelovekov" ("The Fisher of Men")—the cant and smugness of English life were satirized in terms of an amusing grotesque.

During the years of War Communism and the first years of the NEP, Zamyatin played an important part in the literary life of Petrograd. His influence on most of the young writers was decisive. His own output was rather small, but it included some of his best stories: "Peshchera" ("The Cave"), "Mamay," and "Sever" ("The North"), as well as his short satirical tales, *Skazki dlya vzroslykh detey* (*Fairy Tales for Grownup Children*, 1922), reminiscent of Saltykov-Shchedrin's satires. He also began writing for the theater. *Ogni sv. Dominika* (*The Fires of St. Dominic*, 1923) satirized the Soviet Cheka (Extraordinary Commission for Fighting Counterrevolution, the predecessor of the Ogpu) in the form of a historical play, with the action set in Spain during the Inquisition. *Obshchestvo pochotnykh zvonarey* (*The Society of Honorary Bell Ringers*, 1926) was a dramatic variation of "The Islanders," while

Blokha (*The Flea*, 1925) dramatized Leskov's famous story "Levsha" ("The Lefthanded Man"); the latter, done with great farcical verve in the style of the Italian *commedia dell'arte*, enjoyed for many years a great success on the Soviet stage.

Although Zamyatin continued some of the traditions of Russian nineteenth-century literature—part of his work goes back to Gogol and Leskov—he was essentially an innovator. He described himself as a neo-Realist and in an interview he once gave to a French journalist made the following observations on his art:

> What is after all realism? If you examine your hand through a microscope you will see a grotesque picture: trees, ravines, rocks— instead of hairs, pores, grains, and dust. . . . To my mind this is a more genuine realism than the primitive one. To follow up the comparison: while neo-Realism uses a microscope to look at the world, Symbolism used a telescope, and pre-Revolutionary Realism, an ordinary looking glass. This naturally conditions the whole imagery, the entire formal structure.

Zamyatin's method of microscopic realism results in a novel, grotesque vision, akin to surrealism. His short stories, always very carefully constructed, revolve around a complex of interconnected metaphorical images, representing a concentric outgrowth of a central image, of a "mother metaphor," as Mirsky aptly called it ("The Cave" is a very good example of the effective use of this method). His mathematical interests are reflected in his predilection for geometrical images. Many of his characters appear to be drawn by a caricaturist: like Gogol's, they are presented outwardly, with some particular feature grotesquely emphasized. The stories are deliberately pruned of all psychological apparatus. But it would be wrong to think, as some critics have suggested, that there is nothing in Zamyatin beyond his verbal mastery, his love of ornamentalism, and his delight in construction. In stories like "The Cave" and "Mamay" the tragic atmosphere of the years of War Communism is conveyed very effectively, and they only gain from being told with cold and fastidious detachment.

Zamyatin also advocated the method of broken narrative, conducted simultaneously on several parallel planes. He applied it most consistently in his most "surrealistic" story, "Rasskaz o samom glavnom" ("A Story About That Which Matters Most"), a complex multiplanar vision of the Revolution, with an emphasis on its futility. It was denounced by Communist critics as "antirevolutionary" and, together with his novel *We* and his *Nechestivye rasskazy* (*Impious Tales*), contributed most to his reputation of an "inside *émigré*."

In *Navodnenie* (*The Flood*, 1926), a tense story of love, jealousy, and murder, Zamyatin proved his ability to write a good straightforward story with a human interest, free from any satirical intent.

As a craftsman, as a short-story writer, Zamyatin had a great influence on a number of young Soviet writers: Slonimsky, Nikitin, Olesha, Vsevolod Ivanov, and some others were indebted to his "neorealistic" experiments. Of Olesha, who was not one of his direct "pupils," it is perhaps even more true than of the others who sat at his feet in the revolutionary Petrograd of the early twenties.

By nature Zamyatin was a heretic, a nonconformist, a born rebel against the established order of things. Quite early he felt that, under Communism, Russia was not likely to produce a real literature, for

> real literature can exist only where it is produced by madmen, hermits, heretics, dreamers, rebels, and sceptics, and not by painstaking and well-intentioned officials.

Long before Stalin consolidated his omnipotent totalitarian police-state Zamyatin saw the Revolution in Russia heading toward conservatism and stagnation. In 1923 he wrote:

> Let the flame cool down tomorrow or the day after tomorrow. . . . But someone must see this today already, and heretically speak today of tomorrow. Heretics are the only (bitter) medicine against the entropy of human thought."[8]

Earlier he had put the same idea in the mouth of one of his characters in *My (We)*:

> There are two forces in the world: entropy and energy. One means blissful repose, happy equilibrium; the other, the overthrow of equilibrium, painfully infinite movement.

The novel *We* is undoubtedly Zamyatin's most interesting and important work, if not necessarily his best. It is also unique in that, to this day, there has been no complete printed version of it in Russian, though it has been translated into French, English, and Czech. It was written in 1920,[9] and a year later Zamyatin sent a copy of the manuscript to his agent abroad. The book was subsequently published in France (1924), in the United States (1925), and in Czechoslovakia (1927?). By 1924 it became clear to the author that its publication in Russia would

[8] E. Zamyatin, "O literature, revolyutsii, entropii i prochem" ("On Literature, Revolution, Entropy, and Other Things"), in *Pisateli ob iskusstve i o sebe. Sbornik statey No. 1 (Writers About Art and About Themselves: Collection of Essays No. 1)*, 68. The second volume of this collection was never published, it appears.

[9] My authority for this date is Zamyatin's letter printed in *Literaturnaya gazeta (Literary Gazette)* of October 7, 1929. Its full English text will be found in Max Eastman's *Artists in Uniform. A Study of Literature and Bureaucratism*, 87–91.

not be allowed. But its existence could not be concealed: Zamyatin himself had read it at a meeting of the Association of Soviet Writers, and the essay referred to above (see note 8 on page 38) had some lines from it as a motto. Soviet critics were therefore forced to speak of it, and there are references to it in the articles on Zamyatin in the *Great Soviet Encyclopaedia* and in the *Literary Encyclopaedia*. The latter described the novel as "a base libel on Socialist future" and spoke of Zamyatin's "counterrevolutionary tendencies":

> He is in favor of the Revolution but of an . . . infinite revolution. . . . He does not believe in a social revolution . . . because it spells the doom of his class . . . . Zamyatin's theories are merely a disguise for a very matter-of-fact and quite understandable pining of the bourgeoisie after the economic well-being which it has forfeited, and for its hatred of those who have deprived it of that well-being.

The novel is not, on the face of it, concerned with present-day Russia or the Soviet regime as such. It is a satirical fantasy set in the twenty-sixth century. One can see in it the influence of H. G. Wells's scientific romances (in 1922 Zamyatin published a short, sympathetic study of H. G. Wells) and perhaps of Anatole France. It bears a strikingly close resemblance to Aldous Huxley's *Brave New World,* which it preceded by twelve years (the English translation of Zamyatin's novel was published seven years before the appearance of Huxley's). The resemblance is particularly noticeable in some of the minor details, but there is also a similarity of general idea and of the over-all presentation of the standardized state of the future. There are differences, too, due above all to Zamyatin's strong leanings to primitivism and Huxley's rationalist tradition.

In *We* the reader is transported into the twenty-sixth century, into a perfect, modern, standardized state which has no name but is known simply as "The Single State." Its citizens have no names either, but are known by their letters and numbers, consonants denoting males and vowels, females. In this respect Zamyatin was even more logically abstract than Huxley: the latter could not withstand the temptation of showing to advantage his ingenuity and wit in the choice of names for his characters. In general, there is more local description and topical humor in Huxley's novel, while Zamyatin deliberately sticks to universal abstractions. All the citizens of Zamyatin's state wear identical blue-grey uniforms—the novel was written before the appearance of Mussolini's Blackshirts—and badges with their numbers. They are ruled over by the Benefactor (Huxley's World-Controller), and their life is scientifically regulated down to the minutest details. Everything is mechanized and standardized in the Single State, though not quite to the same extent as in Huxley's Utopia: Zamyatin's men of the future have not yet learned to procreate new human beings by means of incubation. But in Zamyatin's state, love is "dehumanized" too, and though promiscuity is the general underlying principle, it is controlled and "distributed," so to speak: special pink counterfoil tickets are issued for its use, which is confined to certain fixed hours, but allows some latitude in the choice of partners. Every "number" of the Single State has also at his or her disposal a few "personal" hours a day, during which he or she is off duty. But even then the "numbers" are not free to do as they like, for the negation of freedom is the very foundation of the Single State:

> Freedom and crime are as closely bound up as, let us say, the motion of an airplane and its speed . . . . If man's freedom is nil, he commits no crimes. So much stands to reason—[10]

thus runs one of the principles of the Single State.

Freedom and happiness are regarded as incompatible, and one must choose between them:

> Happiness without freedom, or freedom without happiness—there is no alternative. Those fools [the men of old] chose freedom and naturally for centuries they yearned for chains. Therein lay human misery: they yearned for chains.

The "personal hour" of the citizens of the Single State is accordingly subordinated to the same mathematically precise rules as the rest of their lives:

> The personal hour which followed lunch [all food in the Single State is, incidentally, chemical—a synthetic product of oil] became in practice an hour of supplementary walk. As usual, the Music Factory performed, through all its loudspeakers, the anthem of the Single State. The numbers, hundreds of thousands of numbers, in bluish unifs, golden badge on their dresses showing the number of each, walked in regular ranks, four by four.

To look after the numbers' morals and behavior—mathematical morals and mathematical behavior though they be—and to save them from all "deviations," there are special "guardians" whose chief task is to spy upon the numbers and who are assisted in this by the voluntary

[10] When I first wrote my book I could not procure the American edition of *We* and therefore translated the quotations from the French version. Since I do not think highly of the American version I let these retranslations stand, with some slight improvements. I have since been able to read the original Russian version, kindly lent to me by Mme Zamyatin, but I could not use it at the time for checking my quotations.

zeal of the well-intentioned numbers. To the law-abiding citizens of the Single State these guardians appear as their guardian angels, and the character in whose name the novel is written remarks with pointed, though unconscious, irony:

> It is extraordinary to discover the number of things of which the Ancients [that is, men of the present era] dreamed and which we have turned into reality.

In the Bureau of Guardians Zamyatin undoubtedly anticipated the evolution of the Cheka (which did not provide him then with an actual example of such thoroughness and efficiency) into the Ogpu and its successors, and the parallel development of the Gestapo in the Nazi state.

The narrator of Zamyatin's novel is one of the chief mathematicians of the Single State—the most privileged category of its citizens—No. D-503, who is completing the construction of a new giant interplanetary flying machine—the *Integral*—which will enable the Single State to establish communications with other planets and win them over to its way of life. He writes "Notes," as he calls them, for the benefit of the inhabitants of those other planets. But as he writes them they gradually become something quite different from what he intended them to be, and we get an insight into a complex psychological change which he undergoes. To put it briefly, he reverts to the old human psychology, to individual consciousness. He discovers that he possesses a soul, something that is regarded in the Single State as an incurable disease: "numbers" are supposed to have no souls and no individual consciousness. "No offense is so heinous as unorthodoxy of behavior"—runs one of the guiding principles of the Single State. Soon he is led to discover that he is no exception—that there are other cases like himself.

The psychological transformation of D-503 is a result of his chance meeting with a woman—No. I-330—who fascinates him and with whom he soon falls in love in the way one is not supposed to fall in love in the Single State (until then D-503 had a normal pink-ticket affair with another woman, O-90). She comes to exercise a strange influence on him; he obeys her slightest and queerest whims, even though they offend his sense of duty as one of the numbers of the Single State. She takes him to the "Ancient House," which is preserved on the outskirts of the State as a historical monument, an illustration of the way the Ancients used to live before the introduction of modern transparent glass houses where everything, with the sole exception of the sex act, is performed in everybody's sight (during the "sexual hour" the blinds are drawn).

In the meantime the process of "humanization," or individualization, of D-503 continues. He is now madly in love with I-330 and has to admit that "all this crazy stuff about love and jealously was not confined to the idiotic books of old." He says of himself: "I no longer lived in our sensible world, but in the ancient morbid world, the world of the square root of minus one." He breaks with O-90 after getting her with child at her own request, for she also seems to have gone off the track and loves him in a way which is not regarded as normal, or approved, in the Single State. "Having a soul" turns out to be an infectious disease.

Then something quite unexpected happens, to the utter dismay and confusion of all law-abiding "numbers." On the so-called "Day of Unanimity," when all the numbers of the Single State are gathered in a huge auditorium to re-elect their Benefactor (the re-election is taken for granted: he has been unanimously re-elected thirty-nine times), some people, with I-330 at their head, dare raise their voice against him. There is a scuffle, "I" is wounded but "D" manages to rescue her and escape. She takes him through the Ancient House to the other side of the wall which circumscribes the boundaries of the Single State (the size and the location of the Single State is a point which Zamyatin leaves vague: one may imagine it as something quite small or as practically coincident with the whole earth). Beyond this wall no number is supposed to penetrate; nor do they know what is on the other side of it. Actually there we find nature untouched by the technical progress of civilization, a dwelling-place of primitive, hairy men. It is the counterpart of Huxley's "Savage Reservation." With these men I-330 and her accomplices, the other "revolutionaries," propose to launch a revolution in the Single State. They all welcome the arrival of D-503, for they plan to make use of his *Integral* for their own ends. There are no very definite ideas behind the revolutionary action of I-330 and her friends, except a primitive, instinctive revolt against the standardized, planned life, in the name of freedom and of change and of newness.

When "D," bewildered by the sight of naked men who live in natural and not mathematical surroundings, asks "I" what it all means, her answer is: "It is the half we have lost," and she adds: "You must learn to tremble with fright, with joy, with wrath and fury, with cold, you must worship fire." But his love for this strange and fascinating woman clashes with his sense of duty and with the deeply absorbed doctrines of the Single State. A curious dialogue takes place between them:

> *He*: This is mad. This doesn't hold water. You don't realize that what you are preparing is a revolution.
>
> *She*: Yes, it is a revolution. Why doesn't it hold water?
>
> *He*: Because *our* revolution was the last, there can be no more revolutions. Everybody knows that.

She: There is no such thing as the last revolution: the number of revolutions is infinite.

This idea of "infinite revolutions," in which the Communist critics saw an echo of Trotsky's conception of "permanent revolution," was apparently very dear to Zamyatin. Its political implications naturally alarmed the Soviet censors, who banned the book.

In the last part of the book the tempo is accelerated almost to the point of incoherence. The day before the proposed flight of the *Integral*, a proclamation is published in the official paper of the Single State, informing all the numbers that the real cause of all recent troubles has been discovered:

> You are ill. Your illness is imagination. This is the last obstacle on the road to happiness. Rejoice, for it has been overcome. The road now lies free. The latest progress made by National Science consists in the discovery of the center of imagination. A triple application of X rays to that center will cure you for ever. You are perfect, you are like unto machines. The road to 100 per cent happiness is open. Hasten ye, young and old.

The proclamation invites every number to undergo the "Great Operation" which will deprive them of imagination, the source of all evil. D-503 sees at first a salvation in this, a way out of his inner conflict. He almost decides to undergo the operation, but changes his mind on realizing that the choice lies between the happiness promised in the proclamation and "I." The trial flight of the *Integral* takes place, but the plot is thwarted—a woman, the caretaker of "D's" house, who is also in love with him, reports the matter to the guardians after prying into his manuscript notes. But she does so without disclosing his own part in the plot. The Single State scores a victory over the revolutionaries. All law-abiding numbers, including "D," who is not suspected, are subjected to the Great Operation: their imagination is extirpated. "I" and the other active revolutionaries are put to torture according to the improved Single State method—they are first placed under the "Pneumatic Bell" and then sent to the "Machine of the Benefactor," a modern improved guillotine. Speaking as a good citizen of the Single State, D-503 thus defends the Pneumatic Bell against the slander of the enemies:

> There were fools who compared it to the old-time Inquisition. But this is just as absurd as to put on the same level a surgeon performing the operation of tracheotomy and a highwayman. Both may be using the same knife to perform the same operation—they cut the throat. Yet one is a benefactor, the other a criminal. One is marked with the "plus" sign, the other, with the "minus."

There is in Zamyatin's novel a prophetic note which distinguishes it from George Orwell's vision in *Nineteen Eighty-Four*: writing in 1948, Orwell had before him all the essential elements of his "Utopia," and one wonders even whether in choosing the date for his title he did not simply play a joke on his readers by merely reversing the last two figures—whether he had in mind not the conditions mankind was heading for but those actually prevailing in a large part of Europe in 1948; this would explain his seemingly arbitrary date. Zamyatin in 1920 needed much greater imagination for his accurate portrayal of the totalitarian state—some of his details anticipate the future with striking fidelity.

Less witty and less scientifically elaborate than *Brave New World*, Zamyatin's novel is more effective as a prophecy of things to come: its very bareness enhances its deadly seriousness.

The story of the campaign against Zamyatin, which led to his subsequent emigration, will be told in Chapter IV.

5. *The Serapion Brothers*

THE contrast between the new Stone Age, so strikingly depicted in Zamyatin's "The Cave," and the conditions created by the New Economic Policy was great. The climate of the NEP proved propitious to a new florescence of a more or less independent literature. For young writers this new flowering of literature was a novel and exhilarating experience. In the history of post-Revolutionary Russian literature an important place belongs to a group of young authors who called themselves "the Serapion Brothers." Their "Brotherhood" was not a literary school, held together by any real or fictitious tenets. What united them was their youth, their zest for life, their eager interest in literature, and their firm belief in the autonomy of art and in the freedom of the writer. They were brought together more or less accidentally, partly topographically, so to speak—through the *Dom iskusstv* (House of Arts), which Gorky set up to counterbalance the influence of the "bourgeois" House of Writers. The House of Arts was situated in the former Eliseyev mansion at the corner of Nevsky Avenue and the Moyka. Fedin in his memoirs says that in the House of Arts "everything was richer, and some things even more distinguished, than in the House of Writers." While the latter considered itself independent, the former was, through Gorky, connected with the Commissariat of Education. According to Fedin, the inhabitants of the two Houses differed also politically: in the House of Arts political views were either foolish or naïve; in the House of Writers survived the old liberal tradition. Much later, Olga Forsh described the House of Arts as "a mad ship."

Gorky and Zamyatin also helped to bring the Serapions together. Several of them were Zamyatin's pupils in his House of Arts literary studio. They looked upon Zamyatin as their master and elder brother, and learned from him to use the tools of their craft. Their debt to him is incalculable, even though today they cannot mention his name. All but one of them (Luntz) are still alive, and four still hold a prominent place in Soviet literature—they are Fedin, Kaverin, Vsevolod Ivanov, and Tikhonov. The others were Zoshchenko, Nikitin, Shklovsky, Slonimsky, Luntz, Gruzdyov, Pozner, and Elizaveta Polonskaya (the only woman among the twelve "brothers").[11] All were quite young: at the time when the Brotherhood came into being, in February of 1921, the two eldest, Fedin and Shklovsky, were twenty-six and twenty-five respectively; the majority were in their early twenties, and three (Luntz, Kaverin, and Pozner) were still in their teens. Most of them were short-story writers; one (Luntz) specialized in drama, but also wrote stories; three were poets (Tikhonov, Polonskaya, and Pozner); and two, literary critics (Shklovsky and Gruzdyov).

They took their name from the "Hermit Serapion," a character in one of E. T. A. Hoffmann's tales, and the significance of this name was disclosed in their literary manifesto and in some of their writings which made a great stir at the time.

In 1922 they published their first *Almanac*, a slender volume printed on wretched paper, which included stories by Zoshchenko, Luntz, Vsevolod Ivanov, Kaverin, Slonimsky, Nikitin, and Fedin. The *Almanac* attracted considerable attention, not because of the outstanding intrinsic value of its contents (though the talent of these young writers was immediately recognized by most critics), but simply because here were several young gifted writers, practically newcomers to literature, coming out as a group and attempting to revive Russian prose fiction. It was their prose fiction which attracted particular attention (of poetry there was more than enough in those years), and one of the critics greeted the appearance of the *Almanac* as heralding the rise of Soviet prose literature. Still, the *Almanac* in itself was hardly an event, and, unlike many of their predecessors, the Serapions did not preface it with any high-sounding declarations. It was only when attention had already

[11] The number of twelve is given by Vladimir Pozner in his *Panorama de la littérature russe contemporaine*. Fedin in his book on Gorky speaks of ten Serapions, excluding Shklovsky and Pozner. The latter he does not mention, while of Shklovsky he says that he "was, indeed, the eleventh, if not the first, Serapion—by the passion he brought into our life, by the wittiness of the questions he threw into our debates." *Gorky sredi nas* (*Gorky in Our Midst*), 115. Pozner's book contains a lively description of the atmosphere in which the Serapions foregathered, which is quoted in William Edgerton's valuable article "The Serapion Brothers: An Early Soviet Controversy," in *The American Slavic and East European Review*, Vol. VIII, No. 1 (February, 1949), 48–49.

been attracted to them that they came out with their literary credo. It appeared in the form of an article by one of the youngest of them, Lev Luntz, and was entitled "Why We Are the Serapion Brothers." It was published, together with their rather unusual, lively, and spirited biographical sketches, as a special supplement to *Literary Notes,* the publication of the House of Writers.[12]

Luntz's article was a courageous declaration of the essential freedom and independence of art: he began by protesting against all rules and regulations which signify coercion and boredom, and explained the meaning of the group's name:

> We have named ourselves the Serapion Brothers because we do not want coercion and boredom; we do not want everyone to write alike, even in imitation of Hoffmann . . . . We proclaim no new slogans, we publish no manifestoes or programs. But for us the old truth has a great practical meaning which has been misunderstood or forgotten, especially among us in Russia. We consider that the Russian literature of our day is amazingly sedate, stuffy and monotonous. We are authorized to write tales, novels, and tedious dramas in either the old or the new style—but by all means on contemporary themes. The novel of adventure is a pernicious phenomenon; classical or romantic tragedies are archaisms or conventions; and the dime novel is immoral. Therefore Alexander Dumas Senior is trash, and Hoffmann and Stevenson are children's writers.
>
> But we consider that our gifted patron, creator of the unbelievable and the improbable, is equal to Tolstoy or Balzac; that Stevenson, the author of pirate stories, is a great writer; and that Dumas is a classic, like Dostoyevsky.
>
> This does not mean that we acknowledge only Hoffmann, or only Stevenson. Almost all of us Brothers are writers of mores [*bytoviki*]. But we know that other things too are possible. A work may reflect the epoch, but it need not do so, and is none the worse for it. Now here is Vsevolod Ivanov, a confirmed realist, describing the revolutionary, oppressive, bloody countryside, who recognizes Kaverin, the author of foolish romantic short stories. And my ultraromantic tragedy lives in harmony with the noble, old-fashioned lyricism of Fedin. For we demand only one thing: that a work should be organic, real, should live its own life. *Its own life.* Not be a copy of nature, but live on a par with nature.

[12] "Serapionovy bratya o sebe" ("The Serapion Brothers about Themselves"), in *Literaturnye zapiski,* No. 3 (August 1, 1922), 25–31. Unable to procure this issue of the magazine, I quote here and below from Edgerton's article, "The Serapion Brothers," with a few changes in translation that seemed advisable to me.

The crux of the "manifesto" was in its proclamation of the writer's freedom from all regimentation and even from his age ("a work may reflect the epoch but need not do so") and the assertion of the organic and autonomous nature of a work of art. The manifesto contained even more daring statements, such as the following:

We have gathered together in days of powerful and revolutionary political tension. "Whoever is not with us is against us," we have been told from the right and from the left.—"Whom are you with, Serapion Brothers? With the Communists or against the Communists? For the Revolution or against the Revolution?"

Whom are we with, the Serapion Brothers?

We are with the Hermit Serapion.

That means—with nobody? That means—morass? Aestheticizing intelligentsia? Without ideology, without convictions? Standing aloof?

No. Each of us has his ideology, his political convictions; each paints his own hut to suit himself. Thus in life, and thus in our stories, tales and dramas. We all together, we the Brotherhood, demand only one thing: that the tone be not false. That we may believe in the work whatever its color.

And further:

Too long and painfully has the public welfare directed Russian literature. It is time to say that a non-Communist story may lack talent, but also it may show genius. And we do not care whom Blok the poet, author of *The Twelve,* was for; nor Bunin the writer, author of *The Gentleman from San Francisco.*

These are elementary truths, but every day convinces us that they must be said over and over again.

Whom are we with, the Serapion Brothers?

We are with the Hermit Serapion. We believe that literary chimeras are a kind of reality, and we will have none of utilitarianism. We do not write for propaganda. Art is real, like life itself. And, like life itself, it has neither goal nor meaning; it exists because it cannot help existing.

To anyone familiar with the present conditions in the Soviet Union it must be clear that today these defiant statements would read like an appeal to a revolution that must be nipped in the bud. And in 1922 Luntz's manifesto provoked the fury of several influential Marxist critics (Lebedev-Polyansky, Kogan, and others), who quite wrongly saw in it a vindication of "art for art's sake," and a stormy controversy arose in which Luntz took a lively part. In replying to his Marxist critics Luntz reiterated the Serapions' artistic credo when he wrote:

Our brotherhood, our "unity of blood," does not lie in political unanimity. We do not care what political convictions each of us holds. But we all believe that *art is real and lives its own special life, independently of where it draws its material from. For that reason we are brothers.*[13]

All the Serapions echoed Luntz's declaration in their spirited auto-biographies. Zoshchenko, who a little earlier had published some amusing and clever parodies of fellow-Serapions,[14] made fun of the "precise ideology" demanded by Communist critics from writers:

> ... being a writer is sort of hard. ... Take ideology—these days a writer has got to have ideology.
> Here's Voronsky now (a good man) who writes: "... It is necessary that writers should have a more precise ideology."
> Now that's plumb disagreeable! Tell me, how can I have a "precise ideology" when not a single party among them all appeals to me?
> I don't hate anybody—there's *my* precise ideology. ...
> In their general swing the Bolsheviks are closer to me than anybody else. And so I'm willing to bolshevik around with them. ...
> But I'm not a Communist (or rather not a Marxist), and I think I never shall be.[15]

We shall see that this frivolous attitude of Zoshchenko's toward ideology was to be recalled, with dire consequences for him, twenty-four years later. At the time, however, this show of political and artistic independence went unpunished.

Several of the Serapions published, in 1921–22, their individual books. These included three volumes by Vsevolod Ivanov, two each by Nikitin and Fedin, and one each by Zoshchenko and Slonimsky. All of them, as well as Kaverin and Tikhonov, were to play an important part in the general revival of literature, and their work will be discussed in greater detail in due place. More should be said here, however, about Luntz and Shklovsky.

Lev Natanovich Luntz (1901–1924) came from a Jewish intelligentsia family. His childhood was happy and secure. At the University of Petrograd, which he entered soon after the outbreak of the Revolution, he studied Romance philology, specializing in Spanish literature.

[13] Lev Luntz, "Ob ideologii i publitsistike" ("About Ideology and Journalism"), in *Novosti* (*News*), No. 3 (October 23, 1922). Reprinted in *Sovremennaya russkaya kritika: 1918–1924* (*Contemporary Russian Criticism: 1918–1924*) (edited by Innokenty Oksyonov), and quoted by Edgerton, "The Serapion Brothers," 54.
[14] See Mikh. Zoshchenko, "Druzheskie parodii" ("Friendly Parodies"), in *Literaturnye zapiski*, No. 2 (June 23, 1922), 8–9.
[15] Quoted by Edgerton, "The Serapion Brothers."

He was supposed to go to Spain on a postgraduate traveling scholarship. His parents emigrated to Germany after the Revolution, and in 1923 he joined them, but his main reason for going abroad was to undergo a cure for some unidentifiable illness which was probably due to under-nourishment and privations during the terrible years of War Communism. He died in a sanatorium near Hamburg soon after his twenty-third birthday.

Luntz's most important contribution to Russian literature—apart from his lion's share in championing the freedom of art on behalf of the Serapions—is his play *Vne zakona* (*The Outlaw*, 1921). It is a romantic tragedy in the Western European tradition, full of incident, with a dynamic, swift-moving plot. Its action is set in Spain. The same "Westernism" characterizes Luntz's two other plays, *Obezyany idut* (*The Apes are Coming*, 1921), and *Bertrand de Born* (1922). *Gorod pravdy* (*The City of Truth*, 1923–24), published posthumously in Gorky's *Beseda,* is a symbolical and philosophical play dealing in abstract terms with some problems raised by the Revolution. Its message is rather ambiguous. In the same number of *Beseda,* Gorky spoke of Luntz as a most promising dramatist who might have renovated the Russian drama and as a man of "rare independence and courage of thought."[16]

In his work, just as in his critical and theoretical pronouncements, Luntz rebelled against the "static" tradition of Russian literature, in drama as well as in prose fiction. He stressed, as we saw, the importance of construction, of plot and incident. His views were stated in a longish essay entitled "Na Zapad!" ("To the West!"), which also appeared in Gorky's *Beseda*[17] and which he had previously read at a meeting of the Serapion Brotherhood.

It is a brilliant and provocative piece of writing which today acquires an added significance. Luntz began by referring to a kind of literature which existed in the West but was regarded in Russia as "unserious if not harmful"—the literature of adventure. In Russia it was tolerated for children; but when the children grew up and were enlightened by their teachers, they hid their Ryder Haggards and Conan Doyles in their bookcases and turned to the "most serious but most boring" Gleb Uspensky.

> We regarded as dime novels and childish fun that which in the West is considered classical. *The plot!* The skill in handling a complicated intrigue, in tying and untying the knots, in twining and

---

[16] Maxim Gorky, "Lev Luntz" (obituary), in *Beseda* (*Colloquy*), No. 5 (June, 1924), 61–62.

[17] No. 3 (September-October, 1923), 259–74.

untwining them—it is acquired by many years of meticulous work, is created by continuous and beautiful culture.

And we Russians, we do not know how to handle plot, we ignore it, and therefore despise it . . . . We do not distinguish between the penny shocker Sherlock Holmes and the real.

We ignore the plot and despise it. But this contempt is the contempt of the provincials. We are provincials. And we are proud of it. There is nothing to be proud of.

Speaking of the Russian theater, Luntz said that it had never existed. Five or six excellent, model comedies, a few, partly forgotten, good dramas-of-manners did not count. Not a single tragedy. He ascribed this state of things to lack of system. Great writers for the theater appear in a bunch, they form a school: so it was in England, in Spain, in France. Intrigue and action are the main things in a play. A dramatic plot must obey rules of dramatic technique. Every dramatic system, whether classicist or romanticist, must have its canons. All these particular rules are subordinated to the general laws of economy of time, economy of space, and economy of action. The drama also demands tradition and training.

That is why dramatic geniuses come out in schools, in pleiades, as a system. One cannot get off in drama with fine psychology, popular speech or social motifs. If the development of the action is defective, the play is no good at all, even though it contain psychological investigations and social revelations of genius.

The Russian theater aspires, above all, after social motifs, after psychological truth, after mores. It ignores the technique of the intrigue, the tradition of the plot. That is why it does not exist. There are fine and original dramas for reading—Turgenev's, Chekhov's, Gorky's. Or there are Futurist, Imaginist and other plays based on mere tricks. Everybody in the theater is shouting about the crisis of the theater, and nobody laments the fact that with us no one knows nor wishes to know how to handle the intrigue, to learn the plot tradition.

Things were different with the Russian novel, went on Luntz, in the sense that it did exist, that there was a Russian "system" of the novel, that the Russian novel had its own "face." This, he said, was due to the fact that, to begin with, there had been more "manure," more precursors, more bad imitators of the West. But the Russian tradition was one-sided, it was realistic. The fine tradition of the historical novel was diverted into juvenile literature. The tradition of the novel of adventure went underground. Dostoyevsky's brilliant attempt to drag it out remained a solitary one. Russian literature does not possess a single first-class historical novel or a single good novel of adventure.

After contrasting this situation with what he saw in the West, Luntz passed over to what he called the "practical" side of his paper— an attack on his fellow Serapions as "typically Russian, provincial, Populist, boring writers," who soon gave up their pious intention to learn how to write interestingly and fell back into the old rut. His behest to his literary brothers was as follows:

> Do what you did before. Be revolutionary or counterrevolutionary writers, mystics or wrestlers with God, but don't be boring. Therefore—to the West!
>
> He who wants to *create* a Russian tragedy *must learn* in the West, for in Russia he has no one to learn from.
>
> He who wants to *create* a Russian novel of adventure *must learn* in the West, for in Russia he has no one to learn from.
>
> But even those who want to *renovate* the Russian realistic novel *I invite to look* to the West . . . . You can, of course, follow the Russian tradition, too, because the Russian novel is majestic and mighty. But I repeat: *Look* to the West, if you do not wish to *learn* from it.
>
> A hard road awaits us. Ahead lies honorable death or true victory. To the West! to the West!

Luntz's essay was the extreme expression of literary "Westernism" in Russia. There is much in his youthful ardor that may sound naïve and much that can be traced back to the influence of Shklovsky and the Formalists. Shklovsky in his *Gamburgsky shchot* (*The Hamburg Count*), published in 1928, wrote: "We miss Luntz very much now, with his mistakes, his despair, and his sure knowledge about the death of the old forms." Luntz's ideas had no lasting effect on Soviet literature. And even the fellow Serapions—with the exception of Kaverin whom he excluded from his attack on them—did not heed his passionate appeal and went, on the whole, their own, Russian, ways. But the appeal itself, in its very extremeness, was symptomatic of the moment when the newborn Soviet literature stood at the crossroads, and the whole literary scene was in a state of turmoil. The editors of *Beseda* (Gorky, Bely, and Khodasevich) accompanied Luntz's essay with a note in which they said that, though not sharing Luntz's opinion about the advisability of "going to the other extreme," they thought his ideas worthy of attention.

Victor Borisovich Shklovsky is one of the most interesting figures in Soviet literature during its first decade. Born in 1893, he was of mixed Jewish-German-Russian descent. His father, a teacher of mathematics, was a pure Jew. His paternal grandmother, who did not learn Russian until she was sixty, wrote her memoirs in Yiddish. His maternal grandfather was a German, by profession a gardener, who married the daughter of a Russian Orthodox priest. Victor Shklovsky's brother also became an Orthodox priest, while his uncle was the well-known journalist, Isaac Shklovsky (Dioneo). At the outbreak of the 1917 Revolution, Shklovsky joined the Social-Revolutionary party and served as a commissar of the provisional government with the armies, first in Galicia and later in Persia. After the advent of the Bolsheviks to power he both fought the Whites and conspired against the Reds. In 1920 he returned to revolutionary Petrograd, but in 1922 escaped to Finland to avoid arrest on charges arising out of his conduct during the Civil War. For a time he lived in Berlin, participating in Russian literary life there, but in 1923, taking advantage of a partial political amnesty granted by the Soviet government, returned to Russia and has been living there since.

His literary career began in 1914. While studying at the University of Petrograd he became one of the leaders of the so-called Formalist movement and one of the founders of *Opoyaz* (Society for the Study of Poetical Language), which had close links with the Futurist movement in literature. Shklovsky's role in the Formalist movement, of which he was the principal theoretician, will be discussed in Chapter III.

Arriving in 1920 in Petrograd, he took quarters at Gorky's House of Arts and was appointed professor at the Institute of the History of Art, where among his students were several Serapions. His influence on them was very great. Like many other writers at that time, he led between 1920 and 1922 a hectic life, managing to write a great deal despite great material hardships; contributing to various newspapers and magazines; lecturing at the Institute and in a number of studios; launching new, and often short-lived publishing enterprises. His first important book was published in Berlin in 1923, after he had left Russia. It was called *Sentimentalnoye puteshestvie (Sentimental Journey)*—the title was a tribute to Shklovsky's favorite writer; for many of his formalistic theories, especially his pet subject of "toying with the plot," he drew upon Sterne's *Tristram Shandy* ("I revived Sterne in Russia, for I knew how to read him," he once wrote). Shklovsky's *Sentimental Journey* is even less "sentimental" than its model. His approach in it to the Revolution and the Civil War and their horrors is as cool, as detached, and as matter-of-fact as that of his pupils, the Serapions, who probably learned their detachment from him. It is a documentary, autobiographical work, covering the period from 1917 to 1923. The first part ("The Front and the Revolution") deals with the author's experiences and adventures during the first year of the Revolution; the second, with his activities in southern Russia towards the end of the Civil War, his life in Bolshevik Petrograd, his escape to Finland, and his life in Berlin.

Shklovsky's manner derives both from Sterne and from Vasily

Rozanov, one of the most original of Russian writers and thinkers.[18] His narrative is broken, fragmentary, full of digressions, irrelevancies and witty, scintillating paradoxes. His deliberate untidiness and casualness, his sprightly, nonchalant personalia may often annoy and even incense the reader, but as a document of that time the book is not only remarkable but unique. Shklovsky's terse, paradoxical appreciations of several of his contemporaries—Gorky, Blok, Gumilyov, and several of the Serapions—are well worth a close study.

Sentimental Journey was followed by another book of personal digressions, more or less in the same vein, but much more affected and therefore less effective, called *Zoo, ili pisma ne o lyubvi* (*Zoo, or Letters Not About Love,* 1923; the title refers to the Berlin Zoological Garden in Tiergarten) and written in the form of an epistolary novel. In the same year there appeared in Berlin his *Khod konya* (*Knight's Move*), a small volume of short essays about art and literature, uneven, but mostly very interesting and clever, with the inevitable personal digressions. After his return to Russia, Shklovsky published another volume of "autobiographical fragments," *Tretya fabrika* (*The Third Factory,* 1926); one more collection of brilliantly paradoxical essays, many of them polemical, *Gamburgsky shchot* (*The Hamburg Count,* 1928);[19] and several theoretical books about literature in defense and illustration of his "formal method." When after 1929 Formalism was proclaimed a dangerous doctrine, Shklovsky devoted himself to literary history and dramatic and film criticism, and also wrote some scenarios. His work after 1930 is of little interest, and in his book of reminiscences, *Vstrechi* (*Encounters,* 1946), he is but a pale echo of his former self.

6. *Maxim Gorky* (1868-1936)

THE name of Maxim Gorky (pseudonym of Alexey Maximovich Peshkov) has become closely linked with Soviet literature and its fortunes. But his attitude toward the Revolution was by no means uniform, and the theme "Gorky and the Revolution" falls into several distinct periods. It also implies much that is still obscure, and it must be left to the future impartial historian of the Revolution, provided he has access to all its archives, to shed light on all these blind spots.

Despite his long personal association with Lenin and with the Bolshevik party in general, and his uncompromising pacifism during World War I, which made him sympathize with the Bolshevik attitude

18 On Rozanov see Mirsky, *Contemporary Russian Literature,* 163–72. In 1920 Shklovsky himself published a curious little book about Rozanov as a writer in which he of course drew parallels between Rozanov and Sterne.

19 The title is taken from boxing terminology, and its bearing on Russian literature is explained in a witty preface.

on the question of the war and its further conduct, Gorky was hostile toward the Bolsheviks between the two revolutions in 1917, and in the early days of the new regime. Later, he exchanged this attitude for one of benevolent neutrality (a Soviet critic described it as "benevolent incomprehension"),[20] and from 1918 to 1921 he devoted himself to the task of saving the remnants of Russian culture and of helping its representatives. It was to him that such institutions as the House of Arts and the House of Scholars (*Dom uchonykh*) owed their existence. He was also instrumental in organizing a vast publishing undertaking known as *Vsemirnaya literatura* (World Literature), which enabled Russian writers and scholars to earn their livelihood by translations during the abnormal years of War Communism. Gorky's personal friendship with Lenin, and his great fame and prestige outside Russia, made it possible for him to take at times an independent attitude toward the new government's policy, and especially to exercise his influence on behalf of some victims of the Red Terror in its initial stages. If we are to believe Zamyatin, Gorky did, for instance, all that he could to save Gumilyov from execution and was terribly upset when his efforts in Moscow on behalf of Gumilyov were forestalled by the authorities in Petrograd, who hastened to carry out the sentence.[21]

Gorky was also responsible for helping and encouraging young writers, in whom he had always taken a great interest. Many of the now famous Soviet authors remember with deep gratitude the encouragement they received from Gorky. It was he who "discovered" Vsevolod Ivanov and helped Fedin on his feet, and in general, the Serapion Brothers as a group owed much to Gorky's sympathetic interest and help.

In 1921 Gorky left Russia for reasons of health (the hardships of War Communism and the heavy load of work he took upon himself in those years had intensified his old tuberculosis) and went to live near Berlin, where he started *Beseda*—"a review of literature and science"— while continuing to contribute to *Krasnaya Nov*. In 1924 he retired to his villa in Sorrento, where he had lived before the Revolution, and there he remained, until 1928, in a kind of self-imposed exile. His attitude toward the new regime during this period was ambivalent: he kept in touch with the Soviet Union and his works were printed there; he never relented in his hostility to its open enemies, both Russian and foreign; but on several occasions he spoke out in frank criticism of it, as for instance in connection with the trial of the Social-Revolutionaries. In his book, published in 1929, Gorbachov wrote of Gorky:

[20] Gorbachov, *Contemporary Russian Literature*, 36.
[21] See Zamyatin's memoir of Gorky in *La Revue de France* (Paris), August 1, 1936.

Gorky in his article about Vladimir Ilyich Lenin (*Russky Sovremennik,* 1924) mentioned somewhat coquettishly ... the fact that he did not quite believe in the good sense of the masses. Gorky hardly ever believed in it in earnest and was always a bad Marxist.

To Gorbachov, Gorky's "romantic Socialism" had little to do with the militant tasks of the proletariat. He saw Gorky as "a revolutionary democrat," a kind of Menshevik, interested above all in fighting for the "Europeanization" of Russia, against the age-old backwardness of her masses.[22]

However, in 1928 Gorky made a short triumphant re-entry into the Soviet Union and was fêted there on the occasion of his sixtieth birthday. A year later he went to Russia again, this time to remain there until his death. His role as the *doyen* of Soviet letters, and as an influential force in all matters of literary policy, facilitated by his new-found friendship with Stalin, was particularly great during the last four years of his life. Certain aspects of Gorky's activities during this last period will be touched upon in later chapters.

As far as his own contribution to Russian literature since the Revolution is concerned, three points are to be noted: (1) Quantitatively speaking, it was not very great and cannot compare with Gorky's pre-Revolutionary output. (2) It was almost entirely retrospective. (3) Its quality was on the whole very high—some of his post-Revolutionary writings will undoubtedly rank among his best. This is true primarily of his nonfiction (I do not mean, however, his political journalism of the last years). His *Vospominaniya o Tolstom (Reminiscences of Tolstoy,* 1919) are justly regarded as one of his masterpieces and as one of the most interesting and penetrating pieces ever written about the great Russian writer. It is not, as D. S. Mirsky rightly pointed out, that Gorky is anything like Tolstoy's intellectual equal, or that he understands Tolstoy better than did some others; it is rather the vividness of his vision of Tolstoy the man, and the brilliant manner in which he conveys certain aspects of Tolstoy to the reader, that matter. Very interesting also, even if not so brilliant and revealing, are his reminiscences of Andreyev and Chekhov, and his portraits of some other of his contemporaries, some of which are to be found in his *Zapiski iz dnevnika (Notes From a Diary,* 1924). *Moi Universitety (My Universities,* 1923) forms a worthy sequel to *Detstvo (Childhood,* 1913) and *V lyudiakh (In the World,* 1915): the whole of this autobiographical trilogy, with its wonderful character drawing and its earthy realism, will remain for posterity as Gorky's most memorable single creation.

After leaving Russia, Gorky published in *Beseda* (1923–25) several

[22] Gorbachov, *Contemporary Russian Literature,* 33–35.

stories. They are also retrospective, but two of them reflect his preoccupation with the problems and inner workings of the Revolution. One is a very interesting study, in the form of a confession, of the mind of a schizophrenic, a revolutionary who betrays his comrades and turns secret police agent. This is "Karamora" ("Daddylonglegs"). Another, "Rasskaz o geroe" ("The Story about a Hero") is of a counterrevolutionary brought up on Carlyle's hero-worship, who might just as well have been a revolutionary, and who ends by becoming a bandit and a hangman. Both stories show Gorky's predilection for unusual characters, for people with a quirk, and both reflect strongly the influence of Dostoyevsky for whom Gorky professed an intense dislike. There are also echoes of Dostoyevsky, especially of his *Notes from the Underground,* in "Rasskaz o bezotvetnoy lyubvi" ("The Story of an Unrequited Love"), one of Gorky's most effective stories.

Delo Artamonovykh (The Artamonov Business, 1925) was Gorky's first regular novel since *Matvey Kozhemyakin* (1911). It was better than any of his middle-period work and showed that, as a novelist, he was by no means a spent force. Its theme and atmosphere recalled *Foma Gordeyev,* but its structure was more firm and more compact. It is the story of a self-made bourgeois family in its three generations. All the characters—the old Artamonov, the founder of the family's prosperity, a strong, self-willed man, one of those to whom Gorky, for all his hatred of the bourgeoisie, felt instinctively attracted; his sons and grandsons, in whom there are already signs of imminent degeneration; their wives; and other episodic characters—are portrayed with Gorky's uncommonly keen gift of observation. As is usual with Gorky, the element of healthy robustness and vitality is combined with an insight into the dark, somber side of life, not only in its outward manifestations, but also in the inner workings of human nature. In spite of the lifelikeness and variety of its characters, of whom Gorky shows not only their darker sides, there hangs about the whole novel that atmosphere of gloom which is so characteristic of Gorky's vision of old Russia and which makes him, in his mature period, despite all his propensity to romanticism, a true representative of critical realism. The same is true of *Zhizn Klima Samgina (The Life of Klim Samgin,* 1927–36). But this long epic of forty years of Russian life (it was to be continued) is one of Gorky's failures. With its multitude of characters and its extremely uninteresting hero, it is diffuse and dull, and it reveals glaringly Gorky's lack of constructive ability.

Gorky's two post-Revolutionary plays, *Egor Bulychev i drugie (Egor Bulychev and Others,* 1931) and *Dostigayev i drugie (Dostigayev and Others,* 1932), which are among his best realistic plays, are also retrospective in nature.

From the above it should be clear that, as an artist, the post-Revolutionary Gorky was looking back and seeking inspiration in the past. His few stories dealing with contemporary Soviet life are of little importance and interest.

The significant role which Gorky played in Soviet letters in the first years of the Revolution does not mean that, as a writer, he had any real influence on young post-Revolutionary literature, no matter what some of its representatives may say now. Mirsky was on the whole right when he wrote, in 1926, that Gorky's work "is profoundly unlike all the work of the younger generation—first of all, for his complete lack of interest in style, and, secondly, for his very unmodern interest in human psychology." The position, however, was reversed soon after Gorky's return to Russia; not because Gorky himself had changed in the meantime, but because post-Revolutionary Russian literature had moved much closer to Gorky—to his realism tinged with revolutionary romanticism. This *rapprochement* will become evident from the further account of developments in Soviet literature.

When Gorky died, on June 18, 1936, his death was lamented throughout the Soviet Union as an irreparable loss to Soviet letters. It was later ascribed to the evil machinations of the enemies of the Soviet Union, the "Trotskyites" and the "Fascists." In a volume of bio-bibliographical information about Gorky we read under the year 1936: "*Winter and spring.* Lives in Crimea, at Tesseli. On the instructions of the worst enemy of the people, the super-bandit and international spy, Judas Trotsky, an anti-Soviet, 'Right-Trotskyite' gang of traitors, spies and assassins sets about preparing the murder of Gorky . . . *May 30.* As a result of the conceived plan of murder and the creation of harmful conditions for Gorky's health he fell ill with influenza at Gorki (near Moscow) . . . . *June 8.* The illness took a turn for the worse in consequence of the saboteur methods of treatment applied by the murderers."[23] This version of Gorky's death was generally accepted in the Soviet Union, and in a report surveying Soviet literature during a quarter of a century Alexey N. Tolstoy spoke of "the murder of Gorky, dictated by the Fascists to their direct agents."[24] This legend about Gorky's death is but part of the general "mythmaking" which plays such an important part in Stalin's Russia. The true facts are still unknown and may not become known for many years to come.

Victor Shklovsky wrote once: "Gorky's Bolshevism is ironic Bol-

[23] S. Balukhaty and K. Muratova, *M. Gorky: Spravochnik* (*Gorky: A Reference Guide*), 75–76.

[24] A. N. Tolstoy, *Chetvert veka sovetskoy literatury: Doklad na yubileynoy sessii Akademii Nauk SSSR 18 noyabrya 1942 goda* (*A Quarter of a Century of Soviet Literature: Report Read at the Jubilee Session of the Academy of Sciences of the U.S.S.R. on November 18, 1942*), 9.

shevism which does not believe in man. By Bolshevism I do not mean belonging to a political party: Gorky never belonged to the Party"; and further: "Gorky does not at all believe in mankind. He does not like all men, but those who write well or work well." These "paradoxes" of Shklovsky's are much nearer the truth than the official "icon" of Gorky the humanist, which has been painted all too often. Gorky is still waiting for someone to strip his true face of artificial hagiographic varnish —to do for him what he did for Tolstoy.[25]

7. *Vsevolod Ivanov*

VSEVOLOD Vyacheslavovich Ivanov, one of the Serapion Brothers, is a typical revolutionary romantic. He was born in Siberia in 1895. His father, a village teacher and a drunkard, was killed accidentally by one of his sons. At the age of fifteen, Ivanov ran away from school to follow a circus. He worked for it as a clown. After a short spell at an agricultural school he became a typesetter, and during summers worked again for the circus in various capacities, including that of "fakir and dervish" (under the name of "Ban-Ali-Bey"). In Ivanov's autobiography we read: "I read a lot, from Dumas to Spencer and from Dream Books to Tolstoy. Books never had a great influence on me, and I read them also from boredom, for I didn't drink vodka."[26]

In the autumn of 1916 Ivanov wrote his first story, and it was printed in the local Siberian paper. Encouraged by this success, he decided to send his next story to Gorky's *Letopis*. Gorky liked the story and wrote Ivanov an encouraging letter, after which Ivanov sat down and wrote, within the next two weeks, twenty stories. Some of them he sent to Gorky, who thought them bad and advised Ivanov to study and read more before he again took to writing. Ivanov says that in the next two years he read more books than he would probably read during the rest of his life, but none of them were about politics; and when the Revolution broke out in 1917, he did not know the difference between the Social-Democrats and the Social-Revolutionaries and so joined both parties at once! In the Civil War he fought first on the side of the Whites (apparently he was conscripted into Admiral Kolchak's army), when he was taken prisoner and barely escaped being shot. After that he fought with the Red guerrillas in Siberia. In 1919 his first book of stories appeared in Siberia, printed and published by himself; and in

25 Something towards this end was done by Gorky's friend, the poet Khodasevich, in his reminiscences of their life at Sorrento. See *Sovremennye zapiski (Contemporary Annals)*, Vol. LXIII (1937).

26 *Pisateli. Avtobiografii i portrety sovremennykh russkikh prozaikov (Writers: Autobiographies and Portraits of Contemporary Russian Prose-Fiction Authors)* (edited by Vl. Lidin), 145.

1920, with Gorky's help, he came to Petrograd. Here he joined the Cosmist group of proletarian writers and, later, the Serapion Brothers. In 1922 he was expelled from the Cosmist for belonging to a nonproletarian literary organization. In 1921 there appeared *Partizany* (*Partisans*), a long story based on Ivanov's experiences in the Civil War. It was followed in 1922 by several books: *Bronepoezd No. 14–69* (*Armored Train No. 14–69*), *Loga* (*Gullies*, a book of stories), and *Tsvetnye vetra* (*Colored Winds*), the last-named a novel. Both Gorky and the Serapions regarded Ivanov as the most talented among them.

In these works and in the novel *Golubye peski* (*Skyblue Sands*, 1923) we find all the characteristics of Ivanov's early work: the spicy, ornamental language, full of dialecticisms; the jerky narrative, interspersed with lyrical refrains; the animistic attitude toward nature, which is made to participate in human joys and sorrows; the obvious influence of Russian folklore; the stress on the cruel, "bestial" aspect of the Revolution, its "blood and sweat"; and the utter detachment with which most horrible things are related. Thus the story called "Polaya Arapiya" ("Hollow Arabia") tells of how the population of a whole village somewhere in eastern Russia, driven by hunger, moves southward to seek "Hollow Arabia," a mythical country of plenty about which they have heard from a crazy woman; of how they are forced to eat rats and horses' manure; and of how they suspect one another of anthropophagic intentions. The story ends with one of them, who is on the point of dying of starvation and exhaustion, hiding under a cart, with the greedy eyes of four of his covillagers on him, watching his every movement, ready to finish him off and devour him. The horror of this story is heightened by the author's detached, matter-of-fact manner. In another typical story, "Dityo" ("The Child"), Red partisans kill two officers who are approaching them in a cart. One of the officers turns out to be a woman. In a basket, tied under the cart, they find a child. After some unsuccessful attempts to feed it on cabbage soup, chewed bread, and other unsuitable things, they decide to make a raid on a near-by Kirghiz camp and steal some cows. At the camp one of them decides also to kidnap a young Kirghiz mother, which he does. The kidnapped mother, without the knowledge of the raiders, brings along her own child. She starts feeding both babies, but soon the partisans discover that she is cheating them and giving preference to her own child. With little thought or hesitation, they kill the "yellow" child so that the "white" one will get enough milk. And they laugh heartily when they see the child sucking vigorously at the breast of the impassive Kirghiz woman.

Shklovsky has pointed out that Ivanov's story may appear at first trite, that it reminds one of some stories by Bret Harte or Leonid

Andreyev or Gorky, but that at the end Ivanov gives it a most unexpected and original twist. It was this *ostranenie* ("making strange"), of which Shklovsky regarded Tolstoy such a superb master, that the Serapions learned from Shklovsky to value as one of the most effective weapons in a writer's arsenal, whether it be in the plot, in description, or in style. In all their early work they were deliberately aiming at this effect of "strangeness" and "freshness," and here there was no difference between the "Westerners," like Luntz and Kaverin, and the "Russians," like Ivanov and Nikitin. In fact, no one sought more these "strange" effects than the last two.

The two novels of Ivanov (*Colored Winds* and *Skyblue Sands*) are novels in name only: they are shapeless, without plot, and full of "ornamental" writing and picturesque local coloring (Siberia, Mongolia)—in fact typical products of the Pilnyak school, but devoid of Pilnyak's intellectualism and free of his historico-philosophical quests. Ivanov is much more genuinely primitive—he has a true pantheistic sense of nature and of man's fusion with it. He brings out forcibly the meaninglessness and aimlessness of life and of human behavior, emphasizing its obscure, inexplicable mainsprings. Characteristic of him is a combination of an instinctive zest for life with a fundamental pessimism. This imparts a somber note to his writings. Like all the Serapions, he is fond of unexpected situations and contrasts, of exoticism, and is given to overnaturalistic descriptions. Life, as Ivanov sees it, is cruel and senseless, and man, a toy manipulated by dark and blind forces. "A man's soul is like a bear's: it don't see its own path," says Ivanov in one of his stories.

In 1923, Ivanov published a short novel, *Vozvrashchenie Buddy* (*The Return of Buddha*), which marked for him a new departure; it was much less "ornamentally" written, was of a less localized interest, and had a plot of adventure. He also tried his hand at a "proletarian" political novel about factory life in *Severostal* (*Northsteel*, 1925), but without success. His book of stories of village life, *Taynoye taynykh* (*Mystery of Mysteries*, 1927), had a mixed reception from Soviet critics. Here, in conformity with the general development of Soviet literature, Ivanov took a step toward psychological realism. His style became more simple and direct; more room was given to the psychology of characters. But Ivanov's attitude toward life remained fundamentally the same: again he showed human conduct as blind and senseless, human beings as possessed by dark and violent passions to which they in the end succumb. Most of the stories in this collection are pervaded with a sense of doom and destruction. As a result Ivanov was accused of mysticism and pessimism, of worshipping blind and cruel fate, of being unable to adjust himself to the Revolution. Some critics spoke of his fundamentally antirevolutionary tendency, in which they saw a legacy of his "petty bourgeois" past. After that, as we shall see, Ivanov did his best to live it down.

8. *Nikitin*

LITTLE is known about the life of another Serapion, Nikolay Nikolayevich Nikitin, except that he was born in the north of Russia in 1897, apparently in a merchants' family, spent most of his childhood in Petersburg, and went to a high school and the university there. In his autobiography he says: "Then the War. Then the Revolution. It would take too long to write about this. Here I learned everything." It is to be assumed that Nikitin fought in the Civil War, but on whose side we do not know. His first story was published in 1922, after he had met Gorky, Shklovsky, Zamyatin (who taught him the art of writing), and the Serapions.

In many ways Nikitin is the most typical representative of Russian prose fiction of this period—more typical even than Ivanov, because his scope is wider, because he is more bookish, and because his manner is less spontaneous and more experimental.

Nikitin's most characteristic early stories are to be found in the first two volumes of his *Collected Works* (1928), entitled respectively *Rvotny Fort* (*Fort Vomit*) and *Polyot* (*Flight*). It is not difficult to see the influence of Remizov, Zamyatin, and Pilnyak on Nikitin. To this list can also be added either as direct or as indirect influences the names of Leskov and Gogol, and, as occasional influences, those of Dostoyevsky and Andrey Bely. From Zamyatin and Pilnyak comes Nikitin's broken, disjointed narrative; from Pilnyak the constant lyrical digressions, the author's personal interventions, the use of "documents" and quotations, the historical landscape, and the intense eroticism of many stories: "Rvotny Fort", "Noch" ("Night"), "Pella," and others; from Leskov and Remizov, the *skaz* manner, with a great variety of spoken intonations and styles: peasants', soldiers', gypsies', and so on; from them too, the predilection for the anecdote, the folklore element, and certain characters such as the hermit Pim in "Fort Vomit." Stories like "Zhizn gvardii sapyora" ("The Life of a Guards Sapper"), "Koshka-sobaka" ("Cat-Dog") and "Chavaly" ("Romanies") read like Leskovian exercises on post-Revolutionary themes, like ingenious pastiches. In a highly concentrated form, nearly all the characteristics of the Russian prose fiction of this period are to be found in Nikitin: the elaborate, affected, mosaic-like style; the hysterically emotionalized diction; the prevalence of incident and action over psychology; the ideological detachment. For a student of this "ornamental," "dynamic" prose with all its good points and all its defects, there is no better material than Nikitin's early stories, written in 1921–23.

Many of these stories deal with the Civil War—in the North, in the South, and in the East. On the whole Nikitin is less interested in the war itself than in its effect on the life of remote Russian villages, where the old and the new clash. Several Soviet critics were right, however, in pointing out that Nikitin was concerned not so much with the new as with the old—with the resistance of the old rather than with the struggle for the new; and that he was much more successful in portraying the old, unchanging aspects of Russia than the new revolutionary heroes.[27] Most of his stories served as an illustration of the thesis that the Revolution had touched only the surface of Russian life and that deep down everything remained as before, almost as it had been a hundred years ago.

One of Nikitin's most typical stories—both stylistically and "ideologically"—is "Night." It is full of literary reminiscences and looks like a mosaic where separate pieces can be traced to various sources: Zamyatin, Pilnyak, Leskov, Remizov, Gogol (his famous comparison of Russia to a troika), Russian folklore, and so on. Its subject is an encounter between two armored trains during the Civil War in the south of Russia. Nikitin is little concerned with the military aspect of the situation, and the final clash is suggested rather than described. What he attempts to do is to suggest the atmosphere of doom, and to present a cross section of both trains—the Red, named after the Hungarian Communist Béla Kuhn, and the White, named after General Kornilov—and their passengers. In a mixture of the tragic and the trivial, the mounting sense of the impending catastrophe (the events of the story take place in one single night) is conveyed very well. The portraits are dynamic and impressionistic: the old general who prays in the solitude of the train's bathroom while his wife is being unfaithful to him with a young subordinate of his whom the Revolution has reduced to drunken cynicism; the young White volunteer Neledin, who writes a naïve and touching letter to his mother and gets indignant with this cynical, drunken officer; the commissar of the Red train, a rugged fellow from Siberia, who makes love to his American secretary. This last pair is, of course, a deliberate parallel to the general's wife and the young officer, illustrating the power which the forces of life have over men at all times. Ideologically speaking, Nikitin refuses to take sides and shows an utter detachment. Both the Reds and the Whites are men—ordinary men—with all their

[27] See Pavel Medvedev's Introduction to volume 1 of Nikitin's *Sobranie sochineniy* (*Collected Works*), 18–19. See also Gorbachov, *Contemporary Russian Literature*, 113–18, and *Ocherki sovremennoy russkoy literatury* (*Studies of Contemporary Russian Literature*), 93 ff.

qualities and all their failings. The old general and young Neledin are certainly meant to inspire sympathy in the reader, more so than any of the Reds. Moreover, the Whites are also shown fighting for their ideas, for the good of the country as they understand it (this is made particularly clear in Neledin's letter home, which has a very genuine ring). To the Reds and the Whites are opposed the "neutral" Cossacks who refuse to fight, who think only of their selfish interests, and after the final catastrophe try to profit by it, collecting scrap iron from the two burned-out trains. Nikitin calls them "the jackals of the Revolution." They are symbolized in Kuzma Fenogenov, a typical Cossack.

> History will call this rabble the jackals. The Revolution also had its jackals who stood aside and waited for profits. But the Revolution itself was beautiful, elemental—like a powerful nocturnal thunderstorm. This is said not to justify it nor is it by any means a poetic image. It is the elements. And about the elements a song must be composed. And each one . . . will compose this song in his own, different way, but not one of them will sing the glory of Kuzma Fenogenov and his droves. . . Cursed be those who warmed themselves at the warm, after-battle ashes.

In another story, "Kamni" ("The Stones"), the implication is that the Revolution and the counterrevolution, the Reds and the Whites, are equally bad and that both bring nothing but misery in their wake. But mostly the Revolution is shown by Nikitin as something mysterious, dark, and incomprehensible, greedy like the sea and intoxicating like the wind (in this respect reminiscent of both Blok and Pilnyak). In the later stories the weekdays of the Revolution, after its comparative stabilization, are contrasted with its early, romantic period—those "wonderful, unforgettable days." Among these stories, "Polyot" ("Flight"), despite its annoying stylistic mannerisms, its Pilnyakian tricks (sudden shiftings of planes, the use of documents and symbolic refrains), and its rather cheap eroticism, succeeds in conveying to the reader the drama of two average old-time officers caught in the revolutionary whirlpool. Some of the scenes describing the madness of Firsov, slightly reminiscent of Bely, are very effective.

Of all the Serapions, no one, perhaps, aimed so persistently at strange, paradoxical effects as did Nikitin. In its most consistent and bare form the method of *ostranenie* is applied by him in "Daisy," the story of a young tigress in captivity and of her ultimate escape. This story, written in the name of the tigress and divided into short chapters, many of them less than half a page, can also be studied as a text illustrating certain favorite devices of the Pilnyak school in Russian literature.

Together with the rest of Soviet literature, Nikitin gradually evolved toward a more realistic treatment of the Revolution and its themes.

9. *Babel*

IN 1923 a writer, whose name was practically unknown till then, attracted the attention of the critics and the public. He was Isaac Babel, soon to be hailed as one of the most talented and original among the younger Soviet writers.

Born in Odessa in 1894 into a typical Jewish middle-class family with strong Jewish traditions, Isaac Emmanuilovich Babel was educated in one of the secondary schools of Odessa. While still at school he developed a great liking for French literature. Flaubert and Maupassant were his first literary masters, and his early youthful stories were written in French. This mingling of the traditional Jewish atmosphere, the study of the Talmud and of Hebrew, with the Latin precision and clarity of the French and their literature, the stylistic fastidiousness inspired by Flaubert (to which was later added the influence of the Revolution seen in its most elemental, "romantic," and cruel aspects), resulted in a strange product, full of contrasts and paradoxes.

Babel's literary career began in 1916, when Gorky, who was then editing *Letopis* (*Annals*), published his first two stories. They were full of eroticism, and Babel and the magazine became involved in judicial proceedings under Article 1001 of the Russian Civil Code, which was aimed at pornography. Gorky, who was quick to see Babel's talent and ready to encourage him, was not satisfied, however, with the next stories which Babel sent him. Influenced by this adverse criticism, Babel stopped writing and did not reappear in literature until 1923. In the early years of the Revolution he took part in the Civil War and in 1920 fought against Poland with the famous cavalry army of Budyonny. Later he held various posts in Soviet administration and worked as a journalist in Tiflis and elsewhere. In an autobiographical note he wrote, he says: "It was only in 1923 that I learned to express my ideas clearly and at not too great a length, and then I took to writing again." In 1923–24 he published a number of short stories. Many of them were included in his *Konarmiya* (*Red Cavalry*, 1926), a volume of stories for which he drew upon his experiences with Budyonny's army in the Soviet-Polish war. In 1927 it was followed by *Evreyskie rasskazy* (*Jewish Tales*) and two longer autobiographical stories, "Istoriya moey golubyatni" ("The Story of my Dovecote") and "Pervaya lyubov" ("First Love").

The *Red Cavalry* stories brought Babel fame: even outside Russia he began to be spoken of as the rising star of the young post-Revolutionary literature. It has been pointed out that Babel was the first among post-Revolutionary writers to revive a definite literary genre—that of the pointed, short *nouvelle* (in which, incidentally, the influence of Maupassant could be easily discerned). Babel's stories, with their clear and distinct outline, their brevity, and their fastidious style, came as something new after the welter of shapeless, loose productions of the Pilnyak school and of the other "dynamic prose" writers. Yet Babel had something in common with them and differed as much as they did from the realists who were about to make their appearance and revive the traditional psychological novel. He had the same predilection for *skaz,* for ornamentalism, and for the exotic and romantic aspects of the Revolution, and the same aversion to psychological analysis. But he differed from Pilnyak and his followers in his feeling for form and his concern with style: even his *skaz* was subordinated to a deliberate stylistic design in which the element of contrast and paradox played a great part. It has been rightly said that it is style which holds his stories together, whether they be tales of the Revolution and the Civil War or pictures of Jewish life in Odessa.

Babel's attitude toward life can be described as purely sensuous and aesthetic. He is attracted by the bright, the picturesque, the unusual in life. His Jewish stories, for all their realism in the portrayal of the peculiarities of life and speech of Odessa Jews, are imbued with the same romanticism and exoticism. Instead of the familiar and traditional middle-class Jewish milieu, Babel shows us something quite out of the ordinary—the world of Jewish gangsters and bandits, who appear to us romantically glamorized and at the same time pathetic and humorous. In the center of this world stands the figure of Benya Krik, the "king" of Odessa gangsters, a character of almost legendary proportions, yet pathetically human and lovable.

In the Revolution, Babel's attention is also centered on the exotic and romantic aspects, on the unusual and paradoxical. All Babel's stories about the life of Budyonny's army have this romantic streak. Babel's keen vision and great sense of line and color, combined with his extreme sensitiveness to cruelty and to all that is excessive and inordinate in life, enables him to depict graphically the Civil War in a series of Goyaesque scenes. He does this with great artistic economy and detachment. He dwells with a certain relish on scenes of plunders, riots, and executions—of senseless, instinctive, almost goodhumored cruelty. It is the almost animal instinct of destruction that he shows above all in the Civil War, and this is why his *Red Cavalry* provoked a strong protest from Marshall Budyonny, who denounced it as a one-sided and distorted picture of his army and its exploits.[28] Babel's stories of the

[28] Budyonny's short retort to Babel appeared in *Oktyabr* (*October*), No. 3 (1924),

Red Cavalry are not, however, realistic snapshots of its everyday life—
they are full of hyperbolism, of romantic contrasts, and of a peculiar
pathos, wherein the cruel and the heroic merge into each other. There
is in Babel a strong element of eroticism which, despite its apparent
naturalism, is also treated romantically and hyperbolically. But many
readers are revolted by the crude and outspoken physiological descriptions which abound in Babel's stories.

Babel's favorite method is that of contrast and paradox. Nearly all
of his stories are based on contrasts, both psychological and stylistic.
Throughout *Red Cavalry* there runs a contrast between the cruelty, the
elemental blindness and crude sensuousness of the scenes described,
and their perception through the spectacles of the narrator, who obviously stands for Babel himself—a typical educated Jew, nearsighted,
physically weak, and psychologically out of tune with his surroundings
and the life he is forced to share, and, in addition, burdened with a
skeptical attitude toward the world. Parallel with this there is the contrast between Babel's poetic descriptions of nature, reminiscent of Gogol
as well as of Imaginist poetry, full of color and hyperbole, and the
crude physiological naturalism of many scenes: the crudeness and
cruelty of human beings and their behavior are set off by this resplendent
theatrical background. Babel's romanticism is tempered—one might
almost say, poisoned—by his irony and skepticism. An unusual "romantic" situation is often set off by small, matter-of-fact details. Here
is a typical passage from the story "Berestechko":

> Right in front of my windows a few Cossacks were executing an
> old silver-bearded Jew accused of spying. The old man was scream-
> ing and trying to tear himself loose. Then Kudrya, of the machine-
> gun section, seized his head and tucked it under his arm. The Jew
> hushed and spread out his legs. With his left hand Kudrya took out
> a dagger and carefully butchered the old man, without bespatter-
> ing himself.

Babel is by no means a painter of everyday life, whether of the Red
Army or of the Odessa Jewry; nor is he a psychologist. He saw the
Revolution as a sort of romantic *décor*, and there is something romantically conventional in most of his characters. Among his contemporaries
he showed himself a great master of the short story. His stories are terse
and compact and have an effective *pointe*. His attitude toward the
Revolution is detached—he has no ax to grind, no message to bring.
The Revolution appears to him as a great elemental force, blind and
cruel, which sweeps along with no regard for the individual. This atti-
under the title "The Womanizing of Babel from *Krasnaya Nov.*" In Russian there is
a pun here, the word for "woman" being *baba*.

tude is reflected in the story called "Gedali." Babel describes in it a conversation with an old Jewish owner of a curiosity shop during the Soviet-Polish War. The old man, Gedali, is ready to say "Yea" to the Revolution, but he refuses to say "Nay" to the Sabbath. He is at a loss to see a difference between the Revolution and the counterrevolution—both shoot and both are cruel to man: "Who can tell Gedali where is the revolution and where the counterrevolution? . . . all we learned men, we fall upon our faces and we cry out loudly: Woe unto us, where is the sweet revolution?"

Gedali asks the author to bring good men to his town—he wants "an International of good men":

> ". . . I want every soul to be kept on the register and be given first category rations. Here, man, pray, eat, and enjoy life. The International, mister comrade, do you know how it should be served?"
>
> "It is served with gunpowder," I answered, "and seasoned with the best blood. . . ."

The story ends with Gedali—"the founder of a fantastic International"—going to the synagogue to pray, "small, lonely, dreamy, in a black top hat, a large prayer book under his arm."

Babel reached the height of his popularity around 1927; his *Red Cavalry* and *Jewish Tales* went through several editions. In 1928 he published a very interesting play, *Zakat (Sunset)*, with the life of Odessa Jews for its setting. During the period inaugurated in 1929 (to be discussed later), his reputation suffered a considerable setback: his romantic irony and detached individualism now proved to be out of place. He ceased publishing. His personal fate is not known, but there is every reason to believe that he fell victim to one of the purges. Nothing has been heard of him since the late thirties. He will be remembered as a typical and brilliant representative of the "romantic" period in Soviet literature.

10. *The Poets: Tikhonov and Aseyev*

WITH the re-emergence of prose fiction, poetry lost something of its monopolistic position. But books of poems continued to appear in great numbers, especially in 1921–23. Mayakovsky and Esenin (see above), both of whom enjoyed great popularity during this period, were echoed by other Futurists and Imaginists. Proletarian and peasant poets were very active, too. Some of the former will be discussed later, for much of their work is characteristic of the next phases in the development of Soviet literature, as will be Boris Pasternak, although one of his best and most important books, *Sestra moya zhizn (My Sister Life)*, appeared in 1922. It is, however, impossible to speak of this period of Soviet literature without saying something about Tikhonov and Aseyev, especially the former, who was not only a member of the Serapion Brotherhood but a true poetic counterpart of the Serapions as prose writers.

Nikolay Semyonovich Tikhonov was born in 1896 into a lower middle-class family. After studying at a trade school, he enlisted in the army as a volunteer and fought with a Hussar regiment on the Riga front, and later with the Red Army in the Civil War. Like many of his contemporaries he also tried his hand at various professions. In 1921 he joined the Serapion Brotherhood and a year later published his first book of poems, *Orda* (*The Horde*). Its principal theme was war. The influence of the Acmeists, especially of Gumilyov and to a lesser extent of Mandelstam, is quite obvious in it. Tikhonov can be described as a romantic realist. His verse of this period has a noble simplicity: there is no pursuit of novelty for novelty's sake. The choice of words is fastidious and precise; the structure of the phrase firm and compact; and the verse has a strong, metallic ring, in keeping with the dominant virile note of fearless acceptance of all the hardships of war, and even of death. Tikhonov's poetry is equally removed from Mayakovsky's coarse and strident rhetoric and from Esenin's mellifluousness. The following typical poem illustrates the influence of Gumilyov and at the same time reflects Tikhonov's fundamentally romantic attitude:

> *Fire, rope, bullet and axe*
> *Like servants bowed and followed us.*
> *And in every drop a deluge slept,*
> *Mountains grew forth from little stones,*
> *And in a twig crushed underfoot*
> *Rustled black-armed forests.*
> *Untruth ate and drank with us,*
> *Church bells pealed from force of habit,*
> *Coins had lost their weight and ring,*
> *And children were not scared of corpses.*
>
> *It was then we learned, for the first time,*
> *Words beautiful, bitter and cruel.*

Or the following famous lines about men of his generation, "simple like iron nails":

> *Life taught me with oar and rifle,*
> *And a strong wind with a knotted cord*
> *Lashed me upon my shoulders,*
> *To make me both calm and nimble,*
> *And simple like iron nails.*

In Tikhonov's second book of verse, *Braga* (*Mead*), the heroic themes of the Civil War predominate, many of them treated in the form of ballads, in which can be seen the influence of English poetry and of Kipling in particular. This form of ballad was taken up not only by Tikhonov, but also by several other disciples of Gumilyov (e.g., Irina Odoyevtseva and Vladimir Pozner—the latter, like Tikhonov, was a member of the Serapion fraternity). Tikhonov's ballads enjoyed great popularity, especially his "Ballad About the Blue Packet" and "Ballad About Nails." The latter, in eighteen laconic lines, sings the heroism of pre-Revolutionary Russian sailors. It ends with the lines:

Nails ought to be made out of these men:
There would be no stronger nails in the world.

The Oriental note, which was later to play a prominent part in Tikhonov's poetry, was introduced in the unrhymed ballad called "Sami." Like the ballads of Kipling in form, it is the story of a Hindu boy in Amritsar who is born to a new life, a new sense of his human dignity, after praying to "Lenni" (Lenin). After this a definite political note is sounded more clearly in the poetry of Tikhonov, who had earlier described himself as an incurable anarchist. It is conspicuous in his next book, *Poiski geroya* (*Quest for a Hero*), where several poems are in the nature of political satires. Even in Tikhonov's earlier lyrical poetry there was nearly always an element of "story," but with time this narrative element became more and more prominent. The three longer poems, written in 1924—"Krasnye na Arakse" ("The Reds on the Araks"), "Litsom k litsu" ("Face to Face"), and "Doroga" ("The Road")—are attempts at creating a new form of revolutionary narrative poem. They reflect the experimental stage in Tikhonov's poetry, when he strove not only after new compositional forms, but also experimented with language and meters, becoming deliberately obscure and difficult; in this period the influence of Gumilyov and the Acmeists gave place to that of the Futurists, of Mayakovsky, and, even more, of Khlebnikov and Pasternak. Tikhonov is one of the very few Soviet poets who turned to creative account Khlebnikov's poetic experiments. Particularly characteristic of this tendency is the poem "Shakhmaty" ("Chess"), one of Tikhonov's most difficult and abstruse poems, in which he attempted to present the Revolution "through a strictly consistent reproduction of all the details of a game of chess" (Gorbachov).

The most important of Mayakovsky's followers during this period was Nikolay Nikolayevich Aseyev (b. 1889), who began writing and publishing before the Revolution. His early poetry was influenced by the Symbolists and Khlebnikov, and a romantic note of rebellious individualism was very strong in it. The influence of Khlebnikov was

70

reflected in Aseyev's archaic stylizations. His acceptance of the Revolution was also colored with romanticism. His hatred of all bourgeois forms, of all philistinism, made him take a hostile attitude toward the NEP. His long poem "Liricheskoye otstuplenie" ("Lyrical Digression") reflects this post-NEP mood of bitter disillusionment.

From 1923 on, Aseyev took an active part in the so-called LEF ("Left Front of Literature"), of which Mayakovsky was one of the leaders and which united mostly Futurists, who sought in it a political basis for their action. In keeping with the program of "utilitarian" art proclaimed by the LEF in their magazine which bore the same name, Aseyev wrote a number of "industrial" and propaganda poems. But romanticism was too strongly ingrained in him, and his narrative poems about the Revolution—*Poema o 26 bakinskikh kommissarakh* (*The Poem About the 26 Baku Commissars*), *Poema o Budyonnom* (*The Poem About Budyonny*), and *Semyon Proskakov* (where a Red Army soldier is contrasted with Admiral Kolchak)—are all full of romantic emotionalism. Aseyev's post-Revolutionary poetry was greatly influenced by Mayakovsky, but on the whole it is simpler and more emotional. Aseyev also took an active part in the literary controversies of the twenties. Some of his theoretical and polemical articles were collected, in 1929, in two volumes: *Dnevnik poeta* (*The Diary of a Poet*) and *Rabota nad stikhom* (*Working at Verse*).

11. *Onguardists* versus *Fellow Travelers. LEF. The Constructivists*

WITH the revival of literature after the end of the Civil War, the antagonism between proletarian and nonproletarian literature reached a new and acute stage. The main part in that revival was played, as we saw, by nonproletarian and non-Communist writers who, in their own way, had "accepted" the Revolution and focused their artistic attention on its processes. Even the majority of the Serapions, despite their insistence on being free to choose their subjects, in point of fact wrote almost exclusively about the Revolution. All these writers who, without being Communists, vaguely sympathized with the Revolution and were certainly hostile to its enemies were dubbed "fellow travelers." The name was first used by Trotsky in one of the essays in his book, *Literature and Revolution* (1923):

> Between the bourgeois art, which is living itself out in repetitions or in silence, and the new art, which has not yet arrived, a transitional art is being created, more or less organically bound up with the Revolution, but at the same time not the art of the Revolution.

After listing a number of writers representative of this art—including Esenin, Pilnyak, Vsevolod Ivanov, and Tikhonov—Trotsky went on:

> Their literary and, generally speaking, spiritual countenance is a product of the Revolution, of that angle of it which has touched them, and they all accept it, each in his own way. But in these individual acceptances they have one feature in common which marks them off sharply from Communism and always threatens to oppose them to it. They fail to grasp the Revolution as a whole, and its Communist aim is alien to them. They are all more or less inclined to look hopefully at the peasant over the head of the worker. They are not the artists of proletarian revolution but its artistic fellow travelers.

The name took root and came to be widely used in all the literary battles and squabbles of the next decade, though the definition was sufficiently vague to allow considerable latitude when it came to deciding whether this or that writer was, or was not, a fellow traveler; thus, some critics treated even Mayakovsky as a fellow traveler. But in a very general way "fellow traveler" became synonymous with "non-Communist," just as "proletarian" came to mean "Communist."

Between 1921 and 1924, fellow travelers dominated the literary scene. Many of the Communist leaders came to look upon them in the way in which they looked upon non-Communist, bourgeois experts in various other fields: in economics, finance, technology, science, medicine, and the like—their superior specialized knowledge and ability made them indispensable. Thus fellow travelers in literature came to be treated as literary *spetsy* (experts). Many orthodox Communist critics willingly admitted their superiority and patronized them. Foremost among these was Alexander Konstantinovich Voronsky (1884–?), the founder and editor of *Krasnaya Nov,* which became the principal refuge of fellow travelers. In the literary battles of 1923–24 it was Voronsky and his review which had to bear the brunt of the attacks on fellow travelers.

These attacks came from the group which called itself "Oktyabr" ("October"); founded at the end of 1922, it took the place of the *Proletkult.* Among its founders were the poet Alexander Bezymensky and the novelist Yury Libedinsky, and its principal spokesmen in the early stages were Semyon Rodov and G. Lelevich (pseudonym of Labory Kalmanson, b. 1901). Affiliated with "October" were two groups of young writers which had earlier clashed with the Smithy: "Rabochaya Vesna" ("Workers' Spring") and "Molodaya Gvardiya" ("Young Guard"). The former was comprised of many non-Communist factory workers;

the latter was connected with the League of Communist Youth. "October" itself had a 100 per cent Communist membership and came out in defense of ideologically-pure proletarian literature. In June of 1923, it began issuing its own magazine, called *Na postu (On Guard)*; and in 1924 another monthly, *Oktyabr (October)*. Both were edited by Lelevich.[29] This group came to be referred to usually as the *"Napostovtsy"* ("Onguardists"). In the first number of *On Guard* appeared the "Ideological and Artistic Platform" of "October." Its main points were as follows:

> In a class society, imaginative literature, just as everything else, serves the objects of a specific class, and only through that class, of the whole of mankind; hence, that literature is proletarian which organizes the psychology and consciousness of the working class and of the wide toiling masses toward the final aims of the proletariat as the reorganizer of the world and the creator of Communist society . . . .
>
> Proletarian literature opposes itself to bourgeois literature as its antipode . . . .
>
> The group "October" asserts the primacy of content. The very content of a proletarian work of literature supplies the verbal and artistic material and suggests the form. Content and form are dialectical antitheses: content conditions form and is artistically formalized through it.

The group refused to give preference to any particular form, or forms, and rejected the one-sided solutions offered by Imaginism, Futurism, and Symbolism. As its final aim it proclaimed the creation of "a new synthetic form of proletarian literature." But "October," too, had its enemies within the ranks of proletarian literature: thus it fought and finally hounded out of existence the old Smithy. At the same time it aimed at creating a united front of proletarian literature and to that end utilized the earlier-founded All-Union Association of Proletarian Writers (known briefly as the VAPP),[30] with branches in Moscow (MAPP) and Leningrad, or Petrograd as it was then still called (PAPP, later LAPP). In these two cities other proletarian literary organizations, such as the "October" itself, were allowed to exist side by side with the branches of the VAPP, but in all other cities the principle of centralization was strictly adhered to.

In January of 1925 there took place the first All-Union Conference of Proletarian Writers, which passed a resolution, on the report of com-

---

[29] Lelevich, who wrote some poetry and in 1926 published a book on Bryusov, was expelled from the Party in 1928 for "opposition."

[30] After 1928 it was known as VOAPP (All-Union Union of Associations of Proletarian Writers).

rade Vardin (pseudonym of I. G. Mgeladze), emphatically proclaiming that literature in a class society, far from being neutral, actively serves a particular class. This, ran the resolution, was doubly true of the present time—in the age of wars and revolutions and in times of acute class struggle. Therefore, all talk about peaceful co-operation and competition of various ideologies in literature was a reactionary dream. In ideology and in literature laws of class struggle operated just as much as in any other field of social life. Hence the necessity of ideological "intransigence" and "intolerance." The resolution contained a violent attack on those who denied the possibility of a specific proletarian culture and literature, and especially on Trotsky and Voronsky as the most consistent opponents of proletarian literature. This negative attitude to proletarian culture was ascribed to the pressure of the petty bourgeois elements, which in 1922–24 found its expression in the opposition within the Communist party—those who were working toward the gradual liquidation of the dictatorship of the proletariat and a return to "democracy." The resolution denied that fellow travelers, who according to Trotsky and Voronsky were to be the main force in literature, were a homogeneous group. It insisted on differentiating between those who honestly, and to the best of their ability, served the Revolution, and the majority of fellow travelers "who distort the Revolution in literature, often slander it, and are imbued with the spirit of nationalism, great-power-mindedness, and mysticism." These "antirevolutionary" elements among fellow travelers must be fought against. The better elements might be made use of, but this could be done only if they were influenced by proletarian literature, only if they were "grouped round a proletarian kernel." It was not enough, went on the resolution, simply to "recognize" proletarian literature; it was necessary to accept the principle of its "hegemony," in order to allow it "to swallow up all species and varieties of bourgeois and petty-bourgeois literature." The resolution ended with the following proud and militant declaration:

> Proletarian literature in the Soviet Union has but one aim before it: to serve the cause of world proletarian victory, to fight ruthlessly all the enemies of the Revolution. Proletarian literature will conquer bourgeois literature, for the proletarian revolution will inevitably destroy capitalism.[31]

Throughout 1923–24 the Onguardists had kept attacking fellow travelers as distorters and detractors of the Revolution, as men who by their creative efforts tried to bridge the gap between the past and the present. In 1924, the controversy reached a high pitch of violence. Trot-

[31] This resolution was printed in *Zvezda* (*Star*), No. 1 (1925).

sky and Voronsky, who had stood in defense of fellow travelers, were attacked even more violently. Ivan Maysky, a former Menshevik, who was later to become Soviet ambassador in London, opened the pages of his review *Zvezda (Star)* to a discussion of the whole subject of proletarian culture and literature. He introduced it with an article entitled "About Culture, Literature, and the Communist Party," in which he sided definitely with the Onguardists and appealed to the authority of Lenin. He was supported by Lelevich, Rodov, and Gorbachov. Among his opponents was G. Yakubovsky, of the Smithy group. A more cautious attitude was taken by Lunacharsky and by the old Marxist critic Peter Kogan.[32]

Since Voronsky's views were to prevail for some time in the official literary policy, his article which provoked the *Zvezda* discussion deserves some attention. Appearing originally in March, 1924, it represented a memorandum submitted to the Propaganda Section of the Central Committee of the Communist party, where the matters of literary policy were usually ventilated and decided. It was divided into twelve "theses," which can be briefly summarized as follows:

(1) After 1905 the main current of Russian literature was individualistic and decadent. The October Revolution cut off the roots which fed this literature. The most prominent among the old writers fell silent, became anemic, or emigrated.

(2) During the Civil War literature was naturally propagandistic. Its main task was to help the Revolution win over its enemies. The services rendered by this propaganda literature in the past were great, and since the Republic of the Soviets remained "a besieged camp" and was obliged to carry an incessant struggle against the bourgeoisie, propaganda literature retained its value.

(3) Following upon the transition from War Communism to peaceful reconstruction, literature was now faced with the problem

32 This discussion was afterwards published in book form under the title *Proletariat i literatura (Proletariat and Literature)*. Maysky prefaced this volume with an Introduction concerning Lenin's views on art, and added the articles of Trotsky and Voronsky which had started the discussion, as well as another polemical article by Voronsky which had appeared in *Krasnaya Nov (Red Virgin Soil)* in reply to Lelevich and himself. Much of this discussion smacks of pedantic scholasticism, while there is also a strong element of personal vituperation, but the issues discussed were of vital interest to a great many writers whose freedom to write more or less as they wished was at stake. English-speaking readers will find a fuller account of this controversy and of Voronsky's subsequent skirmishes with the Onguardists in Hugh McLean, Jr.'s article "Voronskij and VAPP," in *The American Slavic and East European Review*, Vol. VIII, No. 3 (October, 1949), 185–200. The article contains, however, some factual inaccuracies; nor is there any justification for describing Voronsky as one of the most original Soviet critics: Voronsky's chief qualities were his honesty, courage, and comparative broadmindedness; there was nothing original (or even particularly sensitive) in his approach to literature.

of reflecting more truly the revolutionary reality. Propaganda and agitation were not enough. What was expected of literature was the artistic cognition of life. Hence the great revival of prose fiction. The first to reflect the new Soviet realities in prose fiction were the so-called fellow travelers, writers of lower middle-class, peasant, or intelligentsia origin, who grew up during the Revolution, accepted its achievements, observed it at first hand, or even took part in it. They were afterwards joined by some of their seniors. Though motley, ideologically unstable, or even suspect, this literature produced some valuable and significant works reflecting the Revolution, its new men and new mores. Its methods were realistic, though tinged with a peculiar romanticism.

(4) The NEP engendered "constitutional illusions" among a certain section of the bourgeois intelligentsia. These men tried to exploit the literary revival for their own class ends. There were attempts to infuse literature with clericalism and mysticism, to portray the Revolution as a senseless mutiny.

(5) Various groups of proletarian writers were also affected by the literary revival. Many of them were brought down to earth from the heights of abstract industrial romanticism. Several proletarian prose writers emerged from the ranks of the League of Communist Youth.

(6) The Party fought vigorously against all attempts to utilize the NEP for reactionary ends. It gave active assistance to "intermediate," nonparty writers and encouraged the left wing of the fellow travelers. The main fault of the fellow travelers was that they often understood the Revolution as a triumph of the peasants and disregarded the guiding role of the proletariat. Nor were they able to grasp the international character of the Revolution. In helping these writers, the Party exposed the limitations of their outlook. On the other hand, it supported proletarian and Communist writers by helping their publishing enterprises, printing their works in Soviet periodicals, and in other ways. At the same time it combatted all alien influences on them (Andrey Bely, Cosmism, etc.).

(7) Of late, some Communist writers grouped around the magazine *On Guard* began to campaign in favor of a unified Party line in matters of art, in place of the alleged present chaos. They attacked the fellow travelers, the Smithy, the LEF, and even some Communist writers. Their main demand was that proletarian literature should be placed in the center of the picture, while fellow travelers should be relegated to the background. It was true that fellow travelers still held the central position in literary life. It was

due to their numerical and qualitative superiority. But the problem was no longer acute, and the demand of the Onguardists for a "quota" for fellow travelers in literature was unreal.

(8) The growth of Soviet literature in the last three years could not be doubted. The Party's efforts to subordinate literature to its ideological hegemony and to make it serve the cause of the Revolution had borne fruit. But there were also signs of a crisis, of literature being "in the doldrums." They were to be seen in the drying up of romantic enthusiasm, due to the postponement of the social revolution in the West and the unseemly aspects of the NEP; in the artificial, showy optimism of some proletarian writers; in the drunken bohemianism of Esenin; and so on. The urgent problem facing Soviet literature was not the problem of fellow travelers, but the problem of getting out of these doldrums, of helping literature get closer to real life, of saving it from abstract romanticism and from Red hagiography. Vacillating nonparty writers must be oriented toward the Revolution, but their ideological shortcomings must not be glossed over. The sheep must be separated from the goats.

(9) The Party must continue to assist associations of proletarian writers and encourage young Communist writers. But the hothouse atmosphere prevailing in proletarian literary organizations handicapped normal developments. It was therefore desirable to aim at an association on a wider basis, which would include fellow travelers, without encroaching upon the independence of the existing organizations.

(10) It was important to do away with the obvious absurdities and excesses of political censorship which interfered with the artistic evaluation of literary works, regarded satirical portrayal of life as an insult to the Revolution, and demanded Communist ideology from non-Communist writers. A special commission should be set up to mend this situation.

(11) Steps should be taken to alleviate the material hardships of Soviet writers. The problem of living accommodations was particularly acute. Bohemianism in life and its reflections in literature should be combatted.

(12) Though allowing writers full freedom in their search for new forms and styles, the Party considered realism, understood as cognition based on experience, to be most in keeping with dialectical materialism. At the same time the Party called upon writers to produce clear, simple, and intelligible works for the new reading public.[33]

[33] See A. Voronsky, "O tekushchem momente i zadachakh RKP v khudozhe-

Such was Voronsky's moderate, but thoroughly orthodox, Marxist program of the Party's literary policy. It will be seen later that in the main it anticipated the tenets of Socialist realism. He recognized unequivocally the Party's "ideological hegemony" in literature and was uncompromisingly hostile to all alien influences. His thrust at Soviet censorship was mild enough. His desiderata received the implicit official approval when the Press Section of the Central Committee of the Communist party convoked a special conference which, on May 19, 1924, passed a resolution confirming the Party's policy of benevolence toward fellow travelers and their literature. The resolution avoided any specific mention of proletarian literature, preferring to speak of "the art of those peasants and workers who, in the process of cultural elevation of the large masses of the people, become workers' and peasants' writers." But the resolution rebuked the Onguardists and proclaimed that "no literary current, school, or group must come forward in the name of the Party." The majority of ranking Communist leaders opposed, at the time, the claim of proletarian literary organizations to a factual and legal supremacy in literature. Their point of view was tersely formulated by Bukharin when he told the Onguardists: "First you must build, then you can receive." Lunacharsky and Radek took the same attitude. Trotsky had expressed himself even more emphatically when he wrote earlier:

> There can be no question of creating a new culture . . . during the period of dictatorship. The cultural reconstruction, which will begin when the need for the iron clutch of a dictatorship unparalleled in history will have disappeared, will not have a class character. This seems to lead to the conclusion that there is no proletarian culture and never will be one. . . . Such terms as "proletarian literature" and "proletarian culture" are dangerous . . . . They falsify perspectives, violate proportions, distort standards, and further the arrogance of small circles.[34]

History has apparently failed to record Stalin's views on this problem.

The resolution of the Press Section of the Central Committee was embodied in a resolution of the Thirteenth Party Congress which met in May, 1924. A year later, it was laid at the basis of a more explicit resolution of the Central Committee. This resolution of May, 1925, was

---

stvennoy literature" ("About the Current Moment and the Objects of Russian Communist Party in Imaginative Literature"), in *Proletariat and Literature*, 45–52.

[34] *Literature and Revolution*, 185 and 205. (The Russian edition of Trotsky's book appeared in 1923.) I have made slight changes in the translation.

to govern the official literary policy in the next four years, and more will be said about it in Chapter III.

In the heated literary debates which raged during 1923–24, not the least noisy part was played by the former Futurists from the LEF who launched in 1923 a magazine under the same name. Apart from such well-known poets as Mayakovsky and Vasily Kamensky (b. 1884), its regular contributors included some Futurists from the Russian Far East, among them the poets Aseyev and Tretyakov and the literary critic N. Chuzhak (pseudonym of N. Nasimovich, b. 1876).[35] Chuzhak, Osip Brik (b. 1888), Boris Kushner (b. 1888), and Boris Arvatov (b. 1896) were the principal theoreticians of the LEF group. In its program, published in the first issue of the magazine, LEF underlined the revolutionary nature of true Futurism and boasted of the services it had rendered to the Revolution in its initial stages:

> We produced the first things of art of the October era. . . . We organized the newspaper *Art of the Commune,* as well as visits to factories and plants, with debates and recitals. Our ideas won a working-class audience.

The program spoke slightingly and ironically of all rival groups and organizations. It accused proletarian writers of becoming "official" and "academic" and not learning from the Futurists, and referred contemptuously to Pilnyak and the Serapions, as well as to Alexey Tolstoy, who was said to be "scrubbing the white horse of his *Complete Works* in anticipation of a triumphant entry into Moscow." The objects of LEF were formulated in a series of snappy sentences:

> . . . LEF will indoctrinate art with the ideas of the Commune, opening for it the road into Tomorrow.
> LEF will indoctrinate the masses with our art. . . .
> LEF will confirm our theories by active art. . . . It will fight for life-building art.
> We do not claim to monopolize the revolutionary mentality in art. We'll find it out by competition.

In a series of equally bombastic aphorisms LEF announced a revision of its tactics. The battle against the classical heritage in literature was declared to have lost its urgency, the classics having become the

[35] Aseyev, Tretyakov, and Chuzhak belonged to the group *"Tvorchestvo"* ("Creation") in Siberia. Next to those in Moscow and Petrograd, it was apparently the most active Futurist organization in 1919–21. Tretyakov and Chuzhak were later "purged" and disappeared—see the *Bulletin* of the Russian Literary Fund in New York (*Izvestiya Literaturnogo Fonda,* No. 4 [December, 1950], 7). This issue contains a list of Soviet writers, critics, actors, and scholars who were shot or have disappeared. The list is obviously incomplete and is probably inaccurate.

"ordinary textbooks" of the one hundred and fifty millions of Soviet citizens. But LEF promised to go on fighting dead methods in art and relics of the past in post-Revolutionary Russia, and waging war on all those "who for the poetry of one's home substitute the poetry of one's house committee."

> We used to fight the bulls of the bourgeoisie. We shocked people with our yellow blazers and painted faces.
> Now we are fighting the victims of those bulls in our Soviet society.
> *Our weapons are example, agitation, propaganda.*[36]

Throughout the two years of its existence *LEF* magazine championed utilitarian, "purposeful" art, art conceived as "building of life" and "production of things,"[37] opposing this conception to Voronsky's idea of art as cognition of life, as well as to the Onguardists' stress on ideology. It was attacked both on the right and on the left. On the right, apart from Voronsky, its most outspoken critic was A. Lezhnev (pseudonym of Abram Gorelik, b. 1893).[38] Lezhnev rejected the contention of LEF that realism was essentially a bourgeois form of art. For him, it was the art of the rising class. "Every class," he wrote, "which comes to the forefront of history . . . asserts realism in art in one form or another." Soviet literature was therefore irrevocably moving toward realism. The "production art" proclaimed by LEF—art that "makes" life, instead of reproducing or reflecting it—was for Lezhnev a contradiction in terms. Its advocates were faced with the dilemma of either admitting their superfluity, of merging art with technology, of exchanging art workshops for workshops pure and simple, or of creating a new style, conventional and decorative; this was confirmed by the so-called "production" artists. Futurism was for Lezhnev a direct continuation of Sym-

---

[36] *LEF*, No. 1 (March, 1923).

[37] "Art is the production of values (things) needed by the class and by mankind" (Chuzhak). By way of explanation Chuzhak added that there existed two kinds of "things": material objects and "models of things (ideas)." Brik wrote that it was the "purpose" of a thing that determined "the organization of its color and form." In its insistence on form and its hostility to ideology LEF came very close to the so-called Formalists. When Brik wrote that the "history of poetry is a history of the evolution of devices of verbal formalization . . . . A poet is a craftsman of words, a word-maker," he was merely paraphrasing Shklovsky.

[38] Between 1924 and 1929 Lezhnev published several volumes of critical essays: *Voprosy literatury i kritiki* (*Problems of Literature and Criticism*, 1925?), *Sovremenniki* (*Contemporaries*, 1927), and *Literaturnye budni* (*Literary Weekdays*, 1929). Together with D. Gorbov he published in 1929 a survey of the first decade of Soviet literature, *Literatura revolyutsionnogo desyatiletiya* (*Literature of the Revolutionary Decade*). In 1935 appeared an interesting book of meditations on art entitled *Ob iskusstve* (*About Art*). In the late thirties both Lezhnev and Gorbov disappeared from Soviet literature.

bolism, for it implied hypertrophy of form. Futurism stood in the same relation to Symbolism as Symbolism to Naturalism. The so-called "left" art had no right to claim that it was realistic, for realism meant representation of reality and was opposed to formal, fantastic, and abstract art, while "left" art denied the very principle of representation.[39]

LEF was fighting a losing battle. Lezhnev was right in maintaining that Soviet literature was evolving toward realism. Attacked on both sides and aware of its precarious position, LEF, late in 1923, concluded a working arrangement with the Moscow Association of Proletarian Writers for the purpose of fighting "the demoralizing influence of the bourgeois-gentry and would-be fellow-traveling literature" and working out "a sound class policy in art."[40]

The attempt of Futurism to reassert itself in Soviet literary life proved a fiasco: early in 1925 *LEF* magazine ceased publication. Apart from its vociferous campaign for "left" art, its contribution to literature was of small account: a few stories of Babel (whom it introduced into Soviet literature) and some poems of Pasternak, Mayakovsky, and Aseyev are probably all that will be remembered of its output. But, approached retrospectively, its shrill campaigning on behalf of a new art had the merit of freshness and daring. In 1927 *LEF* was revived under the title *Novy LEF* (*New LEF*), but its life was even shorter—more will be said about it in Chapter III.

A kindred group, with a rather vague program couched in appalling jargon (with such critical terms as *"gruzofikatsiya,"* or "loadification"), entered the literary scene in the autumn of 1924. It called itself "The Literary Center of the Constructivists," or LTsC for short. Its manifesto defined Constructivism as "motivated art" and spoke of it as "a stage on the way to the art of Socialism" and as "a reflection of the organizational onrush of the working class."[41] The manifesto was signed by Ilya Selvinsky, Kornely Zelinsky, Vera Inber, Boris Agapov, Evgeny Gabrilovich, D. Tumanny (pseudonym of N. Panov), and Innokenty Oksyonov. They shared LEF's ideas about "purposeful," "technicized" art, but tried to be more specific in their demands on artistic form.

In December of 1924, the Constructivists, following the lead given by LEF, concluded an "agreement" with the MAPP for the object of fighting those literary groups which, "under cover of demands for the artist's technical freedom," tended to "obscure the meaning of our epoch and . . . disorganize the cultural class effort of the proletariat."[42] This

39 "Proletkult i proletarskoye iskusstvo" ("The *Proletkult* and Proletarian Art"), in Lezhnev, *Problems of Literature and Criticism.*
40 *Literaturnye manifesty* (*Literary Manifestoes*) (edited by N. L. Brodsky, V. Lvov-Rogachevsky, and N. P. Sidorov), 245–47.
41 *Ibid.,* 258–60.
42 *Ibid.,* 261.

anxiety of the groups which claimed to stand for "left" art to reinsure themselves by an alliance with the extreme political left was significant, just as was the tendency of various groups to seek theoretical bases, no matter how vague and confusing, for their artistic practices. But it was soon clear that the highway of Soviet literature lay outside these various "fronts" and "centers."

III. The Emergence of a New Literature
1924–29

1. *The Charter of Writers' Liberties*

IN June, 1925, just a year after Voronsky had won his signal victory over the Onguardists, the Central Committee of the Communist party, this supreme policy-making organ of the Soviet state, reaffirmed and clarified its literary policy in a special resolution which came to be spoken of as the "Magna Charta Libertatum" of Soviet writers.[1]

To be sure, the liberties it granted to Soviet writers were relative and limited. The fundamental principle of state and party interference in all matters of art and literature was reasserted quite clearly. The wording did not differ much from that of the resolution passed by the first conference of proletarian writers: point four of the 1925 resolution of the Central Committee laid down that "in a class society there is and can be no neutral art." This statement was, however, qualified by a reference to "the infinitely more varied forms" in which the class nature of art in general, and of literature in particular, is manifested, as compared with politics and economics. The resolution went on to say that it would be wrong to disregard this fundamental fact of Soviet social life—the fact that the working class had conquered power and set up a dictatorship of the proletariat. During the period of proletarian dictatorship the Party was confronted with a number of new problems: the problem of finding a *modus vivendi* with the peasantry while gradually transforming it; the problem of partial co-operation with the bourgeoisie, with a view to slowly ousting it; and the problem of enrolling the intelligentsia in the service of the Revolution and winning it over from the bourgeoisie. The proletariat, while retaining and gradually extending its leadership, must conquer various sectors of the ideological front. The process of infiltration of dialectical materialism into new fields (biology, psychology, natural sciences) has already begun. Sooner or later the proletariat will consolidate its position in literature, too. But this problem is infinitely more complex than many of the others, for "if the proletariat possesses already the unfailing criteria for evaluating the socio-political content of any work of literature, it lacks such ready-

[1] *Ibid.*, 292–98. This resolution was published in all Soviet papers.

made answers to all the problems of artistic form." The resolution denied that proletarian writers had a "hegemony" in literature, but pledged them the Party's support in *"earning* the historical right to such a hegemony." Peasant writers, said the resolution, must be treated benevolently and supported; their peculiarities must be respected.

With regard to fellow travelers the resolution insisted on bearing in mind (1) their differentiation, (2) the role played by many of them as skilled "specialists" in literary technique, and (3) the existence of vacillations among them. The general attitude toward them should be one of tactful care, in order to ensure their speediest adherence to Communist ideology. While sifting away antiproletarian and antirevolutionary elements and combatting all signs of revived bourgeois ideology, the Party must be tolerant toward "intermediate" ideological forms. All this was a restatement of Voronsky's program.

With regard to proletarian writers the resolution recommended that all possible support and assistance be given to them and their organizations, while at the same time discouraging all manifestations of pernicious *komchvanstvo* (Communist snobbery) on their part. "It is precisely because the Party sees in them the coming ideological leaders of Soviet literature that it must fight by all means against a frivolous and disdainful attitude toward the old cultural heritage and toward literary specialists." The resolution also declared war on all attempts at fostering a "hothouse 'proletarian' literature." Communist critics were told to give up their tone of "literary command" and, while fighting mercilessly against all counterrevolutionary tendencies in literature, be tactful and tolerant to "all those literary groupings which can and will march along with the proletariat."

Point thirteen of the resolution confirmed the refusal of the Party to commit itself to any particular literary form. "While guiding literature as a whole, the Party can no more support this or that faction in literature (classifying them according to their different conceptions of form and style) than it can solve problems of the family forms by resolutions, although it does and must guide the building of a new mode of life. Everything leads us to believe that a style in keeping with the epoch will be created by different methods, but the solution of this problem has not yet been suggested. All attempts to bind the Party in this respect, in the present phase of our cultural development, must be rejected." The resolution therefore advocated "free competition of various groups and currents"; any other solution, it said, would be "a bureaucratic pseudosolution." While pledging its moral and material support to proletarian and peasant-proletarian literature, the Party refused to grant legal monopoly to any literary group or organization, not even to the most purely proletarian in its ideology, for this "would mean . . . the undoing of proletarian literature." Taking, apparently, its cue from Voronsky's memorandum, the Party promised to "root out all attempts at crude and incompetent administrative interference in literary matters."

In a way the 1925 resolution of the Central Committee merely sanctioned the existing order of things. Its importance lay in the fact that the claim of proletarian literary organizations to play the leading role in literature and to control the literary production of non-Communists was firmly rejected. Fellow travelers were given more elbow-room and enabled to continue their work in peace. The resolution was interpreted by everybody as a clear-cut victory for them and a defeat for the Onguardists. One of its immediate results was a split within the "On Guard" group. The majority of the group loyally accepted the resolution as the guiding principle and decided to reorient its activities. The name of the group was changed to "On Literary Guard," and its slogans became "Learning, creative work, and self-criticism." In its new work it was led by the young Communist novelist Libedinsky. The obdurate minority, with the critic Gorbachov at its head, withdrew from the group.

The period during which the principles of the 1925 resolution governed literary life in the Soviet Union proved to be rich and fruitful. It was marked in the first place by the revival of the novel as a literary genre, and by that return to realism which Voronsky and Lezhnev had advocated and predicted.

2. *The Revival of the Novel*

CHRONOLOGICAL boundary lines, marking off one period in the evolution of a literature from another, are bound to be somewhat arbitrary. But there are sufficient reasons for regarding the year 1924 as the starting point of a new period in Soviet literature, for it was in 1924 that the Communist party definitely adopted a policy of benevolent encouragement toward non-Communist writers and fellow travelers. And it was the fellow travelers—both the comparatively young newcomers to literature, such as Fedin, Leonov, Kaverin, Slonimsky, and others, and the older pre-Revolutionary writers, like Alexey Tolstoy, Prishvin, and Ehrenburg—who made the greatest contribution to Soviet literature during 1924–29. Indirectly, moreover, the Party's decision to encourage fellow travelers and to snub proletarian writers helped also to stimulate the creative activity of the latter, who, along with the fellow travelers and such Communist and "proletarian" writers as Gladkov, Libedinsky, Fadeyev, and others, had their share in the revival of the novel as a literary form. It is during this period that the novel became the dominant literary genre in Soviet literature, definitely superseding the short story, which had dominated the preceding period. This new formal development implied thematic changes: while most of the writers of the preceding period had dealt with the period of the Civil War and concentrated on recording the incidents of the Revolution and their impressions of it, deliberately discarding the traditional method of psychological analysis and presenting the Revolution as a series of "purple patches," these new novelists aimed at grasping the Revolution as a whole, at analyzing its causes and effects, its makers and victims, at portraying—no longer impressionistically, but realistically —the new *byt* (mode of life, mores) and the sharp conflicts between the old and the new in post-Revolutionary Russia. The scope of literature was widened; though it still dealt predominantly with contemporary themes, the very choice of its themes became wider. At the same time, the writers' treatment of them underwent a considerable change. The earlier combination of ideological detachment and subjectivism no longer satisfied them. The new themes and the new approach favored the medium of the objective social-psychological novel. But thematic changes affected in their turn the character of other literary genres during this period. A number of writers appeared who can be best characterized as chroniclers of post-Revolutionary life, some of them with a strong satirical turn. The period also saw the revival of the historical novel as a legitimate and popular literary genre, no longer to be confined to the domain of juvenile literature.

The striking feature of this period is the richness and variety of its literary production, and an attempt to bring some unity into the picture inevitably involves certain simplification and overgeneralization. In the account that follows I have bracketed some writers together according to certain common characteristics, while departing from the strict chronological order.

NEVEROV AND FURMANOV

Although the rebirth of the novel as the dominant literary genre can be dated from 1924, when Fedin's *Cities and Years,* the first large-scale psychological novel in Soviet literature, was published, this does not mean that there had been no Soviet novels before that. Some of them, however, were novels only in name (those of Pilnyak, Nikitin, and Vsevolod Ivanov); others (those of Semyonov, Tarasov-Rodionov, and Libedinsky) were not characteristic of the period during which they appeared and will be discussed below in connection with their authors' later work. Two writers, however, who died in the early period of Soviet literature, may be introduced here—Neverov and Furmanov.

Alexander Neverov (pseudonym of Alexander Sergeyevich Skobelev, 1886–1923) began writing and publishing before the Revolution. His stories of village life (he was of peasant stock himself) were in the tradition of Populist realism. During the famine of 1920–21 he went to Tashkent and later wrote what became his most celebrated work—*Tashkent gorod khlebny* (*Tashkent, the Bread City*, 1923). It describes the journey to Tashkent of two village boys who are driven from their home by the famine, and gives a forceful picture of famine-ravaged Russia. Neverov also published several plays and stories. His village stories, especially "Andron Neputyovy" ("Andron Good-for-Nothing"), are a truthful reflection of the deep-seated social contradictions which were brought to light by the Revolution. The hero of "Andron" is a village Communist who in his fight for the new mode of life comes up against the stubborn opposition of the peasants.

Dmitry Andreyevich Furmanov (1891–1926) also came from a peasant family, but spent his childhood in Ivanovo-Voznesensk, the "Russian Manchester," where his father kept a pub. In the Revolution his sympathies lay at first with the Social-Revolutionary party, then with the Anarchists, but in 1918 he joined the Bolshevik party and became a member of a provincial executive committee. During the Civil War he served as a political commissar in the army of Chapayev, a colorful peasant guerrilla-leader in the Ural steppes. He earned fame with his *Chapayev* (1923), which Soviet critics often describe as the first important contribution to proletarian prose fiction. Though often referred to as "a novel," it is really a piece of documentary literature. If its historical value is to be doubted, it is not because of any attempt on the part of Furmanov to "fictionalize" history, but because of his very definite political bias. Furmanov showed, however, considerable talent in the portrayal of Chapayev himself and of partisan psychology and methods of warfare. Much emphasis is laid on the political "education" of Chapayev. The novel was later made into one of the most interesting Soviet films about the early period of the Revolution. Furmanov's second novel, *Myatezh* (*Revolt*, 1925), was also a semidocumentary account of the Civil War in Central Asia.

FEDIN

Born in Saratov in 1892, Konstantin Alexandrovich Fedin was older than the majority of the Serapion Brothers in whose almanac he made his literary debut. His early stories reflect the influence of Chekhov and Bunin. This is especially true of the first story of his to attract general attention, "Sad" ("The Orchard"), written in 1920. Its clear, transparent outline, its poetic descriptions, and its well-balanced prose remind one of Bunin, while the treatment of the theme and the characters resembles Chekhov. The subject of this story was one to which Fedin was to return again and again and which runs through much of the early Soviet literature: the clash of the old and the new in the Revolution. This gives the story, which is told in a quiet, measured tempo, a dramatic quality. The principal character is an old gardener, Silanty. His former masters, to whom he is unquestioningly devoted, have been scared away by the Revolution. The old manor house has been made over by the new regime into a children's home: new revolutionary songs echo through its rooms and sound a discordant note. The orchard, which is in Silanty's charge, goes to rack and ruin. In the end, Silanty, taking advantage of the absence of the new occupants, who have gone on some outing, and of his wife whom he deliberately sends on an errand to a near-by town, sets the beloved house and orchard on fire. The same tragic note is sounded in the story "Tishina" ("Stillness," 1924), which is about an old, dispossesed squire. The quiet, realistic flow of the uneventful narrative is broken by the almost fantastic scene of the squire's battle with a flock of rooks for the sake of an old lady whom he once loved and betrayed: the last romantic outburst of a man beaten down by life. "Muzhiki" ("The Peasants"), which relates several episodes in the life of a village shepherd and his daughter, recalls Bunin by its somber portrayal of the cruel and brutal aspects of peasants' life and mentality. The note of cruelty, gloom, and despair is sounded still more clearly in "Narovchatskaya khronika" ("The Chronicle of Narovchat"), told in the name of a half-educated monk and by its *skaz* manner recalling Leskov and Remizov. All of these stories deal with the post-Revolutionary period. There are also a few others, such as "Anna Timofevna" (1922) and "Rasskaz ob odnom utre" ("The Tale of One Morning," 1921), in which the Revolution has no place.

A new and original note was struck by Fedin in his *Transvaal* (1926), a longish story of an odd character with an outlandish name (Swaaker) and an obscure past, who settles down in a Russian village and gradually comes to wield almost dictatorial economic power over the whole neighborhood, marries the daughter of the former squire, and lords over the peasants. He is shown as a cunning, enterprising, thrifty, selfish, and hardhearted *kulak*, disliked and feared, yet respected by all around him. On its publication the story called forth a lively controversy among Soviet critics. Some of them accused Fedin of idealizing his *kulak;* others spoke of his being "blind in the left eye"— that is, of portraying Swaaker as much too powerful and not opposing to him the revolutionary elements in the village.[2]

Fedin, who from the very first had shown that he had close links with the traditions of nineteenth-century Russian literature, was to play an important part in the revival of the novel as a literary genre.

[2] Gorbachov, *Contemporary Russian Literature*, 170–71.

His first novel, *Goroda i gody* (*Cities and Years*), published in 1924, represented the first attempt by a Soviet author to depict the Revolution not in an impartially descriptive or lyrically ecstatic vein—as did Pilnyak, Nikitin, Vsevolod Ivanov, and even Babel—but as a large canvas, combining the elements of a novel of adventure with a psychological novel on a contemporary theme. For one of his mottoes Fedin chose a quotation from Dickens's *A Tale of Two Cities* (". . . we had everything before us, we had nothing before us . . . "). The novel was to be a picture of the first years of the Revolution, an attempt to grasp and analyze its mainsprings and the forces at work in it. Orthodox Soviet critics blamed Fedin for his one-sidedness, for dwelling on inessential aspects of the Revolution and fussing too much about his hero, a spineless and rootless intellectual. The theme of the novel is, in fact, the tragedy of a member of the intelligentsia at grips with the Revolution. Its action covers a period of time from before World War I to 1922. The hero, Andrey Startsov, a young student, is caught by the war in Germany and remains there as a civilian internee. (Here Fedin introduced an autobiographical trait: his own internment in Germany from 1914 to 1918 is the only incident in his otherwise uneventful biography.) Returning to Russia after the Brest-Litovsk Peace, Andrey is drawn into the revolutionary vortex. He fails, however, to find a proper place for himself in the Revolution. His trouble is that he puts personal interests and values before the cause which he is expected, and wants, to serve. He is too sentimental, too vacillating—a modern variant of the *lishny chelovek*—a superfluous man, a misfit, a square peg in a round hole—a character so beloved of the Russian novelists of the nineteenth century. This ultimately brings about his undoing: he is killed by his friend Kurt Wahn, but he is really finished long before physical death overtakes him.

Kurt Wahn, a man of strong will and of action, is shown as a contrast to Andrey. A German by nationality, he is a gifted artist. He and Andrey first meet and become friends in Germany in prewar days, but the moment the war breaks out Kurt's dormant German patriotism awakens, and he breaks with Andrey. Full of enthusiasm, he joins the army and is later taken prisoner by the Russians. They next meet in Moscow in 1918. The years spent by Kurt in Russia as a prisoner of war have turned him into an ardent revolutionary: he is now a prominent member of the Council of German Soldier Deputies, set up after the Bolshevik Revolution. As such he is sent to the small provincial town of Semidol, surrounded by villages with a backward Mordva population, to supervise the repatriation of German war prisoners. He takes Andrey with him. Here one of the important episodes in the plot of the novel takes place: a group of German war prisoners, exploiting the backwardness of the Mordva peasantry and playing on their nationalist sentiments, organizes an anti-Bolshevik detachment. It is led by a German officer, a certain Markgraf von zur Mühlen-Schönau, who is linked up with both Andrey and Kurt: the latter has his own reasons to dislike him, and the former, to be grateful to him. The rebels are defeated by a Soviet punitive detachment. During this short episode Andrey lives through something like a fit of revolutionary enthusiasm; he almost feels to be at one with the Revolution; but this feeling soon vanishes, and later he tries in vain to recapture it. Personal reasons lead him to betray the cause he is serving and help von Schönau escape, by providing him with papers which he steals from Kurt's desk. Before this is discovered, he is sent to Petrograd to take part in the defense against the approaching White Army of General Yudenich. The girl who has fallen in love with him at Semidol follows him there. Another girl, Marie Urbach, with whom he was in love in Germany, comes all the way from Germany to join him. Discovering that she has a rival, she decides to give way and withdraw from Andrey's life. Although Andrey himself could not really decide between the two, this is a great blow to him. Mad with grief, he wanders about Petrograd and afterwards leads a strange secluded life until ultimately Kurt's vengeance overtakes him: all this time Kurt has been dogging him as a traitor. In the end Kurt shoots him.

The construction of this novel is original. It begins with its own denouement—with Andrey's death in 1922 at the hands of Kurt. Then the narrative is switched back to 1919, to Andrey's arrival in Petrograd and the visit which von Schönau, on his way to Germany, pays him there. Much that lies behind these incidents remains obscure to the reader, and this veil of mystery and suspense is lifted only toward the end of the book. Havoc is played with the traditional chronological order of the narrative; it is only with the third chapter that Fedin takes up the exposition of events in their chronological sequence and unravels for us some of the deliberately tangled threads. We are shown Andrey in prewar Germany, his friendship with Kurt Wahn, their life in Nuremberg, the outbreak of war, Andrey's life as a civilian internee in the small Saxon town of Bischoffsberg, and his unsuccessful attempt at escape. There is a whole "chapter of digressions," as Fedin calls it, relating in a flashback the childhood and youth of Marie Urbach, the heroine of the novel, her love affair with von Schönau, her meeting with and love for Andrey. Then the chronological order is reestablished once more, and we are told about the 1918 revolution in Germany; the repatriation of prisoners, including Andrey; his encounter with Kurt Wahn in Moscow; their life in Semidol and the events there. Here again there are some side episodes interpolated into the main story; one of these, a whole novelette, has no direct relation to the main events of the novel and was even published separately before the novel appeared. The novel ends with a chapter describing what happened in Petrograd in 1920: its proper chronological place is between Chapters One and Two.

Although there is a certain disorder—partly deliberate—about *Cities and Years,* it is a work of considerable originality and undoubted literary merits. In point of time it was the first major work in Soviet literature which tried to answer some questions raised by the Revolution. Fedin does not offer any ready-made solutions; he merely shows us the tragedy of a typical member of the intelligentsia caught in the Revolution and swept aside, after an attempt to adjust himself to it and even to play an active role in it. The general suffering and passive attitude of the intelligentsia is well conveyed in a memorable chapter describing the compulsory digging of trenches outside Petrograd, ordered by Trotsky at the approach of General Yudenich's army. The novel combines many traditional elements, which go back to the Russian classics of the nineteenth century (the general theme, the characters, and in parts the manner, recall Turgenev in particular), with formal innovations, for some of which Fedin was indebted to Andrey Bely, while some were his own. This first full-length novel by a post-Revolutionary author at once set quite a high standard.

Fedin's second long novel, *Bratya* (*Brothers,* 1928), has similar peculiarities of construction. It does not begin exactly where it should end, but the real place of the opening chapter is just before the finale. In this opening chapter Fedin introduces, with considerable dramatic skill, in a scene saturated with life and full of psychological intensity, all of the main characters. We are shown at once all the knots of the plot ready to be untied. Fedin then proceeds to demonstrate at some length how these intricate and intertwined knots came into being, and then to undo them in the last section of the book.

The theme of the novel is closely akin to that of *Cities and Years,* and the principal character, Nikita Karev, a gifted composer, is a variation on Andrey Startsov. But besides the issue of purely personal adjustment to the Revolution, he is faced with the additional problem of reconciling with it his artistic vocation. Like Startsov he fails: he cannot find in music an adequate expression for the Revolution, and he also ends by losing, in turn, all the women whom he loved or who loved him.

Fedin's second novel was much closer, in manner, to the Russian tradition of social and psychological realism, but it lacked the exciting novelty and the harmony between form and content of the earlier work.

LEONOV

Another typical representative of the fellow travelers who played an important part in the revival of the novel is Leonid Maximovich Leonov.

Leonov was born in 1899 in Moscow. His father was a peasant, a self-taught poet and journalist. In 1918 Leonov graduated from one of the high schools in Moscow, after which he served for three years in the Red Army. He began writing early, most of his youthful work being in verse. His first story to appear in print was "Buryga" (1922). His early stories are ingenious stylistic experiments. For some time Soviet critics spoke of him as a talented pasticheur. "Tuatamur," a weird and beautiful Oriental poem written in rhythmical prose; "Derevyannaya koroleva" ("The Wooden Queen") and "Bubnovy valet" ("The Knave of Diamonds"), two clever and charming stories where realism, Hoffmanesque fantasy, and quaint Andersenian humor are oddly blended; "Gibel Egorushki" ("Egorushka's Undoing"), a tale of primitive life in the far North of Russia, with a strong element of fantasy—such are some of Leonov's early stories, published before 1924. The influence of Gogol, Leskov, Remizov, Zamyatin, and Pilnyak, together with that of some of the Western romantics, was obvious in most of them. In 1924 appeared two longer works: *Zapiski Andreya Petrovicha Kovyakina* (*Memoirs of A. P. Kovyakin*) and *Konets melkogo cheloveka* (*The End of a Petty Man*). The former, a story of provincial life in the early years of the Revolution, belonged to the Leskov-Remizov *skaz* tradition. *The End of a Petty Man* stemmed from Dostoyevsky and was still largely a pastiche, but it was of more than passing interest and marked the turning-point in Leonov's literary career, for it contained some of the most significant elements of his later, mature work. Its theme was also one that was to play an important part in Soviet literature.

In it Leonov shows us one of the men cast overboard by the Revolution, floating helplessly and aimlessly in the middle of its turbulent stream. He is a scholar, a world-famous paleontologist, Likharev by name, who is engaged on an epoch-making scientific work and is quite impervious to what is going on around him. The action is set during the worst years of War Communism, famine, and misery, against the nightmarish background of revolutionary Petrograd. Likharev is joined by his sister, a consumptive old maid, who comes to minister to his daily needs. He falls ill and is haunted by hallucinations. Every night he is visited by his double, a distant relation of Ivan Karamazov's devil, who comes to converse with him and mock him. There is a powerful rhythm in the succession of mad and terrible scenes. One of the most memorable passages is the description of a gathering of all sorts of *ci-devant* men, the flotsam and jetsam of the Revolution, who engage in futile or crazy discussions of the events. It is after this party that Likharev suddenly becomes aware of the realities and sees that his sister is dying, that there is no bread, nothing left in his larder, that the whole country is going the way of its appointed sufferings. Suddenly there is peace and light in his mind: he is ready to die. But, to make his sacrifice complete, he must destroy the manuscript of his work. His double also urges him to burn it—"maybe something will grow out of its ashes." And there is a note of mockery in the parting words of Likharev's demon when he paints before him a vision of the coming millenium: "Now Russia will rise high, very high. The sky will be paved with concrete, streetcars will furrow the clouds. Bread will be made of air . . . people will wear velvet trousers." At these words Likharev flings himself at his visitor, slips, and loses consciousness. Such is the end of this "petty man," cast away by the Revolution in its implacable course.

Everything in this story—its diction, its characters, its situations— reminds the reader of Dostoyevsky. There are passages that read like plagiarisms, but are probably deliberate parallels—for a long time Leonov, in his treatment of the Revolution, continued to be obsessed by Dostoyevsky and his visions. But for all its dependence on Dostoyevsky, *The End of a Petty Man* is an interesting and powerful work, one of the most interesting in this early period.

Leonov's first long novel, *Barsuki* (*The Badgers*), was published in 1925, soon after Fedin's *Cities and Years*. It reflected the same tendency—away from pure verbal ornamentalism and emotional lyricism, back to psychological and social realism. It had, however, closer ties with the Gogol-Remizov-Zamyatin-Pilnyak tradition. Its language is highly emotional and often stylized; it has frequent lyrical digressions and interpolated stories that have obvious symbolical significance; like Pilnyak, Leonov often suddenly interrupts his narrative to apostrophize the reader, or studs the narrative with exclamations and rhetorical questions. The main theme of the novel is the deep cleavage between town and village, which from this point becomes one of Leonov's favorite motifs: it probably reflects his own background, the double nature of an urbanized offspring of peasant stock.

The novel is a diptych; it falls distinctly into two parts, unequal in length. The first, a shorter one, has for its setting a typical merchant quarter of Moscow not long before the Revolution, a corner of the old world where life runs along a well-established rut. The two heroes of the book, the brothers Semyon and Pashka, grow up amid these surroundings, to which they were brought as small boys from their native village to learn urban ways and be trained in business. But their characters are different and they soon part ways. The elder, Pashka, lame, sullen, unsociable, and willful, rebels against the oppressive, stifling atmosphere of Bykhalov's store where he and Semyon work as errand boys; he runs away, joins the ranks of the proletariat, and becomes a factory worker. During the greater part of the novel the reader loses sight of him, but he reappears toward the end of the book as a Soviet commissar, and plays an important part in the dramatic denouement. The real hero of the book is Semyon. Although he shows himself more adaptable than his brother and remains in Moscow until he is drafted into the army, he cannot delete from his mind the early reminiscences of village life and is nostalgically drawn toward it: at heart he remains a peasant. The Revolution brings him back to his native village as one of the many deserters from the army.

In the second part of the book Leonov shows us Semyon's native village under the impact of the Revolution. The local peasants rise against the Soviets, and on Semyon devolves the leadership of the rebellion. The causes of the rising are to be sought partly in the squabble between two neighboring villages, the squabble that goes back to the pre-emancipation days (this gives Leonov an opportunity for painting some Gogolian scenes of the age of serfdom), and partly in the peasants' grievances arising out of the food tax levied by the new government. The rebellion is ultimately crushed—it fails for lack of any real general purpose and plan behind it and, consequently, of any genuine fighting spirit. Semyon is the only one among the rebels who is actuated by an idea, the idea of an irreconcilable conflict between village and town; the only one who rises above those petty local grievances, who has dreams of a peasant uprising on a national scale, and who is not disheartened by the hardships and privations to which the rebels expose themselves when they retire to the surrounding woods and dig themselves in there (hence their name of "Badgers"). But Semyon, too, when all his followers betray and desert him, is forced to capitulate. In the final scene we see Semyon back from the woods and meeting with his brother. Pashka, now known as "Comrade Anton," heads the punitive detachment sent to suppress the rebellion. Not a word is spoken between them on this occasion (the two brothers had, however, met before in the woods and talked matters over), but the reader is left with the impression that, although capitulating in fact, Semyon does not do so in spirit: his hatred for the town and all that it stands for remains as strong as ever. In a new disguise and under a new name, that of Nikolka Zavarikhin, a young peasant who is on the way to become rich under the NEP, he will come to life again in Leonov's next novel, to personify the same idea and the same everlasting conflict. In *The Badgers,* however, the conflict remains unsolved, and upon that silent meeting between the two brothers, Leonov characteristically lets the curtain fall.

The Badgers was followed in 1927 by another long novel, *Vor* (*The*

Thief), still more ambitious in size and scope, though lacking perhaps the singlemindedness of the earlier novel and the definiteness of its social theme. The Revolution is less obviously felt in it, partly because the novel deals with a period—the era of the NEP—when the Revolution abandoned some of its principles and made a temporary retreat. The hero is Mitka (Dmitry) Vekshin, a curious variety of a Russian Rocambol, who at the same time has not a little in common with some of Dostoyevsky's characters, especially with his namesake in *The Brothers Karamazov* and Raskolnikov. He is one of the "disillusioned" of the Revolution: from a prominent figure in its early stages—a commissar in the Red Army—he becomes under the NEP regime the ringleader of a formidable gang of burglars with a world-wide reputation.

No sooner does the reader begin *The Thief* than he becomes aware of the influence of Dostoyevsky on Leonov. In *The Badgers* it is possible to trace it here and there (in the scene between Egor Brykin and his wife's lover; and in the legend of the Great Kalafat, told by one of the "Badgers" at a campfire), but on the whole this novel belongs to a different tradition. In *The Thief*, however, the impact of Dostoyevsky on Leonov is as obvious as it is in *The End of a Petty Man*. Apart from the general morbid tone and heightened, hysterical style, the predilection for psychological complications and perversities and for delving into the darker sides of human nature, many of Leonov's characters have their models in Dostoyevsky. Thus Masha Dolomanova, nicknamed "The Blizzard," is a direct descendant of Dostoyevsky's "infernal" women—of Nastasya Filipovna in *The Idiot* and of Grushenka in *The Brothers Karamazov*. In old Manyukin there is an obvious resemblance to the old Karamazov. The relation between Mitka and Leonty parallels the relation between Ivan Karamazov and Smerdyakov. Chikilyov, even in name, recalls Shigalyov in *The Possessed*. Pukhov, however, a homespun philosopher with a strong religious coloring, seems to stem from Gorky's "truth-seekers" (just as Katushin in *The Badgers*—the two have much in common); but when Pukhov tells Mitka to steel himself by suffering, one is again reminded of one of Dostoyevsky's favorite ideas. The opening scene of the novel, which takes place on a train, suggests the opening scene in *The Idiot*. The structure of the novel, with its criminological interest, its complicated criss-cross plot, its great number of multifarious characters—representatives of the underworld, former bourgeois, small Soviet employees—is also reminiscent of Dostoyevsky. Leonov still further complicates the already complex structure of the novel by introducing, and making a very clever use of, the device of a novel within a novel, as did André Gide in his *Counterfeiters*: one of Leonov's characters, the writer Firsov, is writing a novel about the characters of *The Thief*. Thus sometimes the reader gets a double vision of the whole thing, through the eyes of Leonov and through the eyes of Firsov.

Leonov excells particularly in drawing the underdogs of life, the "humiliated and injured," the downtrodden representatives of the old world; these he portrays with great insight and much compassion. This compassionate note also allies Leonov with Dostoyevsky and makes him fit in well with the main tradition of Russian literature. *The Thief* is free from political bias, and Leonov is not concerned with any "messages." It is true that the novel ends on an optimistic note: Mitka gives up his gangster life and goes into seclusion somewhere in the country, from where he returns, we gather, a "reformed" character, though how and to what purpose reformed, Leonov does not tell us. This inconclusive ending is typical of Leonov. He is interested not in Mitka's social re-education, but in Mitka as a man, in Mitka's ethical problem, which is to know whether a man has the right to kill a fellow being—the problem that occupied Raskolnikov and Ivan Karamazov. In his revolutionary past Mitka had committed a cold-blooded murder, killing his prisoner, a White officer, in retaliation for his favorite horse. This incident came to be the turning point in Mitka's revolutionary career and the real cause of his subsequent downfall and of all his torments and sufferings.

Leonov is concerned in his novel not with any specific problems of the Revolution, but with life in all its many-sided complexity—life that is reluctant to follow any ready-made grooves and obeys its own laws. Firsov, the novelist in Leonov's novel, says: "After all we [writers] know life better than anyone else. It tastes nice: you eat it—and die without noticing." Through Firsov it is Leonov himself who is speaking, just as to him can be applied the following words: "Firsov was fond of life, of its acrid and coarse smell, of its tart and bitter taste, of its flimsy bulkiness, even of its wise senselessness." It is this smell and taste of life that Leonov tried to convey in his novels, and no wonder Communist critics accused him of "irrationalism." Moreover, to Firsov's irrational zest for life Leonov opposed the views of a certain Chikilyov. The resemblance to Dostoyevsky's Shigalyov is not only in the name. Like his quasi-namesake in *The Possessed*, this insignificant Soviet official, a tax inspector who likes to pry into other people's affairs, preaches the idea of a society based on absolute equality where thought control will be carried to perfection through an all-round system of mutual espionage. Leonov's Chikilyov says:

> Here we are seeking happiness. But we have not yet bethought ourselves of cutting the whole human race to one pattern. Let men be born equal in height, length, weight, and so forth. As soon as

someone starts pushing up, we'll cut his wings short. There will be no trouble, all will dance to the same tune . . . .

In the future state, which will come in a thousand years, there will be no secrets. Anyone, you see, will be able to come to anyone else and watch the other man's life at any time of day or night, say through a magnifying glass. Suppose you are secretly planning to ruin mankind. With those modern scientific achievements—the ray of death, the sneezing gas—you could blow up the whole globe in no time. You must watch the humans, they must not be left to themselves. No little secrets, citizens, come out, come out into the open, and make a clean breast of what you are up to. Then willy-nilly all will be honest. Want it or not, you'll have to stick to it. Suppose I were the ruler of the world, I would fix on to everybody's head a sort of machine, with a kind of telegraph tape. In the morning a specially appointed official would take the reading and affix his resolution. . . . And everybody would be able to peer in the same way into his controller's mind. Thought—that's the source of all suffering.

This is no doubt an intentional parody of Shigalyov's idea of a society which "proceeds from unlimited freedom and arrives at unlimited despotism," as Verkhovensky explains it to Stavrogin:

He has espionage. He has every member of society watching the others, and under an obligation to inform on them. Each one belongs to all, and all belong to each one. All are slaves, and equal in slavery. If need be, slander and murder, but above all—equality. The first thing is to reduce the level of education, knowledge, and talent. A high standard of learning and talent is within reach of higher abilities only—down with higher abilities! Higher abilities at all times seized power and became despots . . . . Slaves must be equal. There has never been freedom or equality without despotism. But there must be equality in a herd, and that's what Shigalyovism means.

It is not surprising, perhaps, that *The Thief* is one of Leonov's works that is never reprinted now.

In *The Thief*, Leonov also reintroduced his favorite theme of the irreconcilable cleavage between city and village. He personified it in Nikolka Zavarikhin, a rival of Mitka in the affections of Masha Dolomanova. Nikolka is young, cunning, energetic, and ambitious. He hates the city and its "idle" inhabitants who sponge on the peasants and their toil, and he dreams of domineering them. He symbolizes peasant vitality and at the same time the unconquerable bourgeois spirit, the lust for wealth and power.

On its publication Leonov's second novel was acclaimed by Soviet critics as a work of indubitable talent and power. But the more orthodox among them stressed Leonov's fundamentally pessimistic attitude toward the Revolution. In the words of Gorbachov,

> The "potent poison of Manyukin's disillusionment" in the "epoch of unheroic weekdays" is diffused throughout Leonov's book.[3]

OLESHA

In 1927 there appeared one of the most interesting and original works in the whole of Soviet literature. Its title was *Zavist* (*Envy*), and its author, Yury Karlovich Olesha. Olesha was born in 1899 in Elizavetgrad and grew up in Odessa, and was thus a countryman of Babel, Katayev, Bagritsky, and some other young writers. Until 1927 he was practically unknown beyond the confines of daily journalism; and even here his activities were limited to the railway men's paper, *Gudok*, for which he wrote topical verse, which he signed "Zubilo" ("Point-Tool"). His name was quite new to most of the critics, but with the publication of *Envy* his literary reputation was established at one stroke. *Pravda* wrote that it had placed Olesha "in the front ranks of those writers who stand close to the circles of proletarian artists." *The Young Guard* called it "a brilliant and profound work." *Revolution and Culture* spoke of the significance of its theme, "one of the central themes of our time." Outside Russia the novel was hailed with equal enthusiasm by several *émigré* critics. The overnight success of this first novel by a hitherto unknown writer could be compared only to that of Dostoyevsky's *Poor Folk*.

There was nothing new in Olesha's theme, however. It was the rather hackneyed theme of the conflict between the old and the new in the Revolution, a conflict which had been explored by Fedin and Leonov, by some of the early revolutionary romantics, by Gladkov, and by many third-rate proletarian novelists. The novelty of the work lay in Olesha's treatment of this theme, in the freshness of form and manner. Instead of portraying this conflict in terms of actual episodes and concrete political or economic problems of Soviet life, Olesha succeeded in raising it to a higher level, in giving it a deeper and more universal meaning.

Envy is a short novel, especially as Russian novels go: some 120 pages. It has only six characters, of whom three stand as it were for the old world, and three for the new. This bareness and simplicity of the structure, reducing the theme to an almost algebraic and symbolic baldness, is obviously deliberate. The characters are Andrey Babichev,

[3] *Ibid.*, 161.

98

director of a Soviet Food Industry combine; his adopted son, Volodya Makarov, a member of the Young Communist League and a noted football player; Valya, a young girl of sixteen, Andrey's niece—these three representing the new world; and Ivan Babichev, Andrey's brother and Valya's father; Nikolay Kavalerov; and Anichka Prokopovich—these representing the old world. Andrey Babichev is a kind of "Americanized" Communist, an embodiment of physical fitness and of moral and intellectual smugness. Volodya is a rather typical young Communist—narrowminded, and strongly oriented toward a machine-made civilization; in the eyes of Andrey he personifies the new generation, the coming man. Valya has also in her something of the modern young woman, healthy and realistic, but at the same time she is endowed with the charm of the eternally feminine. She and Volodya are in love. Ivan Babichev is a gifted good-for-nothing romantic, cast out by the Revolution, who describes himself as "the last dreamer on earth." Kavalerov is also a romantic and a dreamer, but of a different cast. Anichka Prokopovich, a repulsive widow in her fifties, is an incarnation of *poshlost,* of mean vulgarity.

From a formal point of view, the book falls into two parts: in the first, Kavalerov is the narrator; in the second, the author himself takes over. At the beginning we see Kavalerov as an inmate of Andrey Babichev's house where he is, in his own words, the latter's buffoon—one night Babichev, moved by a sentimental recollection of Volodya, his temporarily-absent adopted son, had picked him up in the street where he was lying drunk and had taken him to his home. Kavalerov is quite young, only twenty-seven, but the reader thinks of him as ageless. An individualist who feels out of harmony with his epoch and with the order of things in revolutionary Russia, he dreams of attaining personal fame—of some way of bequeathing his name to posterity—but he can see no opportunity in Communist Russia. His overwhelming, all-consuming emotion is envy. He both envies and hates Andrey, all the more since he realizes that he, Kavalerov, for all his inefficiency, is more intelligent and more gifted than the prosperous and self-satisfied director of the Food Combine—the "sausage-maker," as Kavalerov contemptuously calls him. Babichev, on the other hand, feels for Kavalerov a pity bordering on contempt. One day Kavalerov decides to leave Babichev's house and go back to his old life as a down-and-out loafer. He writes a long sarcastic letter to Andrey, giving vent to his hatred for him and proclaiming his superiority over him. He also expresses his conviction that Volodya, of whom Babichev seems to be so fond, is really in the same position and will never come back. As he takes that letter to Babichev's apartment, Volodya arrives, and Kavalerov sees for himself that Volodya is very much at home there, that there is no similarity in their positions. Realizing his foolishness, he decides to take his letter back, but by mistake picks up Volodya's recent letter to Babichev about himself and thus learns the true motives behind Babichev's hospitality. This makes him hate the "sausage-maker" all the more. He vows vengeance to him.

During his subsequent wanderings through Moscow he comes across Babichev's brother Ivan, whom he had only just seen and overheard in an argument with Andrey. He hails him as his friend, his master, his comforter, for Ivan is Andrey's avowed opponent. A romantic liar, who throughout his childhood kept inventing fantastic gadgets and telling fantastic lies, he speaks also of having invented himself. He laments the disappearance of ordinary human feelings in the new society and wants to organize their parade—"a conspiracy of feelings," as he calls it. In one of the disreputable beerhouses which he now frequents and where he does card tricks, reads people's characters by the lines on their palms, sketches customers' portraits, displays feats of memory, and engages in other dubious occupations, Ivan holds forth before an audience of similar good-for-nothings:

> We are human beings who have reached the uttermost limits of life. Men with strong personalities, men who want to live life in their own way, egoists, single-minded men—it is you I am addressing, for you are the intelligent ones: you are my advance guard! Listen, you in the vanguard! An age is dying. A wave is breaking against the rocks, it boils and then it begins to froth. What do you want? To disappear like the foam of the wave? No, my friends, this should not be your end! No! Come to me and I will teach you . . . .
>
> Be proud! I am your leader, I am king of the rabble. Any man who sings, weeps, rubs his nose on the table when all the beer is drunk and they won't serve him with more—his place is here, by my side. Come, all of you who are laden with grief, all you borne on song. You who are bursting with jealousy and you who are tying a hangman's noose for yourself—I call on you all, children of a doomed age, come to me, vagabonds and dreamers, fathers of families who cherish your daughters, honest bourgeois, men faithful to tradition, who acknowledge the norms of decency, duty and love, who shun the sight of blood and disorder, my dear friends— soldiers and generals alike—let us march out to war.[4]

Babichev is talked about as a new prophet. Marvelous stories are told about him, and rumors make their way "into government offices, the rest homes, and markets."

[4] This and the following quotations are taken, with some alterations, from the English version of *Envy* (translated by P. Ross).

One story concerns an actual episode when Ivan Babichev tries to stop his brother driving in an official car, obstructs the traffic, and is arrested by the Ogpu. It is to the Ogpu examining magistrate that he tries to explain what he means by his "conspiracy of feelings." Here is a part of their dialogue:

"You referred to yourself as a king?" asked the examining magistrate.

"Yes . . . king of the rabble."

"What's that supposed to mean?"

"Well, you see, I am opening a lot of people's eyes."

"What are you opening them to?"

"They must clearly understand that they are doomed."

"You said before, a lot of people. Whom do you include among these people?"

"All those you call decadent. Everybody with a decadent nature. If you'll allow me I'll explain what I mean."

"I'd be grateful if you would."

". . . a whole number of human feelings is about to be eliminated . . . ."

"Which, for example?"

"Compassion, tenderness, pride, zeal, love—in short, almost all those emotions which constituted the soul of man in the age which is now dying."

"I see."

"I take it you understand me. Stung by the serpent of jealousy, the communist is a prey to persecution. . . . We know that the grave of a Young Communist who has committed suicide is alternately covered with wreaths and the curses of his colleagues. The man of the new world says: 'Suicide is the deed of a decadent.' But the man of the old world says: 'He must have committed suicide to save his honor.' Thus we see that the new man schools himself to scorn sentiments that are hallowed by poets and by the muse of history herself."

"So that is what you mean by the conspiracy of feelings?"

"Yes, that is the conspiracy of feelings of which I am the leader . . . . To me has fallen the honor of leading the last parade of human feelings."

The examining magistrate asks Ivan whether he has managed to find any followers. Only one, says Babichev, adding that his name is Nikolay Kavalerov and the emotion he represents is envy.

So Ivan and Kavalerov fight their battle against Andrey together. There is something of a modern Don Quixote in Ivan. When his "con-

spiracy of feelings" fails, he falls back upon the marvelous, all-round
machine of his own invention to which he gives the name of Ophelia—
"the most human, the most touching of all names, . . . the name of a girl
who went mad from love and despair." He intends to use this machine
for the eternal dishonor of the modern, inhuman, mechanized world,
and in particular for the destruction of his brother's "Dime," a gigantic
model canteen which is to provide cheap and hygienic meals for the
population of Moscow and to free housewives from kitchen drudgery.

In the imaginary speech which Ivan Babichev holds at its inauguration he exclaims:

> Do not call upon us. Don't beckon to us, don't tempt us. What
> can you offer us in the place of our capacity for loving, hating, hop-
> ing, weeping, pitying, and forgiving? Here is a pillow. Our coat-
> of-arms. Our banner.

And Ivan brandishes the pillow as a symbol of family life, of the traditional home.

Kavalerov, who acts as a Sancho Panza to Babichev's Don Quixote,
is in fact more romantic, more of an individualist. An obvious kinship
binds him to Dostoyevsky's Man from the Underground. He is worried
by the same problem of self-assertion. The following monologue of his is
reminiscent of the Man from the Underground with his "twice two is
five," of Ivan Karamzov with his "everything is permitted," and of
Raskolnikov's challenge:

> I want to argue. I want to display the force of my personality. I
> want the fame to which I am entitled. . . . If only one could go out
> into the open, do something with oneself, make one's bow: I have
> lived, I have done something I wanted to. . . . If it were only com-
> mitting suicide for no reason. Just out of mischief. To show that
> everyone has the right to act as he thinks fit. Today, let us say. Hang
> myself on your front door . . . .

As a side theme Olesha introduces also the Dostoyevskian theme
of the opposition of Russia and the West. It is not without significance
that Kavalerov, the romantic rebel, the individualist who dreams of
asserting his personality, regrets that he was not born in the West "in
some small French town." "In our country," he says, "the roads to fame
are barred. A gifted man must either dim out or dare lift the barrier
with a great row." It is this last that Kavalerov and Ivan Babichev attempt to do. They end, however, by capitulating and resigning. The
conspiracy of feelings falls flat—even the "Ophelia" fails Ivan. They
are also defeated in their efforts to save Valya from Andrey and Volodya,
and come to realize that she does not want to be saved, that she herself

is part of the new world. For Kavalerov this is the greatest blow, for he is romantically in love with her and imagines himself her knight protector, destined to save her from the usurping designs of Andrey and Valya. In the person of Valya, Olesha may have intended to bridge the world of emotions and the world of new realities. In spite of her modernity and her earthliness, which are seen especially in the scenes of the football match and of the sporting exercises in the courtyard of her house, Valya is drawn in romantically ethereal colors. The sentimental romantic pink is the color accompaniment of her theme. Behind the exterior of a modern Soviet girl, keen on sports and physical culture, Olesha stresses her "eternal-feminine" substance. The key to her personality is in the following phrase which Kavalerov addresses to her and which is repeated as a refrain: "You swept past me like a branch laden with flowers and leaves." Yet, it is not only Andrey and Volodya, but Valya herself who laughs at it. Kavalerov's realization of his failure and defeat lead to his final and utter degradation: he returns to the huge, comfortable double bed of the Prokopovich widow. The same fate awaits Ivan Babichev. In a way, the new triumphs over the old. But only in a way.

Olesha's fundamental theme is the same which occupies many searching minds today, especially among former Communists. We find it restated in Arthur Koestler's *Darkness at Noon* and *The Yogi and the Commissar*. Andrey Babichev, the "sausage-maker," "the model of masculinity," is an embodiment of Koestler's Commissar type. When Rubashov, the hero of *Darkness at Noon,* writes down in his diary— "We have thrown overboard all conventions, our sole principle is that of consequent logic; we are sailing without ethical ballast"—he states, in my opinion, the problem which torments Olesha and which leads Ivan Babichev to organize his conspiracy of feelings. What will be the place of personal ethics, of human emotions and human dreams in this new mechanized, planned, totalitarian society which has discarded all ethical ballast and has proclaimed that the end justifies the means, a society which is represented by Andrey Babichev and his "Dime," that soulless ideal of material comfort and hygiene, and by Volodya Makarov with his cult of "unfeeling, proud machines" and his "Japanese grin"? —such is the main problem of *Envy*. Olesha's romantic rebels are portrayed in all their vulgarity and unattractiveness (one of the merits the Soviet critics saw in it, when they praised the novel on its first appearance, was this showing up of the "enemies of the Soviet regime" in all their naked ugliness). Yet, the unprejudiced reader cannot help being aware that Olesha has a sneaking regard for them—that it is not unintentionally that he endows Kavalerov with talent and imagination; that he sympathizes with his assertion of the worth of the individual and his proud rejection of a fame derived from the manufacture of improved sausages, just as he does with Ivan Babichev for whom "invention is the beloved of reason." For all their vulgarity and meanness the two "negative" characters of *Envy* are human, while the two main spokesmen of the "new world," the world of sausages, machines, and model canteens, are both vulgar *and* inhuman. When Kavalerov returns to Anichka and falls ill, he has a symbolic dream in which he sees Ivan killed by his own "Ophelia." Just as the machine, with a needle protruding from its head, is about to pin Ivan to the wall, he exclaims: "Save him! Surely you are not going to allow a machine to kill a human being?" There is no answer to his agonized cry. "My place is with him," says Kavalerov. "Master! I shall die with you." This dream of Kavalerov is also a symbolic triumph for Valya, the romantic, idealized Valya: charming and beyond reach, she soars above the crowd and the orchestra —"ribbons flew over her head, her dress billowed, her hair streamed upwards." She is apparently the only pledge of redemption for the "new world."

Although Olesha's novel is by no means a perfect work, in it he has succeeded in raising one of the staple themes of early Soviet literature to the level of a modern myth and produced one of the few works which, because of this universal significance, may remain when many other novels about the Russian Revolution will be studied only as documents reflecting a certain interesting period in Russian history.

Among contemporary Soviet fiction the novel also stands out because of Olesha's concern with formal design and verbal texture. Not only has Olesha a keen eye for the world, especially for its material externals, but he also has the gift of presenting them in striking and unexpected images, of making us see them, as it were, with new eyes. There is in his prose a freshness of outlook and vision combined with a freshness and felicity of expression. Like his Ivan Babichev, he is fond of the picturesque and sometimes allows himself to be carried away by his colorful imagery. Some Soviet critics have spoken of the influence of Giraudoux on Olesha's style.

In contrast to the deliberate simplicity of its structure and plot, the verbal texture of *Envy* is rich and complex—at times a little too rich, perhaps. The nervous dynamic style harmonizes well with the tempo of modern urban life, and *Envy* is essentially an urban novel. To the influence of Bely and his school may be ascribed the frequently recurring motifs. Thus Olesha enjoys mirrorlike, reflecting effects, which make ordinary things look new and fresh. Kavalerov himself speaks of the childlike character of his perceptions, of enjoying the vision of things through the wrong end of the binoculars. One of the central moments in the novel is the scene where Kavalerov meets Ivan Babichev, while watching his surroundings reflected in a street mirror. This bizarre, backward, refracted vision of the world, when normal rules of optics and geometry are violated and distorted, is the leitmotif of the whole work, in which the planes of reality and fantasy are displaced and interlocked and the borderline between waking and dreaming obliterated. We are not in the least surprised, therefore, when to Kavalerov's question about his sudden appearance out of nowhere, Ivan Babichev replies: "I invented myself." The motifs of refraction and invention are subtly woven into the very texture of the novel.

That the problem which occupied Olesha in *Envy* continued to interest him is proved by the volume of his stories which appeared in 1929 under the title *Lyubov (Love)*. Two of the three stories in this volume, "Love" and "Liompa," are elaborations of some of the motifs of *Envy*. In "Love" we see a young Marxist, Shuvalov, who falls in love with a girl, and whose vision of the world is suddenly transformed by love. Not only does he see the world differently from the way he saw it before, but his vision of it goes against the grain of his reason. Love turns him from a sober Marxian realist into a romantic. As a foil to him Olesha shows an anonymous, color-blind, black-hatted "citizen" whose vision of the world, except for his color-blindness, echoes the reality. There comes a moment when Shuvalov is so desperate that he is ready to exchange places with his counterpart, to give up the romantic green, the color which has become the dominant color of his world, and to see pears as inedible blue objects. But in the end romantic feelings triumph, and Shuvalov remains with his love and his green vision of the world.

In "Liompa" Olesha develops one of the side motifs of *Envy*—that of the relation between man and the objects which surround him. In *Envy* he contrasted Kavalerov and Andrey Babichev. "Things don't like me," says Kavalerov. "Furniture tries to play nasty tricks upon me. Once I was literally bitten by some varnished angle. My relations with blankets are always involved. My soup never cools. If some silly object, like a coin or a stud, falls off the table, it usually rolls under a piece of furniture which is hard to move. I crawl on the floor and, when I lift my head, I see the sideboard smirk." In "Liompa" we find this theme developed into a whole story. It is the story of a sick man who gradually loses his hold on things and is betrayed by them. Lying on his sickbed the hero of the story, Ponomaryov, thinks:

I thought the outside world did not exist. I thought it would cease to exist with me. But now . . . I see everything turning away from me while I am still alive. After all, I still exist. Why, then, don't things exist? I thought it was my brain which gave them shape, weight, and color, but here they are gone from me, and only their names—useless names having lost their masters—are swarming in my mind.

To this dying man's nominalist vision of the world is opposed the healthy and joyous realism of a small boy:

> Objects rushed to meet him. Without knowing a single name he smiled to them. As he went away a sumptuous trail of objects would flap after him.

In 1930 Olesha published another book of stories, *Vishnyovaya kostochka* (*The Cherry Stone*). It included the stories from *Love* as well as some new ones. Nearly all developed some of the motifs and secondary themes of *Envy*. Also closely related to the main theme of *Envy* was *Tri tolstyaka* (*Three Fat Men*, 1928), a novel supposedly written for children. It is an adventure story, full of delightful whimsicality, telling of certain happenings during a revolution in an imaginary country. The key theme of this novel, which was actually written before *Envy*, is to be found in its concluding lines:

> The three fat men told me: "Take out the boy's heart, and make an iron heart in its place." I refused to. I said that one must not deprive a man of his human heart; that no other heart—whether of iron, or of ice, or of gold—should be given man in the place of the simple, real, human heart.

This theme of the "simple, real, human heart" is also the leitmotif of Olesha's "Strogy yunosha" ("A Strict Youth"), "a play for the cinema," to which reference will be made later.

Several Soviet critics rightly described Olesha as a writer of a single theme. One of them (Lev Levin) defined it as "the theme of a lonely human destiny" and the theme of the "ugly duckling": both definitions were in fact Olesha's own and occur in his play *Spisok blagodeyany* (*A List of Blessings*, 1931), which will be treated at length in Chapter IV. Another critic (Zelinsky) spoke of Charlie Chaplin's "little man" as the real hero of all Olesha's works, and it is true that both Ivan Babichev and Kavalerov have in them something of Chaplin's hero (Babichev's "bowler" is an outward sign of his "Chaplinism"), while in *A List of Blessings* the Chaplin motif plays a very important part. But it would be better to say that all Olesha's writings represent the writer's dialogue with his epoch. This dialogue is significant because it epitomizes the fate of a nonconformist writer in Communist society, and to its later stages we shall return in Chapters IV and V.

The Revival of the Novel

KAVERIN

Veniamin Kaverin (pseudonym of Veniamin Alexandrovich Zilberg, b. 1902) has some affinity with Olesha. But his success was less rapid and spectacular, and he proved to be much more adaptable, so that his literary career was more steady and durable: Kaverin played some part in all the phases of Soviet literature from 1922 to this day.

Coming from a family in which musical talent had been conspicuous for four generations, he also began by studying music. Later he studied Oriental languages and history of literature at the University of Petrograd. He began writing at the age of fifteen and in 1920 sent Gorky his first story, "Odinadtsataya aksioma" ("The Eleventh Axiom"). Soon after that he joined the Serapion Brotherhood, in which, together with Luntz, he represented the "Westernizing" tendency. In his autobiography he described Luntz as his best friend, and also wrote facetiously: ". . . so far I have not had time to make for myself a biography fit for a Russian writer. I neither have tried to shoot myself nor to hang myself, nor did I once go mad."[5] Kaverin's story, printed in the Serapions' *Almanac*, stemmed from E. T. A. Hoffmann, and the whole of his first volume, *Mastera i podmasterya* (*Craftsmen and Apprentices*, 1923) showed the influence of that German romantic and of Edgar Allan Poe (later Kaverin described himself as "a young man who had read Edgar Allan Poe and took every barrel for a cask of Amontillado"). His early stories were often clever experiments for experiment's sake. His interest in plot and composition contrasted sharply with the plotless ornamentalism and shapelessness of most of the writers of this early period. The tendency toward a novel of adventure—this time one can speak of the influence of R. L. Stevenson, another of his and Luntz's idols —is particularly pronounced in Kaverin's first major work, *Konets khazy* (*The End of a Gang*, 1926). It is an exciting story of the Leningrad underworld, of gangsters and anarchists.

Elements of romanticism and grotesque realism à la Gogol are mingled in the stories in *Bubnovaya mast* (*Diamond Suit*, 1927), while the frankly surrealistic *Revizor* (*The Inspector General*) is a parody of Gogol's "The Nose," with a deliberately obscene twist.

On the other hand the novel *Devyat desyatykh sudby* (*Nine-Tenths of Fate*, 1926) reflected the general trend toward reviving the psychological novel. Its theme—the place of the intelligentsia in the Revolution —is reminiscent of Fedin's *Cities and Years*, but the treatment is much more superficial and immature.

In *Skandalist, ili vechera na Vasilyevskom ostrove* (*The Troublemaker, or the Evenings on Vasily Island*, 1928), Kaverin portrays the

5 See *Writers About Art and About Themselves*, 157.

107

academic and literary milieu in Leningrad. Into it he manages to introduce the element of adventure. Much of it reads as a topical pamphlet in the form of a novel *à clef*. One of the main characters appears to have been modeled on Victor Shklovsky, and the literary battles around Formalism are parodied. A note of protest against all restrictions on creative freedom, against all chaperoning of literature, is cautiously sounded, but at the same time Kaverin seems to be settling some personal accounts with the Formalists. The whole tone is too facetious and the message too ambiguous. The problem of the artist's freedom and independence and of his place in society was treated more seriously by Kaverin in his next novel, *Khudozhnik neizvesten* (*Artist Unknown*), which appeared as late as 1931, but was apparently written in 1929–30 and, spiritually, belongs to this earlier period.

There is a great affinity between this novel and Olesha's *Envy*. The similarity can be seen not only in the parallelism of their themes, but also in their form: their brevity, their small number of characters (Kaverin's has only three characters that matter, the rest are mere episodic figures), their simplicity of outline (which, however, in Kaverin's case is complicated by his Sternean toying with the plot), and their concern for form and verbal effects.

The motto to the novel was taken by Kaverin from *Don Quixote*: "And they marveled at the wisdom and folly of this gentleman." With equal appropriateness Kaverin could have chosen for his motto Ivan Babichev's formula: "Invention is the beloved of Reason," which would have suited his hero very well. At the core of *Artist Unknown* lies the problem of artistic consciousness. But it is coupled with the problem of ethics in Communist society. Like *Envy*, *Artist Unknown* is a contemporary myth. Its hero, the artist Arkhimedov, is a modern Don Quixote, an old-fashioned romantic idealist who fights a lonely, losing battle against the new society in the name of forgotten moral values, of artistic freedom and independence. There is a family air of resemblance between him and Olesha's Kavalerov and Ivan Babichev, and one can easily imagine him being drawn into Babichev's "conspiracy of feelings." But, though piteous and ludicrous, he is, unlike them, a lovable character and a tragic figure. The conflict between that which Arkhimedov stands for and the new "technocratic" society is presented in terms of a personal clash between him and his friend Shpektorov, the new-world realist, the man of the Five-Year Plan, a younger and less bourgeois variation on Andrey Babichev. He does not care a hang for Arkhimedov's moral preoccupations and qualms, and attaches more value to a pair of pants than to any moral principles. He is too busy "building Socialism" to bother about such "trifles." He reproaches Arkhimedov for wishing to "incorporate Middle Ages in the Five-Year

Plan." It is indeed to the medieval guilds that Arkhimedov looks back for the ideal of collectivist ethics, when he says:

> In the fifteenth century not a single workshop would accept an apprentice until he swore to perform his work honestly in accordance with the statutes and the aims of State. The weavers of those days used to burn publicly any cloth which had an admixture of hair. Guildsmen guilty of giving false wine measures were thrown off the roofs into the sewers. Just imagine the next session of the Central Executive Committee passing a decree on labor morality. With us there wouldn't be enough sewers for all the unscrupulous guildsmen.[6]

This, in a way, anticipates Arthur Koestler's definition, in his essay "The Yogi and the Commissar," of one of the vaguely formulated but distinct trends of our times as "anti-materialistic nostalgia": "It is allergic to the rationalism, the shallow optimism, the ruthless logic, the arrogant self-assurance, the Promethean attitude of the nineteenth century; it is attracted by mysticism, romanticism, the irrational ethical values, by medieval twilight." "Rationalism," "shallow optimism," "ruthless logic," and "arrogant self-assurance" are precisely the attributes of Shpektorov and of the mentality he represents, just as they express the very essence of Andrey Babichev.

Arkhimedov is not an enemy of the new regime. But, like Ivan Babichev—though much more acutely—he is conscious of a great lacuna in it which must be filled in. To use again Koestler's later definition, he realizes that "a society with no incentives and ethical values will, whatever its economic structure, either dissolve into chaos and anarchy, or become a dumb mass under the whip." Of course, Arkhimedov does not formulate this idea in so many words: after all, Kaverin had to write with an eye on censorship. But it is implicit in Arkhimedov's refusal to surrender his soul and his artistic consciousness to Shpektorov's "new world." It needed a great courage on Kaverin's part to put, in 1931, into the mouth of one of his minor characters, an art student and an admirer of Arkhimedov, the following vehement defense of free art:

> Real art is a perilous business, ruthless, with successes and failures, with revolts against the teachers, with veritable battles in which not only canvases are destroyed but human beings too. It is a battle for one's eye, for an honest eye which will yield to no laws or prohibitions. For its sake, one must accept hunger, cold and mockery. One must pocket one's pride or clench it between one's teeth, and if there is no canvas one must use one's own bedsheets to paint on.

[6] This and the other quotations are taken, with some changes, from the English version of *The Unknown Artist* (translated by P. Ross).

Equally courageous was the denunciation of "little" artists, of typical "conformists":

There are artists who find it easy to work these days. They are the lucky ones who are convinced that time works for them. They seize with a ready hand upon whatever comes their way, because in their artistic household everything seems timely and necessary. There are among them worthy men who have an exceptionally strongly developed instinct of historical self-preservation. And there are the boys who arrive when the meal is over . . . .

Arkhimedov and Shpektorov clash throughout the book. Too much stress, says Arkhimedov, is being laid in Soviet Russia on technique, with the result that morality lags hopelessly behind. "Personal dignity," he contends, "must be an essential ingredient of Socialism." He defends romantic illusions. To Shpektorov, who says that for Soviet Russia "the West is a box of tools without which it is impossible to build even a wooden shed, let alone Socialism," Arkhimedov retorts: "A box of tools is not enough to launch a new era." He insists on fighting "the decline of honor, hypocrisy, baseness, and boredom." Shpektorov just shrugs his shoulders: "Morality? I have no time to stop and think over that word."

The ideological conflict between Arkhimedov and Shpektorov is complicated by their personal relations. Arkhimedov's wife, Esther, and Shpektorov are in love with one another, and a little boy, whom Arkhimedov believes to be his son and whom he named Ferdinand (after Lassalle), is in fact Shpektorov's son. When Esther is faced with the choice between her love for Shpektorov and her pity (and, perhaps, secret admiration) for Arkhimedov, she commits suicide by jumping out of a window. Arkhimedov's clash with Shpektorov ends with Arkhimedov's defeat: he is forced to give up his last and most precious possession, his son and only prospective follower (as in Olesha's *Envy* there is a stress on the childlikeness of romanticism). The boy is officially adopted by Shpektorov, and Arkhimedov renounces all claim to him. This is the crowning blow dealt to him, for he is pathetically attached to Ferdinand. But the epilogue to the novel suggests that his defeat is only on the outward plane. Spiritually, he is the winner, and his passionate and selfless defense of free art is vindicated by his picture—a picture painted by "an unknown artist." The description of that picture, conceived during Arkhimedov's aimless wanderings about the streets of Leningrad after Esther's suicide, forms the epilogue to the novel. It is a picture representing his wife's suicide and the impressions gathered during his wanderings:

Only an artist whose free genius had rejected the cautious, dishonest standards of modern art with its aloofness from the people could have made a success of it. The mixture of the grand style with the trifles, of everyday details with a deep feeling for time, was something which neither living nor dead masters could have taught him. . . . To paint such a picture one had to crush to death.

Arkhimedov's defeat and downfall on the plane of life lead to his triumph as an artist and to the glorious vindication of his conception of true and heroic art. Such was the untimely message of Kaverin's novel, his most interesting work to date.

Like *Envy*, Kaverin's novel is unusual in form. It is begun in the third person, but from the second chapter—Kaverin calls his chapters "Encounters," and, in fact, they all center round some crucial encounter—the author himself intervenes, and after that we see Arkhimedov either through his eyes or as described by those who meet him. Shpektorov is portrayed as the author's former school-fellow, and it is through him that the author meets Arkhimedov. The novel is interspersed with frankly autobiographical material, seemingly irrelevant to the story. Kaverin keeps toying with the plot and resorting to what the Formalist school calls "laying bare the device," which results in some original effects. Some of the most important conclusions about Arkhimedov are reached by the author during a performance of Dickens's *Tale of Two Cities;* and in general, the theater plays a significant part in the unfolding of Arkhimedov's story. Some important scenes are laid behind the wings of the School Youth Theater, and here the important motif of Don Quixote is introduced, thus emphasizing the unreal, romantic, quixotic, "theatrical" nature of Arkhimedov's crusade for true art.

SLONIMSKY

Mikhail Leonidovich Slonimsky (b. 1897) was one of the seven young writers who formed, in 1920, the nucleus of the Serapion Brotherhood (the others, according to him, were Zoshchenko, Luntz, Nikitin, Gruzdyov, Polonskaya, and Pozner; the rest joined them a little later).[7] Like Kaverin and Luntz, he was a Jew and came from a highly cultured family: his father was for many years a regular contributor to the Liberal monthly *Vestnik Evropy* (*Messenger of Europe*); his mother was the sister of Professor Vengerov, the well-known literary historian; his elder brother was a pianist, while the well-known contemporary Polish poet of the same name is a cousin of his. Slonimsky's childhood was spent in a literary and musical milieu. In 1914, he joined the army as a volunteer. When the Revolution broke out in the spring of 1917,

[7] See *Writers About Art and About Themselves,* 313–14.

111

he was still a private in an engineering regiment stationed in Petrograd. The regiment was one of the first to join in the revolt, and more than half of its officers were killed by the men. About this time Slonimsky began to write. In 1918 he was released from military service, and when the House of Arts was founded by Gorky, he began to attend regularly Zamyatin's and Shklovsky's lectures there.

His early stories, collected in the volume *Shestoy strelkovy* (*The Sixth Lancers*, 1922), show a very strong influence of Zamyatin's manner and style: in Slonimsky the training received in Zamyatin's studio is more obvious than in any other of the Serapions. Broken, elliptical narrative; intense aversion to all psychological motivation and analysis; eccentric, odd characters involved in strange situations where the real and the fantastic are intermingled; a predilection for unusual, dramatic incidents—such are the characteristic features of these stories. Nearly all of them have the war and the impact of the Revolution on the army for their setting. The subject is treated in terms of stark realism bordering on the grotesque, and the paramount impression is that of powerful irrational forces playing havoc with human destinies, of senseless cruelty and inescapable doom. One of Slonimsky's merits—especially if we compare him with his two fellow-Serapions, Nikitin and Vsevolod Ivanov—is his ability to tell a story without unnecessary comment.

In 1923 Slonimsky spent some time in the Donets coal basin, editing a miners' paper there. One of the stories he wrote at the time, "Mashina Emery" ("The Emery Machine"), marked, thematically speaking, a new departure. Its hero is a certain Oleynikov, an ascetic Communist of the builder type, for whom personal life is completely overshadowed by his sense of duty toward the collective. Slonimsky fails to make his portrait of this Communist visionary—especially his relations with the girl whom he marries for the sake of her brother's memory—psychologically convincing. But it was one of the first attempts, on the part of a typical fellow traveler, to portray an "ideal" Communist. Oleynikov is shown as a dreamer who lives not so much in the present as in the future when all human emotions, sensations, and desires, everything except man's thoughts, will be mechanized, so that "machines will not only work for men but also rejoice and suffer for them," and human thought, thus freed, "will be able to take mechanized life apart, to separate joy from suffering, and to do away with suffering."

One of the most interesting passages in the story is the letter which Oleynikov receives from his friend Grisha, who, about to commit suicide, asks him to marry his sister. Grisha's letter is the confession of a disillusioned Communist who cannot bring into harmony the two planes of his existence, the two "floors" of life, as he puts it—the ideological and the everyday one. No longer capable of living on the upper floor only, and rejected by the lower floor, he chooses death. Slonimsky shows Grisha as a direct contrast to Oleynikov. As was usual with the Serapions and other writers of this period, he does not go into their biographical antecedents, leaving it to the reader to reconstruct them, but it is clear that Grisha is also a Communist and that their friendship is not purely personal, that they have had a common revolutionary experience. To Oleynikov's single-minded optimism Grisha opposes his doubts and qualms. His schizophrenia is due to ordinary human pity:

> My vision has changed. I used to look at the present through the future and was never sorry for anything. But now I look at the future through the present, and doubts assail me: Are we right? I've been corrupted by the oldest motif in the world—by pity. I remember with horror all I did in 1919. For the future, which you and I know, it was necessary, but what is one to do with pity? Everyday life has eclipsed the aim for which I lived. I feel sorry for all sorts of people—White guards, Communists, all. I want everything to come true now and everybody to be happy. Hence the snag, the vicious circle: in order not to pity anyone, you must rebuild life; in order to rebuild life, you must kill; in order to kill, you must have no pity for anyone; in order to have no pity, you must rebuild life. I can't get out of this vicious circle. I am not up to living on both floors at once. I find myself outside space and time.
>
> Let my case be a lesson to you. Stand on firm ground, don't hang in the air. I know: you'll be up to both floors, you're a strong man.

Here Slonimsky states concisely and bluntly the problem which must have been a very real one for many a Communist. Whether he has succeeded in making his readers share Grisha's faith in the ability of Oleynikov to cope with the problem is another question. For, while Grisha, who does not even appear in the story, is real and human, Oleynikov remains an abstraction.

The story retains many characteristic features of Slonimsky's earlier work—the rapid narrative, packed with incident; strange characters whose actions are disconcerting and unmotivated; rapid dialogue; and little description. Grisha's letter, with its ideological and psychological motivations, is like a foreign body in it. But in it may be seen a germ out of which Slonimsky's later novels grew.

In 1926 appeared Slonimsky's first novel, *Lavrovy* (*The Lavrovs*). It depicts the disintegration of an intelligentsia family. The action of the novel begins on the eve of World War I and goes on into the first years of Revolution. Much of the background—the war scenes, the early days of the Revolution which find the hero serving as a private in Slonimsky's own regiment in Petrograd—is obviously autobiographical and strictly documentary. The novel centers around the figure of Boris Lavrov, who straight from school joins the army as a volunteer, goes through some harrowing experiences at the front, and then is caught in the whirlpool of the Revolution and tries to fix a place in it for himself. To him are opposed, on the one hand, the other members of his family—his vulgar, domineering mother; his meek, henpecked father; his vain, futile brother—and on the other, Foma Kleshnyov, a true Bolshevik, active, sober-minded, resolute, who has a strong influence on Boris and is responsible for the latter's ultimately siding with the Revolution and becoming a small cog in its mechanism. Boris Lavrov has been described by some Soviet critics as a new variety of "superfluous man," once so popular in Russian literature and revived, after the Revolution, by Fedin. This is true up to a point, but at the end Boris is shown on the way to becoming a useful member of Soviet society. However, for a long time he flounders about, unable to grasp the meaning of what is going on around him: the more he thinks about it and about his own actions, the more meaningless it all appears to him. At one moment he thinks that in siding with the Revolution he has attained full freedom, but

> later he realized that there was no freedom anywhere on this earth, not in a single corner of it, and that of all the available unfreedoms he had chosen the one in which his wishes and actions coincided.

Lavrov's search for a place in the Revolution is erratic and psychologically not very convincing, his hold on it rather precarious. One has the impression that in portraying Lavrov's search Slonimsky was either vacillating, afraid to probe deeper into his own hero, or, true to his method of eschewing psychological motivation, was unable at this time, in a novel which purported to be a large-scale picture of the Revolution and its processes, to make a convincing and effective use of his customary medium.

Five years later Slonimsky was to return to his heroes in *Foma Kleshnyov* (1931), a chronological sequel to *The Lavrovs*. Here Kleshnyov, a good, straightforward Communist, is the hero, while Boris Lavrov plays a secondary part and is shown chiefly through his personal preoccupations (his love for Kleshnyov's wife, Liza, and his relations with another girl, Nadya Zhilkina). As a novel the book is a failure.[8] In

[8] In 1949 Slonimsky reissued *The Lavrovs* under a new title: *Pervye gody* (*First Years*). It is a considerably revised version of the original novel, with a number of new characters and new episodes, some of them transferred bodily or in new combinations from another short novel of Slonimsky's, *Proshchanie* (*The Farewell*, 1937). *The Farewell* was meant to complement the picture of the Revolution given in *The Lavrovs*, where Slonimsky had concentrated on the democratic February Revolution,

between *The Lavrovs* and *Foma Kleshnyov,* Slonimsky wrote another
novel, *Sredny Prospekt* (1927).[9] It is quite short and in manner much
closer to the early stories than to the Lavrov novels. Its plot is somewhat
shadowy, certain rather interesting possibilities remain unrealized, leaving loose ends that stick out here and there, but in the main it is a novel
of incident, involving unusual or even absurd situations, and strange,
disconcerting people, who have a habit of appearing from nowhere and
vanishing into thin air. The background is the "unheroic" NEP period
of the Revolution. One of the characters, Mikhail Shchegolev, is a distant relation of Leonov's Mitka Vekshin—a former Red commissar
turned smuggler. Utterly disillusioned, indifferent at bottom to everything, he calmly walks to his doom. The principal character in the novel
is a certain Pavel Lebedev, a "petty man" who becomes a typical hanger-
on of the Revolution. His "success" in life is a combined result of luck
and the animal instinct of adaptation. Though hardly a good novel,
Sredny Prospekt is a good picture of a certain period in Soviet life and
a certain section of Soviet society.

SAVICH

Voobrazhaemy sobesednik (*The Imaginary Interlocutor,* 1928), by
Ovady Savich, appears to be the only work of interest written by this
author, about whom Soviet reference works are silent.[10] It is one of the
very few Soviet novels dealing almost entirely with personal problems
and without political implications. Its hero bears the symbolical name
of Obydyonny, which could be rendered as something like "Mr. Daily"
or "Mr. Everyman," and is apparently meant to represent an average
specimen of Soviet humanity. He is a very ordinary man, an employee
of a provincial trust. The background of the novel and its secondary
characters are all quite real—the daily routine of a Soviet trust, Obydyonny's domestic life, and his relations with his insignificant colleagues. But beyond this background a second, symbolical plane is felt
constantly. The novel is really the story of Obydyonny's gradual transition, on his way to death, to a different plane—of his meaningless, un-

by scenes describing in more detail the October *coup d'état.* Neither the Lavrovs nor
Kleshnyov appeared in it. In *First Years* these scenes were woven into the framework
of the original version and the new characters tied by new ties to Boris Lavrov and
Foma Kleshnyov. Some of these changes were obviously dictated by Slonimsky's desire
to round off and clarify his main hero; others were of a purely "ideological" nature
and will be mentioned in Chapter VII.

9 The novel is so called from the name of a street in Petrograd. The title has
both a direct topographical and a symbolical meaning.

10 The only other work by Savich known to me, outside some magazine stories,
is *My i oni* (*We and They,* 1932) which he wrote together with Ilya Ehrenburg. It is
an anthology of Russian opinions, mainly from literature, about France and the
French.

motivated actions, his deep boredom, and his estrangement from those who surround him. The symbolism is enhanced by the introduction of Obydyonny's "imaginary interlocutor," who now appears as his double, as an exteriorization of his own thoughts and forebodings of death, and now is materialized in the real but mysterious person of a young dancer, Obydyonny's lodger. The novel ends with Obydyonny's death, for which all the rest was merely a preparation. There are in this curious and unusual novel echoes of Tolstoy's *Death of Ivan Ilyich* and also of Dostoyevsky, but the calm, unhurried narrative is quite unlike Dostoyevsky's.

BUDANTSEV

Sergey Fyodorovich Budantsev (b. 1896) began writing before the Revolution, but his first important work, the novel *Myatezh* (*The Revolt*), was published in 1923. Renamed later *Komandarm* (*The Army Commander*), it has for its subject an anti-Bolshevik rising in a provincial town, led by a certain Kalabukhov, a Social-Revolutionary of the left. He is shown as an individualist, a reckless adventurer, capable of personal heroism but opposed to all organization and discipline. He has his own conception of the revolution, which borders on anarchism, and he refuses to accept the Soviet government just as he refused to accept the Brest-Litovsk peace with the Germans and went on fighting them in their rear with his guerrillas. He says: "Your revolution is swallowing me. Yours. Not the one of which I became aware at the front after Brest when I withdrew to the Germans' rear. That revolution was mine, it was eternal, it was against death, it fought death. And yours, which you have mastered in two months, the Communist one, is a change from one form of economic activity to another. A transition, no more."

The somewhat pretentiously named *Povest o stradaniyakh uma* (*A Tale of the Sufferings of Mind*) was written in 1929 and first published in *Novy Mir*. The action of this short novel is set outside Russia and sometime in the past, but it has nothing to do with historical fiction. It has but few characters, and the only one that really matters is the hero, Mikhail Grekov, a brilliant young scientist of the eighteen-sixties, a follower and admirer of Darwin. The story of his childhood, of his scientific and academic career, and of his ill-fated marriage is given in a long flashback. The action proper takes place within a very short time in a Swiss boardinghouse, whose occupants are briefly introduced to the reader as a kind of grotesque backdrop. The narrative centers around Grekov's two attempts at suicide. The first time he takes morphine, but is saved through taking an overdose. The second time he proceeds more elaborately: he takes a scalding bath and then, dressed very lightly, walks out of the boardinghouse with the intention of catching cold. This time he is saved in a not very plausible way—through the combined agency of a friend's timely intervention and of his own suddenly aroused scientific interest in some insects. This artificially contrived rescue ends the novel, leaving the reader to assume that Grekov's suicidal intentions are over and that he will now resume life with a new zest.

The main interest of the novel—an altogether unusual work in Soviet literature—lies, however, in the thorough dissection of Grekov's mind and in the account of his past life. Budantsev was criticized for his unhistoricity and his failure, despite many references to Herzen and other contemporary figures, to portray Grekov as a typical man of the sixties. One Soviet critic spoke of Budantsev's "reactionary individualism." It appears, indeed, that Budantsev's choice of his period was quite arbitrary, or that he chose it by way of disguise, to avoid placing his hero in a contemporary setting. For the problems that occupy him are of no particular time or place; in fact, they might very well be those of a Soviet scholar. Grekov deliberately opposes himself, his personal problems, his meditations on life and death, to the interests of the society at large. In a conversation with his brother he tells the latter that for him his personal problem (the blindness which threatened him at the time) is of infinitely greater consequence than any social injustices. He says:

> Any social cruelty can be straightened out and mitigated. How many institutions that used to oppress mankind have fallen during the past seventy years! But this mitigation did not affect my lot. And the chief thing is: How will you mend the cruelty of Nature, its basic cruelty—death?

The novel is concerned largely with Grekov's grappling with the problem of death. His second attempt at suicide is the result of the cerebral tug of war that goes on within him. His decision to seek death is really a challenge to fate: instead of a simple suicide he must try something which will either finish him off or reawaken in him the desire to live. The ending of the novel suggests this latter outcome, but it is not very convincing.

KLYCHKOV

Sergey Klychkov (pseudonym of Sergey Antonovich Leshenkov, b. 1889) was originally known as a peasant poet. His poetry had points of affinity with Klyuev's and Esenin's, but it lacked the religious and messianic note. Some of its essential themes and motifs are to be found in the volume *Domashnie pesni* (*Domestic Songs*), which is saturated with Russian folklore. The folklore motifs form also an important element of his prose fiction, on which he concentrated after 1924. His novels *Sakharny nemets* (*The Sugar German*), *Chertukhinsky balakir* (*The Prattler of Chertukhino*), and *Knyaz mira* (*The Prince of Peace*), published in the late twenties, are parts of a vast epic of peasant life before the Revolution. Written in rich language, now ornately poetical, now colloquial, they combine a realistic portrayal of village life and types with unbridled fantasy rooted in popular legends, and are peopled with all sorts of quaint goblins, wood spirits, and other whimsies, side by side with peasant characters whose intonations and peculiarities of speech are meticulously reproduced. The best of these novels is *The Prattler of Chertukhino,* in which Klychkov gives free rein to his fantasy. Communist critics, while admitting Klychkov's mastery of the peasant *skaz*, his feeling for Russian folklore, and his clever handling of the plot, stressed his "arch-reactionary romanticism" and his idealization of old Russia.[11] Klychkov ended by disappearing from literature, and there are reasons to believe that he died in a concentration camp.

LAVRENYOV

Boris Andreyevich Lavrenyov (b. 1892) began writing poetry about 1913. In those days he belonged to various Futurist groups. His later poetry, which he went on writing till 1924, was composed under a very strong influence of Gumilyov and, in its romantic and exotic aspect, of Acmeism in general. In 1916, while serving as a cavalry officer in the Russian Army, Lavrenyov wrote his first short story ("Gala Peter"), which, though a little too carefully "made," showed considerable promise. After a spell of revolutionary activity, military and otherwise, he devoted himself entirely to literature, joining the Leningrad group *Sodruzhestvo*. After 1924 his stories and plays earned him an important place in Soviet literature.

In an autobiographical note, published in 1928, Lavrenyov wrote that for him literature filled a gap in life, since there was no longer any romance in life itself.[12] In a later autobiography (1930) he wrote ironically and somewhat defiantly:

> I know my qualities. Also my shortcomings. European literary culture is too strong in me. "Literaturizing." Too much of an inveterate intellectual. Too much of an un-Russian writer. Bred and brought up on French and English writers. I like a sound and firm pattern. I don't like our "literature. . . ."
>
> Literature must be brief, clear and improbable to the point where it can be believed. For truth, there are newspaper reports and chronicle. Literature must excite and captivate. . . .

[11] See Gorbachov, *Contemporary Russian Literature*, 125–26.
[12] *Writers About Art and About Themselves*, 193.

Literature must master *above all* the plot. I have mastered it. To master the rest, is my task for the coming years.[13]

Robust romanticism and concentration on the plot are the salient features of Lavrenyov's work between 1924 and 1926. Quick, dynamic action; plenty of incident; unusual situations; tense, romantically-heightened collisions; and romantic yet lifelike characters with clear-cut social characteristics—these are the essential elements of Lavrenyov's stories, some of which are more like short novels. In many of them the Civil War and the period of War Communism, romantically portrayed, form the background. "Veter" ("Wind," 1924) is the story of the adventures of a sailor whom the experiences of the Civil War turn into a class-conscious revolutionary. After a period of peaceful civilian work, however, he soon gets bored and returns to the romantic life of the front, there to find his death after another exciting (and somewhat improbable) adventure. In "Rasskaz o prostoy veshchi" ("The Story About a Simple Thing," 1924) the hero is an old Bolshevik, chairman of the local Cheka, who is left behind to carry on underground work in a town occupied by the Whites and, after some breath-taking adventures, is caught by them and ordered to be shot. The story, divided into short chapters, proceeds with cinematographic speed from one exciting and psychologically tense situation to another. "Zvezdny tsvet" ("The Starry Flower," 1924) combines an exotic setting (the action takes place in Turkestan) and an exciting story with a sharply contrasting social situation. But the best of these Civil War stories by Lavrenyov is "Sorok pervy" ("The Forty-First," 1924), the heroine of which is a young girl, Maryutka, daughter of a Volga fiisherman, who joins a Red partisan detachment and becomes a first-class sniper. The story tells of the partisans' encirclement by their enemies, and of their laborious retreat through the salt steppes east of the Caspian Sea. On their way they meet a caravan of camels led by some Kirghizes and accompanied by six "Whites." One of these, an officer, who was to have been Maryutka's forty-first victim but whom she had missed, is taken prisoner by the partisans. Later, she is stranded alone with him on a desert island in the Aral Sea, and they fall in love with each other. The story ends with Maryutka shooting her lover when a party of White officers approaches their island: her orders were not to let him go alive. Here, as in some other stories, Lavrenyov makes effective use of some stock literary situations (there are in this story some deliberate echoes of *Robinson Crusoe*) which he instills with fresh content and treats in an original and exciting way.

In some of Lavrenyov's stories the influence of Bely and Pilnyak

[13] *Sobranie sochineniy (Collected Works)*, I, 45–46.

can be discerned—for example, in the lyrical digression about Petersburg in "Wind" and a similar digression about the wolves prowling in the steppe in "The Forty-First." The lyrical paraphrase of passages from *The Lay of Igor's Campaign,* used as an inset in "Wormwood," is likewise reminiscent of Pilnyak. In "Wind" the general symbolism—the wind motif—is also Pilnyakian. But the differences are more striking than the similarities. The digressions are more coherent, more organized: they resemble vignettes worked into the general pattern of the narrative, and Lavrenyov never lets himself be carried away by these irrelevancies, but always has the story in mind. He also knows how to tell a story—rapid, dynamic, well-knit, tense, full of incident. However, for all his avowed aversion to psychological probing and "mystical poking around in one's navel," he is interested in individual characters, and his stories are also social-psychological studies. But he prefers to show his characters in action and dialogue.

After 1926 Lavrenyov turned to subjects taken from everyday Soviet life. His vision of it remained, however, colored by his romanticism. A typical story is "Mir v styoklyshke" ("The World in a Bit of Glass"), subtitled "A Sentimental Story." The characters in it are all "small" people—some of them relics of the world gone by, who live in the past; others live on more or less good terms with the present, but away from the main stream of events. The Revolution serves as a backdrop to the story, but in the center of it stand ordinary human beings and their interwoven human tragedies.

In the stories included in the volume *Shalye povesti (Crazy Tales,* 1926), everyday-life subjects are treated in terms of whimsical humor or grotesque. "Nebesny kartuz" ("The Skyblue Cap"), subtitled "An Improbable Story," is an amusing parody of a Sherlock Holmes story in a Soviet setting. "Vozdushnaya mechta" ("An Airy Dream") is a facetious Leskovian *skaz* of queer happenings in a godforsaken village which the Revolution takes five years to reach: the improbable and the grotesque are intermingled with touches of everyday reality. "Thalassa" (1926), with the ironic subtitle "A Sober Story," tells of the adventures of a meek and modest Soviet employee who gets involved with a pretty smugglers' agent and takes part in a smuggling expedition along the coast of the Black Sea. Beneath its frivolity, however, one can feel Lavrenyov's romantic nostalgia, his aversion to the humdrum realities of Soviet life (Soviet critics accused him of voicing it openly in the short, autobiographical story "Marina").

Sedmoy sputnik (The Seventh Satellite, 1927) was regarded by some critics as a turning point for Lavrenyov. Here he takes the reader back to the period of the Civil War. But his manner is different from his earlier stories of the same period. The narrative is quieter and slower;

the accent is on psychology rather than on incident. It is the story of the gradual transformation of an old general, a former professor of the Academy of Military Jurisprudence, who is arrested as one of the hostages for the murder of Uritsky in 1918, but, unlike many of his fellow prisoners who are shot, is eventually released only to find that his apartment and all his belongings, by the sale of which he lived before, have been confiscated, and he has nowhere to live. After an unsuccessful attempt to get a temporary refuge with one of his old school friends, he goes back to the prison and gets engaged as a laundryman. Later, when a high-ranking commissar discovers his presence there, he is given a judicial post in the Red Army and sent to the front. By this time his sympathies are already on the side of the new regime, and he "accepts" the Revolution out of patriotism, though he does not become a Communist. He admits this when taken prisoner by General Yudenich's White Army, and is ordered to be shot. Lavrenyov's General Adamov, portrayed sympathetically by the author, is probably not untypical of a certain section of the old technical intelligentsia when faced with the Revolution. The story is told in a quiet, subdued manner. The scenes in a Petrograd square, where representatives of the old propertied classes are selling their personal belongings, and in the prison, where some of them are led out to be shot, are very well done.

A place apart in Lavrenyov's work belongs to his novel *Krushenie respubliki Itl* (*The Downfall of the Republic of Itl*, 1926). It describes, in terms of a fantastic satire, foreign intervention in the south of Russia and the establishment there, with the help of England (which is disguised as "Nautilia"), of a democratic Republic. Lavrenyov demonstrates here his narrative skill and sense of humor, but, although he was influenced by Anatole France's *Penguin Island,* his work lacks France's earnestness and has more of a Ruritanian musical comedy about it, as was rightly pointed out by some Soviet critics.

KOZAKOV

Mikhail Emmanuilovich Kozakov (b. 1897) came from a bourgeois Jewish family and spent his childhood in the south of Russia. Before the Revolution he studied medicine in the University of Kiev, but left it without graduating and became a journalist. Later, he graduated from a law school and worked as a defense counsel in a Soviet tribunal. In his autobiography he wrote: "I shall not hide it, I always feel a great moral satisfaction at having been able, in those days, to save a few human lives: acquitted by the Soviet authorities, these people are now, I know, being useful, each in his own way, to state and society." In Kozakov's work there are many echoes of his legal work.

In 1922 Kozakov settled in Petrograd and joined the *Sodruzhestvo* literary group, which was supposed to represent the left-wing fellow travelers. His first book of stories, *Popugaevo shchastye (Parrot's Luck)*, appeared in 1924. In the choice and treatment of characters, it showed a considerable influence of Dostoyevsky. Kozakov approached the Revolution as a landslide which had wrought great changes in the course of daily life, and specialized in the portrayal of the "humiliated and injured" in it. His stories abound in odd characters on whom destiny plays odd tricks. He also shows people in whom the kicks and blows dealt by the Revolution awaken primitive biological instincts and strengthen their instinctive grip on life. Among the more curious characters is Vitos, chairman of the revolutionary tribunal in the story "Tsygarka" ("A Cigarette"), a Dostoyevskian mixture of saintliness and sadism. A good Communist, he displays a great interest in his victims and, after sentencing them, often to death, spends hours questioning them in prison, trying to find out all about them. The author describes this interest as "man's greediness for man."

Kozakov's second book of stories—*Povest o Karlike Makse (The Tale About Max the Dwarf,* 1926)—contained a longish story called "Abram Nashatyr, the Innkeeper." The setting is a Russian provincial town during the NEP period. It is a good picture of everyday Soviet life of that period, but it is also something more than that. The main interest is in the central character, a hardhearted, unscrupulous Jew who rises to wealth and importance through a murder committed, at his instigation, by his brother, and ends by calmly killing that very brother when he reappears on the scene and threatens his peace and happiness.

Kozakov's most interesting work of this period was the short novel *Meshchanin Adameyko (Adameyko the Philistine,* 1927). Its dependence on Dostoyevsky is obvious; it is a psychological detective story, and both its theme and its form recall *Crime and Punishment.* The plot revolves round the murder of Adameyko's neighbor, a well-to-do widow. She is a usurer (a deliberate parallel to Alyona in *Crime and Punishment*), and Adamyeko is a kind of modern Raskolnikov who conceives and plans the murder in order to give life to his idea—his "social fancy" as he calls it—that social justice demands the elimination of all "superfluous" people, of all the "parasites" who have survived the Revolution. Adameyko describes them as the "proud flesh" of life. This is how he formulates his idea to Sukhov, an unemployed printer whom he wants to use as his instrument:

> There are people who should not live. Yet they live, because the Revolution overlooked them, and the Revolution itself is over and will not hurt anyone now: it lies like a cartridge taken apart—the cap here and the case there . . . .

I have in mind—let me put it scientifically—a social fancy. Some people may think it crazy. But why not collect all this "proud flesh" and expose it to one bullet, and use the goods that will be left behind for the benefit of those whom life has injured? . . . I say to myself: If, indeed, it comes to justice, then you, Ardalyon Porfiryevich, justify murder.

(Even the name and patronymic of Adameyko have a Dostoyevskian ring.)

When Sukhov asks him point-blank whether he is personally capable of killing, Adameyko's answer is evasive: he speaks of being capable of "justifying" a murder and of "taking part" in it, but his real intention is to use Sukhov. He does so, and the murder comes off, though actually the victim dies of heart rupture before she is killed.

The narrative follows an unusual pattern: the story is told in jerky zigzags, with constant anticipations of things to happen; but these anticipations and chronological shifts, which do away with the element of "mystery," enhance rather than diminish the psychological interest and suspense. Kozakov's attitude toward his hero is noncommital—he remains true to his maxim: "From myself and from other writers I demand one main thing—that they be *honest* in the literary sense."[14] Adameyko's "idea" has obvious political implications, but his own approach is rather ethical. His attitude toward the Revolution is ambiguous: he is clearly an individualist with Nietzschean leanings, but he is not against the Revolution and emphasizes that he is not of the ruling class, but a "philistine," a man-in-the-street.

Equally original in structure is Kozakov's story "Chelovek, padayushchy nits" ("The Man Who Prostrates Himself," 1928), where newspaper documentation is cleverly worked into the framework of a fictional story. But here the "laying bare of the device" is a trifle too obtrusive. The story is also interesting for its subject matter—various manifestations of anti-Semitism in Soviet life.

In 1929 appeared the first volume of Kozakov's long "historico-political" novel *Devyat tochek* (*Nine Points*), portraying the Russian liberal and revolutionary intelligentsia on the eve of World War I. It was to cover also the post-Revolutionary period, and a sequel to it was published later, but the novel remained unfinished.

[14] *Writers About Art and About Themselves*, 180.

3. Proletarian Novelists

LIBEDINSKY

YURY Nikolayevich Libedinsky (b. 1898) was, chronologically speaking, one of the first "proletarian" novelists. Born in Odessa, he spent his childhood at one of the big plants in the Urals. In 1921 he joined the Communist party and for several years was engaged in political work for the Red Army. He became one of the most active members of the "October" and the "On Guard" groups. In 1922 *The Young Guard* published his first short novel, *Nedelya (The Week)*. It was followed in 1923 by *Zavtra (Tomorrow)*, and in 1926 by *Komissary (The Commissars)*. All three novels deal with the inner life of the Communist party, and their principal characters are average Communists shown in connection with their party work.

In *The Week*, the action takes place in Chelyabinsk in 1920. Libedinsky shows us a number of Communists with different backgrounds, who run the town and have to tackle various problems facing the new government. The central episode is the anti-Bolshevik rising organized by the Whites with the help of the discontented peasants. The rising is suppressed, but most of the Communist leaders perish in it. The novel is interesting as an illustration of the inner workings of the Communist party and as a gallery of lifelike portraits of Communists, drawn objectively though superficially. Its weakest point is its style. Libedinsky himself admitted that he was influenced by Bely, who at one time was his favorite writer. But his attempt to write rhythmical prose, with constant syntactical inversions, in the manner of Bely and Sologub, produces ludicrous results, quite out of keeping with the subject matter and the general realistic manner of the narrative. The descriptions are either vapid or forced and affected. When Libedinsky tries to show his Communists outside their Party activities, he fails signally: as Party members they are sufficiently differentiated, but as human beings most of them lack individuality.

In *The Commissars*, written some three years later, Libedinsky adopted a more simple manner, free from all stylistic pretensions. The action is set in a large, provincial town in 1921, at the critical time of transition from War Communism to the New Economic Policy; the occasion is a refresher course for Red Army political commissars. All the main characters are Communists who played an active part in the Civil War. They are of different social origins: some are factory workers and old Bolsheviks; some are peasants who joined the Party in 1917; while a few come from the middle class. The director of the course is a former officer who was a Menshevik before the Revolution but who is now a good Bolshevik. Some of these former commissars find it difficult to adjust themselves to new conditions, to the discipline which is demanded of them now. Others reveal their essential "bourgeois" nature and have to be purged. The novel is a good picture of a microcosm of the Communist party at a time when the new policy decreed by Lenin produced great bewilderment and confusion among its rank and file. There are scenes of Party meetings, of purges, and of political lectures that have a considerable documentary value. Once more Libedinsky is at his best when he shows his characters in their Party environment. However, as soon as it comes to showing them as human beings facing personal problems, his limitations as an artist become more obvious: neither Lobichev's quest for love nor Mindlov's mental illness, caused by overwork and by separation from his wife who is dying of consumption in the Crimea, is presented in a convincing way. The bourgeois wife of Alferyev, the stern and cold director of the refresher course, is a hackneyed stock character, devoid of flesh and blood. But the psychological conflicts and the clashes of opinions within the Communist elite are shown with considerable objectivity, and for a student of the Communist party and its history and of a certain period of Soviet life, the novel has much to offer that is of undoubted interest.

Tomorrow, which appeared between *The Week* and *The Commissars,* was regarded by Libedinsky himself and by his Communist critics as a distinct failure and, what is more, a great ideological mistake. It reflects Libedinsky's dismay, which he shared with many good Communists, at the sight of the rapid *embourgeoisement* consequent upon the introduction of the New Economic Policy. The action is set in Moscow in 1923. There is a vivid picture of the "demoralization" brought about by the NEP. The plot—if a plot it can be called—is centered around the news of a successful Communist revolution in Germany, which has a heartening effect on many Communist old-timers in Russia. The title of the novel and the way in which the effect of this news is presented justified the critics' inference that for Libedinsky the only way of saving the Revolution in Russia from the morass of the NEP lay through its extension beyond the boundaries of Russia. This was, of course, the way many Communists felt at the time. The novel was therefore denounced as pessimistic and ideologically erroneous. In a postscript to it entitled "Why My *Tomorrow* was a Failure," which accompanied a later edition, Libedinsky admitted that in contemplating the Soviet reality of those days he had arrived at Trotskyism.

In its over-all manner *Tomorrow* is closer to *The Week* than to *The Commissars.* The influence of Bely and of ill-digested modernism is felt in the hysterical, staccato style. Characters are even less individualized, while there is an unsuccessful attempt to show the masses in action. There are some unnecessary episodes which slow down and lengthen the narrative. A failure artistically, *Tomorrow* does not possess the documentary interest of the two other novels.

Fyodor Vasilievich Gladkov (b. 1883) came of a poor peasant family. His early life, amidst poverty, squalor, and wanderings about the country, bears some resemblance to Gorky's. At the age of sixteen he wrote his first story, which was printed in a provincial newspaper. In 1901 he came across Gorky's stories and after that began to imitate him in his work. In 1905–1906 Gladkov took part in the revolutionary movement and was arrested and exiled for three years to Siberia. On returning from exile, he lived in Novorossiysk and there wrote his long story "Izgoi" ("The Exiles"). He sent it to Korolenko who called it "a lunatic asylum,"[15] but advised Gladkov to offer it to the review *Zavety,* where it was accepted. Until 1917 Gladkov worked as a village teacher in the Kuban region. With the outbreak of the Revolution he was again drawn into active political work and stopped writing.

After 1922 Gladkov devoted himself entirely to literature, becoming a member of the "Smithy" and of other proletarian literary organizations. His first major post-Revolutionary work was *Ognenny kon (The Fiery Steed)*, a rather pretentious novel, combining revolutionary ideology with a morbid, amorous psychology *à la* Dostoyevsky and a cheap imitation of modernist style.

However, with the publication of the novel *Tsement (Cement)* in 1925, Gladkov's literary reputation was assured. The novel was enthusiastically received by the Communist critics. It was translated into several European languages, and its sales quickly reached the unheard-of figure of 500,000 copies. On the title page of its early editions one could read the following recommendation reminiscent of the good old times when certain books were approved by the Ministry of Education for inclusion in school libraries: "Recommended by the Chief Department of Political Education for mass public libraries. Admitted by the State Learned Council into school libraries."

In *Cement,* Gladkov tried to write a monumental proletarian novel about the Revolution. Its subject is the transition from the Civil War period, which had disorganized and dislocated the life of the country, to the period of peaceful but unromantic reconstruction. The action is set in a big Black Sea port (which is easily recognized as Novorossiysk), and the novel describes the resumption of work in a well-known cement plant there. Parallel with the story of this reconstruction is shown the disintegration of the old framework of life—the dissolution of family relations, the birth of a new morality and new ways of life. The novel

[15]*Ibid.,* 91.

is full of enthusiasm for revolutionary reconstruction, but one cannot reproach Gladkov for looking at things only through rosy spectacles, for he does not shirk from exposing the seamy side of this new life as well. Gladkov's realism is, however, blended with romanticism. He is fond of contrasts and striking situations, often at the expense of verisimilitude.

The principal characters in the novel are the cement worker Gleb Chumalov and his wife Dasha. Chumalov has spent nearly the whole Civil War at the front and has been decorated with the Order of the Red Banner. On returning to his home town, he takes upon himself the initiative of restarting the cement work. Before he triumphs, he has to overcome a great deal of inertia, of red tape, and of open opposition; much of the novel is concerned with his battle for the cement plant. At the same time Gladkov shows us Gleb's inner conflicts. A good Communist, he has not yet succeeded in discarding some of his old moral instincts and "prejudices." This conflict between his political and his moral nature is one of the psychological pivots of the novel. Gleb clashes first with his wife Dasha, who, during his absence at the front, has been drawn into social work for the Party and has become an "emancipated" woman who believes in "free love," and she now refuses to submit to Gleb's old-fashioned notions of morality and woman's duties. The conflict between Gleb and Dasha is interlinked, through a complex net of relationships, with other characters in the novel: with Badyin, chairman of the local Executive Committee, a drunkard and a debauchee, but a good Party administrator; and with Kleist, an old engineer at the cement plant, an avowed class enemy, who had earlier ordered Gleb's execution but had saved Dasha from death, and who in the end is won over to the cause of restoring the cement plant.

The novel is an interesting document, reflecting a critical period in the life of the Soviet Union and of the Communist party. The atmosphere of confusion and bewilderment is conveyed with great objectivity, and many of the secondary characters are well portrayed. However, the two heroes, Gleb and Dasha, are much less convincing. They lack individuality. Dasha especially sounds stilted, while many incidents in her life touch on cheap melodrama. The principal defect of the novel lies, however, in its style. It is an incongruous mixture of old-fashioned realism, naturalism, and ill-digested modernism, in which the echoes of Dostoyevsky and of Leonid Andreyev are only too obvious. The diction is often shrill and hysterical, and many of the dialogues—especially of the workers—represent an untenable mixture of coarse, naturalistically reproduced dialect and high-sounding, sophisticated rhetoric. Gladkov lacks all sense of measure. In a later, revised edition he tried to smooth out some of these stylistic incongruities.

Among Gladkov's stories written after *Cement* should be mentioned three satirical studies of three different types of "kibitzers" in the Communist party: "Golovonogy chelovek" ("The Cephalopodous Man"), "Neporochny chort" ("The Immaculate Devil"), and "Vdokhnovenny gus" ("The Inspired Goose"). Written between 1928 and 1930, they were republished together in 1936 under the title *Malenkaya trilogia* (*A Little Trilogy*). Told in the first person as episodes in the career of a director of a Soviet plant, they give grotesque portraits of an insolent climber and plotter, a hypocritical prig, and a popular windbag. All three are successfully exposed by the narrator.

FADEYEV

The revival of psychological realism in proletarian literature found its principal expression in the work of Fadeyev.

Alexander Alexandrovich Fadeyev was born in 1901 in a peasant family in the province of Tver, but most of his childhood was spent in the Far East, where his father worked as a surgeon's assistant. In 1918 he became a member of the Communist party and took an active part in the Civil War, fighting against Admiral Kolchak, Ataman Semyonov, and the Japanese. In 1921 he participated in the suppression of the sailors' rising in Kronstadt and was wounded there. From 1921 to 1926 he was engaged in Party work in various parts of the Soviet Union.

Fadeyev's first two stories—"Razliv" ("The Flood," 1924) and "Protiv techeniya" ("Against the Current," 1925)—did not stand out from the general run of "dynamic" prose fiction of that period. Of the former, which had all of the worst stylistic and compositional defects of such writers as Vsevolod Ivanov and Nikitin with none of their merits, Fadeyev himself said later that it was "a slovenly work." "Against the Current" (later renamed "The Birth of the Amgun Regiment"), for all its imperfections, had a greater clarity of design. But it was Fadeyev's third work, the short novel *Razgrom* (*The Rout*), written in 1925–26 and published in 1927, that brought Fadeyev to the forefront of young "proletarian" literature. *The Rout* was very well received and has since gone through several editions (the latest appeared in 1949). It is now regarded as one of the classics of Soviet literature.

There was nothing new in the subject of Fadeyev's novel. It is the story of a Red guerrilla detachment fighting against the Japanese and Admiral Kolchak's White forces in the Far East. The story covers a short period of time and is well constructed. The narrative begins during a lull in the fighting, and this enables Fadeyev to introduce the reader, in the first seven short chapters which form the exposition of the novel, to his main characters. Beginning with Chapter Eight, which is entitled "The First Move," the narrative gathers dramatic momentum and is brought to its inexorable climax when the detachment, at the cost of enormous losses, makes a risky crossing of a bog and breaks out of the enemy encirclement. The surviving eighteen men and their leader are ready for new adventures and new battles.

Unlike Vsevolod Ivanov, Nikitin, and other writers of the Pilnyak school, Fadeyev shows the Civil War not in terms of an elemental movement and a clash of impersonal forces, but in terms of individual psychology. In his novel, men play a more important part than episodes of fighting or ideological problems. His characters are not symbolic tokens, but flesh-and-blood human beings. Levinson, the red-bearded, blue-eyed Jew who leads the detachment; Morozka, the reckless, daredevil miner with rebellious, anarchistic leanings; Varya, his wife, the only woman in the detachment, at once motherly and lascivious, ready to bestow her love on almost anyone; Mechik, a young boy from the intelligentsia who joins the detachment more or less by chance and deserts it at the critical moment; the old man Pika, who reminds Mechik of a picture of a Russian saint; the powerful giant Goncharenko—all are live figures. The only touch of conventional stylization may be seen in the shepherd Metelitsa and his heroic death at the hands of the Whites. Fadeyev himself confessed later that Metelitsa was a kind of afterthought, a complement to Levinson, an embodiment of those characteristics which Levinson lacked for an ideal leader. Hence the disproportion, the hyperbolism of the whole Metelitsa episode.[16] Apart from this, however, the story is remarkable for its objectivity and its psychological verisimilitude, though again there is one jarring note—the final desertion of Mechik, who is shown throughout as a "foreign body" among the partisans: not because the reader does not believe in it, but because here Fadeyev renounces his calm, objective method and passes judgment on Mechik.

Soviet critics lost no time in pointing out that both for his method and his style Fadeyev was indebted to Tolstoy. *The Rout* was, indeed, the first Tolstoyan work in Soviet literature, and, significantly enough, it came from a proletarian novelist. Tolstoy's influence was felt in Fadeyev's method of psychological analysis, in his style, in his descriptions of the battle scenes, and in the very structure of his sentences. Some overenthusiastic Soviet critics went so far as to place Fadeyev on a par with Tolstoy. Fadeyev, they said, had mastered Tolstoy's technique while remaining free from Tolstoy's ideological fallacies, thus giving his work the true proletarian orientation. Other Communist critics

---

16 See Fadeyev's article "Moy literaturny opyt—nachinayushchemu avtoru" ("My Literary Experience—to Beginner Authors"), in *Literatura i zhizn* (*Literature and Life*), 158.

were more cautious and refused to see in Fadeyev anything more than a gifted disciple of Tolstoy. They were right, of course.

Fadeyev's limitations were clearly revealed in his first large-scale work, the novel *Posledny iz Udege* (*The Last of the Udege*), which he began writing parallel with *The Rout*. Unlike *The Rout*, however, which is but a brief episode, *The Last of the Udege* is an ambitious, social-psychological novel with a multitude of characters and a complex, multiplanar plot. It was planned for six volumes, of which three have been published so far, the first part appearing in *October* in 1928. The action is also set in the Far East and involves local intelligentsia, coal miners, and some members of the curious and nearly extinct native tribe of Udege. One of the themes of the novel is the cultural "rehabilitation" of the Udege by the Soviet government and their incorporation into the collective farming system. In the first volumes the action takes place immediately before the Revolution and during the Civil War (originally Fadeyev intended to make *The Rout* part of this novel); the concluding volume must show the same places and the same people fifteen years later, and the changes wrought in them by the Revolution. Since the novel is still unfinished, final judgment on it must be suspended, but Fadeyev himself, in the speech already referred to, admitted quite frankly that he had found the work on this novel very difficult: "Evidently," he said, "one must possess a greater artistic experience than I have to write a big novel with a complex idea, such as I planned."[17]

SHOLOKHOV

Soviet critics and historians of literature usually include among proletarian writers Mikhail Alexandrovich Sholokhov (b. 1905). This inclusion is justified since "proletarian" was always taken to refer, not to class origins (neither Libedinsky nor Fadeyev was a true proletarian in this sense), but to ideological sympathies and Communist party attachments.

Sholokhov was born in the Don Cossack region. His mother was half-Cossack, half-peasant. His father belonged to the lower middle class and came himself from central Russia. Sholokhov has lived most of his life among the Don Cossacks, and nearly all that he wrote is about their life. His secondary education was interrupted in 1918 by the Revolution. Throughout the Civil War when the Don Cossack region was the main scene of hostilities and a large section of the Cossacks actively supported the anti-Bolshevik movement, Sholokhov lived there. There is no evidence of his having fought on either side, but after 1920 he apparently joined the Communist party and worked in Soviet ad-

17 *Ibid.,* 162.

ministration. He began writing in 1923, and his first book of stories appeared in 1925.

It was his novel *Tikhy Don* (*The Quiet Don*), however, that made Sholokhov famous throughout the Soviet Union.[18] He began work on it in 1926, and the first three volumes appeared between 1928 and 1933 (a fourth volume was added in 1940). The novel went through more than one hundred printings, and over five million copies of it were sold in Russia and abroad. There is no doubt that Sholokhov became the most popular writer in the Soviet Union. In 1936 he was elected deputy of the Supreme Soviet and in 1939 awarded the Order of Lenin. He was also elected to the Soviet Academy of Sciences.

Like Fadeyev's *The Rout*, *The Quiet Don* was an expression of the "back to Tolstoy" trend in Soviet literature. It is a vast canvas of Cossack life on the eve of World War I, during it, and in the first five years of the Revolution; in fact, all things taken into consideration, a Cossack *War and Peace*. It is a realistic novel, brimful with life, with a great number of characters. It is a chronicle of the war and the Revolution, with a particular stress on their effect on the Cossacks and their life. Without a plot in the strict sense of the word, it is written in a colorful, racy language that is sometimes spoiled by an excessive tendency toward ethnographical naturalism. Sholokhov is particularly good when he deals with the Cossacks and their life, a subject with which he is particularly familiar. Much weaker are those parts where the non-Cossack element is introduced. Here one feels Sholokhov losing his grip on his material and realizes the enormous distance that separates Sholokhov from Tolstoy. Like *War and Peace*, *The Quiet Don* is a combination of a family chronicle and a historical epic (with the difference, however, that Sholokhov has a clear-cut central hero in the person of Grigory Melekhov): alongside a multitude of fictitious characters there appear in it several historical personages, such as Generals Kornilov and Alexeyev, the Cossack Ataman Kaledin, the Bolshevik leader Podtyolkov, and other prominent actors of the Civil War drama. Unlike Tolstoy, Sholokhov avoids philosophizing about history. His presentation of the period is on the whole objective and balanced. He neither idealizes all his Reds as heroes nor portrays all the Whites as unmitigated villains. One of the most idealized figures is the Communist agitator Bunchuk, who becomes leader of a machine-gun section and is in the end shot by several Cossacks who have gone over to the Whites. But even Bunchuk is shown as a three-dimensional figure—with all the human failings—and

18 The author of a recent book about Sholokhov reveals that Sholokhov had some difficulty in getting his now famous novel accepted by *Oktyabr,* and that there were rumors at the time, which even found their way into the press, that *The Quiet Don* was written not by Sholokhov but by a White army officer who was killed and whose manuscript Sholokhov "stole."—I. Lezhnev, *Mikhail Sholokhov*, 12.

not as a paragon of Communist virtues. Nor does Sholokhov attempt to deny heroism in the opponents of Bolshevism; there is a touch of grandeur in the description of the death of the Cossack officer Kalmykov, who is shot by Bunchuk. The Cossack Ataman Kaledin, who collaborated with the Whites, is also portrayed without the usual prejudice and hostility, and there is sense of real tragedy in the scene preceding his suicide. Sholokhov's principal character, Melekhov, with whom the author is obviously very much in sympathy personifies the deep cleavage among the Cossacks. He is shown changing sides and deserting the Reds, and in the third volume we even see him fighting on the side of the Whites. The fourth volume was written with the specific object of setting this straight and of showing Melekhov's final change of heart, but the ending is somewhat ambiguous, and Melekhov's adherence to the new order of things somehow incomplete. Throughout the novel one feels that Sholokhov himself, while his reason approves the Communist Revolution, cannot help subconsciously regretting the loss of much in the traditional mode of the Cossack life which the Revolution has swept away. While the novel has unquestionably been overpraised, and many defects of its language and composition overlooked, it is, if not a classic, a work of great breadth, giving a truthful and impartial picture of the revolutionary blizzard that swept over Russia, carrying with it many human lives and affecting individual destinies.

Sholokhov's second major work will be discussed in the next chapter.

TARASOV-RODIONOV, MALYSHKIN, AND OTHERS

Alexander Ignatyevich Tarasov-Rodionov (b. 1885), a Bolshevik since 1905, took an active part in the 1917 Revolution and commanded Red Army divisions in the Civil War of 1919–20. After demobilization he worked for a time as examining magistrate attached to the Supreme Tribunal of the Republic. His novel *Shokolad* (*Chocolate,* 1922) was one of the first Communist contributions to the revival of prose fiction. Its theme aroused a good deal of controversy. It is the story of the framing of a certain Zudin, chairman of a local Cheka, who becomes innocently entangled with a beautiful girl, a former ballerina and a counterrevolutionary agent, to whom out of pity he gives a job in his office. Suspicions are aroused among his colleagues, and an investigation ordered from the center. Although Zudin's friends and colleagues who are appointed to the commission that is to investigate his "crimes" are convinced of his fundamental innocence, they agree with the investigator sent from Moscow who demands that Zudin be shot. Their motives are rather involved: the working masses, they say, will never believe in Zudin's innocence, and it is their duty to impress on the masses that the Revolution spares no one who betrays its cause, no matter how highly placed. The novel ends with Zudin bidding farewell to his wife: to comfort her, he pretends that the Party, while announcing his execution, is sending him on a long and secret mission to Australia. Soviet critics regarded the author's main thesis—the sacrifice of a good and honest Communist to the ignorance and prejudice of the masses—as an ideological error, and the novel was attacked for being untrue to life. While not without interest for the light it throws on the early workings of the Cheka, *Chocolate* is poor literature. The characters, beginning with Zudin himself, are unreal; the story smacks of cheap melodrama; the style is poor: Tarasov-Rodionov's hashed, pseudo-poetic prose obviously belongs to the Pilnyak school, but he lacks utterly Pilnyak's sense of language.

In 1928 Tarasov-Rodionov published *Fevral (February)*, the first volume of *Tyazhelye shagi (Heavy Steps)*, which was intended as a vast chronocle of the Revolution of 1917. Tarasov-Rodionov was later denounced as a Trotskyite and disappeared.

Alexander Georgievich Malyshkin (1890–1938) attracted attention in 1924 with his *Padenie Daira (The Fall of Dair)*, which was written in 1921. As its subject it had one of the principal episodes of the Civil War—the Red Army break-through at Perekop, which brought about the end of the last organized center of anti-Bolshevik resistance in the Crimea. This work is a typical specimen of "dynamic" prose: there is no psychology in it, no individualized characters; the center of interest is in the masses, in the clash of the Red and White forces, which is shown with something of epic grandeur. The heightened, rhythmical diction is derived from Bely and Pilnyak; however, along with other Soviet writers, Malyshkin later evolved towards realism. In his novel *Sevastopol* (1929), he gave a picture of the Revolution as it affected the Black Sea fleet. Its hero, Shelekhov, is a sailor from the intelligentsia who gradually, but not without some relapses, comes to espouse the cause of the Communist Revolution. Malyshkin's main thesis is that men like Shelekhov can find their place in the Revolution, provided that they give up aspiring for high positions and accept being useful but inconspicuous pawns in the new order.

Artyom Vesyoly (pseudonym of Nikolay Kochkurov, b. 1899) is one of the few true proletarians in the ranks of proletarian literature. His father was a Volga stevedore, and Vesyoly himself worked as a factory hand and drayman. A member of the Communist party, he fought in the Civil War, and most of his work before 1928 has the Civil War as its subject. His characters are soldiers, sailors, peasant guerillas, and other "instinctive" revolutionaries. In his stories, which are collected in two volumes, *Gorkaya krov (Bitter Blood)* and *Dikoye serdtse*

133

(*The Wild Heart*), Vesyoly concentrates on the elemental, irrational, and destructive aspects of the Revolution. He prefers the first person narrative and the *skaz* manner. In his novels—*Strana rodnaya* (*My Country*) and *Rossiya krovyu omytaya* (*Russia Washed in Blood*)— verbal ornamentation plays a more important part than the plot. Of all the proletarian writers he stands closest to Pilnyak (except for his Communist orthodoxy), while in some of his earlier stories his short staccato sentences recall Mayakovsky's verse. *Russia Washed in Blood* is a colorful picture of the first phase of the Revolution, in the center of which stands the mass desertion of soldiers from the front.

Sergey Alexandrovich Semyonov (b. 1893), son of a Petersburg factory worker, is another true proletarian. He joined the Communist party in 1917 and made his debut in literature in 1922 with the novel *Golod* (*Hunger*), written in the form of a diary and giving a naturalistic description of starving workmen in revolutionary Petrograd. This was followed by a number of stories of workers' life. Considerable attention was aroused by Semyonov's long work *Natalya Tarpova* (1927). It is a social-psychological problem novel, dealing with the life of the Communist party and with the problems of marriage, family life, cultural work, ideology, etc. Its heroine is a woman, an active member of a Communist organization, who is shown both in her political and private life against the background of the NEP. As in the case of Libedinsky's novels, its value is mostly documentary.

4. *Some Pre-Revolutionary Writers*

AFTER 1921 several pre-Revolutionary prose writers, whom the Revolution had at first silenced or driven away, made a gradual reappearance in literature. There were also those who from the very first had sympathized with the Revolution, but did not come to play a part in post-Revolutionary literature until it had reverted to traditional realism. The work of the most important among these older writers, who can now be justly regarded as part of Soviet literature, will be discussed in this section.

ALEXEY N. TOLSTOY

Count Alexey N. Tolstoy (1882–1945) joined the ranks of Soviet writers in 1922. Before that, he had taken sides with the anti-Bolshevik "White" movement. In 1919 he emigrated abroad and lived first in Paris and then in Berlin. His return to Russia in 1923 was dictated largely by personal considerations, in which the purely financial difficulties of *émigré* existence played not a small part. But it was also connected with the so-called "Change-of-Landmarks" movement among the émigrés, when a comparatively small number of them—scholars, writers, and journalists—decided to bow before the Revolution as a force that had won the day and accept it as a fact, without, however, subscribing to its Marxist ideology. Tolstoy's return was a great acquisition for the young Soviet literature. A man of great natural gifts, a master of excellent Russian prose, one of the principal representatives of that neo-realism which combined the best traditions of nineteenth-century Russian literature with some modernist achievements, Tolstoy could certainly count on being lionized in the country where the dearth of good prose fiction was still badly felt.

However, it took Tolstoy a long time to find a real place for himself in Soviet literature. He was always at his best in describing real life, especially the life he knew well. His pictures of the decaying gentry in *Khromoy barin* (*The Lame Squire*), and in numerous pre-Revolutionary stories and plays, were his best work. His post-Revolutionary work was handicapped, for a long time, by his inability to hit upon a congenial theme. Fundamentally a man of the past, a cross between a country gentleman and a literary bohemian, he felt lost in the melting pot of post-Revolutionary Russia. As a former *émigré* he had to tread warily. Reluctant to draw upon the recent past, he wisely abstained at first from portraying and interpreting the unfamiliar present. Hence his escapes into the realm of fantasy and attempts to clothe fantastic plots with revolutionary ideas. In *Aelita* (1922), a combination of a Wellsian scientific romance with a Russian psychological novel, the plot revolves round the arrival of a Soviet scientific expedition on Mars and an attempt to start a social revolution there. Upon this social fantasy are superimposed two other themes: of love being stronger than death or than any sense of revolutionary duty, and of elemental, irrational revolt. The former, one of Tolstoy's favorite themes, is exemplified in the love affair between the leader of the expedition, the engineer Los, and the beautiful Martian woman Aelita. The second theme is embodied in Gusev, a demobilized Red Army man who joins the expedition out of sheer boredom and thirst for adventure and places himself at the head of the Martian proletariat: Soviet critics objected, however, that Gusev was neither a proletarian nor a Communist. Actually, Gusev is a true Russian; when he arrives on Mars, his first thought is to proclaim its annexation to Soviet Russia. In his Bolshevism there are elements of anarchism, and one feels that it is his nationalism and anarchism that make Tolstoy sympathize with him.

The same strain runs through *Rukopis, naydennaya pod krovatyu* (*A Manuscript Found under a Bed*, 1923), where an old, degenerating squire cannot help admiring the broad, elemental, purely Russian sweep of the Revolution, although he really hates all that it stands for.

The same idea dominates *Golubye goroda* (*Skyblue Cities,* 1925) where two forces are shown at grips in post-Revolutionary Russia: the force of rational organization and planning, and the force of elemental, biological life. In the end it is the irrational force of life that triumphs, and the hero, a Communist dreamer and planner, has to admit his defeat. Any other solution would have been contrary to Tolstoy's nature. In a sympathetic essay on Tolstoy, Voronsky once pointed out that Tolstoy's main characters were often dreamers and idealists who came to a bad end after a clash with reality. Tolstoy's most infectious quality is his zest for life, his craving for full-blooded things, his earthy realism, which is excellently served by his rich, racy, full-blooded Russian.

During this period Tolstoy continued also to work on his long novel *Khozhdenie po mukam* (*The Way Through Hell*), which he began when still an *émigré* (the last volume was completed in 1941). It is a vast canvas of Russian life on the eve of World War I, during it, and in the first year of the Revolution. The story is well told, the characters are lifelike and varied. The picture of pre-Revolutionary Russia is painted in dark colors, with a strong emphasis on its futility, its spiritual confusion and disorientation. The work is spoiled by the author's persistent tendency to philosophize about the historical destinies of Russia and the meaning of the Revolution, and by his petty spitefulness in the portrayal of the literary Bohemia—here Tolstoy shows his lack of taste and his intellectual and moral inferiority to the other and greater Tolstoy, Leo.

Infinitely more satisfactory is *Detstvo Nikity* (*Nikita's Childhood,* 1921), written shortly before Tolstoy's return to Russia. This story of a child's life on a pre-Revolutionary Russian estate, of obviously autobiographical inspiration, is worthy to stand beside Leo Tolstoy's *Childhood* and Aksakov's autobiography. Tolstoy the realist, who is in love with life and its pleasures and knows how to describe it truthfully and yet poetically, is here at his best. Its beautiful Russian—simple, limpid, and yet picturesque—makes it into one of the unquestionable masterpieces of post-Revolutionary Russian literature. It was first published outside Russia, but has since been reissued many times in the Soviet Union and has come to be considered part and parcel of Soviet literature—the one and only true example in it of the old gentry tradition, and therefore hardly in keeping with the rest of it.

Tolstoy's literary output in the late twenties was large and uneven. Constant attacks on him as a "bourgeois" writer forced him to look frantically for the right line to follow. In the fantastic genre *Aelita* was followed by *Giperboloid inzhenera Garina* (*Engineer Garin's Hyperboloid,* 1925), later revised and renamed *Garin the Dictator* (1927). Garin is a "superman," a "Fascist," who dreams of organizing and ruling the world on the principle of caste division: the upper caste will govern and create; others will perform the function of procreation; still others, free of all emotions and ideas, will be mere robot slaves; and the unnecessary surplus will be exterminated.

Sem dney v kotorye byl ograblen mir (*Seven Days in which the World was Robbed*) is a mixture of social satire with science fiction. It tells the story of a conspiracy of a group of American capitalists who succeed in scaring the world into submission by bombing and splitting the moon. In the end their dictatorship is overthrown. Written with gusto, it is one of Tolstoy's lighter works. The same may be said of *Priklyuchenia Nevzorova ili Ibikus* (*The Adventures of Nevzorov, or Ibicus*, 1925), a grotesque picture of *émigré* life within the framework of an adventure story. *Émigré* life is also the subject of *Chornoye zoloto* (*Black Gold*), later revised and renamed *Emigranty* (*The Émigrés*). Here foreign and *émigré* intrigues around Soviet oil form the center of a melodramatic plot. The picture of *émigré* life is one-sided, and some of the characters not very real. Everyday Soviet life of the NEP period was handled by Tolstoy in "Vasily Suchkov," the story reflecting the widespread mood of disillusionment during the aftermath of the heroic period of the Revolution.

Some of Tolstoy's later works will be discussed in their proper chronological context.

EHRENBURG

Another pre-Revolutionary writer who came to play a conspicuous part in Soviet literature was Ilya Grigoryevich Ehrenburg (b. 1891). A Jew of middle-class origin, he lived from 1909 to 1917 abroad, mostly in Paris. In 1911 appeared his first book of poems: at the time he felt an aesthetic attraction toward Roman Catholicism and even thought of entering a monastery. During World War I, after an unsuccessful attempt to join the Foreign Legion in France, he covered the war on the French front for one of the big Russian dailies. The Bolshevik Revolution inspired him to write "A Prayer for Russia," a powerful poetic diatribe against the Bolsheviks as modern barbarians. During the Civil War, Ehrenburg lived in the south of Russia under the Whites. On his return to Moscow he was arrested but soon released. *Razdumya* (*Meditations*), a book of poems published in 1921, marked his "acceptance" of the Revolution. But Ehrenburg was none too anxious to remain in Russia, and in the same year he went back to the bohemian haunts in Montparnasse where he had spent his carefree, happy-go-lucky exile. Soon, however, he was deported by the French police. After a short stay in Belgium, he went to Berlin where he also contributed to the periodical *Nakanune*. In 1923 he was back in Russia. Later he was allowed to revisit France and for several years lived in Paris. In 1936-37 he covered the Spanish Civil War on the Loyalist side for Soviet newspapers, and the outbreak of World War II found him again in Paris. Of all Soviet writers, Ehrenburg knows Western Europe best and is at heart attached to Western ways of life, feeling particularly at home in the café land of Montparnasse.

The work which started Ehrenburg's career as a successful, versatile, and prolific Soviet novelist was his *Neobyknovennye priklyucheniya Julio Jurenito (The Extraordinary Adventures of Julio Jurenito)*, written in 1921, during his enforced stay in Belgium, and published in Berlin in 1922.[19] It is perhaps to this day Ehrenburg's best work, the one in which he managed to find the most adequate form of expression for his cynical nihilism, his unprincipled mockery of everything. In a note he contributed to a collection of autobiographies of contemporary Russian writers, Ehrenburg said of it: "It is my only book 'in earnest'; it seems that neither the critics, nor the readers, nor I myself, nobody can define precisely where mockery ends in it." It is primarily a ruthless, satirical indictment of modern European civilization, in which no country, no nationality, and no aspect of that civilization is spared. But Soviet Russia—where Ehrenburg's "Master," the Mexican Julio Jurenito, the great *"agent provocateur,"* whose mission is to unmask the sham and evil of modern civilization, ends his life—does not fare any better at Ehrenburg's hands. It is this corrosive, all-pervading, nihilistic cynicism, apparent in all his best work, that is Ehrenburg's principal attribute as a writer. It is the only thing in him that seems genuine and sincere, all the rest—his enthusiasm for Soviet achievements on various "fronts," which he voiced later in *Den Vtoroy (The Second Day)* and in *Ne perevodya dykhaniya (Without Stopping to Draw Breath)*, or his patriotic effusions during the Soviet-German War—are mere pose. And yet behind this cynical, wholesale negation one senses the tragic dualism of a man whose real roots are in that very civilization he so ruthlessly yet lightheartedly exposes.

To give here even a brief analysis of all Ehrenburg's writings between 1921 and 1929 is impossible. All I can do is to mention a few of the more important ones, leaving some of the later ones to be mentioned in due course. *Zhizn i gibel Nikolaya Kurbova (The Life and*

19 The full title of Ehrenburg's novel is long and elaborate: *The Extraordinary Adventures of Julio Jurenito and of His Disciples: Monsieur Delhaie, Karl Schmidt, Mr. Cool, Alexey Tishin, Ercole Bambucci, Ilya Ehrenburg, and Aysha the Negro, in the Days of Peace, War and Revolution in Paris, Mexico, Rome, Senegal, Kineshma, Moscow and other Places; As Well As Various Opinions of the Master about Pipes, about Death, about Love, about Freedom, about the Game of Chess, about the Jewish Race, about Reconstruction, and about Many Other Things.* The number of books published by Ehrenburg since 1921 is well over two score; they include novels, stories, plays, poetry, essays, travelogues, and journalistic reports.

Undoing of Nikolay Kurbov, 1923) is the story of an "ideal" Communist, purposeful and rigidly ascetic, who succumbs in a clash with the irrepressible "biological" forces of life. *Trest D. E.* (*Trust D. E.*, 1923) is an "inverse Utopia," telling the story of how Europe is conquered, in 1940, by the soulless, capitalist civilization of America. Ehrenburg's versatility is illustrated by such works as *Lyubov Zhanny Ney* (*The Love of Jeanne Ney,* 1923), a sentimentally melodramatic story of a love affair between a respectable French girl from a bourgeois family and a Russian Communist; and *Rvach* (*The Grabber,* 1925), a satirical picture of the Soviet scene during the NEP. The same period is depicted in *Leto 1925 goda* (*The Summer of 1925,* 1926), which is the most personal, sincere, and earnest of all Ehrenburg's works. It was denounced by Soviet critics as a cynical expression of the post-NEP mood of depression and disenchantment. Another picture of everyday Moscow life is *V Protochnom pereulke* (*In Protochny Lane,* 1927), where the characters are less schematic and more real than is usual with Ehrenburg. *Trinadtsat trubok* (*Thirteen Pipes,* 1923), a volume of short stories, is a good example of Ehrenburg's storytelling gift.

Ehrenburg's talent is undeniable, but most of his works suffer from the rapidity with which they were produced. Too often the journalist is to the fore in him, and some of his novels and stories are clever pamphlets in fictional form. But he knows how to handle a thrilling plot and has undoubtedly learned from Western detective fiction. His caustic intelligence makes his satires witty and pointed. He is good at parody—in *Julio Jurenito* there is some obvious parody of Dostoyevsky and Anatole France. But his characterization is crude and simplified. He is fond of sharp contrasts and often uses stock characters who are either paragons of abstract virtue or unmitigated scoundrels. Although violently denounced by orthodox Communist critics as a typical degenerate bourgeois, a cynic who holds nothing sacred, Ehrenburg enjoyed in the twenties considerable popularity among Soviet readers, which was in no small measure due to the "exoticism" of his non-Russian subject matter and his ability to tell a good story.

PRISHVIN

Mikhail Mikhailovich Prishvin (b. 1873) is something of a Russian W. H. Hudson. A trained specialist in agriculture, he first attracted attention in 1907 with *V krayu nepugannykh ptits* (*In the Land of Unscared Birds*), which contained some wonderful descriptions of nature and animal life in the Far North of Russia. A poet of nature, he is also a great master of racy and picturesque Russian. His first important post-Revolutionary work was *Kurymushka* (1924), which he described as his first "real story of a man." It is a novel of obviously autobiographical inspiration, though written in the third person, and describes the hero's childhood with remarkable insight into the inner workings of a child's mind. Further parts of it appeared later under the title *Kashcheyeva tsep* (*Kashchey's Chain*). In Russian folklore Kashchey is the legendary embodiment of evil, and the title symbolizes the fetters of moral and social prejudices from which man must free himself. Prishvin's manner resembles Remizov's, but his outlook of manly and robust optimism marks him off from some of the dominant tendencies of Russian literature. He is a passionate sportsman and at the same time an animal lover, and in many of his stories of the Soviet period he continued to explore the theme of nature. Some of them—for example in the volume *Lesnaya kapel* (*Forest Thaw*, 1945)—are more like short poems in prose, combining descriptions of nature with lyrical meditations.

VERESAYEV

V. Veresayev (pseudonym of Vikenty Vikentievich Smidowicz, 1867–1946) was before the Revolution a typical old-school realist, a scrupulous and observant witness of the social and psychological processes of his time. He gained fame with his nonfictional *Memoirs of a Physician* (1901). A documentary value attaches also to his two post-Revolutionary novels. In *V tupike* (*In a Blind Alley*, 1924) he draws a picture of the democratic and socialist intelligentsia confronted with the Revolution and with the problem of its terroristic excesses. It is a painstakingly objective work. Veresayev shows both the young and the old, both those who accept the Revolution and those who reject it. The heroine, Katya, a typical young girl from the revolutionary intelligentsia, morally pure and intellectually honest, frank in her democratic rejection of the antidemocratic Bolshevik Revolution, is a memorable creation. To her is opposed Leonid, a Bolshevik who justifies the Red Terror on grounds of expediency, rejects contemptuously the "old yardsticks" of "our dear, sensitive intelligentsia," and recognizes but one criterion: "Does the Revolution need it?" The novel is a truthful, if by no means a comprehensive, picture of the period and its problems.

The same can be said of Veresayev's *Syostry* (*The Sisters*, 1933), which portrays two girls from the old intelligentsia belonging to the Young Communist League and their reactions to the policy of forcible collectivization. The novel is written in the form of their joint diary. One accepts Communism unquestioningly, the other passes through a crisis of individualism and becomes a prey to doubts. But it is the latter who, with her intuition and common sense, proves to be more farsighted than her sister who adheres blindly to Party instructions and finds herself behind the times when Stalin springs upon the country

Some Pre-Revolutionary Writers

his famous article "Giddiness from Success," which denounces the excesses of collectivization and decrees a slackening of its tempo. The novel was at first warmly acclaimed by Soviet critics, but soon it was realized that Veresayev's picture of the inner life of the Young Communist League was far from flattering, while the ending seemed to suggest that Party members had better ignore instructions and follow their own intuition.

The Sisters was Veresayev's last contribution to fiction. After 1933 he concentrated on literary history, publishing *Pushkin in Life* and *Gogol in Life,* and wrote his *Memoirs,* which are characterized by the same scrupulous veracity. He also returned, toward the end of his life, to his old love (he was a classical scholar besides being a doctor of medicine) and undertook a translation of *The Iliad.*

SERGEYEV-TSENSKY

Sergey Nikolayevich Sergeyev-Tsensky (b. 1876), one of the outstanding representatives of Neo-Realism in pre-Revolutionary literature, published in 1923 *Valya,* first in a series of novels meant to constitute a vast canvas of Russian life between the eve of World War I and the present day. Gorky thought it one of the best works in modern Russian prose fiction. It is a work of intense psychological realism, with many interesting, uncommon characters and a rather intricate plot. It was followed at rather long intervals by other volumes of the same series; several of them dealt with World War I and will be discussed later; their connection with *Valya* is somewhat tenuous, and the general pattern of the whole series—the title of which is *Preobrazhenie (Transfiguration)*—remains obscure. Of Sergeyev-Tsensky's post-Revolutionary stories, *Rasskaz professora (The Professor's Tale,* 1924), is a narrative within a narrative. Although told in 1920 by a Red Army commander, it has a pre-Revolutionary subject and is a psychological study of the makings of a murderer. In the volume called *Zhestokost (Cruelty),* the long title story tells of the death of six Bolshevik commissars in a clash with peasant rebels during the Civil War.

Sergeyev-Tsensky also wrote several historical novels which will be discussed later.

SOBOL

Andrey Mikhailovich Sobol (1888–1926) began his literary career shortly before the Revolution. Coming from a Jewish middle-class family, he left home at the age of fourteen, worked as a prompter in an operetta theater, and tried several other professions. In 1905–1906 he took part in revolutionary activities. Sentenced to four years of penal servitude in Siberia, he managed to escape and emigrate. In 1915 he

141

returned, illegally, to Russia and enlisted in the army under an assumed name. His first novel, *Pyl (Dust)*, was published in 1915 and acclaimed by critics. After the Revolution he wrote a number of stories. Some of the best are to be found in the volume *Oblomki (The Wreckage,* 1923). Many of them are psychological studies of "superfluous men"—of revolutionaries disappointed in the Revolution, or of counterrevolutionaries who no longer believe in their cause. Sobol is a realist, but his realism has a nightmarish, fantastic quality, and his manner is impressionistic. His fantastic realism is particularly effective in such stories as "Oblomki" ("The Wreckage"), describing a group of odd inmates of a Crimean boardinghouse during the Civil War, in whose midst appears a Dostoyevskian "petty demon" in human disguise; or "Panoptikum" ("Panopticon"), a story of strange happenings in a commune organized by "egocentric anarchists" in a provincial town, where human beings and wax figures are equally real (or unreal). The whole Revolution appears to Sobol as a gigantic panopticon.

The longest story in the book, "Salon-vagon" ("The Pullman Car"), is more deeply psychological, though also told in a rapid succession of impressionistic scenes. It is the story of an old special railway coach which was once upon a time at the disposal of a governor-general in Central Asia and which is now (in 1917) occupied by a special commissar of the Provisional government, an old revolutionary, who travels to and fro over the whole vast expanse of Russia, from one front to another, in a desperate effort to stem the wave of mass desertions and save the Russian Army from complete disintegration. Sobol succeeds in conveying both the fantastic nature of events and the inner drama of the Commissar, who sees his long-desired Revolution turn into a grim and cruel reality. When the hero of the story tells the girl with whom he falls in love and for whom the blue Pullman car is a symbol of her happy childhood, that

> One must not be afraid of pity. It is, perhaps, the most beautiful of all human sentiments bequeathed to us,

it is the author himself who speaks through him: nearly all of Sobol's stories are imbued with pity for those whom the Revolution has crushed or led off the track. In this he was a true heir to the traditions of nineteenth-century Russian literature.

One of Sobol's last stories, "Povest o golubom pokoe" ("The Tale of a Blue Chamber"), was an unexpectedly light-hearted picture of non-Russian life, which had nothing to do with the Revolution. Soon after writing it, he committed suicide in a Moscow street, himself one of the spiritual victims of the Revolution.

SHAGINYAN

Before the Revolution, Marietta Sergeyevna Shaginyan (b. 1888) was known as a minor poet of the Symbolist school and author of modernistic stories. Of Armenian descent, she had a variety of interests and studied philosophy, music, and science, and later textile weaving; after the Revolution she taught some of these subjects. Most of her post-Revolutionary work consisted of prose fiction. The novel *Svoya sudba* (*One's Own Fate*), written before the Revolution but published in 1923, described life in a mental home. *Peremena* (*The Change*, 1924) and *Priklyucheniya damy iz obshchestva* (*The Adventures of a Society Lady*, 1925) are pictures of Soviet life during the Civil War. Considerable interest was attracted by her attempt to create a Soviet detective novel by combining a thrilling plot with revolutionary ideology.

Strange though this may appear today, in 1925–26 Soviet critics kept complaining that the public preferred foreign novels to the home product. The magazine *Zhurnalist* (*The Journalist*) lamented, in 1925, the fact that the statistics of lending libraries and railway newsstands showed that Soviet readers preferred translations of foreign fiction to works by Soviet writers. None other than Gorky volunteered the following interesting explanation of this state of things:

Jack London, Conrad, and O. Henry are read more readily. . . because they write more "romantically," with more stress on the plot, and about unfamiliar things. . . . The reader wants romanticism, no doubt about it. He wants to be told about things familiar in an interesting and unfamiliar way, he wants his own experiences to be somehow deepened and beautified. He can see that contemporary reality is more interesting than its representation in books, and he feels that books leave something unsaid, while some of them gloss over or hide certain things.[20]

Three years later the Soviet critic Lezhnev had to admit that foreign fiction still constituted the bulk of Soviet reading and that Jack London and Upton Sinclair remained "the most widely read authors." The demand for "romanticism" which Gorky mentioned was satisfied in part by such writers as Ehrenburg. It was with this need in mind that Marietta Shaginyan wrote her two novels, *Lori Len—metallist* (*Laurie Lane, the Metal Worker*) and *Mess Mend ili yanki v Petrograde* (*Mess Mend, or the Yankees in Petrograd*). They appeared in 1925 and 1926 under the pen name of "Jim Dollar," their supposed narrator being an American worker in Russia. The novels caused some stir and enjoyed popularity with the public at large, but Soviet critics disapproved of this attempt to "sovietize" Nat Pinkerton. In Gorbachov's opinion,

[20] No. 10 (1925). Quoted by Lezhnev, *Literary Weekdays*, 10.

Shaginyan's detective novels were neither fish nor fowl: for good thrillers there was too much propaganda in them; at the same time the author failed to overcome her "bourgeois" approach. Thus the attempt to produce a literature both entertaining and ideologically sound ended in a fiasco.

In 1929 Shaginyan published a curious experimental novel called *K. i. K. (K. and K.)*. The story of a missing Soviet commissar was told in four different versions by four authors, who were themselves characters in the novel. The epilogue contained an amusing critical examination of their works—a poem, an unfinished *nouvelle,* a verse melodrama, and a "scientific film"—which was put into the mouth of the missing commissar. The work was marked by original composition, clever handling of the plot, and good characterization.

SERAFIMOVICH

Of the "proletarian" pre-Revolutionary writers the best-known was Alexander Serafimovich (pseudonym of Alexander Serafimovich Popov, 1863–1949), who began writing as far back as 1888 when he was a political exile. A Don Cossack by origin, he stood close to the Social-Democratic party and was one of the pillars of Gorky's *Znanie* group of writers. One of the first to adhere to the new regime, he contributed to the *Izvestia* of the Moscow Soviet and wrote various political leaflets. For this he was expelled from the literary society *Sreda* and from the Writers' Publishing House in Moscow, a fact that serves to illustrate the anti-Bolshevik mood which prevailed among Russian writers in 1918–21.

Serafimovich's principal post-Revolutionary work is the novel *Zhelezny potok (The Iron Torrent,* 1924), now regarded as a Soviet classic. It tells of the march of a partisan army across the Caucasus during the Civil War. Their leader is something of a legendary figure, but the real hero of the novel is the partisan mass, the object of the author being to show mass action and mass mentality. He depicts the heroic exploits of these fighters for the Revolution, but also shows their calm, unreflecting cruelty. In form it has been compared to an Eisenstein film: mass scenes alternate with brief close-ups, with no attempt to treat the characters psychologically or to show their antecedents; we see them only in action and as parts of a bigger whole. Communist critics praised the novel for its "truthfulness" and its "clear understanding of the class essence of the Civil War."

5. Writers of Everyday Life and Satirists

AMONG the many fellow travelers who lent richness and variety to the Soviet literary scene during this period there were several writers whose main interest lay in their reflection of Soviet mores. They did not belong to any single literary school and reflected different aspects of Soviet life. Some of them were straightforward chroniclers of post-Revolutionary Russia; others approached life from a satirical angle. It is somewhat arbitrary to bracket them together and to discuss some of them apart from those who contributed to the revival of the novel. They had, however, this in common—that they were out to chronicle the everyday realities of the Revolution, with the emphasis on its second, unromantic phase. Most of them specialized in short stories rather than in novels. Their literary merits are unequal, but many of them held at one time an important place in Soviet literature, and some are still active in it.

Chroniclers of the Revolution
SEYFULLINA

Lydia Nikolayevna Seyfullina (b. 1889) came into literature rather late. Of mixed Russian-Tartar descent, she was a school teacher by profession. Her first stories appeared in 1921 in the local press in Siberia. One of them was favorably reviewed by Petrograd and Moscow critics, and in 1923 she moved to Moscow and devoted herself to literature.

Most of Seyfullina's early stories had for their setting the village during the Revolution and portrayed its social conflicts. Her best-known work, which went through several editions, was *Peregnoy* (*Mulch,* 1923), a long short story. Its hero is a good-for-nothing peasant who is completely transformed by the Revolution. Parallel with his inner transformation, Seyfullina shows the general impact of the Revolution on village life. In *Virineya* (1924), a counterpart to *Peregnoy,* Seyfullina portrays the new type of peasant woman emancipated by the Revolution. Both stories were written in the old-time realistic manner and differed greatly from the romantic portrayal of the Revolution in the work of Vsevolod Ivanov and Nikitin. They set a pattern for many stories about the beneficent effects of the Revolution on the backward Russian peasant. Both were later dramatized and successfully staged. In *Pravonarushiteli* (*Lawbreakers,* 1921) Seyfullina gave an equally unpretentious, realistic portrait of a homeless boy, one of the great army of waifs and strays who wandered about Russia in those years. Although lacking imaginative power, Seyfullina has a gift of observation, and her stories of post-Revolutionary rural Russia retain a documentary value.

ROMANOV

Panteleimon Sergeyevich Romanov (1884–1940) was even older than Seyfullina, but only a few of his stories appeared in print before the Revolution. He wrote two long works, one an autobiography— *Detstvo (Childhood,* 1928)—the other a long and ambitious novel about pre-Revolutionary Russia entitled *Rus (Russia,* 1924–26); but it was his novels and stories of contemporary Soviet life that gave him a place of his own in Soviet literature and made him widely known outside Russia. The best-known of these was the novel *Tovarishch Kislyakov (Comrade Kislyakov,* 1930), known to non-Soviet readers under the title *Three Pairs of Silk Stockings.* This novel, and the earlier *Novaya skrizhal (The New Table of Commandments,* 1927), as well as many of Romanov's short stories which are collected in the volumes *Bez cheryomukhi (Without Cherry Blossoms)* and *Voprosy pola (Problems of Sex)* deal with Soviet youth, with love and marriage, and with the problem of reconciling the romantic impulses of human nature with the new morals and the stern demands of Communist ideology. Problems of sex particularly interested Romanov. He showed the new type of young men and women, mostly students, reflecting sexual laxity and cynicism characteristic of the early period of the Revolution, when new Communist morality was equated with the lifting of all taboos and inhibitions. As the heroine of "Without Cherry Blossoms," one of Romanov's most typical stories, puts it:

> Among us there is no love, there is only sexual intercourse, because we relegate love contemptuously to the domain of "psychology," and it is only physiology that counts.

In most of Romanov's stories there is a touch of vulgarity and unhealthy sensationalism, and their success was largely due to their subject matter, but there is no doubt that they mirrored faithfully a certain phase in the evolution of Soviet society when traditional moral values were held in contempt and the old family and marital relations were rapidly disintegrating.

LIDIN

Vladimir Lidin (pseudonym of Vladimir Germanovich Gomberg, b. 1894) made his debut in literature shortly before the Revolution with some stories in Chekhov's manner. After the Revolution he wrote several novels and numerous stories. In these he often described the milieu of the Soviet employees, of the old and the new bourgeoisie—the so-called "Nepmen," the new rich of the NEP period. He is pre-eminently a short-story writer, and owes much of his technique to Chekhov, Bunin, and Maupassant. One of his would-be novels, *Idut korabli* (*Ships Are Sailing*, 1926), is really a collection of short stories running parallel, or rather alternately, loosely connected with one another, with settings in Moscow, Italy, Germany, and the Arctic region. The two most important of these stories have for their respective heroes a certain Ivan Kostrov, a convinced and sincere Communist, and Glotov, the cashier of the plant of which Kostrov is the manager. The interest of the Glotov story lies mainly in the vivid picture of a somewhat unusual aspect of life in Soviet Moscow: the racecourse, the restaurants and night clubs, and so on.

In *Otstupnik* (*The Renegade*, 1928), a regular problem novel, Lidin portrayed the milieu of Soviet students. Its hero, Bessonov, is involved in a murder and passes through a series of moral trials. The novel ends with his regeneration. At the last moment he gives up his plan of escaping abroad and decides to make a clean breast of his part in the murder. When he makes this decision, he suddenly realizes anew the beauty of life and rejoices at the thought of going back to his own world, where he will learn "the values of life, of human blood, of toil, and of love." Once more the novel is an interesting picture of Soviet life and mores of the NEP period.

KATAYEV

Valentin Petrovich Katayev was born in Odessa in 1897, where his father was a schoolmaster. He began writing at the age of nine, and his first poem was printed when he was twelve. In 1914 he met Ivan Bunin and, in his own words, became his "conscientious pupil." In 1915 he joined the army as a volunteer, and was wounded, shell-shocked, and gassed. During the Civil War in the Ukraine he was tossed between the Reds and the Whites and spent at least eight months in various prisons. In 1922 he settled in Moscow and devoted himself to literature.

His early post-Revolutionary work consisted of short stories about everyday life and stories of adventure. Some of his best early stories are to be found in the volume *Otets* (*The Father*, 1928). The title story is about an old man who carries on a quiet but joyless existence in one of the great South Russian ports where he is a schoolmaster. His sole joy in life is his son, a former officer who is imprisoned in the same town as a counterrevolutionary. When he is at last released, he turns out to be quite unworthy of his father's care and affection: he manages to get a snug job for himself and lives comfortably while the old man loses his job and is forced to drag out a miserable existence. In the end the young man goes to Moscow, leaving his father to die a lone death. The story is a study of two different types—men of two different genera-

147

tions. It also gives a good picture of daily life in a large provincial city under the Soviet regime.

There is in many of Katayev's stories a strong lyrical strain which distinguishes him from other everyday-life writers. He is also more versatile and has tried his hand at other genres. *Ostrov Ehrendorf* *(Ehrendorf Island,* 1924) is a novel of adventure, while *Rastratchiki* *(The Embezzlers,* 1927) is a gay caricature, describing the adventures of two employees of a Moscow Trust who abscond with a sum of money and go on a spree. Justice overtakes them in the end, but in the meantime the two men have plenty of fun and meet all sorts of queer people. Told in a quick tempo, full of amusing incidents, this novel treats Soviet life in lighthearted, satirical terms. About the same time Katayev wrote several gay, farcical plays about everyday Soviet life and its problems which will be mentioned in the section on the drama.

OGNYOV AND OTHERS

Considerable attention was aroused in 1926–27 by *Dnevnik Kosti Ryabtseva (The Diary of Kostya Ryabtsev).* Its author was N. Ognyov (pseudonym of Mikhail Grigoryevich Rozanov, 1888–1938). His earlier stories, such as "Shchi Respubliki" ("The Cabbage Soup of the Republic") and "Evraziya" ("Eurasia"), were written under a strong influence of Pilnyak, whom Ognyov once acclaimed as a daring challenger and destroyer of old forms. The interest of *The Diary of Kostya Ryabtsev* lay, however, not in its form, but in the novelty of its subject. Written in the form of a schoolboy's diary, it gave an extremely interesting and vivid picture of life in revolutionized Soviet high schools at the time when the old principles of education and methods of instruction were cast to the winds, and schools became miniature revolutionary republics run by the students. The picture was based on a thorough inside knowledge—Ognyov himself had taught in Soviet schools—and for a historian of Soviet education it is a document of great value, all the more interesting since the principles of education in the Soviet Union have now undergone a radical change. Ognyov also wrote a sequel to it, *Iskhod Nikpetozha (Exit Nikpetozh),* describing Kostya Ryabtsev's college days, but it is less interesting either as literature or as a document of the period.

The life of Soviet students, with an emphasis on its more unsavory aspects, is the subject of *Kommuna Mar-Mila (The Mar-Mila Commune,* 1926), a novel by Sergey Grigoryev (b. 1875).

An equally somber picture of the mores of the Young Communist League was given by Nikitin, one of the Serapion Brothers, in his novel *Prestuplenie Kirika Rudenko (The Crime of Kirik Rudenko,* 1928), where drunken debauchery, sexual laxity, and crime play a prominent part. The novel gave rise to a controversy, Communist critics accusing Nikitin of laying on the black paint too thickly.

Provincial life was vividly portrayed in Sergey Zayaitsky's *Baklazhany* (*Eggplants,* 1928), in which he introduced some members of the clergy under the Soviet regime—a subject seldom touched upon in those days by Soviet writers.

The Satirists

ZOSHCHENKO

Mikhail Mikhailovich Zoshchenko, one of the original Serapions, was for many years the most widely-read Soviet writer, and his popularity among the Russians outside Russia rivaled his popularity in the Soviet Union. In the biographical dictionary of Soviet writers, published in 1930, we read: "The name of Zoshchenko, a most popular Soviet humorous writer, enjoys widest fame. His stories are read even by those who, as a rule, do not follow contemporary literature."[21]

Born in 1895 in Poltava, Zoshchenko was the son of an artist. He studied at the Law School of the University of St. Petersburg but did not graduate, and in 1915 enlisted as a volunteer in the army. He was wounded and gassed, but this did not prevent him from volunteering again, in 1918, for the Red Army. His literary career began in 1921 when he joined the Serapion Brotherhood.

Zoshchenko gradually evolved a style and manner of his own, which mark him off from all other Soviet writers and make his writings easily and instantly recognizable. It was based on *skaz,* which was popular in the early period of Soviet literature. But of all the writers who, in the years 1920–23, used the *skaz* form so lavishly and with so little restraint, Zoshchenko was the only one who stuck to it after it had gone out of fashion with the revival of the novel and a return to psychological realism. Zoshchenko not only retained the *skaz* form, but modified it and put it to a new use.

His early stories, included in the book *Rasskazy Nazara Ilyicha gospodina Sinebryukhova* (*Stories Told by Nazar Ilyich Mr. Sinebryukhov,* 1922), were typical of that period. They were about the war and the Civil War, and were put into the mouth of a semieducated noncom whose language was a mixture of natural raciness and a hideous, artificial lingo. Both the subject and the language were exotic and the presentation highly stylized. It is obvious that Zoshchenko's masters were Leskov and Remizov, and to a certain extent Zamyatin; but beneath these influences it is possible to discern individual notes and unmistakable signs of literary mastery.

21 V. Tarsis, *Sovremennye russkie pisateli* (*Contemporary Russian Writers*), 86.

With both the *skaz* manner and the exotic subjects going out of fashion, Zoshchenko had to evolve a new manner to suit both his artistic personality and the requirements of the times. He passed through an intermediate period, writing a number of short stories in which the comic effects were achieved through the subject matter, through improbable and ridiculous situations, involving comic characters. These stories were written in the third person, in the ordinary, "educated" language. Then he began writing short humorous stories which stood on the border line between imaginative literature and newspaper *feuilleton*. Their subjects were usually topical: they exposed the so-called "minor defects of mechanism" in various branches of Soviet administration and satirized Communist red tape, corruption, inefficiency, and so on. Gradually, Zoshchenko evolved a new manner—a combination of his earlier *skaz* stories and his purely comic anecdotes. It was largely a question of finding a proper "mouthpiece" for the *skaz*—a good substitute for the author—who would no longer be exotic, but would fit in with the normal course of daily Soviet life. Such a mouthpiece was found by Zoshchenko in the Soviet man-in-the-street, the average Soviet citizen who passively accepts the Revolution, but vaguely regrets the good old times and longs for bourgeois comforts. Zoshchenko's narrator speaks the inimitable jargon of a semieducated man, with a strong admixture of the specific Soviet journalese which was, at the time, rapidly inundating and disfiguring the Russian language. He is a synthetic portrait of the Soviet philistine.

Although Zoshchenko's situations are often improbable and grotesque, the label of "everyday-life writer" suits him more than it does anyone else. He gives a true picture of Soviet weekdays, stripped of all romantic and heroic varnish, of all pretension and make-believe. Some of the orthodox Soviet critics were from the outset at a loss what to make of Zoshchenko. In turn they praised him for exposing so mercilessly the petty-bourgeois weaknesses of the average Soviet citizen—the spirit of *embourgeoisement* invading large circles of Communist society, including the Party itself—and denounced him as a vulgar "bourgeois," identifying him with his own characters.

Zoshchenko is a most prolific writer: his stories, most of them quite short, form many volumes, some of the titles of which are: *Uvazhaemye grazhdane (Esteemed Citizens)*, *O chom pel solovey (What the Nightingale Sang About)*, *Nervnye lyudi (Nervous People)*, and *Siren tsvetyot (Lilac Is in Bloom)*. Most of them went through several editions. Their popularity with the mass of Soviet readers rested probably on their outward comic effects and on the familiarity of the subject matter. But it is their second, hidden meaning and their technical excellence that make the best among them into real literature. Stylistically, some of them are genuine gems. At his best Zoshchenko reminds one simultaneously of two great masters of Russian literature, so dissimilar on the whole, but so alike in one thing—in their keen vision of the mean vulgarity and insipidity of life: Gogol and Chekhov. It is the pettiness, the vulgarity of life, the essential incomprehensibility of one man to another, that forms the keynote of Zoshchenko's stories. In some of the best—in "Wisdom," for instance—one can sense a deep feeling of tragedy beneath and beyond the humorous and grotesque presentation of a humdrum, vulgar life. The most hilarious of modern Russian writers is at heart a thorough pessimist, and for a discerning reader his comic stories must inevitably leave an aftertaste of sadness. Often one feels that Zoshchenko is speaking with his tongue in his cheek, and it is not surprising that Communist critics were baffled by him.

Like Gogol and Leskov, Zoshchenko is one of the most difficult Russian writers to translate, for so many of his effects are based on verbal jugglery, on inimitable peculiarities of speech. It is as difficult to translate Zoshchenko into English or American as it would be to translate Damon Runyon or Edward Lear into Russian.

Since Zoshchenko's work is all more or less of a piece, it is not improper to discuss here one of his later works—his first "novel," *Vozvrashchonnaya molodost (Youth Restored,* 1933). Although he called it a novel, it differs little, except in length, from his typical stories. It is written in the same colloquial, facetious style. Its very short chapters, each containing a typical Zoshchenko situation or anecdote, make it into a succession of short stories, held together by the unity of characters and a slender plot. It falls into two parts, with the first seventeen chapters forming a kind of preface in which the author makes his pseudo-scientific and subtly irrelevant comments on the subject of his story. The work was written at the time when the need of bringing science and literature together was urged by Soviet critics. In reading Zoshchenko's "preface," the reader cannot help feeling that the author is laughing at science, at Soviet critics, at his own ridiculous characters, and at the reader. Describing his "novel" as a cross between an ordinary novel which the reader picks up of an evening "in order to dispel his daily worries and become engrossed in other people's lives, other people's motions, and other people's thoughts," and a scientific treatise written "in the simple, incoherent, everyday language," Zoshchenko goes on in the same would-be naïve but actually jeering vein:

> Well, if this is not a scientific work, if, suppose, the Academy of Sciences or, say, the Section of Scientific Workers, having come to an agreement with the Municipal Committee and the Writers' Union, refuses to find here any signs of a scientific work, or, while

finding such signs, will not regard the author as having duly mastered the Marxist-Leninist conception, then, in such a case, this book could be described by a more neutral name, a more harmless one, so to speak, which would not annoy the eyes and ears of certain citizens and organizations. Let this book, say, be called an educational film. Let it be, say, such an educational film as we have had on the screen: *Abortion,* or say, *Why Does It Rain?* or *How Silk Stockings Are Made,* or finally *What Is the Difference Between Man and Beaver?* There are such films on great contemporary scientific and industrial subjects, worthy of study. Just as in those films, we shall first have a scientific argument with various footnotes and references to this and that, and all sorts of comments which will definitively clear up the matter. And only after that the reader, slightly tired and dazed by other people's thoughts, will receive his share of entertaining reading matter, which will serve as a sort of visual illustration to the above-mentioned thoughts and considerations.

The story itself concerns an aging, almost decrepit Soviet professor of astronomy, vaguely hostile to the present regime but just as vaguely in sympathy with Socialism in general. He laments his lost youth and finally succeeds in restoring it by an effort of will. He deserts his wife, marries a young girl, flighty and vulgar, who "at the age of nineteen has already managed to change five husbands and undergo seven or eight abortions," and goes away to the Crimea with her. Soon she tires of him and begins to flirt with young men. One day the Professor finds his Tulya in the arms of one of these young men. He has a stroke, and one side of his body is paralyzed. In the end he is cured and even manages to preserve his restored youth. He returns to his wife and family, but deep in his heart never ceases to pine after Tulya.

All the situations and characters in the novel are grotesque, and the work reads like a sort of synthetic parody of many Soviet works, with their stock situations and ready-made themes. Here is Zoshchenko's description of the happy marriage of the Professor's daughter, who, herself an enthusiastic Communist, marries a Communist—for reasons of work they have to live apart, meeting once in every five days:

> Lida, feeling a little sorry at heart, and at the same time surprised by the haste with which he had married, consented to wait a little, agreeing that the search for an apartment, the removal, and various domestic affairs and cares might unfavorably affect the course of his work. He praised her for her common sense and political maturity, saying that he now realized quite well that he had made no mistake in choosing her, and that, indeed, he would per-

haps be unable to find at present a better wife. And Lida, pleased with his praises, looked at him with admiring eyes and said that, maybe, she too could not have a better husband. They were happy in their own way, and in no hurry to disturb their happiness with kisses and embraces.

The most amazing thing about Zoshchenko's novel is that it was taken seriously as an attempt to introduce science into literature and bring the two together. Several discussions were organized on this subject, in which some eminent Soviet scientists, such as Professor Yoffe, the famous physicist, took part, and it did not occur to anyone that Zoshchenko was pulling everybody's leg.

The element of parody and legpulling played also a large part in Zoshchenko's *Golubaya kniga* (*Light-Blue Book,* 1934), which he dedicated to Gorky, who had first suggested that Zoshchenko should write a humorous "History of Civilization." In a letter to Gorky with which he prefaced the book, Zoshchenko said that what he had written was not so much a "History of Civilization" as "a short history of human relations." It is a collection of usual Zoshchenko stories, over forty of them, written in the inimitable chatty style of Zoshchenko's semiarticulate philistine "hero." The stories are arranged under five main headings: "Money," "Love," "Perfidy," "Failures," and "Remarkable Happenings," and are linked together by historical and pseudohistorical anecdotes, illustrating the part played in human life and relations by money, love, and so on. Each section has a short "preface" and "postface," in which Zoshchenko gives free play to his irony. The book ends with a short "postface" to the whole volume, and two sections entitled "Taking Leave of the Bourgeois Philosopher" and "Taking Leave of the Reader." The unity which Zoshchenko tried to impart to this volume of some four hundred pages gives his humor a "monumental" quality. The reader is free to take these humorous stories at their face value or to read into them a deeper meaning and message. Zoshchenko himself refrains from laying his cards on the table, and some of his cards are certainly "marked." His delight in laughing at life and at the follies of mankind knows no bounds. But, as usual, his is not a simple, hearty laughter, and the reader cannot help feeling uncomfortable.

More about Zoshchenko will be found in Chapters VI and VII below.

BULGAKOV

Among the writers in the late twenties and early thirties who acquired, like Zamyatin, the reputation of an inside *émigré* was Mikhail Afanasyevich Bulgakov (1891–1936). Born in Kiev, he came from an intelligentsia family, studied medicine but did not practice it, and engaged in journalism before turning to literature. His first work to attract attention was the novel *Belaya gvardiya* (*The White Guard*), which in 1924 was serialized in *Rossiya* (*Russia*), one of the more independent magazines which specialized in publishing the work of fellow travelers. Apparently the novel did not meet with approval in the higher spheres, for it was never published in book form in the Soviet Union; several editions of it were, however, issued outside Russia. Later it was dramatized by Bulgakov and, under the title *Dni Turbinykh* (*The Days of the Turbins*), had a somewhat checkered career on the Soviet stage. By 1930 Bulgakov had the reputation of a "neo-bourgeois writer" belonging to the "right wing" of Soviet literature.

Bulgakov used to say that of all his works he liked *The White Guard* best. But its value as literature is not very great. It is written simply, in the realist manner, without any stylistic or compositional refinements. Its interest lies in its subject matter and in the author's attitude toward his characters. The action is set in Kiev in 1918, when the Ukraine was under the semi-independent, German-sponsored government of Hetman Skoropadsky. The novel describes the events leading up to Skoropadsky's downfall and the subsequent occupation of Kiev, first by the Ukrainian nationalists of Petlyura and then by the Bolsheviks. In Soviet literature it has the unique distinction of having no Communists in it, all its principal characters being White officers, some of them Monarchists, and all avowed enemies of Bolshevism. They are portrayed sympathetically—as honest, chivalrous, disinterested men who fight the Bolsheviks not for personal, selfish reasons, but in the name of patriotism and of their principles. This is true above all of the brothers Turbin, who stand in the center of the picture: the liberal-minded but disillusioned Alexey, the elder brother, chivalrous and courageous, but lacking in will power; and the young, romantically inclined Nikolka, who bears a certain resemblance to Petya Rostov in *War and Peace*. Bulgakov's approach is detached and objective, and not all the Whites are painted in these attractive colors. The Turbins end by accepting Bolshevism, but Bulgakov shows them doing so for purely patriotic reasons, as the lesser of the two evils, for in the struggle between the Bolsheviks and Petlyura's bands, the former stood for the unity of Russia.

Bulgakov's novel apparently enjoyed a great success with the readers. Communist critics tried to explain it away by the craving of the average Soviet reader for "exotic" and "thrilling" matter. But there was probably more to it than that, and a still greater success awaited the dramatization of Bulgakov's novel on the stage of the Moscow Art Theater. Here the alleged "counterrevolutionary" elements of the novel, especially the chivalry and personal heroism of its "White" heroes, were brought into still greater relief. The success of this play, which included the performance on the stage of the old Russian national anthem, was so staggering that after a time the government was forced to ban the play, at any rate in Moscow. The ban was temporarily lifted in 1932, but soon after that Bulgakov got into trouble again with some other plays of his, and *The Days of the Turbins* disappeared again from the Soviet repertoire. By 1934 Bulgakov was virtually ousted from literature. His last known work was an adaptation of Gogol's *Dead Souls* for the Moscow Art Theater.

Bulgakov's book of stories, *Dyavoliada (Devilry,* 1925), was also denounced as hostile to the Revolution. It consists of five stories of uneven length. Both in subject matter and in manner, these stories differ from *The White Guard.* They all deal with contemporary Soviet life, but with two small exceptions do so in terms not of realism but of fantasy or of satirical exaggeration. It is these stories which entitle Bulgakov to be regarded as a satirist.

The first story, which gave the book its title, begins on a realistic plane but passes imperceptibly into the realm of fantastic satire, where the real and the unreal are hopelessly intermixed. It is based on a trifling anecdote about Soviet red tape and tells the story of the undoing of a small Soviet clerk who gets fired because he mistakes the name of his new boss for the word "pants," and issues, as a result of that mistake, a nonsensical instruction. In his efforts to vindicate himself he loses his name and identity and encounters all sorts of queer and grotesque people. His fantastic adventures give us odd glimpses of the Soviet bureaucratic mechanism. Bulgakov deliberately discards here all realism and psychology: his characters are grotesque puppets, his world the Gogolian world of fantastic reality. The story particularly calls to mind Gogol's *Nose.* But "Devilry" is at the same time a satire on the inefficiency of Soviet bureaucratic institutions, told with almost too much gusto.

There is a more clearly drawn boundary line between the real and the fantastic in the longest story in the book, "Rokovye yaytsa" ("The Fatal Eggs"). It is a sort of scientific satire, and the reference in it to H. G. Wells's *Food of the Gods* is not accidental. The story is told against the background of a satirically presented picture of Moscow life in 1925, but its plot is purely fantastic. A certain Professor Persikov, a zoologist of world-wide reputation, in the course of his routine work makes an important scientific discovery—a new kind of red ray possessing an enormous life-giving and procreating capacity. His experiments with it, conducted on frogs, coincide with a mysterious epidemic which almost wipes out the poultry population of the Soviet Union. Against Persikov's wish and at the suggestion of a Communist whose name is

Rokk (the name sounds exactly like the Russian word *rok,* fate—hence the untranslatable pun in the title), it is decided to use Persikov's discovery in the breeding of new hens in the Soviet Union. A special farm is allotted for this purpose, and Rokk placed in charge of it. Hens' eggs are ordered from Germany, and the experiment begins. It ends, however, in disaster. Because of an error on the part of some Soviet institution, Rokk receives, instead of hens' eggs, several crates containing eggs of ostriches and huge anacondas and crocodiles, which Persikov had ordered for his scientific experiments, while the hens' eggs arrive at Persikov's address after much delay, when it is too late to avert the disaster: snakes, crocodiles, and ostriches, hatched artificially on the "Red Ray Farm," come out of those eggs, grow within a few hours to giant dimensions, multiply with unheard-of rapidity, and cause havoc, panic, and destruction all around. They begin by swallowing Rokk's wife and killing all the inhabitants of the farm. They then proceed to invade the province of Smolensk, laying eggs by the thousands as they move eastwards toward Moscow, and procreating at an extraordinary rate. All the resources of the Republic—the Red Army, the Air Force, the Chemical Warfare Society, the fire brigades—are mobilized to fight this terrible invasion. Towns and villages on the way to Moscow are seized with panic; thousands of people perish; Moscow itself is in a state of alarmed expectation. The anger of the mob turns against Persikov, who is held responsible for the disaster. A crowd led by Rokk, who has gone mad after his wife's death, storms the Zoological Institute and kills Persikov and his faithful attendants. In the end the terrifying progress of the gigantic reptiles is stopped by an unexpected circumstance: a severe frost grips Russia one night in the middle of August, and the reptiles and their eggs freeze to death. Nature intervenes to save the Soviet Union from complete destruction: this climax in itself sounded a counterrevolutionary note.

Apart from the fantastic plot, in "The Fatal Eggs" there is no such mingling of the real and the fantastic as in "Devilry." But the reality is portrayed from a satirical angle. Beginning with Rokk—an antiquated Communist, in the past a flautist in a cinema orchestra, who in 1925 still wears the symbolical leather jacket of a hidebound Communist—down to the episodic figures of several Soviet journalists, all the characters in the story are obviously satirized. Irony permeates the whole story, but Bulgakov's own attitude is difficult to make out: he uses this all-round irony as a sort of safety valve.

The third important story in this collection is entitled "The Adventures of Chichikov" (this was the title which the censorship imposed on Gogol's *Dead Souls*). The subtitle is "A Poem in Ten Points with Prologue and Epilogue" (Gogol also called his *Dead Souls* "a

Poem"). The story introduces Chichikov and several other characters from Gogol's immortal work and transplants them to the Soviet Union, the obvious implication being that in contemporary Russia there is plenty of scope, both for the cunning rascals and rogues like Chichikov and for some of Gogol's inefficient bunglers. The point which Bulgakov seems to make here is that, beneath the surface and beyond the Communist appearances, life in Russia remains much as it used to be in Gogol's days. On entering the gate of the very hotel which he left one hundred years ago at the end of Gogol's novel, Chichikov finds that everything is exactly the same:

> Cockroaches were peeping out of the crevices and even seemed to have become more numerous. But there were some slight changes, too . . . . Thus, for instance, the sign bearing the word "Hotel" was now replaced by a poster with the inscription "Hostel No. So-and-so." Also, needless to say, dirt and filth were such as Gogol could never have imagined.

Chichikov's adventures in modern Russia are humorously described though the humor is a trifle too obvious and superficial. He easily adjusts himself to the new surroundings and circumstances and plays a number of cunning tricks on the silly and inefficient Soviet administration. The first thing they ask him to do is to fill out a questionnaire containing one hundred tricky questions. It takes him only five minutes to do so, but when he hands it in, his hand trembles:

> "Well," he thought, "presently they will read it and will see what sort of a bird I really am, and . . .
> But nothing happened at all.
> First of all, no one read the questionnaire. Secondly, it got into the hands of the filing clerk who did the usual thing with it: she entered it as an outgoing document instead of an incoming, and then immediately shoved it somewhere, so that the questionnaire vanished into the thin air, as it were.
> Chichikov grinned and started upon his job.

It was only after Chichikov had played all sorts of ingenious tricks and these had been laid bare, thanks to Nozdryov, that his questionnaire was unearthed with great difficulties, and this is how it ran:

> *Name*: Paul. *Patronymic*: Ivanovich. *Surname*: Chichikov. *Social standing*: Gogol's character. *Pre-revolutionary occupation*: Buying up dead souls. *Relation to military service*: Neither this nor that nor devil knows what. *To what party are you affiliated?* Sympathizer (but with whom, goodness knows). *Have you been under trial?* Curved zigzagging line instead of an answer. *Address*: Turn

into the courtyard, third floor on the right, ask at the enquiry office for the officer's wife Podtochina, and she will know.

Finally, the author himself intervenes, volunteers to catch Chichikov, has him dissected, finds inside him stolen "people's milliards" in the form of diamonds, and orders him to be drowned in an ice hole. As a reward he asks for Gogol's *Complete Works*.

Then follows the ironical epilogue, which dismisses the whole story as a bad dream:

> . . . of course, I woke up. And there was nothing: no Chichikov, no Nozdryov, and what is more, no Gogol. . . .
>
> "Well, well," I thought to myself, and began to dress. And once more life paraded before me in its everyday attire.

Commenting on Bulgakov's picture of Soviet life, Communist critics said that it boiled down to the assertion that the Revolution had changed nothing below the surface of Russian life, and they compared Bulgakov to his countryman Shulgin, with his famous formula: "Everything the same, but slightly worse."[22]

ILF AND PETROV

In 1928 appeared a long novel which was soon to become one of the favorites with the Soviet public. It was called *Dvenadtsat stulyev* (*Twelve Chairs*), and was signed by two unknown names: Ilf and Petrov.

Ilya Arnoldovich Ilf (1897–1937) and Evgeny Petrov (pseudoym of Evgeny Petrovich Katayev, younger brother of Valentin Katayev, 1902–1942) were both born in Odessa. But they first met in Moscow, where they began their literary career as journalists, on the railwaymen's paper *Gudok*. Everything they wrote between 1927 and 1937 was written jointly. In their joint humorous "autobiography" (which contained a great deal of truth, said Petrov later) they wrote:

> It is very difficult to write together. It was easier for the Goncourts, we suppose. After all they were brothers while we are not even related to each other. We are not even of the same age. And even of different nationalities: while one is a Russian (the enigmatic Slavic soul), the other is a Jew (the enigmatic Jewish soul).

[22] In 1926 Shulgin, former editor of the Monarchist daily *Kievlyanin* (Kiev), one of the leaders of the "Progressive Bloc" in the Fourth Duma and one of the most brilliant *émigré* journalists, paid a sensational "secret" visit to the Soviet Union and published an interesting account of it in the book called *Tri stolitsy* (*Three Capitals*). Later, it turned out that the organization which had arranged Shulgin's "conducted tour" of the Soviet Union was an offshoot of the Soviet secret police, organized for the purpose of infiltration into the anti-Soviet groups abroad, and that the manuscript of Shulgin's book was actually edited and proof-read in the offices of the Moscow Ogpu. The same organization was later responsible for the kidnapping of General Kutepov in Paris.

In his "Recollections of Ilf" (written in 1939), Petrov has told the curious story of the genesis of *Twelve Chairs*, their first joint product. One day Valentin Katayev, who used to write comic verses for *Gudok*, came to the editorial offices and announced: "I want to become the Soviet Dumas-père." To Ilf's question "Why?" he answered: "It is high time to launch a Soviet novel workshop. I'll be the Dumas-père and you'll be my Negroes. I'll give you the themes, you will write the novels, and I'll polish them up. I'll just go over your manuscripts once or twice with my master's hand—and there it is. Like Dumas-père. Eh? Who's game? But remember, I'll give you a rough treatment." They exchanged a few more jokes on the subject, and then Katayev said quite seriously: "Here is an excellent theme: chairs. Imagine that money is hidden in one of the chairs. It must be found. Isn't it a good adventure novel? There are also other themes. Eh? Do agree. Seriously. Let Ilya write one novel, and Zhenya, another."[23]

Thus was born the idea of *Twelve Chairs*. Ilf and Petrov decided to write it together and the very same day drew up the plan. This was in August or September, 1927, and by January, 1928, the novel was completed. It was written together by the two of them, in the most literal sense of the word—that is, they sat beside each other and collaborated on every sentence. When the first part of the novel was shown to Katayev, he liked it and said: "You'll do without the Dumas-père. Continue to write on your own. I think the book will be a success."[24] And so it was.

Twelve Chairs is a gay picaresque novel. It is also a satire. In the center of it stands the irrepressible Ostap Bender, who was originally meant as a purely episodic character, but grew into a real hero. He is one of the most memorable creations in Soviet literature, a modern Chichikov, a cunning and ingenious rogue, who leads the fantastic, breath-taking race for the diamonds which their pre-Revolutionary owner hid in one of a set of twelve chairs. The set having been dispersed, the search for the right chair takes Bender, his assistants and his rivals, among whom is a former priest, through all sorts of fantastic and farcical adventures. All this against the background of grotesquely satirized Soviet life of the NEP period. The hunt for the chair has an appropriate ideological ending: the chair with the diamonds in it turns out to have become the property of a Soviet club and the money used for cultural purposes. As for Bender, in an attempt to escape from Russia across the Dniester into Rumania, he meets his death. The authors afterwards regretted having disposed of their hero and decided to bring him back to life in their second novel, *Zolotoy telyonok* (*The Little*

23 E. Petrov, "Iz vospominaniy ob Ilfe" ("From my Recollections of Ilf"), in *Zapisnye knizhki* (*Notebooks*), 14–15.
24 *Ibid.*, 19.

Golden Calf, 1931). This sequel to *Twelve Chairs* is just as entertaining and just as recklessly fantastic, while the satire in it is even more serious and biting. It also has a neater and better balanced plot, revolving round several competing pretenders to the role of the son of Lieutenant Schmidt, the famous hero of the *Potyomkin* mutiny in 1905, with Ostap Bender acting as the sponsor and impressario of one of these pretenders. Here again everyday Soviet life can be seen through a grotesquely distorting mirror.

In *Twelve Chairs* and its sequel we see a procession of Soviet gangsters, confidence men, corrupt and unscrupulous officials, and gullible, ordinary citizens. The authors let their fancy run loose, while at the same time drawing upon real life for their characters and situations. As the Communist review *October* put it, life in *Twelve Chairs* is "grotesque, confused, improbable, and yet real."

Ilf and Petrov also wrote together a number of humorous and satirical stories, again for the most part satirizing various aspects of Soviet life. However, two of the stories in the volume *Tonya* (1935) are satires on American life: "Tonya" describes the first steps of a young Soviet couple in America and contrasts American and Soviet life (it is written more seriously than is usual with Ilf and Petrov and is spoiled by its obvious didacticism); while "Kolumb prichalivayet k beregu" ("Columbus Puts To") is an amusing short skit on modern United States, describing what happens to Christopher Columbus when he rediscovers twentieth-century America, with her reporters, her publicity, her burlesques.

Ilf and Petrov's last major joint work, *Odnoetazhnaya Amerika* (*One-Storied America*, 1936), was also about the United States: it is a witty, satirical account of their visit to the United States and their transcontinental car trip. In writing it, they adopted a new method: twenty chapters were written by Ilf, twenty by Petrov, and seven by both of them in the old way. Today the book would not be passed by the Soviet censor: its satire was rather mild, and there were many things in American life that appealed to the two Soviet authors.

When Ilf died of tuberculosis in 1937, this successful tandem team came to an end. Left to himself, Petrov did not produce anything worthwhile. He was killed in 1942 in the Crimea, while reporting the war for Russian and American newspapers.

In 1939 there appeared, posthumously, Ilf's *Zapisnye knizhki (Notebooks)*, short notations of an observant artist, containing both the laboratory material for satires and "lyrical" fragments.

6. The Historical Novel

STRANGE though this may appear at first glance, historical fiction as a specific literary genre took a new lease on life in post-Revolutionary Russia—a Russia which was supposedly looking to the future and doing away with the past. Some of the historical novels published in the Soviet Union during the period under review represented a new departure and constituted a distinct contribution to literature. To understand this, a brief survey of Russian historical fiction before the Revolution may not be out of place here. It was the influence of Walter Scott and the quickening of national-patriotic sentiments after the Napoleonic wars that gave rise to historical novels in Russia. The novels of Zagoskin (who was often called the Russian Walter Scott though he was certainly inferior, both in talent and in scope of historical vision, to the famous Scot novelist) as well as Pushkin's historical novels and Gogol's *Taras Bulba,* much as they differ from each other, represented the fruits of Scottism on the Russian soil. The well-known Russian critic Apollon Grigoryev (1820–64) went so far as to say that the whole of the National-Romantic period in Russian literature was influenced by Sir Walter Scott. The art of the historical novel became in the eighteen thirties the subject of a curious controversy between two Russian critics, Belinsky and Senkovsky (Sekowski). Belinsky had an unqualified admiration for Scott, while Senkovsky, the Polish-born *enfant terrible* of Russian literary criticism, who was a notable Oriental scholar and possessed an infinitely greater historical erudition than his opponent, came forth as a detractor of Scott and of historical fiction as a literary genre, calling it "a bastard, counterfeit art."[25]

Zagoskin had several successors. The best-known of them was Lazhechnikov, whose novels were built on more solid historical foundations than Zagoskin's costume pieces and were at the same time quite readable. But the traditions of Scottism were not carried on in great Russian literature. Turgenev's six major novels, while "historical" in the sense that they mirror successive stages in the evolution of Russian society, do so in terms of imaginary characters and do not come within the strict meaning of historical fiction. The only instance of a historical novel in the great Russian literature of the second half of the nineteenth century is Tolstoy's *War and Peace.* But *War and Peace,* this "river of a novel" (*"roman-fleuve"*), is a genre in itself. While it is, of course, a historical novel, it is also something more than that—a vast epic of Russian life, a family chronicle, and a masterpiece of individual

[25] For some details of this controversy see Peter Struve, "Walter Scott in Russia," in *The Slavonic and East European Review,* Vol. XI (January, 1933), 397–410.

psychological analysis. What is more, this "historical" novel is eminently antihistorical in spirit and sets out to shatter the traditional view of
history. Tolstoy's great work has therefore remained a solitary, isolated
fact in Russian literature, even though it did influence some second-
and third-rate novelists. After Tolstoy, historical fiction was for a long
time relegated to the lower regions of literature or regarded as juvenile
reading (typical examples of it are Alexey K. Tolstoy's colorful costume
novel *Prince Serebryany* and the novels of Vsevolod Solovyov). More
important was the handling of historical themes in the drama, where
the Shakespearean tradition of Pushkin's *Boris Godunov* was continued
by the same Alexey K. Tolstoy in his famous trilogy—*The Death of
Ivan the Terrible, Tsar Fyodor Ioannovich,* and *Tsar Boris.* Alexander
Ostrovsky, the principal representative of Russian dramatic realism,
also wrote some historical plays.

An attempt to revive and renovate historical fiction and give it a
higher status in literature was made by the Russian Symbolists—in the
novels of Merezhkovsky and Bryusov and in the stories of some less important writers like Kuzmin, Sadovskoy, and Auslaender. The interesting new element in Merezhkovsky's historical novels—those which form
his celebrated trilogy, *Christ and Antichrist,* as well as his later novels
from Russian history—was that, contrary to the traditional historical
novel brought into fashion by Walter Scott and to Tolstoy's great
masterpiece, the central parts in them were assigned to historical, not
fictitious, characters. Julian the Apostate, Leonardo da Vinci, Peter the
Great, and Alexander I of Russia are the key characters in Merezhkovsky's novels. But in Merezhkovsky the novelist was subordinated to the
thinker: in terms of historical facts and characters he gave expression to
his historical, philosophical, and religious ideas. His novels were "his-
toriosophical" novels *à thèse.* They combined an attempt—not always
successful—at archeological accuracy with a modernization of history,
but lacked true historicity. This is particularly obvious in the last part of
the trilogy, *Peter and Alexis.* In a way it was therefore natural for
Merezhkovsky to give up, finally, the historical-novel form and turn to
a nonfictional treatment of historical themes and characters.

In Bryusov's historical fiction (*The Fiery Angel* and *The Altar of
Victory*) the impulse was purely literary: they were an outlet for the
general tendency of the Symbolists to get away from contemporary life,
which, in their eyes, lacked color and variety, and to seek inspiration
in the past or in exoticism, as did the romantics. After Merezhkovsky
and Bryusov came a new interval which lasted until after the Revolution, when the historical novel was once more revived both in Soviet
Russia and in *émigré* literature (Mark Aldanov).

The Social-Historical Novel

It is possible to distinguish two principal varieties of historical fiction in post-Revolutionary Russia: the social-historical novel and the biographical novel. The former originated in the desire to relate the present to the past; the latter was prompted largely by a desire to escape from the present into the past.

It is also necessary to bear in mind that the general orientation and significance of Soviet historical fiction underwent a considerable change in the mid-thirties. In the present section, going beyond the strictly chronological limits of this chapter, I shall discuss the novels which appeared prior to 1937; those which appeared later will be mentioned in Chapters V, VI, and VII.

It has been said that revolutions are propitious to historical studies and to the spirit of history.[26] It is very doubtful, however, whether this statement, without serious qualifications, is applicable to the Russian Revolution. In its later phases especially, the Revolution proved to be much more propitious to the revision, and even falsification, of history. It is nevertheless true that so far as the literature of the Revolution tried to grasp the meaning of events and not merely to record them, it had to analyze their genesis and treat them in historical perspective. A Soviet critic stressed the influence of the present on the interpretation of the past when he wrote in 1936:

> Popular mass movements are legitimately becoming the principal theme of the Soviet historical novel. The *reassessment of the historical role of the people,* the rehabilitation of its past heroes—all this has been suggested to our novelists by the present-day practice of millions of toilers.[27]

The same critic said that "the pedigree of the Revolution" was naturally one of the main subjects of Soviet historical fiction.[28]

Hence, during the period under examination, especially in its early part, there were a number of Soviet novels containing historical material about the Revolution of 1917 itself and of purely historical novels about its more or less distant antecedents. This type of novel is exemplified by Tarasov-Rodionov's *February* and Sholokhov's *The Quiet Don.* Still closer to contemporary history stands Furmanov's *Chapayev.*

The Revolution of 1905 and the revolutionary movement which preceded it also quite naturally attracted the attention of Soviet novel-

26 D. S. Mirsky, "Der russische historische Roman der Gegenwart," in *Slavische Rundschau,* No. 1 (1932).

27 M. Serebryansky, *Sovetsky istorichesky roman* (*The Soviet Historical Novel*), 50–51.

28 *Ibid.,* 53.

ists. It was the subject, for instance, of *Kolokola* (*The Bells*, 1926), by
Ivan Evdokimov (b. 1887), and of *Goryachy tsekh* (*Hot Workshop,*
1932), by Olga Forsh (of whom more will be said later).

The same period is treated in *Tsushima*, a novel about the Russo-
Japanese War by Alexey Novikov-Priboy (1877–1948). A professional
sailor, he began writing long before the Revolution, but his first book
of stories did not appear until 1917. He was known mostly as the author of vivid but unpretentious sea yarns written from a revolutionary
standpoint. The subject of *Tsushima* is the notorious disaster of the
Russian fleet. The novel is an eyewitness account of the progress of
Admiral Rozhestvensky's fleet around the world toward its doom at
Tsushima. The first part gives a detailed, realistic picture of the sailors'
daily life and routine. The second part is centered around the battle
itself, in which the author was taken prisoner by the Japanese. It is
almost nonfictional in its documentary character and does not aim at a
creative interpretation of history.

Some Soviet writers sought subjects for their historical novels in
the revolutionary movements of the more remote past. Their novels are
more strictly historical, but they are also essentially revolutionary in
inspiration and approach. To these historical-revolutionary novels belongs *Odety kamnem* (*Clad with Stone*, 1927), by Olga Dmitrievna
Forsh (b. 1875), who before the Revolution wrote stories using the
pseudonym of "A. Terek." *Clad with Stone* is a novel about the Russian
revolutionaries of the eighteen seventies and eighties, written in the
form of a diary. In Forsh's approach to historical fiction may be seen
some influence of Merezhkovsky and the Symbolists, and her historical
novels are never purely historical for they also contain philosophical
and psychological elements.

Alexey Pavlovich Chapygin (1870–1937), a pre-Revolutionary
writer of peasant origin, first attracted attention in 1915 with his novel
Bely skit (*White Hermitage*), of which Gorky thought very highly. In
1926–27 Chapygin made a spectacular comeback to literature with his
long, thousand-page historical novel *Stepan Razin,* about the picturesque brigand leader of the Cossack rebellion in the seventeenth century, who is one of the favorite heroes of Russian folk poetry. Chapygin
paints a vast canvas of one of the most turbulent periods in Russian history—a period which he not only knows but also feels. The novel is
spoiled, however, by overminute descriptions and a highly stylized language, while the figure of Razin is also stylized and idealized. Chapygin's second historical novel, *Gulyashchie lyudi* (*Itinerant People,*
1935), also had the seventeenth century for its setting and a popular revolt for its subject. Almost as long as his first novel, it gave an interesting picture of the religious struggle and social unrest in that period.

The Historical Novel

In *Povest o Bolotnikove* (*The Tale about Bolotnikov,* 1929), by Georgy Storm, we are taken still further back in Russian history. Bolotnikov was one of the leaders of the rebel Cossacks and peasants during the "Time of Troubles" on the threshold of the seventeenth century. Storm's novel is much shorter than Chapygin's and the writing much more impressionistic. It is a series of graphically told episodes set against a background of rapidly changing scenery. Most of its characters are historical, but since historical documentation is often wanting for them, the author took some liberties in attempting their psychological reconstruction. This is especially true of the colorful figure of Bolotnikov himself. History and fiction are skillfully blended, and ingenious use is made of passages from historical documents. Freely used archaic terms lend the language a spicy flavor, but on the whole stylization is kept within bounds.

Another historical "mass" novel is Artyom Vesyoly's *Gulyay-Volga* (1934), which is a chronicle of Ermak's expedition to Siberia. Written in a lyrical vein, as is usual with Vesyoly, it is stylized to resemble folk songs, while Vesyoly's characters are patterned on his revolutionary partisans but unfortunately lack both individuality and historical verisimilitude.

The life of runaway Siberian peasants and of workers in state mines under Catherine II was the subject of a novel by Anna Karavayeva (b. 1893), called *Zolotoy klyuv* (*The Golden Beak*). Karavayeva belonged to the proletarian "October" group and had earlier specialized in describing social collisions in the post-Revolutionary village. In her historical novel she made considerable use of little-known historical documents.

Non-Russian revolutionary subjects came in for a lesser share of attention. Among the novels which dealt with the French Revolution may be mentioned Ehrenburg's *Zagovor ravnykh* (*The Conspiracy of Equals,* 1928), the subject of which is the Babeuf movement; and *Chorny konsul* (*The Black Consul,* 1931), by Anatoly Vinogradov (b. 1888), which tells the story of Toussaint L'Ouverture's rising in Haiti. The Paris Commune of 1870 is the subject of Peter Pavlenko's short novel *Barrikady* (*Barricades,* 1932), which is imbued with a true revolutionary spirit.

The Biographical Novel

To the second group of Soviet historical novels belong many novelized literary biographies or novels about prominent figures in literature, art, and science. Many of them were "escapist" in character, that is, their authors did not feel inclined or capable to deal with contemporary life and its problems—either because they feared to walk

165

where angels tread, or because, like their predecessors the Symbolists, they failed to find inspiration in contemporary life.

It is interesting to note, however, that the authors of these biographical novels included several literary scholars. The novel which launched the fashion for literary-historical novels—the Soviet counterpart of Lytton Strachey and André Maurois—was *Kukhlya* (1925), by Yury Nikolayevich Tynyanov (1894–1944). A literary historian of note, one of the leaders of the Formalist school in literary science and an authority on the Pushkin period, Tynyanov brought to this new genre of fiction his great literary erudition and his feeling for the period. The hero of *Kukhlya* was Wilhelm Küchelbecker, one of Pushkin's schoolfellows and friends, himself a poet and playwright, who became implicated in the Decembrist conspiracy of 1825 and was exiled to Siberia. Tynyanov's work was based on a meticulous study of the documents. But with all its unquestionable historicity, the novel was also an interesting psychological study of a literary and political Don Quixote, a kindhearted but muddleheaded idealist, lovable and ridiculous, whose life contained the seeds of tragedy: because of the discrepancy between his lofty aspirations and his inadequate powers of self-expression, he ended in failure and frustration. Küchelbecker's fate is shown also as part of the social pattern of the period. Pushkin, Griboyedov, Zhukovsky, and other well-known historical figures appear in the novel, and the whole background-picture is excellently drawn.

Tynyanov's second novel was *Smert Vazir-Mukhtara (The Death of Wazir-Muchtar,* 1929). "Wazir-Muchtar" was the official Persian title of Alexander Griboyedov, the famous author of *The Misfortune of Being Clever* and Russian minister to Persia, one of the most interesting and enigmatic figures in Russian literature. Tynyanov's novel, published in connection with the centenary of Griboyedov's death (he was assassinated by the Teheran mob in 1829), was not a full-length biography, but covered only the last year of Griboyedov's life, from the moment when he returned from Persia with the Treaty of Turkmanchay in his pocket: at this moment his reputation as a diplomat—so different from his posthumous fame as a writer—had reached its climax. By concentrating on this last year of Griboyedov's life, which marked the beginning of a steady progress toward the inevitable doom, Tynyanov tried to emphasize the tragic essence of Griboyedov's personality, to convey that "acrid smell of fate" which Griboyedov diffused around him. But he failed in what André Maurois regarded as the most essential thing in the art of biography—namely, in discovering the keynote to the life and personality of the model. Instead of a portrait, he gives us a mirror broken into many fragments, in which we see reflected separate features of his model, but no synthesis is achieved. Instead of conveying

166

a sense of doom, Tynyanov relates but a series of disjointed anecdotes in which can be discerned only a persistent tendency to caricature and to mock. Tynyanov's historical characters are helpless puppets, and his attitude toward history a caricature of Tolstoy's. The style is reminiscent of Andrey Bely's, but Tynyanov's "Belyisms" are at times annoyingly obtrusive. For all its defects, however, *The Death of Wazir-Muchtar* is an interesting and original work, more original even than *Kukhlya*. Its very defects result from the author's attempt to rise above the ordinary level of historical fiction, to present the problem of Griboyedov as the tragic problem of the individual battling with his own destiny.

Tynyanov's third and last historical novel was *Pushkin* (1936–37), a full-length fictional biography of the great Russian poet. As the new fashion demanded, it was written much more simply and realistically than the Griboyedov novel, but lacked its originality as well as the poetic unity and inevitability of *Kukhlya*. Tynyanov also wrote three shorter historical stories—"Podporuchik Kizhe" ("Lieutenant Kizhe"), "Maloletny Vitushishnikov" ("Minor Vitushishnikov"), and "Voskovaya persona" ("The Wax Figure")—set respectively in the reigns of Paul I, Nicholas I, and Peter the Great. All three stories are highly stylized; in these the author's primary concern is neither with history nor with psychology but with style.

Tynyanov's *Kukhlya* had a large progeny. Within the next few years appeared several novels and stories about Lermontov (by Pilnyak, Sergeyev-Tsensky, Pavlenko, and others), but none of them matched the high standard set by Tynyanov's work. Pushkin, too, naturally attracted attention, especially in connection with the centenary of his death, which fell in 1937. Among the more satisfying biographical novels about him may be mentioned *Pushkin v Mikhaylovskom (Pushkin at Mikhaylovskoye)* and *Pushkin na yuge (Pushkin in the South)*, by Ivan Novikov (b. 1879), a pre-Revolutionary writer of the Turgenev-Bunin landed-gentry school. *Zapiski d'Arshiaka (Memoirs of d'Archiac, 1937)*, by Leonid Grossman (b. 1888), a noted literary scholar, was based on the fictitious memoirs of the Vicomte d'Archiac, who was Danthès' second in his duel with Pushkin. Severely criticized by Soviet critics, it was a well-told story of the last months of Pushkin's life. Grossman also wrote a novel about Dostoyevsky's gambling in Germany *(Roulettenburg, 1932)*, and a novel about Loris-Melikov and the last years of Alexander II's reign—*Barkhatny diktator (The Velvet Dictator, 1933)*.

After Tynyanov, the most important contribution to the literary-historical novel was made by Olga Forsh, mentioned above. In *Sovremenniki (The Contemporaries, 1927)*, she describes Gogol's life in Rome and his friendship with the religious painter Alexander Ivanov. The theme of the novel is the artist's place in society, and to present it more completely, the author introduces the fictitious character of another painter, Bagretsov, but the interest is focused on Ivanov. In *Simvolisty* (*The Symbolists*, 1933)—later renamed *Voron* (*The Raven*)—the subject is the Russian literary scene before the Revolution. It was intended as part of a wider work about that epoch in Russian life. Social-historical and biographical elements were combined in her later three-volume novel *Radishchev* (1934–39): *Yakobinsky zakvas* (*The Jacobin Leaven*), *Kazanskaya pomeshchitsa* (*The Squiress of Kazan*), and *Pagubnaya kniga* (*The Nefarious Book*). Its hero is Alexander Radishchev, the author of *A Journey from St. Petersburg to Moscow* (for which he was exiled to Siberia by Catherine II). The novel has a definite bias, to fit in with the official Soviet view of Radishchev as a precursor of the Russian revolutionary movement, but is well written and gives an interesting picture of the period.

Another combination of the social-historical and biographical novel is Storm's *Trudy i dni Mikhaila Lomonosova* (*Labors and Days of Mikhail Lomonosov*, 1932), in which Lomonosov's life is projected against the contemporary Russian and European scene.

Russian and foreign literary figures were brought to life in Anatoly Vinogradov's novels *Dva tsveta vremeni* (*Two Colors of Time*, 1930) and *Povest o bratyakh Turgenevykh* (*The Tale about the Brothers Turgenev*, 1932). The former is about Stendhal and his part in Napoleon's Russian campaign. It is an entertaining narrative: as a fiction writer Vinogradov is better than as a scholar, for his studies of Mérimée, Stendhal, and Franco-Russian literary contacts are full of errors. The novel about the brothers Turgenev, based in part on unpublished material, is centered around the lives of Nikolay and Alexander Turgenev and their associations with Russian freemasonry. Vinogradov also wrote a novel about the life of the famous Russian chemist Mendeleyev, *Khronika Malevinskikh* (*The Chronicle of the Malevinskys*, 1934).

Tynyanov's and Vinogradov's literary novels are connected with a large nonfictional literature of literary biographies constructed on the principle of *montage*, of piecing together bits of contemporary evidence from letters, diaries, memoirs, and the like. To a certain extent all these literary biographies reflected the same tendency—to escape from contemporary, topical themes.

Alexey Tolstoy's Peter the First

A place apart among Soviet historical novels belongs to Alexey N. Tolstoy's ambitious but unfinished novel *Pyotr Pervy* (*Peter the First*). Gorky, in 1931, called it "the first real historical novel in our literature."

The Historical Novel

Romain Rolland admired this "gigantic epic, huge, dense and intricate like a forest with its roads, bogs, gaps of sky and shadows."

From the time of Pushkin, the outsize figure of Peter the Great, the reformer of Russia, had attracted Russian writers. Pushkin's unfinished *The Negro of Peter the Great, Poltava, The Bronze Horseman*, not to speak of several lyric poems, have Peter for their hero. Toward the end of his life Pushkin was collecting material for a history of Peter's reign, and, just as his *Captain's Daughter* was a by-product of his historical study of the Pugachov revolt, this historical work might well have produced a novel dealing with Peter's times. Leo Tolstoy also thought of writing a historical novel about Peter, but gave up the idea. Most of the minor historical novelists of the nineteenth century felt drawn towards this exciting period in Russian history, and in many of their novels Peter appears as a secondary character. Merezhkovsky made Peter the central figure in the last—and least satisfying—part of his trilogy, but with him the historical personality of the great Emperor was distorted and twisted to suit his own ideas about Russian history. This is even more true of Boris Pilnyak, whose stories about Peter are made to fit in with his neo-Slavophile concepts.

Pilnyak's attitude toward Peter was frankly hostile, and closer to Merezhkovsky's than to Pushkin's and the nineteenth-century literary tradition. The same hostile approach is obvious in Alexey Tolstoy's two early stories from Peter's times: "Navazhdenie" ("Obsession") and "Den Petra" ("Peter's Day"), both written in 1917. In the first Peter himself does not appear; in the second he is the hero. The story describes an ordinary day in Peter's life. Tolstoy deglamorizes Peter, stressing all of his bad qualities, both physically and spiritually: his ugliness, his coarseness, and his almost bestial cruelty. Peter's reforms are interpreted as the personal whim of a willful barbarian despot. This story was strongly denounced by the great Russian historian Platonov as a distortion of historical truth. Yet much of this early hostile attitude can still be seen in Tolstoy's play *Na dybe (On the Rack*, 1929) where, like Merezhkovsky and some of his predecessors, Tolstoy contrasts Peter and his son Alexis and builds the tragedy out of the conflict between personal and impersonal forces. Here, however, Peter appears already as a statesman for whom the good of his country is the supreme law to which everything else must be sacrificed.

In the same year, 1929, Book One of Tolstoy's novel was serialized in *Novy Mir*. Book Two was published in 1933. Book Three did not appear until 1944-45. After Tolstoy's death in 1945, the remaining part (six chapters) was published in the same year. During this period Tolstoy also wrote dramatic versions of the first two parts, and the scenario for a film which enjoyed great success in Russia and abroad.

169

Unlike most traditional historical novels, *Peter the First* is primarily a biography of a great historical figure set against the vast background of the period. There are in it some fictional characters who help diversify the plot, but the main interest is centered on Peter and the Russia of his time. Peter is the true hero of the novel. The story begins with his childhood and is carried down to the battle of Narva (1701); Tolstoy apparently intended to end the novel with the great victory over Charles XII of Sweden at Poltava (1709).

The Peter of the novel is quite different from the Peter of the earlier story and the play. He is portrayed as a great man, a genius, who performed great deeds and changed completely the face of Russia. Without idealizing his hero, Tolstoy no longer shows him as an assemblage of physical and other monstrosities. This change of attitude may have been in part due to a change in the official Soviet approach to Peter (this, however, came to light only when Tolstoy was engaged on the second part of the novel), but in part it was no doubt the result of a more careful and thorough study of historical sources. It is clear that extensive research underlies Tolstoy's novel, although, unlike Merezhkovsky's work, it never gives the impression of a wax museum or a record office.[29] Nor, on the whole, are Tolstoy's characters mere vehicles for certain ideas and points of view. They are alive and real. He is equally good in individual characterization and in the portrayal of this turbulent and critical period in Russian history, which he paints with great gusto. The novel is brimful with life, it has a multitude of characters, a richness and variety of settings, and a great width of social, historical, and geographical scope. Written in excellent, full-blooded Russian, with no attempt at reproducing pedantically the language of the period, it is a fine example of historical realism.

The question whether Tolstoy tried to read the present into the past and deliberately suggested parallels between Russia in the process of "Sovietization" and Russia being forcibly "Europeanized" by Peter is not easy to answer. The first volume is, on the whole, free from such a tendency. In the subsequent volumes it is felt here and there, especially in the treatment of Peter himself. But in the end Tolstoy's artistic sense and flair for life saved him from the pitfall of reading too much of the present into the past, which cannot be said of his later play about Ivan the Terrible (see Chapter VI below).

[29] For an appraisal of Tolstoy's handling of documentary sources see I. I. Veksler, *Alexey Nikolayevich Tolstoy: Zhiznenny i tvorchesky put* (*A. N. Tolstoy: Life and Work*), 359–72.

7. The Poets

AFTER 1925, poetry, which had dominated the earlier Soviet literary scene, receded into the background. Some poets, in keeping with the prevalent trend in literature, turned to prose fiction (Tikhonov and, to a lesser extent, Pasternak) or to play writing (Mayakovsky); or tried to bring poetry and prose closer to each other, either in content or in style (Pasternak in his narrative poems and Selvinsky). Few new poets came to capture the attention of the critics and the reading public. This does not mean, however, that no good poetry was produced during this period.

Of the poets who had made a name for themselves earlier, the most notable were Mayakovsky, Pasternak, Mandelstam, and Tikhonov.

MAYAKOVSKY

The last five years of Mayakovsky's life were uneasy and hectic, and his poetry full of contradictions. No longer unequivocally recognized and accepted as the leader of revolutionary literature, he was attacked by orthodox Communists for his individualism and "formalism." In 1927 he revived the magazine *LEF* under the title *The New LEF*, but a year later parted ways with it and issued the slogan "To the Left of LEF." In 1929 he organized the group REF (Revolutionary Front), but the attacks on him did not cease, and in February, 1930, two months before his death, he joined the Russian Association of Proletarian Writers, the bulwark of Communist orthodoxy, which at that time called the tune in Soviet literary life. After 1926 he took an active part in daily journalism, becoming a regular contributor to *Komsomolskaya Pravda,* for which he wrote political and propaganda verse.

Mayakovsky's principal works written after 1924 were the long poems *Vladimir Ilyich Lenin* (1924), *Khorosho! (It's Good,* 1927), and *Vo ves golos (With Full Voice;* unfinished, published posthumously in 1930). All three are regarded today in the Soviet Union as being among Mayakovsky's masterpieces. All three are essentially political, imbued with enthusiasm for the work of Lenin and the achievements of the Soviet Union under Stalin. In all three, Mayakovsky's usual qualities and defects are displayed.

But Mayakovsky's political enthusiasm was not without reservation, and a counterpart to his poems glorifying the new order of things were his satirical poems and his two biting and clever satirical plays, *Klop (The Bedbug,* 1928) and *Banya (The Bathhouse,* 1929). In these two plays he gave vent to his passionate protest against the smug philistinism that was invading Soviet life and against the hypertrophied bureaucratism that was becoming increasingly characteristic of the new state. The figure of Pobedonosikov, the director of the Department of Co-ordination, in *The Bathhouse,* is a brilliant satire on Soviet bureaucracy. Both plays are "expressionistic" and full of unusual scenic devices. Mayakovsky himself took an active part in their production.

Between 1926 and 1930 Mayakovsky made three trips abroad and regularly toured the Soviet Union, giving lectures and recitals of his poems in fifty-two towns.

Toward the end of this period a personal, lyric note reappeared in his poetry—a note of unwonted bitterness and disillusionment. It may have been because of new complications in his love affair with Lydia Brik, the wife of his friend the LEF critic; but the attacks of those who still doubted his wholehearted attachment to the Revolution and regarded him as a mere fellow traveler must have had some share in it, too. A few days before his death he stated in public: "They hang so many dogs on me, and accuse me of so many sins . . . that at times I feel like going off somewhere for a couple of years, only not to listen to abuse." On April 14, 1930, Mayakovsky shot himself through the heart. He left a note, addressed to his mother, his sisters, and his comrades, in which he apologized for what he was about to do and asked them to abstain from gossip; and a poem in which he spoke of his "love boat" having smashed against "everyday life" *(byt)* and of being "quits" with life.

This suicide of a man who, five years earlier, had in a poem severely reprimanded Esenin for taking his own life and had written, paraphrasing Esenin,

> *In this life it is not hard to die—*
> *To mold life is far more difficult*

came quite unexpectedly to his many friends and admirers—as well as to the official circles in the Soviet Union. The immediate reaction was one of shocked stupefaction. The keynote of all the obituaries in the Soviet press was that the very idea of suicide was "incompatible" with Mayakovsky. Lunacharsky, Koltsov, Khalatov, Demyan Bedny—all with one voice repeated that they never expected it from Mayakovsky.[30] The official version attributed the suicide to Mayakovsky's illness: a disease of the throat combined with overwork and nervous breakdown.

[30] Among the numerous reactions to Mayakovsky's death one of the most interesting is Roman Jakobson's essay "O pokolenii, rastrativshem svoikh poetov" ("About the Generation Which Squandered Its Poets"), in *Smert Vladimira Mayakovskogo (The Death of Vladimir Mayakovsky);* this little book contains also an essay by D. S. Mirsky. One of the early leaders of Russian Formalism and a friend of Mayakovsky, Jakobson stresses the persistence of the suicide motif in Mayakovsky's poetry and gives an interesting analysis of his "mythology," which included a belief in bodily immortality somewhat akin to Nikolay Fyodorov's religion of resurrection.

Unofficially, it was blamed largely on disappointment in love. But there can be no doubt that, his professions of official optimism notwithstanding, Mayakovsky was feeling at the time more and more out of tune with the surrounding realities.

Today Mayakovsky's "individualistic" and "formalistic" deviations are forgotten, as is his final "un-Communist" act of escaping from the insoluble tangle of his own contradictions through voluntary death. He is regarded as the greatest Soviet poet—this estimate has the sanction of Stalin himself—the classic of Soviet literature, the bard of the Revolution. Even if timid attempts to question his poetic heritage and his value as a model for young Soviet poets are made occasionally, they are quickly cut short and his detractors immediately called to order (this happened as recently as 1949). Whether all of Mayakovsky's work can be fitted in with the narrow tenets that now govern literature and art in the Soviet Union, and whether he himself would be at home in present-day Soviet society, are altogether different questions. The fact remains that he took his voluntary exit from that society in 1930.

PASTERNAK

Boris Leonidovich Pasternak (b. 1890) is undoubtedly the most significant of the living Soviet poets. Son of a well-known portrait-painter who was a friend and illustrator of Leo Tolstoy, Pasternak grew up in a refined artistic and intellectual atmosphere of Moscow. His mother was a gifted musician, and he too devoted several years to a serious study of music. Later he studied philosophy at the University of Moscow and at Marburg, the center of German Neo-Kantianism. As a young man he joined one of the many factions of the Futurist movement. His first two books of poetry—*Bliznets v oblake* (*A Twin in a Cloud*, 1913) and *Poverkh barryerov* (*Over the Barriers*, 1917)—showed considerable talent, but it was only after his third book, *Sestra moya zhizn* (*My Sister Life*), published in 1922 but written some five years earlier, that he was hailed as a new star on the Russian poetical horizon. A year later, with the appearance of his next book of verse, *Temy i variatsii* (*Themes and Variations*), Pasternak was recognized as the outstanding younger poet of post-Revolutionary Russia. In 1925 Pasternak published a book of short stories, some of which had earlier appeared in magazines. In 1926 and 1927 appeared two long narrative poems: *Spektorsky* and *1905 god* (*The Year 1905*); in 1931, a piece of autobiographical prose called *Okhrannaya gramota* (*The Safe Conduct*); and in 1932, another book of lyrical verse, *Vtoroye rozhdenie* (*The Second Birth*). After that several collections of his verse, including occasional new poems, appeared at various dates. At the same time he was engaged in translating Shakespeare, enriching Russian literature with new poetic versions of *Hamlet, Othello,* and *Romeo and Juliet.* He also translated extensively the Georgian poets, old and modern; but these translations were apparently done not from the originals but from word-for-word prose translations. It was only in 1943 that a new and slender volume of Pasternak's original poetry made its appearance.

A romantic and an individualist, Pasternak has never been quite at home in Soviet literature. His talent was never disputed, his influence on a number of young Soviet poets, as well as on several *émigré* poets, was very great (among those who were influenced by him at this or that stage of their career may be named Tikhonov, Bagritsky, Selvinsky, Sayanov, and Antokolsky), but he was periodically attacked for being out of tune with the new Soviet state, for his individualism, for his "chamber" poetry. Unlike so many other Soviet writers, he was constitutionally incapable of prostituting his Muse, of writing to order. Hence his long silences, his translations of Georgian poets, and his escape into Shakespeare.

Pasternak is not a poet for the many; rather, he is a poets' poet. He is neither easy nor simple, and many people find him obscure. His capricious syntax, his elliptical language, his associative method, which involves sudden metaphorical jumps, all demand an imaginative effort on the part of the reader. His rhythms are vigorous, infectious, and varied; his poems have a long breath. His startling freshness and originality are due both to the novelty of his vision and to the originality of his idiom. Things that may appear ordinary and trite he approaches from a new perspective and presents in a new way. To use Coleridge's words, he "lends the charm of novelty to things of every day." The Formalists would say that his favorite method is that of *"ostranenie"* ("making strange"). He likes unexpected contrasts and bold and paradoxical metaphors. He has no fear of vulgarisms, of prosaic locutions, or of technical terms, but uses them without destroying the poetic, and even the romantic, effect. In a way quite different from Mayakovsky's, without recourse to purely tonic verse, without doing violence to classical meters, he approximates poetry to prose, gives his verse the intonations and cadences of ordinary colloquial speech, and yet achieves wonderful musical and rhythmical effects. He is nothing if not a musical poet. Some of his best poems (for instance, the remarkable short lyric beginning "The boat is thumping in my drowsy breast") may appear to defy normal semantic analysis, but as the reader is carried along on the waves of their sound magic, their hidden and profound meaning is revealed to him. Yet there is in Pasternak nothing of the effeminate musicality of a Zhukovsky, a Fet, a Balmont, or a Verlaine. The texture of his verse is taut and muscular. His prosaisms, his bold enjambements, his paradoxical juxtaposition of poetic and unpoetic words, destroy

174

the automatism of perception and enhance the effect of novelty and freshness. He has been compared with Donne, with G. M. Hopkins (without his religion), and with Rilke (without his mysticism), but one might as well find in him parallels with T. S. Eliot and Dylan Thomas —and if poetry could develop untrammeled in the Soviet Union, his influence on the younger generation of poets would certainly be comparable to Eliot's.

In passionate intensity Pasternak has also been compared with Lermontov. His kinship with the romantic tradition in Russian poetry is beyond question. He has something of Tyutchev's intense cosmic feeling, and the ordinary phenomena of nature—the succession of seasons, the rain, the snow, the thunderstorm—receive in his poetry a novel and original response. One cannot say of Pasternak, as one can of many other poets, that he is a poet of thought alone or of feeling alone: in him the two are blended. In this he is akin, among the Russian poets, to Baratynsky. Allusive and elusive, he is yet never vague. He is infinitely more sophisticated, more cultured, more subtle than Mayakovsky. At times one can feel the burden of culture weighing down on him, and one can see him trying pathetically to escape his own complexities and contradictions. It is easy to realize that the literary climate of the Soviet Union was for most of the time hardly propitious to such a poet.

It was especially in his two longer narrative poems, "Spektorsky" and "The Year 1905," that Pasternak tried to overcome the pure individualism of his lyrical poetry, in which nature and the spiritual, rather than social life, were the principal source of inspiration. "Spektorsky" is a kind of lyrical autobiography unrolled against the background of contemporary life, a tale in verse, relating some episodes in the life of a young Moscow intellectual and introducing facts of Pasternak's own life. Here and there Pasternak shows a fine gift of observation and description, but in the main he is concerned with the inner life of his hero, his amatory and intellectual preoccupations. Once or twice he apologizes, as it were, for having chosen as his hero an "insignificant" personage. The lyricism of the poem, full of happy discoveries, is very characteristic of Pasternak, but the narrative thread is both too slender and too involved, and as an attempt to outgrow lyricism and create a modern epic, the poem is a failure. It is nothing more than one of Pasternak's extended lyric poems, a sequence of lyrical scenes.

"The Year 1905" (1927) is also a series of disjointed fragments, presenting various aspects of the 1905 Revolution. The central episode deals with Lieutenant Schmidt and the famous "Potyomkin" mutiny in the Black Sea Fleet. But here again Pasternak fails in his effort to overcome his individualism and to treat a social theme. The best parts of the rather uneven whole are the purely lyrical sections which reflect the poet's personal vision of the 1905 Revolution in Moscow.

Attempts to get outside himself, to reconcile his own personal views with the demands which Soviet society makes on its poets, were reflected also in some poems in *The Second Birth* (1932), but they too ended in failure. All that Pasternak could say of Socialism was that its remoteness appeared to him "close by." But this ambiguous and paradoxical statement did not satisfy his Communist critics, who again accused him of keeping aloof from the problems of the day.

Many of the poems in *The Second Birth* have the Caucasus and its majestic nature for their background and echo Lermontov. One of the best describes, with true Pasternakian felicity and freshness of expression and an acute sense of sound associations, a vision of Tiflis from the mountains. But it is characteristic of Pasternak that from the majestic splendors of the Caucasus he longs to go "back home, to the vastness of the sadness-inspiring apartment," that he is yearning for "the sedate life, such as it is." He aspires to simplicity and even dumbness, voicing these sentiments in a poem which echoes Tyutchev's famous "Silentium":

> *There are, in the experience of great poets,*
> *Elements of such naturalness,*
> *That, once having tasted of them,*
> *It is impossible not to end in utter dumbness.*
> *Having established one's relationship with all that is,*
> *And being familiar with life in the future,*
> *It is impossible not to fall, ultimately, as into a heresy,*
> *Into an unheard-of simplicity.*

After the publication of *The Second Birth*, for over ten years Pasternak published almost nothing except translations. Then, in 1943, appeared a little book called *Na rannikh poezdakh (On Early Trains)* containing twenty-six poems, of which eleven were written in 1936 and fifteen in 1941. Some of them were inspired by the war. In 1945 another book appeared, entitled *Zemnoy prostor (The Terrestrial Expanse)*; it consisted in part of a reprint of selections from the 1943 volume, and in part of new poems, all of them written during the war and suggested by it. The chief characteristic of the poems in these two little volumes was their greater simplicity and directness—of themes, of emotions, and of structure. Some Soviet critics welcomed Pasternak's "more human attitude toward life," but in 1946 he was again attacked for his individualism, for being out of tune with the Revolution. Of these attacks more will be said in later chapters.

Pasternak's prose is very much like his poetry. It is characterized by the same freshness of vision and felicity of expression. It consists of several short stories—first published in book form in 1925; then reprinted in 1933 under the title *Vozdushnye puti (Aerial Ways)*, with the addition of a new prose fragment, distantly related to "Spektorsky" —and an autobiographical work entitled *The Safe Conduct*. Of all the stories, only one, "Aerial Ways," has any relation to the Revolution, and in this the Revolution forms only the background to its psychological theme. Of the others, the longest, the most characteristic, and the most satisfying is "Detstvo Luvers" ("The Childhood of Luvers"). It is a story of a few years in the life of a girl on the verge of puberty. The story is quite plotless. Outward events are described only so far as they are in correspondence with the inner states of the heroine's mind. In portraying them, Pasternak alternately proceeds from the inside outwards and from the outside inwards, thus recording the deep subterranean currents in the girl's mind while at the same time describing the objects outside her that take part in her life and affect her. He uses the method of accumulating infinitesimals, somewhat reminiscent of Proust's, but Pasternak is both more concise and more elliptical. There is also some influence of Rilke's *Aufzeichnungen des Malte Laurids Brigge*. As a boy, Pasternak met Rilke when his father painted Rilke's portrait. Later Rilke corresponded with the elder Pasternak and followed with interest the beginnings of his son's career. For his part, Boris Pasternak was always a great admirer of Rilke's poetry. This admiration is reflected in *The Safe Conduct*, an autobiographical work that deals mainly with the poet's years of study in Germany and has all the qualities of Pasternak's highly original prose style. It is also interesting as the confession of a romantic individualist up against a fundamentally hostile world.

MANDELSTAM

One of the leaders of pre-Revolutionary Acmeism, Osip Emilievich Mandelstam (1891–1942?), belongs as a poet to the pre-Soviet period of Russian literature. But he was the only poet of that brilliant period who not only survived the Revolution but for fifteen years continued to hold a small but distinguished place on the Soviet literary scene. Mandelstam's first two books of poems, *Kamen (The Stone,* 1913) and *Tristia* (1922), revealed him as a poet of great originality, a subtle and fastidious craftsman, steeped in classical and Western European culture. In the words of Mirsky, "Mandelstam's diction attains sometimes to splendid 'Latin' sonority that is unrivaled by any Russian poet since Lomonosov."[31] His poetry has a somewhat "bookish" appearance—he is often stimulated by literary and historical themes, by music and architecture

[31] Mirsky, *Contemporary Russian Literature,* 259–60.

—but these bookish themes are lyrically reinterpreted and transmuted, and through them pierces a deep personal experience. Their form is always original and arresting.

Throughout the Revolution, Mandelstam remained a detached and somewhat bewildered spectator. Not a prolific writer at any time, he published little after 1922. In 1928 appeared his last volume of poetry, *Stikhotvoreniya (Poems)*, containing his two earlier books and twenty new poems written between 1921 and 1925. In some there are distant and very personal echoes of the Revolution, but the latter is seen *sub specie aeternitatis*. In several of these poems the influence of Pasternak can be felt, though Mandelstam remains throughout a more careful, more restrained, and more classical artist. Until 1933 Mandelstam continued to publish his poems, now and then, in various Soviet magazines that were broad-minded enough to admit a poet so obviously uncongenial to the Revolution. Some very interesting poems appeared in 1932 in *Novy Mir*, and in 1933 *Zvezda* carried a sequence of twelve poems about Armenia. But Mandelstam apparently took no part in Soviet literary life, and it is not clear whether he ever became a member of the Union of Soviet Writers.

Like Pasternak, Mandelstam wrote some interesting prose, though purely nonfictional. Of his pre-Revolutionary essays Mirsky said that they contained "perhaps the most remarkable, unprejudiced, and independent things that have ever been said on modern Russian civilization and on the art of poetry."[32] Although this is something of an exaggeration, and Mandelstam is at times a little involved and obscure in his essays, his ideas are interesting and stimulating. His one post-Revolutionary volume of prose, *Shum vremeni (The Sound of an Epoch, 1925)*—later enlarged and renamed *Egipetskaya marka (The Egyptian Stamp)*—consisted of short pieces written in a distinctive, personal manner. Mandelstam recalled in them his childhood and adolescence, trying to recapture the flavor of that period— "the sound and growth of an epoch." He succeeded very well in doing so: the Russian *fin de siècle*, the stately splendor of the Imperial St. Petersburg (especially in "Childish Imperialism"), the peculiar, stuffy atmosphere of the bourgeois Jewish home in which he grew up, the modern "anglicized" school in which he was educated—everything is inimitably brought to life. One of the best pieces is "Knizhny shkap" ("The Bookcase"), where, through a description of his family bookcase and its successive "geological strata," he paints a suggestive, synthetic portrait of the Russian and Russian-Jewish intelligentsia of the nineties. This portrait grows out of a recollection of a book of Nadson's poems, which Mandelstam aptly describes as "the key to the epoch."

32 *Ibid.*, 260.

Like many of his poems, the book reveals Mandelstam's acute feeling for history and for the passing of time. It is his ability to contain the general within the concrete that gives particular value to his picture of the *temps perdu*. When many of the better-known Soviet writers will have been forgotten, Mandelstam's slender volume of prose, together with his poetry of the Soviet years that will one day be unearthed from the old Soviet magazines, will retain its place in Russian literature.

After 1934, Mandelstam disappeared from literature. His exact fate is not known. According to a story that was given wide currency in Russia, he was arrested for writing an epigram about Stalin. He is said to have died in a concentration camp, but his death was never officially announced, and reports concerning its date, place, and circumstances vary.

TIKHONOV

Nikolay Tikhonov's development in the late twenties was complex and devious. Constantly on the lookout for new forms, he fell under a strong influence of Khlebnikov, Mayakovsky, and Pasternak. At the same time he tried to move closer to Soviet realities. Temperamentally romantic, he fell in love with the Soviet East, and many of his poems of this period have for their setting the Caucasus and central Asia. He was attracted both by their exoticism and by the pioneering efforts to bring modern civilization to Lermontov's "drowsy East." The old Orient satisfied his romantic craving for the picturesque, while the work of the new Soviet "Kulturträgers" appealed to his innate desire for adventure. Even when he voiced orthodox Communist sentiments and glorified the civilizing mission of the Soviets, he romanticized and hyperbolized the reality.

In 1935 Tikhonov published a book of poems called *Ten druga* (*The Shadow of a Friend*). Its title was suggested by the well-known poem of Batyushkov, an early nineteenth-century poet, and the first poem had a line from it for its motto ("I was leaving the misty shores of Albion"). The book recalls Batyushkov (as well as the Acmeists) by the plasticity of its imagery and the classical clarity of its diction. But its spirit is quite different from Batyushkov's. It is a lyrical diary of a visit to various European countries—Poland, France, Belgium, and England—which are seen through Soviet spectacles. The last poem is called "The Gas Mask": the poet sees the gas mask—"this head, neither a fish's nor a bird's, looming, tongueless, on man's shoulders" replacing "the living human countenance"—as the uncanny symbol of the epoch:

Gas mask!
Within your sticky rubber

Enclosed is Europe's head,
And there is no more laughter or smile,
The forests do not murmur, and the grasses do not rustle.

There are evocations of Parisian crowds, of English miners, of Nazi victims in Germany, of "Asturian heroes," and of Abyssinians sharing the last drop of water with the deceived Italian soldiers. Beside all them the poet places the name of "the land of lands" and voices his faith that the day will come when, stuffed with straw, the gas mask will be hung on the door as a target for children's games, just as the Assyrians used to hang motley masks "to drive away sickness and the devils." This optimistic faith, rooted in Soviet patriotism, inspires the whole book. Europe is shown as a contrast to "the land of lands." But, whether or not one shares Tikhonov's political outlook, one cannot help appreciating the poetic quality of the best among these poems.

It was also in the late twenties—and parallel with his development toward realism—that Tikhonov began to use more and more the medium of prose. He wrote once, "When a poet writes prose he merely extends the range of his work," and these words can well apply to him: in his prose he remains true to his romantic realism. He showed this in his first book of stories, *Riskovanny chelovek* (*The Venturesome Man*, 1927). Not content with the elementary, superficial truth of real life, Tikhonov perceives beyond it another and different truth: it is, in his own words, "the truth of artistic perception which merges into the subtle art of artistic lie" and which transforms everyday life, so that from a mere accident it is turned into something many-sided and general. Tikhonov's art is based on a vision of reality, but the reality is condensed and turned into something almost fantastic. He likes sharp, definite outlines, bright colors, and dramatic situations, and he prefers to show his characters in action. Like the earlier revolutionary romantics of the dynamic prose period, he has an aversion to psychological analysis. Curiously enough, while in his poetry he tended to become less of a romantic and more of a realist, in his prose he was moving in the opposite direction. A story like "Klyatva v tumane" ("An Oath in the Fog," 1933), with its Caucasian setting, is full of romanticism, of adventures, of unusual characters. What distinguishes Tikhonov from writers like Vsevolod Ivanov and Nikitin is his interest in the plot, his careful construction, and his orderly narrative. This is particularly noticeable in his stories about the war and the Civil War—in *Voyna* (*War*) and *Klinki i tachanki* (*Blades and Chariots*).

Tikhonov's style is in keeping with his romantic realism: it is compact, robust, and picturesque; in its wise economy one feels the influence of his poetic training, of his Acmeist heritage. He is also in no small degree indebted to Kipling, both in the technique of his stories and in the spirit of romantic realism which pervades them. Like Kipling's, many of his stories deal with military life, and often their action is set on the eastern fringes of Russia. His characters also have a Kiplingesque touch.

SELVINSKY AND CONSTRUCTIVISM

The movement in poetry away from the romantic and lyric toward the realistic and concrete found its expression, in the late twenties, in the school of Constructivism. Its chief theoretician and critic was Kornely Zelinsky (b. 1896); its principal exponent in poetry, Ilya Lvovich Selvinsky. Born in 1899 in a bourgeois family in Simferopol, he studied at first in a Catholic monastery school in Constantinople, then in the high school at Evpatoria. He took part in the Civil War, served as a sailor and worked in a factory, and then went to the University of Moscow. His first book of poems was published in 1926, and he soon became the acknowledged leader of the Constructivists.

Constructivism as a movement was rather vague and heterogeneous. It had some points in common with Futurism, especially in its admiration of modern technology, but it did not share the Futurists' wholesale rejection of the art and culture of the past. It laid a great stress on the principle of "organization" in a poetic work and tried to introduce into poetry the methods of prose. It advocated what it called the "local method," which consisted in subordinating the word pattern of a poem to its subject, in "localizing" it stylistically. Of all the nominal practitioners of Constructivism, Selvinsky was the only one who tried to practice consistently what he preached.

His principal works during this period were *Ulyalaevshchina* (*Ulyalaevism,* 1927), *Zapiski poeta* (*Notebooks of a Poet,* 1928), *Pushtorg* (1929), and *Pao-Pao* (1932). They are all long, narrative poems, with a plot and a number of characters. *Ulyalaevshchina* is almost a novel in verse, with a complicated plot line, describing the partisan and bandit movements in eastern Russia and portraying several cleverly drawn and sharply individualized characters. The plot is somewhat blurred in its complexity—this is one of the defects of the poem—but in itself the tendency toward plot, away from purely lyric forms, is characteristic of Constructivism as it was understood by Selvinsky. Selvinsky is a realist, or rather a naturalist, and *Ulyalaevshchina* reveals his greediness for life. One critic has described him as a "temperamental rationalist." His vocabulary, his syntax, and his irregular meters were strongly influenced by Mayakovsky. But he also introduced some innovations of his own, such as using queer typographical devices, punctuating his words with periods and question marks to indicate pauses

181

and changes of intonation, and mixing Latin characters with Russian. Some of these innovations looked like experiments for the sake of experiment, but some had inward justification and showed a feeling for words and a sense of rhythm. Both in *Ulyalaevshchina* and in the autobiographical *Notebooks of a Poet*, Selvinsky resorts to dialogues and introduces long discourses on political and aesthetic subjects. In *Notebooks of a Poet* he displays his gift as a parodist in clever and pointed parodies of several Soviet poets.

Pao-Pao is a play in verse and was supposed to be a contribution to the Five-Year Plan literature. It is the story of an ape, who symbolizes simultaneously the low, animal instincts of men and bourgeois culture. Introduced into the beneficent proletarian environment of a Soviet factory and discovering there Marxism, the only true ideology, Selvinsky's ape becomes human. Taken at its face value, the poem, though it has some clever points, is absurd. But Selvinsky may have written it tongue in cheek.

BAGRITSKY

Another Constructivist was Eduard Bagritsky (pseudonym of Eduard Georgievich Dzyubin, 1897–1934), a Jew and a native of Odessa, one of the most talented and attractive poets of his generation. His first poems appeared in print in 1914. In 1917 he was with the Russian Army on the Persian front and during the Revolution fought in the Red Army. His first volume of poetry, *Yugo-zapad* (*South-West*, 1928), in some points resembled Tikhonov's early romantic realism. It was possible to trace in it the same influences—of Gumilyov and the Acmeists, of the English ballads (which he translated), and of Kipling. One of his favorite heroes seems to have been Tyll Eulenspiegel. A decided romantic who looked at the Revolution from outside, Bagritsky saw it as something strange and alien, but recognized its elemental, sweeping force. In one of his best lyric poems, in which one feels the winds of the Revolution blowing about, he speaks of "strange constellations rising above us," of "strange banners unfurling over us," and likens himself to "a rusty oak leaf" bound to follow in the wake of these strange banners. In some of his poems, however, he tried to draw closer to the Revolution and to portray it other than subjectively. Such is his famous *Duma ob Opanase* (*The Lay About Opanas*), which for a long time was regarded by Soviet critics as one of the masterpieces of Soviet poetry. It is a long poem, in which the lyric and the narrative elements are intermingled, telling the story of a simple Ukrainian peasant, Opanas, who flees from a Communist food-requisitioning detachment commanded by a Jew, Kogan. While fleeing, Opanas encounters the "Green" anarchist band of Makhno and is forced to join it. When Kogan falls into the hands of Makhno, Opanas is ordered to have him shot. He decides to let Kogan escape, but Kogan refuses the offer and chooses death, which he faces with proud indifference. Later on, the Makhno bands are defeated by the Reds, and Opanas is taken prisoner. Questioned by the Red commander Kotovsky, he admits having shot Kogan and submits docilely to his own execution.

The Lay About Opanas is a heroic revolutionary poem. The underlying romanticism of its conception is unquestionable. In form it has been influenced by Ukrainian folk poetry and by Taras Shevchenko, the national poet of the Ukraine. Its free and quick-changing meter recalls Ukrainian folk songs. There are in it some beautiful evocations of the Ukrainian landscape. In its combination of naïve simplicity and romantic hyperbolism it also derives from folk poetry.

In his later poems, collected in *Pobediteli* (*The Victors*) and *Poslednyaya noch* (*The Last Night*), Bagritsky tried to identify himself even more closely with the Revolution and Socialism, but at heart he remained a romantic; his sense of life, and zest for it, saved him from becoming didactic or doctrinaire. In the autobiographical narrative poem *Fevral* (*February*), which was published posthumously, the romantic note is again sounded very clearly. But *South-West* (for which Bagritsky made a careful and small selection from the poems written during the first ten years of his poetic activity) remains, I think, his best book, full of genuinely spontaneous poetry and striking a distinct personal note. Such poems as "Pigeons," "The Watermelon," and "The Cigarette Box" deserve a place in any anthology of modern Russian literature.

Bagritsky belonged nominally to the Constructivist group, but his connection with it was rather tenuous, though he did apply the "local method." His premature death in 1934 was a great loss to Soviet poetry.

BEZYMENSKY AND OTHER PROLETARIAN POETS

Unlike the earlier "Cosmists" of the "Smithy" group, the younger proletarian poets—those born between 1898 and 1904—represented the realistic trend. At one time the leading role among them was played by Alexander Ilyich Bezymensky. Born in 1898 in Zhitomir, he began working for an underground Social-Democratic organization in 1916, and a year later joined the Communist party. He played an active part in various proletarian literary organizations and in the early twenties was one of the ringleaders of the opposition to fellow travelers. He became the recognized bard of the Communist party and the Young Communist League and the principal rival of Demyan Bedny for the unofficial poet-laureateship.

If the nineteenth-century "civic" poets followed the famous dictum of Nekrasov that "A poet you need not be but you must be a citizen," Bezymensky went one better, proclaiming that he was first a member of the Communist party and only then a poet. In one of his poems he uses the much publicized formula: "I carry my Party membership card not in my pocket but inside myself." To the traditional "sentimental" themes of the "bourgeois" poets he opposed the matter-of-fact realities. Let others think of spring, he said,

> But I, as I walk along, keep thinking
> Of the cost price of Soviet goods.

He expressed his contempt for love poetry when he wrote defiantly:

> Some fear for girlish lips,
> And I, for smoking stacks.

His predominant mood was one of joyful optimism. In one of his poems he wrote that "if the heart of a Communist cell could for a moment become a fifty-kopeck piece, it would contain two kopecks' worth of bitterness and forty-five kopecks' worth of joy" (what happens to the remaining three kopecks is not clear). One of his books was called *Tak pakhnet zhizn* (*That's What Life Smells Like*). But he saw the chief aim of a proletarian poet as the discovery of World Revolution "behind every small trifle."

Bezymensky was strongly influenced by Mayakovsky and did his best to imitate the latter's declamatory style and coarse language. In his longer poems, such as *Komsomolia*, he uses, like Mayakovsky, a rapid succession of different contrasting meters. But he totally lacks Mayakovsky's sense of rhythm and keenness of vision: he explains and describes things rather than shows what he sees. Much of his poetry is mere rhymed journalism. In his earlier verse the life of the Communist party was almost the only subject. Later, in *Puti* (*Pathways*, 1925), his field of vision was somewhat enlarged and his official optimism mitigated by the sudden realization of the tenacity of old-world instincts beneath the Communist surface of Soviet life.

Bezymensky reached the height of his popularity in 1929–31. His play in verse, *Vystrel* (*A Shot*, 1930), caused a sensation—but of a political, rather than a literary, nature—and gave rise to a general discussion about the methods of proletarian literature. It was deliberately a-psychological and propagandistic; its characters were schematic embodiments of various problems of Soviet life. It was meant as a satire but lacked the pungency and brilliance of Mayakovsky's satirical plays. *Noch nachalnika politotdela* (*The Night of a Chief of Politsection*) was another purely political poem, dealing with the work of the political instructor on a collective farm. It lacks structural and stylistic unity and is a rather incongruous mixture of Mayakovsky with Koltsov and Nadson. It is both more realistic and more sentimental than Bezymensky's earlier work. In line with the general evolution of Soviet literature Bezymensky discarded his earlier experimental proclivities and called upon Soviet poets to learn from Pushkin and other Russian classics.

Closely akin to Bezymensky was another poet of the Young Communist League, Alexander Zharov (b. 1904). His early poetic style also derived from Mayakovsky, while his choice of themes was similar to Bezymensky's, with more stress on everyday realities.

More talented, and at the same time less political and more personal, were Mikhail Golodny (pseudonym of Mikhail Epstein, 1903–48) and Mikhail Svetlov (b. 1903). Svetlov's Civil War poem "Grenada," with its folk-song accents and lilting rhythm, enjoyed great popularity and foreshadowed the later trend toward songs.

Iosif Utkin (1903–42), a Jew born in Manchuria, attracted attention with his poem *The Tale about the Redheaded Motele, Mr. Inspector, Rabbi Isaiah and Commissar Bloch,* which described the impact of the Revolution on provincial Jewish life and was full of Jewish local color. Utkin's lyric poetry was characterized by heightened emotionalism. Soviet critics spoke of the influence of Esenin on him. He was killed during the Soviet-German War.

Somewhat apart from these proletarian poets stood Vissarion Sayanov (pseudonym of Vissarion Makhnin, b. 1903). Son of a political exile in Siberia, he joined the Communist party as a young man and fought in the Civil War. Later he was active in the LAPP. His early poetry had little in common with Bezymensky's. His main theme was the Civil War, and he treated it romantically and heroically, in a spirit of virile optimism reminiscent of Gumilyov. His careful handling of form was also influenced by the Acmeists. His predilection for classical meters, at the time when most young poets followed Mayakovsky and took liberties with Russian prosody, singled him out among his contemporaries. Later he turned to political and social themes, but in these poems (which include the inevitable poem about Lenin) one misses the attractive personal accent of his more youthful poetry. Sayanov also wrote a narrative poem, with a detective adventure plot, called "Kartonazhnaya Amerika" ("Cardboard America").

INBER AND OTHERS

It is impossible to enumerate all the poets who were active in the late twenties and early thirties. With some of them we shall meet later, but a few may be mentioned here briefly.

Vera Inber (b. 1893) began publishing before the Revolution, imitating Akhmatova, but lacking Akhmatova's sincerity and depth. In the twenties she joined the Constructivists, but, like Bagritsky's, her connection with the movement was superficial. She exchanged her intimate lyricism for revolutionary themes and showed a tendency toward narrative poetry, which is particularly noticeable in the book entitled *Synu, kotorogo net* (*To the Son Who Does Not Exist,* 1927).

Another Constructivist was Vladimir Lugovskoy (b. 1901), whose first book of poems, *Spolokhi* (*Sheet Lightnings*), appeared in 1926. Most of his early poems were about the Civil War, and there were both Acmeist and Futurist influences in them, but like so many others he later moved toward revolutionary realism and in 1930 joined the RAPP. He wrote some charming poems about children.

Pavel Antokolsky (b. 1896) is another poet on whom the Acmeists (in his case Mandelstam, rather than Gumilyov) had a considerable influence. He is a man of culture and his poetry wears a somewhat bookish air: he often draws inspiration from history and world literature and has made many translations.

Futurism during this period had lost much of its appeal and popularity. Next to Mayakovsky and Aseyev it was represented by Sergey Tretyakov (b. 1892) who was, in the twenties, one of the principal theoreticians of the LEF group and an ardent advocate of "factual literature," of which more will be said later.

A curious figure among the Soviet poets of this period was Nikolay Zabolotsky. Some poems of his, with their mixture of whimsical hyperbolism and matter-of-factness, read like parodies or frank nonsense verse. In others there may be some subtle satirical intent. At one point Zabolotsky's "case" was seriously debated in the Soviet press, and Tikhonov said that Zabolotsky was faced with the alternative of either "committing an artistic suicide" or completely "reorganizing his poetic household" and attuning himself to Soviet realities. Zabolotsky apparently chose the first alternative and disappeared from Soviet literature for quite a time, re-emerging many years later with much more orthodox though not uninteresting poems. These included a verse translation of *The Lay of Igor's Campaign.*

8. *The Drama*

A Glance at the Russian Theater

THOSE who visited the Soviet Union in the twenties brought back the impression that here was the only country in Europe where there was no crisis in the theater. Theatrical life seemed to be in full swing and the art of the theater blossoming in all its fullness. The names

of Stanislavsky, Meyerhold, and Tairov were known all over the world
and their art discussed in Paris, Berlin, and London.

It must, however, be noted that the different and even diametri-
cally opposed tendencies they represented were not purely of Revolutionary growth, that they were all rooted in the pre-Revolutionary
Russian theater, and that some of them merely received a fresh impetus
from the Revolution. The intense psychological realism of Stanislavsky's Moscow Art Theater, with its tendency to extend the psychological treatment of characters in a play beyond its actual limits and to
create, as it were, their personal biographies; the Constructivism of
Meyerhold, with his sharply pronounced tendency to subordinate the
author and the actors to the supreme will and caprice of the producer;
the "pure" theater of Tairov, which was just as hostile to psychological
realism and naturalism as Meyerhold's, but differing from the latter in
its tendency toward aesthetic "theatricalization" of reality—all these
different theatrical currents had in substance existed before the Revolution. As far as Stanislavsky and Tairov are concerned, the Revolution
did not affect to any noteworthy degree their main line of development.
But it was not quite so with Meyerhold; the Revolution supplied him
with new social and political contents, resulting in what came to be
known as "socio-mechanics": the constructivist technique was subordinated to the class idea.

Stanislavsky (The Moscow Art Theater), Tairov (the Kamerny
Theater), and Meyerhold (with the theater which bore his name) represented, then, the three main currents in modern Russian theater. All
the other theaters, especially those which sprang up after the Revolution, were either an extension of one of them or represented an attempt
to combine some of their principles. Thus the Vakhtangov Theater
combined the methods of Stanislavsky with those of Meyerhold; while
the Theater of the Revolution (Alexey Popov), the Realistic Theater
(Ohklopkov), and the Leningrad Dramatic Theater (Akimov) followed
more or less in the path of Meyerhold, though the influence of Tairov
on them could also be discerned. The Theater of the Revolution in
particular aimed at a synthesis of different methods. It was also the
most consistent in choosing for its productions modern plays with a
definite social and political significance. The same stress on modern
repertoire was given by the Trades Unions' Theater, but here the
method was more realistic.

The Revolution undoubtedly gave a new impetus to theatrical
life in Russia. There were several reasons for this. There is no denying,
of course, the efforts expended by the Soviet government in fostering
theatrical culture, especially in the first years of the Revolution, when
it was clearly conscious of the power of the theater as a weapon of propa-

ganda. But also must be taken into account the inherent theatrical instinct of the Russian people, with its love of the spectacular. If anything, this theatrical instinct was intensified in the first years of the Revolution, when the theater became one of the means of escaping from the hard and sordid realities of life. Even during the worst years of famine and general misery, theaters in Moscow were crowded; while the numerical increase in theaters and in the number of theatergoers since the Revolution has been extraordinary. Factory and village-club theaters, children's theaters, theaters of various national minorities (Jewish, Georgian, Armenian, Gypsy, and others)—all these represented either a new departure or a new development in the life of the Russian theater.

The weak spot of the post-Revolutionary Russian theater has been the lack of good new dramas. The Russian theater as such has always been infinitely more interesting and significant than the dramatic literature on which it had to rely, but never was the scarcity of good dramatic literature so strikingly laid bare and illustrated as in the modern Russian theater, especially since the Revolution. .

The problem of creating a new revolutionary repertoire has been worrying the leaders of the Soviet theater from the very outset. Even before the Revolution the Russian theater, more than any other, had to rely to a large extent on foreign repertoire plays; and what there was of original dramatic literature was, with a few exceptions (such as Gogol's *Government Inspector*), eminently undramatic and untheatrical. Such was, after all, practically the whole theater, not only of Chekhov, but also of Ostrovsky. This explains, in a large measure, the fact that the modern Russian theater, in aspiring toward "theatricalization," went so far in denying the role of the playwright in the art of the theater and either tried to do without him or took the utmost liberties with the dramatic text: hence Meyerhold's well-known fanciful and often distorted adaptations or "stylizations" of classical Russian plays such as Gogol's *Government Inspector* and Ostrovsky's *Forest*. Meyerhold proclaimed the supremacy of the producer over the author and the actor. In this he was not alone: his ideas were echoed by Max Reinhardt in Germany and Granville-Barker in England, both of whom saw the way to a rebirth of the art of the theater in its emancipation from the author. This tendency was further increased by the competition which the sound motion pictures offered to the theater. But it was Meyerhold who not only pioneered the idea, but tried most consistently to bring it to life.

In the Soviet Union, however, parallel with Meyerhold's experiments on this "authorless" path and with the development of the theater along the line of mass performance and of revolutionary festivals (which in a way meant the revival of the ancient and medieval conception of the theater as a mass mystery), the problem of a new repertoire continued to preoccupy those who were concerned with the destinies of the Soviet theater.

In 1927, surveying the achievements of the Soviet theater during the first revolutionary decade, Vladimir Wolkenstein, one of the leading Russian dramatic critics and himself a dramatist of some merit, wrote: "The problem of the new theater is above all the problem of a new repertoire." In summing up the results of ten years of dramatic activity, he was rather optimistic, emphasizing especially "the growing interest taken by the public in the new plays." But Wolkenstein undoubtedly erred on the side of official optimism: three or four years later Cecil de Mille was still asking Zamyatin, "Where are your new plays?" and Zamyatin had to agree with him that there were none. In 1933 the dearth of good contemporary plays was still the keynote of Soviet dramatic criticism. And while Wolkenstein had earlier noted that the public clamored for new plays, Soviet critics now admitted that the theatergoers were tired of what they were being offered in the way of new Soviet plays and showed a renewed interest in classical drama.

Soviet Playwrights

Soviet dramatists of the twenties can be roughly divided into three principal groups. The first and most numerous group consisted of older writers who had established themselves before the Revolution and represented different currents: Realism, Neo-Realism, Romanticism, and Futurism. Among them we find Maxim Gorky, Alexey Tolstoy, Zamyatin, Mayakovsky, Trenyov, Lunacharsky, and Wolkenstein. For the majority of these, playwriting was only a sideline to their other activities. In fact, of those named above, only Wolkenstein devoted himself entirely to the drama. Lunacharsky was more important as a literary critic and as the man who in the first years of the Revolution was responsible for the new government's literary and artistic policy. In this capacity he contributed measurably to the development of theatrical culture in the rural areas. His own plays, now justly forgotten, are full of high-sounding revolutionary romanticism and cheap symbolism: their literary and dramatic value is mediocre. Of the remaining authors, it can be said that their contribution to the post-Revolutionary drama was secondary to the rest of their literary output. Gorky's two post-Revolutionary plays—*Egor Bulychev i drugie (Egor Bulychev and Others)* and *Dostigayev i drugie (Dostigayev and Others)*—are frankly retrospective in character and represent variations on one of Gorky's favorite themes: the decadence of the Russian bourgeoisie. In technique they are superior to some of Gorky's earlier plays; and in sureness of characterization recall some of Gorky's best prose fiction, such as *The*

Soviet Russian Literature

Artamonov Business to which they are allied in theme. The success of *Egor Bulychev* was greatly helped by the excellent productions of the Moscow Art Theater and the Vakhtangov Theater. But neither of these plays represents a new development in drama.

Alexey Tolstoy's plays written in the twenties are, on the contrary, greatly inferior to those of the earlier period when, of all the Neo-Realists, he showed himself the most capable of handling well the dramatic form. Two of these post-Revolutionary plays—*Zagovor imperatritsy (The Empress' Conspiracy)* and *Azef*—were written in collaboration with the literary historian Pavel Shchogolev and dealt with recent Russian history, which was distorted to suit the official interpretation. Later, Tolstoy specialized in historical drama, writing a play about Peter the Great and dramatizing his novel about him. Toward the end of his life he wrote a play about Ivan the Terrible, of which more will be said later.

Mayakovsky's *Mystery-Bouffe* was the first signal success of Soviet drama. It was an impressive grand-scale political satire, with a multitude of characters, both real and allegorical, and was designed for mass action. Its first production provided Meyerhold with an opportunity for bold experiments in stagecraft, but it did not hold its place on the Soviet stage for long, partly because of the technical difficulties of production and partly because its spirit was soon no longer in harmony with the prevalent tendency for realism. Mayakovsky's two pungent satires—*The Bedbug* and *The Bathhouse*—were technically more manageable, but also contained a number of ingenious tricks and novel devices. These fitted in well with Meyerhold's idea of "socio-mechanics" and were fully exploited on the stage.

Konstantin Andreyevich Trenyov (1884–1945), who before the Revolution was known as a second-rate realist of the Gorky school, scored a great success with his *Lyubov Yarovaya*, a tense psychological drama enacted against the background of the Civil War. Its heroine is a village teacher, a convinced Bolshevik, who is married to a White officer. This play was one of the big successes of the Moscow Art Theater. Trenyov also wrote some historical plays.

The second group of playwrights consisted of younger writers, mostly fellow travelers, who came into literature after the Revolution. For the majority of them, too, playwriting was subsidiary to other activities. Among these were Vsevolod Ivanov with his *Bronepoezd No. 14-69 (Armored Train No. 14-69)*, a dynamic play of the Civil War, the first purely Soviet play to be produced by the Moscow Art Theater and one of its greatest post-Revolutionary successes; Bulgakov with his *The Days of the Turbins;* Katayev with *Kvadratura kruga (Squaring of the Circle)* and other satirical plays of Soviet life; Lavrenyov with *Dym*

The Drama

(*Smoke;* originally called *Revolt*) and *Razlom* (*The Break*), two well-
constructed plays portraying the dramatic conflicts arising during the
Revolution and the Civil War; Fedin with his *Bakunin v Drezdene*
(*Bakunin in Dresden*); Seyfullina with her dramatization of *Virineya;*
Olesha with his dramatized versions of *Envy* (retitled *A Conspiracy of
Feelings*) and *The Three Fat Men,* and his *Spisok blagodeyaniy* (*A List
of Blessings*); Gladkov with his *Vataga* (*The Gang*); Neverov with his
dramatization of his own novels, *Baby* (*Womenfolk*) and *Smert Zak-
hara* (*Zakhar's Death*); Babel with his symbolically-realistic plays of
Jewish life, *Zakat* (*The Sunset*) and *Maria;* Leonov with his *Untilovsk*
and the dramatizations of his novels (*The Badgers, Skutarevsky*); Zayaitsky with several plays for the Children's Theater; and others.

Katayev's plays were for the most part gay, light-hearted comedies,
satirizing various aspects of Soviet life. *Squaring of the Circle,* which
had a great though not lasting success in the Soviet Union and was
well received abroad (in Paris, for instance, it was successfully revived
in the 1949–50 season), is an amusing satire on Soviet marriage and a
grotesquely realistic picture of the post-Revolutionary student milieu.
Other aspects of Soviet life were treated by Katayev in the same farcical
vein in *Doroga tsvetov* (*The Primrose Path*).

The satire in Bulgakov's plays *Zoykina kvartira* (*Zoyka's Apartment*) and *Bagrovy ostrov* (*The Crimson Island*) was even more grim
and serious; as a result both these plays were soon taken off the repertoire, and Bulgakov was forced to dramatize other people's works (Gogol, Dickens). His dramatization of Gogol's *Dead Souls* enjoyed a great
success at the Moscow Art Theater.

The third group of playwrights consisted of younger writers who
more or less specialized in writing for the theater. The most prominent
among them were Alexander Afinogenov (1904–41), Vladimir Kirshon
(b. 1902), Nikolay Pogodin (b. 1900), Vsevolod Vishnevsky (b. 1900),
Alexey Fayko (b. 1893), Boris Romashov, and Nikolay Erdman (b. 1902).
Most of the writers of this group continued to write in the thirties, and
some of them we shall meet later. All were realists and wrote almost
exclusively about contemporary Soviet subjects. Of plays popular in
the twenties may be mentioned Fayko's *Chelovek s portfelem* (*The Man
with the Briefcase*), a social-psychological problem drama, and Erdman's *Mandat* (*Mandate*), a satirical comedy, full of Gogolian verve,
produced by Meyerhold. Its author became later a victim of one of the
purges.

On the whole, the evolution of the Soviet drama followed the general trend of developments in literature. In the early period the romanti-
cally-heroic treatment of revolutionary themes prevailed. There was
also a large number of naïve and primitive propaganda plays, most of

which soon vanished into oblivion. They dealt with topical subjects, were stuffed with political speeches, and portrayed crude black-and-white characters. Among the later propaganda plays of better quality may be mentioned Sergey Tretyakov's *Rychi, Kitay! (Roar, China!)*, influenced by Mayakovsky's conception of poster art.

The second period was marked by pronounced realistic tendencies in the treatment of contemporary subjects—the Civil War, the changed ways of life, and various problems raised by the Revolution. As in literature, there was a reversion toward psychological realism in the drama.

9. *Literary Criticism and Literary Controversies*

The Formalists

IN keeping with the quantitative and qualitative growth of Soviet literature in the mid-twenties, and with the variety of currents represented in it, this period was characterized by a variety of critical opinions and by sharp clashes of conflicting points of view. Today, in retrospect, when the deadening influence of the uniform Party line is felt in every nook and cranny of Soviet cultural life, the variety and vitality of the Soviet literary scene in the twenties appears quite amazing.

Not a small part in these literary controversies was played by the so-called Formalism, or, as some of its partisans preferred to call it, the "formal method" in the science of literature and in literary criticism. Until the end of the twenties the Formalists were the most consistent and active opponents of the officially sponsored Marxist, sociological approach to literature.

The origins of Formalism can be traced back to two main Russian sources. On the one hand, it was influenced by the two schools in the Russian *Literaturwissenschaft,* which are linked respectively with the names of two great nineteenth-century scholars: Alexander Veselovsky (1838–1906) of St. Petersburg and Alexander Potebnya (1835–1891) of Kharkov. The former initiated in Russia the so-called school of "historical" poetics and made an important contribution to the study of comparative literature. The latter, who was primarily a specialist in linguistics, founded the school of linguistico-psychological poetics. Both broke sharply away from the prevalent nineteenth-century tradition, felt equally in literary criticism and in literary scholarship, which had attached paramount importance to the social content and message in literature.

On the other hand Formalism was greatly indebted to modern Russian poetry, to Symbolism and its subsequent outgrowths. Chronologically speaking, Formalism as a distinct school in the science of literature originated more or less simultaneously with Futurism, and some of its more extreme representatives were closely connected with the latter. But the bases of the formal method, in the broad sense of that term, had been laid down first by the literary-historical and linguistic studies of Veselovsky and Potebnya—as well as the kindred movements outside Russia, especially in Germany—and secondly by the poetry and poetics of Symbolism, more particularly in the person of Andrey Bely (and, to a lesser extent, Bryusov). Bely's studies of Russian prosody marked an epoch and exercised a decisive influence. Despite Bely's errors in some particulars and the fallacy of some of his too sweeping conclusions, his work in this field, based on formal analysis and statistical evaluations, still retains its value and interest. The method first applied by him to the study of Russian verse was further exploited and extended by the Formalists.

What in the case of the Symbolists had been a more or less casual and limited expression of their natural interest in problems of literary form and had been confined almost exclusively to poetry, Formalism as a school tried to work out into a theory applicable to all literary facts. Its aim was to construe the science of literature along the same lines which are adopted in approaching other arts. It viewed literature as an evolution of literary styles and genres and was bent on rejecting all extraliterary criteria and approaches—ideological, sociological, psychological, biographical, or any other. Literature, the Formalists maintained, was primarily one of the arts, and therefore literary science and literary criticism must in the first place deal with the specific devices (*"priyom"*) of that art and not with its philosophical, sociological, psychological, or biographical contents and implications. In the main, their approach was analogous to Croce's formula: *"Lo fatto estetico é forma e niente che forma."*

The beginnings of Formalism as a distinct school date from the early years of World War I, when a group of young students of literature organized in Petrograd the so-called "Opoyaz" (Society for the Study of Poetic Language) and began to issue its non-periodical publication, *Poetics.* The leading role in it was played at the time by Victor Shklovsky, who later became the principal theoretician of extreme Formalism. Among other regular contributors were Roman Jakobson (b. 1896), L. Yakubinsky, O. Brik, and others. In the first miscellany published by Opoyaz there appeared Shklovsky's article entitled "Transsense Language and Poetry," which testified to the close relationship between Formalism and Futurism as a reaction against Symbolism, in the name of what the Futurists called the "self-sufficient word." In their revolt against all literature in which words were subordinated to meaning, the Futurists went so far as to demand a universal "trans-sense" language. One of the best Soviet literary scholars, Boris Eichenbaum (b. 1886), who in the twenties joined the Formalists, says that "the main slogan which brought together the original group of Formalists was the slogan of the emancipation of poetic words from the fetters of philosophical and religious tendencies to which the Symbolists were more and more succumbing."

The principal tenets of Formalism have been stated with great dogmatic clarity, fullness, and detachment in Boris M. Engelhardt's little book *Formalny metod v istorii literatury* (*The Formal Method in the History of Literature,* 1927).

The main fallacy of the traditional approach to art is seen by Engelhardt in our failure to overcome the dualistic conception of the "object expressed" and the "means of expression," or—to use the ordinary terminology—of form and content. The result is that, instead of studying a beautiful *work of art,* we study *the beautiful* in a work of art. It is necessary, says Engelhardt, to do away with this dualism: "In a work of art, studied on the aesthetic plane, there can be neither a system of means of expression nor an expressed object, and this not only in the sense of the famous opposition of form to content, but also in the sense of the broader antithesis of the 'language of art' and the aesthetically significant object of expression. From this point of view there is no such thing as an aesthetically significant object expressed in one or another way in a work of art, but only the work of art as an object of aesthetic study." In every such object, continues Engelhardt, two elements must be distinguished: (1) the aesthetic significance as such, and (2) the work itself as a concretely determined structural entity. Thus approached, the process of artistic creation is reduced to the molding of an aesthetically indifferent concrete material (the object of creation) into an aesthetically significant one (the work of art). Defining the object of aesthetic study as actual material *plus* aesthetic significance, the Formalists determine the boundaries of the science of literature and its auxiliary branches. The problem of aesthetic significance per se belongs to the competence of general aesthetics. The material as it exists before it is subjected to the process of aesthetic remolding must come within the corresponding nonaesthetic branch of study. Since the material of literature is words, it falls within the purview of linguistics. The object of the specific aesthetics of a given art is to assess the aesthetic function of different elements of the organized concrete material. Thus, the object of the aesthetics of literature is, first, to define, on the basis of general aesthetics, the meaning of aesthetic significance per se; secondly, on the basis of general and specific linguistics, to establish the primitive characteristics of verbal material in its preaesthetic state; and, finally, to elicit the specific meaning of that material in its aesthetically organized form. Therefore, the study of a literary work consists in demonstrating how the aesthetic factor transforms original verbal material into a work of art.

In their definition of aesthetic significance the Formalists follow the school of Hamann and Jonas Kohn, which defines it as "self-value." There are, they say, two ways of perceiving an object: the nonaesthetic, which has a practical purpose behind it; and the aesthetic, which is purposeless. This may be illustrated by the different ways in which the same river landscape is seen by the pilot who is piloting the boat, and the passenger of that boat who simply enjoys the view. For the pilot each detail of the river has a meaning and an interest so far as it has a bearing on his task. For the passenger the whole landscape is interesting and valuable in itself. In order to turn the raw material into a self-valuable work of art, it is necessary first to eliminate all collateral meanings attached to it, while, at the same time, since an object devoid of collateral meanings ceases to attract attention to the same degree as before, it is necessary somehow to increase its power of being perceived. Thus, the process of aesthetic reshaping is a twofold one: it implies aesthetic *neutralization* and aesthetic *condensation*. The aesthetic interpretation of a work of art consists in explaining this twofold process.

For the solution of the problem of the other element of an aesthetically organized entity—the element of words—the Formalists turn to linguistics. Accepting the theory that language is an organ of communication, they distinguish in it two elements: (1) that which is being communicated, and (2) a system of means of communication. These means or vehicles of communication consist of words. Therefore, for the Formalists a poetical work is a complex of words. This leads one of the theoreticians of Formalism, Roman Jakobson, to the statement that poetry is indifferent to the object of expression, that it is concerned only with the shaping of self-valuable words which stand in the same relation to it as sounds, colors, and lines stand to music, painting, and architecture. In practice, therefore, the extreme Formalists reduce the study of a work of art to the study of its devices, by which they mean words or the separate elements of verbal structure in their aesthetic function, *e.g.*, the rhyming words taken as rhymes or the syntactical patterns taken as an element of construction. Devices, as the Formalists understand them, include also the choice of subjects and the treatment of plots, and Formalism has done much for the study of these aspects of prose fiction. According to Zhirmunsky, who did not share all the excesses of left-wing Formalism, the unity of these devices constitutes the style of a literary work. Before that, Shklovsky had coined his provocative formula, proclaiming that a work of literature represents "the sum of its stylistic devices" and nothing else. The Formalists reject automatically Potebnya's theory of poetry as "thinking in images." Words, they say, not images or emotions, are the real material of poetry. Their poetics is built on the opposition of two systems of language—the poetical and the everyday. To the ordinary everyday speech, which aims at the greatest possible economy, fluency, and accuracy, they oppose the deliberately obstructed, complicated, and twisted poetical speech, which aims at creating the greatest possible effect by overcoming the automatism of perception. In accordance with this, they lay stress in literature on what they call *"ostranenie"* (*"making strange"*), the object of which is to enhance the effect by presenting ordinary things in an unusual form or in an unusual perspective. Shklovsky took pains to demonstrate how frequently Tolstoy had resorted to this device. The Formalists naturally welcomed the same tendency in Mayakovsky and Pasternak. Some of the younger Soviet writers, such as Kaverin and Slonimsky, both of whom were influenced by Shklovsky's ideas, practiced the *"ostranenie"* method on an extensive scale and shunned simplicity.

Tynyanov, who was in the twenties one of the leading Formalists, evolved the theory of verse language as a constant violation of automatism through the ascendancy of one specific factor which dominates all other elements and tends to deform them; thus, the meter of a poem tends to deform its syntax and meaning. According to Tynyanov, poetic language implies a continuous clash of various elements. The impression of a deliberate verbal whole is achieved through various violations, interruptions, brakings, and digressions, which all help to destroy the automatism of perception.

The more extreme Formalists not only disregarded altogether the element of content in the usual sense of the word, and studied the naked form of a work of literature, but they also had a tendency to deny all causal connection between literary facts and all the other concomitant facts. Above all, they denied all connection between a work of literature and the personality of its author. Thus, Boris Eichenbaum in one of his articles wrote:

> The mind of the artist, as someone who experiences this or that mood, remains, and must always remain, outside his work. A work of art is always something made, shaped, invented, not only artistic but artificial in the good sense of that word, and therefore there neither is nor can be any place in it for the reflection of the inner empiric world of its author.

Just as emphatically Eichenbaum denied all causal connection between art on the one hand, and life and social environment on the other.

For the Formalists the evolution of literature consisted primarily in a succession of styles, forms, and genres. Boris Tomashevsky (b. 1890), in his *Teoriya literatury* (*Theory of Literature*), said that the value of a work of literature lay above all in its novelty and originality. Shklovsky in his *Teoriya prozy* (*Theory of Prose Fiction*) wrote: "Forms of art are accounted for by their artistic lawfulness (*zakonomernost*). A new form appears, not in order to give expression to some new contents, but in order to replace the old form which has lost its artistic value." The same idea was voiced by Eichenbaum when he said that art subsisted "by crossing and contrasting its own traditions, by developing and modifying them on the principle of contrast, parody, shifting, and sliding." This is why the Formalists were particularly interested in certain minor writers in whom the new genre characteristics were more conspicuous. But in laying down this principle the Formalists failed to specify the laws which govern this dialectics of art, this "lawful" succession of forms. Nor did they bother to explain why this or that particular form, and not another, succeeds and supplants this or that old form. This gap in the theory developed by Shklovsky, Eichenbaum, Tomashevsky, Tynyanov, and Jakobson was pointed out by their "fellow traveler," the most moderate and cautious among the Formalists, Professor Victor Zhirmunsky (b. 1891), author of a number of valuable theoretical and historical studies and originally a specialist on German Romanticism. It was he who drew a distinction between the broadly understood "formal" method and the "extravagances" of Shklovsky and consorts, which he described as "formalistic." In his introduction to the Russian translation of Oskar Walzel's little book *Die künstlerische Form des Dichtwerks* (1919), Zhirmunsky set forth a number of points on which he disagreed with his fellow Formalists. The formula of art as device seemed to him acceptable only as a method of aesthetic study.

Side by side with it there could exist other equally legitimate formulae: art as a product of mental activity; art as a social fact and factor; art as a moral, religious, or educational fact; and so on. Syncretic forms of art are to be met not only in the primitive stages of civilization. Zhirmunsky cited some works of Novalis, Nietzsche's *Zarathustra,* and the writings of Andrey Bely as examples of philosophico-poetical syncretism in modern literature. The same is true of all so-called tendentious literature, where the artistic object is coupled with moral or social sermonizing. Zhirmunsky even conceded that "tendentiousness" in a wide sense—that is, understood as a certain moral tendency or orientation—was characteristic of a great majority of literary works.

Once it is granted that device is not the only thing that matters in a poetical work, it follows that it is not the sole factor of literary evolution. Zhirmunsky therefore flatly rejected Jakobson's formula of

197

device as "the sole hero of literature." He maintained that Joseph Bédier was perfectly right when, in his standard work on French heroic legends, he studied the influence of monastic civilization, the problems of monastic and ecclesiastical policy, and the way of life in monasteries. One would be equally justified, when studying Nekrasov as a poet, in considering the influence of Belinsky's ideas on him.

Zhirmunsky objected also to the explanation of the succession of literary forms on the principle of contrast. Such an explanation, he said, was too broad and meaningless; it did not account for the direction of the historical process, since most widely dissimilar trends could arise by contrast. Nor did Zhirmunsky accept the view of literature as a purely formal, objectless art. Poetry, he said, just as painting and sculpture, and as distinct from music and ornamental drawing, is one of those arts which *have* an object. Modern poetics was wrong in giving preference to problems of composition over those of thematics. Poetics cannot be confined to problems of prosody, instrumentation, syntax, and plot construction. The aesthetic evaluation of a work of literature is not complete unless it embraces poetic themes—what is known as "content" or "message"—considered from the point of view of their aesthetic effectiveness.

Finally, Zhirmunsky established another important point of divergence between himself and the extreme Formalists, and thus introduced some clarity into the area where great confusion had reigned before. He refused to treat a lyric poem and a modern psychological novel on the same footing, insisting that the relation between composition and theme in the two is quite different. While a lyric poem is, indeed, a work of verbal art, wholly subordinated to the aesthetic design, a novel by Tolstoy or Stendhal makes use of words in their neutral capacity and subordinates them, as in everyday speech, to their communicative functions. Such a work, even if it be considered a work of verbal art, can be so regarded only in a sense quite different from the one which applies to a lyric poem. Zhirmunsky admitted the existence of purely formal prose fiction, in which the elements of style and composition predominated, and cited examples of such "ornamental" prose fiction in modern Russian literature (Gogol, Leskov, Remizov, Andrey Bely). But it was precisely when confronted by such "ornamental" works that one became fully aware of their fundamental difference from the novels of Tolstoy, Stendhal, or Dostoyevsky, in which words are used "neutrally" or, to use the Formalist terminology, are perceived not in their "self-valuable" meaning, but with all the collateral accretions of meaning.[33]

[33] Zhirmunsky's views are quoted by Engelhardt, *The Formal Method in the History of Literature.*

Zhirmunsky's strictures on his erstwhile colleagues were a stab in the back of Formalism. It came at a time when Formalism, under the growing impact of hostile criticism on the part of orthodox Marxists, was beginning to disintegrate. For a few years the Formalists were able to voice their views more or less freely, but the great majority of orthodox Communist critics, including the most moderate among them, not to speak of the Party leaders, were openly hostile to them. It was under this pressure that the Formalists gradually modified their views. The change became more or less imperative when it came to expressing their attitude toward contemporary literature. All that has been said above of the Formalist views refers primarily to Formalism as a school of literary science, and not as literary criticism properly speaking. But their theoretical views were bound to influence their judgments on contemporary literature—and so much was admitted by Engelhardt in his book—although he drew a distinction of principle between the science of literature and literary criticism. The latter, he said, does not investigate literature but is its complement, its final stage. Its object is to assimilate a given work of literature to the artistic consciousness of the reading public. The criterion of scientific objectivity cannot be applied to criticism; it is always subjective, for the criticized work has to be sifted through the personality of the critic, who represents a certain historical and social environment. Yet it would be absurd to deny the inevitable connection between literary science and literary criticism and to demand that they use totally different criteria. Literary criticism need not be absolutely objective; it can introduce certain modifications into the hard-and-fast rules laid down by the literary historian; and it can take into account facts and elements which literary history leaves out. But how can a literary critic who accepts in principle the theory of Formalism resist the temptation of applying purely formal criteria in his own critical work? In the second half of the nineteenth century, Russian literary historians were strongly influenced by the "civic" and utilitarian tendencies of literary criticism; now it was the turn for literary history or science to exercise its influence on literary criticism.

But the upholders of Marxist views on literature could not eye with indifference the attempts of the Formalists to apply their theoretical views to the criticism of contemporary literature. Nor did the Formalists themselves dare approach Soviet writers with purely formal criteria. So, after 1927, they began to modify their theory. We have already seen the important reservations that were made by Zhirmunsky. Shklovsky and Eichenbaum, too, made concessions to the sociological method and began to include within the scope of their studies problems concerning the social and historical genesis of literary facts. This change of attitude found an expression in a number of articles by Eichenbaum

Soviet Russian Literature

and in Shklovsky's work on Tolstoy's *War and Peace* (1929). Eichenbaum spoke openly of combining the formal method with the sociological. But the enemies of the Formalists remained wary and suspicious. A certain Professor Efimov, of Smolensk, in a pamphlet entitled *Formalizm v russkom literaturovedenii* (*Formalism in Russian Literary Science,* 1930) showed himself very skeptical of the value of the Formalists' "sociologism." It was not real, he said, for it denied the causal genetic connection between social and economic facts, on the one hand, and literary facts, on the other.

Some of the early extreme Formalists, including Shklovsky and Brik, tried at one point to conclude an alliance with proletarian literature and to direct the latter into their channels. Both were regular contributors to Mayakovsky's *LEF* and *New LEF,* and Shklovsky even came to advocate the "literature of fact," of which the "Lefists" became the most ardent partisans.

Whatever may have been the errors and excesses of extreme Formalism with its one-sided and unrealistic deification of form in literature, there can be no doubt that, in its uncompromising reaction against the social-utilitarian tradition of the nineteenth-century criticism and the subjective impressionism of some modern critics, on the whole its effect on Russian literary studies was beneficent. It drew attention to many problems traditionally despised by Russian literary historians and critics; it studied actual literary facts, instead of indulging in extra-literary investigations and futile generalizations; and finally, it tried to put literary history and literary criticism on a sound scientific basis and do away with critical dilettantism. In the twenties it was the most productive school in literary science, and even its adversaries could not but succumb to its influence: with a few exceptions, the representatives of the sociological school of the twenties and early thirties paid infinitely more attention to problems of form than did their "civic-minded" predecessors in the nineteenth century. At no other period was the study of literature in Russia so productive, so rich in both theoretical and historical works, as when Formalism reigned supreme. Among the theoretical works published between 1921 and 1927 we find: Zhirmunsky's *The Rhyme,Problems of Poetics, Introduction to Metrics,* and *The Structure of Lyrical Poems;* Shklovsky's *Theory of Prose Fiction;* Tomashevsky's *Theory of Literature;* Tynyanov's *The Problem of Verse Language;* Griftsov's *Theory of the Novel;* Grossman's *Method and Style;* Vsevolodsky-Gerngross' *Theory of Intonation;* Reformatsky's *An Essay in the Analysis of Novel Composition;* and Eichenbaum's *Verse Melody.* Works dealing with Russian literature and its specific problems include Zhirmunsky's study of Pushkin and Bryusov; Eichenbaum's books on Tolstoy, Lermontov, and Akhmatova; Grossman's,

Dolinin's, Zeitlin's and Victor Vinogradov's books on Dostoyevsky; and Vinogradov's studies of Gogol and Akhmatova. Major works in the field of comparative literature include Zhirmunsky's *Byron and Pushkin*, Piksanov's *Griboyedov and Molière*, Shklovsky's *Pushkin and Sterne*, not to count numerous essays on Pushkin in his relation to English and French literature by Yakovlev, Yakubovich, Tomashevsky, Kozmin, and others.[34] Though not all of these works came from the pen of the Formalists proper, it was Formalism which gave the impetus to all the studies of this kind, and therein lies its undoubted merit.

The Marxists and Other Sociological Critics

The sociological method in literary criticism and history and theory of literature, which was the principal method opposed to Formalism, was comprised of several trends of which orthodox Marxism was only one. Among its not strictly Marxian followers were to be found some of the older historians of literature, such as Pavel N. Sakulin (1868–1926)[35] and Nikolay K. Piksanov (b. 1878). Both accepted the teachings of the Formalists up to a point, and Sakulin even tried to combine the formal method with the sociological approach. He agreed that history

[34] This list is far from complete. Those who are interested in the subject will find further references in Balukhaty's *Theory of Literature,* Tomashevsky's *Theory of Literature,* and Vladislavlev's *Russkie pisateli (Russian Writers),* which has a special section on "Problems of Poetics" (434–38). There are also two French articles on the subject: B. Tomashevsky, "La nouvelle école d'histoire littéraire en Russie," in *La Revue des études slaves,* Vol. VIII (1928); and N. Gourfinkel, "Les nouvelles méthodes d'histoire littéraire en Russie," in *Le Monde slave* (February, 1929). English-speaking readers may refer to the informative articles by A. Voznesensky, "Problems of Method in the Study of Literature in Russia," in *The Slavonic Review,* Vol. VI (June, 1927); and M. Kridl, "Russian Formalism," in *The American Bookman* (1944). The literary output of the Formalist school, especially in the field of theory, dwindled after 1927, but some interesting works continued to appear; among them may be named Andrey Bely's *Ritm kak dialektika i Medny Vsadnik (Rhythm as Dialectics and the Bronze Horseman)* and *Masterstvo Gogolya (Gogol's Craftsmanship).* Bely also left a number of unpublished studies on poetics. The publication of works on literary history went on undiminished. Numerous new literary documents and memoirs of great value have been published since the Revolution. Of particular value are such publications as *Literaturnoye Nasledstvo (Literary Heritage)* and *Zvenya (Links).* The former, launched in 1931, is a nonperiodical publication which still continues to appear. It has published special volumes devoted to Pushkin, to Goethe in Russia, to Franco-Russian literary contacts, to Tolstoy, Herzen, Lermontov, Griboyedov, Belinsky, and Saltykov-Shchedrin, and several miscellaneous volumes. It is a mine of priceless information. *Zvenya,* also nonperiodical, appeared between 1932 and 1936 and contained a number of valuable studies and previously unpublished documents in the field of Russian literature and Russian culture. Some valuable materials have also been published under the auspices of the State Literary Museum, including the correspondence between Alexander Blok and Andrey Bely.

[35] His works include *The Synthetic System of Literary Studies, The Theory of Literary Styles,* and an ambitious sociological study of the evolution of literary styles in Russia, volume 1 of *Russian Literature.*

of literature was primarily a history of styles and forms, but looked for a sociological explanation of their succession.

The older orthodox Marxist critics were represented, in the nineteen twenties, in addition to such pillars of the Communist party as Trotsky, Bukharin, and Lunacharsky, by Mme Lyubov Axelrod-Orthodox (1868–1940?), Vladimir M. Fritsche (1870–1929), Peter S. Kogan (1872–1932), Alexander Voronsky, Vyacheslav Polonsky (1886–1932), Valerian Polyansky (pseudonym of P. I. Lebedev, 1882–1948), and Vladimir F. Pereverzev (b. 1882). Among the younger ones may be named Isaac M. Nusinov (b. 1889), Pavel N. Medvedev (b. 1891), A. Lezhnev, Dmitry A. Gorbov (b. 1894), G. Gorbachov (b. 1897), and Leopold L. Averbach (b. 1903). Some of the older Marxists, especially Kogan and Fritsche, took an uncompromisingly hostile attitude toward Formalism and stuck to their old-fashioned guns. Thus Kogan, author of *Literature of These Years* and of several other works, voiced this extreme anti-Formalist view when he wrote:

> I am little attracted by formal investigations. I take no interest in Mayakovsky's syntax or in discussions about composition, imagery, epithets, etc. I could never understand why these boring questions should be thrashed out in public.

Kogan thus came closest to the traditional attitude of Russian "utilitarian" criticism, with its neglect of, and even contempt for, problems of form—an attitude that had been already discarded by Plekhanov, the founder of Russian Marxism and the first to apply consistently Marxist principles to the study of literature. Kogan's attitude was not, however, shared by all the older Marxist critics. Both Trotsky and Lunacharsky recognized the value of some of the Formalists' studies. This was even more true of the younger Marxist critics. Some of them attached great importance to questions of form and style, but sought to explain different forms and styles by economic and social causes and stressed the class nature of art.

All their differences apart, those who adhered to the Marxist method had a common ground. They all proceeded, of course, from the doctrine of historical materialism. As distinct from the aesthetic method in all its varieties, which *describes* aesthetic facts, the Marxists aimed at *explaining* and *interpreting* literature. For them, each given complex of literary facts is a product of the social environment in which the literary work is produced. The Marxist approach implies, therefore, three consecutive stages. It begins by analyzing the economic structure of society. Thence it proceeds to explain social conditions and class differentiation. Finally, from the economic and social data it deduces the social psychology of a given society, its mental and intellectual state, which is a result of the complex interaction of economic and social factors. Where the Marxists vary is in the assessment of the relative importance of those three elements—the economic basis, the social structure, and the social psychology. For some of them the social psychology of a society is the immediate source of its art and literature, while economic and social facts have no direct bearing on literature, but exercise their influence through the intermediary of the psychological factor and merely condition the society's psychology. For others the economic factor pure and simple, especially the "prevalent form of production," is the one that directly influences and determines the evolution of art and literature.

This latter extreme wing of Marxism was represented in the Soviet Union by Pereverzev, author of works on Gogol and Dostoyevsky. Pereverzev did not neglect problems of style and even studied the stylistic "devices" of the authors with whom he was concerned, but he sought to explain them by the underlying economic conditions and, above all, by the process of production. Dostoyevsky's art, for instance, became, in his interpretation, an expression of the grievances and aspirations of the lower middle class. For a short time Pereverzev's Marxist interpretation of Russian classical literature was very much in vogue, but soon he was attacked by leading Marxist critics who accused him of "vulgarizing" and distorting Marxism. "Pereverzevism" was proclaimed a dangerous heresy that had to be stamped out, and he and his followers were hounded off the literary scene. The campaign was carried on with great vituperation, the word "Pereverzevism" was bandied about in the columns of Soviet periodicals, and Marxist critics of various brands vied with each other in denouncing those who were guilty of it. Not the least vocal in this campaign were the faithful watchdogs of the proletarian purity of Soviet literature from the former "On Guard" group. Particularly vicious attacks on Pereverzev were made by Gorbachov, one of the early pillars of that group and one of the most intelligent younger critics. The precariousness of a Soviet critic's position was strikingly illustrated by the speedy fall from grace of Gorbachov himself, whose name, in the late thirties, was joined to the list of "missing."

As in the case of Formalism, it is necessary to distinguish between the application of the sociological method to the study of literature, especially of its past phenomena, and its manifestations in current literary criticism. As far as the former is concerned, the sociological school has produced some interesting and valuable works (those of Sakulin, Piksanov, and even Pereverzev). But its critical output is of little value, for it was too much influenced by the constant variations in the official literary policy of the Communist party.

203

Literary Controversies

We have seen that, when in 1925 the conflict between the "On-guardists"—those extreme partisans of proletarian hegemony in literature—and the more moderate elements within the Party, who took the fellow travelers under their wing, came to a head, the moderates won. Fellow travelers were given elbowroom and enabled to work more or less unhampered. It was their share in Soviet literature that made the period discussed in the present chapter a period of fruitful diversity.

The new orientation of the "On Guard" group, known now as the "On Literary Guard" (with a magazine of the same name), brought it closer to the principal spokesmen of the fellow travelers in literary criticism. They spoke of raising the quality of proletarian literary production, of learning from the classics of nineteenth-century realism and from Tolstoy especially, and of showing the "live" Soviet man, instead of ideological abstractions. Their enemies delighted in pointing out how little difference there was now between some of the critics of *On Literary Guard* (e.g., V. Ermilov) and such advocates of fellow travelers as Voronsky, Polonsky, and Lezhnev. These enemies turned up on the extreme left of literature, in the LEF group, which, after an interval of four years, in 1927 launched *The New LEF*. Its pillars were Chuzhak, Tretyakov, Brik (all former Futurists), and Victor Shklovsky, and its slogan became "literature of fact" (or "factography," to use the word later coined by them). They attacked equally the fellow travelers and the proletarian psychological realists, and spoke no less slightingly of Gladkov's *Cement*, Fadeyev's *The Rout*, and Semyonov's *Natalya Tarpova* than of Leonov's *The Thief*.

In 1929 there appeared a volume of their articles written during the two previous years. Edited by Chuzhak, it was called *Literature of Fact*[36] and contained articles by the editor, Brik, Shklovsky, Tretyakov, V. Pertsov, P. Neznamov, V. Trenin, and T. Grits, most of them contributing several articles (there were five by Chuzhak, seven by Tretyakov, and eight by Shklovsky). All spoke of the death of fiction, of "plot literature," and acclaimed the advent of "factual literature." Chuzhak called fiction "opium for the people" and saw in factual literature an antidote for it.[37] He spoke of "activizing," "concretizing," "techniciz-ing," and "rationalizing" literature—of shifting the center of gravity from human emotions to the organization of society. It was no use, he said, learning from the classics, for old literature was throughout individualistic and idealistic. There was no room for inspiration in art,

[36] *Literatura fakta. Pervy sbornik materialov rabotnikov LEF'a.* (edited by N. Chuzhak).
[37] *Ibid.,* 28.

since art was a matter of "skill" and of "knack" (this was the old Formalist notion of art as "a sum of devices," presented from a class angle).

Tretyakov ridiculed the pessimists who were lamenting the absence of "Red Homers and Red Tolstoys" and the optimists who regarded the appearance of Communist Tolstoys as a matter of time. His answer to those who demanded or expected Soviet Tolstoys was: "There is no need for us to wait for Tolstoys, because we have our own epics. Our epics are the newspapers."

What the Bible was for the medieval Christian—a guide for all occasions of life; what the novel with a message was for the Russian liberal intelligentsia, the newspaper is today for the Soviet activist,

wrote Tretyakov; and he added:

What is the good of talking about book novels, about something called *War and Peace,* when every morning as we snatch our newspaper we turn over a new page of the most astounding novel called "Our Today." The characters in this novel, its authors and its readers are we ourselves.[38]

Chuzhak rejected emphatically the idea that the object of literature was cognition of life and repeated the old LEF slogan about literature as "life-building." Most Soviet novels were no more than conscientious attempts at "cognizing" life and proceeded from the obsolete notion that literature must approach life at a certain distance in time in order to allow life to settle down before it became the subject of literature. This notion was shared by Gorky, and this was the great defect of his fictional work, though Chuzhak had nothing but praise for Gorky the publicist. Among post-revolutionary writers, Chuzhak singled out for praise Furmanov and Tynyanov who came quite close to "factography," the former in his *Chapayev,* the latter in his historical novels. The field of "factography," as Chuzhak and his fellow "Lefists" understood it, was wide: it embraced newspaper sketches and reports, biographies, memoirs, autobiographies and human documents, diaries, essays, law reports, travelogues, reports of meetings, speeches, pamphlets, parodies, satires, and even "artistic (that is, masterful) scientific monographs."[39] Chuzhak listed some achievements in this field, allocating the first place to John Reed's *The Ten Days That Shook the World.* His list also included Veresayev's *Pushkin in Life,* Shklovsky's *Sentimental Journey,* Mayakovsky's *How I Wrote My Esenin,* the memoirs of the old revolutionaries Nikolay Morozov and Vera Figner, Voronsky's autobiography (although as a literary critic Voronsky was one of

38 *Ibid.,* 31–33.
39 *Ibid.,* 60.

the bugbears of the "factographers"), Tretyakov's books about China, and Arsenyev's *In the Jungles of the Ussuri Region* (this book of travel and hunting adventures in the Russian Far East was often cited by the "factographers" as superior to much of Soviet fiction and as a proof that fiction was dying out). He also named purely journalistic writings of Koltsov, Zaslavsky, Radek, Zorich, and others.[40]

Similar ideas were developed by Shklovsky, Tretyakov, and Pertsov. Shklovsky insisted on the importance for the writer of having another profession which would provide him with material for writing. Journalists and reporters therefore had an advantage over professional fiction writers. He also raised his voice against the prevalent tendency to imitate the classics, saying that "the traditional psychological novel is not easily acclimatized in Soviet conditions, for its plot formulae are of no use in the conditioning of new material."[41]

Tretyakov demanded "biographies of things" and wrote: "Such books as Forest, Bread, Coal, Iron, Flax, Cotton, Paper, Railway Engine, Factory, remain unwritten. We need them and they can be done most satisfactorily by using the method of 'a biography of a thing.' "[42] As an example of this factographic literature he quoted the French writer Pierre Hamp.

The idea of "artistic realism" as the proper style of proletarian literature was rejected by Pertsov, who said that the critics of *On Literary Guard* did not know the meaning of realism, let alone of "proletarian realism"; all that they could say was that it meant the way the classics wrote, Tolstoy in particular.

Literature of Fact contained a number of sarcastic judgments about some of the greatest successes of Soviet literature. Thus Brik wrote that in Gladkov's *Cement* all the ingredients were taken from the best cookery books, but the result was "inedible," because the ingredients were not cooked—"only for appearance's sake were they kneaded into a kind of literary paste."[43] Similar attacks were made on Fadeyev and Leonov, on Bagritsky and Utkin.

Tretyakov in *The New LEF* accused all the leading fellow travelers and proletarian novelists of being "Passeists," of looking toward the past instead of the present and the future.

The New LEF, attacked on all sides, ceased appearing in 1928, and the LEF group soon came to an end. Its place was taken by the REF (Revolutionary Front), launched by Mayakovsky. But its independent existence was of short duration, and it ended by merging with the RAPP

40 *Ibid.,* 61–62.
41 *Ibid.,* 130.
42 *Ibid.,* 70.
43 *Ibid.,* 87.

(Russian Association of Proletarian Writers) as part of a larger body of proletarian literary organizations.

In May of 1928 took place the first Congress of all associations of proletarian writers (VOAPP). Its leading lights were Fadeyev, Libedinsky, Averbach, and Ermilov, and its proceedings were reflected in a volume of articles edited by Averbach.[44] Fadeyev's report, read at the Congress, was reissued later as a separate pamphlet, under the title *The Highway of Proletarian Literature*.[45] It contained attacks both on Voronsky and Lezhnev and on LEF. The former were attacked for their "irrationalism," their interest in the subconscious. The same charge was leveled against a number of writers, including Pilnyak, Leonov, and Vsevolod Ivanov. The "Lefists" were criticized for their ultra-rationalist approach to literature. Their worship of facts was ascribed to their inability and reluctance to interpret the world that surrounded them. "We must take down what we see, let others come and make it all out" —such was, according to Fadeyev, the LEF formula. Their proclamation of the supremacy of form over content, their insistence on "ideological form" were ascribed to the same reason. Fadeyev defended against LEF the two main tenets of the proletarian neo-realists: the portrayal of "live" men instead of schematic abstractions, and the learning from the classics of realism, from writers like Tolstoy and Flaubert who, for all their "bourgeois" limitations, had attained the maximum objectivity that was possible under the circumstances. Learning from the old literature was not, however, enough in itself, said Fadeyev; the foremost duty of a Soviet writer was to learn from life itself.

44 *Tvorcheskie puti proletarskoy literatury. Vtoroy sbornik statey* (*The Creative Paths of Proletarian Literature. Second Collection of Articles*). An earlier collection appeared in 1928 and contained reports and addresses delivered at the 1927 Moscow Conference of proletarian writers by Averbach, Libedinsky, Bezymensky, Fadeyev, Zonin, and Ermilov.

45 *Stolbovaya doroga proletarskoy literatury.*

IV. Literature Puts on Uniform
1929-32

1. *"Social Command"*

IN 1929 fellow travelers and all independent writers came once more under concentrated fire, this time with results that were disastrous to Soviet literature as a whole. The period of comparative freedom was at an end, and to it succeeded what came to be known as the dictatorship of the RAPP, which was headed unofficially by that most virulent of critics, Leopold Averbach. This period lasted about three years and coincided with the early years of the first Soviet Five-Year Plan of industrialization and collectivization, to which everything else in the country was subordinated. Literature, too, was enlisted in its service. The leading role in it was given to Communist writers and purely "proletarian" organizations. RAPP assumed dictatorial powers and laid down the policy which all writers had to follow if they cared to survive in literature.

The inauguration of this policy of subordinating literature (and other arts) to the requirements of the Five-Year Plan was preceded, in 1928-29, by a lively controversy in the Soviet press on the subject of "social command," in which a number of prominent writers and critics took part.

In a sense, "social command" (*"sotsialny zakaz"*) had always been taken for granted in the Soviet Union. But it was understood broadly as the implicit command of the ruling class. Even some orthodox Communist critics were ready to admit, for instance, that Pilnyak and the Serapions, in describing the Revolution and its impact on Russian life, were carrying out this implicit social command, despite their own, studiedly detached attitude. But this time social command was to be understood much more narrowly—as specific assignments to be executed by writers. The first to use the formula and to give it this meaning were the former Futurists from LEF. The RAPP extremists, led by Averbach, followed suit, though Averbach himself was moderate at first and did not recommend "dictating directly" to writers. Most of those who took part in the 1928-29 controversy, writers and critics alike, protested against this narrow interpretation of "social command."

Gladkov, himself a Communist, described the LEF formula as "fundamentally alien" and harmful to proletarian literature. The point of view of its opponents was clearly voiced by Polonsky, the editor of *Pechat i Revolyutsiya,* who wrote:

> The theory of "social command" marks an attempt, on the part of a group of writers and artists of the extreme left, who are severed from the proletariat, to establish a link with it, while preserving their independence as makers of ideological values. Having assigned to the working class the role of "social commander" . . . they keep for themselves the humble role of "artisans" . . . of producers of "ideological" things. . . . It is easy to notice that while they throw a sop to the working class they remain in reality on the other side of the fence. For the theory of "social command" does not furnish that organic link with the proletariat which . . . is precisely what our epoch demands of the master who aspires to be the proletarian artist of the proletarian revolution and the proletarian spokesman of our wonderful age.[1]

Polonsky opposed the theory of social command from the Marxist point of view. But before a few months had passed he was himself proclaimed a counterrevolutionary and divested of his leading position in Soviet magazines. The theory of explicit social command, sponsored by the extremists of RAPP, then received official approval. It was decided to place literature in the service of the Five-Year Plan, to make use of writers in the furtherance of it, and to involve them in "Socialist emulation" which was becoming so popular in industry. Writers were expected to become "shock workers" *("udarniki"),* to form "artistic brigades," to join various construction projects and collective farms and describe them in factual sketches *(ocherki).* In fact, RAPP, which had hitherto fought LEF, now took a leaf out of the latter's book and proclaimed the superiority of "literature of fact" to all other forms. Fiction was frowned upon, and several leading fellow travelers—Alexey Tolstoy, Kaverin, and others—became journalists and *ocherkists.* Some continued, however, writing novels and stories. But these had to reflect various aspects of the Five-Year Plan. Collective writing also became fashionable. The idea was encouraged by Gorky, who sponsored two big collective literary undertakings—a *History of the Civil War* and a

[1] V. Polonsky, "Spor o sotsialnom zakaze" ("The Controversy about Social Command"), in *Pechat i revolyutsiya (Press and Revolution),* No. 2 (1929), 23. This article served as an introduction to a discussion in which O. Brik, P. Kogan, G. Gorbachov, Z. Steinman, I. Nusinov, V. Pereverzev, and N. Zamoshkin took part. In the same number appeared short statements on the same subject by Gladkov, Leonov, Pilnyak, Selvinsky, Fedin, and Karavayeva. All of them protested against the idea of "social command." In the next issue Polonsky replied to his critics, of whom Brik, Kogan, and Pereverzev were the most outspoken. *Pechat i revolyutsiya,* No. 3 (1929).

History of Factories and Plants. As part of the latter, appeared a volume describing the construction of the Stalin Canal linking the White Sea with the Baltic and built with forced labor of common-law criminals and political prisoners. Several well-known writers and critics collaborated on this volume (Alexey Tolstoy, Zoshchenko, Katayev, Inber, Zelinsky, Averbach, and others).[2]

Averbach and Bezymensky who played the leading roles in RAPP set about instilling new political blood into a literature that had become too objective and apolitical. The old dream of the "Onguardists" came true: the supremacy of proletarian literature was officially recognized. RAPP was to set the line, and everybody had to toe it. The result was a drying-up of the creative sources of Soviet literature, a narrowing-down of its themes, and a tightening of controls over individual writers.

Pilnyak in Hot Water

Two literary incidents which, in 1929, involved Pilnyak and Zamyatin, served well to illustrate the limitations on the writer's freedom in the U. S. S. R. The Pilnyak incident was caused by the publication of the author's short novel *Krasnoye derevo* (*Mahogany*). Following the not unusual practice—for reasons of foreign copyright—Pilnyak had his novel first published (in Russian) in Berlin, by a firm which had contacts with the Soviet State Publishing House. In the meantime the book was apparently turned down by Soviet censorship[3] and its publication abroad unleashed furious attacks on Pilnyak, which led to his expulsion from the Association of Soviet Writers.[4] Later Pilnyak tried to redeem himself by revising *Mahogany* and incorporating it in his Five-Year Plan novel, *The Volga Flows into the Caspian Sea.*

In more than one way *Mahogany* is a typical work of Pilnyak's, with no plot and almost no action. It is a static picture of the two-faced modern Russia—of the old world encased within the new, with the main attention on the old. The scene is set in an old small town in provincial Russia, which Pilnyak describes as "Russian Bruges and

[2] A detailed account of the way in which literature was placed in the service of the Five-Year Plan will be found in Harriet Borland, *Soviet Literary Theory and Practice during the First Five-Year Plan: 1928–1932.* This informative study appeared when my book was already completed.

[3] The exact workings of Soviet censorship are surrounded with mystery, and its history offers numerous puzzles. In the main its functions are exercised by *Glavlit*, or the Central Department of Literary Affairs. Some, though very inadequate, information about its procedures will be found in George Reavey, *Soviet Literature Today.* Some interesting data about the activities of Soviet censorship will be found in the article by a former Soviet citizen, V. Zavalishin, "Sovetskie tsenzory za rabotoy" ("Soviet Censors at Work"), in *Narodnaya Pravda* (*People's Truth*), Paris, No. 11–12 (November, 1950).

[4] For details of this incident see Eastman, *Artists in Uniform.*

Russian Kamakura." In the center of the novel stands the Skudrin family. Yakov Skudrin himself is a typical relic of the past, a cunning and clever embodiment of the surviving counterrevolutionary tendencies. With a quaint irony he lists the Tsars he has outlived, from "Nikolay Pavlovich" (Nicholas I) to "Nikolay Alexandrovich" (Nicholas II), adding to them "Vladimir Ilyich" (Lenin) and concluding: "I am also going to outlive Alexey Ivanovich," that is Rykov, the then chairman of the Council of People's Commissars who was to perish later as a victim of the opposition purges. Skudrin develops a counterrevolutionary theory—behind which one can feel Pilnyak's own views—of the imminent extinction of the proletariat as a result of the progress of mechanization: "all proletarians will become engineers." His brother Ivan, who hates Yakov and has changed his last name to Ozhogov, is a romantic revolutionary for whom the clock stopped in 1919. With a few others like himself he has founded a primitive commune; they live in a dugout in a factory yard and preach a variety of Communism based on charity:

> "Communism is primarily charity, an eager interest of one man in another, friendship, co-operation, collaboration. Communism means giving up things, and for a genuine Communist love, respect for men, and men as such stand above all other things,"

says Ivan, lamenting the loss of this genuine Communism.

Yakov's youngest son, Akim, an engineer, whose short visit to his native town forms the single "incident" in the otherwise static story, has some affinity with Ivan. He is also a Communist, but belongs to the Trotskyite opposition and has fallen out with the "general line" of the Party. At heart he is, in Pilnyak's own words, "the flesh of the flesh" of his uncle. The reader can feel that Pilnyak's own sympathy lies with these two romantic revolutionaries, and it was this tendency toward romantic idealization of Trotskyism that led to the banning of the book. When, later, a good deal of *Mahogany* was bodily transposed by Pilnyak, as a minor episode, into his novel *The Volga Flows into the Caspian Sea,* the whole episode with Akim was excluded, and several other characters, bourgeois wreckers and ideal Communists, were opposed to Ivan Ozhogov, the last of the idealists of romantic Communism. In *Mahogany* we see only the representatives of the old world, relics of the seventeenth-century Russia, and those two antiquated Communists. At the end of the book their obsoleteness is symbolized in Akim missing his train: "Akim the Trotskyite missed his train just as he had missed the train of time."

Apart from the two romantic revolutionaries, who in 1929 sounded anachronistic and frankly counterrevolutionary, critical notes crop up here and there in the book. Thus, Pilnyak emphasizes the inefficiency of Soviet provincial administration based on "the slow squandering of pre-Revolutionary wealth." The trade-union membership card is represented as the pivot of the town's life and a key to its elementary comforts: "Those who are disfranchised receive no bread, nor do their children."

In *Volga vpadayet v Kaspiyskoye more* (*The Volga Flows into the Caspian Sea*, 1930), Pilnyak set out to put right the ideological fallacies of *Mahogany*. Yet, the real significance of the novel had little to do with the avowed task of glorifying the Five-Year Plan. It is true that the Five-Year Plan forms the background of the book. But it is not by chance that Pilnyak conceives his industrial project on a somewhat fantastic and hyperbolical scale. The novel tells the story of the building of a gigantic dam at Kolomna, not far from Moscow, with the object of reversing the Volga and making the river Moscow navigable to big Volga steamers (on a more modest scale this project was realized a couple of years later in the form of the Volga-Moscow canal).

The book is interspersed with a great deal of technical matter. It opens with a long passage which would be more in its place in a textbook of hydraulics (a good example of the "factual literature" demanded by Chuzhak and Tretyakov). One of the chapters, even, has attached to it in the form of an appendix a complete issue of the wall newspaper published at the Kolomstroy, which the gentle reader is politely asked to read, but which, from the point of view of the story, can be just as well left unread. But Pilnyak is interested not in the technical achievements of the Five-Year Plan but in the clash of the old and the new world in Soviet Russia. His artistic attention is centered on the depiction of the forces which the old world arrays in this battle. Side by side with the Soviet Union of the Five-Year Plan, Pilnyak shows us the half-Asiatic, pre-Petrine Russia. This Russia is symbolized in the Marina Mniszek tower in Kolomna, which forms a sort of refrain running throughout the book. Pilnyak develops here his favorite conception of the historical duality of Russia, her Januslike face turned simultaneously toward West and East. But Pilnyak does not confine himself to a symbolical demonstration of the essential duality of Russia. With a picturesqueness which reminds one of Gogol, he depicts, next to the model Communist city of Kolomstroy, built according to plan, the little old town of Kolomna, which drags on its unchanging, sluggish, sleepy life, with pigs wallowing in the mud in the middle of the streets —just as in Gogol's Mirgorod. (Here again Pilnyak was in fact repeating himself, for in one of his earlier stories he had written: "In the market square a puddle, not a Gogolian, but an all-Russian one. At the corner of the puddle the inn called 'Europe.' ")

And side by side with the ideal Communist Sadykov, simple and straightforward, and therefore the least interesting for the author, Pilnyak shows us a number of complex and twisted characters who obviously attract him much more. Some of them are outspoken enemies of the Soviet regime, counterrevolutionaries and wreckers (an important part in the novel is played by a wreckers' conspiracy—a fashionable and topical subject in nearly all Five-Year Plan novels and plays).

But the most important character—and the one who is obviously nearest and dearest to Pilnyak's heart—is again Ivan Ozhogov, old Skudrin's brother, half-workman and half-tramp, who introduces himself as "a Communist of the year 1919." He is another character brought over from *Mahogany,* but in the framework of this novel he acquires an added symbolical significance. He personifies the romantic and heroic period of the Revolution, the period of storm and stress when the elemental forces were let loose and swept like a gale across Russia. Pilnyak's Ozhogov is not the only representative of this type of romantic Communist in Soviet literature. In Gladkov's *Cement,* two ardent Communists, the young girl Polya Mekhova and the typical intellectual Sergey Ivagin, are possessed by the same mood, the same disillusionment, and the same pining after the epoch of War Communism. But *Cement* was written at the very beginning of the NEP when, from the Communist point of view, such moods were much more comprehensible and excusable. With Pilnyak, this revolutionary romanticism is opposed, not to the semibourgeois reality of the NEP, but to the realism, both heroic and everyday, of the Five-Year Plan, of Socialist reconstruction. His Ozhogov is therefore, from the point of view of an orthodox Communist, an unpardonable anachronism. Yet Pilnyak cannot conceal his sympathy with Ozhogov: the latter embodies for him all that is best in the Revolution. His death in the waters of the river when the new dam is opened, while it fittingly disposes of an anachronistic relic of the past, symbolizes also the death of those best elements in Communism.

Pilnyak went all out to glorify the Five-Year Plan and to remove the bad impression which *Mahogany* had created in Communist circles, but, filled with romanticism and heavily flavored with Dostoyevskian scenes, the novel misfired completely.

Pilnyak's recantation after the publication of *Mahogany,* which has been described as "abject," was not the only one in his literary career. In 1926 he went to Japan, one of the objects of his visit being to set up the Japanese branch of the Russo-Japanese Literary Society. A result of this trip was a book called *Korni yaponskogo solntsa (The Roots of the Japanese Sun).* It was full of the usual Pilnyakian fireworks, of relevant and irrelevant reflections, of interesting observations and half-baked generalizations. With his *Kitaysky dnevnik (A Chinese*

Diary) it was included in the seventh volume of his Collected Works issued by the State Publishing House. In 1932 Pilnyak revisited Japan, and in 1934 appeared another book, this time entitled *Kamni i korni* (*Stones and Roots*). It consisted largely of quotations from the earlier book, with additions, comments, and self-refutations. It also contained a renunciation of the earlier book, worded so astonishingly that one might easily suspect Pilnyak of speaking with his tongue in his cheek. Pilnyak wrote here:

> The writer Pilnyak informs his readers that his *Roots* (1926) are no good. The writer Pilnyak of 1932 asks his readers to throw out from their shelves the seventh volume of the GIZ edition of his Collected Works. As for the translations of this book, Pilnyak asks that its Japanese translation be destroyed first of all. This must be done out of respect for the author.[5]

Not content with this formal disavowal of his book, Pilnyak went on to advocate in even more astonishing terms a strict control of writers:

> ... A writer is like a geologist or a traveler to uninhabited and undiscovered lands .... Writers must be treated like geologists, for writers can certainly muddle up things no less than the latter. In Soviet literature, too, it is necessary, after reregistering all writers and cutting down their number ... to create an Institute of Literature, an Institute of Artistic Prospecting and Equipment, without whose diploma writers could not have the status of a writer and get published, by analogy with the Institutes of Mining Prospecting which equip the geologist for his work. This Institute, in qualifying a writer, should demand from him, beside the ability to write and general knowledge, moral good faith which characterizes the writer in his public work and his home life .... And if a writer makes a mistake (this also happens to geologists), his mistake will be an accident and a matter for regret rather than abuse. For, given the diploma of the Literary Prospecting Institute and the writer's honesty, there will be no doubt about the accidentally vexatious nature of the mistake. And the mistakes will be much fewer, although God alone is never mistaken because He does not exist. .. , while those who make most mistakes are the geologists because they discover things hitherto undiscovered and because they are not tourists who follow beaten paths. Tourist writers, in particular those who travel from Moscow to the Dneprostroy of Socialism in the mail coaches, dormeuses and railway carriages of

---

[5] *Stones and Roots*, 51. In the 1935 edition this and other similar passages were transposed from the third person to the first.

Tolstoy, Dostoyevsky and Bunin, travel like tourists and will never get anywhere.[6]

This amazing passage, which is a good specimen of Pilnyak's elaborately nonchalant manner (popularized at one time by Victor Shklovsky and going in part back to Rozanov), defies comment. The actual nature of Pilnyak's mistakes, factual and "political," which he made in 1926 and deemed it necessary to rectify in 1932, is immaterial. One is left wondering whether Pilnyak was making here an abject act of submission to whatever control the omnipotent Soviet state had chosen to exercise over him as a writer, or, like Slonimsky's hero, Boris Lavrov, merely electing "the best of all available unfreedoms," or simply pulling his readers' and censors' leg by piling up his subtle irrelevancies. The only possible way of commenting upon his unprecedented proposal is by juxtaposing it with the following extracts from Pilnyak's 1923 diary, published in lieu of a special article in the volume entitled *Writers About Art and About Themselves*:

> . . . I am not a Communist and therefore do not admit that I must be a Communist and write as a Communist, while I admit that the Communist power in Russia is determined, not by the will of the Communists, but by the historical destinies of Russia, and, inasmuch as I want to trace those destinies (as best as I can and as my conscience and my intellect prompt me), I am with the Communists, that is, inasmuch as the Communists are with Russia I am with them, too. . . . I admit that I am much less interested in the fate of the Russian Communist party than in the fate of Russia, the Russian Communist party being for me only a link in the history of Russia. I know that I must be absolutely objective, must not bring grist to anyone's mill, must not delude anyone, and I admit that I may be wrong in everything, but I also know that I cannot, nor know not how to, nor ever shall, write otherwise than I do, even if I wanted to do violence to myself. . . . In recent years our state has been setting up incubators for Party literature, providing them with food rations, and nothing came of it, or rather bad things came of it, for when these people touched art they stopped being politicians, without becoming artists. . . . Hence another conclusion: I believe that a writer must care only about his manuscripts, about their being *good,* and the honesty and validity of his Party-school-social membership card is his own personal business which has nothing to do with literature.[7]

6 *Ibid.,* 57–58.
7 *Writers About Art and About Themselves,* 83–85.

Pilnyak's pathetic attempts at adjusting himself included also *O-Kay* (1931). Described as an "American novel," it was really not a novel at all, but the usual Pilnyakian assortment of facts, impressions, and relevant and irrelevant reflections, all gleaned on his short visit to the United States. In the main it was a denunciation of capitalist America, one-sided and biased, and Pilnyak had no reason or occasion to refute it, although here and there his admiration for the achievements of American material civilization can be felt. This admiration did not, however, conflict with the Party line of the moment, for one of the popular slogans of the Five-Year Plan period was "Let us catch up and overtake America," and the stress was very much on technical progress.

The Zamyatin Incident

The incident with Zamyatin, which led to his resignation from the All-Russian Writers' Association, also happened in 1929. It was caused by the publication of his novel *We,* in a shortened Russian version, in the *émigré* magazine *Volya Rossii* (Prague). The publication was preceded by an editorial note explaining that the Russian version represented a retranslation from the Czech. Unlike Pilnyak, Zamyatin behaved in this incident with great dignity. He disclaimed all responsibility for the publication of this Russian version, and when the Writers' Association, yielding to the vociferous campaign launched in the Communist press, passed a vote of censure on him, he resigned his membership. In a letter he wrote to the Association he said that it was impossible for him "to belong to a literary organization which, albeit indirectly, takes part in the persecution of a fellow-member."[8]

But the campaign against Zamyatin, led by RAPP, continued; he was denounced as an "inside *émigré*" and reduced to silence. In 1931, somewhat unexpectedly (and probably not without Gorky's influence), he was allowed to leave the Soviet Union. He settled down in France where he died in 1937, after publishing the first part of his novel about Attila, *Bich Bozhy (The Scourge of God).* The posthumous edition of *We* in its original Russian form was about to appear in 1939, but the publication plans were upset by the outbreak of the war, and the book has not been published to this day. At the moment of writing there is some hope of its being serialized in a Russian periodical in New York.

The Campaign Against Voronskyism and the "Pereval" Group

The year 1930 was marked by violent attacks on all the more or less independent writers who failed to follow the Party line. One of the

8 For details see Eastman, *Artists in Uniform.*

most bitterly attacked groups was "Pereval" ("The Pass"). "Pereval"
came into existence in 1924 as a result of the secession of a number
of writers—mostly poets—belonging to the "Young Guard" group,
from "October." These younger writers disagreed with the anti-fellow
traveler policy of the leaders of "October" and went over to Voronsky's
Krasnaya Nov. The "Pereval" group later was joined by such older
writers as Prishvin, and by several peasant poets, including Klychkov.
Among its most talented younger members were Ivan Katayev (b. 1902,
no relation of Valentin) and Andrey Platonov (b. 1896). Its chief critics
were Lezhnev and Gorbov. For several years Voronsky was associated
with the group and supported its policy of *rapprochement* between
proletarian writers and fellow travelers. In fact the group itself represented an attempt to merge the two. In literature it advocated realism
and the Russian tradition of humanism. The peasant element was
strongly represented in it, but many of its members were good and
honest Communists and Marxists. The list of members of "Pereval,"
published in one of its collections (1930), included such an orthodox
Communist as Pavlenko, as well as such writers as Malyshkin, Amir
Sargidzhan, and Marianna Yakhontova, of whom the two latter acquired subsequently fame as historical novelists.

The campaign against Voronsky reached its climax in 1927, when
he was expelled from the Party and apparently banished to Siberia.[9]
In 1930, when Leopold Averbach, who had been responsible for Voronsky's downfall, was ruling dictatorially over Soviet literature, Voronsky
recanted. He was permitted to return to Moscow and readmitted to the
Party. After that he did not play any conspicuous part in Soviet literature; and in 1937 he "disappeared" again, this time for good. But
"Voronskyism" was constantly used as a term of abuse in the campaign
against "Pereval" and other nonconformists. It was identified with
"Bergsonian idealism," and the "Pereval" writers and critics were accused of "idealistic humanism," of "irrationalism," of subjectivism, of
betraying the principles of class war, of being soft to the class enemies,
and of supporting the *kulaks.* Among the works of the "Pereval" writers
singled out for attack was Ivan Katayev's novel *Moloko (Milk,* 1930).
Katayev was accused of approaching the class conflicts from a sentimental standpoint and of treating the class enemies too mildly and humane-
ly.

Throughout these years the "Pereval" stuck courageously to its
guns. At the height of Averbach's campaign against Voronsky in 1927
its members published their "Declaration," in which they stressed their
part in the Revolution and the fact that they had fought on its side in

---

[9] For an account of the 1927 campaign against Voronsky see McLean, "Voronskij
and VAPP," 199–200.

the Civil War. They also spoke of humanism and sincerity as the underlying principles of literature. In 1930 they reasserted these principles in a volume called *Rovesniki* (*Contemporaries*).

After 1930 "Pereval" virtually ceased to exist as an organized group, but its final self-liquidation did not come until 1932. Ever since, it has been described as "a reactionary phenomenon," and later its activities were linked up with those of the "Trotskyite" opposition. Several of its writers, including Ivan Katayev and Klychkov, disappeared from the literary scene. Some continued to appear in print individually but later were also banned from literature; while still others, like Golodny and Svetlov, recanted and were pardoned.

But there was no unity within the RAPP itself, and the charge of Voronskyism was readily used in inter-RAPP polemics. Thus, an article in *Pechat i Revolyutsiya* brought this charge against Libedinsky for his theory of "direct impressions"—for opposing art to science and saying that "direct impressions lie at the basis of art; they are the common link uniting the creator at the moment of creating a work of art and the perceiver at the moment of perception."[10] Similar charges were brought against such a hidebound RAPP stalwart as Ermilov, who had praised Libedinsky's new novel *Rozhdenie geroya* (*The Birth of a Hero*, 1930). This novel, which Ermilov and some other RAPP critics had described as "a model of proletarian literature," aroused a bitter controversy. It was written as a specific response to the demand for showing the "live" Soviet man. Libedinsky's hero was Shorokhov, a Communist commissar. The author showed him in his personal and family life (thus supplementing, as it were, his earlier novel *The Commissars*) with all his foibles and contradictions—with all the temptations, especially of the flesh, lurking in wait for him. In the end the author made him overcome these temptations and foibles: Shorokhov was "reborn" as a true proletarian hero, a living example to the men of the future. One RAPP critic described the novel as Freudian and characterized Shorokhov's experience as a fight with his libido. Calling Shorokhov "a newfangled Party Hamletkin," the critic wrote: "All Libedinsky's characters are pale and impotent shadows of reality, for whom the material world, class struggle, Socialist reconstruction in our country are merely the idealistic creation of self-developing shadows."[11]

Those who criticized Libedinsky's novel won the battle, and the author himself had to admit that it was one of his greatest failures, better to be forgotten.

10 See D. Tamarchenko and N. Tanin, "Napostovstvo ili voronshchina?" ("Onguardism or Voronskyism?"), in *Pechat i revolyutsiya*, No. 5–6 (1930), 40–47.

11 See A. Kamegulov, "Pismo tovarishcham" ("A Letter to Comrades"), *ibid.*, 29–40.

2. Olesha's Inner Dialogue

TO recount in all details the RAPP campaign of vituperation against all noncomformist writers and critics would be an impossible and dreary task. But the tragic plight of a talented Soviet author trying to preserve his artistic individuality and to reconcile his conception of literature with the demands of the "ruling class" on him may well be illustrated by the case of Yury Olesha.

The publication of Olesha's *Envy* in 1927 was hailed by nearly all Soviet critics as an event of great literary importance; even diehard proletarian critics from VAPP and RAPP joined in this chorus of praise. Particular enthusiasm was displayed by V. Ermilov, who missed Olesha's irony and chose to see in Andrey Babichev a portrait of a good Communist and of the new Soviet man. The fallacy of this view was soon exposed by more perspicacious critics. Ya. Chernyak, in an article in *Pechat i Revolyutsiya* (1928, V.), wrote that Communism would ultimately reject Babichev, although for the time being it still needed him and his model canteen. Lezhnev, in 1929, spoke of Babichev as "an Americanized businessman," while Polonsky called him a "parody" and said that he was as much of a bourgeois as his antipode Kavalerov. Polonsky continued to regard *Envy*, as a work of literature, very highly, and voiced the opinion that Olesha's artistic success in "objectivizing his own inner lyrical world" (this meant, of course, identifying Olesha with Kavalerov) implied "the possibility of conquering it."[12] Olesha's subsequent works, however, showed that he was obsessed by but one theme—and that an essentially individualistic one.

In his story "The Cherry Stone" (written in 1929), in which there are many allusions to his "controversy" with his age, Olesha compared art to wandering in an invisible country, "the country of attention and imagination." The wanderer is not alone, he is accompanied and held by the hand by two sisters: "One sister is called Attention, and the other, Imagination." There is also much that is revealing in Olesha's autobiographical fragments. In his very interesting "Zapiski pisatelya" ("Writer's Notes"), written in 1931 and included in the 1934 volume of his *Selected Works* (which also included *Envy*), Olesha speaks of the artist as a magic photographer who sees the world afresh and transforms it: "One must see the world in a new way. It is very good for a writer to engage in this kind of magic photography. This is not a trick, nothing to do with Expressionism. On the contrary, it is the purest, the healthiest Realism."

---

12 V. Polonsky, "Preodolenie zavisti" ("Overcoming of Envy"), in *Novy Mir* (*New World*), No. 5 (1929), 196. Later Olesha himself admitted this when he said: "Yes Kavalerov looked at the world with my eyes."

Two other autobiographical fragments, both written in 1928 and included in *The Cherry Stone*—"Ya smotryu v proshloye" ("I Look Into the Past") and "Chelovechesky material" ("Human Material")— showed that Olesha was anxious to overcome his individualism, to unburden himself of his "bourgeois" past, and to attune himself to the Revolution. In the latter he wrote:

> I seize myself in myself, I seize by the throat the me that wants to turn suddenly and stretch its hands toward the past. The me that thinks that the distance between us and Europe is but a geographical distance. The me that thinks that everything that is going on is only his life, unique and unrepeatable—*my* all-embracing life, the end of which cuts short all that exists outside me.
>
> I want to crush within me my second I, my third I, and all the I's that are crawling out of the past.
>
> I want to destroy all small feelings within me.
>
> If I cannot be an engineer of the elements, I want to be an engineer of human material.

In "I Look Into the Past," Olesha spoke of solitude, of "a lonely human destiny," and of "being alone everywhere and in everything." Such a lonely man, he said, is called a dreamer, people laugh at him and make him laugh, too, and then explain it by his being "worthless and officious," while he "walks on, lonely, his head drawn into his shoulders, and in his mind vanity, haughtiness, self-humiliation, contempt for human beings, alternating with tenderness, and thoughts about death produce a never-subsiding storm. It never breaks out of this sickly skull, the man tames it, drawing his head into his shoulders, but now and then he turns round to look at those who laughed, and they see then that the face which always made them laugh is bared in a dog's scowl." This tragic self-portrait of a lonely artist appeared in print when optimism and collective enthusiasm were the order of the day in Soviet literature, and it was no wonder that Soviet critics began to speak of Olesha's lack of harmony with "the great era of Socialism."

In 1931 appeared Olesha's play *Spisok blagodeyaniy* (*A List of Blessings*). Its dramatic structure had many weak points, but it was very interesting as a further development of the theme of loneliness and of other favorite motifs of Olesha's. Full of literary reminiscences and allusions (motifs from *Hamlet,* from Andersen's "The Ugly Duckling," and from Chaplin's films play an important part in it), it was quite unlike the contemporary run-of-the-mill Five-Year Plan plays, with their glorification of Socialist construction and their vilification of its enemies, the wreckers, and their sharp, black-and-white division of characters into heroes and villains. Olesha's play, with its Symbolist undercurrents and its close interweaving of personal and social motifs, reminded one rather of Ibsen.

The central figure of the play is a famous Soviet actress, Elena Goncharova. The play is divided into eight scenes. It begins with a prologue which shows the theater after a performance of *Hamlet*. The performance was followed by a post mortem, and now Goncharova, who played the title role, and who is about to leave for abroad, has to answer written questions. Her answers to some of them represent clues to certain problems, which Olesha then sets out to develop in dramatic form. One of the questions is: Why is *Hamlet*, this old foreign play, "written evidently for the intelligentsia" and which the working-class spectator cannot understand, being shown? Goncharova's answer is: "*Hamlet* is the best thing produced by the art of the past. So I believe. In all probability, *Hamlet* will never be shown to Russian audiences. I decided to show it to our country for the last time." To the question: "Why produce *Hamlet*? Are there no contemporary plays?" Goncharova answers: "Contemporary plays are schematic, false, devoid of fantasy, rectilinear." On the note which reads: "In the period of reconstruction, when everybody is seized by the frenzied tempo of building, it is disgusting to listen to your Hamlet's wearisome soul-searchings," Goncharova's comment is: "I believe that in the period of quick tempi an artist must think slowly." A more personal question, which runs: "You're a famous actress, you earn well. What do you miss then? Why on the photographs is there such a restless expression in your eyes?" elicits the following candid reply from Goncharova: "Because it is very difficult for me to be a citizen of the new world." One of the notes handed to her Goncharova tears up without reading. The last note contains a request to repeat the flute scene between Hamlet and Guildenstern. She accedes to it, and this gives Olesha an opportunity to state, in Shakespeare's words, his own artistic credo. When Goncharova recites Hamlet's answer to Guildenstern:

> Why, look you now, how unworthy a thing you make of me. You would play upon me; you would seem to know my stops; you would pluck out the heart of my mystery; you would sound me from my lowest note to the top of my compass; and there is much music, excellent voice in this little organ, yet cannot you make it speak. 'Sblood, do you think I am easier to be played on than a pipe? Call me what instrument you will, though you can fret me, you cannot play upon me,

it is Olesha himself who answers his epoch, his country, and its Guildensterns from the Communist party.

Just as Goncharova finishes the monologue, one more note falls on the stage at her feet. She picks it up and reads: "What was written in the note which you tore up? Answer honestly." She says that she was asked whether she would return from abroad and that her honest answer to that question is: "I shall."

Scene Two shows Goncharova and a friend of hers, Semyonova, also an actress, preparing a farewell party on the eve of Goncharova's departure for Paris. On the wall hangs a large portrait of Charlie Chaplin. Goncharova asks her friend to dust it from time to time, and then addresses the portrait:

—Chaplin, Chaplin! Little man in frayed trousers. I am going to see your famous films. Katya . . . I shall see "The Circus" and "The Gold Rush." The whole world went into raptures about them . . . Years have passed, and we still have not seen them . . . .

She visualizes herself arriving in Paris on a rainy day, when sidewalks, umbrellas, and capes will shine "in Maupassantish slush," and she will go to see and cry over a Chaplin film in some small Parisian cinema. Then she remembers a notebook she wants to entrust to her friend's care during her absence. She wonders whether she should not take it with her and sell it abroad. Semyonova thinks it must be her diary, the diary of an actress, but Goncharova corrects her: "No, it isn't the diary of an actress. It is the secret of the Russian intelligentsia . . . . The whole truth about the Soviet world." Goncharova shows her friend the book and explains:

—Look, the book is divided into two halves. Two lists. Here is the first half: a list of crimes of the Revolution.

To which Semyonova advises her to hide the book away, but Goncharova retorts:

—Don't be afraid. You think, these are crude complaints about the shortage of provisions? Don't be afraid, it's something different. I speak about the crimes against personality. There are many things in the policy of our government which I cannot put up with. Come here. Look: here, on the other side is a list of blessings. You think I can't see and understand the blessings of the Soviet government? Now let us put the two halves together. This will be me. You see? It is my anxiety, my ravings. Two halves of one conscience, a confusion which drives me crazy. I'll hide it in this suitcase. It mustn't be left here. Anything may happen. Someone will find it. Awful. They'll interpret it in a vulgar way, they'll say: a counterrevolutionary!

"Why not really sell it abroad?" suggests Semyonova. Goncharova is indignant.

—What? Tear off one half? Only the crimes. For abroad they won't pay a penny for a list of blessings of the Soviet government. Show only the items of malice and pass over in silence the items of enthusiasm? No. This notebook cannot be torn. I am not a counter-revolutionary. I am a creature of the old world who is arguing with herself.

The scene ends with the appearance of the director of the theater and a young man who brings Goncharova a large bouquet from workers as a token of gratitude for her acting. Goncharova asks the young man to thank them and tell them that she would soon be back and that she is proud to be an actress in the land of the Soviets.

In the next scene the action switches to Paris and becomes rather melodramatic. Paris is shown as a city of contrasts, typical of the crisis that eats away at the heart of capitalist Europe—of luxury and pleasure-hunting, on the one hand, and poverty and unemployment, on the other. The contrast is symbolized in the International Artists' Ball, or-ganized by the banker Lepelletier as a diversion amidst the economic slump, and a demonstration of the unemployed that is being prepared simultaneously. Goncharova, the famous Soviet actress, is expected to appear at the ball. She is tempted to buy on credit a beautiful even-ing dress from a Russian *émigré* dressmaker; and a White Russian journalist, who discovers by chance and steals her secret notebook with its two lists, publishes in his paper her list of crimes of the Soviet gov-ernment, alleging that Goncharova sold it to him for four thousand francs (the price of the evening dress). In support of this allegation he produces Goncharova's receipt written on the back of the newspaper's letterhead paper. This receipt he sends, together with the notebook, to the Soviet Embassy, and some Soviet officials whom Goncharova meets in Paris believe the whole story and treat her as a traitor. There is also a grotesquely improbable scene between Goncharova and Mar-geret, the director of a French music hall in which she hopes to appear in the flute scene from *Hamlet* and thus earn the money she owes for the dress. The whole dialogue between them is at cross-purposes. Mar-geret has no use for the scene from *Hamlet*. Thinking that Goncharova is a flautist he suggests that she should appear as a special attraction on the program. She will begin by playing a minuet on the flute, then will swallow the flute. The audience will gasp. "Then you will turn your back to the audience and it will appear that the flute is sticking out from a place from which flutes never do. This will be all the more piquant since you're a woman . . . . Then you will begin to blow on the flute from the other end, so to speak—and this time not a minuet, but something jollier." The scene ends with Goncharova leaving the theater alone, depressed and humiliated, and soliloquizing:

—I want to go home . . . My friends, where are you? . . . My youth . . . I wanted to sell my youth . . . I dreamed of you, Paris. I sought your fame . . . how could I have forgotten that there is no greater fame than the fame of those who rebuild the world . . . . I want to go home . . . . My country, I want to hear the noise of your discussions. Workman, it is now only that I understand your wisdom and your generosity, your face turned toward the starry sky of science. I looked askance at you and I was afraid of you as a foolish bird is afraid of the one who feeds it . . . Forgive me, Land of the Soviets, I am going back to you . . . I don't want to go to the ball . . . I want to go home . . . I want to stand in a food line and cry.

In the street she meets a lamplighter and a man who turns out to be a workman dismissed by Margeret. She gives him some money. When she is gone and the lamplighter has lit the street lamp, the other man turns out to be a perfect likeness of Chaplin—with his shock of hair, his moustache, his bowler, his big boots, and his cane.

The play ends on a rather shrill, melodramatic note with Goncharova's death in an attempt to protect a Communist leader of the unemployed from the police. She is killed by a crazy Russian *émigré* who was hired to assassinate the Communist leader.

As a drama the play has many weak points, while, ideologically speaking, it lacks consistency, and the symbolic ending is rather artificial. However, the very fact that Olesha uses the method of symbolic realism is significant. But the main interest lies in those bits of dialogue in which Olesha carries on the argument with himself. One of the most important passages is a conversation between Goncharova and Fedotov, a Soviet trade official who is on his way home from the United States. Fedotov asks her what she does in Paris. She says she spends her time just walking about, and then goes on:

Sometimes I stop and look. I see my shadow lying. I gaze at it and I think: my shadow is lying on the stones of Europe. I live in a new world. Now tears well up in my eyes when I see my shadow on the stones of the old world. I recall my personal existence in the world which you call new. What did it consist of? Only of thinking. The Revolution deprived me of the past and did not show me the future. So my thoughts became my present. To think. Think. I did nothing but think—with my thought I wanted to grasp what I could not grasp with my sensations. A human life is natural only when thoughts and sensations are in harmony. I was shorn of that harmony, and therefore my life in the new world was unnatural. With my thought I fully grasped the idea of Communism. With my brain I believed that the triumph of the proletariat was natural and lawful. But my feelings spoke against it. I was torn asunder. I fled here from this double life—had I not done so I would have gone crazy. In the new world I was like a broken sliver of glass of my country. Now I have come back, and the two halves have been joined together. I live a natural life, I have recovered the present tense verbs. I eat, I touch, I look, I walk . . . . A speckle of dust of the old world, I am deposited on the stones of Europe. They are ancient, mighty stones. They were laid down by the Romans. No one will move them.

To which Fedotov replies with true Communist fervor:

They will soon be wrenched out of the ground, and barricades will be built of them.

He is indignant when Goncharova tells him that for three weeks she has been resting from thoughts of the Revolution and that it is natural for a human being to think about his or her own self. When Fedotov denounces this as "a man-in-the-street's attitude," Goncharova corrects him: "In other words, human." I am an actress, she says, and

an actress becomes great only when she gives flesh to a democratic theme, which everybody understands and by which everybody is moved.

When Fedotov retorts that Socialism is such a theme, she disagrees, and to his question: "What is, then?" replies:

The theme of a lonely human destiny. Chaplin's theme. An ugly man wants to be beautiful. A beggar wants to be rich. A lazy man wants to receive a legacy. A mother wants to join her son.

There is hardly any doubt that much of what Goncharova says reflects Olesha's own innermost thoughts. It is he who suffers from the dichotomy of thoughts and feelings, he who yearns for a "democratic theme" by which all would be moved. This was understood by many Soviet critics and more or less admitted by Olesha himself.

There is also much that is interesting in what Tatarov, the White Russian journalist, says of Goncharova:

She was allowed a great deal. She produced *Hamlet*. Think only: *Hamlet* in a country where art has been reduced to the status of propaganda for pig-breeding, for digging silage pits. . . . And yet

... her most ardent desire was to flee here. ... Through her ... I shall prove once again, and most convincingly, that there is slavery in Russia. There has been talk of it throughout the world. But what does the world hear? It hears the grievances of lumberjacks, the obscure bellowing of slaves who can neither think nor shout. And now I can extract a complaint from a highly-talented creature .... A famous actress from the country of slaves will shout to the world: Don't, don't believe my fame! It was a price paid for my refusal to think. Don't believe my freedom; I was, after all, a slave.

This passionate denunciation of Soviet slavery is put, of course, into the mouth of an enemy, of one of the villains of the play, but it has a ring of sincerity.

On the face of it, the play was a denunciation of the old decadent bourgeois world which Goncharova (just as Kavalerov) had idealized from afar: at contact with it she experienced a change of heart. For her list of crimes of the Soviet government she substituted a list of the crimes of capitalism. And Olesha made her into a tragic victim who, by her death on the ancient stones of Europe, expiates her temporary betrayal of the new world. But subsequent events showed that for Olesha himself the tragic dilemma was by no means solved, and the inner dialogue went on.

In 1932 the magazine *30 Days* published a short piece by Olesha entitled "Something from the Secret Notebooks of the Fellow Traveler Sand."[13]

Modest Sand, a Soviet writer, a fellow traveler, is obviously Olesha's alter ego, and the whole piece must be (and was) taken as a barely disguised personal confession. Sand-Olesha begins by saying that he is very fond of looking at himself in a mirror, that while some men never even dream of doing it, he would not miss a cupboard with a looking glass that was being loaded on to a furniture van.

This introduction sets the appropriate note of extreme individualism and introspection. Sand continues then:

When you think that you are a writer and that you live in an epoch when a new class is rising, and when you begin to check yourself, to look around, to weigh up what you have done, it becomes clear that your doings, which at moments seem to you so important, are in fact extremely insignificant by comparison with the majestic character of all that forms the history of these years and days.

13 "Koe-chto iz sekretnykh zapisey poputchika Zanda," in *30 dney*, No. 1 (1932), 11–17. I have chosen the spelling "Sand" in English because of a reference there is to George Sand.

Sand mentions a picture at which he likes to look. It shows Schiller being given a triumphant ovation by the people after the first perform-ance of his *Kabale und Liebe*:

> It is the rising class greeting its poet . . . . I am a poet, too. How can I help dreaming about my own *Intrigue and Love*—about a new drama which would shake the proletariat just as once upon a time Schiller's drama shook the burghers? How can I not dream about strength? Not to crave passionately, to the point of howling, to the point of tears, for strength which a writer must have when a new class rises?

Quoting Benvenuto Cellini's words about his envy of other masters, Sand speaks of his "noble envy" of several writers: of Jack London ("I could write equally fine things, since life itself, by creating such circum-stances, favors me in this"); of Balzac ("The wizard who sees the way all the people around him live, what they want, and what they think"); of Pushkin ("He should be envied more than anybody, because when he was twenty-four, he wrote *Boris Godunov*, a tragedy . . . which at-tains such perfection as has not existed either before or after him"). There is also Tolstoy, says Sand, but one cannot envy him, "because he just *was*, as natural phenomena are—stars or waterfalls," and he chose the mightiest adversaries to fight, before whom the rest of man-kind lay prostrate: Napoleon, Death, Christianity, Art, and Life itself, since he wrote *The Kreutzer Sonata*. "Envy and ambition are forces that aid creation," says Sand. He describes then his friend Kolotilov, a strong man, a scientist.

> I think, for instance, that art is the chief thing in life. Like the sky it envelops my life. But Kolotilov asserts that life is vast, and that art is only part of it, just as his science is.

That man is strong, continues Olesha, whose attention is focused on the outer world. For Kolotilov this outer world is experiment, matter.

> While for me, a writer, this outer world is the epic. Yes, yes, the epic! To portray events, characters, passions—to be outside.
> Passions? But how can I portray another man's passion without inoculating myself with its germ? If I wish to portray greediness or something else . . . I must stir up in myself, pull out, and straighten out the sprout of that passion! The sprout, unless it is already flowering in me! And in stirring it up I shall set in motion all the others—all the tissues of my mind. So it means again turn-ing the attention to oneself, to the inner world. That's what it is. My very profession—the profession of the writer—is such that my attention cannot belong to the outer world alone . . . .

Sand-Olesha states here his dilemma with the utmost clarity and candor and exclaims passionately: "I don't want to be a writer." Then he makes a vow:

> Never to look in a mirror! Never! To get away from the miserable, infantile habit of scrutinizing oneself. It is a characteristic of the weak. A child in a bathtub examines its hands, its feet, its little body . . . .
> I want to cross out of my consciousness everything that bespeaks weakness. I want to become completely re-educated.[14]

At the end of his "Notes" Sand introduces his friend Bazilevich, a Bolshevik newspaper editor. Sand tells him of the difficulty of being a writer, of his "lofty desires" and his "agonizing perplexity." Bazilevich does not look long for an answer. "You must merge yourself with the life of the masses," he says. Sand comments upon this answer:

> An official phrase . . . . But he utters this phrase with living conviction. Then, if a phrase is official, it does not mean yet that it is not an expression of life. I exclaim that I want to write a new *Intrigue and Love*. It is a highsounding phrase. But I utter it with living conviction, and this phrase is part of my life . . . . A highsounding phrase is then also an expression of life. And these two phrases meet.

The fragment ends with a variation of Bazilevich's phrase: "You must fuse with the masses!"

In the same number of *30 Days* was published a Communist critic's reply to Olesha.[15] He accused Sand of "slandering history" by implying that it used to be more lenient and that now it "oppressed and debased man." Sand was also slandering his country and depreciating that "majestic something which constitutes the history of these years and days." He demanded the right to utter highsounding phrases—"*Any* highsounding phrases!" exclaimed the critic indignantly. In his opinion the whole thing was "quite simple": instead of repeating after Bazilevich that "You must fuse with the masses," Sand should say "*I* must fuse with the masses."

Olesha's dialogue with himself was now brought into the open, and the same magazine printed an "Open Letter" which a workers' literary group addressed to him. They wrote:

> . . . Instead of helping us, you are actually hindering us. You sow panic. You raise alarm. Instead of joining the proletariat in the

14 In Russian the word *perestroitsya* is used—literally, "to reconstruct oneself."
15 I. Bachelis, "Nash otvet poputchiku Zandu" ("Our Answer to the Fellow Traveler Sand"), in *30 dney*, No. 1 (1932), 18–20.

depiction of the petty bourgeoisie, you share the attitude of Sand, you pull out of yourself the "sprouts" of his passions and "straighten them out" in yourself. . . . In your works, comrade Olesha, there is still no working class, you have not shown our production . . . . You are now concerned with problems of art and of fellow-traveling . . . . You stand before a mirror, consumed by Benvenuto Cellini's "noble envy."[16]

Two months later Olesha published his reply to this letter. It was entitled "The Necessity of Re-educating Myself Is Clear to Me."[17] Here are the salient points from this candid and courageous statement:

> In the course of years themes grow and develop inside the writer. Suddenly, one fine day, he sees that the themes which were his life are not wanted. This is a monstrous shock to him. One theme turns out to be unwanted, another untimely, still another reactionary or demobilizing, and so on.

The writer deletes those themes from his notebook, but this is really no solution:

> A deleted theme can rise and stand athwart the brain. A graveyard of themes arises. They rot—these individualistic corpses—and poison the brain. They cannot be brought out . . . .
>
> Half the talent consists of memories. And what is a memory? It includes the philosophy I read, under the influence of which I was brought up—I who was born into the world of private property . . . . One must accumulate new memories, . . . learn to know the workman as I know Sand . . . . This cannot be done all at once . . . . I realize clearly the necessity of re-educating myself. But I am first of all a writer. In other words, imagination has a great power over me. I am even ill with the elephantiasis of imagination, that is, hyperbolism . . . . Do not identify me with Sand. He is only one half of my memories. The other half began to be accumulated by Zubilo.[18] I am still young, there is plenty of time ahead of me, many victories . . . . I know that I shall reach this future . . . along my own ways but I shall reach it . . . . And there is nothing more important for an artist than his own ways.

But this was precisely what the Communist supervisors of litera-

---

[16] "Otkrytoe pismo rabochego litkruzhka 'Dvoretsstroya' pisatelyu Yuriyu Oleshe," ("Open Letter of the Workers' Literary Group of 'Dvoretsstroy' to the Writer Yury Olesha"), in *30 dney*, No. 3 (1932), 63–64.

[17] "Neobkhodimost perestroyki mne yasna: Otvet Yuriya Oleshi litkruzhku Dvoretsstroya," in *30 dney*, No. 5 (1932), 67–68.

[18] This was Olesha's pen name when he wrote satirical verse for *Gudok*. At that time he enjoyed a great success with his numerous working-class readers.

ture would not grant Olesha. They wanted him to follow their ways. The editors of *30 Days* prefaced Olesha's confession with a statement that, while admitting the necessity of re-education, he continued "to think and feel along the old lines." They expressed the hope that the tempo of Olesha's "re-education" would be speeded up by this discussion.

In the next number the same magazine published a scene from Olesha's new play *Chorny chelovek* (*The Black Man*), the hero of which was to be Modest Sand, the author of the "Secret Notebooks." In a short note Olesha explained the idea of the play. Sand dreams of becoming the writer of the ruling class. To attune himself to his epoch he must reject a number of themes, themes that may be wonderful in themselves but are "not wanted for our times" or are even harmful— "reactionary, pessimistic, demagnetizing." A writer must delete such themes from his notebook. But this is not a solution, for, cast out of the writer's notebook, the theme will dwell in his brain and interfere with his creative effort:

Driven in, it will twist itself and crawl out onto the paper.

If Sand tackles a new, great, living, joyful, "sunny" theme, that black lizard of a theme will nevertheless, one way or another, thrust out its stinking tail or its venomous head through his new work . . . . How is one to kill the lizard theme? . . . The severed parts of the lizard's body will grow again. There are many such themes, a whole nest of poisonous lizards.

Olesha's Sand is obsessed by the theme of murder. He wants to kill a man and does so in a dream. To rid himself of that obsession he decides to consult the Black Man, a graphologist and chiromantist ("a cynic, a quack, a poisoner," adds Olesha). This symbolic character was to be, according to Olesha, a synthetic parody of Freud, Spengler, and Bergson, and of their ideas, a caricature of decadent European thinkers, "a parody of those who write today about the doom of progress and the end of mankind which lies prostrate at the feet of machines." The idea of the play was to show Sand's clash with the Black Man— "the conflict of the idea of death in creation with the idea of rebuilding the world through creation." Whether the play was ever finished or not, no more of it was published, and Olesha's inner dialogue went on in silence.[19] We shall return to its last stages later.

[19] In an article about Olesha's art, this play is spoken of as "unfinished." See Lev Levin, "Tema odinokoy sudby" ("The Theme of Lonely Destiny"), in *Literaturny sovremennik* (*Literary Contemporary*), No. 7 (1933), 119–42. In this article, written a year after the above discussion, the author, after analyzing Olesha's obsession with his "lizard themes," comes to the conclusion that Olesha has not yet rid himself of them, and advises him to "open the window" and let in "the fresh wind of real life." Levin was later accused of "Trotskyism."

3. *Some Five-Year Plan Novels*

A MONG the outstanding Five-Year Plan novels, apart from Pilnyak's *Volga,* were those of Leonov, Katayev, and Sholokhov.

In Leonov's *Sot* (1931), the Five-Year Plan forms the background of the story which deals with the construction of a huge paper mill on a small river among the dense forests of northeastern Russia, in a remote, out-of-the-way country, barely touched by civilization and preserving its old way of life. In carrying out their industrial project the Communists come up against the resistance not only of nature but also of the forces representing the old world. As in his earlier works, it is in this conflict between the old and the new that Leonov is primarily interested. The old is represented by three main elements. First, there is the large mass of conservative peasants who instinctively stick to the old and fear the new. They are supported and inspired by the monks from a neighboring forest hermitage, who represent the force of religion and superstition and its sway over the peasant mass. Finally, there are some individual enemies of the Soviet regime who are engaged in deliberate sabotage.

Among the monks Leonov places a young man, Vissarion by name, a former officer of the White Army. He is an active ideological enemy of Communism, with strange and confused ideas of his own. He preaches the coming of a new Attila, the destruction of modern mechanistic civilization, and the resurrection of the "human soul." The reader cannot help feeling that to some extent Leonov sympathizes with these ideas, that they echo the anti-urban utterances of Semyon in *The Badgers* and of Zavarikhin in *The Thief.*

The principal Communist in the novel, Uvadyev, combines belief in reason with revolutionary instincts. "Everything is all right," he says, "everything is always all right in the world, but there are still some things in it that need blowing up."

Among the several types of technical specialists in the novel the most interesting is the old engineer Burago, a man of great culture and intelligence who loyally serves the new government but is far from sharing its ideology. The worm of culture is eating away at his heart. But he believes in Russia as a country where anything is possible (Gorky's formula, which many fellow travelers used to justify their acceptance of the Revolution). Another engineer, Renne, is shown as a selfish, narrowminded enemy of Communism, a saboteur, whose only aim is to wreck the construction.

In the end, Socialism triumphs—all technical and political obstacles are surmounted, Vissarion is murdered, and Renne commits suicide when he realizes that his plans of sabotage have failed. But Leonov is interested not so much in showing the technical success of the Five-Year Plan project as in depicting a tense social conflict, against the background of which he weaves a complex pattern of individual psychology.

Leonov's second Five-Year Plan novel, *Skutarevsky* (1932), has a much more primitive pattern. The "social command" is more clearly felt in it, and the plot has a touch of melodrama. Leonov introduced into it the fashionable element of industrial sabotage organized from abroad. Its topical character was further emphasized by the fact that Leonov chose for the subject of his novel the wrecking activities in electrical industry—at the moment when the famous trial of British engineers in Moscow was taking place. Again, however, Leonov is primarily interested in the psychological conflict. There is the inevitable element of family opposition. The hero of the novel is Professor Skutarevsky, an old man of pre-Revolutionary training and an international celebrity in the field of electricity. The saboteurs include his son.

Skutarevsky's proletarian origins are duly emphasized. He is not a Communist but is vaguely in sympathy with the new regime and works for it as the head of the Institute of High Frequencies, which has been created at Lenin's personal wish and which is now engaged in secret research work. But Skutarevsky's mentality is on the whole alien to the official Communist ideology (though he is not quite so much of a "fossil" as Pilnyak's Professor Poletika), and Leonov's main purpose is to show how he gradually but inevitably rallies to it and even joins the Party. His ideological transformation is closely interwoven with the events of his personal life—the discovery of his son's implication in the sabotage plot, and his own strange and abortive love affair with a young Communist. But as is often the case with Leonov, the novel ends abruptly at the moment when Skutarevsky is about to turn over a new leaf in life.

Katayev's *Vremya, vperyod!* (*Forward, Oh Time!*) is a more genuine Five-Year Plan novel, concerned primarily with production processes, and not with social and individual psychology. Instead of inventing a fictitious setting, Katayev described one of the real industrial projects, the gigantic coke-chemical combine at Magnitogorsk. This element of reality was introduced deliberately—Katayev even called his novel "a chronicle." Where in Pilnyak's *Volga* the wall newspaper was merely a literary trick (similar to those which the *avant-garde* painters before World War I used when they introduced into their pictures three-dimensional objects), the insertion by Katayev of a long article from one of the Soviet papers about the production of high-grade concrete has a different function, and the article is in all probability authentic. Generally speaking, purely technical matter plays a large part in Katayev's novel.

Some Five-Year Plan Novels

Forward, Oh Time! differs also from Pilnyak's and Leonov's novels in that it is imbued with real enthusiasm for Socialist reconstruction, with that somewhat naïve Americanism, that cult of machinery bordering on fetichism which was characteristic of Russian Communism at the time. While Pilnyak and Leonov were concerned primarily with human beings and their intellectual and emotional problems, in Katayev's novel purely technical problems play the major part in the plot. The subject is the breaking of the world record for concrete-mixing by an enthusiastic brigade of Magnitogorsk workers. The action of the novel takes place all in one day. Round this subject Katayev has strung a number of diverse characters, drawn vividly but superficially, without any attempt at deep psychological probing. The description of how the brigade of a certain Ishchenko, under the supervision of the young Communist engineer Margulies, breaks the record set by the workers of Kharkov, is vivid and dynamic.

The whole novel, with its quick cinematographic tempo, its rapidly shifting scenes, bears traces of the influence of John Dos Passos, who at the time enjoyed great popularity in the Soviet Union and was regarded as a revolutionary, not only ideologically, but also technically speaking. The saboteurs, who had become almost a fixture in the Five-Year Plan literature, are absent from Katayev's novel, and this in itself is a refreshing feature. By comparison with Pilnyak and Leonov, the general tendency of Katayev's theme is much more optimistic. There is no hint of the sharp cleavage between the old and the new in the Soviet Union. It is significant that to the enthusiasm and zeal of his 100 per cent Communists Katayev opposes the philosophy of an American industrial magnate who visits Magnitogorsk as a guest and tourist. The magnate lacks faith precisely in that in which the Russian Communists have come to believe with the zeal of converts—in the power of machinery, in mechanized civilization. For him the salvation of mankind lies in a return to God and Nature. The American capitalist does not sound very convincing, but it is perhaps on purpose that Katayev put those unpopular ideas into the mouth of a foreigner and a capitalist. Among his Russians the skeptical note is sounded only by the old engineer Nalbandov, but he is just an opportunist, who easily adjusts himself to all conditions and circumstances, and not an active enemy of Communism. Only one of the workers, Sayenko, a drunkard and a gambler, is shown as a negative character and a real counterrevolutionary; all the rest are full of Socialist enthusiasm and willing to sacrifice their interests to the common cause. Occasionally there is a slight touch of satire, but there is a great difference between this novel and *The Embezzlers* or Katayev's satirical plays, and one feels that Katayev must have deliberately blunted the point of his satire. The satirical ele-

233

ment is particularly conspicuous in the conversations between the American millionaire and Nalbandov, where the author treads on safe ground.

Another aspect of the Five-Year Plan is depicted in Sholokhov's long novel *Podnyataya tselina* (*Virgin Soil Upturned*), the first volume of which appeared in 1931. Written in a more simple, less picturesque style than his vast Cossack epic, it gives a striking and powerful picture of forcible collectivization of agriculture among the Don Cossacks, and of the Cossacks' overt and covert resistance to it—when they hid their stocks of grain, slaughtered their cattle, and so on. As a work of literature this novel may be inferior to *The Quiet Don*, but its interest and value as a social document are unquestionable. It is written with the maximum possible objectivity. There is nothing of Katayev's light-hearted optimism in it. The tragedy of the dispossessed peasants, the conflict between their inborn proprietary instincts and the doctrine of Communism, and the harsh process of so-called "de-kulakization," are shown in all their stark reality and acuteness. Most of the characters are Cossacks, and there are many finely-drawn portraits of various types. The only outsider is Davydov, a workman from Leningrad, whom the Party sends to supervise and speed up the collectivization campaign and who becomes involved in sharp clashes with the Cossacks. It has been rightly said that this novel of Sholokhov's does more to help understand the realities of collectivization than all official Soviet literature on the subject put together.

A more orthodox treatment of this subject we find in *Bruski*, a long novel by Fyodor Vasilievich Panfyorov (b. 1896), the first two volumes of which appeared in 1930. Its success at first was enormous; it had very large sales, and the Soviet press was almost unanimous in praising it. Several literary groups claimed Panfyorov as their spokesman. Officially, he stood closest to Libedinsky's "On Literary Guard" and was regarded as a true proletarian writer.

Bruski is a long, rather tedious, and almost plotless novel with a multitude of characters (most of whom fail to come to life) and a strong political bias, since one of the main objects of the author was to demonstrate the advantages of collective farming over individual tenure of land. The novel takes its title from the name of an estate somewhere on the Volga. Its owner died before the Revolution and it was on the point of passing into the hands of a rich peasant, a *kulak*, when the Revolution occurred. It was then seized by the village poor, who eventually turned it into a collective farm. The hero is a certain Kiril Zhdarkin. Demobilized after the war, he returns to his native village and is struck by the poverty and ignorance of his fellow villagers. He takes to his farming with great zest, but gradually comes to realize that if he limits his interests to it, he will himself degenerate into a *kulak*. He gives up his farm, goes to the city, and becomes a factory worker. Here the truth dawns on him, and he understands that the only salvation for the peasants lies in doing away with individual ownership of land and organizing farming on collective lines. Returning to his village, Zhdarkin organizes a commune in Bruski.

Although biased, the novel is not grossly one-sided and is of some documentary value: it portrays minutely and faithfully the class conflicts and differentiation among peasants. But its value as a work of art is insignificant. Speaking of the third volume, then still in preparation, Panfyorov said somewhat defiantly that he had more to learn from technical works on peat industry than from Tolstoy or Dostoyevsky. Panfyorov's artistic shortcomings were from the very first realized by some critics, but this did not prevent them from proclaiming his novel a classic of Soviet literature. But *habent sua fata libelli,* and a few years later, during the campaign for raising the standard of Soviet literature (of which more will be said in the next chapter), Panfyorov's novel became one of the principal targets for attack. The signal was given by Gorky, who singled out *Bruski* as a glaring example of the low standard of craftsmanship and language in contemporary Soviet literature. A controversy ensued in which Gorky was opposed by Serafimovich and several others, but the great majority of Soviet writers and critics sided with Gorky, and a veritable hurricane of criticism and even abuse was unleashed against Panfyorov and his novel.

Among the novels dealing with the industrial aspects of the Five-Year Plan may be mentioned also Gladkov's *Energiya (Power)* and Shaginyan's *Gidrotsentral (Hydrocentral)*, both describing, at great length and with minute detail, vast construction projects.

There were also numerous Five-Year Plan plays, all of them built more or less on the same pattern—with good, honest Communists for heroes, and spies, wreckers, and saboteurs for villains. All had the inevitable happy ending, the villains being unmasked and duly punished. Of these plays, Kirshon's *Bread* and some others enjoyed a considerable but ephemeral success.

In poetry, too, the Five-Year Plan subjects were exploited by Bezymensky, Selvinsky, Aseyev, Kirsanov, and other poets.

But the end of the RAPP period in literature came about soon in a sudden and spectacular fashion.

235

V. Literature in the Doldrums
1932-41

1. The "Reform" of 1932

THE reversal of literary policy came as a bolt from the blue on April 23, 1932, when the Central Committee of the Communist party took what was almost immediately described as its "historic" decision. In substance it meant the disbanding of all proletarian (and other) literary organizations and the creation, in their place, of a single Union of Soviet Writers. This step was motivated by the "achievements of Socialist reconstruction," which made the existence of separate proletarian literary and artistic organizations superfluous. The Party decided that, having succeeded in breaking in literature and subordinating it to its plan, it had achieved a sufficient degree of homogeneity which could be maintained in future. This reversal of policy meant doing away with the very conception of fellow travelers. For some time the more moderate among the Communist writers and critics had been insisting that it was wrong to lump all fellow travelers together—that those who were known under this name could really be divided into two main groups: (1) enemies of the Revolution, whether open or disguised, and (2) its allies. This was in substance the point of view advocated from the very first by Voronsky; and just as, on the political and economic plane, Stalin, after denouncing Trotsky's views and disposing of him, adopted much of the policy championed by him, so now, on the literary plane, much of the denounced and abused "Voronskyism" was actually carried into practice. The majority of the fellow travelers were raised to the rank of full-fledged allies. Averbach and his followers were completely disavowed, their policy was declared harmful, and those who had suffered in silence from the mailed fist of their dictatorship felt now free to attack them and heap abuse on them: Soviet newspapers and magazines for the latter part of 1932 are full of violent denunciations of "Averbachism." It was only later, however, that Averbach's activities were officially connected with those of the enemies of the Soviet regime, the Trotskyites and "Fascist agents," and Averbach's literary dictatorship presented in a new light as part of a subtle Machiavellian plot against the very foundations of the Soviet state and its internal and external security. What happened to Averbach personally is not known for certain: officially his name did not figure in any of the opposition purges.

The 1932 resolution of the Central Committee did not explicitly denounce the literature of the Five-Year Plan period. On the contrary, it emphasized that in the past few years literature and art in the Soviet Union had grown, both quantitatively and qualitatively speaking, and this growth was ascribed to the successes of Socialist reconstruction. The resolution recalled how, a few years earlier, when "alien elements" were still active in Soviet literature and proletarian literature was still weak, the Party had helped, by every means in its power, in the fostering of special proletarian organizations. "But now"—went on the resolution—"that the rank-and-file of proletarian literature has had time to grow and assert itself and that new writers have emerged from factories, plants, and collective farms, the framework of the existing proletarian literary and artistic organizations is becoming too narrow and hinders the proper development of artistic work." There was a danger, therefore, of these organizations being turned into a means of cultivating exclusive coteries and of diverting a large body of writers and artists from contemporary political problems. It can be seen, then, that behind the Central Committee's "historic" decision lay not so much the concern for the writers' and artists' freedom as the realization that Averbach's tactics of dictatorial regimentation of art was not bringing fruit, and that other methods had to be tried to ensure that literature should follow the Party line, without at the same time impairing its quality.

An important role in this reversal of policy was played by Gorky. He was one of the first to draw attention to the noticeable lowering of literary standards after 1929. In his campaign for raising the standard of literature he was supported by the most talented among the Communist writers, such as Sholokhov and Fadeyev. After the passing of the 1932 resolution, Gorky's voice in all literary matters became particularly authoritative, and more than ever he came to be looked upon as the *doyen* of Soviet letters.

From the practical point of view, the most important part of the 1932 resolution of the Central Committee was that which decreed the creation of a single Union of Soviet Writers. This step was designed primarily to put an end to factional squabbles and to create a body that would be more or less homogeneous, held together by officially approved bylaws and hence more easily controllable. The Union was to comprise all Soviet writers who accepted the general policy of the Soviet government, supported Socialist reconstruction, and adhered in their work to the method of Socialist realism. This last restriction was the most important. However ill-defined may have been this method (as we

237

shall see below), its use circumscribed the writer's scope by imposing on him the obligation to deal in his work with "Socialist realities." By the very fact of adhering to the Union of Soviet Writers—and this, though formally a voluntary act, was too closely bound up with all sorts of material and other advantages to be really regarded as such—a Soviet writer limited, of his own accord, the range of his creative work and agreed to serve the Soviet state and its ultimate policies in his capacity as a writer. In a way, this meant going back on the amount of freedom which the famous resolution of 1925 accorded to those who were then termed fellow travelers; not to speak of the earlier period of more or less spontaneous literary creation, when such a document as the manifesto of the Serapion Brothers, proclaiming that literature need not reflect the epoch and that a writer had a right to be politically detached, was still conceivable. Henceforth it was enough to prove that a work of literature (or any other work of art, for that matter) was incompatible with the spirit of Socialist realism—that it contained a slight admixture of "poisonous idealism," or "formalism"—to place it outside the pale of Soviet literature. This, a priori, imposed on the writers a great circumspection in their choice of themes and their treatment of them. The political factor remained decisive, and although writers were no longer expected to write purely industrial or political novels, they were expected to adhere to Socialist realism or face ostracism. The Union of Soviet Writers was thus a typical by-product of totalitarian regime; it was not an ordinary professional organization, for all its members were not only obliged to subscribe to a definite political program, but were also tied down to a specific literary method.

Since one of the principal objects of the 1932 reform was to ensure homogeneity in Soviet literature—or, in other words, complete compliance of the writers with the demands made on them by the Party—considerable importance attaches to the Literary Institute which was created as an adjunct to the Union of Soviet Writers. Its function was to train and indoctrinate young Soviet writers. Many of the younger writers now active in Soviet literature (Simonov, Aliger, and others) studied at this Institute, of which Gorky was the principal sponsor. After Gorky's death there was some question of abolishing it, but, as one of its former students—now in the United States—has informed the present writer, it was "saved" through the personal intervention of Stalin.

2. Socialist Realism: Theory

THE statute of the Union of Soviet Writers provided that all its members should apply in their work the method of Socialist realism. As with everything in the Soviet Union, the coining of this formula was ascribed to Stalin himself, who was also said to have formulated the role of Soviet writers as "engineers of human minds."[1]

The same statute defined as the object of Socialist realism "the creation of works of high artistic significance, saturated with the heroic struggle of the world proletariat and with the grandeur of the victory of Socialism, and reflecting the great wisdom and heroism of the Communist party . . . , the creation of artistic works worthy of the great age of Socialism."

In itself this directive was, apart from the obvious political implications, sufficiently vague to allow a variety of interpretations; and, to begin with, Socialist realism was interpreted by Soviet commentators as implying a considerable latitude of styles. However, so far as the stress was on the word "realism," this formula was directed against "romanticism," on the one hand, and against all sorts of "formalistic" experiments, on the other. Thereby it merely sanctioned the tendency which had already been dominant in Soviet literature ever since 1925. "Back to realism" was the slogan, launched by Voronsky and Lezhnev, underlying the revival of the novel after 1924. As time went by, this tendency became even more pronounced in the work of the proletarian writers, most of whose novels were nearer to old-fashioned realism than the early works of Fedin and Leonov, let alone of Pilnyak. It is significant that the invitation to learn from the classics came not only from Gorky and Fadeyev but also from Bezymensky, the early proletarian disciple of Mayakovsky.

But if, by proclaiming realism to be the dominant trend of the new age, Soviet leaders merely consecrated the status quo, by qualifying it as "Socialist" they hardly helped make matters clearer. The question arose at once wherein lay the difference between Socialist realism and realism pure and simple? Was it only in the Socialist contents of a work, in its Socialist message? But why, then, was it necessary to speak of a new literary method and style? Some Soviet critics drew a parallel between Socialist realism and what a Russian critic of the eighteen seventies, Shelgunov, had described as "popular realism," which he opposed to the "aristocratic realism" of the majority of Russian writers of the nineteenth century (Turgenev, Tolstoy, Goncharov, Pisemsky). A typical representative of popular realism was seen by Shelgunov in one of the minor "populist" novelists of the sixties, Reshetnikov. He described the essence of popular realism as preoccupation with social psychology above all. Instead of individuals and representatives of the upper classes its writers focused their attention on the "masses," on the middle class, and on the peasants.[2] According to Soviet critics,

---

[1] See, however, above, Page 220, what Olesha said, in 1928, about his wish to be an "engineer of human material."

popular realism, which had survived in different forms till the October Revolution, could no longer meet the situation. And like their predecessors in the eighteen sixties, after the emancipation of the peasants, the realist writers were now confronted with the task of discovering a new realistic method that would fit in best with the historical realities of the moment. First of all, they had to realize that this new variety of realism must oppose itself to popular realism as typical of the obsolete small-bourgeois mentality. Socialist realism was called upon to reflect *Socialist* realities and *socialistic* mentality. It was thus, historically speaking, a legitimate successor of popular realism. In the opinion of Pereverzev, who advanced this view, the value of the term "Socialist realism" lay in the fact that it naturally and inevitably presupposed its historical antithesis which was at the same time its inexorable premise, namely, popular realism. One can see that this attempt at tying socialist realism with its historical antecedents did not lead very far.

Other critics opposed Socialist realism to bourgeois, or critical, realism. The traditional bourgeois realism, they said—the realism of a Balzac and of the great Russian nineteenth century novelists—was rooted in a critical, more or less negative, attitude toward reality. It was born of a protest against that reality and was therefore potentially revolutionary. Socialist realism, on the contrary, was founded on a positive attitude toward the new realities of a collectivized society. It was fundamentally optimistic, it said "yea" to life, while the old bourgeois realism was fundamentally pessimistic and often implied an unhealthy, morbid attitude toward the world.

Gorky, in his report to the First Congress of Soviet Writers in 1934, said: "While we do not at all deny the vast and enormous work performed by critical realism and highly appreciate its formal achievements in the art of word-painting, we must understand that we need this realism only for throwing light on the relics of the past, for fighting them, for eradicating them. But this form of realism has never served and cannot serve to educate a socialistic personality, for, while criticizing everything, it never affirmed anything or, at worst, it went back to the affirmation of what it had criticized."[3]

One of the younger Marxist critics, Nusinov, whom we shall later meet in a different context, contrasted Socialist realism with the methods of psychological realism used by Dostoyevsky and Tolstoy. The aim of Socialist realism was the exact opposite, he said, of Dostoyevsky's

[2] *"Populisme"* in France, in the early nineteen-thirties, was somewhat similar to popular realism thus understood. One of its exponents, Eugène Dabit, author of *Hôtel du Nord*, was very popular in the Soviet Union and died while on a visit there.

[3] M. Gorky, *O literature. Statyi i rechi 1928–1936 (About Literature: Articles and Addresses 1928–1936)*, 471. A translation of this report will be found in *Problems of Soviet Literature* (edited by H. G. Scott).

psychologism, for Dostoyevsky reduced man's actions to the struggle within him between the forces of good and evil, and sought for it a religious solution and explanation. But it was wrong to think, as did some Soviet writers, that Tolstoy's psychological method was any nearer to Socialist realism. There was only one point in which they met, and that was Tolstoy's moral optimism. But Tolstoy, too, like Dostoyevsky, showed human beings as individuals and not as parts of a social body: for Tolstoy, man was an embodiment of good as long as he was left to himself, but became an agent of evil whenever he was, or felt himself to be, part of a social whole. This made Tolstoy's method even more dangerous than Dostoyevsky's, for the latter at least "showed the man of the past in all his iniquity." A Socialist writer, before assimilating Dostoyevsky's and Tolstoy's psychological methods, must substitute for their non-class and unhistorical attitude, rooted in religious pessimism and abstract ethics, his own social and historical interpretation. Therefore, of the classics of bourgeois realism, Balzac and Stendhal, with their social and historical approach to their themes, were much closer to Socialist realism than either Tolstoy or Dostoyevsky. At the end of his article Nusinov offered, however, the following purely political formula of Socialist realism: "The main object of Socialist realism is the struggle for the destruction of the world of property and the triumph of Socialism."

Finally, an attempt was also made to oppose Socialist realism to the revolutionary romanticism which characterized the work of many Soviet writers in the early period, and to which some of them still clung. There was a long and heated discussion on the relation between Socialist realism and revolutionary romanticism, the outcome of which was that the latter was recognized as an essential ingredient of Socialist realism. This view was advocated by Gorky, in whose own work elements of "revolutionary romanticism" had always been very prominent, and he was supported by such romantically inclined Soviet writers as Lavrenyov. Gorky himself went even further when, in one of his articles published in 1934, he proclaimed that revolutionary romanticism was merely "a pseudonym of Socialist realism."

After gallons of ink had been spilled in fruitless and somewhat scholastic attempts at defining Socialist realism, a compromise formula, which reconciled Socialist realism with revolutionary romanticism, was agreed upon, but the dispute about the relation between them was revived again after the war.

From the very first it was clear that the negative aspects of Socialist realism were more tangible than the positive. It was fundamentally a reaction against certain existing trends and practices (or malpractices) in literature—as it turned out, a two-pronged reaction. It was a product of the "reform" which had swept away "proletarian" literary and artistic organizations and aimed at raising the general level of Soviet literature. Those who were instrumental in bringing about that reform had in mind an all-round improvement of Soviet literature. They wanted to improve the language and style which had become slipshod and sullied with colloquialisms and dialecticisms (this was one of the chief reproaches Gorky made to Panfyorov); they wanted to do away with the barrenness resulting from the uniformity of themes and their one-sided treatment; and they also wanted to reinstate *man* to his rightful place: novels, stories, and plays about production and productive processes, about new construction projects and collective farms, were to give place to works which would focus their main interest on human beings, on ordinary Soviet men and their personal life. This element of humanism in Socialist realism was strongly emphasized by several speakers at the first Pan-Soviet Congress of Writers, of which more will be said below. Theoretically speaking, Socialist realism aimed at greater objectivity. By comparison with the immediately preceding period it did enlarge the writer's scope. On the other hand, by imposing on the writer the task of portraying the new Socialist reality and the new Soviet man, and by emphasizing at the same time the heroic nature of the new era of Socialism, it set them on a hunt for new heroes. If in 1930 Libedinsky had called his novel *The Birth of a Hero,* the most usual title for a critical article or a book about Soviet literature in the late thirties became "In Search of a Hero." There were, however, very few heroes who satisfied the exacting Communist critics, and the frantic search for "a hero of our times" continued.

Nevertheless, so far as Socialist realism contributed toward greater objectivity and helped raise the literary standards, it showed its progressive facet. But it had also a conservative, or even reactionary, aspect, for it was also a reaction against what was described, sweepingly and therefore meaninglessly, as "bourgeois Formalism." This phrase was used to include all experiments with form and technique, and much of earlier Soviet literature came under this description. While in the first stages of the Revolution the *avant-garde* artists were treated as its natural allies, now those who were responsible for running the most "advanced" state in the world suddenly turned conservative and began to look askance at all revolutionary experiments in art, dubbing them as "bourgeois Formalism." The formula was widely used in the thirties and applied to all fields of art. In visual arts the ban on "Formalism" and the insistence on representational realism led to a frank revival of stiff and lifeless "Academicism" of the worst variety. In the theater Meyerhold and Tairov, who were responsible for the most interesting and daring theatrical experiments, became the principal targets for attack. Tairov after a time managed to work his way back into the fold, but Meyerhold, who was first deprived of his theater, eventually disappeared from the scene and apparently either committed suicide or met his end in a concentration camp. In music one of the first conspicuous victims was Dmitry Shostakovich, whose opera "The Lady Macbeth of Mtsensk"—until then regarded as one of the most notable achievements of Soviet music—seems to have incurred, in 1935, the displeasure of Stalin himself, with the result that a storm of criticism was unleashed against Shostakovich in the Soviet press, both general and musical, and various musical bodies passed resolutions condemning the opera as an expression of "rotten bourgeois Formalism." For some time Shostakovich was forced into retirement, but he emerged later with his Fifth Symphony, winning back his place in Soviet music. During the war he reaffirmed his position by his Seventh (the Leningrad) Symphony. His subsequent tribulations are well known. Since Shostakovich was highly regarded outside the Soviet Union and his opera was performed with success in several European countries, his case aroused much interest: it was the first clear demonstration of what Communist totalitarianism in art meant.[4]

3. The First Congress of Soviet Writers
Literature as Handmaiden of the State

IN August, 1934, the new Union of Soviet Writers called its first Pan-Soviet Congress in Moscow. The government spokesman at the Congress was Andrey Alexandrovich Zhdanov (1888–1948), who later the same year replaced the murdered Kirov as head of the Communist organization in Leningrad and subsequently acquired great notoriety by his cultural "purges." In his inaugural address at the Congress, Zhdanov stated quite plainly that literature in the Soviet Union could not but be tendentious. He said:

> Our Soviet literature is not afraid of being accused of tendentiousness. Yes, Soviet literature *is* tendentious, for in the age of class struggle a non-class, non-tendentious, would-be apolitical literature does not and cannot exist.

[4] For some details of the Shostakovich case see the interesting article by Gerald Abraham, "Shostakovich: A Study of Music and Politics," in *Horizon*, Vol. VI, No. 33 (September, 1942). In the light of what happened to Shostakovich and Meyerhold—and since then to so many others—it is interesting and appropriate to recall what Gorky wrote in 1930 apropos the Pilnyak incident and other similar cases: "We have a stupid habit of dragging people up to the belfry of fame and throwing them down into the mud after a while. No need for me to specify examples of such absurd and cruel treatment of people, everybody knows them. They remind me of the scenes of 'lynching' of pickpockets in 1917–18." See "The Working Class Must Rear Its Masters of Culture," in *About Literature*, 49.

And I think that every Soviet man of letters can say to any thick-headed bourgeois, to any philistine, to any bourgeois writer who will talk of the tendentiousness of our literature: "Yes, Soviet literature is tendentious, and we are proud of its tendentiousness, because our tendency consists in liberating the toilers, the whole mankind from the yoke of capitalist slavery."[5]

There was, of course, nothing new in what Zhdanov said: as early as 1905, Lenin, in one of his articles, had stated that under the dictatorship of the proletariat literature must become "Party-minded."

Zhdanov went on to emphasize the fact that the Congress was convening at a moment when the main obstacles on the way to Socialist reconstruction had been overcome, when the policy of industrialization and collectivization had been vindicated, when the Socialist system had "finally and irrevocably triumphed in our country under the guidance of the Communist party, under the leadership of genius of our great leader and teacher, comrade Stalin." The international weight and prestige of the Soviet Union was growing, said Zhdanov, and so was "its importance as the shock brigade of the world proletariat, as the mighty bulwark of the coming proletarian world revolution." The difficulties still facing the Soviet Union would be overcome with the aid of "the great and invincible doctrine of Marx-Engels-Lenin-Stalin." Soviet literature was the youngest of all literatures of the world, but it was also the richest in ideas *("samaya ideynaya")*,[6] the most progressive, and the most revolutionary. Its successes reflected the achievements of the new Socialist system. It was superior to bourgeois literature which reflected faithfully the decline and decay of the capitalist system, was characterized by "an orgy of mysticism, clericalism, and pornography," and for its "heroes" had thieves, detectives, prostitutes, and hoodlums. Things were different in the Soviet Union:

> Our Soviet writers draw for the material for their works of art, their themes, their images, their speech, upon the life and experience of the men of Dneprostroy and Magnitostroy. . . .
>
> In our country the chief heroes of literary works are the active builders of a new life: working men and women, collective farmers, engineers, members of the Komsomol, pioneers. . . . Our literature is saturated with enthusiasm and heroism. It is optimistic, but

---

[5] A. Zhdanov, *Sovetskaya literatura—samaya ideynaya, samaya peredovaya literatura v mire (Soviet Literature—The Richest in Ideas, the Most Progressive Literature in the World)*, 12. This pamphlet reproduces Zhdanov's address at the Congress. An English version of it will be found in *Problems of Soviet Literature* (edited by H. G. Scott).

[6] The Russian word *ideyny* defies exact translation.

not through any zoological instinct. It is fundamentally optimistic, because it is the literature of the rising class of proletariat, the only progressive and advanced class.

Zhdanov gave the following definition of Socialist realism:

> Comrade Stalin described our writers as engineers of human minds. What does it mean? What duties does this title impose on you?
>
> It means, above all, to know life in order to depict it truthfully in works of art, to depict it not scholastically, not lifelessly, not just as "objective reality," but to depict real life in its revolutionary development.
>
> In so doing, truthfulness and historical concreteness of artistic depiction must be combined with the task of ideological remolding and re-education of the toiling people in the spirit of Socialism. This method in fiction and in literary criticism is what we call Socialist realism. . . .
>
> To be an engineer of human minds means to stand with both feet firmly planted on the ground of real life. This, in its turn, means breaking away from old-type romanticism, from that romanticism which depicted nonexistent life and nonexistent characters, diverting the reader from the contradictions and oppressions of life into a world of the impossible, a world of Utopia. Our literature . . . must not shun romanticism, but it must be a romanticism of a new type, revolutionary romanticism . . . . Soviet literature must know how to portray our heroes, it must be able to look into our tomorrow.

Declaring the proletariat to be the only heir to the best treasures of world literature, Zhdanov called upon Soviet writers to "collect, study, and critically digest" the literary heritage "squandered" by the bourgeoisie. He also warned them that Soviet literature had still to live up to the demands of its epoch: its weak spots reflected "the lagging of consciousness behind economics." But all the prerequisites for producing "works attuned to the epoch" were there.[7]

Zhdanov's address set the keynote to the Congress. Most of the writers who took part in its deliberations subscribed to his thesis about the "tendentiousness" of Soviet literature. Vsevolod Ivanov, who as a member of the Serapion Brotherhood had earlier protested against all tendentiousness in literature and demanded from the latter only one thing—"that its voice should not ring false"—could be heard confessing that life had taught him wisdom and that he realized now that

7 All these quotations are from Zhdanov, *Soviet Literature,* 6–14.

245

"Bolshevik tendentiousness" was an indispensable weapon in a Soviet writer's literary armor.

The principle that literature was *ancilla rei publicae,* which underlay Zhdanov's speech and had always been in fact the unshakeable basis of the Communist party policy in literary matters, was fully endorsed by the Congress. The latter paid special attention to the problem of producing "national defense literature" to help the Red Army and boost its martial spirit. Vsevolod Vishnevsky, a Communist playwright, author of several plays dealing with the Red army and navy life, urged his "friend Olesha" not to overlook, "amidst his dreams about a better future," the more immediate need of being ready to defend, arms in hand, the Soviet Union against the imminent "imperialist" aggression. In its address to Voroshilov, the commissar for defense, the Congress undertook "to arm the country and the Red Army with new models of literature," depicting both the Red Army in all its "heroic simplicity and unmatched strength," and its potential enemies, the nature of their objectives and their "anti-human" aims.

Olesha's Plea for Humanism

Vishnevsky's appeal to Olesha referred to Olesha's speech at the Congress, one of the most sincere and interesting. Once again, it was a candid personal confession of a Soviet writer who, while doing his best to adjust himself to the new world and meet its demands, was conscious of his ties with the "old world," of the "Kavalerov" in him. It was both frank and pathetic. Olesha began by saying that in every human being there were both good and bad things and that he could not visualize a man incapable of understanding what it meant to be vain, cowardly, or selfish. In an artist this characteristic is particularly developed and he knows how to pull up the seedlings of the most diverse human passions and turn them into trees. An artist cannot describe a character without becoming that character, at least momentarily. Very often the artist is asked how he knows this or that, or whether he has just "invented" it. The answer is that the artist "invents" everything. He cannot invent that which does not exist in Nature, but Nature has no secrets from him, it is more communicative with him than with anyone else. It would be possible to write a book called "The Machine of Transmutations," which would demonstrate how life impressions are transmuted by the artist into images of art. An artist's relations with the good and the bad, with vice and virtue, are none too simple. When he portrays a negative character, all that is negative in him comes up to the surface. Goethe is reported to have said: "I felt like rereading *Macbeth* but dared not. In the state in which I then was, I was afraid that this reading might kill me." That was true, added Olesha: "An image can kill an artist." He

246

recalled his own *Envy* and what was said about the kinship between the author and his hero. He admitted that Kavalerov's vision of the world was his own and that when Kavalerov was denounced as an epitome of vulgarity, he was shocked.

I could not believe that a man with a keen eye and a gift of seeing the world in his own way could be vulgar and worthless. I said to myself: "It means that all this ability, all these things of your own, which you regard as your strength, are worthless and vulgar. Can that be so?" I wished to believe that the comrades who had criticized me (they were Communist critics) were right, and I believed them. I began to think that what I took for a treasure was in fact a sign of poverty. Thus the conception of a beggar was born in me . . . . My artist's imagination came to my aid, and under its impulse the naked concept of social futility began to take on the form of fiction, and I decided to write a novel about a beggar.

The novel remained unwritten.[8] It was only later that Olesha understood why he did not write it, understood that it was not he who mattered but that which was around him:

While I was thinking over the theme of the beggar and recapturing my youth, my country built factories. It was the first Five-Year Plan . . . . This was not my theme. I could have gone to a construction project, lived at a factory among workers, described them in a reportage, even in a novel, but it was not my theme, it wasn't the theme that was connected with my bloodline, with my breath. I wouldn't have been a true artist had I chosen this theme. I would have lied and invented. I did not have what is known as "inspiration." It is difficult for me to understand a worker, a revolutionary hero. I cannot become one. It is beyond my power, beyond my comprehension. That is why I don't write about it. I felt terrified and began to think that I was unwanted . . . and thus arose in me the terrifying image of the beggar, the image that was killing me.

Meanwhile, continued Olesha, there grew up a young generation that knew nothing of the old world, and the sight of this new generation brought about the miracle of his own rejuvenation. As an artist he became fascinated by these new, young Soviet men and women:

. . . a young Soviet man is growing up in our country. As an artist I rush to him. "Who are you? what colors do you see? do you ever have dreams? what do you daydream about? what do you feel yourself to be? how do you love? what feelings do you have? what do you reject and what do you accept? what predominates in you—

8 This novel was even announced for publication in one of the Soviet magazines in 1931.

feeling or reason? do you know how to cry? are you tender? have you understood all the things that terrified me and that I could not grasp? what are you like, young man of the Socialist society?" I cannot write without discovering an analogy between us. I want to create the type of the young man, endowing him with all that was best in my own youth.

Declaring that a writer must be "an educator and a teacher," Olesha announced his intention of writing plays and stories about young people who will be concerned with moral problems, and added:

> Somewhere there lurks in me the conviction that Communism is not only an economic but also a moral system, and the first to embody this aspect of Communism will be our young men and young women.

> I shall endeavor to embody in these works all my sense of beauty, of gracefulness, of nobility, my whole vision of the world . . . in order to prove that the new socialistic attitude to the world is a human attitude in the purest sense of the word. Such is my rejuvenation. I did not become a beggar . . . .

To many sober-minded Communists Olesha must have appeared as a dreamer and an idealist. But his plea for humanism struck some responsive chords. Shklovsky, the one-time cold and calculating Formalist and later an ardent advocate of "factography," spoke of the birth of new proletarian humanism, of the coming era of "a new sensibility." Vera Inber, the former Constructivist, stressed the failure of Soviet literature in portraying "positive" characters, and attributed it to the tendency of Soviet writers to draw their characters flat, without all their human flaws and foibles.

A curious and somewhat naïve document was quoted by one of the delegates from Georgia, the novelist Dzhavakhishvili.[9] It was a "letter of instructions" to the Congress from a group of readers, subscribers to a municipal lending library in Rostov-on-Don. Among other things it urged writers

> . . . to write more about love, about marriage, to depict ordinary life, without exaggeration, but also without underrating its importance. . . . Give us striking and unforgettable types of heroes of our days, both positive and negative. . . . More historical novels

---

[9] Delegates of various national minorities played an important part at the Congress which proclaimed, as one of the urgent tasks, a closer interpenetration of Russian and other national literatures of the Soviet Union. The difference of languages, it was said, should not conceal the *ideological unity* of Soviet literature thus widely understood. Similarly, a closer intercourse with international revolutionary writers was urged by the principal spokesmen of the Congress.

are wanted. The reader needs them greatly. . . . What is more, we want to laugh. Give us a chance to laugh heartily and not just smile gingerly. . . . We want a literature that would be read and that one would feel like reading. . . . Write in simple, correct language. Learn it from the classics.

This document seems to be a fair reflection of the desiderata of the average Soviet reader who was bored by Five-Year Plan literature with its ready-made patterns, its neglect of ordinary human beings and of their personal problems, and its overemphasis of the ideological element. Dzhavakhishvili himself, in commenting upon this letter of instructions, said that he would put an end to all talk about "forbidden" subjects which was still sometimes heard: to his mind all subjects were good—if treated in the spirit of Socialist realism.

Many of the speeches at the Congress reflected the widespread dissatisfaction with the state of things in Soviet literature in the period preceding the "reform" of 1932. An official statement by Nakoryakov, of the State Publishing House, described 75 per cent of the literary works produced during the years 1929–31 as worthless![10]

It will be seen that much of what was produced in the years that followed went to satisfy the demands of the Rostov-on-Don library subscribers.

Olesha himself tried to give life to his idea of the artist's duty to portray young people and their problems in his short film scenario "Strogy Yunosha" ("A Strict Youth"), published in 1934 in *Novy Mir.* Its hero was a young Communist, and its theme the problem of "qualitative inequality" in Socialist society, of the place which talent and brains must occupy in it. Olesha's thesis here was that Socialism means inequality and that one must "live up" to those who create spiritual values—music, pictures, ideas, and beauty. Olesha also brought in his favorite theme of "feelings": his young Communist champions some of the feelings which Communists have come to regard as "bourgeois prejudices," but which, he maintains, are really all-human. He devises a new code of Komsomol ethics, based on such qualities as modesty, truthfulness, generosity, altruism, and even sentimentality. This skeleton of a play, almost masquelike in its symbolic delineation of characters, was received coolly by Soviet critics, who detected in Olesha's conception of ethics a dangerous touch of idealism. The film, though made, was never shown. This "play for the cinema" was Olesha's last major contribution to Soviet literature.

[10] This statement was quoted by Gorky in his address at the Congress. See *About Literature,* 480. It is curious to note that Professor L. Timofeyev, in attacking the British edition of my book in the Soviet publication *Culture and Life,* referred to this statement and called it "unfounded."—*Kultura i zhizn* (March, 1947).

Bukharin Sums up Soviet Poetry

One of the most interesting reports at the Congress was made by Nikolay Ivanovich Bukharin (1888–1938), the ablest and the most erudite of the theoretical exponents of Soviet Communism, who, four years later, was to be arrested, tried, and executed on charges of conspiring against the security of the Soviet Union.

Bukharin surveyed the development of Soviet poetry and examined the problems facing it in the era of Socialist realism. He distinguished three main periods in the evolution of Soviet poetry. The first period was a period of new slogans, when new principles of life were proclaimed to the working masses of all countries. Its poetry was declamatory, full of sweeping ideas, of cosmic concepts. But it had no flesh and blood; it was a kind of "poetical blueprint," heroic and abstract—"insofar as one can speak of abstract poetry at all." The second period was characterized by a transition to constructive everyday work when specialized knowledge and skill were in demand. Poets turned their attention to the minutiae of life. Cosmic visions of "World Sovnarkoms" gave place to minute depiction of empiric realities. It was a dialectical negation of the preceding period: universalism passed into its opposite, synthesis gave place to analysis. The third period was just beginning. It was conditioned by the growing complexity of life:

> The problem of mastering the technique of production has not been solved yet, though much has been done. Cultural needs have expanded to an extraordinary degree. Interests have become incomparably more diversified. There is a tremendous desire to know everything, a desire to *generalize,* to rise on a *new* basis to the understanding of the process as a whole. Hence the need that is felt for synthesizing poetry and synthesizing literature in general . . . . This is not just a return to the starting point, not a reversion to declarative, schematic poetry, but a new synthesis which can only arise out of previous analytical work.[11]

Bukharin examined also in detail the work of individual Soviet poets. While admitting that Pasternak shunned topical themes, he spoke of him as "one of the most remarkable craftsmen of verse in our days" and made flattering references to his formal achievements. At the same time he criticized such orthodox Communist poets as Demyan Bedny and Bezymensky for being "elementary" and "old-fashioned,"

[11] This and subsequent quotations are taken from N. Bukharin, *Poeziya, poetika i zadachi poeticheskogo tvorchestva v SSSR* (*Poetry, Poetics and Tasks of Poetic Creation in the U.S.S.R.*). An English version of Bukharin's report will be found in Scott (ed.), *Problems of Soviet Literature,* 185–260.

and even made some strictures on Mayakovsky. Underlining the need for raising the general level of poetic culture, he pointed out that those poets who were ideologically above suspicion often tended to be "elementary" and went on as follows:

Yet one of the hallmarks of a significant work is the wealth of associations and emotions it evokes, of ideas and allusions it contains. If you compare the work of many of our poets with that of Verhaeren you will see how many ideas the latter has . . . , how much culture he possesses. And with us a rhymed slogan often passes for poetry. You may mention Mayakovsky. But to some extent time has set its stamp on him, too, for life has grown infinitely more complex, and we must march forward. Culture, culture, and once more culture!

Bukharin's strictures on Demyan Bedny, Bezymensky, and even Mayakovsky, especially next to his praise of Pasternak, Tikhonov, and Selvinsky, and his derogatory references to certain aspects of "proletarian" poetry, provoked some spirited protests from several delegates. Bedny and Bezymensky rose to defend themselves, while others, whom Bukharin in his reply described sarcastically as "Mayakovsky's poor relations," took up the defense of the late poet. Replying to Kirsanov, Surkov, and others who had accused him of brushing aside Mayakovsky's propaganda poetry, Bukharin said:

Pardon me, but I rate Mayakovsky very highly, and I used a formula which says that he has become "a classic of Soviet poetry"; but this does not mean that even such a great man as Mayakovsky must be idolized. For you are idolaters and fetishists if you do not understand that *life keeps moving forward*. I am not against propaganda poetry as such, I am not against tendentious poetry in the good sense of that word . . . . I said that propaganda itself must undergo a change now, that the conception of topicalness has changed, that a mere rehash of editorials and minute operative slogans in verse satisfies no one, that we must aim at a synthesis, at creating a powerful, rich, and diversified art.[12]

Besides his Marxist analysis of various trends in Soviet poetry, Bukharin made an attempt at clarifying the concept of Socialist realism. He said that it was absurd to oppose romanticism to Socialist realism; that while old realism was to a certain extent antilyrical and old lyric poetry to a certain extent antirealistic, there was no such discord between Socialist realism and lyric poetry; that Socialist realism, while

[12] It is significant that the pamphlet reproducing Bukharin's report, as well as his "Last Word" in reply to his opponents contains also a "Statement" in which he apologizes for his polemical brusqueness and says that his estimates of individual authors must not be understood as "directive and compulsory."

definitely anti-individualistic, must be "oriented toward man." Bukharin rejected flatly the formula of "Communist individualism" suggested by André Gide in a letter he addressed to the Congress; such a formula, he said, was a contradiction in terms.

Socialist Realism versus James Joyce

Another very interesting and controversial report was read before the Congress by Karl Radek (1885-?) who, like Bukharin, was subsequently "purged" as a Trotskyite and "Fascist agent." It was entitled "Contemporary World Literature and the Tasks of Proletarian Art."[13]

Three capital events of recent times, said Radek, determined the evolution of contemporary world literature: the World War, the October Revolution in Russia, and the advent of Fascism to power in several European countries. In the light of these events and their reflection in literature, Radek proceeded to analyze the contemporary literary scene. He spoke of the birth of a young proletarian literature in Western Europe and in Asia, of the bourgeois writers who were rallying to the cause of the proletariat, such as André Malraux and Jean-Richard Bloch in France, Johannes Becher and Ludwig Renn in Germany, and Theodore Dreiser in the United States;[14] he referred sympathetically to such proven friends of the Soviet Union as Romain Rolland, Bernard Shaw, and Upton Sinclair, and mentioned the recent "change of heart" on the part of André Gide, whom he called "a great French poet"; he analyzed the output of Italian Fascist literature and admitted the possibility of Fascism's producing talented writers. In his reply to his critics he stressed the split in bourgeois literature, its division into openly Fascist literature and literature attempting to defend bourgeois democracy but "slowly creeping towards Fascism," while there was also a group of bourgeois writers who were openly siding with Soviet Communism. As a typical example illustrating the disintegration of bourgeois literature, Radek quoted Céline's *Journey to the End of the Night*. Tomorrow, he said (prophetically, it may be added), Céline might become a Fascist. But today he was reflecting the despair of those elements of petty-bourgeois intelligentsia which saw no way out of the crisis and were profoundly disappointed in capitalism. This was something to be welcomed:

[13] Like the other major reports at the Congress it was immediately issued, together with Radek's reply to his opponents, in pamphlet form: Karl Radek, *Sovremennaya mirovaya literatura i zadachi proletarskogo iskusstva*. An English translation of it will be found in Scott (ed.), *Problems of Soviet Literature*, 73–184. All the quotations that follow are made from the original Russian text.

[14] Several foreign writers, including Jean-Richard Bloch, André Malraux, Theodore Plivier and others, attended the Congress as foreign guests. André Gide sent his greetings.

252

Literature of disintegration is not our literature, but it is a good thing when your enemy is disintegrating, when one part of the petty bourgeoisie ceases to believe in bourgeois leadership. When the petty bourgeois masses see a dark night ahead of them, this may lead to their seeking a way out of this state of things alongside of us. . . .

Literature which is still hostile to the revolution but is already hostile to Fascism is of great importance to us.

But particularly interesting was what Radek had to say about the advanced antibourgeois writers of the West and the desirability of learning from them. For some time this problem had been occupying Soviet writers and critics. Several of them were looking for models in the West. This was especially true of some of the fellow travelers. Many critics pointed out the debt which Olesha's vision and method of presentation owed to Jean Giraudoux. Some influence of Proust could also be discerned in his work. (Olesha himself admitted his admiration for H. G. Wells's *The Invisible Man*.) And Katayev, in his novel *Forward, Oh Time!,* was certainly influenced in his technique by John Dos Passos. But the most discussed literary figure in the West was naturally James Joyce, although little of his work was at the time accessible to those Soviet writers and critics who could not read him in the original. Joyce came to be regarded as the epitome of the antibourgeois spirit in bourgeois literature and as a literary revolutionary, and in the early thirties a bitter controversy about his significance for Soviet literature flared up.

Paradoxically, the campaign against Joyce and what he stood for was launched by Prince D. S. Mirsky (b. 1890). During the Civil War, Mirsky fought in the ranks of Denikin's and Wrangel's White Armies. With their collapse he emigrated and with the help of the late Maurice Baring, who knew his family well, found his way to London. Here he became lecturer in Russian literature at the School of Slavonic and East European Studies and published, in 1926–27, his excellent two-volume book on Russian literature. He also contributed articles on Russian literature to the *Times Literary Supplement* and to various "highbrow" and *avant-garde* English and French periodicals (such as *Echanges,* for example). A man of great erudition, of broad views and pungent personal style, he was at home not only in Russian but also in classical and Western European literature and soon won for himself a position of respect and authority in English letters. To many people his conversion to Communism (about 1931 he became a member of the British Communist party) came as a surprise. But to some who knew him well this about-face seemed a natural result of his love of intellectual mischief and his instinctive nonconformism, and when in 1932 he went back to Russia, these people confidently predicted that he would end badly. At first Mirsky's knowledge of European, especially English, literature and his personal ties with a number of English and French left-wing intellectuals were taken advantage of: he was entrusted with editing English classics, writing introductions to various volumes, and acting as liaison officer for various foreign guests of honor who visited the Soviet Union. He also published a malicious book on the British intelligentsia.

In 1934, however, just before the Congress of Soviet Writers, he got into a bad scrape as a result of an article which he printed in *The Literary Gazette* (June 24, 1934) about Fadeyev's novel *The Last of the Udege*. In this article he reproached Fadeyev for trying to win back the sympathies of the intelligentsia whom he had "offended" by his portrayal of Mechik in *The Rout*. Mirsky spoke slightingly of Fadeyev's part in Soviet literature and called his novel "an artistic blunder." Fadeyev's novel was at the time freely criticized by various critics, and the article did not attract much attention. But a month later the *Literary Gazette* was obliged to recant and "accept the responsibility for Mirsky's blunder." Mirsky himself was taken severely to task by some orthodox Communist critics who pointed out that a recent convert from "White-Guardism" had no right to criticize Communist writers. The fact that Mirsky had criticized Fadeyev from the ultra-left standpoint and had showed himself to be *plus royaliste que le roi même*, was disregarded. For a time Mirsky's name disappeared from *The Literary Gazette*, but in January, 1935, somewhat belatedly, none other than Gorky came to his defense. He pointed out that Mirsky had been quite right, because "everyone knew" that Fadeyev's novel was bad, and it was anyway not Mirsky's fault if he was born a prince. Gorky was answered by Panfyorov who, in an article published simultaneously in *Pravda* and *Izvestia*, once more accused Mirsky of unfair methods of criticism. The controversy around this incident gradually died out, but in the summer of 1935 Mirsky was arrested on unspecified charges. A few months later, apparently as a result of some intervention from abroad, he was released, but removed from Moscow. The latest ascertainable news about him was that he was editing a local newspaper in some out-of-the-way town in Siberia. In 1936 and 1937 his signature still appeared under some articles in Soviet publications, but apparently they were articles written before his "mishap."[15] After that his name was never mentioned, and it is not known whether he is alive or not.

[15] Thus we find an ultra-Marxist article by Mirsky in the Pushkin volume of *Literaturnoye Nasledstvo* (*Literary Heritage*) (1937). In the same year the Leningrad magazine *Zvezda* began to publish Mirsky's biography of Pushkin, about which it even printed a special advance notice. After the first two installments, however, the publication was discontinued without any explanation. Earlier, Gorky had enlisted

The anti-Joyce campaign took place before the Fadeyev incident. Early in 1933 Mirsky published several articles on the problem of the relationship between Soviet literature and contemporary European writers.[16] He charged some "formalizing" Communists with trying to interest Soviet writers in Joyce's decadent art, and with regarding newfangled art forms as an absolute virtue. Among those whom he criticized was the Communist playwright Vsevolod Vishnevsky, and the latter replied to him in an article entitled "We Must Know the West!"[17] He reminded his readers that one of the first to raise the issue of mutual Western and Soviet influences was the famous film-producer Sergey Eisenstein, who met Joyce in Paris and became interested in Joyce's methods. Eisenstein himself said that he realized, while working on the film based on Dreiser's *An American Tragedy*, that new methods and new devices were needed for a deeper understanding of images and characters, and that the new social treatment of images had a great effect on purely formal devices. It was from this idea, he said, that his conception of "inner monologue" in films had originated.

Propping himself on the authority of Eisenstein, Vishnevsky boldly took up the cudgels on behalf of Joyce. He described *Ulysses* as "a perfectly outspoken portrayal of men of the capitalist era," and spoke of Joyce as having "revealed the amazing secrets of the life and mentality of the people of the dying epoch." Free from all usual literary tricks, from an entertaining plot, from Zolaesque naturalistic twists, *Ulysses* was "a stunning, avalanche-like, epochal work," which faithfully recorded the epoch and its human multitude. It gave rise to new literary currents in France, England, the United States, Italy, and other countries.[18]

> *Ulysses* is remarkable for the great tension in which it holds the reader. It is the nervous tension . . . of Western life. *Ulysses* is musical. It creates multiplanar life, and makes you aware not only of the "hero," but also of the world, of cosmos. *Ulysses* is amazingly exact, often scientifically exact, opening the road to a kind of supernaturalism . . . . *Ulysses* reflects a tremendous linguistic culture— Joyce is a rare linguist . . . .

Mirsky's collaboration in the collective *Istoriya fabrik i zavodov* (*History of Factories and Plants*). According to the list published in the *Bulletin* of the Russian Literary Fund in New York, Mirsky died in his Siberian exile.

16 For instance, "Dos Passos, sovetskaya literatura i zapad" ("Dos Passos, Soviet Literature and the West"), in *Literaturny kritik* No. 1 (1933); and two articles about Joyce and Proust in *God shestnadtsaty* (*The Sixteenth Year*), Nos. 1 and 2 (1933).

17 "Znat Zapad!" in *Literaturny kritik* (*Literary Critic*), No. 7 (1933), 80–95.

18 Vishnevsky gave here a rather strange assortment of names representing the Joyce "school" in European literature. His list included Valéry Larbaud, Montherlant, Drieu de la Rochelle, Dos Passos, Hemingway, Walter [Waldo?] Frank, Thornton Wilder, Virginia Woolf, and Aldous Huxley.

Six hundred pages of Joyce's book are brimful with hatred for the old capitalist Britain. Joyce is one of those "witnesses" of whom Lenin spoke. Lenin knew very well how to handle any material with which literature, journalism and statistics provided him. How barbarous and medieval Mirsky sounds when he says: "We have no use for Joyce and Proust." Another step and Mirsky . . . will evidently make a bonfire of their books.

Describing Joyce as "a monstrously powerful realist," Vishnevsky accused Mirsky of failing to understand the objective value of what one found in Joyce and his followers, "decadents" and "nihilists" though they be; for, socially speaking, their experiments were parallel to those of the Russian Futurists and, like the latter, these Western intellectuals, "these lonely souls," these "protestants" were still blind to the fact that their real "customer" was the revolutionary proletariat. But

time will come when they will see it. Some of them will join the revolution, others the counterrevolution. It is a great pity that Mirsky in advance brands all these seeking, embittered, radical lonely souls as candidates for the camp of the counterrevolution.

Vishnevsky also defended Dos Passos and quoted Olesha's opinion of the new currents in literature as "progressive" and as implying "a generous conception of life." Vishnevsky also mentioned a questionnaire of *The Literary Gazette,* which showed that among Soviet writers Dos Passos was the most widely read author.

The controversy about Joyce and Dos Passos, and the value of literary innovations in general, continued throughout the year.[19] Radek's report to the 1934 Congress of Soviet Writers contained a summing up and the final verdict.

One section of Radek's report was entitled "James Joyce or Socialist Realism?" With his usual biting irony Radek said that Soviet writers were not familiar with foreign literatures and when they heard of this or that novelty they asked "with morbid interest" whether it might not contain "a great key to art." Whenever they heard that a book eight hundred pages long, without full stops or commas, appeared abroad, they said: "Maybe this is the new art that is being born out of chaos?" It would be absurd, went on Radek, for Soviet writers to refuse to learn from foreign artists. From the point of view of form an average French writer certainly wrote as well as a very good Soviet writer. There was nothing surprising in this—a French or English workman also could

[19] Several articles about Joyce, of whom little was really known in the Soviet Union (in this respect Mirsky had an enormous advantage over his opponents), appeared about this time in Soviet magazines. Among them may be mentioned a detailed and serious study by R. Miller-Budnitskaya in *Literaturny kritik,* No. 1 (1934).

handle his tools better than his Soviet comrade. Therefore there was much that Soviet literature could learn, not only from the old classics but also from the literature of dying capitalism. The question was not whether one should learn from a great artist like Proust the art of depicting all the minutiae of man. The question was whether Soviet literature should go along its own "highway" or follow in the footsteps of foreign "seekers."

Two names represented the search for new forms in literature. One of them was Marcel Proust, who "wants to present the psychology of his heroes, the heroes of the French drawing room, by laying bare their minds, by subtly dissecting their tissues, by sniffing at all their motions." Compared to Proust's, however, even the meanest of Dostoyevsky's characters are giants of suffering.

> . . . The drawing-room heroes of Proust seem to be saying that there is no need to analyze them, that no analysis will get anything out of them.

The other "hero" of contemporary bourgeois literature was James Joyce, "the mysterious author of *Ulysses,* a book which is loudly discussed but little read." His "originality" consisted in attempting to depict a day in the life of his characters "motion by motion—the motions of the body, the motions of the mind, the motions of the feelings in all their shades—from conscious feelings to those which rise up in the throat like a spasm." His writings were like cinematographic shots which omitted nothing in the life of the hero.

> One thought clings to another; if it leads him astray the author runs after it. His hero, while drunk, is assailed by hallucinations. The author breaks off the narrative and relates these hallucinations. More than eight hundred pages are devoted to one day in the hero's life.

Dismissing Joyce's "intricate web of allegories and mythological allusions," his "madhouse phantasmagorias," Radek went on to examine the essence of the "new method" which, in his opinion, "reduced naturalism to clinical observation, and symbolism to delirious ravings." He saw the quintessence of Joyce in

> his conviction that there is *nothing great in life—no great events, no great people, no great ideas,* and that the writer can give a picture of life by just taking "any hero any day" and photographing him carefully. *A heap of dung, teeming with worms and photographed by a motion-picture camera through a microscope—that is Joyce.*[20]

[20] The italics throughout are Radek's own.

Radek denied that Joyce, for all his minute portrayal of every single motion of his hero, was an impartial recorder of life:

He has selected the piece of life which he is portraying. His selection is determined by the fact that his entire world lies between a bookcase full of medieval books, a brothel, and a pothouse. For him, the national revolutionary movement of the Irish middle class does not exist, and therefore the portrait which he draws is wrong, despite its semblance of detachment.

While the Joycean method might be considered fit for depicting small, insignificant, worthless people and their actions, thoughts, and emotions, it "would prove utterly bankrupt the moment the author were to approach the great events of the class struggle, the gigantic conflicts of the modern world."

Radek attributed the "morbid interest" some Soviet writers evinced in Joyce to the fact that he was almost untranslatable and practically unknown in the Soviet Union, but added also the following significant explanation:

This interest in Joyce reflects unconsciously *the craving of the right-wing writers, who have adjusted themselves to the Revolution but do not understand its greatness, to get away from Magnitogorsk and Kuznetskstroy, to get away from the great deeds of our country to "great art" which shows small doings of small men; to escape from the stormy seas of the Revolution to the stagnant waters of a little marshy pond where frogs live.*

Radek ended his report by advising Soviet writers to learn from the best masters of proletarian literature abroad, and to portray not only Soviet factory workers and collective farmers, but also the underground revolutionaries in Nazi Germany and the Chinese coolies.

Radek's report provoked several retorts, mostly from foreign guests at the Congress. His chief opponent on the subject of Joyce was a certain Herzfelde,[21] who said that Joyce was a great artist who photographed not a heap of dung but "his own inside." Radek thought this correction immaterial and provoked general laughter and applause by pointing out that "a man's inside also contains various component parts of a heap of dung." In a more serious vein he said that an artist had no business to look into his inside at the moment when the Fascists were preparing "to stifle the last remnant of culture" and "to throttle the Soviet Union." For Radek the historic role of Joyce lay not in any inventions of literary technique:

Joyce's form is in keeping with his content, and *his content is a reflection of all that is most reactionary in the petty bourgeoisie.*

21 I could find no information about this writer, apparently a Czech.

Joyce may curse at God, he may curse at imperialist England, but he does not lead the artists the right way . . . . *The only things that appeal to Joyce are the medieval, the mystical, the reactionary in the petty bourgeoisie.*

As for Dos Passos, Radek admitted that he was "a great revolutionary artist." If he had not yet reached his full stature, it was because he was under the influence of Joyce and not under the influence of Marx and of the great artists of realism. His formalistic innovations, which some Soviet writers admired so much, were his main weakness:

He inserts newspaper clippings in order to paste together the background which he is incapable of portraying.

Radek finished by opposing Socialist realism to all these bourgeois attempts to find new forms. Socialist realism did not mean indiscriminate photographing of life. It selected what was essential, as its very name implied.

Joyce stands on the other side of the barricades . . . . There is nothing fundamental we can learn from Joyce. If you mean learning from Joyce his technique, I am not going to argue. I don't write novels, but if I did I think I would learn how to write them from Tolstoy and Balzac, not from Joyce.

I wish to say to Soviet and foreign writers: *"Our road lies not through Joyce, but along the highway of Socialist realism."*

Radek, not yet exposed as an agent of Hitler and an enemy of the Soviet Union, was speaking as an official representative of the Party, and his verdict on Joyce, Proust, and Dos Passos bore the stamp of finality. Soviet writers accepted it in silence, or even joined in the attack on Joyce and the "decadent" bourgeois literature. Even Vishnevsky did not come up in defense of Joyce, preferring to rebuke his friend Olesha, to whose opinion about Joyce he had appealed against Mirsky. The vicissitudes of Soviet literature are illustrated by the fact that today, when Joyce is more than ever held to be the epitome of Western decadence, both Mirsky and Radek have disappeared from the scene while Vishnevsky occupies a place of honor in Soviet literature.

Thus the "highway" of Soviet literature was clearly traced: a close alliance with revolutionary proletarian literature abroad; learning from the old masters like Balzac and Tolstoy; and no traffic with modernists and innovators who were in search of new forms. Yet, compared with what we shall see later, the general tone of Radek's report and of the entire debate on the relations with the West was quite broadminded, and the program of Socialist realism as outlined by the Congress left the writers some scope.

4. Changes in Soviet Outlook

On the Road to Totalitarianism

SOCIALIST realism was but one of the manifestations of far-reaching changes in the official Soviet outlook which took place between 1932 and 1939. These changes could not but affect the development of literature. Some of them were determined by external factors—by Hitler's advent to power and the growth of the Nazi state in Germany and of what came to be known as the "Fascist menace" to the existence of the Soviet Union. In the face of it Soviet leaders began to look for allies among the Western democracies. Hence the more conciliatory attitude toward the Socialist parties in Europe and the encouragement given to the policy of the so-called "Popular Fronts"; hence also the entry of the Soviet Union into the hitherto despised League of Nations. To what extent this policy of international co-operation was sincere and genuine and to what extent it was dictated by the desire to play out the opposing camps in Europe cannot be discussed here. What matters is that, from 1933 on, the Soviet Union and its leaders became increasingly "national-minded." While it would be a gross mistake to think that the old idea of world revolution, which inspired the Bolsheviks in 1917 and underlay the conception of both Lenin and Trotsky, was now given up, there is no doubt that for the time being it gave place to Stalin's conception of "Socialism in one country." The survival of the Soviet regime in Russia was no longer regarded as contingent on the immediate social revolution in other countries, the chances of which appeared remote. It was therefore important to ensure the external security of the Soviet Union and to increase its military might, while at the same time consolidating the Soviet regime internally. It was in the thirties that the Soviet Union became the thoroughgoing totalitarian state it is now. Viewed retrospectively, the literary reform of 1932, which did away with proletarian and other organizations and set up a homogeneous writers' organization pledged to support the domestic and international policies of the Soviet government, was a clever step in the direction of suppressing all nonconformism and establishing a totalitarian control over all manifestations of spiritual and cultural life.

Revising Russian History

In 1934 the leadership of the Communist party launched a significant campaign against the views of the leading Soviet historian, Mikhail Nikolayevich Pokrovsky, who had died in 1932. For many years Pokrovsky, who had received his historical training before the Revolution, was the principal exponent of the Marxist interpretation of history. He was fond of describing history as "politics projected into the past" and of denying the very existence of such a thing as "objective history." In the words of his followers, "All scholarship is Party scholarship, the tenet about non-Party scholarship is one of the most harmful perversions of Marxism, pregnant with direct consequences. As for history, it must be politically oriented to the maximum degree and more Party-minded than any other science." The years 1929–31, which in literature were marked by the RAPP dictatorship, witnessed a violent and concentrated attack on the "class enemy on the history front."[22] Eminent historians were accused of "bourgeois objectivism." Several of them, including Platonov and Tarle, were arrested and exiled. By 1930, with the reorganization of the Soviet Academy of Sciences on the Marxist basis, the school of Pokrovsky had won the battle. Under Pokrovsky's influence the teaching of history was practically discontinued in Soviet schools and colleges and replaced by vulgar sociology. Such things as chronology, facts, and historical personalities were completely disregarded. In the words of a later critic, "living people have almost disappeared from our curriculum and teaching."[23]

The reaction came in 1934. It was a complete about-face. Pokrovsky, by now dead, was denounced as a "vulgarizer" of Marxism, guilty of empty sociological schematism, of perverting and distorting Russian history, of failing to see the positive achievements of the Russian people, and of approaching the past solely from the point of view of vulgar opposition between the people and the state. Pokrovsky's works, which had hitherto served as the principal textbooks of Russian history, were discarded, and Stalin himself, assisted by Kirov and Zhdanov, drew up observations that were to guide the compilers of new textbooks. A contest for a new school textbook of Russian history was announced, with several prizes. None of the contestants was adjudged worthy of the first prize, but the second prize was awarded to Professor Shestakov, whose *History of the U. S. S. R.* became the officially adopted textbook.

The attitude toward Russia's past was fundamentally revised. A good Soviet citizen had to be a Soviet patriot. And patriotism no longer meant pride in the "conquests of the Revolution" (the popular phrase of the twenties); it also implied pride in Russia's past, in her military glory, in her territorial expansion, in her historical achievements, and in her military heroes. This new patriotic spirit and new attitude toward the past brought forth a number of historical novels which differed greatly from the earlier Soviet historical fiction, especially in their choice

[22] This was the title of a book by R. Seidel and M. Zwieback: *Klassovy vrag na istoricheskom fronte: Tarle i Platonov i ikh shkoly* (*The Class Enemy on the History Front: Tarle and Platonov and Their Schools*).

[23] From an article by Yu. Bocharov in *Istorik-Marksist* (*The Marxian Historian*), quoted by B. H. Sumner, "Soviet History," in The *Slavonic and East European Review*, Vol. XVI (April, 1938), 601.

of subjects. The interest was now focused on critical moments in Russian national life, on the periods when Russia fought for her very existence against external enemies.

Historical Novels with a Difference

Among these new historical novels, one of the earliest and most ambitious was Sergeyev-Tsensky's *Sevastopolskaya strada* (*The Ordeal of Sevastopol*), which was first serialized in 1937-38. The author set himself the task of painting the picture of Russia in 1854-55 against the general background of contemporary history, of doing for the Crimean War what Tolstoy did for the Napoleonic wars of 1805-12. The result was a novel of some fifteen-hundred pages. There is in it, of course, more war than peace, because, unlike the period covered by Tolstoy, the whole of the period chosen by Sergeyev-Tsensky was taken up by the war. We see Sevastopol preparing for the attack, the scuttling of the Russian fleet in the bay, the battles of Alma and Inkermann, the siege of the city, and the famous charge of the Light Brigade. We also see the background of the war—in St. Petersburg, London, and Paris, with Nicholas I, Queen Victoria, and Napoleon the Little all making their appearance on the scene. There are full-length portraits of several historical figures, including Pirogov, the great Russian surgeon who was responsible for the activities of the first Russian Red Cross nurses at the front. Some of the battle scenes are quite well done; the description of the scuttling of the Russian fleet is particularly good. Interlocked with the historical narrative are stories of some personal destinies, in the course of which the author takes the reader to the "rear," to an estate in the province of Kursk, and shows us provincial Russia and its reactions to the war. The novel is not free from an anti-British bias, but is on the whole much more objective than some of the earlier Soviet novels on historical themes.

The period of the Napoleonic Wars and its leading individual figures naturally attracted the attention of Soviet novelists and playwrights. Here, perhaps, the existence of Tolstoy's unique masterpiece deterred many writers from attempting to treat the subject on a large scale (even Sergeyev-Tsensky's novel about the Crimean War invites some invidious comparisons). But there were many works dealing with individual figures and separate episodes. One of the most successful was Vladimir Solovyov's play *Fieldmarshal Kutuzov* (1939). There were also novels and plays about Suvorov and Bagration.

Of the earlier periods in Russian history, the one to attract particular attention was the period of the struggle against the Tartars, with its climax in the famous battle of the Kulikovo Field (1380) in which Prince Dmitry Donskoy defeated the Tartar host of Khan Mamay and paved the way for Russia's final liberation from the Mongol yoke. Dmitry Donskoy is the central figure in the historical novel of that name by Sergey Borodin (pseudonym of Amir Sargidzhan), but its real hero is the Russian people. For his novel Borodin was awarded a Stalin prize. He also wrote a short biography of Dmitry Donskoy which enjoyed wide circulation during the war.

The struggle with the Tartars, seen partly from the other side and on a vaster plane, was the subject of a historical trilogy by V. Yan (pseudonym of Vasily Yanchevetsky). The first two parts of it (*Genghiz-Khan* and *Batu*) had the two great Mongol war captains for their central figures, while the third part dealt with Alexander Nevsky. The whole was a colorful work for which the author drew on various historical sources, both Russian and Oriental, making also large use of Russian folklore.

Of the later rulers of Russia, the two that were reappraised and extolled now were Peter the Great and Ivan the Terrible. Peter was seen both as a man who revolutionized Russia from above and did not stop before harsh coercive measures and as the creator of Russian military might—the man who made Russia a powerful factor in European politics. Soviet literature paid tribute to him through Alexey Tolstoy's novel which has been discussed in an earlier chapter. As for Ivan, he was acclaimed as a precursor of Peter, who realized the necessity of westernward expansion of Russia, and as a great Russian patriot and a wise statesman.

Exterminating the Enemies

In the approach to Ivan as a farsighted patriot and great statesman and not merely a cruel and perverse tyrant, there was nothing essentially novel: this view had already been advanced by some Russian nineteenth-century historians. If there was anything new in the Soviet approach it was the tendency to idealize the personality of the Tsar and to justify his ruthless treatment of his enemies. This vindication was not accidental, for under Stalin's absolute, despotic rule Russia was in many respects going back to the times of Ivan the Terrible, even though those who stress this parallel are often guilty of forgetting the historical perspective and of drawing unwarranted conclusions.

In literature the glorification and idealization of Ivan found its expression during and after the war, and more will be said of it in Chapter VII. Here it should suffice to point out that this particular piece of historical revision was closely bound up with one of the cardinal features of the Soviet scene during this period: the consolidation of Stalin's absolute power, the cunning and ruthless extermination of all opposition in a series of framed-up trials, during which Lenin's Old

Guard, the leading figures in the Comintern and the Communist party, and the front-rank generals of the Red Army were all eliminated on fantastic charges of conspiring with the Germans and the Japanese for the destruction of the Soviet Union. Not the least fantastic feature of these trials was the abject docility with which the accused themselves confessed to their fantastic crimes and the readiness and violence with which the intelligentsia, including writers, denounced them. In September, 1936, the leading article in *October* magazine—entitled "The Vermin is Squashed!"—denounced the sixteen accused in the trial of the "Trotskyite-Zinovievite gang" in the following terms:

There were sixteen of them in the dock. Sixteen base hirelings of Fascism. Sixteen active members of the Trotskyite-Zinovievite gang. Sixteen murderers, who had stained their hands with the blood of the best son of the people, Sergey Mironovich Kirov, came on trial before the people, before history. . . . The Fascist curs confessed their criminal deed. They admitted that they were direct agents of the Gestapo, that they had co-operated with the Fascists.
. . .

The despicable gang of murderers, whose names will be cursed through ages, has been crushed. The sentence of the Court has been carried out. It is easier to breathe now that the Trotskyite-Zinovievite vermin has been squashed.

And so on and so forth, with many bloodthirsty quotations from Vyshinsky, who acted as the chief prosecutor in the trial. The same article denounced the enemies of the people who had "entrenched themselves on the literary front." Among these were included the dramatic critic Pikel, who "for many years operated in the field of 'criticism,' carrying out with impunity his counterrevolutionary deeds" (and who was sentenced to death by the Court); the writer Galina Serebryakova, author of a biographical novel about Marx, who organized a literary salon "with the object of covering up her filthy deeds and connections"; Tarasov-Rodionov, author of *Chocolate*, described now as "a graphomaniac Trotskyite"; the influential critics Selivanovsky and Maznin; the novelists Ivan Katayev, Boris Guber, and N. Zarudin (all of whom belonged to the "Pereval" group), who "gave material assistance to the Trotskyites and 'visited' them in exile."

The editors of *October* continued indignantly:

Enemies of the Party and the people infiltrated themselves into the editorial boards of magazines, into publishing houses, into the Union of Writers, wherever they could, carrying out their infamous, vile, base deeds, taking advantage of rotten liberalism and sometimes of direct connivance.

Then came the inevitable element of self-accusation:

It was a bad mistake on our part and a sign of blunted vigilance when the counterrevolutionary degenerate Friedland and the inveterate Trotskyite terrorist Ter-Vaganyan took part in the discussion about the historical novel organized by *October* magazine in the spring of 1934, and when their speeches were published in our magazine; or when our magazine published *Marx's Youth* by the enemy Serebryakova.

In 1934 Kamenev's henchman Chernyak worked for several months in *October* magazine. The editorial board unmasked and expelled him, but he was immediately invited to work in *Krasnaya Nov.* . . .

Were not a number of bad mistakes, committed by the *Krasnaya Nov* magazine, and consisting in the publication of insolent, frankly counterrevolutionary articles by Vaganyan, due to the blunting of vigilance? Or the publication of such works as *Seekers of Glory* by Orlov, etc., about which *Pravda* wrote indignantly?

To this day Kamenev's henchman Elsberg, who prints his articles in *Krasnaya Nov* and works in the *Academia* publishing house, is active in literature.[24]

The article ascribed these and other facts, which testified to "lack of Bolshevik vigilance," to the "group spirit" which prevailed in literature and overshadowed broad political interests, and proclaimed (in capital letters) the following principle:

The interests of the Party and of the people are the immutable supreme law governing the work and conduct of every truly Soviet writer. There is no justification for our mistakes, for the blunting of Bolshevik vigilance. We are taught vigilance every day and every hour by our Party, by our leader of genius—Stalin.

Joining their voices to the national chorus of wrath against the Trotskyite-Zinovievite gang, Soviet writers have with one accord condemned the Trotskyite agents on the literary front and expelled them from their ranks.[25]

A few months later another Soviet periodical published a special article on "Trotskyite Agents in Literature" in which several literary critics were specifically denounced as Trotsky's agents: Voronsky was called "Trotsky's armsbearer," Mirsky was described as "Averbach's henchman," Lev Levin as "Averbach's envoy in Leningrad," and Oksman (a

---

[24] This "henchman of Kamenev's" reappeared in Soviet literature and was even awarded a Stalin Prize in 1949 (see Chapter VII).

[25] See "Gadina razdavlena!" in *Oktyabr*, No. 9 (1936), 3–8.

well-known historian of literature and specialist on the Pushkin period) as "a swindler and adventurer."[26]

The Cult of Stalin and Mythmaking

The already-quoted *October* article ended on a note that was becoming more and more usual in Soviet literature in those days—of undisguised adulation for Stalin:

> Workers on the literary front—writers, critics, editors, publishers—together with the entire people, are turning their eyes, full of affection and devotion, toward Stalin.
>
> All the thoughts and feelings of our great people are turned toward him, the father of the Soviet Union, the bright sun of humanity, the greatest genius of our age, toward our dear Stalin. His name is uttered by the toilers of the whole globe with immense affection and joy, as a symbol of new and beautiful life.
>
> With the banner of Stalin our country is vigorously and confidently striding from victory to victory.[27]

This cult of Stalin, which gradually acquired truly mythological proportions, became a distinctive feature of Soviet society in the thirties: no parallel to it can be found in the early history of the Soviet Union during Lenin's lifetime; and even the posthumous myth of Lenin pales before the living legend of Stalin. The idolatrous sentiments for Stalin were voiced on all possible occasions, but more especially in connection with the trials and purges of his enemies and on the occasion of the promulgation of the Stalin Constitution in 1936, which provided the Soviet Union with a democratic façade and a most liberal constitution on paper (never, however, has the gulf between what was decreed on paper and the reality been so wide). This cult of Stalin found also its reflection in literature: in the poems of Prokofyev, Shchipachov, Dolmatovsky, Lebedev-Kumach, Surkov, and many others whose reputation was established in the thirties will be found numerous adulatory references to Stalin. Older writers, too, could not escape the contagion. A few of those who apparently refused to "conform," in one way or another, to the new ideological outlook were forced to silence and eventually disappeared from the literary scene. They included those who were openly denounced as "Trotskyite agents" and "enemies of the people," but there were also some who "faded out" silently, without much ado. Thus, nothing was heard, after 1937, of Babel and Pilnyak. The latter was credibly reported, outside the Soviet Union, to have been arrested

[26] L. Plotkin, "Trotskistskaya agentura v literature" ("Trotskyite Agents in Literature"), in *Zvezda*, No. 7 (1937).
[27] "Gadina razdavlena!" in *Oktyabr*, No. 9 (1936), 3–8.

Changes in Soviet Outlook

and shot in 1937, but officially his death was never announced. Babel
was known to have been in a concentration camp, but again there is no
official information, and it must be left to the future historian of Soviet
literature to ascertain the exact circumstances of their "disappearance"
from literature and their personal fate. There is no parallel anywhere
in modern times to such complete disappearance of writers of the caliber
of Pilnyak and Babel. Mystery surrounds also the fate of Olesha. Not a
line of his was published in the leading Soviet literary magazines between 1938 and the outbreak of the war. During the war, when most
Soviet writers contributed to the war effort as front-line correspondents,
and when even Pasternak and Akhmatova wrote poems inspired by the
war, Olesha's name was never mentioned. It reappeared again after the
war, when at least one of his stories was published in *Ogonyok*, a weekly popular magazine. But he soon disappeared again.[28]

To list all the Soviet writers who "faded out" in the thirties would
be a hard task, requiring meticulous research and access to all Soviet
publications. One more major disappearance may be mentioned here,
however—that of Mikhail Koltsov (b. 1898), the well-known Soviet
journalist, renowned for his sharp style and his biting denunciations of
the "bourgeois" enemies of the Soviet Union. The last important job
he did for *Pravda* was to cover the Civil War in Spain. His *Ispansky
dnevnik (The Spanish Diary)* appeared in 1938.

Connected with the cult of Stalin and the denigration of his enemies, particularly of Trotsky and the alleged "Trotskyites," was the
falsification of recent history undertaken in literature. A typical example of it was the already mentioned novel *Bread,* by Alexey Tolstoy,
written obviously for the purpose of glorifying the role of Stalin in the
Civil War at the expense of Trotsky. History was travestied in a similar
way in a film called "The Defense of Tsaritsyn," which dealt with the
same period of the Civil War. Needless to say, all more or less compli-
mentary references to Trotsky in the early works of Soviet literature
are being expunged from recent reissues.[29]

[28] Without access to all periodicals and other Soviet publications it is impossible
to ascertain the exact dates of these "disappearances." The last story by Pilnyak that
has come to my notice was published in *Literaturny sovremennik*, No. 2 (1937); the
last story by Babel, in *Krasnaya Nov*, No. 7 (1937). Several short stories and sketches
by Olesha (of little intrinsic interest) appeared in 1936 in *30 dney*, a magazine devoted to short stories, poetry, and literary criticism. In 1937, both *30 dney* and *Zvezda*
published fragments from a film scenario written by Olesha and A. Macheret (it was
called "Walter" and its subject was the persecution of political enemies in Nazi Germany). In 1938 there appeared in *30 dney* (No. 4) a short, journalistic piece by Olesha
entitled "Nasha rodina—Rossiyskaya sotsialisticheskaya respublika" ("Our Country—The Russian Socialist Republic"). Ironically, it appears that it was after this
loyal (and very trite) expression of Soviet patriotism that Olesha disappeared for a
long time from Soviet literature.

[29] Typical of this attitude was an article by Colonel E. Boltin, "Lenin and

After the 1937 trial of the "right wing" opposition, in which the principal accused—Bukharin, Rykov, Krestinsky, and Yagoda—were described as "the frenzied slaves of the German-Japanese-British-Polish intelligence services" (this hyphening in itself was a priceless example of Soviet "incantation formulae") and accused, among other crimes, of the murder of Kirov and Gorky, the theme of foreign "spies" and "diversionists" provided many a Soviet novelist and playwright with material, and even some of the best writers hastened to make use of it.

The Soviet Union Going Conservative

Parallel with the growing conservatism in art, the rehabilitation of the historical past and its heroes, the emergence of Soviet patriotism, and the sedulous cultivation of the Russian species of "Führerism" ("vozhdizm"), went the process of what has been described as the birth of the new respectability.[30] It meant, in the first place, the restoration of the family as an object of respect and as the mainstay of the state. Divorce laws were tightened, abortions made illegal, and sexual laxity strongly condemned. In matters of education there was a marked return to old-time, pre-Revolutionary methods. An end was put to all experimenting with progressive education. Discipline came back into its own, and with it such old-fashioned "bourgeois" institutions as grades, examinations, certificates, gold medals, uniforms, segregation of sexes, military schools modeled on the old cadet academies and named after Suvorov, and so on. This retrogressive process was slow and gradual, and some of the changes mentioned here were enacted only in the forties. It goes without saying that, under the new dispensation, one of the distinctive features of the early Soviet educational system—the large part allotted to students in the management of schools—went overboard. Today Ognyov's novel about a Soviet school of the twenties (see Chapter III) reads like a glaring anachronism.

The reappearance of economic inequality was another feature of the period. It was the natural result of the encouragement given to personal incentive in industry and collective farming which is associated with the famous Stakhanov movement. It is also curious to note that in the pre-World-War II world, the Soviet Union was the only country in

Stalin, the Organizers of the Red Army and Inspirers of its Victories," in *Novy Mir*, No. 2-3 (1940), 274-85. All the credit for the creation of the Red Army was given to Stalin, while Trotsky was mentioned only once as "Judas Trotsky."

[30] The expression is not mine. It was used by the late Sir John Maynard, a benevolent student of the inner processes in the Soviet Union, as a chapter heading in his book *Russia in Flux*. He himself borrowed it from John D. Littlepage and Demaree Bess, who in their book *In Search of Soviet Gold* say: "A new kind of respectability is emerging, which sometimes seems almost as extreme in one direction as the previous ideas in the other." This phrase aptly describes the Soviet processes in the thirties.

Europe where domestic servants were not a vanishing institution but a fixture of everyday life—not a privilege within the reach of a few rich, but a right to which the Soviet intelligentsia, officialdom, and technocracy felt justly entitled.

This is not the place to study all these new facts and trends in detail; they belong to the domain of the sociologist and student of politics. But they must be recorded, for they not only were reflected in Soviet literature of this period, but also affected its character. The official slogan—"Life has become gayer, comrades!"—was taken up by Soviet writers who vied with each other in describing "the new and beautiful life."

It should also be mentioned that this period saw a gradual relaxation of the antireligious campaign which had reached its climax in the early thirties. A characteristic incident occurred in 1937 when the one-time poet laureate of the Soviet regime, Demyan Bedny, was officially rebuked for the opera libretto he wrote, entitled *Bogatyri* (*Epic Heroes*), because he spoke in it slightingly of Russia's conversion to Christianity in the tenth century. The authority of Karl Marx was invoked to show that this historical event was a progressive factor of great moment. The opera was withdrawn.

These processes, which have sometimes been described as the Russian "Thermidor" (though they bore little resemblance to the original French Thermidor), were of dual nature. Up to a point, they represented a genuine concession to the unspoken desires and sentiments of the masses which had grown tired of the Revolution and the sacrifices it imposed on them in the name of long-distance goals—hence the promise of gayer life, of less austerity, and of greater personal comforts and amenities, which played such an important part in the government propaganda in the late thirties. To some extent the fostering of national feelings and the rehabilitation of the past also represented a sop to the population which could not be roused by the prospect of the world triumph of Communism. On the other hand, these processes meant a tightening of the Party's totalitarian hold on the country—by strengthening the discipline and by suppressing all manifestations of nonconformism while at the same time creating new large groups of people interested in the maintenance of the existing regime. Behind all these ideological changes could be detected the one all-powerful motive which demanded the preservation of the totalitarian single-party dictatorship. The worship of the Soviet state had replaced the worship of the old abstract ideal of world revolution. But the ideal remained. And the importance of literature as a docile instrument of the Party policy was realized more clearly than ever. A repetition of the literary chaos of the twenties could not be allowed.

5. Socialist Realism: Practice

Types and Heroes

ONE of the objects of Socialist realism in literature was described by some of its advocates as the creation of *types*—of typical characters of the revolutionary epoch—a task in which until then most Soviet writers were believed to have failed. On the other hand, there were also those partisans of Socialist realism who stressed the search for *heroes* and the reflection of the heroic features of the great revolutionary age, again maintaining that literature had hitherto failed to do so. These two aspects of Socialist realism, as it was understood by Soviet writers and critics, were reflected in the literary output which followed the "reform" of 1932.

Among the early achievements of Socialist realism Soviet critics counted Sholokhov's *Virgin Soil Upturned,* although it was largely written and even published in the earlier period of the Five-Year Plan. Among the works of that era it stood out through its greater objectivity. Sholokhov succeeded in realistically depicting a whole sector of Soviet life and in portraying a number of typical characters. Davydov, a Leningrad workman whom the Party sends into the South to supervise collectivization and who has to fight the small-bourgeois, possessive instincts of the Cossacks; Nagulnov, who represents the left-wing deviations within the Party and ends by being expelled from it; Ostrovnov, a thrifty farmer who, in joining the collective farm and even becoming its manager, pursues in reality his personal ends; and the colorful old man Shchukar—all these are memorable character creations, typical and individualized at the same time. Davydov was probably meant by the author to serve as the embodiment of revolutionary heroism, but as a model hero he did not come off.

Another achievement of Socialist realism was seen by the critics in Bruno Jasieński's novel *Chelovek menyaet kozhu (A Man Sloughs His Skin,* 1934).

Jasieński (b. 1901) was one of a number of international Communists who found their spiritual, and later also physical, home in Moscow. Of German-Polish descent, he belonged apparently to the cosmopolitan group of artists in Paris and wrote his first works in French (among others, *Je brûle Paris,* a Utopian revolutionary novel). His fate was not unlike that of many other foreign Communists who came to worship at the shrine of Lenin: he was accused of Trotskyism and "liquidated."

The principal character in *A Man Sloughs His Skin* is a young American engineer who is shown as gradually shedding his bourgeois nature and becoming a true friend of the Communists. The action of the novel is set against the background of Socialist reconstruction in central Asia, with flashbacks into the pre-Revolutionary past. There are many diverse characters including several American engineers, one of whom is a disguised British intelligence agent (in his story Jasienski deliberately mixed facts—or what he believed to be facts—and fiction). The novel had a well-organized plot and was competently written. Whether it was written directly in Russian is not clear, but on its first edition there is no mention of its being a translation, and by rights it belongs to Soviet literature.

A place apart belongs to *Kak zakalyalas stal* (*That's How Steel Was Tempered,* 1935) by Nikolay Ostrovsky (1904–1936). Like Furmanov's *Chapayev* and Serafimovich's *Iron Torrent,* it is regarded as a major Soviet classic. Frankly autobiographical, though not told in the first person, it describes the formation and growth of a young Communist of working-class origins, his childhood, his part in the Civil War, and his share in the subsequent reconstruction effort. The hero, Pavel Korchagin, an embodiment of true-red Communism and revolutionary heroism, became one of the most popular characters in Soviet fiction, at least if one is to believe official Soviet information. The element of Socialist "uplift," which came to be regarded as one of the indispensable ingredients of Socialist realism, played an important part in Ostrovsky's "novel," in which the influence of Gorky can be clearly seen. Its popularity was partly due to the appeal of the author's personality. Blind and bedridden during the last years of his life, he battled heroically against these handicaps, dictating his novel, taking an active interest in life, and receiving visitors. At the seaside resort of Sochi in the Caucasus, where he lived, he became almost a kind of institution and an object of devout pilgrimages. To what extent Ostrovsky's nationwide popularity was spontaneous and what part was played in it by deliberate mythmaking is difficult to say.

Among the other works boosted during this period may be mentioned Anton Makarenko's semifictional *Pedagogicheskaya poema* (*Educational Epic,* 1934) and its sequel, *Kniga dlya roditeley* (*A Book for Parents,* 1938). Makarenko (1888–1939) was a noted Soviet pedagogue who specialized in juvenile delinquents, of which there were a great many in the Soviet Union. *Educational Epic* (translated into English as *Road to Life*) described in detail Makarenko's educational venture in the famous Gorky colony for the waifs and strays of the Revolution. For the most part it has a sincere ring and is of considerable interest to a student of Soviet education, though probably it does not tell the whole story or the whole truth. In its sequel the tendency to idealize the reality is much more pronounced. This is even more true of Makarenko's novel *Flagi na bashnyakh* (*Flags on Towers,* 1939).

*

Older Writers' Contribution to Socialist Realism

LEONOV

Leonid Leonov's only major prose fiction during this period—his first since *Skutarevsky*—was a long novel entitled *Doroga na Okean* (*The Road to the Ocean*, 1935). Like nearly everything Leonov wrote, it is an interesting work. Its complex, unwieldy structure, with numerous intersecting lines of plot and a great number of characters bound together by intricate ties, is further complicated by the curious superimposition of three temporal planes in the narrative: the present, the past, and the future. Leonov is in fact carrying three parallel narratives. In the first, which unrolls in the present—about 1934—the background for the action is provided by the life, political and other, of the Volga-Revizan railway, of which Kurilov, the novel's principal character, is the political director. The railway, however, forms only the setting; the main interest of the novel is psychological, and as usual Leonov is concerned primarily with complex human relationships.

Kurilov takes a notable place in Leonov's portrait gallery: it was his first attempt to place a real Communist in the center of the picture, to make him the pivot round which the story revolves. Kurilov is an active Communist with a distinguished Party and Civil War record, with a past that obliges and a responsible position in the present. He is an *"otvetstvenny rabotnik,"* a high-ranking Communist official. Communist critics reproached Leonov for underrating the political aspect of his "hero" and dwelling on his "human, all too human" feelings and failings. But it is no accident, perhaps, that Leonov shows us Kurilov from this "human" angle, at grips with an incurable disease and gradually realizing, at the approach of death, how little personal enjoyment he has had from life. Hence his mild platonic "affairs," his interest in other people's lives, his unexpected tolerance for one of his bitterest class enemies, his brother-in-law Omelichev, whom he discovers among the employees of his railway. In the end Kurilov dies after an unsuccessful operation performed by the famous surgeon Ilya Protoklitov.

Leonov's characteristic predilection for showing human relationships as complex tangles is revealed in the fact that Ilya is the husband of Liza, in whose life Kurilov comes to play a very important part: after meeting him, her whole life and outlook are completely transformed. Ilya also has a brother, Gleb, who, next to Kurilov, is the most important character in the book. A former White Army officer, he is an active enemy of Communism. By clever deceit he worms his way into the Communist party and secures for himself an important post under Kurilov. In Kurilov he sees the main danger to his far-reaching designs, and by a series of clever moves tries to forestall him. Later, Gleb very nearly suggests to his brother Ilya (who as Liza's husband has a personal grudge against Kurilov) the idea of a surgical murder. Gleb's undoing comes during a periodical purge in the Communist cell of his railway depot. Despite his clever tissue of lies, despite an artistically faked proletarian autobiography, he fails: at the last moment his own brother unmasks him.

Parallel with this plane runs the story of the past, which is concerned with the pre-Revolutionary antecedents of the same railway, with its construction and the concomitant interplay of private interests and unsavory speculation. Leonov introduces a young Communist journalist, Peresypkin, a friend of Kurilov's, who unearths this past story of the Volga-Revizan railway from forgotten archives and oral legends. The link which connects the past story with the present is a certain Pokhvisnev, who happens to be the uncle of Liza Protoklitova. But this story of the past, told with many unsavory details, in that Dostoyevskian vein of which Leonov is so fond, seems a rather artificial adjunct to the main story, and its *raison d'être* is not very easy to detect.

Superimposed on these two stories, which jostle and interfere with each other and make the reader at times lose his bearings among the welter of names and incidents, is a third story. This is a Utopian picture of the world of the future, of Ocean, "the mother of the cities of the future" (situated apparently somewhere in the Far East), to which the author himself accompanies Kurilov and Peresypkin, and which is presented simultaneously as the author's and Kurilov's vision and as a reality of the future. Much of this story is given in long footnotes which sometimes run into pages—an original but most annoying device. Particular stress is laid on the military events of the future, on the war between the Federated Soviet Republics and the non-Sovietized remainder of the world. Soviet critics reproached Leonov for having thus circumscribed his vision and failed to visualize the man of the future and the kind of life he was going to live. Even more important was Leonov's failure to blend organically his Utopia with the rest of the novel; the footnote device was clear evidence of this. As a whole, the novel was a failure, but even so it was more interesting than some of the so-called "achievements" of Socialist realism.

FEDIN

Fedin's principal work published during this period was *Pokhishchenie Evropy* (*The Rape of Europe*, 1934–35). The interval which elapsed between the publication of the first and the second volume accounted for a certain shift of emphasis and the resulting lack of unity.

Originally one of Fedin's objects seems to have been to contrast the bustling Soviet Union of the Five-Year Plan with the quiescent and

decadent bourgeois West. In the first volume the action is set in Western
Europe: in Norway, Holland, and Germany. Europe is shown through
the eyes of a Communist journalist, Rogov, who has some traits in
common with two of Fedin's earlier heroes, Startsov and Nikita Karev,
with the difference, however, that he is a Communist and is not faced
with the problem of adjusting himself to the Revolution.

The bourgeois world is personified in the van Rossoems, a family
of Dutch timber merchants who held vast interests in Russia before the
Revolution and obtained from the Soviet government a concession for
their former forests. Philip van Rossoem, the younger brother, who is
responsible for the firm's dealings with the Soviet Union, stands for
modern progressive spirit in business; knowing Russia and the Russians
well, he likes the country and has no prejudice against the new regime.
To him is opposed his elder brother and partner, Lodevijk, who dis-
likes the very idea of trading with "those godless Bolsheviks" and looks
askance at the extension of the firm's trading business in Russia, especially as the affairs of the concession run far from smoothly and there
are growing signs of the Soviet government's unwillingness to prolong
it on the old basis. But Lodevijk's health is failing (he dies later in the
book), and Philip is allowed to have his way. The third representative
of the van Rossoem family is their nephew, Frans, who is the firm's
agent in Russia and is married to a Russian woman with a somewhat
romantic past: dissatisfied with her drab life in the Soviet Union, Klavdia Andreyevna escaped across the Finnish border and joined the
émigrés, adopting the career of a night-club dancer. Frans von Rossoem
met her in a Riga night club, fell in love with her, and took her back to
Russia as his wife. At the time Rogov arrives in Holland she is there
on a visit to Phillip van Rossoem. Rogov falls in love with her and they
go back to Russia as lovers.

To Philip and Lodevijk van Rossoem—one of them modern, progressive, broad-minded, the other conservative and old-fashioned but a
model of gentlemanly urbanity—Fedin opposes another capitalist type
in the person of Sir Justus Elderling-Geyser, in whom Soviet critics saw
an intentional likeness of Sir Henry Deterding: it is true that although
Fedin took some pains to disguise his name, that of the "Shell Oil Company" appears in the novel without any disguise. Whereas the van
Rossoems are portrayed as three-dimensional human beings with their
individual characteristics, Elderling-Geyser resembles a crude *Pravda*
cartoon of a capitalist "shark."

There is little incident or movement in the first volume of the
novel. Much of it is taken up with descriptions, some of which—such
as the urban landscapes of Bergen and Amsterdam, done in the Flemish
manner—are very good. But there is about the whole novel that static

quality which characterized also Fedin's second novel, *The Brothers.* Only here it is more accentuated.

In the second volume the pace is even slower, while the action moves to Russia to a place on the White Sea coast, and then to Leningrad and Moscow. At the end of the first volume Philip van Rossoem sails for Russia to discuss the affairs of his concession; the second volume opens with his arrival. There we see Philip and Frans fighting a losing battle over their concession, which is finally annulled: the Soviets are now strong enough to dictate their own terms, and Philip has to be satisfied with the role of a mere timber broker for the Soviet Union. His business defeat is compensated by his "conquest" of Klavdia whom, after Frans's death in a motor accident (or was it suicide?), he takes back with him to Holland.

The main defect of the novel is the lack of unity of design between the two parts, with the result that the second volume represents a series of scenes with no backbone to them. In the first volume such a backbone is supplied by the satirical picture of decaying Europe. But there is no corresponding counter-picture of the Soviet Union. The mythological title is somewhat obscure and sounds farfetched. In the first volume it might have referred to Rogov's "abduction" of Klavdia, but in the second volume Klavdia is in turn "abducted" by Philip van Rossoem. At the same time, there is no real justification for the title if it is to be understood politically or ideologically.

Another work Fedin wrote during this period was a very short novel (rather a novelette) called *Sanatory "Arktur"* (*Sanatorium "Arcturus,"* 1936). Its action is set in Davos in a sanatorium for tubercular patients. The principal character is a young Russian who is recovering from tuberculosis. He is one of Fedin's favorite "reasoning observers." There is very little action—Fedin's static technique is suited by this picture, painted in subdued tones, of semireal existence on the confines of death.

KAVERIN

The element of personal life, the portrayal of which was implied in Socialist realism, played a large part in Kaverin's new novel *Ispolnenie zhelany* (*The Fulfillment of Desires,* 1934–35). The problem of the individual's integration in society had always interested Kaverin, but this time he showed more interest in the people themselves and their personal problems. The hero of the novel is Trubachevsky, a young student of literature who makes a literary discovery. His friend Kartashikhin, who is of proletarian origin, is contrasted to him and shown as a more useful and purposeful member of society. Another character, Novodvorov, introduces the political-detective element, for he is an enemy in disguise, a secret agent of some anti-Soviet *émigré* organization (the persistence of this motif in the Soviet novels of the mid-thirties serves well to illustrate the potency of the "social command"). The characters include also an old professor of literature for whom Trubachevsky works, his son (another class enemy and a friend of Novodvorov), and his daughter; the latter is in love with Kartashikhin and supplies the romantic element.

The novel is much more simple and straightforward in outline than *Artist Unknown*. There is no toying with the plot of which Kaverin used to be so fond and which now might easily have been interpreted as "bourgeois Formalism." The message of the novel, if any, is not very obvious: perhaps it is to be sought in the ultimate winning back to the community of Trubachevsky, who for a while goes astray and is shown as preoccupied too much with things of little importance in a Socialist society.

This novel of Kaverin's was followed by *Dva Kapitana* (*Two Captains,* 1939). It is a story of adventure, with a mild detective interest, woven round the pre-Revolutionary Arctic explorings of a Russian captain, but involving also its post-Revolutionary echoes and aftermath. Compared with the majority of contemporary Soviet novels, it has a pleasant accent of freshness and novelty. Kaverin's interest in the plot, in adventure, is certainly refreshing. The book is somehow reminiscent of Arthur Ransome's juvenile sea yarns (plus the inevitable ideological element), and although it first appeared in a regular literary magazine, most of its subsequent editions were issued by the Children's Section of the State Publishing House (*Detizdat*). It is, in fact, a book for children which can be read and enjoyed by grown-ups.

KATAYEV

Katayev's *Beleyet parus odinoky* (*Lone White Sail,* 1936) is one of this author's most attractive works. Its autobiographical background is obvious. The action is set in Odessa, where Katayev himself grew up and where his father was a schoolmaster. The principal characters in the book are two boys: one, Petya Bachey, the son of a high-school teacher; the other, Gavrik, a little fisherman. The novel takes place in 1905, against the background of the first Russian Revolution, and this gives Katayev a chance to introduce elements of exciting adventure. We catch glimpses of the Potyomkin mutiny, of a typical Jewish pogrom, of street fighting and strikes in Odessa. But these revolutionary activities merely form the background; the main interest and charm of the novel derive from the fresh and delightful presentation of the two boys—one of them a typical intelligentsia boy, the other a little Odessa street Arab—and of their half-childish, half-adult experiences and adventures.

In Petya's case the grown-up element is introduced by the Revolution, which suddenly encroaches upon his uneventful everyday life. Here and there the author forgets that he is showing us the Revolution of 1905 through the eyes of two nine-year-old boys, and there are passages—for example about religion and the Church—which must jar on the readers' ears whatever their views; but such passages are few, and against them can be set such wholly delightful pages as the opening description of Petya's last day on a seaside farm in Bessarabia; the picture of Petya's school entrance examinations when he is deeply disappointed by not being allowed to recite right through Lermontov's poem about the "lone white sail"; the whole episode of the street game of "buttons," of which Gavrik is a recognized champion, and how this involves Petya in petty larceny, lies, and other misdeeds; or the wanderings of the two boys about the city in the early days of the Revolution, when Petya unwittingly carries in his school satchel cartridges which he believes to be Gavrik's spoils at "buttons." These and some other scenes have about them an accent of freshness and spontaneousness and in their genuinely deep insight into children's psychology are worthy to rank with some of the best things written about children in Russian literature. The novel was turned by Katayev into a very successful play for the Children's Theater in Moscow and later made into a film which had some memorable acting by child actors in the principal roles.

Katayev's short novelette *Ya, syn trudovogo naroda* (*I, the Son of the Toiling People,* 1937), based on his experience in the early days of the Civil War, is of little interest.

ALEXEY TOLSTOY, MALYSHKIN, ZOSHCHENKO, VSEVOLOD IVANOV, NIKITIN, AND OTHERS

Alexey Tolstoy's chief contribution to Socialist realism literature—apart from his historical novels and plays—was the last part of his long novel *The Way through Hell,* which has already been mentioned. Another work of his, the novel *Bread,* revealed an important and distinctive aspect of Socialist realism: the tendency to rewrite recent history to fit in with the latest Party line. There is no doubt that in writing *Bread* Tolstoy was carrying out an assignment. Its subject was the Civil War, more specifically the defense of Tsaritsyn (Stalingrad) against the Whites in 1919. The author's principal object was to glorify the role played by Stalin and Voroshilov and to expose Trotsky's "treacherous" conduct. This Tolstoy did to the best of his considerable natural ability, but despite some good characterizations and vivid descriptions the novel did not add any new laurels to his crown.

The statute of the Union of Soviet Writers stipulates that Socialist realism must aim, not only at describing the realities of the new world, but also at remolding men and educating them toward Socialism. Its literature must provide edifying examples. This "Socialist uplift" became an integral part of Soviet literature in the nineteen thirties. Several writers tackled the theme of moral and political "reformation" of hostile elements. Thus Zoshchenko, in *Istoriya odnoy zhizni (The Story of One Life,* 1935) chose for his setting the construction of the White Sea–Baltic (Stalin) Canal, which was built with the forced labor of common law criminals and political prisoners, under the supervision of the Ogpu, and described the moral regeneration of an ordinary criminal working on that construction. Soviet critics welcomed Zoshchenko's book as a new step towards the portrayal of a positive character, and a renunciation of his customary satirical method and approach. But the book, with its sentimental idealization of the Ogpu men, is one of Zoshchenko's weakest: he was obviously out of his element. The same subject, on a wider scale, was dealt with in Pogodin's play, of which more will be said later.

The "reforging" of hostile or indifferent elements—to use the formula popular in the Soviet press of the time—was also one of the themes of Malyshkin's *Lyudi iz zakholustya (People from the Backwoods,* 1938). This work was planned as a long and ambitious novel, with a great number of characters and two parallel lines of action, one in Moscow, the other at a big construction project in the Urals. The action is set during the first Five-Year Plan at the height of the reconstruction fever. Unfortunately, only the first volume was written, the author dying soon after its publication. It is an interesting, though uneven, work. Several of the characters—Peter Soustin, Zhurkin, and Tishka—are quite well done, and most of the chapters dealing with the Krasnogorsk project and its life are good: well written, vivid, and free from all idealization.

In the late thirties two former Serapions, of whom little had been heard for some time, made a comeback. Nikolay Nikitin published a long novel, *Eto nachalos v Kokande (This Began at Kokand,* 1940), describing the period of Socialist reconstruction in Central Asia; and Vsevolod Ivanov wrote a long and colorful autobiographical novel entitled *Pokhozhdeniya fakira (The Adventures of a Fakir,* 1935). In 1938 Ivanov published *Parkhomenko,* a biographical novel about a noted Civil War leader, which heralded a revival of the Civil War theme in literature. The new approach to it, however, contrasted sharply with the romantic hyperbolism of Pilnyak and his followers. It was more realistic and more historical, even though history, as in Alexey Tolstoy's *Bread,* was often distorted to suit the official Party line of the moment. Among these "socialist-realistic" novels about the Civil War may be mentioned another biography of a Red Cossack leader, *Kochu-bey* (1937), by Arkady Perventsev (b. 1905).

Some Newcomers

PAVLENKO

At the 1934 Congress of Soviet Writers great stress was laid on the need for creating special "national defense literature." Several works were written to meet this demand. A typical example was *Na vostoke* (*In the East,* 1937) by Peter Alexandrovich Pavlenko, formerly a member of the "Pereval" group.

Pavlenko was not exactly a newcomer to Soviet literature. Born in 1899, he spent his childhood and youth in the Caucasus. Between 1919 and 1924 he was engaged in active Communist work in the oil city of Baku, developing there a strong hatred for Britain and the British. In 1924 he went as a delegate to the Communist party congress in Moscow, and in the summer of the same year was sent on some vague mission abroad which took him to Turkey, Syria, Greece, Italy, and France. About this time he also made his literary debut with a book called *Aziatskie povesti* (*Asiatic Tales*), exotic in subject matter and florid in style. Among his later works mention has already been made of *Barricades,* a novel about the Paris Commune. But it was not until 1937, when *In the East* appeared, that he made a real hit in Soviet literature.

Pavlenko's novel has no "hero" in the ordinary literary sense of the word. In a different sense, most of its many characters—with the obvious exception of the enemies of the Soviet Union—are heroes in their respective walks of life. Its underlying idea is that small and seemingly inconspicuous doings are just as "heroic" under the circumstances as the most startling exploits. The real hero of Pavlenko's novel is the Soviet Far East with its spirit of daring, enterprise, and enthusiasm. Soviet men are shown here, on the remote fringes of the vast Soviet territory, blazing new trails and building a new life. The book had a definite propaganda object and value since it portrayed the work of reconstruction and military preparations on the Soviet Far Eastern frontier in anticipation of a Japanese attack. To many people in the Soviet Union the menace of Japanese aggression seemed at the time more immediate and real than the menace of Nazi Germany.

The first two parts of the novel, the action of which starts in 1932, deal mostly with peaceful activities—with the building of new cities in Siberian forests, the carrying out of new and daring projects by young Soviet men whom Pavlenko characterized in the following words:

> And so they came out there in hundreds of thousands and in millions in order to keep pace with the Revolution and not lag a

step behind it. Their fathers had burned down estates, had defended scores of fronts, had lost their wives and become disused to their children, while the sons were building cities and setting up stable families, were getting used to sleeping eight hours and eating three meals a day.

It is a picture of stabilization, of the Revolution settling down to peaceful work after a hectic period of struggle and destruction, yet losing none of its zest and enthusiasm. A whole procession of builders, explorers, collective farm managers, military commanders, and Ogpu officials, passes before our eyes, while we also get glimpses of frontier skirmishes, of Chinese and Korean guerrilla leaders, and of Japanese and White Russian spies who cross the frontier from Manchukuo. In fact, peaceful reconstruction is but one side of the picture. Gradually, military activities and military preparations are thrust to the forefront. Part Four of the novel, where the action is set at some future though not very distant date—"the year 193."—describes the war between the Soviet Union and Japan, started by the latter and won by the former: Tokyo is bombed and destroyed from the air, the Japanese fleet is defeated by Soviet submarines, while the Japanese land attack fails thanks to some mysterious and deadly new weapon invented by the Soviets. The rising of the Japanese workers and the insurrection in China combine to make the military rout of Japan complete and final. The last part of the book describes the feverish building of a new town, to be called Sen Katayama after the well-known Japanese revolutionary, which is to house seventy thousand Japanese, Chinese, Korean, and Manchu war prisoners, as well as its Russian builders, and thus symbolize the triumph of international brotherhood. One of the episodes of this last part of the novel describes the trial, in Sen Katayama, of the chief villain, the old and astute Japanese arch-spy Marusima, but strangely enough the outcome of the trial is not mentioned.

Pavlenko's novel gives some interesting glimpses of Soviet life and activities in the Far East, but it shows traces of hasty writing, and the episodes dealing with the Japanese and White Russian spying activities smack of a cheap thriller and are unconvincing.

It is interesting to note that although the novel appeared at the time when the outside world labored under the illusion that the Soviet Union had abandoned its dream of world revolution and was evolving along purely nationalist lines, Pavlenko did not hesitate to sound the "internationalist" note. "There are a million Communists in Europe— the war will be to the bitter end," says one of the characters in the novel. England is shown by Pavlenko as the symbol of the old capitalist world which is bound to collapse:

Whole nations were dying before people's eyes. Political systems established in the course of centuries crumbled to pieces. England was tossing in agony, and the young nations, her laborers, stood by, their mouths agape with joy and happiness. With England, a whole era in the history of mankind was passing away. If it were possible to impersonate political systems we would have seen a decrepit gentleman posing as a diplomat and an educator, who, after his death, turned out to be only a secondhand dealer and usurer. And as always happens in the life of men, no sooner had this enterprising merchant died than a hungry shoeblack emerged and, on the strength of a certain similarity in their biographies, claimed to be the historical successor of the deceased.

Pavlenko's "hungry shoeblack" was Japan.

HERMAN

Yury Pavlovich Herman (b. 1910) published his first major work in 1936, when Socialist realism was in full swing. It was a novel called *Nashi znakomye (Our Friends)*. The book had an immediate success, partly because it satisfied a widespread demand for pictures of everyday life and ordinary people. Its very title was apparently designed to convey the idea that people in the book were the kind that every reader could meet in everyday life. Almost throughout the book—which is long, somewhat old-fashioned in construction, and tries to be very "true to life"—the author succeeds in maintaining an accent of quiet, unobtrusive veracity and only toward the end cannot withstand the temptation of sliding into sentimental idealization.

Our Friends is a story of an attractive Soviet girl, Antonina Staroselskaya, a dreamer in search of a meaning of life. This she finally finds in social work and in a marriage (her third, the first two having been failures) to an Ogpu official, who twice crosses her path before she really gets to know him.

The story begins in 1925, during the NEP period (there is a clearly detectable undercurrent of hostility in the author's portrayal of NEP conditions, reminiscent of the attitude of Gladkov's ideal Communists). Antonina, a sixteen-year-old girl, is left alone after the death of her father, an accountant in some Soviet institution. She gives up school, sells her father's belongings, and starts looking for work. At one of the labor exchanges she meets a famous and popular actor and falls in love with him, dreamily and romantically. He takes her to supper in a luxurious restaurant, and this constitutes the climax of Antonina's romance; the next day the actor goes away, leaving Antonina to her dreams of him.

After that she drifts, more or less against her will, into marriage with Skvortsov, a merchant seaman who is engaged in smuggling activities, and becomes his unwilling accomplice. When Skvortsov is caught by the Ogpu, Antonina is summoned and questioned by Altus, the Ogpu official, whom she had met casually before. Skvortsov is sentenced to three years of hard labor, but Antonina is let off. She finds work as a hairdresser's assistant, but continues to lead the same half-dreamy, half-real existence, unconscious of its purpose but vaguely feeling that some such purpose will be found. A neighbor of the Skvortsovs, Pal Palych Shvyryatykh, a former waiter, maître d'hôtel and director of restaurants under the old regime, now in charge of one of the Soviet canteens, falls in love with Antonina. An elderly man who lost in the Revolution not only his fortune but also his dream of becoming a landowner, he is at bottom not bad and is full of gentle and genuine solicitude for Antonina and her little son. In his friendship Antonina finds an outlet from her solitude. Skvortsov, whom Antonina had divorced in the meantime, returns after having served his term, and she has not the heart nor the will to refuse him. For a time they live together; then Skvortsov is run over by a car, and just as she had drifted into marriage with Skvortsov, Antonina now drifts into marriage with Pal Palych. Outwardly their marriage is happy at first: he is full of love and tenderness for her, while she, without loving him, feels that she owes him a debt of gratitude. But at heart she is still dissatisfied with life and tormented by vague yearnings. All this leads to a stupid affair with one of Pal Palych's former customers, a representative of the old bourgeoisie. It culminates in a repulsive scene during which Pal Palych beats his rival almost to death, while Antonina realizes how stupid and undignified her behavior was. She makes up with Pal Palych and falls back into the old, smooth groove. They plan a journey to Crimea, when suddenly this frail structure of Antonina's existence is upset by an unexpected visit from Tatyana, former caretaker of the house where she used to live. Tatyana is also Skvortsov's former mistress, but now is running a stockbreeding farm somewhere in the country. For a few days Tatyana—this new and changed Tatyana, a useful member of society—stays with Antonina, and after seeing her off, the latter decides to break with Pal Palych. This escape from Pal Palych and the atmosphere of peaceful smugness concludes the second part of the novel. The third part tells of Antonina's "regeneration" through learning and work and of the ultimate happiness she finds in her marriage with Altus. The dreamer becomes a socially useful member of the community. The ending strikes a false note, and Altus himself, this guardian angel from the Ogpu, cuts a very unreal figure. Nor is the novel by any means free from tearful sentimentality.

Of Herman's other works the most interesting is a long story called "Alexey Zhmakin." Its hero is an escaped criminal who is tracked down by an energetic and virtuous Ogpu official, bent on "reforming" his quarry rather than on bringing him to bay. Both the character of Zhmakin and the situations in this story are unusual; there is an atmosphere of tension and the interest is sustained throughout, even though the reader can hardly believe in Herman's virtuous Ogpu man. The latter (his name is Lapshin) appears also in another story where he is the principal character and is even less credible.

VIRTA

Another newcomer to Soviet literature in this period was Nikolay Evgenyevich Virta (b. 1906).[31] He made his name with his first novel, *Odinochestvo (Solitude,* 1936), which was to be the first part of a trilogy dealing with some important phases of the political history of the Soviet Union. In *Solitude* the subject is the famous peasant rising, led by Antonov, in the province of Tambov in 1920. At the time it was a cause of great concern to the Soviet government, and its suppression was regarded as a matter of prime importance: the troops sent to crush it were commanded by Tukhachevsky, the future marshal and the principal victim of the Red Army purge in 1937.[32] Incidentally, the theme of Leonov's *Badgers* was probably also inspired by the Antonov rising, though the novel was not an exact portrayal of it.

In Virta's novel the hero is a real personage—Peter Storozhev, a well-to-do peasant who becomes one of Antonov's principal lieutenants. The interesting subject, the acuteness of the conflict portrayed, the variety and wealth of characters involved, and the skillful handling of the material made *Solitude* a memorable first novel. Its last part, entitled "The Wolf," had true accents of tragedy: it described the collapse of the Antonov movement and showed Storozhev roaming like a lonely wolf around his native village, striking the last desperate blows at his enemies. Although Virta was at pains to present Storozhev as a villain and an enemy of the people, he could not deny him a certain grandeur. Nor was Antonov himself painted in uniformly black colors.

Soviet critics were at first cautious in their comments on Virta's book, but it appears that soon the word went round that Stalin himself thought very highly of it, and praises were showered on the practically unknown writer. The novel went through several editions in a short time. In 1937 Virta wrote a play based on it called *Zemlya (Land).* Later he was awarded a Stalin prize for the novel.

[31] Virta's real name was apparently Severtsev. His father was a village priest in the province of Tambov.

[32] In later editions of *Solitude,* subsequent to Tukhachevsky's liquidation, his and Uborevich's names were expunged from the book.

The second volume of Virta's trilogy appeared in 1937 under the title *Zakonomernost (Lawfulness)*. Through several characters and plot threads it is connected with *Solitude*. Storozhev himself does not appear in it, except in a flashback, but hovers in the background and is an important factor in the story. The same part of Russia is the scene of action, but at a much later period, in the late twenties. There are frequent references to Antonov and his movement, and the survivals of "Antonovism" among the peasants and the anti-Soviet elements of Soviet intelligentsia and officialdom are stressed. Their links with the old Social-Revolutionary party are pointed out.

At the beginning of the novel we are introduced into the household of Nikita Kagarde, a village schoolmaster and one of Antonov's former henchmen, and are told his story, which involves his relations with Storozhev. His son, Lev Kagarde, who is shown first as a boy and then as a young man, is the hero of the novel. An ambitious youth, who inherits his father's hatred for the Soviet regime, he becomes the center of a sabotage group in the small town of Verkhnerechensk. Intelligent, unscrupulous, with a gift and a craving for leadership, he succeeds not only in drawing into his net some of the anti-Soviet elements in Soviet institutions, but also in corrupting several representatives of the younger generation who, dissatisfied with drab realities, are on the lookout for ideals and adventures. Kagarde provides them with both. Most of these young people, who ultimately find their way back into the fold, are shown as innocent victims of Kagarde's charms and cunning. Kagarde himself, unmasked and held at bay, disappears in the nick of time from the town. He goes to Moscow where for a time he changes his methods and tactics without, however, giving up his final anti-Soviet aims. He imagines himself to be safe, while in fact all the time his footsteps are dogged by the vigilant organs of political security. He meets his end while on his way to a tryst with Storozhev on the Polish frontier: Storozhev, according to the novel, has been living in Poland all this time, awaiting a signal from his partisans to cross over into Russia and lead a general anti-Soviet uprising.[33]

Virta's second novel (the third part of the trilogy was never published) was, as far as I know, the first important Soviet work of fiction

[33] In fact Storozhev never went to Poland; he remained in Russia and was shot soon after the publication of Virta's book. Virta must have known him personally as a boy. From the scanty biographical data attached to the 1947 edition of *Solitude* we learn that the village in which Virta grew up joined in 1921 the Antonov rebels and that his father's house, the best in the village, was used by the rebels as their headquarters. Of Virta's father this short biography says that he was "more inclined to politics than to priestly duties." There is also a dark hint at a family tragedy which took place in 1921 after which Virta became the head of the family: apparently Virta's father was shot with other rebels. In his novel the village priest is shown as an enemy of Communism and a friend of Storozhev.

to deal with the background of the wreckers' and opposition trials that swept the country in the late thirties. It is very interesting since it shows the variety of the characters involved in anti-Soviet activities and especially the diversity and complexity of the motives ascribed to them. It is true that Virta does his best to show Lev Kagarde—this miniature caricature of Trotsky and embryonic "Führer"—in all his repulsiveness. But some of Kagarde's victims, willing and unwilling, are very attractive. The picture painted by Virta is on the whole objective but, of course, is far from complete. Some of the riddles presented by the famous "trials" are left unsolved; and certain aspects of the affair are completely ignored. The moral of the tale, as the author sees it, is given in the purely political epilogue, which has for its motto a line from Sophocles: "That which is coming . . . ." Here is a passage from it:

> We have come out on the right road and we know where it leads us. Everything is behind and everything is ahead, everything is known, everything is understood, time has lifted its veils.
>
> The Bogdanovs, murderers and hirelings of murderers, have been caught and brought to book from their stinking underworld, and the world recoils in horror from this abyss of baseness. Their repugnant road is ended—they died the death of mad dogs. But have all of them been caught and brought to trial before the people?
>
> We must learn to distinguish between enemies and friends, learn to search and to find, to love and to hate. Let us be prepared— storms are still ahead of us.

The epilogue explains the title of the novel: it refers to the lawful course of the Revolution and the relentless lawfulness of its nemesis.

Virta's novel may be regarded as a good specimen of what is expected of Socialist realism, for it combined edifying purpose with a sufficiently detached portrayal of realities.

KRYMOV

Another younger writer whose first novel was a great success was Yury Krymov (pseudonym of Yury Solomonovich Beklemishev, 1908–1941). Born in Petrograd, he came of an intelligentsia family (his mother was a writer, too), but before entering literature he worked for many years as a technical expert in various branches of Soviet industry. His first novel, *Tanker "Derbent"* (*The Tanker "Derbent,"* 1938), was greatly praised by Soviet critics and was soon translated into several foreign languages. Its setting is laid in a Caspian Sea port and on board an oil tanker which is engaged in "Socialist emulation," or "Stakhanovism," so popular in those days. Krymov succeeds in making the story of the tanker's part in this contest not only readable but even exciting.

His characters are sufficiently original and interesting. The hero, Basov, is somewhat unusual: surly, quarrelsome, seemingly unattractive, he is snubbed by his superiors and disliked or mistrusted by most of those who work with or under him, which does not prevent him from showing his mettle in the end and proving a true Stakhanovite hero. The central episode in this short realistic novel, based on a thorough knowledge of the life it describes, is the fire on another tanker whose survivors are rescued by the *Derbent*. In keeping with what was regarded as one of the essential features of Socialist realism, the story of human relations, and in particular of Basov's matrimonial mishaps, is cleverly interwoven with the social aspect of the novel.

Krymov's literary career was cut short when he was killed in battle with the Germans in September, 1941. His biography mentions that on the eve of his death he joined the Communist party.

Socialist Realism in Drama

During the Five-Year Plan period the drama, more than any other form of Soviet literature, suffered from the deadening effects of "social command." And with the advent of Socialist realism the reaction against it took a twofold form: on the one hand, there was a tendency toward greater objectivity in the portrayal of social collisions and toward a more realistic presentation of complex characters, instead of aligning them in two opposite camps, as flawless Soviet heroes and unmitigated anti-Soviet villains; on the other hand, to plays dealing with purely social themes and situations were added plays about ordinary Soviet citizens and their everyday personal problems. Some of them struck a gay note and were built around farcical situations. A typical example was *Chuzhoy rebyonok (Another Man's Child)*, by Vasily Shkvarkin (b. 1893), which enjoyed a great success and brought its author a fortune. With real drama, however, it had few affinities.

POGODIN

Representative of the new trends in the Soviet drama were the plays of Nikolay Pogodin and Alexander Afinogenov. Pogodin came into literature via journalism, and all his plays reflect an interest in topical problems of Soviet life. The first three—*Tempo, Snow,* and *Poema o topore (Poem About an Axe, 1930)*—were written before the advent of Socialist realism. *Tempo* and *Poem About an Axe* are, in the main, typical Five-Year Plan production plays. *Tempo* has for its subject the construction of the Stalingrad tractor plant, and its characters, all of whom are superficially drawn, include Communist enthusiasts, anti-Communist saboteurs, and an American engineer who is at first horrified by Russian slovenly methods and then amazed by the tempo of construction which eclipses all American records. The play actually lacks all plot; Pogodin's method is that of documentary naturalism: thus since the American, Mr. Carter, knows no Russian, his speeches are given in English, but to make them understandable to Russian readers and spectators each sentence is duplicated in Russian. Pogodin himself, in writing of *Tempo,* said that nothing in his play was "invented" —that Carter was modeled on a Mr. Kidler who built the Stalingrad plant, that other characters were also drawn from life, and that everything that happened to Carter had actually happened in real life. And, in keeping with the views prevalent at the time, Pogodin declared: "The theater has to do with documentary dramaturgy, and it would not be a bad thing to try to bring this documentariness, this truthfulness home to the spectator."

Poem About an Axe deals with the discovery of nonrusting steel at a Soviet plant and was built in much the same way as *Tempo,* with almost the same assortment of characters. *Snow* has for its subject a scientific expedition, somewhere in the Caucasus (the location is deliberately vague), with the object of "conquering" mountain snows and utilizing them for industrial purposes. There are the usual stock characters: the enthusiastic communist leader of the expedition; the skeptical, egocentric and absent-minded professor who ends by espousing the Communist cause; the engineer, who as a class enemy tries to sabotage the whole expedition; a young Communist girl-journalist who keeps unmasking "enemies"; two young natives, brother and sister, who defy their tribe's hostility to the expedition; an operatically-wicked native sheikh; and so on. *Snow* differs from the two earlier plays in being less "documentary"; it even has a touch of symbolism. Another novel feature in it is the inclusion of a Prologue in which the two leading actors give humorous comments on the play and its characters. They also reappear several times during the play, interrupting the action with their comments and humorous asides. In Act Two, after a slapstick scene in which the wicked sheikh is duped by the girl journalist, they butt in with the following dialogue to make fun of the run-of-the-mill Soviet plays:

> *The Second*: I don't like this play.
> *The First*. Why?
> *The Second*. This play is like nothing on earth. In fifteen years I have got used to plays which resemble each other like a pair of overshoes. The spectators know in advance where to clap, where to laugh, and where to go to sleep.
> *The First*. What about crying?
> *The Second*. Nowadays you don't cry during the play, you do so after the play.

287

Generally speaking, Pogodin's Five-Year Plan plays differed from the typical products of that period by their element of humor, though more often than not this humor was somewhat primitive.

Pogodin's first play written after the 1932 "reform" was *Moy drug* (*My Friend*). Written in 1932, it was produced by the Theater of the Revolution in 1934. Largely, it repeats the pattern of his earlier plays— it shows a Soviet plant under construction and the efforts of its director to overcome all sorts of difficulties. But the play is less episodic, less journalistic, and dramatically more compact. There is also an attempt to give a more rounded-off portrait of the central character, Gay, the director of the plant. He is the new Soviet man, the positive hero, one of the builders of Socialism. All the other characters are there merely to set him in relief and are for the most part as conventional as those in Pogodin's earlier plays. This is particularly true of Gay's enemies, those who, guided by various motives, hinder the construction. In the words of one of the leading Soviet dramatic critics, Yuzovsky, who was on the whole quite favorable to Pogodin, "Pogodin's negative characters do not come off. . . . They are mannequins disguised as saboteurs and wandering about the play because one can't dispense with them."

In *Posle bala* (*After the Ball*), written in 1933 and produced also in 1934, the negative characters are either comic or melodramatic, and the whole play is a rather incongruous mixture of *kolkhoz* heroics, slapstick humor, and melodrama, with a dash of romantic calf-love—all against the background of a hectic sowing campaign on a collective farm.

Pogodin's most successful play was *Aristokraty* (*Aristocrats*). Described as "a comedy in four acts," it was written in 1934–35. The scene is the construction of the Stalin White Sea-Baltic Canal, which was dug with forced labor, and the main characters are three "Cheka-men" (*chekisty*), as they are described in the list of characters, and numerous prisoners, of whom four are described as "Specialists" and the rest as "Bandits, thieves, prostitutes, fanatics, *kulaks*, etc." The play lacks real plot. In a series of rapid, colorful episodes, some of which no doubt must have been very effective on the stage of Okhlopkov's Realistic Theater, it tells the story of the winning over of these class enemies and social outcasts, most of whom refuse at first to work or submit to discipline. Psychologically it is unconvincing, and the Cheka-men, in their saccharinity, are particularly unreal. But many of the minor characters are real enough, and the dialogue, spiced with thieves' slang, is quite vivid. Among the multitude of characters there are two who stand out. One is Sadovsky, an engineer sentenced to forced labor for his anti-Soviet wrecking activities; the other, Kostya the Captain, a glib, irrepressible gangster, full of humor and vitality. While Sadovsky is a pale abstraction, Kostya is real enough so long as he refuses to work, behaves rebelliously and cracks his gangster's jokes, but his conversion into an enthusiastic Stakhanovite is not very easy to believe. Mr. van Gyseghem, in his book *Theatre in Soviet Russia,* has described Pogodin's *Aristocrats* as "a modern miracle play," giving a very interesting account of its production by Ohklopkov's Realistic Theater, which he called "the last word . . . in the direction of a stylized convention."

In *Chelovek s ruzhyom (The Man With the Rifle,* 1937), Pogodin tried to apply the principles of Socialist realism to recent history. The play represents a series of episodes which show Lenin (or the Soviet myth of Lenin) in October, 1917. The play owed its great success largely to the lifelike performance of Lenin's role by Shchukin. In 1941 Pogodin followed this up with another play about Lenin—*Kremlyovskie kuranty (The Kremlin Chimes).* Whereas in *The Man With the Rifle* the stress was on Lenin the man, here Lenin the statesman was to the forefront.

AFINOGENOV

Afinogenov, who belonged to the *Proletkult,* began by writing in the twenties a number of mediocre plays. Typical of them was *Malinovoye varenye (Raspberry Jam,* 1926), a Communist melodrama, complete with bourgeois villains, spies arriving from abroad, camouflaged telephones, invisible ink which a hysterical woman drinks instead of sedative drops, and a young Komsomol heroine. The artistic value of this play (and some other of Afinogenov's early plays) is nil; its characters are quite unreal and its humor often in bad taste. It has, however, some documentary value, since it sheds considerable light on certain aspects of Soviet life of that period. This is still more true of *Chudak (The Eccentric,* 1928), the hero of which is a young enthusiast of Soviet production who has to fight against indifference, red tape, favoritism, anti-Semitism, and other evils rampant at a Soviet paper mill. Though not free from some melodramatic moments and occasional lapses of taste, this play gives a more realistic picture of life, and its characters are psychologically more plausible.

Afinogenov's first popular success was scored with *Strakh (Fear,* 1931), a somewhat overpraised problem play about an old scientist who becomes a more or less willing tool of anti-Soviet elements but ends by repenting. The play has some interesting ideological moments since it deals with the problem of freedom of science, but the characterization is poor and the form conventionally old-fashioned.

A great success awaited also the play *Dalyokoye* (1936; in English translation *Distant Point;* actually the title is the name of a small railway siding on the Trans-Siberian Railway). It is in the true Chekhovian, undramatic tradition: a record of twenty-four hours in the life of several inconspicuous Soviet people working at a tiny station lost in the Siberian forests at which the special coach of a high-ranking Red Army commander, proceeding from Vladivostok to Moscow, is forcibly delayed. After Pogodin's plays there is a refreshing absence of saboteurs and class enemies, and although there is the inevitable amount of declamatory phrases and breezy official optimism, several of the characters are sufficiently attractive as ordinary human beings. Afinogenov has more phychological finesse than Pogodin but he lacks Pogodin's sense of the theatrical. A sequel to *Dalyokoye,* called *Vtorye puti* (*The Second Track,* 1939), where the same characters (and some new ones) are shown a few years later, is much weaker.

Afinogenov's last play was *Nakanune* (*On the Eve,* 1941), about the early phase of the Soviet-German war. Afinogenov was himself one of its early victims: he was killed in the winter of 1941 during an air raid on Moscow.

LEONOV'S PLAYS

Much more interesting are the plays of Leonov. His dramatic works before 1932 included a dramatization of his own novel, *The Badgers,* and three original plays: *Untilovsk* (1928), *Provintsialnaya istoriya* (*A Provincial Episode,* 1928), and *Usmirenie Badadoshkina* (*The Humbling of Badadoshkin,* 1929). In all three the theme was the survival of the "old Adam" in the new world. Just as in his novels, Leonov's approach to this theme was psychological and ethical, rather than social or political. The most characteristic feature of his plays was their tenseness, their strain. There was nothing ordinary about them: strange, unusual, often pathetic characters, full of quirks and twists, were involved in strange situations and engaged in weird conversations, full of allusions, of symbolic undercurrents, in which things left unsaid mattered more than what was actually said: a mixture of Chekhov, Ibsen, and Dostoyevsky. It was this symbolism and this tendency to generalize that raised Leonov's plays above the level of the average Soviet dramatic productions. In *Untilovsk,* for instance (the name itself—that of a small town—is significant), Leonov tried to portray in a microcosm the vulgarity of life. The characters are a gallery of "has-beens" and castaways, some of them pathetic, some despicable, but all of them drifting futilely, away from the main stream of life. Chervakov, who is described in the list of dramatis personae as "an Untilovsk homunculus," was apparently meant by Leonov as the embodiment of all that was mean and evil in the old world. Soviet critics saw in him "the psychological quintessence of counterrevolution," but Leonov was not really interested in any political issues, and there is very little in the play to indicate when its action takes place. Untilovsk itself is a psychological symbol, not a geographical term, while Chervakov is a distant descendant of the Karamazovs, a cross between the old Karamazov himself and Smerdyakov.

Both dramatically and ideologically speaking, Leonov's plays are inconclusive; there are too many loose ends in them and too little unity of action. But his superiority to such acknowledged Soviet dramatists as Pogodin and Afinogenov is revealed in his characters and his dialogues. His characters may strike one as queer, as too complex and twisted, too Dostoyevskian, but they are infinitely more interesting, especially in *Untilovsk,* than those of Pogodin and Afinogenov. And Leonov is a great master of Russian: his language is rich and flexible, his dialogues remind one at once of Leskov and Dostoyevsky; however, he sometimes lets these run away with him to the detriment of purely dramatic considerations. His plays also have a great gamut of moods— from tragic pathos to grim humor. In *Polovchanskie sady (The Orchards of Polovchansk,* 1936–38) and *Volk (The Wolf,* 1938)—the latter also known as *Begstvo Sandukova (Sandukov's Flight)*—the dramatic effect is achieved by a close interweaving of family and social conflicts. In both, Leonov comes somewhat closer to the Soviet realities of the day, but his method remains that of symbolic realism. There is an obvious influence of Ibsen and Chekhov, while at least one Soviet critic has noted an affinity between Leonov's plays and the symbolic theater of Maeterlinck.

In *The Orchards of Polovchansk,* there is an almost classical unity of place and time, the drama unfolding within a day or two during a family reunion of the Makkaveyevs. The old man, Makkaveyev, is director of a famous state orchard. In addition to the two children who live with him, he has five sons by his first marriage, who represent the flower of Soviet manhood and a variety of occupations. One of them does not appear in the play, although mentioned in the list of characters. But in a way he is the real hero of the play: the news of his death while on an important mission in the Arctic comes during the family reunion celebrations, over which he presides, as it were, in spirit, as a symbol of patriotic duty and vigilance. The dramatic knot of the play is tied around the appearance, during the family reunion, of a former friend of the family who turns out to be an enemy agent. There are some well-drawn, slightly grotesque, minor characters, but on the whole the play differs from Leonov's earlier ones in that nearly all the characters are wholesome and more or less attractive people and not a collection of cranks and monstrosities. Even the villain is not too overdone. However, despite the excellent dialogue and the subtle atmosphere of suspense, as drama the play fails. Is it because, as one Soviet critic has suggested, Leonov is at his best only when he portrays unhappy people? *The Wolf* has many points in common with *The Orchards,* but here the theme of the exposure of enemy agents is more to the fore and is handled much more melodramatically. With it again is interwoven the theme of family conflict. The play is full of symbolism, of significantly allusive dialogues, of understatements and mysterious hints, but one cannot help feeling that Leonov has been wasting these Ibsenian subtleties on a theme that was not worth it. As usual with Leonov, there are several finely drawn characters, especially some of the minor ones. All Leonov's characters have depth and leave scope for the actor's imagination, so that his plays must gain considerably on the stage.

Throughout this period Soviet critics continued to complain about the dearth of good Soviet plays. With one or two exceptions Soviet theaters preferred to produce plays by pre-Revolutionary or foreign authors, and this undoubtedly reflected the playgoers' preference. In his book on the Soviet theater Mr. André van Gyseghem, the well-known British theater director who paid four visits to the Soviet Union and spent a year working with Soviet producers, gives a list of plays which ran in the leading Moscow theaters during the 1935–36 season. If we exclude the Jewish State Theater and the Gypsy Theater with their specific repertoires, there were forty-nine Soviet productions as compared with seventy-two foreign and pre-Revolutionary Russian. They represented forty individual plays by thirty-one Soviet authors. The only authors with more than one play running were Afinogenov, Fayko, Kirshon, Pogodin, Pervomaysky, and Mikitenko. Of these, the last two were Ukrainian-language writers, while Kirshon was soon to be exposed as a Trotskyite and an enemy of the people, and his plays banned.

Socialist Realism in Poetry

Simplicity, realism, and accessibility to the masses came to be regarded also as the main virtues in poetry, and several new poets whose work satisfied these requirements gained recognition and popularity in the thirties.

PROKOFYEV

Alexander Andreyevich Prokofyev (b. 1900) came of the Northern peasant stock (his father was a fisherman on Lake Ladoga). He joined the Communist party in 1919 and fought in the Civil War. His first books of poetry appeared in 1931, but he became particularly popular in the latter part of that decade. In 1939–40 he took part in the war against Finland as a newspaper correspondent. During World War II he worked in the Political Administration of the Leningrad front. In 1944 he was awarded a Stalin Prize for his poem "Russia."

Socialist Realism: Practice

Prokofyev's early poems were written under the influence of Mayakovsky and were characterized by bombastic diction, by "grand" revolutionary themes, and by affectedly-crude language. There were also in them some survivals of proletarian Cosmism, with its grandiloquence and its predilection for capital letters. In a poem called "The Epoch," Prokofyev spoke of "the young Epoch overtaking constellations in the impetuous train of Fame." In the poem "We" (1930) he referred to his generation of Soviet men as being famed "from the White Sea to San Diego." Referring to the Allied intervention in Russia in 1919, he recalled "Lord Churchill" who "led the bandits" and expressed the pious wish that "the entrails of his swinish soul may be scattered by the wind," that in his hour of death "he may tear the earth with his teeth," for "such vermin must be quartered." In the same poem Prokofyev spoke of the existence of "two Englands," one of which could not live while the King was alive, and so "the second England will emerge after hanging the King."[34]

In the late thirties Prokofyev became less political minded and began to write simple poems about his native country, about village life, and about love, in which he revealed his unquestionable inborn gift of song. It is in these simple poems, strongly influenced by folk songs and village ditties and asking, as it were, to be accompanied on the accordion, that Prokofyev is at his best. His range is limited, he is often naïve and sentimental, but his best poems are infectiously melodious.

SHCHIPACHOV

The emphasis on simplicity and melodiousness became very pronounced during this period, and several of the poets who gained popularity in the late thirties developed along the same lines as Prokofyev. Many of them were of humble origin and had joined the Bolsheviks when still quite young. One of these, Stepan Petrovich Shchipachov (b. 1899), came of a poor peasant family and began earning his living when still a boy. In 1919 he volunteered for the Red Army and joined the Bolshevik party. Later he taught in military schools, but in 1931 enrolled in the Institute of Red Professors where he studied literature. His poems began to appear in print in 1926 and his first book was published in 1931. By 1947 he had some twenty books of poetry to his credit. During World War II he worked for an army newspaper at the front.

Shchipachov's poetry is simple in themes, in structure, and in rhythms, but his simplicity is more studied than Prokofyev's, and his lines lack melodious infectiousness. Soviet critics have spoken of the "philosophic note" in Shchipachov's poetry, but his "philosophy" is

[34] In the 1947 edition of Prokofyev's *Selected Poems*, this passage about "Lord" Churchill and the two Englands was omitted.

293

elementary and shallow—one should rather speak of his inclination to rationalize, of which Prokofyev at his best is free. Soviet critics have a high opinion of Shchipachov's poem about Lenin's house in Siberian exile—"Domik v Shushenskom" ("The Little House at Shushenskoye") —but by absolute poetic standards it is a mediocre work.

DOLMATOVSKY

A much younger poet is Evgeny Aronovich Dolmatovsky (b. 1915), a true offspring of the Revolution. His first poem was published in *Pioneer Pravda* when he was fifteen. In 1933 he worked as a volunteer on the construction of the Moscow subway, about which he wrote several poems. A year later his first book of poems was published. In 1937, after graduating from the Gorky Literary Institute, he went to the Far East and published a whole book of *Far Eastern Poems*. In 1939 he took part in the Soviet invasion of Poland, and in 1940 he served in the war against Finland as a war correspondent. During World War II Dolmatovsky served again as a war reporter on various fronts, received nine decorations, and published several books of poems. Like Shchipachov, he is simple and unsophisticated, but more virile and optimistic. He is the author of many popular songs that have become part of the everyday Soviet repertoire. They are typical of the tendency, prevalent in the thirties, to return to simple, traditional forms and to write poetry with mass appeal.

SURKOV

Alexey Alexandrovich Surkov (b. 1899) also came of a poor peasant family; his childhood was spent in his native village in the province of Yaroslavl. From 1912 to 1918 he worked at various trades in St. Petersburg; later he served in the Red Army and did Party work in the Volga region. In 1934 he graduated from the Institute of Red Professors. In the invasion of Poland, the war with Finland and World War II Surkov did political and newspaper work at the front. His first book of poems appeared in 1930 and has since been followed by nearly thirty others. In Surkov's prewar poetry reminiscences of the Civil War play a large part, and woven into them is the motif of implacable hatred for the enemies. The fighting note is clearly sounded in his poems; he speaks of "the joy and fatigue of battle" and of the "acrid smoke of unquiet campfires"; he has no use for "warmth and quiet." In a program poem entitled "The Hero," Surkov speaks of himself as "a soldier of world revolution," "an anonymous guardsman of the rebel class," who learned under fire "to hold his rifle and his heart at ready." In another war poem —"Sovremenniku" ("To a Contemporary")—dedicated to his friend and fellow poet Mikhail Isakovsky, Surkov wrote:

Socialist Realism: Practice

> *We grew old before we realized it,*
> *As though we had been fighting all life.*

The poem spoke of their generation as having suffered enough for five future generations, and ended on a defiant note:

> *Let the roads into the new epoch*
> *Be unexplored and dangerous,*
> *We refuse to exchange for anything*
> *Our draughty destiny.*

This stern acceptance of one's lot, coupled with Communist loyalty and patriotic pride, is the keynote of Surkov's poetry. It is free from that mawkish sentimentality which colors much of Shchipachov's and Dolmatovsky's work. There is in it a manly note, reminiscent of the early Tikhonov and going back to Gumilyov. The very texture of his verse is firm and compact. His military songs were among the most popular in the Red Army.

TVARDOVSKY

Alexander Trifonovich Tvardovsky (b. 1910) lived until the age of eighteen in a backwoods village. In 1928 he went to Smolensk and began writing for newspapers. His first book of poems—*Put k sotsializmu (The Road to Socialism)*—appeared in 1930; it described the rise of collective farms. Fame came to Tvardovsky with the publication, in 1936, of his long poem *Strana Muraviya (The Land of Muravia)*; in 1941 he was awarded a Stalin Prize for it. In the meantime Tvardovsky graduated from the Institute of History and Philosophy in Moscow and, joining the Red Army, took part in the invasion of Poland and in the war against Finland as a war correspondent. In 1941, when Hitler invaded the Soviet Union, Tvardovsky resumed his work for army newspapers. He did not become a member of the Communist party until 1938.

Tvardovsky's principal prewar work was *The Land of Muravia*. It is a narrative poem of over two thousand lines, divided into nineteen chapters. Its hero is a "middling" peasant, Nikita Morgunok, who refuses to join a collective farm. Leaving his family, he sets out with his horse and cart in search of the fabulous land of Muravia, the Land of Cockaigne of peasants' dreams where he can truly own and till his own land, where everything will be his, where he need not ask anyone's permission, where there will be no communes and no collective farms—a land that is true to peasant traditions. The poem describes Nikita's fruitless quest and the various adventures and incidents that befall him on the way: he partakes of the carousing of the dispossessed *kulaks* who hold a wake for their deported covillagers; his horse is stolen by a former *kulak* who sells it to an itinerant priest, and Nikita has to drag his cart for the rest of his journey; in a prosperous collectivized village he attends a wedding feast; and he sees with his own eyes the misery and poverty of a village where individual tenure still prevails. His last encounter is with an old man who had gone on the last pilgrimage to the holy places of Kiev but is now returning, without having reached his destination, suddenly convinced that even if God exists He has no more power in this world. He tells Morgunok that there is no such thing as Muravia Land, that it has "grown over with grass and sward." "Why should anyone need this Land of Muravia when there is such life all around you?" he asks. So the only thing that is left to Morgunok is to join a collective farm. The political moral of Tvardovsky's poem is thus quite orthodox. But it is not a propaganda poem. The author has an understanding for, and sympathy with, the personal proprietary instincts of the average Russian peasant personified in Morgunok. The scene of the carousing, dispossessed peasants has a tragic accent. One of them sings a song about a little bird which refuses to eat or sing and asks for its cage to be opened. The charm of the poem lies in its blend of realism and whimsical fancy, of spicy satire and gentle humor. It is a modern counterpart of *Who Lives Happily in Russia?*, Nekrasov's great epic of peasant life; like the latter it is saturated with the genuine spirit of folk poetry. Tvardovsky not only uses the racy peasant speech which fits naturally into his easy-flowing verse, but also handles skillfully various folklore devices and especially the motifs and meters of the *chastushka* (village ditty). Folklore motifs are worked, for instance, into the imaginary speech which Morgunok addresses to Stalin, asking the latter to be allowed to keep for a while his holding and promising to join the *kolkhoz* later.

LEBEDEV-KUMACH, ISAKOVSKY, AND GUSEV

The genre of song became the specialty of several poets who wrote almost exclusively poems that were meant to be sung rather than read. Some of them were written in collaboration with the composers who set them to music or as lyrics for popular films. This is especially true of Vasily Lebedev-Kumach (1898–1948), author of the popular "Pesnya o Rodine" ("Song of the Motherland"), which was treated as a sort of unofficial national anthem and became the signature tune of Radio Moscow. He also wrote such popular "hits" as the song about the wind from the film "The Children of Captain Grant," or the march from the film "The Gay Kids." These are simple, catchy, and melodious.

Great popularity was also enjoyed by the songs of Mikhail Isakovsky (b. 1900) and Victor Gusev (b. 1909). Both were influenced by Russian folk songs and responsible for some successful imitations: Isakovsky's humorous "I kto ego znayet?" ("Why on Earth?") and Gusev's "Polyushko," popularized by the Red Army Choir, have found their way back to the people, just as did some early nineteenth-century imitations of folk poetry by Merzlyakov, Neledinsky-Meletsky, Tsyganov, and others.

SIMONOV, BERGHOLZ, AND ALIGER

In the thirties there also began to appear in Soviet magazines the names of three poets, two of them women, who were to become much better known during the war. The poetry of all three reflected the new interest—now not only tolerated, but even encouraged from above—in personal themes. At the same time all three were more sophisticated and technically more fastidious than the song writers like Dolmatovsky or Lebedev-Kumach.

Konstantin (Kiril) Mikhailovich Simonov (b. 1915) from the outset divided his attention between personal love-themes and historical-patriotic subjects. Typical of the former is the poem entitled "Pyat stranits" ("Five Pages," 1938) which tells, in the form of an unmailed letter forgotten in a hotel room, the story of the unfolding and withering of a love between two people. It reveals a feeling for form and words, and is emotionally tense, though at times it smacks of cheap sentimentality. Its refreshing feature is its complete freedom from all political and social didacticism. Simonov's patriotic poems included a long poem about Suvorov (1939), a poetic recreation of several episodes in the career of the great Russian soldier, and a poem about the famous "Ice Battle" which Alexander Nevsky won against the Teutonic Knights. There was, in Simonov's handling of his material, in his stress on visual imagery, some influence of Acmeism and of its leader, Gumilyov.

Another Acmeist, Akhmatova, influenced the early poetry of both Olga Bergholz (b. 1910) and Margarita Aliger (b. 1915). Both sounded clearly a personal, feminine note. Bergholz, who represented the Leningrad school of poets, was more austere and intellectual; Aliger, more emotional. Both occasionally introduced a topical social note. Of their and Simonov's war poetry more will be said in the next chapter.

VI. Literature on War Service
1941–46

1. *Prelude to the War*

IN the late nineteen thirties the theme of "Fascism" and its evils (the term "National Socialism" was deliberately avoided in the Soviet Union) and of the implied Hitler threat to the Soviet state became one of the staple themes of the Soviet press. There were also frequent references to it in Soviet literature, mostly, however, in its internal aspect, the stress being laid on the activities of "Fascist agents" in the Soviet Union. At the same time the indirect effect of the Nazi menace was felt in the growth of patriotic literature—of novels and plays dealing with great national crises in Russian history and extolling the heroism of the Russian people and even of its leaders and rulers. In 1939, however, appeared a curious little book by an almost unknown author, which described the first twenty-four hours in the coming war between the U. S. S. R. and Germany. It was called *Pervy udar* (*The First Blow*), and its author was Nikolay Shpanov.[1]

The First Blow is a short novel. It has a somewhat tenuous love story, but its center of gravity is in the description of the air-war operations. All the characters are members of the Soviet Air Force, bomber pilots and navigators, paratroopers, and others. Shpanov shows a Soviet bomber force undertaking, within a few hours after the outbreak of the war, a long-distance raid on important industrial targets in Nuremberg. Great havoc is wrought there, and after returning safely to their base, the Soviet bombers prepare for another raid. The book gives some interesting glimpses into the life of the Red Air Force, but the characterization is slight and superficial. An introductory chapter describes the international situation which precipitates the war. Here Shpanov was as wide of the mark as he was in his description of the initial air operations. According to him, the Soviet Union, the first victim of the Nazi aggression, had to face this aggression alone, although at the end of the introduction there is a hint that at the very last moment France,

---

[1] I could find no biographical data about Shpanov. Soviet magazines published several stories of his in the thirties, and during the war he wrote war stories and sketches.

under the pressure of the "Popular Front" movement, is about to throw in her weight on Russia's side. Great Britain, on the other hand, is shown as taking an attitude of friendly neutrality toward Germany, while Poland comes in on Germany's side as her half-willing ally. An interesting point about Shpanov's book is that it does not mince words: although some of the names of German generals are fictitious, Germany herself as the aggressor is named *en toutes lettres,* and the description of the first Soviet raid on Nuremberg is given with an abundance of topographical detail.

It is to be presumed that three months after its publication (it was signed for the press in May of 1939) Shpanov's book, copies of which had just had time to reach foreign countries, was withdrawn from circulation, for Shpanov's forecast of events had completely miscarried: instead of the combined German-Polish aggression against the Soviet Union, encouraged by British neutrality and French hesitations, came the Stalin-Hitler friendship pact, which shocked the outer world and probably surprised the Soviet people themselves. It was followed by the German attack on Poland, the declaration of war by Britain and France, and, at the proper moment, the Soviet stab in Poland's back. This latter was presented as a move to liberate the oppressed Russian and Ukrainian minorities from the yoke of Polish Fascists, and this war of liberation was glorified in many poems, stories, and sketches. The delicate topic of the Molotov-Ribbentrop pact and of Nazi-Communist collaboration was studiously avoided by Soviet writers, but many of them had no difficulty in changing their tune and replacing their denunciations of German Nazis by attacks on Polish "Fascists" and Anglo-French "Imperialists."[2]

2. *Literature as Part of the War Effort*

L ESS than two years later (with the Soviet-Finnish War interlude again giving rise to considerable "patriotic" literature), the tune had to be changed again. For most Soviet writers the Nazi attack on the Soviet Union was probably as much of a surprise as the friendship pact of August, 1939, but there can be no doubt that this time they faced about more willingly and sincerely.

From June, 1941, on, literature in the Soviet Union, as behooves a totalitarian country, became part of the total war effort. It was regarded as an important war weapon. Many Soviet writers joined the fighting forces as war correspondents and devoted themselves almost entirely to war reportage. Those who for various reasons remained behind wrote

[2] Recently Shpanov published a novel called *Podzhigateli* (*The Incendiaries,* 1950), in which the blame for World War II is laid on the Western democracies.

stories, poems, and sketches about the war or boosted morale by writing patriotic historical novels, biographies of national heroes, patriotic pep articles, and the like. The place and function of literature in wartime were clearly and succinctly defined by *Literature and Art,* the official mouthpiece of the Union of Soviet Writers and of the government Committee on Arts, when it wrote:

> What is of paramount importance today, as it has never been before, is the *activizing* function of art which possesses the invaluable faculty of inspiring men to fight, of helping them in the struggle.
>
> The expression "military theme" is inaccurate. What we need is not military literature, but *militant* literature. We want not just ordinary "military" art but *fighting* art (*voyuyushcheye iskusstvo*).[3]

In another leading article the same official journal wrote:

> Always bound up closely with the life of the people, Soviet art had entered, since the outbreak of war, upon a new phase of its development. From now on, it was called upon to serve one single aim—the cause of victory over the enemy. It was meant to become a weapon in the hands of the soldiers who rose to defend their country. It had to foster the fighting spirit of the people, to consolidate the force of patriotism, to fan the hatred for German-Fascist invaders, to call for revenge. It was to show the moral greatness of the Soviet people, their tenacity, their faith in the coming victory.[4]

3. *War Fiction*

SOVIET wartime literature is enormous in bulk. Much of it is of that ephemeral variety of which Ehrenburg wrote in one of his wartime articles: "A writer must know how to write not only for the centuries but how to write for the one short second if the fate of his people is to be decided in that second." Most of this literature consists of short works: short stories and front-line reports. But there are also many plays and several novels, mostly written in the latter part of the war. In the list of war authors many well-known names will be met, though some strike one by their absence. There were also a few newcomers.

Among the few regular novels about the war written while it was still fought should be mentioned those of Simonov, Fadeyev, Leonov, Sholokhov, Nekrasov, Gorbatov, Grossman, and Perventsev.

[3] *Literatura i iskusstvo* (*Literature and Art*), September 19, 1942. This publication represented the wartime merger of *Literaturnaya gazeta* and *Sovetskoye iskusstvo* —*The Literary Gazette* and *Soviet Art.* Toward the end of 1944 they resumed separate publication.

[4] *Literatura i iskusstvo,* October 17, 1942.

Simonov's *Dni i nochi* (*Days and Nights,* 1944) is a story of the Stalingrad battle. As a picture of one of the most important and decisive events of the war it is quite good. But it is not great literature and cannot even stand comparison with Plivier's novel about Stalingrad. The characters are quite conventional, and the fictional story, especially the love episode, is trite. But there is throughout an appealing absence of bombast.

Another novel about Stalingrad is *V okopakh Stalingrada* (*In the Trenches of Stalingrad*), by Victor Nekrasov, written in 1945 and published in 1946. Free from Simonov's fictional adornments and based on first-hand experience, it is of greater documentary value, simple, sincere, and free from politics.

Fadeyev's *Molodaya gvardiya* (*The Young Guard,* 1945) is centered around the activities of an underground group of members of the Young Communist League under German occupation. It is based on actual facts that were disclosed during the war. Fadeyev succeeded in investing his heroes (in both the real and the literary sense of the word) with flesh and blood and creating memorable characters. The novel is competently written and well put together. It was enthusiastically hailed by Soviet critics, but later came in for criticism on the ground that the author had minimized the role of Party leadership and overrated that of his young patriotic heroes.

Much was expected of Sholokhov's war novel, his *Quiet Don* being still the most widely popular single work in Soviet literature. So far only fragments of this novel, entitled *Oni srazhalis za Rodinu* (*They Fought for Their Country*), have appeared, and it is premature to judge it. Sholokhov is a slow-working writer, and he apparently understands that in order to write a work of wide compass about an event of such national magnitude as the war of 1941–45, a writer must approach it at same distance in time. During the war he was much less prolific than many other writers, though he did write some war stories and sketches, of which "Nauka nenavisti" ("The Science of Hatred," 1942) aroused considerable attention.

Of the other front-rank Soviet writers, Leonov, in addition to his war plays which will be discussed later, wrote *Vzyatie Velikoshumska* (*The Taking of Velikoshumsk,* 1944). Only 150 pages long, it can hardly be described as a novel. It deals with an episode in the life of a Soviet Tank Corps during the Red Army's successful offensive in the Ukraine. The writing is fragmentary and impressionistic. As in Leonov's earlier work, the realism has a symbolic quality. Even such a small, and on the whole natural, detail as the fact that the commander of the Tank Corps, the driver of one of his tanks, and a peasant woman in one of the liberated villages all have the same name—Litovchenko—is apparently meant as a symbol of the unity, nay identity, of the Soviet people in the hour of national calamity. Leonov begins by describing the tour of inspection which General Litovchenko makes of the sector of the front to which his corps has just been assigned. He finds himself near his native town of Velikoshumsk, recently taken by the Red Army, retaken by the Germans, and now about to be recaptured from them.

The description of the General's journeyings and encounters with various people is reminiscent of Leo Tolstoy's manner: suffering from a feverish chill, he is in that state of befuddlement where, although he retains complete lucidity of thought when it comes to military matters, as soon as he is left to himself, recollections of childhood, impressions of gruesome reality, and dreamlike anticipations of a meeting with his old teacher in Velikoshumsk will mingle together. In the course of his peregrinations we are introduced to tank No. 203, which with its crew of four men and one kitten, becomes the main character in the story. The greater part of the story describes the nocturnal progress of this tank and her final destructive but suicidal attack on a German column, in which two members of her crew meet their end. The characters of the four members of the tank crew are etched very sharply. One of the best passages in the story is the whimsical fairy tale which the tank commander tells his crew while they are holding night watch over their temporarily disabled tank.

Nepokoryonnye (The Unconquered, 1943), also known as *Semya Tarasa (Taras's Family),* by Boris Gorbatov (b. 1908), deals with the war reactions of a Soviet family in the Kuban region after it has been overrun by the Germans. The author seems to have deliberately modeled his family set-up—an old father and two sons—on that in Gogol's famous romance *Taras Bulba.* There are some descriptions of the fighting, but Gorbatov is primarily concerned with human beings and the heroism and patriotism of ordinary Soviet citizens.

On the other hand, in *Narod bessmerten (The People Immortal,* 1943), by Vasily Grossman (b. 1905), are portrayed various types of Soviet fighters—officers, political commissars, and men. Grossman entered the ranks of Soviet writers in 1934 and began before the war the publication of a long novel *(Stepan Kolchugin)* dealing with pre-Revolutionary times and World War I.

Katayev's short novel *Syn polka (The Son of a Regiment,* 1945) tells the adventures of an orphan boy adopted by a front-line regiment.

The only major novel dealing with the war in the West was Ehrenburg's *Padenie Parizha (The Fall of Paris,* 1941). It was written before the German invasion of Russia and gave a picture of France between 1935 and 1940, together with an analysis, through a variety of characters representing various strata of French society, of the causes of France's collapse. It is a social-political novel, and the journalistic approach, always present in Ehrenburg's novels, is evident here. A man of no strong or stable convictions, Ehrenburg has a keen, versatile, and observant mind and is quick to respond to topical themes. Having lived in France off and on for years, he knows the country and on the whole loves the people. He stayed in Paris throughout the tragic days of the debacle and was able to see much for himself. His character studies of French politicians of various shades, of industrialists, intellectuals, and workers, are fundamentally true to life, even if they are psychologically not very profound. The over-all picture is, however, colored by a definite bias, his thesis being that the salvation of France lay in her working class and, more especially, in the Communist party as its most vocal and active spokesman. Most of Ehrenburg's characters serve to illustrate and prove this thesis. Michaud and Denise Tessat (who gives up her own class and family to work for the people), and Pierre Dubois and Agnès, who, though belonging to the middle class, also come to be with the people, are those who represent true France. To them are opposed most of the politicians (those of the People's Front are shown in an even more unpleasant light than some of the right-wing ones like Ducamp, in whom at least there is a healthy core of deep-seated French patriotism), industrialists, and unhinged young intellectuals like Lucien Tessat, who moves from one extreme to another and from a left-wing intellectual Communist becomes a Fascist and an admirer of Franco. Of those whom Ehrenburg portrays sympathetically, Denise and Michaud, who love each other, are the only ones to survive: unswerving in their loyalty to Communism, they look forward to coming battles and the better future which will be forged in them. Much stress is laid by the author on their unshakable faith in the distant land of Socialism. But the picture drawn by Ehrenburg is incomplete and ambiguous, since he deliberately passes in silence such an important factor in the situation as the Soviet-German pact of 1939 and the havoc it wrought in the ranks of European Communists, especially in France. The problem of reconciling their hatred of the Germans with their allegiance to Moscow simply does not arise for Ehrenburg's good Communists.

Wartime short stories were numerous, but few of them have literary distinction and lasting interest; usually, the less fictional, the more documentary they are, the greater is their value. Such are, for instance, Tikhonov's sketches of Leningrad during the siege—*Cherty sovetskogo cheloveka* (*The Traits of the Soviet Man,* 1943). In one of the stories an old history teacher, in a conversation with a chance street acquaintance, compares Leningrad to ancient Troy, and most of the stories tell of the simple heroism of its defenders and are more like documentary sketches.

In *Morskaya dusha* (*Soul of the Sea*, 1942), a volume of stories by Leonid Sobolev (b. 1898), are to be found portraits of typical Soviet sailors and episodes of naval war. Sobolev had written earlier, among other things, a long novel about the pre-Revolutionary Russian navy— *Kapitalny remont* (*Capital Refitting*, 1933). Volumes of stories by Kaverin, Pavlenko, Paustovsky, Gabrilovich, Ilyenkov, and Stavsky may also be mentioned here.[5]

Some interest attaches to Yury Herman's story "Be Happy!" (the original title is English, transliterated into Russian characters). It is written in the form of a diary of a Russian girl attached to an aerodrome used by the British near the supply port of Murmansk, and its characters include several R. A. F. pilots who are portrayed with considerable sympathy and warmth.

4. War Plays

OF the many war plays the most interesting are those of Leonov: *Nashestvie* (*Invasion*, 1942) and *Lyonushka* (1943). For each of them the author was awarded one of the annual Stalin prizes for literature.[6]

Written in Chistopol on the Kama, the great and majestic tributary of the Volga, far from the turmoil of the war, *Invasion* is full of dramatic tension and poignant scenes. Most of the action is set within the household of Dr. Talanov, a slightly Chekhovian country doctor, in a small town situated along the road of the German advance on Moscow in 1941. The central character is Fyodor Talanov, Dr. Talanov's prodigal son who has been serving a sentence for a criminal offense and returns to his native town, unexpected by his family, on the eve of the Germans' entry. Broken physically and morally, he adopts a cynical pose behind which can be felt the tragedy of a man who has lost himself and his

[5] Konstantin Paustovsky (b. 1892) published many stories before the war. He had a leaning toward romanticism which he did not conceal. Evgeny Gabrilovich had early connections with the Constructivists, but first attracted attention with his Five-Year Plan sketches of collective farming. Among his war stories "Pod Moskvoy" ("Before Moscow") is one of the best. Vasily Ilyenkov (b. 1897) wrote one of the much-discussed Five-Year Plan novels, *Vedushchaya os* (*Driving Axle*, 1933), and another novel about Socialist reconstruction, *Solnechny gorod* (*The Sun City*, 1935). Vasily Stavsky, author of lively war reportages, particularly from the Moscow front, was one of the early casualties of the war.

[6] Annual Stalin prizes for the most outstanding works of fiction, drama, poetry, and literary criticism (there were also parallel prizes for outstanding achievements in other fields of art and various branches of learning) were instituted at the end of 1939 and have since been awarded annually. In each category there are several prizes, the first prize representing a handsome sum of 100,000 roubles. Among the early recipients of prizes for literature were Alexey Tolstoy (for the third part of his *A Way Through Hell*), Sholokhov (for the third volume of *The Quiet Don*), Ehrenburg (for *The Fall of Paris*), Virta, Simonov, and Tikhonov.

place in life and is capable now only of some desperate action, for good or for evil. Beneath this cynical bravado he is trying to conceal his despair and emptiness. It is around Fyodor's spiritual rebirth that Leonov ties the main knots of his play. The Germans in the town are terrorized by the underground activities of a group of partisans led by Kolesnikov, the former secretary of the local executive committee: every day some Germans in the town are killed, and a note is pinned to their bodies with the words *"Dobro pozhalovat"*—"Welcome to you." This phrase becomes the symbolical leitmotif of the play: it is used by different people under different—and sometimes most dramatic—circumstances. Fyodor Talanov, whom Kolesnikov refuses to take into his group, kills some German officers on his own and when caught poses as Kolesnikov—a deceit in which his parents bravely concur. The play ends with the Russian paratroops retaking the town just after Fyodor and two other partisans have been hanged by the Germans.

Even if Leonov's play does not quite hit the mark, it has the makings of a really fine play, with effective dramatic situations, emotional suspense, and tense, significant dialogues which convey more than their surface meaning. As usual with Leonov, the play has depth, an undercurrent of symbolism, and it is this that saves Leonov from lapsing into cheap melodrama although at times he skirts dangerously close to it.

Some of Leonov's characters and situations will be familiar to readers of his novels and earlier plays. Fyodor, for instance—a man with no place in life, with an empty soul, lost but not beyond recall—is a distant relative of Mitka Vekshin in *The Thief*. The homecoming of the prodigal son also recalls similar situations in Leonov's plays (Pylyaev in *The Orchards of Polovchansk,* Sandukov in *The Wolf,* and Syrovarov in *Blizzard*, though, unlike them, Fyodor is not a political enemy). Another character who can be traced back to Leonov's earlier works is Fayunin, a former local capitalist who returns with the Germans and becomes the mayor of the town under them. He can claim more or less direct descendance from Manyukin in *The Thief* and *Untilovsk.* But Fayunin is more clearly a class enemy and not just an outcast. He is weak and cowardly, but Leonov is obviously at pains to hint at some redeeming feature in his make-up. Is it to be found in his instinctive, ineradicable Russianness? He is playing the Germans' game, he serves loyally his German masters, but one can feel that there is no love lost between them, and the Germans simply despise him and treat him like dirt. There is almost a note of admiration in Fayunin's voice when he describes Mrs. Talanov as "an iron old woman" after the scene in which Fyodor pretends he is Kolesnikov.

Of the "positive" characters, the Talanov couple are Leonov's greatest success: ordinary Russian people, not Communists, they are the "unheroic heroes" of the war. But even in the portrait of Kolesnikov, Leonov has managed to avoid hagiographic approach. The Germans in the play are deliberately contrasted with the other characters and are shown as mechanical robots, not human beings.

Leonov has a true sense of the theater, but his plays, like Ibsen's, can also be enjoyed as literature. His characters' speech is so sharply individualized that they are immediately recognized by their voices: as one Soviet critic put it, "one can listen to his plays with one's eyes shut." His stage remarks are an integral part of the play.

Leonov's second war play, *Lyonushka,* described as "A people's tragedy in four acts," has many points in common with *Invasion,* but is even more intensely dramatic. It presents a group of partisans in the German rear, each of them a sharply-outlined, individual character. The plot follows two intersecting lines: one of them involves a traitor who appears among the partisans; the other is concerned with the love of Lyonushka, the heroine, the only girl among the partisans, for a handsome tank lieutenant whom she meets as they move out of their village and who is later brought to their headquarters in the woods as a half-burned live corpse. Once more Leonov uses the method of symbolic realism and manages to achieve great dramatic suspense without resorting to declamatory effects.

Konstantin Simonov's play *Russkie lyudi (The Russians,* 1942) deals with a war episode on the Southern front. Part of the scenes are laid on the Russian side of the front, part in the German-occupied area. The main characters are a group of ordinary people whose unassuming bravery and contempt of death are symbolic of the whole Russian people. There are also some Germans in the play and a Russian traitor. The title is significant: throughout the play the stress is on *Russian* patriotism, a fact for which Simonov had to apologize later. The romantic element is furnished by the hero's love for the young girl driver Valya whom he has to send on dangerous reconnaissance work behind enemy lines.

Simonov's play is much simpler than Leonov's, written along straightforward realistic lines. Its chief merit lies in its lifelike characterization; several of the minor characters are particularly good. The play was a great success during the war and made Simonov's name familiar outside Russia.

Alexander Korneychuk (b. 1910), a Ukrainian dramatist, caused a sensation with his wartime problem-play *Front (The Front,* 1942).[7]

---

7 The original Ukrainian spelling of the name is "Korniychuk." Most of his plays were written in Ukrainian and translated into Russian. It is not clear whether this was the case with *The Front.* Another of his plays, *Gibel eskadry (The End of a Fleet,* 1934), was awarded a second prize in the All-Union dramatic contest.

Unlike Leonov, Korneychuk is concerned not with deep and tense human conflicts but with a problem of military-political nature. He shows two different types of Red Army commanders. One, Ivan Gorlov, an old soldier of the Revolution, still thinks in the antiquated terms of the Civil War and scorns the modern idea of technical warfare. He has personal courage and a distinguished revolutionary record, but he does not fit in with the new requirements of a total war and surrounds himself with men who also are inadequate. Korneychuk portrays this entourage of Gorlov in a deliberately satirical, even grotesque, vein— even their names are expressive of their character, in the old, eighteenth-century tradition. To Gorlov is opposed Ognyov, a much younger man. Gorlov is inclined to look down on him because he was a mere boy when Gorlov was fighting with Budyonny's Red Cavalry in Poland. Ognyov, however, understands much better what is needed in the war against Nazi Germany, and in the end is appointed in Gorlov's place. Korneychuk intensifies the dramatic conflict by introducing two other Gorlovs into the play, Ivan's son and brother. Both of them are opposed to Ivan and are instrumental in bringing about his downfall.

Korneychuk was praised by the Soviet press for fearlessly tackling an important and topical problem: during the first year of the war many of the older commanders who had acquired experience in the Civil War stuck obstinately to the old notions of revolutionary warfare. They included Marshals Budyonny and Voroshilov, both of whom had to be replaced. Korneychuk's exposure of these romantics of the Civil War at a time when the Soviet Union was suffering serious reverses caused resentment in some quarters. But the play, one of the most widely discussed events of the 1942 theater season, met with official approval. One may even suspect that its writing was suggested in the highest spheres.

5. *War Poetry*
SIMONOV

IN poetry, too, patriotic war themes predominated during these years —almost to the exclusion of all others.

Among the most popular wartime poets were Konstantin Simonov and Alexey Surkov, both of whom spent the greater part of the war with the Russian armies. The war also took Simonov outside Russia, and when it was over, he visited most of the European countries as well as the United States and Japan. One of Simonov's most popular and most characteristic war poems (it is also one of his best) was dedicated to his friend and fellow poet, Surkov. Beginning with the line "Do you recall, Alyosha, the roads of the Smolensk region," and recalling poignant scenes of the Russian retreat before the Germans during the early phase of the war, it was full of deep love for one's country, of Russian, rather than Soviet, patriotism (the word "Soviet" is not once mentioned in the poem), and this explains why it became so popular with Russian *émigrés* outside Russia. As the poet recalled the road of Russian retreat ("Villages, villages, villages and churchyards"), he had a vision of the dead rising from their village graves to pray "for their grandsons who no longer believed in God."[8] And he voiced his pride in being born a Russian:

> *Up till now, my friend, the bullets have been kind to us,*
> *But three times when I thought that death was at hand,*
> *I was full of pride that I had been born a Russian,*
> *I was proud of our dear, our terrible land,*
> *Proud it was a Russian mother who gave birth to me,*
> *Proud it was my fate for such a land to die,*
> *Proud that a Russian woman had given me the threefold*
> *Embrace in Russian fashion when she bade me goodbye.*[9]

Even more widely popular was Simonov's short poem "Zhdi menya" ("Wait for Me"). Its poetic value was little and its appeal chiefly sentimental, for it voiced, in a simple if somewhat naïve form, the feelings of a soldier at the front who wants his wife (or his beloved) back home to wait for him even when all the others—parents, friends, and relatives —despair of his return.

Like his earlier work, Simonov's war poetry is very uneven: now, as in a poem written during the battles on the Voronezh front, at the height of the Russian retreat in 1942, he succeeds in investing his emotions, bordering on despair, with powerful poetic accents; now, as in *"Ubey ego!" ("Kill Him!")*, a poem inspired by savage hatred for the enemy, he remains cold and prosaic. Too often his poetry is marred by a tendency towards journalism. His best poems are those where the patriotic and the personal notes are mingled. The volume *S toboy i bez tebya (With and Without You,* 1944) is composed mostly of purely personal love poetry. Some of these poems, for which Simonov—of all people!—was criticized as an "individualist," are very good, but in the final analysis Simonov seems to lack that indefinable something, that magic which turns merely good poetry into great poetry.

SURKOV

Surkov, on the contrary, is better when he is more impersonal, when he speaks of collective deeds of heroism. Poems like "Rossiya"

---

8 These two lines were deleted from some later editions.
9 Translated by Vivian da Sola Pinto, in *The Road to the West: Sixty Soviet War Poems.*

("Russia") and "Rodina" ("My Country") evoke the glorious past of Russia and the wars she fought in olden days. The poet refers to Russia as "immortal, undying, enigmatic in her wise simplicity." He recalls the battle of the Kulikovo Field (in 1380) and the Polish, Swedish, and French invasions. Like other Soviet poets he voices his hatred for the enemy, and one of the sections of his book *Dekabr pod Moskvoy (December Before Moscow*, 1942), in which the German onslaught on Moscow at the end of 1941 is evoked, is entitled "I Sing Hate." Some poems strike, however, a more personal, intimate note.

Surkov also wrote several popular war songs, such as "Pesnya smelykh" ("The Song of the Bold"), written on the day the Germans invaded Russia, with its famous refrain: "The bold strike fear into bullets,—The bold are unscathed by the bayonet"; "Pesnya zashchitnikov Moskvy" ("The Song of the Defenders of Moscow"), and "Zastolnaya" ("The Drinking Song").

PROKOFYEV, DOLMATOVSKY, SHCHIPACHOV, AND TVARDOVSKY

Alexander Prokofyev, Evgeny Dolmatovsky, and Stepan Shchipachov all contributed their quota of patriotic war poetry—much of it rather indifferent "slogan poetry"—each more or less following his personal bent. So did Tvardovsky, the author of *The Land of Muravia,* which he tried to parallel in another humorous epic, *Vasily Tyorkin*. Its hero is a kind of synthetic Russian soldier—cheerful, humorous, resourceful—embodying both the inherently homely wisdom of the Russian people and certain specific Soviet characteristics. The poem deals with his adventures, grave and gay, at the front and follows him almost to the gates of Berlin. It was written and published in installments over a period of several years (1941–45) and lacks the unity of *The Land of Muravia,* but has many of its qualities: its humor, its mastery of racy Russian, its variety of meters, and its wealth of memorable lines.

ALIGER AND BERGHOLZ

Special mention should be made of the war output of the two young women poets, Margarita Aliger and Olga Bergholz. Both of them grew in stature during the war. Of the two, Bergholz is perhaps the more accomplished poet. Her best war poems, collected in *Leningradskaya tetrad (The Leningrad Notebook,* 1942), reflect the heroic siege of Leningrad, throughout which she stayed in the city, doing regular broadcasts on the radio while it functioned. She is essentially a lyric poet, and her approach throughout is personal, but it is in the combination of the trivial and the majestic, in the fusion of the personal and the impersonal, that she is at her best: her poetry reflects not only the misery of the war-ravaged city where hunger and disease were rampant, not only the nobility of its heroic spirit, but also its historic grandeur. In its austere clarity her poetry is in the classical tradition.

Aliger is more romantic, more emotional, and more spontaneous. Her choice of words is less fastidious, her diction more blurred. One of her best war poems is "Moya pobeda" ("My Victory"), a long lyric poem in which the general theme of the war and the personal theme of a woman's destiny are closely interwoven. In "Zoya" she attempted a non-personal narrative poem: its heroine is Zoya Kozmodemyanskaya, a young girl who was tortured and executed by the Germans.

TIKHONOV AND INBER

Two older poets, Nikolay Tikhonov and Vera Inber, also found their inspiration in the heroic siege of Leningrad, its misery and grandeur. Tikhonov's long poem *Kirov s nami (Kirov Is With Us)* earned him one of the Stalin prizes. It described Kirov, the Communist boss of Leningrad who was assassinated in 1934, going the rounds of blockaded Leningrad on a dark, cold night. In another poem, in which he deliberately imitated the majestic numbers of Pushkin and went for inspiration to Russian history, Tikhonov drew a poetic parallel between Leningrad and Moscow.

Vera Inber, who came to Leningrad at the beginning of the war and stayed there for nearly three years, wrote during the siege her long poem *Pulkovsky meridian (The Pulkovo Meridian,* 1943), for which she was also awarded a Stalin prize. Classical in form and realistic in content, this poem of 816 lines, divided into 136 six-line stanzas with sonnetlike rhyming scheme, gives a picture of everyday life in the blockaded city, alternating with the author's comments on the events. The result is somewhat uneven, which is not surprising in a poem of such length. Inber is best when she is most concrete; the weakest parts of the poem are those where she generalizes and rationalizes. Here is one of her typical stanzas:

> *How painfully—still worse, how swiftly—can*
> *Faces grow old these days. The features stand*
> *Out, cut to birdlike sharpness by the hand,*
> *It seems, of some ill-omened make-up man.*
> *A pinch of ashes and a little lead—*
> *And faces look like faces of the dead.*[10]

[10] Translated by Alexander Kaun and Dorothea Prall Radin in Kaun, *Soviet Poets and Poetry,* 197.

War Poetry

Of the other established poets who made their contribution to war poetry, mention should be made of Pasternak and Anna Akhmatova. Neither published much during the war. Pasternak's little book, *On Early Trains,* which included a group of war poems, has been mentioned before (see page 176). These poems were subsequently included with some others in *Terrestrial Expanse* (1945). As usual, they were characterized by a freshness of approach and expression, but some critics accused Pasternak of remaining too individualistic and aloof in his treatment of war themes. Others doubted whether his new "un-Pasternakian" simplicity really suited him. The former Constructivist Zelinsky wrote, however, that:

> ... having turned to the war, this chapter in the history of our today so oversaturated with clatter and iron, Pasternak was able to say some intelligent and poetic, if somewhat belated, things about it. Pasternak's war poems are not the best of their kind, but they are imbued with love and respect for the Soviet man, the fighter, the victor.[11]

Soon, however, he and some other critics were to be rebuked for praising Pasternak.

Anna Akhmatova, the only survivor of the second Golden Age of Russian poetry, made her reappearance as a poet in 1940 when several of her poems were published by the Leningrad magazine *Zvezda.*[12] The same year a collected edition of her poetry entitled *Iz shesti knig (From Six Books)* was published: it contained all her earlier books of poems (of which the last had appeared in 1922), to which some slight additions had been made, plus one new book called *Iva (Willow Tree)* consisting of a score or so of poems written between 1936 and 1940.[13] These new poems showed no weakening of poetic power: some, in fact, were among her best. The volume was coolly received, however, by Soviet critics, who emphasized that Akhmatova had remained true to her old self—

[11] See K. Zelinsky, "O lirike" ("About Lyrical Poetry"), in *Znamya (Banner),* No. 8–9 (1946), 184.

[12] Akhmatova's name had, however, reappeared somewhat earlier. In 1933 *Zvezda* published her study of the connection between Pushkin's *The Golden Cockerel* and Washington Irving's "Alhambra," and in 1936 another Pushkin study (about Pushkin's debt to Benjamin Constant's *Adolphe*) appeared in a special Pushkin publication. It was also in 1936 that *Zvezda* published Akhmatova's translation of the poem "Pervy grekh" ("The First Sin") by the Armenian poet D. Varuzhan (1884–1915).

[13] It is not quite clear whether, prior to the publication of *From Six Books,* the new poems making up *Willow Tree* were published separately under that title, also in 1940. Judging by a review in *Literaturnaya gazeta,* this was apparently the case.

311

that the Revolution had not affected her in the least. Her poetry never-theless continued to appear in Soviet magazines. During the war Akh-matova enjoyed the privilege of being evacuated by air from besieged Leningrad to Central Asia, but she was back in Leningrad by 1945.

Of newcomers of promise there were few during the war. Perhaps one may single out Mikhail Dudin, who in 1945 published a book called *Kostry na perekryostkakh* (*Bonfires at Crossroads*). Though lacking originality, he showed himself to be a careful craftsman rather in the Acmeist tradition. Some good war poetry was written by Nikolay Braun, another Leningrad poet.

6. War Reportage and War Diaries

A great many Soviet writers worked as war correspondents, and their front-line reports appeared regularly in the Soviet press or were broadcast by Radio Moscow. Among them we find Simonov, Ehrenburg, Evgeny Petrov (of the Ilf-Petrov team), Grossman, Gorbatov, Stavsky, and others. Simonov was one of the most active and prolific; his front-line reports covered the whole vast extent of the front, as was indicated by the title of the volume in which some of them were collected: *Ot Barentsova morya do Chornogo* (*From the Barents Sea to the Black Sea*). Simonov's *Voennye dnevniki* (*War Diaries*) were published in the magazine *Znamya* and also issued in book form, as was the *Frontovoy dnevnik* (*Front-line Diary*, 1942) of Evgeny Petrov, who was killed in 1942 near Sevastopol. Grossman's *Stalingradskie ocherki* (*Stalingrad Sketches*), later included in his book *Gody voyny* (*The Years of War*, published in 1946), was one of the earliest coherent accounts of the great Stalingrad battle. The siege of Leningrad found its documentary reflec-tion, in addition to the stories and poems already mentioned, in Fade-yev's *Leningrad v dni blokady* (*Leningrad in the Days of the Blockade*, 1944) and Inber's *Pochti tri goda: Leningradsky dnevnik* (*Almost Three Years: A Leningrad Diary*, 1945). Inber's *Diary* gives a realistic picture of life in the blockaded city, with its mixture of nightmare and reality; but there is something rather unpleasant about the affected tone and patronizing attitudes the author strikes now and then, for example, when she speaks about the workers of Leningrad. Fadeyev's sketches are more simple, impersonal, and straightforward.

There was also some interesting nonliterary war reportage. One of the earliest works to attract attention and to be published also outside of Russia was Polyakov's *V tylu vraga* (*In the Enemy's Rear*, 1942). Alexander Polyakov (1908–1942) served as a political commissar in the army and at the same time a correspondent of the Red Army news-

paper *The Red Star*. He was attached to Major-General Galitsky's in-
fantry division, which, after dealing heavy blows to German tank columns in the very early days of the war, was encircled by the enemy and
was forced to fight its way out of the encirclement, for which purpose
it was divided into several detachments. Polyakov accompanied one of
these detachments and his book is a day-by-day account of their east-
ward march.

Later, partisan activities behind the German lines provided one of
the most exciting subjects. In 1944 appeared P. Ignatov's *Dnevnik
partizana* (*The Diary of a Partisan*). It described the activities of a
guerrilla detachment in the Kuban Region, covering the period from
1941 to May, 1943. In 1945 the magazine *Znamya* began the publication
of the work called *Lyudi s chistoy sovestyu* (*People With a Clear Conscience*), by Petro Vershigora (b. 1910?); the next year it appeared in
book form. Vershigora, a young Ukrainian film producer, was mobilized
at the very beginning of the war. The early chapters of the book give
some idea of the military unpreparedness of the Soviet Union and of
the summary methods of training: less than a month after he was mobilized, Vershigora, utterly untrained and inexperienced, was command-
ing a platoon in action. The bulk of Vershigora's book consists, however, of an interesting and patently truthful account of the raids made
behind the enemy lines by the famous partisan army of Sidor Kovpak,
which Vershigora joined in 1942. These raids took them through the
enemy-occupied Belorussia and Ukraine and as far west as the Carpa-
thians. Their object was to harass the Germans, to disrupt their lines of
communications, to undermine their morale, and to boost the spirit of
the population. While pointing out the "romantic" nature of their activities and the fact that those who joined the partisan army were
"romantics," Vershigora writes simply and realistically, and his book
throws light on one of the most interesting and peculiar aspects of the
war on the Soviet-German front, the existence of "Partisania," a separate country within the vast German-occupied Soviet territory. Vershigora himself does not use the term "Partisania," but he constantly
speaks of "Great Land" (*"Bolshaya Zemlya"*) to refer to the nonoccupied
part of the Soviet Union, while designating the territory held by the
partisans as "Little Land" (*"Malaya Zemlya"*);[14] the contact between
the two was maintained almost entirely by radio, though there were
also exchanges of flying visits, and Kovpak himself—a colorful, old
Ukrainian who took part as a sergeant in the first World War and later
distinguished himself in the Civil War—paid a visit to Stalin in the
Kremlin to receive instructions. It is interesting to note that here and

[14] The expression "Great Land" was also used in besieged Leningrad to refer
to the rest of the Soviet Union.

there Vershigora voices the partisans' resentment against the Red Army on account of its retreats. Thus he writes:

Let us put it bluntly: before the battle of Stalingrad we all tendered our accounts to the Red Army. Many bitter words were said, many bitter thoughts thought. After all we were battering the Germans in their rear and moving forward, while they kept so far retreating. . . .

They abandoned towns, villages, rivers. They abandoned them with a heavy heart, perhaps, but nevertheless behind them lay a country which was being more and more filled with the Stalinist will to victory, and they felt it. They had the rear, the mighty Soviet rear. And we, an army with no rear and no flanks, we saw only the bitter fruits of the retreat, its seamy side. We saw Belorussia thrown into dust, we saw the Ukraine trampled underfoot, bloodstained. And we also knew the thoughts and angry words of a certain Order of the Day, and more than anybody else, we, the civilians, schoolmasters, accountants, collective farmers, and musicians who had taken to arms, we had the right to hurl reproaches at the men who were retreating eastwards.

Vershigora adds, however, that many of them understood that they owed their victories to the fact of being opposed by the weakest units of the enemy while the bulk of Hitler's forces and resources was being used against the Red Army.

Like other Soviet writers who wrote about the war, Vershigora abstains from analyzing more closely the causes of the catastrophic Russian retreat in 1941 and 1942. Today, from the revelations of numbers of Russian displaced persons, of so-called "nevozvrashchentsy" ("irrepatriates")—Soviet citizens who refused to be repatriated when the war was over—we know (and this is something that many people suspected at the time, but no one dared say aloud) that in 1941 there were mass desertions from the Red Army and that the population of the occupied territories welcomed the Germans with bread and salt and with pealing of church bells. At this time the phrase "Welcome to you!" upon which Leonov built his play had quite another meaning. The large-scale partisan movement among the people began later, when the Nazis had exasperated the population by their behavior. True, Vershigora does portray "traitors" and hint at disloyal behavior of village population, but such cases are presented as individual, not as a mass phenomenon. In approaching Soviet war literature—whether fiction or documentary works—we must always bear in mind that, no matter how truthful it is (and Vershigora's book certainly gives the impression of truthfulness), it never tells the whole truth. This limits its documentary value for the future historian. An interesting proof of the fact that some Soviet writers themselves were aware of the danger of the optimistic concealment of the whole truth may be seen in an article which Fyodor Panfyorov published in *October* in 1946.[15] A loyal and sincere Communist, the author of *Bruski* spoke here of people who tend to simplify the complex problem of the war and of the Soviet victory, who insist that there was no such thing as the retreat of the Red Army, that it was but "a planned withdrawal, wearing down the enemy"; and who, when reminded that there was a time "when the fate of our country hung by a thread," tell you to "forget it."

Panfyorov's frank outburst was subsequently criticized as a manifestation of pessimism and despondency, unworthy of a good Communist.

7. Wartime Journalism: Tolstoy and Ehrenburg

AFTER the outbreak of the war the Soviet government made full use of the patriotic Russian spirit it had been assiduously fostering since the late thirties. The great national figures of the past—Dmitry Donskoy, Alexander Nevsky, Minin and Pozharsky, Suvorov, Kutuzov —became objects of a veritable patriotic cult. They were all mentioned by Stalin in his first wartime public pronouncement—the radio speech he made on July 3, 1941. In this speech, after the usual "Comrades," he used the truly Russian old form of address: "Brothers and sisters." The war against Germany became officially known as "The Second War for the Fatherland" (*Vtoraya Otechestvennaya Voyna*)—the first was the one Russia fought against Napoleon in 1812. This stress on Russian, rather than Soviet, patriotism, which we have already noticed in Soviet literature, was no doubt dictated to the government by the realization that to make the war really popular and to arouse the masses it had to be presented as a war for national existence and national heritage. For the first time in many years the word "Russia" was readmitted into the Communist vocabulary and freely used in the press. The taboo was lifted even from the past achievements of the Russian state: in a wartime broadcast of Pushkin's great poem *The Bronze Horseman,* the poem was referred to as a poem about St. Petersburg—"that magnificent embodiment of Russian military glory and of Russian statecraft."

Characteristic of this revival of Russian patriotism were the wartime articles of Alexey Tolstoy and Ilya Ehrenburg. Both were pre-Revolutionary writers, both had taken a patriotic attitude during World War I, both had proved themselves to be eminently adaptable opportunists, and both found no difficulty in taking the new line, especially

[15] No. 5 (1946), 151–62.

315

since in the case of Tolstoy it answered his innermost leanings: his acceptance of the Revolution had been, in part at least, dictated by his inborn Russian patriotism, and the task of reconciling the Soviet regime with the historical development of Russia appealed to him. He wrote eloquently of Russia's glorious past, of her epic heroes and her great historical figures, of the "Russian psyche" which was an unknown quantity to foreigners and even to many Russians and which was now revealed as "the psychology of the Soviet, and above all Russian, man who, having drunk of the drink of freedom, has discovered that . . . under the vivifying sun there exists higher justice inscribed with golden letters in the Stalin Constitution and that there also exists our Soviet Motherland—the country of our fathers and forefathers, destined for the happiness of our children and grandchildren."[16]

Tolstoy's wartime articles were collected in two volumes: *Rodina* (*Motherland,* 1942) and *Chto my zashchishchayen* (*What We Are Defending,* 1942).

Ehrenburg was even more prolific than Tolstoy: his articles written between June, 1941 and March, 1943 were collected in two volumes of nearly four hundred pages each, entitled *Voyna* (*The War,* 1942 and 1943.) The first volume is divided into four sections, entitled "Germans," "Hirelings," "Friends," and "Our War." The second is similarly arranged. Many of his articles were written in defense of the common heritage of European civilization; and many of the things which he said in them were to become highly unpopular four or five years later. Thus, in an article published on July 20, 1941, he spoke of the courage of London as "the first victory of human dignity over the barbarity of Fascism," of England being "left alone in the ranks," and of "the brotherly front of the three great Powers." In another article, dated September 20, 1941, referring to German attempts to sow discord among the allies, he wrote:

> We are not going to tell the Germans how much war equipment was and will be delivered to us by our allies. Our business is to kill the Germans—it does not matter how, whether on our fighters or on American, whether in our tanks or in British. Our business is to kill the Germans on our front. The British will see about the second front. . . . There has never been a stronger alliance than the alliance of peoples against Hitler.

On July 14, 1942, Ehrenburg wrote: "Soviet patriotism is a natural continuation of Russian patriotism. The Russians were never given to despising other peoples." And he went on to speak of the Russians'

16 "Za Sovetskuyu Rodinu!" ("For the Soviet Motherland!"), in *Pravda,* February 23, 1942. Reprinted in A. Tolstoy, *Rodina* (*Motherland*).

learning from Europe, of Peter the Great's going to school in Holland, of Voltaire's influence on Russian freethinkers, of the Decembrists' debt to the French Revolution, of Pushkin's passionate attachment to foreign poets, of the influence of Hegel on Herzen and Belinsky, of Mechnikov's learning from Pasteur, and even of the Russian proletariat's profiting by the lessons of the European labor movement. True, he also spoke of Europe's debt to Russia, to her literature. But the main idea, which Ehrenburg kept driving home in his articles, was the indivisibility of European cultural heritage:

> We never separated our culture from that of Europe, we are bound up with it not by wires, not by rails, but by blood vessels, by convolutions of the brain. . . . The destinies of European culture are infinitely dear to us. We remember that the Decembrists were inspired by the Declaration of the Rights of Man, that Turgenev was a friend of the best French writers. We cannot look at the tragedy of Europe from the side—

he wrote on March 19, 1943.

This theme runs through many of Ehrenburg's wartime articles. It was obvious that he was glad to be able to vent his inherent cosmopolitanism and in particular his attachment to French culture. On the other hand he gave free rein to his hatred for the Germans. His anti-German articles had no equal for venomous mordancy, Alexey Tolstoy coming in second best. A moment came, however, when a sudden stop was put to these anti-German effusions of Ehrenburg: in the spring of 1945 *Pravda* published an article entitled "Comrade Ehrenburg Exaggerates." It accused Ehrenburg of overdoing the "hate-the-Germans" stuff and pointed out that there were both "bad" and "good" Germans. The article came from a high quarter—it was signed by Georgy Aleksandrov, head of the Propaganda Section of the Central Committee of the Communist party—and Ehrenburg had no alternative but to take the cue and change his tune; for a time he simply stopped writing. The change of tactics implied in Aleksandrov's article was, of course, dictated by military-political considerations. Had Alexey Tolstoy been alive then (he had died a little earlier, in February, 1945) Aleksandrov's injunction would have been applicable to him, too.

8. *Historical Novels and Plays*

THE vogue for historical novels and plays, as well as for biographies (straightforward or novelized) of national heroes, continued during the war. Heroes of the Napoleonic wars naturally enjoyed great popularity, and there were several biographies of Suvorov, Kutuzov, Bagration, and other Russian generals.

317

Alexey Tolstoy, in addition to resuming his work on *Peter the First* (see Chapter III), wrote also two plays about Ivan the Terrible. They formed two parts of *Ivan Grozny (Ivan the Terrible)*, which was subtitled "A dramatic tale." The first part was called *Oryol i orlitsa (The Eagle and His Mate,* 1942), the second, *Trudnye gody (The Hard Years,* 1943).[17] Soviet critics regard this play as one of the greatest achievements, not of Tolstoy only, but of Soviet dramaturgy also. In the words of one of them, Tolstoy "for the first time applied the principles of Shakespearean dramaturgy as understood by the founders of Marxism."[18]

The two plays overlap chronologically, covering respectively the periods 1553–69 and 1566–71. In the first, the stress is on Ivan the man; in the second, on the statesman who subordinates everything to the interests of the state as he understands them. Tolstoy deliberately commits certain anachronisms and takes some liberties with history, but on the whole his "dramatic tale," just as his great novel, is based on a careful study of historical material, and several documents of the period are skillfully incorporated into the play. With great mastery Tolstoy reproduces the spirit of the Tsar's language as we know it from his writings, with its combination of biblical solemnity and crude colloquialism. But the tendency to read the present into the past, or at least to suggest a parallel between the two, is much more obvious here than in *Peter the First.*

The play is meant to be an apologia for the cruel and tyrannous Tsar, not only as a statesman who, in ruthlessly suppressing the boyar aristocracy and in establishing his absolute rule, had at heart the long-range interests of the Russian state, but also as a personality. In this, Tolstoy is poles apart from his namesake and distant relative, Count Alexey K. Tolstoy (1817–75), who portrayed Ivan in his tragedy *The Death of Ivan the Terrible* and in his novel *Prince Serebryany.* In direct contradiction to the literary and historical tradition, the Soviet author proceeds to whitewash also Ivan's most cruel henchman, Malyuta Skuratov, while presenting in an unfavorable light the noble figure of Metropolitan Philip, one of Ivan's victims. In his interpretation of Ivan's personality Tolstoy is at variance with the nineteenth-century historical tradition and is closest to the more recent interpretation of Ivan the Terrible in the work of R. Wipper, whose book about Ivan, first published in 1923, was reissued in 1944 (an English translation of it appeared in Moscow in 1947). In his literary autobiography, published in 1943 in *Novy Mir* (No. 1), Tolstoy said that the age of Ivan the Terrible

---

[17] These were limited, privately printed editions (see Veksler, *A. N. Tolstoy,* 446–47). The play in its revised version was published in *Oktyabr,* No. 11–12 (1943).
[18] That is, Marx and Engels. See Veksler, *A. N. Tolstoy,* 472.

attracted him as "one of the tragic and creative epochs during which the Russian character was formed." In a later variant of the same autobiography he pointed out that in writing his play he was stimulated by the humiliations to which the Germans had subjected his country: "I called to life out of nowhere that great and passionate Russian character—Ivan the Terrible—in order to arm my own 'infuriated conscience.' "[19]

In the first part of Tolstoy's dramatic diptych an important place is occupied by the story of Ivan's love for his Circassian wife, Marya Temryukovna, in whose portrayal Tolstoy also departs from the historical tradition. In general, while it has many literary merits, viewed as history Tolstoy's play is either a piece of skillful propaganda or a feat of subtle leg-pulling.

A similar tendency toward whitewashing Ivan can be discerned in Vladimir Solovyov's play *Veliky Gosudar (The Great Sovereign)* and in the three-volume novel, *Ivan Grozny (Ivan the Terrible,* 1941–45), by Valentin Kostylyov (1888–1950). The latter focuses attention on the wars that Ivan fought to secure for Russia an outlet to the Baltic.

More recent periods of Russian history also attracted several writers. In the light of the armed conflict with Germany some eyes were naturally turned to World War I. The veteran novelist Sergeyev-Tsensky published during the war three novels dealing with this period: *Brusilovsky proryv (Brusilov's Breakthrough,* 1943), *Pushki vydvigayut (The Guns Are Brought Out,* 1944), and *Pushki zagovorili (The Guns Have Spoken,* 1945). All three form part of the author's *Transfiguration* (see page 141 above), designed as a vast epic of Russian life, comparable in scope to Jules Romains' *Les Hommes de bonne volonté.*

As historical novels, Sergeyev-Tsensky's World War I novels are in the tradition of Leo Tolstoy's *War and Peace,* rather than of Alexey Tolstoy's *Peter the First*: their heroes are fictitious, while historical characters are assigned subordinate roles. *Brusilov's Breakthrough,* which deals with the 1916 offensive of the Russian armies against Austria-Hungary, recaptures very well the atmosphere of "patriotic anxiety" which prevailed in Russia on the eve of the Revolution. The central character is Lieutenant Liventsev (he reappears also in the sequels to the novel), a young, intelligent, and sensitive officer; through his reactions the author presents the events to us. There are also a number of other characters, both historical (Emperor Nicholas, Brusilov, Ivanov, and other generals) and fictitious, but the author is primarily concerned with depicting the social psychology of the Russian people dur-

19 "Kratkaya avtobiografiya" ("A Short Autobiography"), in A. Tolstoy, *Povesti i rasskazy.* 1910–1943 *(Tales and Stories:* 1910–1943). See also Veksler, *A. N. Tolstoy,* 444–45.

ing the war. The novel is remarkable for its objective, and even sympathetic, treatment of the conflict which Lenin and his fellow Bolsheviks (including Stalin) had denounced as "imperialistic": this would have been unthinkable before 1941. On its publication Sergeyev-Tsensky's novel was warmly acclaimed by Soviet critics, but as soon as the war was over, it was attacked for its objectivity and its unorthodox approach.

Brusilov (who was one of the few old-time war leaders to rally to the Soviet regime and to give his blessing to its war against Poland in 1920) was the hero of another novel (which bears his name) by a pre-Revolutionary writer, Yury Slyozkin (1887–1947). Its first installments appeared in *October* in 1944, but for some reason the publication was interrupted and the complete novel did not appear in book form until 1947. Soviet critics favorably contrasted Slyozkin's political interpretation with that of Sergeyev-Tsensky. Still another work about Brusilov was Selvinsky's play *General Brusilov* (1943). A reissue of Brusilov's *Memoirs* also marked this temporary revival of interest in World War I.

The Russo-Japanese War also came in for its share of attention. It was the subject of *Port-Arthur* (1944), a long and rather dull novel by Alexander Stepanov. Inferior to Novikov-Priboy's *Tsushima* as literature, it made up for what the latter lacked in patriotism.

A place apart among the wartime historical novels belongs to *Pugachov* (1943–44), a very long novel by Vyacheslav Shishkov (1873–1945) about the famous eighteenth-century rebel. It is a colorful work, with a multitude of characters, written in the realistic tradition. Shishkov died before completing it. An engineer by profession, Shishkov lived most of his life in Siberia, and many of his earlier works had that part of Russia for their background. One of the most interesting was *Vataga* (*The Gang,* 1923), a novel about a group of Old Believers who became revolutionary partisans during the Civil War.

Non-Russian history provided material for *Staraya Angliya* (*Old England,* 1943), by Evgeny Lann, a novel about Jonathan Swift and the contemporary political struggle in England. This was one of the signs of an increased interest, favored by wartime alliance with the West, in the Anglo-Saxon world.

9. *Zoshchenko, Fedin, and Herman on the Carpet*

Zoshchenko's Before Sunrise

SOME nine hundred Soviet writers, in one form or another, took part in the war, and it is small wonder that they wrote about almost nothing else. A work dealing with a subject entirely unrelated to the current events, or to something that could be regarded as their antecedent in the past, was a *rara avis* in the Soviet periodicals of those days. Such a rarity was Zoshchenko's "novel" *Pered voskhodom solntsa* (*Before Sunrise*), which began to appear in *October* in 1943 (Nos. 6–7 and 8–9). Two installments of it were printed, totaling sixty-eight pages, whereupon the publication was discontinued without any explanation. No. 8–9 of *October* was signed for the press on September 27, but No. 10 was not signed until December 27. The delay may have been due to ordinary wartime causes, but it is significant that in the meantime Zoshchenko's work was attacked by a certain L. Dmitriev in *Literature and Art*[20] and made subject for discussion in the Praesidium of the Union of Soviet Writers—a not unusual procedure.[21] Dmitriev described Zoshchenko's work as "vulgar," "harmful," and "remote from the life of the people." At the discussion in the Union of Soviet Writers it was criticized by Fadeyev as "antinational" and "antiartistic," while the critic Yudin called it "amoral" and said that it "went against the fine traditions of Russian literature." A feeble attempt to defend Zoshchenko was made by Olga Forsh, who evoked Rousseau's *Confessions*.[22] Before long, more guns were brought into action against Zoshchenko: *Bolshevik*, the authoritative Party organ specializing in higher exegesis, published a short article signed by four individuals who described themselves as "average Leningrad readers." The article protested against Zoshchenko's "vulgar philistinism" and deliberate disregard of the great struggle in which his country was engaged. In the next number of *Bolshevik*, Tikhonov, in an article about Soviet literature and the war, spoke of Zoshchenko's novel as "a phenomenon profoundly alien to the spirit and character of Soviet literature."[23]

What exactly was Zoshchenko's crime?

Before Sunrise is not an easily definable work. Zoshchenko subtitled it *"povest,"* which is usually translated as "tale," but is in fact used in Russian to designate a genre intermediate between a story and a novel, something like a short novel. Zoshchenko's work is, however, neither a story nor a novel in the accepted sense of the word. It bears a certain resemblance to his *Youth Restored* (see page 151 above), which Zoshchenko himself recalls in his "Introduction." The similarity lies chiefly in the introduction of the element of science: Pavlov's physiological theories form an integral part of the work, while there are also refer-

---

20 "O novom romane Zoshchenko" ("About Zoshchenko's New Novel"), in *Literatura i iskusstvo*, December 4, 1943.

21 This took place on December 6, 1943.

22 For more details see Reavey, *Soviet Literature Today*, 118–20.

23 "Ob odnoy vrednoy povesti" ("About a Harmful Story"), in *Bolshevik*, No. 2 (January, 1944), 56–58. See also Tikhonov's article "Otechestvennaya voyna i sovetskaya literatura" ("The War for the Fatherland and Soviet Literature"), in *Bolshevik*, No. 3–4, (1944).

ences to Freud's interpretation of dreams. This time, however, the scientific aspect is treated more seriously while the element of fiction—in the proper sense of the word—is completely absent (at least in the published parts) and is replaced by short autobiographical fragments recalling various incidents in the author's life. These fragments cover first the years 1912–26; then the years 1900–15 (that is, when Zoshchenko was between five and fifteen years of age); then the still earlier childhood, first from the age of two to the age of five; and then before the age of two. Zoshchenko begins by saying: "I am unhappy and I don't know why," and the object of this retrogressive excursion into his past is to discover the true cause of his unhappiness, of his melancholy and life-weariness. But to the reader the real meaning of all this devious probing into his youth and childhood is not very easy to see. Many of the autobiographical incidents are indeed trivial or even vulgar. Very few have a real intrinsic interest. The psycho-pathological significance of some is doubtful. But what shocked the Soviet critics was the frankly introspective character of the whole work, the author's exclusive and unashamed preoccupation with his ego, coupled with his flippant attitude toward the "epochal" events of his time. There is nothing in the work, however, to justify the charge of fundamental hostility to the Soviet regime or even of incurable and decadent pessimism: in fact Zoshchenko hints that he succeeded in the end in curing himself of his melancholy and that he was helped in this by Pavlov and his theory of conditioned reflexes. How this was achieved would probably have been told in the subsequent installments. As for Freud, who is *persona ingrata* in the Soviet Union, Zoshchenko showed no leaning towards him; on the contrary, he tried to beat him with Pavlov.

As it stands (though perhaps one should not judge it in this incomplete form), *Before Sunrise* is not one of Zoshchenko's successes. One wonders, however, whether, like *Youth Restored*, it was not meant to be a gigantic hoax. The most interesting thing in it are a few confessions that throw light on Zoshchenko as a writer, Zoshchenko the unhumorous humorist.

Zoshchenko's *Before Sunrise* was to be recalled three years later when he was "purged" from Soviet literature (see Chapter VII). At the same time it was pointed out that throughout the war he had stayed in Alma-Ata and made no contribution to the literary war-effort. It is true that, but for *Before Sunrise*, the name of Zoshchenko is conspicuously absent from the Soviet wartime periodicals. (Zoshchenko himself says a little flippantly that during the first year of the war he was "busy writing various scenarios on subjects needed in the days of the great war for the Fatherland," and in 1942 began working on *Before Sunrise*, for which he had been collecting materials for ten years.)

Fedin's Literary Reminiscences

Another interesting work that had no relation to the war was Fedin's book of literary reminiscences, *Gorky in Our Midst,* which has already been mentioned in connection with the Serapion Brothers. Its first part was published in 1943 and was highly praised. Coming as it did from the pen of one of the most distinguished Soviet writers and dealing with the earliest period of Soviet literature, it was of great literary interest. The second volume appeared in 1944, with the subtitle *Ukhodyashchy Peterburg (The Vanishing Petersburg).* It contained some interesting portraits of such writers as Sologub, Remizov, Volynsky, and others. But this time it was Fedin's turn to come under fire: he was accused of being "objective" (objectivity is a crime from the point of view of Socialist realism!) and "dispassionate," of having completely left out of account the historical-political background. "How can one be outside politics during the war for the Fatherland?" exclaimed Vsevolod Vishnevsky, while I. Lezhnev significantly accused Fedin of having been carried away by the fashionable tendency toward a "revaluation of values" and therefore ready to "revise the very foundations of our outlook." Marietta Shaginyan spoke of Fedin's "soft benevolence" and of his "distortion of the past"; and Tikhonov reproached Fedin for misinterpreting Gorky's position.[24] The second volume of Fedin's memoirs was accordingly taken off the shelves as a work that, in the official view, reflected no credit on Soviet literature. Later, the first volume was included in the condemnation. Fedin, still recognized as one of the best Soviet writers, took it in his stride and in 1945 published an interesting full-size novel—his first since *The Rape of Europe* —which also had nothing to do with current events; together with its postwar sequel it will be discussed in the last chapter.

Herman's Story Suppressed

A Soviet critic smugly wrote once that for Soviet literature there were no "forbidden subjects."[25] Her tacit implication might have been, however, that there were forbidden approaches and forbidden attitudes,

[24] All these opinions were voiced at the routine post-mortem on Fedin's book in the Praesidium of the Union of Soviet Writers and were reported in *Literatura i iskusstvo,* September 9, 1944. See Reavey, *Soviet Literature Today,* 121. Previous to that, however, the same L. Dmitriev who had attacked Zoshchenko published an article in the same paper (August 5, 1944), in which he described Fedin's book as "a defense of the attitude of a contemplative artist [and] of apolitical art."

[25] E. Knipovich in *Znamya,* No. 2 (1947), 173. The article was a review of some stories which had appeared in *Novy Mir.* The phrase was used in connection with a story by Andrey Platonov, which Knipovich criticized for its picture of postwar relations in a Soviet family. Platonov, a former member of the "Pereval" group, had been in trouble before for his outspoken descriptions of collectivization.

and the history of Soviet literature, especially since 1929, affords ample proof and illustration of this. A postwar case of a work by a well-known writer suppressed for being out of tune with the official outlook may be mentioned here. In 1949 *Zvezda* began the publication of a short war novel by Yury Herman, *Podpolkovnik meditsinskoy sluzhby (Lieutenant Colonel of the Medical Corps)*. The first installment, of some forty pages, appeared in No. 1, and the conclusion was to follow. It did not, however, appear in No. 2. On the last page of the next number *Zvezda* printed Herman's "Letter to the Editor" in which he wrote that in view of the readers' "just criticisms" he had decided to stop the publication of his novel which needed "radical reworking from the first chapter to the last." "It had been pointed out," Herman explained, "that the hero of the novel, Dr. Levin, lived isolated in his tiny circumscribed world, was completely engrossed in his own sufferings, and had no right to be described as a positive character. The psychological self-probing of the decadent hero, the complexity of his attitude toward life—all this taken together has led to a wrong picture of the life of the hospital and the garrison." To this letter of self-criticism the editors of *Zvezda* added a short postscript to the effect that they now realized the error they had made in publishing Herman's novel—"in which the main character is portrayed as an aloof, decadent, morbidly irritable individualist," and were not going to print any more of it. Of the six members of the editorial board of *Zvezda*, one was Herman himself. Comments seem superfluous, even though it will be argued that both the author and the magazine yielded to the *readers'* demands for cheerful, optimistic works.

VII. Toeing the New Party Line
1946–50

1. *Putting the Screw On*

NO sooner was the war over than the tightening of ideological controls in the Soviet Union became apparent to most people. Actually, these controls were never relaxed very much; that is, the government
never really let out of sight its long-range aims, and the seeming concessions to popular feelings were of a purely tactical, opportunistic
nature.

Even during the war there were enough signs to show that the
Communist party would never allow the "revaluation of values" to go
too far and that as soon as the proper bounds were overstepped, it
would clamp down on the transgressors. This was the meaning of the
attack on Zoshchenko in 1943 and of the rebuke to Fedin in 1944, as
well as to Ehrenburg in 1945. There were other similar cases. Thus,
Aseyev and Selvinsky, one a former Futurist and the other a former
Constructivist, were accused of "ideological mistakes" in their poems
about Russia. Selvinsky's mistake (in a poem called "Whom Russia
Lullabied") consisted in depicting Russia as too "soft" and broad-
minded. Pasternak was criticized for keeping aloof from the war and
devoting himself almost entirely to new translations of Shakespeare
(somewhat inconsistently, another poet, Mikhail Lozinsky, was praised
for accomplishing his excellent translation of Dante's *Divine Comedy*
to the accompaniment of guns and bombs, and this was even adduced
as a proof of the artist's freedom in the U.S.S.R.). Certainly those in the
West who spoke of the "Great Retreat" of the Soviet regime and expected the war to bring about far-reaching internal changes in Russia
were soon undeceived. The concessions which the Soviet government
made before the war, and even more so during the war, to Russian
patriotism and to Russian national feelings, were no doubt dictated by
the consideration that patriotism and national feelings could be used
to advantage in an all-out conflict with Nazi Germany. Once this new
national spirit was aroused, it was not easy to exorcise it, but it was possible to make use of it as a weapon of domestic and international policy,
to channel it *ad majorem gloriam* of the Soviet state.

Soviet Russian Literature

The ever growing tendency toward *statism*, the glorification of the Soviet state, endowed with all the attributes of unlimited autocracy, is one of the salient features of the recent ideological evolution in the Soviet Union. So far as there was, and is, a revival and a rehabilitation of the past and its traditions, there appears a predominant tendency to strengthen the authority and prestige of the state: old ranks, orders and decorations, uniforms (not only schoolboys and schoolgirls, but even schoolteachers wear them now), strict enforcement of the discipline in the army and in schools—such are the characteristic features which distinguish Stalin's Russia from Lenin's. The historical figures that are particularly glorified today also represent the same trend: Ivan the Terrible, Peter the Great, Suvorov, Kutuzov, and other great military leaders. It is true that this cult of absolute power and military leadership is somehow still combined with the continuing veneration of the outstanding figures of Russian democratic and revolutionary intelligentsia, such as Radishchev, Belinsky, Chernyshevsky, and Dobrolyubov, and of the great Russian men of letters, Pushkin, Lermontov, Tolstoy, Nekrasov, and Chekhov.[1] But this veneration is no more than lip service: the true meaning of what all these men stood for—especially of their unflagging stand for freedom of the mind—is either grossly distorted or disregarded to suit the current Party line with which it is utterly incompatible. Never before in the history of Russia has a grosser deceit been practised than this appropriation by her present rulers of the names of Pushkin and Lermontov, of Tolstoy and Chekhov, of Radishchev and Herzen, of Belinsky and Nekrasov, and of so many others, as the spiritual ancestors of "Soviet culture." To be able to do so, they are—as we shall see—cutting them to their measure, shearing

[1] As a rule Dostoyevsky is not included in the list of great Russian writers. Although much study was done in the Soviet Union of Dostoyevsky's life and writings (especially by such scholars as Dolinin and Grossman), Gorky's view of him as a harmful and dangerous writer prevailed. During the war, however, even Dostoyevsky was affected by the general "revaluation of values," and on September 5, 1942, the editor of *Literatura i iskusstvo*, V. Ermilov, a former die-hard critic of the On Guard and RAPP groups, published in his paper an article entitled "A Great Russian Writer: F. M. Dostoyevsky." Dostoyevsky was shown as a national thinker, an ethical teacher, a preacher of humanism, and thus fundamentally an "anti-Fascist" writer. Dostoyevsky's well-known hatred of Prussianism was stressed, and he was represented not as a precursor of Nietzsche, but as a denouncer of Nietzschean morality *avant la lettre*, a prophet who had foreseen the advent of Nazi barbarity. Dostoyevsky's *The Possessed* was interpreted by Ermilov as a prophecy of the Nazi political "gangsterism." Although Ermilov studded his article with numerous reservations, his conclusion was that Soviet people had much to learn from Dostoyevsky, and even more from Dostoyevsky the teacher of true humanism than Dostoyevsky the novelist. This reappraisal of Dostoyevsky—a typical example of Soviet "doublethink"—was of short duration, however, and Soviet critics soon reverted to the traditional Gorky view. Ermilov himself had to live down his "heresies" and gave a public lecture on Dostoyevsky's "reactionary ideas," which was published in pamphlet form in 1948.

326

them of some of their essentials, or creating myths about them. But in doing so, they often cannot help contradicting themselves or unsaying what they have said before.

The cult of the state which characterizes Stalinite Russia is, of course, in flagrant contradiction, not only to the credo of the "revolutionary-democratic" thinkers whom the present-day Russian Communists still pretend to regard as their predecessors, or to the early trends of Russian Bolshevism, but also to the teachings of Marx, Engels, and Lenin about the "withering away" of the state. That this glaring inconsistency is puzzling some minds in the Soviet Union may be seen from the fact that in August, 1950, Stalin deemed it necessary to publish in *Bolshevik* an authoritative explanation of why the Marx-Engels-Lenin thesis is no longer applicable to the Soviet Union of today.[2] In his statement he pokes fun at the "doctrinaires and Talmudists" who imagine that it is enough to memorize Marxist formulae by heart and recite them forwards and backwards.

During the war many people also made much of the concessions which the Soviet government accorded to religion, and to the Orthodox church in particular. The antireligious campaign was gradually slackened after the mid-thirties. This change of policy—if not of heart—undoubtedly represented a concession to popular feelings which paralleled the concessions to the people's patriotism and was dictated by the interests of the Soviet state in the event of an international conflict. One of the Soviet government's first acts when the war broke out was to close down the antireligious journal *Bezbozhnik* (*The Godless One*), of which Demyan Bedny used to be a regular contributor, to abolish the society for propagation of atheism, and to seek the support of the church in the all-out national effort. In wartime literature the religious sentiments of the people were often reflected (Simonov's poems, Leonov's dramas). The fact that village priests took part in the guerrilla movement was duly emphasized. After the war the policy of concessions to the church was continued. To some extent, no doubt, this policy did represent a genuine retreat and an admission, on the part of the Communist leaders, of their defeat on the religious front, the original plan of exterminating religion by open persecution having proved a failure. But the price paid by the church for these partial concessions was a heavy one, for they resulted in making the now officially recognized Orthodox church subservient to the state and even turning it into a useful instrument of the Kremlin's foreign policy—in the Near East and in the Balkans. The traditional enmity of the Orthodox hierarchy to Roman Catholicism was skillfully fostered by the professedly atheist government of Communist Russia. Unable to indoctrinate the Russian

2 *Bolshevik*, No. 15 (August, 1950).

masses with the idea that religion was opium for the people, Stalin took the cue from Ivan the Terrible and Peter the Great and subordinated the church to the state. The important difference between them was that neither Ivan nor Peter professed to be an atheist. With the church well under control, it was possible after the war to resume antireligious propaganda, which is now mainly directed toward young Communists, among whom religion seems to have won many recruits.

With the war at an end it soon became increasingly clear that the precarious and uneasy alliance between Stalin's totalitarian police-state and the democracies of the West, known as the alliance of all "freedom-loving" nations (the word when used by the Soviet leaders and their press and radio always smacked of hypocrisy), was cracking at the seams. During the war Soviet leaders perforce had to acknowledge the role of their Western allies in the victories won over Nazi Germany. On June 13, 1944, a week after the landings in Normandy, Stalin spoke in glowing terms of the Allied invasion of the Continent, saying that "the history of warfare knows no other undertaking comparable in breadth of conception, grandeur of scale, and mastery of execution."[3] But as the war drew closer to its conclusion, the achievements of the Western allies began to be played down. The 1946 edition of the officially approved textbook of Soviet history, which was speedily brought out to replace the 1945 edition, spoke briefly and somewhat grudgingly of the Allied contribution to the victory over Germany, representing the Soviet Union as "the savior of civilization and progress in Europe and the whole world."[4] Stalin's tribute to the Allies' invasion of Germany disappeared from the 1946 edition. So did, very significantly, the account of the dissolution of the Communist International in 1943, which the West had hailed as the final break with the old Communist policy of fomenting world revolution. In a speech on February 9, 1946, Stalin outlined the new Party line with regard to the war and the victory—the latter was presented as a triumph for the Soviet social and political order and as a proof of its superiority to the non-Soviet order. The speech heralded the return to the old Bolshevik conception of two irreconcilably hostile worlds. The wartime alliance of freedom-loving nations (which in truth was not more than a cobelligerency) was to give place to a total ideological war in which the Soviet Union was to stand opposed to its wartime democratic allies. This ideological war was soon to reach an unheard-of pitch of violence and acerbity and to

[3] I. Stalin, *O velikoy Otechestvennoy Voyne Sovetskogo Soyuza (About the Great War for the Fatherland Waged by the Soviet Union)*, 137.

[4] A. M. Pankratova (ed.), *Istoriya SSSR (A History of the U.S.S.R.)*, 390. This textbook for high schools, published under the auspices of the Academy of Sciences of the U.S.S.R., was compiled by Professors K. Bazilevich, S. Bakhrushin, A. Pankratova, and A. Vogt.

eclipse completely anything that was ever said or written in the Soviet Union against "Fascism." Significantly enough, the first attacks in this all-out war of ideologies were launched on the literary front.[5]

2. *The Zhdanov "Bombshell"*

ON August 14, 1946, the Central Committee of the Communist party passed a resolution which, although it dealt with some specific cases of literary "heresy," marked the starting point of a new era in Soviet literature which has become associated with the name of Andrey Zhdanov.

The resolution, known as the resolution "On the magazines *Zvezda* and *Leningrad*," came to most people outside the Soviet Union as a bolt from the blue; nor was it apparently expected by the Soviet writers. It took many people quite a long time to understand its full purport. It dealt with the unsatisfactory manner in which the above-named two Leningrad literary magazines were run.[6] *Zvezda* was accused of publishing recently several "ideologically harmful" works and specifically of "providing a literary tribune" for Zoshchenko, a writer who had "long since been specializing in writing empty, fatuous and vulgar stuff, and in preaching rotten lack of ideas (*bezideynost*), vulgarity, and apoliticalness, designed to lead our youth astray and to poison its consciousness." Zoshchenko was described as "scum of literature," and his story "Priklyucheniya obezyany" ("The Adventures of a Monkey"), published in 1946 in *Zvezda* (No. 5–6), was singled out for attack. It was characterized as "a vulgar lampoon on Soviet life and Soviet people." Zoshchenko was accused of "anti-Soviet innuendoes," and his "unworthy behavior" during the war, when he published such a "disgusting" work as "Before Sunrise," was recalled.

The resolution further accused *Zvezda* of "popularizing" the work of Anna Akhmatova, who was described as "a typical representative of empty poetry which is devoid of ideas and alien to our people." Her poems were said to be "imbued with the spirit of pessimism and decadence," expressive of "the tastes of the old drawing-room poetry . . . of bourgeois-aristocratic aestheticism and decadence, of 'art for art's sake,'" and "harmful to the cause of the upbringing of our youth."

[5] The switch in the Soviet attitude to the war and to its allies is discussed at some length, with numerous quotations, in George S. Counts and Nucia Lodge, *The Country of the Blind: The Soviet System of Mind Control*. It is a very thorough and illuminating account of the "Zhdanov era."

[6] *Zvezda* was a monthly founded in 1924. It was regarded as the organ of the Leningrad branch of the Union of Soviet Writers. In the thirties it was one of the best Soviet literary periodicals. *Leningrad* was a fortnightly magazine of more recent origin.

Akhmatova's poetry, said the resolution, was "not to be tolerated in Soviet literature." By publishing Zoshchenko's and Akhmatova's work, the magazine—went on the resolution—had wrought "ideological havoc" among the Leningrad writers. Similar accusations were proffered against the other magazine, *Leningrad*, which also had published Zoshchenko and Akhmatova as well as "a number of works imbued with the spirit of servility before everything foreign." The editorial boards of both magazines were charged with having forgotten the fundamental maxim of Leninism which proclaims that

> our magazines, whether scientific or literary, cannot be apolitical . . . . Our magazines are a powerful weapon of the Soviet state in the task of educating the Soviet people, and especially of the young, and must therefore be guided by that which constitutes the essence of the Soviet order, namely its politics. The Soviet regime cannot tolerate the education of the young in a spirit of indifference to Soviet politics, in a spirit of pooh-poohism and of ideological neutrality . . . . All preaching of ideological neutrality, of apolitical-ness, of "art for art's sake," is alien to Soviet literature.

The resolution further accused the Union of Soviet Writers and its chairman, Tikhonov, as well as the Leningrad City Committee of the Communist party, of condoning the political mistakes of *Zvezda* and *Leningrad* and of taking no steps for the improvement of those magazines. The editors of *Zvezda* were ordered to "liquidate" these "mistakes and shortcomings" and to stop printing Zoshchenko, Akhmatova, and "suchlike" writers. A. M. Egolin, deputy chief of the Propaganda Section of the Central Committee of the Communist party, was appointed editor-in-chief of *Zvezda*, while *Leningrad* was simply suppressed.[7]

A week later, Zhdanov—who during the next two years was to play the role of the Communist cultural "boss"[8]—made reports on the situa-

---

[7] The resolution of the Central Committee was first published in *Kultura i zhizn.* It was reproduced in *Pravda* and other Soviet newspapers and in all literary magazines. Some of them accompanied it by editorial comments and embroiderings, and additions to the list of "harmful" works. Thus *Znamya* attacked its own editorial board, in particular for publishing Grossman's prewar play *Esli verit pifagoreytsam* (*If One Is to Believe the Pythagoreans*) as reflecting an "alien philosophy." The play is not devoid of interest, but its "philosophy" is not easily detectable. Its moral seems to be that a good old Liberal of the Tsar's days who swears by Pythagoras is a more valuable individual than a bad Bolshevik who values his material well-being above everything else. *Znamya* added to the list of "harmful works" Vsevolod Ivanov's novel *Pri vzyatii Berlina* (*At the Taking of Berlin*), Fedin's *Gorky in Our Midst*, Kirsanov's "formalistic" poem about Alexander Matrosov, etc. See "Vyshe znamya ideynosti v literature!" ("Higher the Banner of Ideas in Literature!"), in *Znamya*, No. 10 (1946), 27–37.

tion arising out of the Central Committee's resolution before the Leningrad branch of the Union of Soviet Writers and the Leningrad City Committee of the Communist party, developing and clarifying the main points of the resolution and laying down the new Party line in matters of art and literature.[9]

Zoshchenko and Akhmatova were discussed by Zhdanov at some length. He denounced Zoshchenko as "a vulgarian" who was "accustomed to mocking at Soviet life, Soviet conditions, and Soviet people, while disguising his mockery under a mask of empty entertainment and fatuous facetiousness." Zoshchenko's story about the ape he characterized as "the epitome of all that is negative in Zoshchenko's literary production," adding that Zoshchenko deliberately portrayed Soviet life as ugly, grotesque, and vulgar "in order to put into the mouth of a monkey the vile, poisonous, anti-Soviet statement to the effect that life in a zoo is better than life at large, and that in a cage one can breathe more freely than among Soviet people."[10] Zhdanov then recalled Zoshchenko's contribution to the Serapion Brothers' autobiographies and made a general attack on the Serapions for preaching "rotten apoliticalness, philistinism, and vulgarity."

From Zoshchenko, Zhdanov passed on to Akhmatova, whom he characterized as an out-and-out individualist, a representative of the "reactionary literary morass," a "cross between a nun and a whore." Her poetry was described as "remote from the people," as "the poetry of the upper ten thousand of the old Russia of the landed gentry," a relic of the irrevocable past, which could only breed depression and pessimism and a desire to escape into the narrow world of personal emotions, and thus poison the minds of the young people.[11]

8 The fact that at the same time Zhdanov played an important political role and in 1947 was entrusted with the leading part in the revived Communist International (the so-called "Cominform") shows what importance was attached at this juncture to the "cultural front."

9 A combined and condensed stenographic version of Zhdanov's reports was printed in all Soviet newspapers and most literary periodicals. For a more complete English translation of it see Counts and Lodge, *The Country of the Blind*, 84–97, where it is, however, mistakenly described as a report made at the First All-Union Congress of Soviet Writers (which took place in 1934). This slip inadvertently serves to emphasize the identity of some of the things Zhdanov said in 1934 and 1946: his 1946 speech did not inaugurate a fundamentally new policy, it was merely an accentuation and a development of the line laid down earlier. The curbs announced in 1946 derived from the principles proclaimed in 1934. The quotations that follow were translated from the Russian text printed in *Znamya*, No. 10 (1946), 7–26.

10 Zoshchenko's story described, in his usual satirical vein, the adventures of an monkey which had escaped from a zoo. His quips at Soviet conditions of life were neither more nor less venomous than in most of his satirical stories. Zhdanov also mentioned and quoted a poetic satire on Soviet conditions, written in the form of an amusing parody, a sequel to Pushkin's *Evgeny Onegin*, by A. Khazin.

11 The obvious inference is that the moods voiced by Ahkmatova and by other

Soviet Russian Literature

It is not an accident [went on Zhdanov] that the literary magazines of Leningrad showed an enthusiasm for the cheap modern
bourgeois literature of the West. Some of our writers have come
to look upon themselves not as masters but as pupils of the bourgeois-philistine writers, adopting the tone of servility and admiration toward philistine foreign literature. Does this servility become
us, Soviet patriots, us who have built up the Soviet order, which is
a hundred times better than any bourgeois order? Does this servility before the narrow bourgeois-philistine literature of the West become our progressive Soviet literature which is the most revolutionary literature in the world?

At the root of the grave blunders committed by the editors of
Zvezda and *Leningrad* lay the fact that they had forgotten some of the
fundamental Leninist principles, said Zhdanov. And he reminded his
audience of Lenin's article of 1905 in which he wrote that literature of
the Socialist proletariat must become "Party-minded" *("partiynaya")*.
It was the same phrase which Zhdanov had recalled in his speech at the
1934 Congress of Soviet Writers (see page 244 above).

Zhdanov also uttered a warning to those who, spurred no doubt by
the encouragement given to Russian patriotism during the war, were
going too far in their "revaluation of values." He said:

We all love Leningrad . . . . [It] must not become a refuge for all
kind of literary kibitzers and adventurers who want to use Leningrad for their own purposes. Zoshchenko, Akhmatova, and their
like do not hold Leningrad dear. They want to see in it the embodiment of a different social-political order, of a different ideology.
Old Petersburg, the Bronze Horseman as a symbol of this old Petersburg,[12] this is what looms before their eyes.

Zhdanov accused the Leningrad City Committee of the Communist party of forgetting the importance of the ideological front and
emphasized the international aspect of the whole affair. This international aspect was soon to overshadow all the rest. Said Zhdanov:

The bourgeois world resents our successes both at home and in
the international arena. As a result of World War II the positions
of Socialism have been strengthened. The question of Socialism is
on the agenda in many countries in Europe. The imperialists of
all breeds resent it. They are afraid of Socialism, they are afraid
of our Socialist country which serves as a model to all progressive

"pessimists" and "individualists" found a response among Soviet audiences and caused
Communist leaders considerable worry.
[12] See above, p. 169.

332

mankind. The imperialists and their ideological henchmen . . . try their best to slander our country, to show it up in a wrong light, to slander Socialism . . . . The task of Soviet literature is not only to reply, blow for blow, to all these infamous calumnies and attacks . . . but also to castigate and attack boldly bourgeois culture which is in a state of decay and corruption.

It did not become Soviet patriots, went on Zhdanov, to worship at the shrine of bourgeois culture and play the part of its pupils. Soviet literature stood for a higher culture and had the right to teach all the others. Soviet writers were "in the front line of fire" at a moment when the ideological front was becoming more important than ever.

The resolution of the Central Committee concerning *Zvezda* and *Leningrad* initiated a movement that went on gathering momentum and had far-reaching repercussions on Soviet literature. It meant much more than the eclipse of Zoshchenko and Akhmatova or even their expulsion from literature: before a few weeks had passed, both were in fact officially expelled from the Union of Soviet Writers,[13] and the latter cleansed its administration, relieving Tikhonov of his presidential post and appointing Alexander Fadeyev as secretary-general, to be assisted by four other secretaries: Simonov, Tikhonov (who was thus demoted but not ostracized), Vishnevsky, and Korneychuk. The Praesidium of the Board of the Union of Soviet Writers also passed a resolution in which it voiced its full support of Zhdanov and the Central Committee and listed with gusto its own sins. The Central Committee was right, said the resolution, in pointing out that the board of the Union of Soviet Writers and its chairman took no steps to improve the working of *Zvezda* and *Leningrad* and that, far from fighting the harmful influences of Zoshchenko and Akhmatova and other "un-Soviet" writers, they encouraged "the infiltration of alien tendencies and morals into Soviet literature." *The Literary Gazette,* the official organ of the Union of Soviet Writers, was guilty of publishing an interview with Akhmatova

[13] As far as it is possible to ascertain, for over three years not a line of Akhmatova's was published in the Soviet press. Her whereabouts were unknown. But in April of 1950, seven poems over her signature appeared in the popular illustrated weekly *Ogonyok (Flamelet)*, No. 14, April 2, 1950. The poems bear a general title "Iz tsikla 'Slava miru' " ("From the 'Glory to Peace' Cycle"). Stalin is hailed as the incarnation of freedom and peace, "foreign lies" are denounced, and the land of the Soviets is described as the country where poets' voices "sound more fully." The poems were apparently meant as Akhmatova's contribution to the Stockholm Peace Petition campaign. Their poetic quality is very low, and one hesitates to believe that they were written by Akhmatova.

As for Zoshchenko, a year after his disgrace some patriotic war stories of his appeared in *Novy Mir*, No. 9 (1947). They did not read like genuine Zoshchenko and passed unnoticed. A few short pieces were published over Zoshchenko's signature in the summer of 1950 in *Krokodil*, the Soviet magazine of satire and humor.

in 1945, as well as her portrait. The leadership of the Union was also responsible for the "wide diffusion" given to Pasternak's "apolitical poetry, devoid of ideas and severed from the people's life." It was guilty also of encouraging such "ideologically harmful" works as Sergeyev-Tsensky's *Brusilov's Breakthrough* and of tolerating "the morbid delectation in suffering" which characterized the work of some of the young poets.

The resolution stressed further the "un-Soviet spirit of servility before the bourgeois culture of the West . . . which was particularly conspicuous in the drama," and lashed out against the dramatic critics. It pointed out that there was no satisfactory program for the teaching of the history of Soviet literature in the Union's Institute of Literature. Harmful "bourgeois-nationalist tendencies" were said to exist in some national Republics (the Ukrainian, Tartar, and Bashkir in particular). Several Soviet writers were accused of "keeping aloof from the fundamental problems of the day," of "ignoring the life and the needs of the people," and of "not knowing how to depict the best traits and qualities of the Soviet man." The resolution insisted on a "radical change" in the "ideological life and work" of the Union, on focusing attention on contemporary themes, and on the necessity to "castigate servility, expose the true nature of the capitalist environment, combat its demoralizing influences, and lay bare the character of modern imperialism with its implied threat of new bloody wars."[14]

Fadeyev made an attack on Pasternak, saying that, although he had grown up under the Soviet regime (which was not quite exact—Pasternak was twenty-seven at the outbreak of the Revolution), his work stood for "that individualism which is profoundly alien to the spirit of our society." Surkov accused himself of lack of "vigilance" in allowing the publication of Akhmatova's poems in *Ogonyok,* of which he was editor-in-chief. Vishnevsky, one of the editors of *Znamya,* voiced his amazement at Akhmatova's "silence" in the face of "the judgment of the people and of the Party" and proposed to expel Akhmatova and Zoshchenko from the Union of Soviet Writers, reminding his colleagues what they owed to the Party, which had always shown its concern for literature and had always come to its aid.

In the meantime the Central Committee of the Communist party followed up the resolution on *Zvezda* and *Leningrad* by two others: one was entitled "On the Repertoire of Dramatic Theaters and Measures for Its Improvement" and the other "On the Motion Picture 'Big Life.' "

The resolution on the theaters signalized the unsatisfactory condition of the Soviet theaters, whose main weakness was the almost com-

[14] See *Oktyabr,* No. 9 (1946), 182–87.

plete absence of plays by Soviet authors on contemporary themes. The resolution listed some theaters and said that out of their 117 current productions 25 only were contemporary Soviet plays. Of these some were described as ideologically worthless. The authorities responsible for the choice of plays were also criticized for their "passion" for staging historical plays, irrespective of their value, and for "introducing plays by bourgeois foreign dramatists." The Committee on Art Affairs was specifically rebuked for distributing to theaters such plays as Somerset Maugham's *The Circle,* Pinero's *The Dangerous Age,* Kaufman and Hart's *The Man Who Came to Dinner,* Bernard's *Le Petit Café* and so on. The production of these plays, said the resolution, had turned the Soviet stage into a sounding-board for the propaganda of reactionary bourgeois ideology and morals. It meant an attempt "to poison the consciousness of the Soviet people with hostile ideology and to revive the vestiges of capitalism in consciousness and life." This was a gross political error. The resolution called upon the Committee on Art Affairs and the Union of Soviet Writers to concentrate on the creation of a contemporary Soviet repertoire:

> Playwrights and theaters must reflect in their plays and performances the life of Soviet society, . . . must contribute in every way to the further development of the best aspects of the character of Soviet man.

The task of Soviet playwrights and producers was described as the training of Soviet youth "in cheerfulness and joyousness, in devotion to their country, and in confidence in the victory of their cause." "At the same time," the resolution continued, "the Soviet theater is called upon to show that these qualities are characteristic, not just of a few chosen persons, of heroes, but of many millions of Soviet people."

The second of these resolutions dealt specifically with the shortcomings of Pavel Nilin's film "Big Life," mentioning also other "unsuccessful and faulty" films, such as the second part of Eisenstein's "Ivan the Terrible," Pudovkin's "Admiral Nakhimov," and Kozintsev and Trauberg's "Simple People." Of Eisenstein's film it was said that he had "exhibited ignorance of historical facts by portraying the progressive army of the *oprichniki*[15] as a band of degenerates, similar to the Ameri-

---

15 The *oprichniki* (from *Oprichnina*—the Apart, the Peculium) were a special army or police force created by Ivan the Terrible as part of his policy of exterminating the Boyar opposition. They carried a dog's head and a broom attached to their saddles as the emblems of their job which was to "bite and sweep out the traitors to the Tsar." The Soviet Encyclopaedias, both the "Little" (1930) and the "Great" (1939), while pointing out that the earlier historians had distorted the class nature of the *Oprichnina* and presented it as a cruel whim of the cruel Tsar, emphasized its oppressiveness for the mass of the peasants (*the Great Encyclopaedia*) and spoke of the cruel methods of the oprichniki who did not spare even children (*The Little En-*

can Ku Klux Klan, and Ivan the Terrible, a man of strong will and character, as weak and spineless, resembling Hamlet in his irresolution. The showing of "Big Life" was prohibited, and its author hastened to recant. Eisenstein, too, made a groveling confession, dutifully agreeing that he had distorted historical truth. The second part of his film was withdrawn. Pudovkin, for his part, refashioned his "Admiral Nakhimov," removing from it all that was objectionable.

One of the echoes of these resolutions on the drama and the motion pictures was an address made by Simonov at the All-Union Conference of Theater Leaders and Playwrights in November, 1946, in which he declared that "a playwright must be a politician," that "Soviet art" was not a mere "geographical conception," and that everything written and performed on the territory of the Soviet Union was not automatically Soviet literature:

> The struggle with capitalism, with alien ideologies, is not merely an external struggle. It is also our internal struggle with the "birthmarks" of capitalism within our society.[16]

Simonov also called upon Soviet dramatists "to reveal . . . to the entire world the ideological superiority of our people." His whole speech was a fiery call to arms, to an "active, merciless, and unceasing attack on our enemies." These enemies were to be sought on the "ideological front" where "a tremendous battle is being waged on a world scale and with unparalleled violence."

The response to Zhdanov's new line went on rapidly mounting in pitch and violence.

3. The Anti-Westernist Witch-Hunt

IT was the accusation of "servility before the West" (or even "before everything foreign"), contained in the resolution of the Central Committee, elaborated by Zhdanov in his reports, and taken up by the Union of Soviet Writers in its resolution of September 4, that was to become the keynote of the new Party line in cultural matters and the "theme" of the Zhdanov era in Soviet literature. The autumn of 1946 marked the beginning of this era. Viewed retrospectively, this beginning now appears somewhat modest: the Central Committee resolutions, the Zhdanov reports, and the first reactions of the Soviet writers to them can be compared to a few instruments in an orchestra tuning up. But

cyclopaedia). By 1946, the Oprichnina came to be looked upon as a wholly "progressive" phenomenon. Any taunts at it could easily be construed, of course, as veiled attacks on the Soviet secret police.

[16] Sovetskoye iskusstvo (Soviet Art), November 22, 1946.

before long the whole orchestra of Soviet totalitarian propaganda, obeying its invisible conductor, was performing at full blast, and in an ever growing crescendo, what might be called "The Anti-West Symphony." A student of present-day Russian literature cannot help recalling the title of a Russian book published in 1884: *The Fight Against the West in Our Literature.* It was written by Nikolay Strakhov (1828–1895), a friend of Dostoyevsky and Tolstoy and one of the latter-day Slavophiles. This is not the place to recapitulate the Westernist-Slavophile controversy which, from the middle of the nineteenth century on, left its indelible imprint on Russian political, social, and philosophical thought, and which in a modified form is being revived now. But briefly, however, it was a controversy between those who thought that Russia was essentially a member of the Western family of nations and as such was bound to follow along the same general lines of development and those who believed in Russia as a world apart, superior to the decadent, selfish, legalistic, and individualistic West, and drawing its strength from the adherence to pure, uncontaminated traditions of Eastern Orthodoxy and of the communal pattern of life.

To compare the present day Soviet anti-Westernists to the Slavophiles, especially the early ones, among whom were some of the most brilliant Russian minds (Khomyakov, Ivan Kireyevsky), is to insult the Slavophiles. Communist ideologists have much more in common with the "Nihilists" of the eighteen sixties who were extreme utilitarians and materialists and whose ideas were borrowed from the West. They themselves would reject indignantly any attempt to link them up with Slavophilism. But the fact remains that they have revived today the two fundamental Slavophile themes: the fight against the West and Russia's superiority to the bourgeois world. Even the terminology is very much the same: such expressions as "the decadent (or rotten) West" are as popular today as they were with the Slavophiles in the middle of the nineteenth century. One of the great paradoxes of the situation is that Russian Marxists (including Lenin) always regarded themselves as heirs to the Westernist tradition of Russian thought and were opposed to Slavophilism in all its forms, objecting to the conservative Slavophilism of Khomyakov, Kireyevsky, Dostoyevsky, and others as much as to the revolutionary Slavophilism of Herzen (in the last period of his life) and of the Populists. Today it is they, or their descendants, who, in the name of Marx (an out-and-out Slavophobe!) and Lenin (who prided himself on being a "Westernist"), are staging in Russia their gigantic mockery of Slavophilism, in which the Slavophile idea of Russia's mission in the world is mated to the anticultural tradition of Russian nihilism.

To give a detailed account of the anti-West campaign which, in

337

the last four years, has rapidly permeated all the fields of Soviet life, would require a separate volume. All that can be done here is to indicate its main phases and facets as far as literature is concerned and to give some of the more striking illustrations.[17]

The campaign went in three principal directions: (1) ferreting out those guilty of "servility before the West," to whom the term "rootless cosmopolitans" *("bezrodyne kosmopolity")*[18] soon came to be applied; (2) direct attacks on, and denunciations of, the "decadent West," especially of the United States of America; and (3) glorification of everything Russian and assertion of Russian superiority in every field.

The Hunt for "Rootless Cosmopolitans"

In the spring of 1947 the Board of the Union of Soviet Writers held one of its periodic conferences at which Fadeyev, in his capacity of secretary-general, read a report on the tasks of Soviet literary theory and literary criticism. He stressed the superiority of Russian realism over its Western European counterpart and attacked those who regarded Russian realistic literature as "a sort of appendix to Western European literature." He spoke with particular venom of a book published in 1941 by one of the most prominent Soviet critics of the thirties, Isaac Nusinov, an orthodox Marxist and Communist. Fadeyev called the book "a very harmful one." The book was entitled *Pushkin i mirovaya literatura (Pushkin and World Literature)* and discussed the relation between Pushkin's "Little Tragedies" and contemporary European literature. Nusinov advanced the thesis that Pushkin was "a European" and

[17] From literature the fight against "servility before the West" spread rapidly to other fields: music, art, linguistics, science, etc. By 1949 even Soviet circuses were denounced by the official *Soviet Art* for their tendency toward "bourgeois cosmopolitanism" and "formalism." For more details of this anti-Western witch-hunt in fields other than literature see Counts and Lodge, *Country of the Blind*, especially chapters V ("Music as a Weapon"), VI ("Science as a Weapon"), and VII ("Education as a Weapon"). In linguistics there was a most remarkable about-face when Stalin himself, in the summer of 1950, came up with a denunciation of the linguistic theories of Marr, whose opponents had been for over two years hounded as "bourgeois cosmopolitans." Stalin's "contribution" to linguistics was hailed as "a work of genius" by many Soviet scholars and critics.

[18] The exact rendering of this phrase is "cosmopolitans without kith or kin," and one is almost tempted to translate it as "bastard cosmopolitans." I have not been able to ascertain when, where, or by whom it was first used. It figured in *Pravda's* editorial on January 28, 1949, with reference to the "plenary meeting" of the Board of the Union of Soviet Writers early that month at which an attack had been made on "a certain antipatriotic group of theater critics." These critics were described as "bearers of a rootless cosmopolitanism, profoundly repugnant and alien to Soviet man." After that the phrase became common currency. Its possible anti-Semitic implications will be discussed below. The expression "bourgeois cosmopolitanism" had been used earlier in connection with the attack on "Veselovskyism." Later, "rootless cosmopolitans" were also described as "passportless tramps."

that in his plays he owed a great deal to foreign stimuli. There was nothing novel in Nusinov's ideas, but for Fadeyev they were now tantamount to the crime of *lèse-majesté*. Fadeyev quoted a passage from the book in which Nusinov said that Pushkin had not attracted so much attention in the West because he was "incomparably more of a European writer than Tolstoy and Dostoyevsky" who "negated the West, opposing to it their Oriental ideals, the ideals of Russia." Fadeyev's comment upon this rather platitudinous statement was as follows:

> The book proceeds from the conception that the light shines from the West and that Russia is an "Oriental" country. Pushkin is denationalized, turned into something universal, pan-European, pan-human . . . . Nusinov is preaching the eternal "universal" themes which seem to have an abstract existence. Pushkin for Nusinov is a genius only because he has his own solutions for these abstractly existing universal themes. Therefore, throughout his chapters, there flashes before us a series of names of writers and poets of Western Europe, and Nusinov hops, carefree, from one century into another . . . . The book has nothing to do with Marxism.[19]

After thus tearing to pieces Nusinov's six-year-old book, which at the time of its publication aroused no special objections, Fadeyev proceeded to look for the roots of Nusinov's "heresies" and found them in the theories of Alexander Veselovsky, a great Russian nineteenth-century literary scholar and one of the pioneers of the comparative method in literature. Veselovsky was looked upon as their master by many leading Soviet literary scholars, especially of the Formalist school.[20] But even outside that school he was held in great esteem: in 1938 the centenary of his birth was commemorated with great pomp, all Russian literary scholars and critics, including orthodox Marxists (e.g., V. Desnitsky) paying tribute to him; in 1940 one of Veselovsky's major works —*Istoricheskaya poetika (Historical Poetics)*—was reissued with an introduction by Zhirmunsky; and even as late as 1946 the Leningrad University published a little book by Professor V. Shishmaryov on *Alexander Veselovsky and Russian Literature*, in which Veselovsky was spoken of as a pathbreaker in the field of literary studies. But now Fadeyev, from the heights of his official position, fulminated against Veselovsky and his followers as the true originators of "servility before the West." His attack unleashed a veritable storm: all leading Soviet periodicals carried a spate of articles against "Veselovskyism" and its survivals in the Soviet Union, of which many examples were cited. The name of

[19] Fadeyev's report appears in *Problemy sotsialisticheskogo realizma (Problems of Socialist Realism)* (edited by B. Byalik), 24.
[20] For Veselovsky's influence on the Formalists, see above, page 192.

Veselovsky was bandied about in the Soviet press, and "Veselovskyism," identified with "cosmopolitanism," "comparativism," and "bourgeois liberalism," became a term of abuse, like the earlier "Bogdanovism," "Voronskyism," and "Pereverzevism." At the end of 1947, *October* magazine published a long article by the well-known critic Kirpotin, in which the charges against Veselovsky and his school were summed up.[21] In the same number two feeble voices of protest were raised. One belonged to the former Formalist and Futurist Victor Shklovsky, the other, to Shishmaryov, whose booklet on Veselovsky Fadeyev had attacked.[22] Shishmaryov timidly suggested that Veselovsky's detractors might have confused him with his less important brother, Alexey, author of a well-known book on Western influences in Russian literature.

But in the next issue of *October* (January, 1948), Kirpotin published a thundering reply under the following long and elaborate title: "About Servility Before the Capitalist West, about Alexander Veselovsky, About His Followers, and About Things that Matter Most."[23] Here Veselovsky was portrayed as one of the ideologists of the pre-Revolutionary ruling classes (Veselovsky was in fact a democratic liberal, with strong inclinations toward Comtian positivism). He was blamed for inculcating into the minds of Russian intelligentsia the notion of Russia's inferiority and the idea that the Russians must look upon Western Europeans as their "masters." The name of Veselovsky, said Kirpotin, was made use of "to blunt the revolutionary and social acuity of the heritage of Russian classical criticism." His followers fell back on it in order to pass off their "mimicry of Marxism" for the genuine article: under Veselovsky's label "comparativism" was smuggled into Soviet literary scholarship and disguised as Marxism. From Veselovsky a direct line could be traced to "historical fatalism with all its spiritual diseases: passivism, contemplativeness, skepticism, 'pure scholarship.' "

A month later Anatoly Tarasenkov, who had been earlier accused of favoring Pasternak and probably had to make good for his "sin," followed up with an even more violent attack on Veselovsky in *Novy Mir*.[24] Whatever timid voices had been raised in defense of Veselovsky were finally silenced in March, 1948, when *Culture and Life,* the official mouthpiece of the Central Committee of the Communist Party, au-

---

[21] See *Oktyabr,* No. 12 (1947). Kirpotin's "big gun" was supported by two smaller-caliber guns, I. Dmitrakov and M. Kuznetsov.

[22] *Ibid.* At this time the editors of *Oktyabr* (and they included Kirpotin himself) still regarded a "discussion" about Veselovsky as permissible. Later they were blamed for such misplaced "liberalism."

[23] "O nizkopoklonstve pered kapitalisticheskim Zapadom, ob Aleksandre Veselovskom, o ego posledovatelyakh i o samon glavnom," in *Oktyabr,* No. 1 (1948), 3–27.

[24] An. Tarasenkov, "Kosmopolity ot literaturovedeniya" ("Cosmopolitans in the Science of Literature"), in *Novy Mir,* No. 2 (1948), 124–137.

thoritatively pronounced the "excommunication" of Veselovsky and his school. But the anti-Veselovsky witch-hunt continued in the Soviet press, and Soviet critics and journalists vied with each other in denouncing various manifestations of "comparativism" (which now became synonymous with "Veselovskyism") in literary history and literary criticism. *The Literary Gazette,* the official organ of the Union of Soviet Writers, easily broke all the records in this respect, but even serious scholarly publications tried to keep pace with it. The denouncers were obviously anxious to curry favor with those who shaped the literary Party line on the higher level, but often were themselves denounced in turn, and no one could feel immune in the face of this inquisitorial competition.[25]

Here are some typical examples, chosen more or less at random, of accusations that were to be found in *The Literary Gazette* and other Soviet periodicals during 1948 and 1949. Authors of the first volume of the new *History of French Literature* (published by the Academy of Sciences in 1946), a joint effort of several leading Soviet scholars, were taken to task for constantly referring to the well-established fact of the influence of such French authors as Boileau, Molière, and La Fontaine on Russian eighteenth-century literature. A similar accusation was brought up against the joint authors (again all of them leading specialists in their field) of the new *History of English Literature*: their crime consisted of mentioning the influence of Swift, Richardson, Fielding, and Sterne on Russian literature. They had even dared speak of Gorky's debt to Fielding—an unpardonable sacrilege![26] Boris Eichenbaum, au-

25 Thus such critics as L. Subotsky, J. Altman, and A. Isbach, all of whom wrote articles against "servility before the West," were later branded in their turn as "rootless cosmopolitans." The examples could be easily multiplied, but the whole matter seems to pertain rather to the field of psychopathology than of literary history. Many of the critics attacked in 1948–49 must have recalled the skit which Alexander Raskin published in *Novy Mir* (No. 10–11, 1946) at the very beginning of the anti-Western witch-hunt. It was in the form of extracts from the diary of a Soviet critic who, after waiting for two years and four months for his "indignation" to mature, attacks a book "according to all the rules of etiquette" and then discovers that the book was in fact good and his article a piece of "downright opportunism." The diary contained the "ten commandments" of a Soviet critic, among them the following: "1. Do not be the first to speak out! 2. Do not be the second! 3. Be the third! 4. Confess the mistakes of your fellow-critic! 5. Quote! 6. Avoid appraisals! A cheap appraisal may cost you dear. 7. It is better to overblame than to underpraise. 8. If you have been smitten on your right cheek, protect the left."

26 Whether Gorky was influenced by Fielding or not, the fact remains that his famous article "O tom kak ya uchilsya pisat" ("On How I Learned to Write," 1932) was a glowing tribute to Western European literature and a frank acknowledgement of the influence exercised on him by French writers. He wrote here: "The real and deeply educative influence on me as a writer was exercised by the 'great' French literature—by Stendhal, Balzac, and Flaubert. I would very much like to advise the 'beginners' to read these authors."—*About Literature,* 215. On the strength of this statement Gorky could be easily denounced today as "a rootless cosmopolitan."

thor of some very good works on Tolstoy, was accused of regarding Schopenhauer, "that reactionary obscurantist," as Tolstoy's principal philosophical master and of looking to the French novels of adultery as one of the sources of *Anna Karenina.*

Authors of a program of courses for Soviet theatrical institutes were accused by *The Literary Gazette* of "insulting" the great Russian dramatist Ostrovsky by suggesting that in his play *Bez viny vinovatye (The Guilty Without Guilt)* he had used the well-worn device of "recognition" which he took from the Greek comedy via Molière and other European dramatists. A certain Veronica Motylevskaya, of whom nobody had heard before, detected dangerous "comparativist" tendencies in the standard history of the Russian theater by Vsevolodsky-Gerngross (first published in 1929): describing the author, in an article in *The Literary Gazette,* as "an idealist and a formalist, an inveterate representative of the 'comparativist' school . . . a true disciple and follower of Alexey Veselovsky and of Perets . . . a fierce, militant champion of foreign, and especially German, influence on the Russian theater," she accused him in particular of associating the origins of the Russian theater in the seventeenth century with the German troupe of Pastor Gregory—a fact that will be found even in most general textbooks of Russian history.

Even the authors of the officially approved *History of the U. S. S. R.,* by Pankratova and others (1947 edition), were found at fault in mentioning the influence of Leibnitz, Helvetius, Rousseau, Mably, Raynal, and other European thinkers on Alexander Radishchev.

No period in the history of Russian literature was left untouched by Zhdanov's witch-hunters. One of the most glaring examples of this literary inquisition was the case of Professor V. Propp, whose book on the sources of magic folk-tales was published by the University of Leningrad in 1946 and favorably reviewed at the time by Zhirmunsky and others. But when the witch-hunt was in full swing, Professor Propp's book was brought out of oblivion and its author put on the carpet. He was accused of quoting abundantly from such international authorities on folklore and anthropology as Frazer, Lévy-Bruhl, Boas, Kroeber, Frobenius, and others, and his book was indignantly compared to a London or Berlin telephone directory. His statement that folklore was essentially an international phenomenon was declared to be "un-Marxian" and "a survival of Veselovskyism." His whole conception, it was said, was vitiated by a complete "disregard for nations and classes."

An obscure Soviet critic (a certain Sergev Ivanov) attacked Leonid Grossman, author of a number of valuable studies of Dostoyevsky, Tyutchev, and other writers, for suggesting that in Lermontov's poetry can be traced many biblical and Oriental motifs.

There is no point in multiplying these examples. It is enough to say that "comparativism" in literary studies is regarded today in the Soviet Union as a mortal sin. At least this is true so far as foreign influences on Russian literature are concerned. The "comparative" approach is permitted, however, in reverse, so to speak—that is, in order to demonstrate the influence of Russian, and especially Soviet, writers on Western European and American literature. Soviet scholars and critics are enjoined to study, for instance, the influence of Gorky on Jack London, Upton Sinclair, and Dreiser. Such a well-known "comparativist" as Grossman, cut off from his proper field of studies, published in 1948 an article about the influence of Mayakovsky on Louis Aragon.

An important aspect of the Zhdanov inquisition is to be seen in the sinners' "confessions" and "recantations," which remind one of Galileo's trial. These recantations are perhaps the saddest feature of this newest phase of Soviet mind control: in character and in scope they far exceed anything that happened during the 1929–32 period when Averbach tried to boss Soviet literature, and are the best proof of the totalitarian subjection of literature. Perhaps the most glaring example of this was the mass recantation of literary scholars accused of "Veselovskyism," in the big auditorium of the University of Leningrad in April, 1948. Zhirmunsky, Eichenbaum, Dolinin, Azadovsky, Propp, and others mounted the rostrum in turn and abjured their "comparativist" sins, renouncing their old and valuable works and promising to "reform." The most pathetic of all was the declaration made by Dolinin for his book *V tvorcheskoy laboratorii Dostoyevskogo (In Dostoyevsky's Creative Laboratory,* 1947), an interesting and stimulating study of the genesis of Dostoyevsky's novel *A Raw Youth,* had been attacked. Dolinin, who had devoted most of his time to the study of Dostoyevsky, making a most valuable contribution to it, announced now his intention of "giving up" Dostoyevsky and of turning his attention to Belinsky, Dobrolyubov, Chernyshevsky, and other "revolutionary democrats."[27]

The campaign against "rootless cosmopolitans" reached the highest pitch of intensity during 1949, when literally dozens of literary and dramatic critics were "purged." The peculiar feature of these new purges was the divulging of the critics' real names whenever they happened to use pseudonyms. By this process it was revealed that a great many of those who were specifically branded as "rootless cosmopolitans" bore Jewish names. Since at the same time certain Jewish cultural organizations were subjected to persecution for propagating

[27] A more detailed account of this remarkable university meeting will be found in my article "The Soviets Purge Literary Scholarship," in *The New Leader,* April 2, 1949, 8–9.

Jewish cultural separatism and sympathizing with Zionism, and the last Jewish newspaper was closed down,[28] it came to be widely believed outside the Soviet Union that the campaign against "cosmopolitanism" had a definite anti-Semitic angle. While it is not to be denied that in their campaign against the West the Communist rulers of Russia may have deliberately played on the anti-Semitic sentiments of certain sections of the Russian population, especially in the Ukraine (and this must be the explanation of the unprecedented practice of divulging the real names of Jewish critics), the three following facts must also be borne in mind: (1) many of those who were described as "rootless cosmopolitans" were not Jews; (2) there were also Jews among their accusers; and (3) other national minorities in the Soviet Union were similarly charged with harboring bourgeois-nationalist tendencies and their cultural organizations persecuted alongside the Jewish ones. Tartar and other writers were accused of idealizing their historical heroes, many of whom had been historical enemies of Russia, and of thus emphasizing their apartness. When the Russian Jews were accused of considering their literature as part of a general Jewish literature and not as one of the components of Soviet literature, it was a similar phenomenon, and its causes are to be sought not in any specifically *Russian* nationalism, but in the supranational Communist ideology. To speak of the revival of governmental anti-Semitism in the Soviet Union is at least premature. But given the existence of anti-Semitic feelings among the population, the effect of certain proceedings resorted to in the campaign against cosmopolitanism could not but be premeditated.[29]

The anticosmopolitan theme naturally found its reflection in litera-

28 Among the disbanded Jewish organizations was the Jewish Anti-Fascist Committee. One of its leaders, the great actor Michoels, director of the Jewish State Theater in Moscow, was posthumously denounced as a cosmopolitan. The Jewish poet Fefer, who accompanied Michoels on his wartime visit to the United States and Great Britain, was also involved in the anticosmopolitan purge and disappeared from the literary stage.

29 In view of the international implications of the present Soviet campaign against "cosmopolitanism" it is possible to presume that certain sections of the Jewish population appeared to the Communist rulers of Russia suspect from the point of view of their Western, and more particularly American, sympathies. It is also significant that many Soviet cartoons depicting "Wall Street warmongers" gave the latter exaggeratedly Semitic facial characteristics. There were also anti-Zionist cartoons which in olden days might well have adorned the pages of some reactionary anti-Semitic paper. The political and international significance of the campaign launched by Zhdanov in 1946 was later emphasized by himself and by Georgy Malenkov, another member of the Politburo, at the first Cominform meeting in Poland in 1947. In his address there Malenkov said: "Kowtowing and servility before the West represent at this juncture a serious threat to our state inasmuch as the agents of international reaction are endeavoring to make use of people who are infected with the feeling of servility and kowtowing before the bourgeois culture for the purpose of weakening the Soviet state."

ture, in novels, stories, and plays. A typical example of it is a novel by a comparative newcomer to Soviet literature, Grigory Konovalov, called *Universitet* (*The University*, 1947). It portrays the life of students in one of the newer Soviet universities. Its hero, Ilya Kozharov, is a young scholar, a scientist turned philosopher, who sees his vocation in demonstrating the originality of Russian philosophy and its superiority over that of the West. By "Russian philosophy" he means primarily the revolutionary-democratic thought of Belinsky, Chernyshevsky, and Dobrolyubov, and the teachings of Russian materialistic scientists. When one of his elder colleagues writes an article about Belinsky, Chernyshevsky, and Dobrolyubov and entitles it "Russian Feuerbachians," Kozharov grows indignant: to describe these thinkers as Feuerbachians is to underrate their original contribution to Russian thought.[30] Some of Kozharov's colleagues, good Communists though they are, sound a little skeptical about his unqualified enthusiasm for Russian philosophy. A great friend of his, a chemist, asks: "But where are the philosophers? Stalin alone, but then he is an all-embracing genius. Name me at least one modern philosopher. . . . There are chemists, there are biologists, there are constructors, but where are the philosophers?" But the author's sympathy is obviously on Kozharov's side, and he shows him energetically sweeping through the university like a new broom and getting the better of his opponents. This ideological theme of Konovalov's otherwise rather trite novel anticipated the attack which was launched in 1947 on Georgy Alexandrov, former head of the Red Army Propaganda Section, for his book on Western philosophy, in which he was said to have overrated the influence of Hegel and other Western philosophers on Russian thought.

The anticosmopolitan theme was also exploited by Simonov in his novel *Dym otechestva* (*The Smoke of Home Fires*, 1948), which, however, left Communist critics dissatisfied. But particularly numerous were the plays on this subject, since the theater was always regarded in the Soviet Union as an effective weapon of political propaganda. In Romashov's *Velikaya sila* (*A Great Force*, 1948) the main characters are two scholars. One of them, Lavrov, is a good Soviet patriot; the other, Milyagin, an admirer of things foreign. On his return from the United States, Milyagin is full of admiration for the American way of life: "They have comfort, they know how to live," he says. He also denies

[30] The influence of Feuerbach, a left-wing German Hegelian and a philosophical precursor of Marx, on the Russian "revolutionary democrats," was previously commonly taken for granted (among others, by Lenin). But the complete originality of Belinsky became the dominant theme of the vast 1948 jubilee literature about him. One Soviet critic went so far as to say that it was high time to stop speaking of Belinsky as a Westerner. Before a year had passed this unfortunate critic (Johannes Altman) was himself denounced as a rootless cosmopolitan.

the existence of any specific Soviet science: for him science is international, universal, it "belongs to the whole world." In the end Milyagin is, of course, unmasked and removed. In A. Stein's play *Zakon chesti* (*Point of Honor*, 1948) the villain is a Soviet scholar, Professor Losev, who goes to the United States, is feted there and agrees to sell the secret of his medical discovery (a pain-killing remedy). He is exposed, however, by a colleague of his who accuses him of being ready to "cede the priority of Soviet science to an American firm." Soviet patriotism and vigilance triumph over "cosmopolitan machinations."

Some Soviet critics pointed out the many weaknesses of these plays, especially the unconvincingness of their "villains." For one of them (Efim Kholodov, pseudonym of M. Meyerovich), Milyagin was let off too lightly by the author. But less than a year later Kholodov himself was denounced as "a rootless cosmopolitan" and his pseudonym duly divulged.

Simonov's play *Chuzhaya ten* (*Someone Else's Shadow*, 1949) represents a variant on the same theme: here Professor Trubnikov, an old-fashioned individualist, communicates his scientific discovery—a means to put an end to epidemic disease—to his foreign colleagues. An old-fashioned humanist, he finds it somewhat difficult to believe, when his "vigilant" collaborators point out to him that he has committed a crime. But when it is explained to him that American scientists might avail themselves only of the first part of his discovery and breed microbes for use in future war, he realizes the "monstrosity" of what he has done.

Another cosmopolitan-minded scholar was portrayed by A. Sofronov in his play *Karyera Beketova* (*Beketov's Career*, 1949). Highly praised at first, this play was subsequently denounced as crude and unrealistic. But the anticosmopolitan theme continued to be regarded as topical and important and at the meeting of the Board of the Union of Soviet Writers in January, Fadeyev said:

> Greatly mistaken are those who think that the fight against cosmopolitanism is but a short-term campaign. It is a war of principles and ideas which must be fought continuously and intransigently.

An impartial observer of the Soviet literary scene cannot help reflecting with dismay on the fact that not a single voice of dissent, let alone protest, was raised against this total subjection of literature to the line dictated from the Party heights. Yet—as one subservient Soviet critic thought it appropriate to recall in 1947—when, in 1925, the Communist party adopted its famous resolution on literary policy whereby a *modus vivendi* was established with the so-called fellow travelers, many writers openly disapproved of it and regarded it as an uncalled-for interference with literature.[31] But when Zhdanov died in 1948, all Soviet literary magazines carried glowing obituary tributes to him, and he was hailed as "the great, wise, exacting and benevolent friend of Soviet literature."[32]

Denouncing the "Decadent West"

Parallel with the unmasking of "rootless cosmopolitans" at home went the denunciation of the decadent bourgeois West, of the "Anglo-American imperialists" and "warmongers" and their "satellites." The memories of the wartime alliance against Hitler were quickly thrown to the winds, and the Western democracies portrayed as the "capitalist encirclement," as the implacable enemies of the Soviet Union, plotting day and night for its destruction. If during the first Five-Year Plan, Soviet literature was placed in the service of industrialization, now it was openly made into a weapon of Soviet postwar foreign policy. The purely literary content of *The Literary Gazette,* the official organ of the Union of Soviet Writers, was reduced to a minimum, and it was filled instead with purely political articles in which Tikhonov, Simonov, Lavrenyov, Surkov, Gorbatov, and many others denounced the United States of America and Great Britain (and later Tito's Yugoslavia) and fulminated against President Truman, Ernest Bevin, Léon Blum, Jules Moch, and (later) Trygve Lie. Contemporary European and American literature was represented as rotten to the core. The only exemption from the wholesale condemnation was accorded those writers who showed themselves friendly to the Soviet Union. As soon as this or that writer changed his attitude toward the Soviet Union to an unfavorable one, he lost favor with his Soviet admirers: thus it was with Lion Feuchtwanger, Upton Sinclair, Sinclair Lewis, Richard Wright, and J. B. Priestley. The last was rather popular in the Soviet Union until his "Open Letter" to Ehrenburg (published in April, 1950), when Simonov denounced him as "a warmonger" for refusing to sign the Stockholm Peace Petition. Jean-Paul Sartre and Henry Miller took the place of Joyce and Proust as the incarnation of all that was evil in modern European culture. But whereas in the thirties there were at least some more or less serious studies of Joyce and Proust in Soviet magazines,

31 See L. Plotkin, "Partiya i literatura" ("The Party and Literature"), in *Zvezda,* No. 10 (1947), 161. Plotkin referred specifically to Veresayev who had expressed his regret that such pre-Revolutionary writers as Sologub, Voloshin, and Akhmatova were "doomed to silence" under Soviet conditions; to Andrey Sobol who had written that "tutelage and art were incompatible"; to Ivan Novikov who had said that the very notion of "guidance" in matters of literature was beyond his comprehension; and to Pasternak who had "polemized with the resolution of the Central Committee with undisguised hostility, . . . maintaining that we were passing not through a cultural revolution but through a cultural reaction."

32 See L. Plotkin, "A. A. Zhdanov i voprosy literatury" ("A. A. Zhdanov and Problems of Literature"), in *Zvezda,* No. 1 (1949), 121.

sheer abuse was now the only recognized method of polemic. Sartre and Henry Miller and their followers were described as "spiritual lechers," William Faulkner as "flesh of the flesh of a decaying society." John Steinbeck's works were "putrid, lurid, and antihuman." Eugene O'Neill was "a degenerate." And no language was strong enough when it came to former Communists or former Communist sympathizers. Arthur Koestler was described by Ivan Anisimov as "a literary *agent provocateur*" whose writings "stank."[33] George Orwell was called "a charlatan," a "suspicious individual," a former police agent and yellow-press correspondent who passed in England for a writer because there was "a great demand for refuse there." André Gide and André Malraux were also denounced as "renegades" and "American agents."

The anti-Western, especially the anti-American, theme was exploited by Soviet writers to their heart's content. Among the plays with this (to put it mildly) anti-American bias may be named Simonov's *Pod kashtanami* (*Under the Chestnuts of Prague,* 1947) and *Russky vopros* (*The Russian Problem,* 1947)—the former about the liberation of Czechoslovakia, the latter about an American journalist who misinforms his public about the Soviet Union but later repents, with dire consequences to himself; Anatoly Surov's *Nezadachlivy galantereyshchik* (*The Ill-Starred Haberdasher,* 1948)—a crude satirical comedy comparing President Truman to Hitler; and Lavrenyov's *Golos Ameriki* (*The Voice of America,* 1949), which is very violent in its denunciation of American "warmongers" but stresses the existence of "two Americas."

In Sergey Mikhalkov's[34] play *Ya khochu domoy* (*I Want to Go Home,* 1949) the British are the villains: this crudely sentimental play deals with the fate of Soviet children in D.P. camps whom the British "refuse" to repatriate. Both the British and the Americans are shown as treacherous, dishonest, and callous in Vitaly Sobko's *Za vtorym frontom* (*Behind the Second Front,* 1949).

In poetry, too, anti-Westernism became the staple theme. It is the keynote of Simonov's little book *Druzya i vragi* (*Friends and Foes,* 1948), in which he lashes out mostly at the Americans but makes also a savage attack on Léon Blum. The book is an obvious but unsuccessful attempt to imitate the satirical invectives of Mayakovsky. The verse is crude and prosaic. Anti-Americanism characterizes also a group of poems by Dolmatovsky entitled "Slovo o zavtrashnem dne" ("The Word About To-

---

[33] *Oktyabr,* No. 10 (1938). Anisimov specialized before World War II in Western European literature.

[34] Sergey Mikhalkov (b. 1913) is the coauthor (with El-Registan) of the new Soviet national anthem. He also wrote some good poetry for children and some clever political fables on topical subjects, imitating the great Russian fabulist Krylov.

morrow"), which were published in *Novy Mir* (1949, No. 7). In one of these poems the poet visualizes a new Nuremberg trial which will take place in Moscow (apparently after World War III and a successful Communist revolution in the United States), when the "working-class of America will stand by our side," when "neither prayers nor the Bomb will save our enemies," and when the new warmongers will follow in the footsteps of Ribbentrop and Goering. The "exhibits" before the Court will include the atom bomb and "an engraved dollar bill—the coin of treachery." The judges—among whom will be Spanish prisoners, Chinese soldiers, and lynched Negroes—will pass a death sentence on the "warmongers" and "This will be the last execution on earth." In another poem Dolmatovsky refers to a mysterious explosion somewhere in Soviet Asia, designed to "move mountains" and to serve "as a warning to our enemies on foreign shores." This first poetic hint of the Soviet atomic explosion appeared in print a few months before President Truman's disclosure startled the world.

Anti-Western ingredients play also an important part in Pavlenko's novel *Schastye (Happiness,* 1947), which was awarded one of the annual Stalin prizes. Most of the action is set in Crimea in 1945. There are chapters dealing with the background of the Yalta Conference of the Big Three, with glimpses of President Roosevelt and Mr. Churchill. While Roosevelt, in accordance with the view assiduously fostered in the Soviet Union, is portrayed on the whole sympathetically, Pavlenko is much less kind to Churchill. One of the characters, a Soviet wine-expert, is used by Pavlenko as a foil to an American visiting journalist, in order to demonstrate the superiority of everything Soviet over everything Western and to pour contempt on the Allies' conduct of the war. In the chapters dealing with the Red Army's march through Europe, the anti-Allied sentiments characteristic of 1947 are clearly voiced. In one scene Pavlenko introduces an American major who is obviously supposed to epitomize the spirit of the United States Army. For this major, a peacetime businessman, war is just another chance of furthering his business interests. He boasts:

"I have adapted myself well to the front conditions. I always carry with me half-a-score of prospectuses and price lists and a dozen ready-made contracts. I hit upon it in Alexandria. . . . We flooded the Egyptian market with our goods, right under the enemy fire, so to speak. . . . In North Africa . . . we landed with ammunition and samples of merchandise—we captured towns and conquered markets all in one. In Italy the procedure was, naturally, still further improved. On my tanks I wrote in Italian: 'Buy SANIT soap, the best in the world.' "

The operations of the Allied armies during the final phases of the war are dismissed by Pavlenko in a few colorfully contemptuous sentences:

> The Americans were hurrying towards the frontiers of Austria. The British were capturing, in the backyards of the war, some scared Nazi generals and singing praises, both in prose and in verse, to their "Monty," as though Montgomery's soldiers were the only ones on the battlefield.

Pavlenko's novel was first serialized in 1947 and published in book form in 1948. Since then Soviet writers, journalists, and military experts have gone even further in minimizing the contribution of their erstwhile allies to the common victory over the Germans. The popular weekly *Ogonyok* published in April, 1950, an article by Lev Slavin, author of the Civil War play *Interventsiya (Intervention)* and various other works, about Field Marshal Montgomery. The article is entitled "An Orderly as a Field Marshal." It presents Montgomery as an "errand boy" of his American "bosses" and describes the famous Dunkirk operation as "Hitler's miracle": according to Slavin, Hitler deliberately let the British escape in the hope of enlisting Great Britain's help against the Soviet Union.

Another well-known Soviet writer, Gennady Fish, in a volume of anti-American propaganda entitled *Sovetskaya byl i amerikanskie skazki (Soviet Facts and American Fairy Tales*, 1948), wrote of American Lend-Lease:

> ... the Americans sent us a bit of their harvest. Did their harvest not come from the seeds carried from Russia? So they did not give us a loan; it would be more exact to say they paid their old, old debt ... of which we did not remind them.[35]

---

[35] Quoted by W. W. Kulski in "Can Russia Withdraw from Civilization?," *Foreign Affairs*, Vol. XXVIII (July, 1950), 631. In 1949 a book called *Vot ona Amerika! (Here She Is, America!)* was published in Moscow. It contained excerpts from the writings of Gorky, Mayakovsky, and Bill-Belotserkovsky (a Soviet playwright who at one time lived and worked in the United States and published a volume of *American Stories*), as well as from two Soviet journalists. The object of the book was to present the United States in as black colors as possible. Mikhail Koryakov, a former Soviet journalist, pointed out in an article in *Novoye Russkoye Slovo* (New York) that extracts from Mayakovsky were carefully pruned of all more or less flattering references to things American. The book was suitably illustrated with drawings picturing various "horrors" of American life. The artist received a Stalin prize of 50,000 roubles. Those interested in the picture of the United States through the Soviet spectacles may consult the novel *Delovye lyudi (Businessmen*, 1939), by Boris Dmitrievich (alias Dmitry) Chetverikov (b. 1896). The prologue to the novel begins with the sentence: "America has been discovered more than once"; while the epilogue to it ends as follows: "America has been discovered more than once. But the

This systematic falsification of recent history reached its peak up to date when a film called "Secret Mission," with music by Aram Khachaturian, was shown in Moscow (August, 1950). It showed Mr. Churchill revealing to the Germans in 1944 the secret of the coming Red Army offensive, which was to save the Allies from their difficulties in the Ardennes, and the Americans concluding a secret deal with Himmler!

It is highly significant that Soviet denunciations of German National-Socialism and of Italian Fascism never reached the degree of frenzy and violence of the present campaign against the democracies of the West, not even during the Spanish Civil War. Nor were Soviet writers ever made to participate so unreservedly in the anti-Fascist campaign as they are now in the campaign against the "Anglo-American warmongers." Back in the thirties *The Literary Gazette* still preserved its literary appearance: today at least one page out of the four in each issue is almost wholly devoted to frenzied outbursts against the United States and its "lackeys," among whom Marshal Tito now holds a prominent place.

"Sowjetrussland über Alles"

"Cosmopolitanism," authoritatively wrote the leading Soviet philosophical review in 1948, "is a reactionary ideology which preaches renunciation of national traditions, contempt for the distinctive features in the national development of each people, and renunciation of the feelings of national dignity and national pride. Cosmopolitanism preaches a nihilistic attitude of the individual toward his nationality— toward its past, present, and future .... The ideology of cosmopolitanism is hostile to, and in radical contradiction with, Soviet patriotism— the basic feature which characterizes the world outlook of Soviet man."[36]

If "Soviet patriotism" is thus proclaimed to be the basic feature of

real discovery of that fine country will be made by the armed revolutionary proletariat." The novel was an exposure of American capitalism.

My book was already in the press when there appeared a valuable study of Soviet attitudes toward America, more especially during World War II and after it, by Professor F. C. Barghoorn: *The Soviet Image of the United States: A Study in Distortion.* The most interesting thing in Mr. Barghoorn's book is his account, based on personal experience between 1942 and 1947, of the attitudes of the ordinary Soviet people to America. And he is absolutely right in some of his basic conclusions, as when he says that the susceptibility of the Soviet people to "alien influences" is "ultimately in large measure the result of discontent among Soviet people with the conditions of life in the U.S.S.R.," or that "It is a safe rule in evaluating Soviet propaganda to assume that the volume devoted to a particular theme is a key to the resistance which it encounters among the Soviet public." This is the only comforting aspect of the rabid postwar "anti-Westernism" in the Soviet Union.

[36] See "Protiv burzhuaznoy ideologii kosmopolitizma" ("Against the Bourgeois Ideology of Cosmopolitanism"), in *Voprosy filosofii* (*Problems of Philosophy*), No. 2 (1948).

the new Soviet outlook, it is in turn based on the glorification of everything Russian. Russian superiority in every field of human endeavor
is broadcast to the world, and Russian priority claimed for nearly every
modern—and not so modern[37]—invention. The blowing of its own
trumpet, in which the Soviet Union has been indulging for the last few
years (though its modest beginnings go back to the immediate prewar
period), is the necessary logical counterpart of the denunciation of the
West, and is designed to boost Soviet patriotism and to build up the
concept of a self-sufficient, superior world.

A pride in the achievements of one's country is a natural appur-
tenance of healthy patriotism. But when, as in the Soviet Union today,
it acquires "apocalyptic" dimensions and, what is more, is indoctrinated
with totalitarian thoroughness and with jingoist intolerance, it becomes
both ridiculous and revolting. There is something utterly naïve in the
daily staking-out of Russian claims to the priority of various inventions (radio, telephone, telegraph, bicycles, airplanes, tanks, tractors,
even the printing press), which has become a regular feature of the
Soviet press and radio propaganda. In themselves, some of these claims
may not be so fantastic and would bear a closer investigation (there is
much to be said, for instance, for the priority of Baron Schilling in inventing the electric telegraph, just as for Yablochkov's precedence over
Edison), but the preposterousness of some of the others and the ob-
viousness of the political motive behind all of them make the whole
thing appear absurd in the eyes of the outside world. Soviet writers are,
however, expected to glorify everything Russian and to defend the
honor of Russian science, just as they must decry everything foreign:
such is the demand of the newest Party line. Parallel with propagating
in their works the idea of Soviet all-round superiority, they are carefully building up the myth of the prevalent anti-Western trend in nineteenth-century Russian literature and progressive thought, to the complete distortion of truth. This anti-Western mythology presided over
the 1948 commemoration of the centenary of Belinsky's death and the
1948 sesquicentennial celebrations of Pushkin's birth. The narrow na-
tionalistic approach to Pushkin, the complete denial of his essential
"Europeanness," which characterized the 1949 jubilee literature, was
particularly significant and contrasted sharply even with the 1937
Pushkin commemoration, although at the time patriotism had already
become part of the official Soviet outlook. But it was then more broad-
minded and did not imply a wholesale rejection of everything foreign,
so that even in 1941 it was possible for Nusinov to describe Pushkin as
"a European" and to say that he "continued and deepened Western

[37] It is claimed, for instance, that bookprinting was known in Russia before
Gutenberg.

culture" and could not conceive Russia's future "outside the Western paths." Six years later, as we have seen, these commonplaces were rigged up as dangerous heresies, and Nusinov was ostracized from literature.

4. *Reappraising Soviet Literature*

IN their whitewashing of the historical past the Communist leaders of Russia sometimes get involved in inextricable contradictions. They are well aware of the risk of Soviet patriotism being confused with Russian patriotism and that of the good points of the "good old times" being exaggerated. From time to time writers are warned of these dangers. Immediately after the war there was a sharp revulsion from the indiscriminate hero-worship practiced during the war. Writers were sharply reminded that it would not do to seek escape in historical themes, that such themes must be chosen with great discretion, and that it was imperative for them to pay more attention to contemporary Soviet subjects, to the portrayal of postwar reconstruction problems and of peacetime home-front heroes. A number of novels were, indeed, written in response to this injunction—some of them will be mentioned in a later section of this Chapter.

A characteristic echo of the overdoing of the historical rehabilitation theme is found in the already mentioned novel by Grigory Konovalov, *The University*. Its hero, Ilya Kozharov, after he wins his academic battle and is appointed to supervise the work of Ph.D. candidates, is shocked by the general trend of Ph.D. theses submitted to the faculty, by their remoteness from the realities of the day, their concentration on minor issues of the past, and especially their lack of that

> concretely historical, scholarly approach which we are wont to describe as the Party spirit. He just couldn't put up with it. In this respect one thesis stood out. . . . [Its author] was writing about poetry at the time of Peter the Great. . . . Coming across dithyrambs to Peter, Ilya could not help thinking: "All this was written not by a candidate who had lived in a Soviet family and studied in a Soviet school and was engaged in propaganda work at a factory, but by some sort of a Liberal."

Proceeding along this path, Kozharov thought, one might easily arrive even at whitewashing Nicholas I.

In 1949 the Soviet critic A. Leites published a study of University dissertations submitted during the past five years, pointing out that while 212 of them dealt with Russian pre-Revolutionary literature and 158 with foreign literature, only 24 dealt with Soviet literature. Leites ridiculed the choice of subject for her dissertation of a certain T. Vasilyeva who wrote about "the little-known English writer [Walter Savage] Landor." Referring later to this dissertation in his report at the conference of Soviet writers in January, 1950, Fadeyev said: "I also think that our young people could do for the time being without Landor." Apropos of another dissertation on Rainer Maria Rilke and Russian literature, Fadeyev exclaimed: "And who is Rilke? An extreme mystic and reactionary in poetry."

Some thorny problems are also involved in the Soviet claim to the classical heritage of Russian literature. In 1948 an interesting discussion took place in the course of which Soviet literary historians and critics were reminded that the Soviet period of Russian literature must not be treated as just another link in a continuous chain of development (this was known as the "theory of a single stream"), that the October Revolution of 1917 represented a sharp break with the past and the beginning of a new era. In a report "On the Teaching of Soviet Literature in High Schools," read at a meeting of the Praesidium of the Leningrad Branch of the Union of Soviet Writers early in 1948, A. Dementyev and E. Naumov came out with a sharp attack on Professor L. Timofeyev's standard high-school textbook of Soviet literature.[38] He was accused of the fundamental fallacy of regarding Soviet literature as part of modern literature, or "so-called 'contemporary literature' which continues the Russian classical literature of the nineteenth century," and of ignoring it as "a completely new phase in the development of Russian and world literature." Timofeyev was also accused of denying the very existence of a history of Soviet literature; for him, said Dementyev and Naumov, only a few Soviet writers existed, such as Gorky, Alexey Tolstoy, Mayakovsky, Sholokhov, and Fadeyev, but there was "no history of Soviet literature." The same accusation was leveled against the Russian literature curricula in Soviet universities. The authors concluded their report by suggesting that the literature curricula should be "refashioned" by the Ministry of Education "in such a way as to give Soviet literature its rightful place in schools" and that a new textbook

---

[38] A shortened version of this report was printed in *Zvezda*, No. 3 (1948), 182–88, under the title "Uluchshit prepodavanie sovetskoy literatury" ("Improve the Teaching of Soviet Literature"). The so-called "theory of the single stream" was mentioned again by Fadeyev in his 1950 report "On the Tasks of Literary Criticism," published in *Literaturnaya gazeta*, February 4, 1950. He claimed that it had been successfully disposed of, and that in doing so Soviet writers and critics had to repeat that Dostoyevsky was a reactionary writer, that there were also reactionary sides to Tolstoy's work, that it was wrong to gloss over Chekhov's "apoliticalness," and that even Gorky had made big mistakes which he set straight "under the enormous ideological influence of Lenin and Stalin." At the same time Fadeyev made several thrusts at the well-known Hungarian Marxist critic Georg Lukacs for "denying the possibility of Party guidance in literature" and for being too lenient to Existentialism and other hostile movements in the capitalist world.

of Soviet literature should be produced—"it must be competent, bright, and lively and must teach our youth to love the remarkable Soviet literature—the most progressive, the richest in ideas, the most revolutionary literature in the world."

For many years the necessity of producing a competent and comprehensive *History of Soviet Literature* had been urged in the official and literary circles. Before World War II a special committee was set up under the chairmanship of Alexey Tolstoy for this purpose, but it is not known how much progress it made. To this day the latest comprehensive account of Soviet literature—apart from high-school textbooks —is Gorbachov's *Contemporary Russian Literature,* the second edition of which appeared in 1929.[39] It was written by a former "On Guard" critic (who was later disowned and discredited as a Trotskyite) whose views certainly do not reflect the present-day official standpoint. The same is true of the *Literary Encyclopedia,* which began to appear in 1930 under the auspices of the Communist Academy (not to be confused with the Academy of Sciences) and of which eleven volumes were published covering about nine-tenths of the Russian alphabet. Among its editors and collaborators were prominent Trotskyites and other "oppositionists" (Kamenev, Bukharin, Radek, and others), and it is no wonder that today it figures on the Soviet *Index librorum prohibitorum* as an expression of heretical views. But the complaints which Soviet leaders and Soviet writers voice about the absence of a good history of Soviet literature must sound insincere and absurd to any impartial outsider. How is it possible to undertake the compilation of a comprehensive book on Soviet Literature after 1918 when recent history is being constantly subjected to ideological revision in a way that was admirably satirized by George Orwell in his *Nineteen Eighty-Four,* so that the compilers of such a history could never be sure that by the time it was ready for the press a number of writers and literary works would not have been wiped out of existence in accordance with the latest Party line! In Gorbachov's book many pages are devoted to Pilnyak, and his index contains references to thirty-eight titles of Pilnyak's works. To-day Pilnyak's name is quite unlikely even to be mentioned. In any history of Soviet literature appearing in the early thirties, considerable space would have been given to Babel and Olesha, but in Alexey Tolstoy's little wartime survey of the first twenty-five years of Soviet literature their names are absent. The same would be true today of Zoshchen-

39 The fact that a new impression of Gorbachov's book appeared as late as 1931 under the imprint of the State Publishing House is an interesting illustration of the slow grinding of Stalin's mills in those days, for Gorbachov had been denounced as a Trotskyite much earlier. In 1931 Kirpotin and others protested in *Zvezda* against the reissue of Gorbachov's book, but in 1933 *Zvezda* published an article by him. Eventually he was purged.

ko and many others. The process of revision and obliteration of the past is going on all the time, and since the war a number of well-established literary reputations have been questioned or exploded. Thus, late in 1948 *The Literary Gazette* came down upon the editorial board of the "Sovetsky Pisatel" publishing house for reissuing Ilf and Petrov's satirical novel *The Twelve Chairs,* one of the greatest early successes of Soviet literature, insisting that if the authors had been alive, they would never have allowed their novel to be published in unrevised form. More recently, the soundness of Bagritsky's "romantic" poetry was questioned by zealous Communist critics, and particular aspersions were cast on his once most popular work, *The Lay of Opanas.* Today Bagritsky's romanticism and political detachment seem incompatible with Socialist realism. In 1949 an attempt was made to question even the validity of Mayakovsky for the present generation of Soviet poets, and *The Literary Gazette* carried a long and rather bitter controversy on this subject. In the end Mayakovsky was vindicated and his "detractors" pointedly reminded that Stalin himself had proclaimed him the greatest Soviet poet.

In the case of living authors there is a definite tendency to forget or gloss over their past sins. It is all the more surprising, therefore, to see a Communist critic display a sudden concern for historical truth and solemnly remind Soviet editors that "history is history," that it must not be tampered with, and that it is no use concealing the fact that such "eminent" Soviet authors as Ehrenburg, Fedin, and Aseyev wrote once upon a time dubious or harmful works, and that Fedin had the misfortune of belonging to the Serapion Brotherhood, the true "un-Soviet" nature of which was exposed by Zhdanov.[40]

5. *"Stalin the Great"*

THE picture of Soviet literature today would be incomplete without another reference to the cult of Stalin the Leader (the Russian word *vozhd* is, by the way, the exact equivalent of the German *Führer* and the Italian *Duce*). Since the war this cult has acquired unprecedented dimensions and has penetrated deeply into Soviet literature. "The Greatest Man of our Time," "The Teacher," the "Father of the Peoples," the "Coryphaeus of all sciences," the "all-embracing genius" —such are the names which Soviet writers freely bestow on Stalin. Parallel examples of such abject adulation would be difficult to find in modern history. There is hardly a novel, a story, a play, or a poem on a contemporary Soviet theme which does not illustrate this truly Oriental

[40] L. Plotkin, "A. A. Zhdanov i literatura" ("A. A. Zhdanov and Literature"), in *Zvezda,* No. 1 (1949), 121.

worship of the all-powerful ruler who is endowed with all imaginable qualities and faculties. A few instances should suffice here.

In Pavlenko's novel *Happiness*, the hero, Voropayev, is received by Stalin in Livadia, the former Imperial residence in the Crimea, during the Yalta Conference. The chapter describing their meeting is a real gem of Communist hagiography. When Voropayev, a Communist of long standing with an excellent war record, first saw Stalin at a little distance, "he could not budge—his legs did not obey him." Stalin was engaged in a friendly conversation with an old gardener and advising him to "experiment boldly" with grapes and lemons. The gardener looked at Stalin "in bewilderment and at the same time with a kind of childish admiration." This idyllic scene was interrupted by Voropayev's appearance, and suddenly Voropayev saw "with horror" [?] that Stalin

> was going toward him, with outstretched arms, smiling his all-pervading smile. . . . Stalin was calm to the point of improbability. . . . Voropayev thought that Stalin had not aged since he had seen him last at the parade on November 7, 1941, but had changed sharply in a different sense. His face, still the same, familiar to its slightest fold, had acquired new features, features of solemnity, and Voropayev was glad when he noticed them. Stalin's face could not but change and become a little different, because the nation was going toward him, with outstretched arms, smiling his all-tion had changed and become even more majestic.

Molotov, who happened to be present at the interview, though busy with diplomatic papers, helped Stalin and Voropayev to break the ice. During the conversation Stalin of course revealed his warm and kindly nature, his interest in men, his amazing grasp of the situation.

The finale of the scene is quite priceless and deserves being quoted at least in part in Pavlenko's own words:

> Moved infinitely by this soul-burning conversation Voropayev put his hand into the pocket of his greatcoat and, together with the handkerchief, pulled out and dropped on the ground the morning posy of snowdrops.
>
> [The posy had been given Voropayev that morning by a little girl he met on the road "for Stalin." On hearing the story, Stalin ordered a basket of cookies for the girl and after it was brought dismissed Voropayev with a few encouraging words.]
>
> And as he looked straight into Voropayev's eyes, his face seemed to sparkle as though a ray of sun had whisked across it.

The tone of Pavlenko's description, as though parodied from Tolstoy, makes the whole scene sound still more incongruous.

357

A different aspect of the Stalin cult will be found in I. Popov's play *Semya (The Family;* published in *Novy Mir,* 1950, No. 1). Here we have a deliberate attempt to enhance the historical importance of Stalin in the Bolshevik movement and to link him more closely than ever with Lenin. The action of the play takes place between 1886 and 1897, partly in Simbirsk during Lenin's school years and partly in St. Petersburg. The last scene shows a group of Social-Democratic workers discussing the tactics of the labor movement and the strike that is breaking out in Petersburg, and the name of Stalin is introduced in the following conversation:

> *Shelgunov.* . . . The working people are waking up everywhere.
> *Babushkin.* Even from the distant Transcaucasia there come tidings. Thousands of miles from here, at the other end of the country, they follow the same line as Vladimir Ilyich [Lenin] here.
> *Nikitich.* There, too, the movement is putting forth new and remarkable men.
> *Stryapunov.* Name them.
> *A Voice.* Who?
> *Babushkin.* Stalin. Victor Kurnatovsky writes us about him, and so does Mikhail Kalinin. They all mention him. Just like Vladimir Ilyich he is for the militant line, for the creation of a centralized workers' party.
> *Shelgunov.* And he also denounces mercilessly everything that stands in the way to our great goal.

Just before the curtain falls Lenin himself makes a dramatic entry —he has just been released from prison—and Stalin's name is once more brought in:

> *Vladimir Ilyich.* . . *(With sudden ardor).* And have you heard about Transcaucasia?
> *Voices.* We know, we know! We have just heard it from Babushkin.
> *Vladimir Ilyich.* But do you know all about Transcaucasia?
> *Voices.* Stalin is there!
> *Vladimir Ilyich.* Splendid. Ivan Vasilievich, pass on my firm and friendly handshake to comrade Stalin.

The play ends with Lenin's announcing the coming foundation of "a great, powerful and unshakable party." But one is almost inclined to suspect that Mr. Popov wrote his play about Lenin with the object of outdoing his fellow writers and firmly affixing Stalin's star on the historical firmament alongside with Lenin's as far back as 1897 (when Stalin was seventeen years old)—a matchless example of Communist mythmaking. In reviewing the first performance of the play in *The Literary Gazette* (January 21, 1950), the novelist Vera Smirnova wrote: "Thus for the first time, at the cradle of the Party, are linked together the two great names dear to us."

When earlier works of fiction are revised by Soviet writers, one finds inserted in them the previously absent references to Stalin. Thus, in Slonimsky's *First Years*, the revised version of *The Lavrovs* (see page 113 above) a conversation between two characters is introduced in which Stalin is mentioned as Lenin's right-hand man in the October, 1917, *coup d'état*. Slonimsky also took an opportunity of removing from *The Lavrovs* some disparaging references to Lenin and some compliments to Plekhanov.

As for poetry, the poems and songs that sing and extol Stalin the Great in all the languages of the Soviet Union are countless, and few are the poets who have not made their contribution to this treasury of Staliniana. Among the more curious examples may be cited a poem by Vsevolod Azarov entitled "Velikaya kniga" ("The Great Book"), published by *Zvezda* in 1949 (No. 5). It is a twenty-four-line paean to the official *History of the Communist Party,* in which "every word was created by Stalin" and which is described as

> *The simple, the great, the wise book,*
> *The immortal chronicle of our victories.*

6. *The Postwar Literary Output*

THAT literature can still exist under the above-described conditions of relentless mind control from above and continuous mind-reading by fellow writers and critics is not a little surprising. Yet, in quantity at least, the output of the four years that have passed since Zhdanov's bomb exploded over the heads of Soviet writers is considerable, though the quality is mostly very low. No more than a brief catalogue of the more important works which appeared during this period in fiction, drama, poetry, and literary history can be given here.

The Novel

Several of the older Soviet writers have added, during the past four years, to their lists of novels; among them may be mentioned Fedin, Kaverin, Katayev, Ehrenburg, Pavlenko, and Panfyorov.

Fedin's "dilogy"—*Pervye radosti* (*First Joys*, 1945–46) and *Neobyknovennoye leto* (*Unusual Summer*, 1948)—is, perhaps, the most outstanding literary event of the postwar period. The two novels are separated chronologically but linked together by the same characters. In *First Joys* the action is set in Saratov, on the Volga, on the eve of World

War I. The principal characters are a young boy, Kirill Izvekov, a budding revolutionary, and an older revolutionary and factory worker, Ragozin. But an important part is also played by two representatives of the intelligentsia, the writer Pastukhov and the actor Tsvetukhin, and there are a number of other characters representing various strata of Russian pre-Revolutionary society. The novel is written in a broad, realistic manner, much closer to the classical tradition than Fedin's earlier works. This is even more noticeable in *Unusual Summer,* where the period portrayed is more or less the same (though chronologically more limited) as in his *Cities and Years*: the action passes during the summer of 1919. But here there is no experimenting with form; the narrative is steady and straightforward. Politically speaking, the novel is also more orthodox. Kirill Izvekov, who toward the end of the first novel was arrested and imprisoned for his subversive political work, is shown now in the prime of his revolutionary activities. Ragozin and Pastukhov also play an important part. Much is made of Stalin's leading role (now part of the generally accepted Stalin myth) in halting Denikin's White Army's successful offensive. Apart from this inevitable homage to Stalin, there is no attempt at political or psychological simplification. The characters are sufficiently complex and well drawn; the writing has a rich, full-bodied quality. If the two novels lack the freshness, originality, and independence of *Cities and Years,* they have a new maturity and are certainly superior to such a work as *The Rape of Europe.*

Of Kaverin's novel *Otkrytaya kniga* (*The Open Book,* 1949), so far only the first part has been serialized (in *Novy Mir*). Whether it will be continued and published in book form may be doubted: having evoked some protests, it has been since adjudged "a mistake." The first protest came from a group of Leningrad University students who protested against Kaverin's portrayal of Soviet youth as engaged in trivial problems of personal life, in amorous pastimes, and so on. The novel is a first-person narrative told by a young Soviet girl, who is a few years older than the Revolution and grows to be a famous bacteriologist. An important role in the early part of the novel is played by an old and eccentric doctor with a revolutionary past who makes an important discovery about viruses. The heroine becomes involved in the loss of his manuscripts which she undertook to preserve after his death. Here Kaverin displays his passion for a plot of adventure, and this overcomplicated plot (into which the reader at any moment expects to see introduced the machinations of "bourgeois cosmopolitans") must obviously serve as a compensation for the otherwise realistic texture of the novel.

Another work that was severely criticized on its appearance in *October* magazine was Katayev's novel *Za vlast Sovetov* (*For the Power of the Soviets,* 1949). The novel portrayed the underground wartime activities of the Odessa partisans, whose headquarters were located in the famous catacombs under the city. Katayev introduced into it the two principal characters of his *The Lone White Sail,* the boys Petya Bachey and Gavrik, both of them middle-aged men now, Petya with a son of his own, very much like the boy-hero of the earlier novel. The novel lacks the peculiar attraction of *The Lone White Sail,* but is well written and has an exciting story. The criticism of it came from a fellow writer, Mikhail Bubyonnov, who wrote a letter to the editor of *October* charging Katayev with minimizing, and even disfiguring, the role of the Communist party in the partisan movement. Several other critics chimed in somewhat belatedly, and at the plenary conference of the Board of the Union of Soviet Writers early in 1950 the novel was described as a "political blunder."

No such charges were made against Pavlenko's *Happiness,* some aspects of which have been discussed already. Its anti-Western tendency was, of course, well in keeping with the official line. So also was its rather primitive political moral, that personal happiness can only be reached if it is subordinated to, or at least combined with, an unselfish service to the common good of the country and an unflinching devotion to the Party. The novel is largely concerned with wartime reconstruction problems facing the Soviet Union. One of the problems treated in it is the resettlement of a large number of Kuban Cossacks in the Crimea, but no mention is made of the fact that the bulk of the native Tartar population of the peninsula were deported for siding with the Germans during the war—a good illustration of that *suppressio veri* which is an essential characteristic of Socialist realism.

Gladkov's *Povest o detstve (Story of My Childhood,* 1949), for which he was awarded a second Stalin Prize, is a straightforward autobiography. Free from some of the shortcomings of his fiction, it will probably rank as his best work; in this it resembles Gorky's autobiographical series, and Gorky's influence is strongly felt in it, all the more so since Gladkov's childhood, full of hardships, was not unlike Gorky's.

Ehrenburg's *Burya (The Storm,* 1948) is a long and ambitious novel about the war, with a parallel action in Russia and in France. It has a multitude of characters—Soviet people from all walks of life, Frenchmen, British and American officers, and Germans. Superficial but colorful, it displays Ehrenburg's knack for happy phrases, for a quick summing-up of a situation, as well as his matchless ability to respond, when necessary, to the prevalent official line. The contrast between the two worlds, the Soviet and the non-Soviet, is stressed throughout the novel. As one of the Soviet critics who praised Ehrenburg's novel said, speaking of his portrayal of the British and the Americans: "The reader unmistakably recognizes [in them] the familiar faces of people who have sold their honor, their conscience, and their opinions for ringing dollars."[41] To those who remember the Ehrenburg of *Julio Jurenito* and of *The Summer of 1925* his enthusiasm and his indignation sound equally spurious.

Fyodor Panfyorov's long novel *V strane poverzhennykh* (*In the Land of the Vanquished*, 1948), a sequel to his earlier *Borba za mir* (*The Struggle for Peace*, 1946–47), has an improbable, melodramatic plot, involving the diversionary work of a young and beautiful Soviet girl among the Germans. The characters are equally unreal, especially the Germans, portrayed as vile and inhuman in the highest degree.

Arkady Perventsev's patriotic war novel *Chest smolodu* (*Watch Your Honor*,[42] 1948), in reflecting the dismay which the early reverses of the Red Army caused among the Soviet people, strikes a more sincere note. It also has a long and pleasant autobiographical flashback about the hero's childhood among the Kuban Cossacks.

Of the newcomers to Soviet literature, Vera Fyodorovna Panova (b. 1905) attracted attention with her short novel *Sputniki* (*Traveling Companions*, 1947). This unpretentious tale, describing a group of people working together during the war on an ambulance train which evacuates the wounded from the front, struck a genuinely human note and was remarkable for its objective characterization and its detached tone reminiscent of Chekhov. Panova's next work—*Kruzhilikha* (1948; the title is the name of a factory)—dealt with some problems of transition from wartime to peacetime conditions in Soviet industry, but Panova's chief concern was again with human beings and their relationships. Though not as good as the earlier work, it had the same quality of detachment and understatement. *Kruzhilikha* led to a curious and typical controversy, during which some critics blamed Panova for this very quality. One of them complained, with naïve earnestness, that Panova did not "decipher" her characters enough, that no sooner did the reader come to like a character than he discovered that the author meant that character to be a "negative" one, and vice versa, thus "shouldering upon the reader the responsibility for appraising her characters."

Why is Panova so merciless to good people as to floodlight all their shortcomings, making us several times change our attitude toward her characters and in the end remain perplexed? Why is she so kind to wicked people as to floodlight their slightest good characteristics?

41 Vl. Dmitrevsky in *Zvezda*, No. 6 (1948).

42 The title comes from a Russian saying: "Watch your honor while still young," which Pushkin used as a motto for his *Captain's Daughter*.

The Literary Gazette complained that at a critical discussion of *Kruzhilikha* the novel was used by some critics "to preach non-Party spirit in literature." The critic Munblit was quoted as saying that the principal charm of Panova's novel lay in the fact that "one cannot tell which character is positive and which negative . . . . I find it interesting to meet such imperfect people who change and toward whom my attitude changes." This, said *The Literary Gazette,* was the statement of an aesthete, "aimed at the principle of Party-mindedness in our literature." Although both of Panova's novels were singled out for Stalin awards, several critics maintained that her "detachment" was incompatible with Socialist realism.

Panova's third short novel, *Yasny Bereg* (*The Clear Shore,* 1949), described life on a large stockbreeding state farm. She was awarded another Stalin prize for it.

Other newcomers who have attained celebrity since the war are Mikhail Bubyonnov, Semyon Babayevsky (b. 1909), and Vasily Azhayev. Bubyonnov's *Belaya beryoza* (*The White Birch,* 1948) is a long and tedious war novel, with conventional characters and situations. Babayevsky received the 1948 and 1949 Stalin Prizes for his *Kavaler zolotoy zvezdy* (*The Knight of the Golden Star*) and the sequel to it, *Svet nad zemlyoy* (*Light over the Land*). Their hero is a war veteran who returns to his native village and engages in collective farm work. These novels responded to the insistently voiced demand for the portrayal of postwar reconstruction and peacetime heroes and are characteristic examples of conscientious and orthodox Socialist realism, of little literary distinction. The same may be said of Azhayev's *Dalyoko ot Moskvy* (*Far from Moscow,* 1948), which describes the heroic feat of the building of an oil pipe line in eastern Siberia within one year in 1941. The novel is naïve, long (over seven hundred pages), and formless, but the author manages to communicate to the reader his enthusiasm for the everyday heroism of his characters.

Since the interest in contemporary Soviet themes is particularly encouraged today, six similar novels were awarded Stalin Prizes in 1949 (in addition to Babayevsky's *Light over the Land,* which had the distinction of a first prize). They were *Zemlya Kuznetskaya* (*The Land of Kuznetsk*), about the life of Siberian coal miners, by Alexander Voloshin; *Marya,* about women's part in collective farming, by Grigory Medynsky (pseudonym of Pokrovsky); *U nas uzhe utro* (*With Us It Is Morning Already*), about fishermen's life in Southern Saghalien, by Alexander Chakovsky; *Ivan Ivanovich,* about an ordinary Soviet family in the Far North, by Antonina Koptyaeva; and *Bolshaya doroga* (*The Highway*), by Vasily Ilyenkov. On the other hand, only one war novel had the distinction of a Stalin award—*Vesna na Odere* (*Spring on the*

Oder) by Emmanuel Kazakevich, which describes the last stages of the Soviet offensive against Germany.

Boris Polevoy's *Povest o nastoyashchem cheloveke* (*The Tale of a Real Man*, 1947), enthusiastically acclaimed by the critics, told the dramatic story of the adventures of one of the real heroes of the war, a Soviet airman who lost his legs in a forced landing, but managed to crawl out of the enemy lines and later rejoined the air force. Polevoy's volume of sketches *My, sovetskie lyudi* (*We, the Soviet People*, 1948), was also based on true-life stories.

To the documentary literature about the partisan movement were added Ivan Kozlov's *V Krymskom podpolye* (*In the Crimean Underground*, 1947); Leonid Korobov's *Malaya zemlya* (*The Little Land*, 1948), the impressions of a *Pravda* correspondent with Kovpak's army, supplementing Vershigora's book; and A. Fyodorov's *Podpolny obkom deystvuyet* (*The Underground Regional Committee is in Action*, 1947).

The vogue for historical fiction continued after the war even though writers were enjoined not to withdraw too much into the past. In postwar historical novels the stress is on the great military (and naval) exploits of the past. Typical examples are Leonty Rakovsky's *Generalissimo Suvorov* (1947); Marianna Yakhontova's *Korabli vykhodyat v more* (*The Ships Sail Out*, 1948), dealing with the Russo-Turkish War under Catherine II; and Alexander Yugov's *Ratobortsy* (*The Champions*, 1949), a long parallel novel about two Russian medieval princes, Alexander Nevsky and Daniel of Galicia. In Rakovsky's novel about Suvorov the anti-British bias is very prominent. The anti-American theme was exploited by Ivan Kratt in his novel *Koloniya Ross* (*The Ross Colony*, 1950), about the Russians in California, with Colonel Rezanov as its hero.[43] Many historical, literary, and scientific biographies, permeated with the antiforeign spirit and designed to foster the sense of Russian national superiority, continue to appear. Typical of them is *Povest ob ukradennoy idee* (*The Story of a Stolen Idea*, 1948) by Yury Weber, a biography of Alexander Popov, from whom Marconi is alleged to have stolen the idea of radio.

The Drama

Many postwar dramas have already been mentioned in the sections dealing with the fight against the West and with new Soviet nationalism. These anti-Western and anticosmopolitan plays constitute the bulk of postwar dramatic production. To those that have been mentioned before may be added Nikolay Virta's *Zagovor obrechonnykh* (*The Con-*

43 The same author's earlier novel about the Russians in Alaska, *Ostrov Baranova* (*Baranov's Island*, 1945), was free from this anti-American bias.

spiracy of the Doomed, 1949) and Sergey Mikhalkov's *Ilya Golovin* (1949). The action of Virta's play takes place in Czechoslovakia, and it exposes the "intrigues" of the American "warmongers" in "People's Democracies." Mikhalkov's drama denounces a cosmopolitan-minded artist. The same anticosmopolitan spirit colors many biographical plays about Russian artists, writers, and scientists. The *Literary Gazette* has been complaining of the overproduction of these biographical plays and of the dearth of good plays on contemporary Soviet themes—a complaint of which Soviet leaders and critics never seem to tire.[44] One of such topical plays—Vadim Kozhevnikov's *Ognennaya reka* (*River of Fire,* 1949)—was praised by most critics until *Culture and Life* came down upon Kozhevnikov and his flatterers with a thundering article, denouncing his ignorance of Soviet life and of the technicalities of his subject (the play dealt with some new technological invention in Soviet metallurgy), as well as his conventional characters and pretentious style. With wonted alacrity, all Soviet critics, as well as fellow writers, took their cue from *Culture and Life* and began to speak of Kozhevnikov's play and its publication as "a big mistake." A similar play by Anatoly Surov—*Zelyonaya ulitsa* (*Green Street,* 1948)—escaped condemnation, as did also Virta's *Khleb nash nasushchny* (*Our Daily Bread,* 1947), written in response to a demand for portraying everyday heroes of collective farming.

Yet, a look at the last page of *Pravda* or *Izvestia* today will show that the majority of Moscow theaters are still showing pre-Revolutionary plays, either Russian or foreign. Thus, for instance, on March 7, 1950, *Pravda* listed plays by Gogol, Ostrovsky, Naydyonov, Goldoni, Oscar Wilde (*The Ideal Husband*), Shaw (*Pygmalion*), and so on, as against no more than two or three plays by Soviet writers, not one of them dealing with a contemporary subject. The inference seems inevitable that Soviet theatergoers still prefer plays by Gogol and Goldoni, by Ostrovsky and Shaw, to plays about "Soviet realities," whether they be by Virta and Surov or by Kozhevnikov. It is significant that, of the plays which were awarded Stalin Prizes in 1949, one dealt with the Civil War and was obviously written to glorify Stalin and extol his part in the defense of Petrograd against General Yudenich in 1919 (this was Vishnevsky's *Nezabyvayemy 1919*—*The Unforgettable 1919,* the only play deemed worthy of the first prize), while four were devoted to the exposure of "enemies" inside and outside the Soviet Union (Simonov's *Someone Else's Shadow,* Lavrenyov's *Voice of America,* and Mikhalkov's *Ilya Golovin* and *I Want to Go Home*).

[44] See, for instance, A. Anastasyev and G. Gaydovsky, "Bolshe pyes o stroitelyakh kommunizma" ("More Plays about Builders of Communism"), in *Literaturnaya gazeta,* January 18, 1950.

Poetry

To use popular Soviet terminology, poetry is today, more than ever, the "bottleneck" (*"uzkoye mesto"*) of Soviet literature. Here the deadening influence of the Party line and of "social command"[45] is particularly telling. Pasternak has been silent since 1946. Akhmatova, as we saw, after three years of silence was forced to toe the line—with lamentable results. Bergholz, Aliger, and Inber have not written anything that can be compared with their war poetry. Simonov, who in 1947 showed a great deal of courage in defending, in his capacity as editor-in-chief of *Novy Mir*, Margarita Aliger against accusations of writing poetry that was "too personal" and "despondent," has himself been producing nothing but propaganda poetry and plays since that time. Prokofyev, Dolmatovsky, and Shchipachov (of whom Prokofyev alone has the makings of a genuine poet) have also been anxious to conform to the latest Party line and have fallen below their prewar and wartime level. Tvardovsky's only long postwar poem, *Dom u dorogi* (*The House by the Roadside*, 1946), was written before the Zhdanov era. It forms a sort of complement to his *Vasily Tyorkin* and tells of the peregrinations and sufferings of a simple soldier's wife who is captured by the Germans and sent to a forced labor camp. It has the same genuine accents as his earlier work and is refreshingly free from Party politics.

The new stars on the Soviet poetic horizon are Nikolay Matveyevich Gribachov (b. 1910) and Alexander Yashin (pseudonym of Alexander Yakovlevich Popov, b. 1913). Both have been awarded Stalin prizes: Gribachov in 1948 for his narrative poem *Vesna v "Pobede"* (*Spring in "Victory"*—"Victory" being the name of a collective farm); and Yashin in 1949 for his *Alyona Fomina*, another *kolkhoz* poem glorifying the work of women in collective farming. Judged by strictly poetic standards, both poems are mediocre. They are greatly inferior, for instance, to Tvardovsky's *Land of Muravia*. But they are full of joyful optimism, and that is what matters most today: in many postwar literary discussions, ever since Zhdanov's attack on pessimism, young poets have been accused of despondency and preoccupation with their personal problems, and even harping on wartime experiences has sometimes been interpreted as an escape from the realities of today.

Literary Criticism and Scholarship

After all that has been said in this chapter there is no need to explain why nothing of real value has been added since the war to literary

---

45 Although this expression was launched by Mayakovsky, Soviet critics today prefer to avoid it, or take care to explain that it does not mean real "command."

criticism or why even literary research into the past has been most un-
favorably affected. In both, the theme of anti-Westernism and anti-
cosmopolitanism has effectively drowned everything else, and even the
publication of literary materials—a field in which much was done in
the Soviet Union in the first twenty years—has been governed by the
same bias.

In 1949, three literary critics and historians were awarded a Stalin
prize of the second magnitude. The choice fell upon works that com-
plied with the prescribed Party line. One of them was Ermilov's revised version of a book on Chekhov: the revision consisted in bringing
into due prominence Chekhov's deficiencies, especially his political neutrality. Another was Yakov Elsberg's book on Herzen which, by stressing one-sidedly Herzen's hostility to bourgeois Europe, duly met the
demands of the Zhdanov era. For Elsberg to receive a Stalin prize was a
great advancement: twice before he had been in hot water, once in the
early thirties and then again during the anticosmopolitan campaign.
The third work awarded a prize was S. Makashin's study of Saltykov-
Shchedrin.

Another award under the same category had somewhat unexpected
consequences, which cannot but confound those who are not initiated
into the mysterious workings of the Communist party machinery. A
prize of the third order was awarded to an Azerbaidzhanian man of
letters, M. Husseinov, for a study of the movement of ideas in Azer-
baidzhan in the nineteenth century. In announcing the awards, the editorial in *The Literary Gazette* (March 8, 1950) described the book as
a valuable contribution to the study of an Azerbaidzhanian progressive
thinker. Before long, however, the award was adjudged a mistake and
withdrawn, and the book denounced for its dangerous "deviations."

The postwar peroid saw also a revival of the old controversy about
Socialist realism, of which a little more will be said by way of concluding this study of Soviet literature.

Conclusion—The True Meaning
of Socialist Realism

OFFICIALLY, the era of Socialist realism, inaugurated in 1932, continues in Soviet literature. Yet, even after so many years of its enforced practice, its meaning continues to be a subject for discussion.

In 1948, there appeared a volume of essays, to which reference has already been made, entitled *Problemy sotsialisticheskogo realizma* (*Problems of Socialist Realism*).[1] Its object was to bring Socialist realism in line with Zhdanov's 1946 "directives." It contained, among other things, Fadeyev's address on "The Tasks of Literary Theory and Criticism," Motylyova's essay establishing the superiority of Soviet literature over the bourgeois, and Ya. Fried's denunciation of European decadent literature.[2] There was also a long essay by B. Byalik on "Gorky and Socialist Realism,"[3] in which Gorky's thesis about Socialist realism as a combination of realism and revolutionary romanticism was revived and expanded. This led to a further futile debate on this well-worn subject. The consensus of Soviet critical opinion went against Byalik— for the time being romanticism was under suspicion and believed to be fraught with dangers. Byalik was accused of misunderstanding and misinterpreting Gorky.

[1] One of the editors of this volume, L. Subotsky, was subsequently denounced as "a rootless cosmopolitan."

[2] "Sotsialistichesky realism i sovremennaya dekadentskaya literatura" ("Socialist Realism and Modern Decadent Literature"), in *Problems of Socialist Realism*, 347–93. This is a comparatively serious study of certain trends in modern European literature, without any attacks on "American warmongers" and without a specific anti-American bias, most of the writers mentioned being French or British. Apart from the inevitable references to Proust, Joyce, Dos Passos and Sartre, the author mentions as "decadents" Henry de Motherlant, Paul Valéry, François Mauriac, Valéry Larbaud, Jean Giraudoux, André Gide, Jules Romains, Julien Benda, André Malraux, Albert Camus, André Breton, Romain Gary, Kafka, Edwin Muir, Stephen Spender, Norman Nicholson, Ronald Latham, Owen Barfield, and William Faulkner. To them he opposes Soviet writers and a few "Progressives" in the West (Romain Rolland, Theodore Dreiser, J. B. Priestley, Jean-Richard Bloch, Jean Cassou, Louis Aragon, and Paul Eluard).

[3] "Gorky i sotsialistichesky realizm," in *Problems of Socialist Realism*, 115–16.

Conclusion

There is no need to go into the details of that controversy here. Some interest attaches, however, to an article by A. Belik, a minor critic who managed to survive the anticosmopolitan purge. It appeared in *October* magazine in February, 1950.[4] Belik began by dealing out blows right and left, saying that he was interested, not in what had been achieved by Soviet literary scholars, but by "what has not yet been done, or is being done in a wrong way." The chief sin of Soviet literary scholars was their "lagging behind life." There were no "objective" causes for such lagging, said Belik, the reason was therefore purely "subjective": namely, the inability of the scholars and critics to grasp fully the precepts of Leninism. Belik put much of the blame at the door of Alexandrov and his book on Western philosophy, which, though denounced by the Central Committee of the Communist party and exposed by Zhdanov, continued to exercise its harmful influence. Belik saw its influence, and a dangerous tendency toward liberalism, in the writings of A. M. Egolin, who was largely responsible for the Party line in literature, even though on the face of it Egolin came out against Alexandrov in his pamphlet "Itogi filosofskoy diskussii i zadachi literaturovedeniya" ("The Results of the Philosophical Discussion and the Tasks of Literary Scholarship," 1948).[5]

Belik also attacked several other literary scholars and critics, among them Kirpotin, Tarasenkov, Belchikov, I. Lezhnev (for his book on Sholokhov), Veksler (for his book on Alexey Tolstoy), and Timofeyev (for his *Theory of Literature*). All of them were guilty of persisting in Alexandrov's main sin, that of "vicious objectivism"; Alexandrov's book was "unscholarly," said Belik, because it was "permeated with objectivism." Timofeyev was also accused, more specifically, of advancing the erroneous and "condemned" theory of the "combination of romanticism and realism as the essence of Socialist realism." As is usual with Soviet critics, Belik tried to beat his victims with their own stick by reinterpreting their own quotations from Lenin and by appealing to the supreme authority of Stalin in literary matters. He advised literary scholars and critics to take guidance from the recently published letters of Stalin to Gorky and Felix Kohn, in which all the problems facing Soviet literature were neatly solved. It was Lenin and Stalin, said Belik,

---

[4] "O nekotorykh oshibkakh v literaturovedenii" ("About Certain Mistakes in Literary Science"), in *Oktyabr*, No. 2 (1950), 150–64.

[5] In 1946 Egolin was entrusted with the reorganization of *Zvezda*. In 1948 his lecture-pamphlet *Za vysokuyu ideynost sovetskoy literatury* (*For the High Ideological Content of Soviet Literature*) was given wide publicity as an authoritative statement of the official Party line in literature (there was an American edition of it, see Bibliography). An earlier work by Egolin—*Osvoboditelnye i patrioticheskie idei russkoy literatury XIX veka* (*The Ideas of Liberation and Patriotism in Nineteenth Century Russian Literature*, 1946), was criticized by Belik for its crypto-liberalism.

who had "laid down the firm theoretical foundations of Socialist literature by establishing the principle of Party-mindedness as the fundamental law of Socialist realism." Falling back on quotations from them, Belik frankly equated Socialist realism with a "Party-minded attitude toward Socialist realities." It was therefore absurd, in his opinion, to pretend that everything published now in the Soviet Union was *ipso facto* in accord with Socialist realism, as though the latter were "a badge issued to every Soviet writer for the mere fact of being one." As a work that did not fall within the meaning of Socialist realism Belik cited Katayev's latest novel, *For the Power of the Soviets.* He also attacked Tarasenkov for his broad interpretation of Socialist realism as allowing of "different literary manners"[6] and reminded whomever it might concern that as late as 1945 Tarasenkov had been praising Pasternak as a true Soviet poet.[7] While not denying that writers were free to follow "different creative paths," Belik suggested, quite logically, that if Socialist realism were "the true and predominant method of Socialist literature," then "there must exist manners, media of expression, laws of composition, of the plot, of image-building, etc., which correspond to that method," just as, conversely, "there exist manners, media of expression, etc., which contradict Socialist realism."

Belik's article soon came under the fire from the big guns of Party leadership: on March 31, 1950, *Culture and Life* printed an editorial accusing Belik of attempting to revive the bad days of RAPP and Averbach. Yet there was really nothing new in what Belik had said: he was merely following faithfully the latest official line. His real crime consisted in revealing, wittingly or unwittingly, the fact that the king was naked, by openly equating Socialist realism with the current Party line. For, as the foregoing account of the fortunes (or misfortunes) of Soviet literature since 1932 must make clear, that is what Socialist realism really means. Hence the various accretions to it since its inauguration in 1932. When the current Party line decrees militant anti-cosmopolitanism, it immediately becomes part and parcel of Socialist realism. If the Party line so wills it, romanticism is made the essential ingredient of Socialist realism; if not, romanticism is declared a dangerous and alien perversion.[8]

With realism in its original sense, Socialist realism has little to do,

6 In his book *Idei i obrazy sovetskoy literatury* (*Ideas and Images of Soviet Literature*). This book includes also Tarasenkov's article against Veselovsky and the "cosmopolitans," which Belik praised.

7 This is only one of the many examples of the Soviet critics' common practice of "informing" on their colleagues.

8 Very symptomatic is the popularity enjoyed in the Soviet Union, both during his lifetime and posthumously, by A. Grin (pseudonym of Alexander Grinevsky, 1880–1932), author of romantic and fantastic adventure stories and novels and creator

Conclusion

at least with realism as it was understood by Chekhov when he said that "imaginative literature . . . depicts life as it really is," and that "its aim is truth—unconditional and honest." There is no need to stress here again the fact that whole vast tracts of Soviet reality are taboo for Soviet literature, that one would look in vain to it for even a dim reflection of such phenomena as forced labor and concentration camps, or the anti-religious campaign before the late thirties and especially the opposition it met with, or the mass desertions of the Red Army in the early stages of the war against Germany.

Gorky once said that Socialist realism was but a pseudonym for revolutionary romanticism. Selvinsky suggested more recently (perhaps without realizing all the implications of his suggestion) that it be re-named "Socialist symbolism." But one would be much closer to the truth in describing it as a pseudonym for Stalinism. It is in fact merely a device designed to enlist art and literature in the service of the Soviet state and its aims. Its actual contents may therefore vary, its framework may be expanded or contracted, but the one thing it is and will be in-compatible with is the true freedom of the artist. The history of Soviet

of the make-believe country of "Grinland." Grin began writing before the Revolu-tion when he was regarded as a second-rate imitator of Anglo-Saxon writers of ad-venture stories. After the Revolution he continued to write in the same vein and somehow managed to keep his work free from politics. It was his romanticism that accounted for his success with Soviet readers who were fed up with the ordinary literary fare they were served and wanted something more spicy. Grin was also held in great esteem by many Soviet writers. He seems to have had an engaging personality and was a good storyteller. Paustovsky introduced him into one of his stories, while Leonid Borisov wrote a whole book about him entitled *Volshebnik iz Gel-Gyu* (*The Wizard from Gel-Gyu*, 1945). In 1950 Grin was posthumously denounced as a typical cosmopolitan and debunked as a worthless imitator of Stevenson, Edgar Allan Poe, Conan Doyle, etc., in an article by Victor Vazhdayev entitled "Propovednik kosmopoli-tizma. Nechisty smysl 'chistogo iskusstva' Aleksandra Grina" ("A Preacher of Cos-mopolitanism: The Impure Meaning of Alexander Grin's 'Pure Art' "), in *Novy Mir*, No. 1 (1950), 257–72. Much of what Vazhdayev says about the literary value of Grin's work is valid, but the true meaning of the popularity of this "militant reactionary and cosmopolitan" who was "no innocuous dreamer" escapes the Communist critic. For Soviet readers and many Soviet writers Grin and his "Grinland" filled a sorely felt gap: even a tenth-rate Stevenson would have satisfied them. Grin's aloofness from politics, and the fact that he never wrote on contemporary subjects, made him at the same time free from suspicion in their eyes. The same craving for romanticism is reflected in the growing popularity today of science fiction and adventure stories: both genres are being encouraged now but an attempt is made to channel them into the service of Communism and to use them as weapons against the West. Some in-formation about this branch of Soviet literature will be found in Sergey Ivanov's article "Fantastika i deystvitelnost" ("Fancy and Fact"), in *Oktyabr*, No. 1 (1950), 155–64. Among the earlier scientific romances may be mentioned *Strana shchastlivykh* (*The Country of the Happy*, 1931), by Ya.Larry, a mixture of H. G. Wells with Com-munist ideology. A good example of this Soviet "scientific adventure" literature is Efremov's "A Meeting over Tuscarora," which has been translated into English (see Bibliography). But this particular story was denounced by Ivanov for its "cosmopoli-tanism."

literature from 1918 to 1950, as here unfolded, is a story of the gradual but inevitable extinction of that freedom. It is also a story of the steady decline of culture, of its relentless leveling-down. Complete cultural and spiritual isolationism is the hallmark of the Stalin era in Russia. Konstantin Leontyev, that brilliant Russian nineteenth-century thinker, in visualizing this anticultural trend resulting in dead uniformity, associated it with "progress," with modern ideas of political and social democracy. Today in Russia this leveling-down and uniformization of culture is being achieved at the cost of suppressing all democratic institutions, of a return to the sixteenth-century absolutist ideal of Ivan the Terrible. To quote from a recent book, which every foreign student of Russia should read, what is at stake today is the very spiritual existence of Russia.[9]

[9] "Le véritable problème qui se pose à la Russie trente ans après la révolution . . . c'est le problème de son existence spirituelle, et *par conséquent* du régime qui puisse lui en restituer la possibilité." Wladimir Weidlé, *La Russie absente et présente,* 197.

Bibliography

NOTE. Except for Sections I and V this Bibliography does not aim at completeness.

In Section II are listed the most important bibliographical sources of general and specific nature, and the reader may refer to them for further information. Information about all books published in the Soviet Union may be obtained from the monthly *Book Records* (*Knizhnaya Letopis*) issued by the State Publishing House in Moscow.

Section III contains a selective bibliography of the most important general works about Russia, her history and her literature, and of works on the Soviet Union. As far as the latter are concerned, only a small portion of a vast and rapidly growing literature of very unequal value has been included; in making the selection, particular attention was paid to those works, irrespective of their point of view, which bear on the problems discussed in the present book.

Section IV–a is again but a small (though representative) fragment of the vast Soviet literature about literature. Included in it are works characteristic of different phases of Soviet criticism. In Section IV–b an attempt was made to give as full a list as possible of works about Soviet literature available in English. As a rule magazine articles are not listed, but there are a few included that seemed of special interest. References to some others will be found in the body of the book. A few of the more important works in languages other than English are also included.

Section V represents to my knowledge the most complete list as yet available of Soviet literature in English translations. Wherever possible, account was taken of both American and British editions. For this list I am greatly indebted to the bibliographies of Mr. Philip Grierson and of Mr. A. Ettlinger and Miss J. Gladstone (see Section II). But excellent though they are, they contain some gaps. No attempt has been made to list translations of Soviet authors which appeared in periodicals. Nor have the stories included in various anthologies and collections been listed separately, as was done in the Ettlinger-Gladstone bibliography. Whenever the title of the English translation differs considerably from the Russian, the exact English rendering of the original title is supplied in brackets. In case of the leading Soviet authors, such as Gorky, Ehrenburg, and some others, the nonfictional works are also included. So are the documentary war books, since these are often mentioned in the text. I have no doubt, however, that even so there are gaps in my list, too; in particular, many translations published by the Foreign Languages Publishing House in Moscow must be missing.

Section 1. Books cited in footnotes

Balukhaty, S. *Teoriya literatury. Annotirovannaya bibliografiya. i. Obshchie voprosy* (*Theory of Literature: An Annotated Bibliography. i. General Problems*). Leningrad, Priboy, 1929.

Balukhaty, S., and K. Muratova. *M. Gorky: Spravochnik* (*M. Gorky: A Reference Guide*). Leningrad, Gos. Izd. Khudozhestvennoy Literatury, 1938.

Barghoorn, Frederick C. *The Soviet Image of the United States: A Study in Distortion*. New York, Harcourt, Brace, 1950.

Borland, Harriet. *Soviet Literary Theory and Practice during the First Five-Year Plan: 1928–1932*. New York, King's Crown Press, 1950.

Brodsky, N. L., V. Lvov-Rogachevsky and N. P. Sidorov (ed.). *Literaturnye Manifesty* (*Literary Manifestoes*). Moscow, Federatsiya, 1929.

Bukharin, N. *Poeziya, poetika i zadachi poeticheskogo tvorchestva v SSSR* (*Poetry, Poetics and Tasks of Poetic Creation in the U. S. S. R.*). [Moscow], Gos. Izd. "Khudozhestvennaya Literatura," 1934.

Byalik, B. (ed.). *Problemy sotsialisticheskogo realizma* (*Problems of Socialist Realism*). [Leningrad], Sovetsky Pisatel, 1948.

Chukovsky, K. *Aleksandr Blok kak chelovek i poet* (*Alexander Blok as Man and Poet*). Petrograd, A. F. Marks, 1924.

Chuzhak, N. F. (ed.). *Literatura fakta. Pervy sbornik materialov rabotnikov LEF'a* (*Literature of Fact: The First Collection of Materials of the Workers of LEF*). Moscow, Federatsiya, 1929.

Counts, George S., and Nucia Lodge. *The Country of the Blind: The Soviet System of Mind Control*. Boston, Houghton Mifflin, 1949.

Dymshits, A. L., and O. V. Tsekhnovitser (ed.). *Vladimir Mayakovsky. Sbornik I*. Moscow-Leningrad, Izd. Akademii Nauk SSSR, 1940.

Eastman, Max. *Artists in Uniform: A Study of Literature and Bureaucratism*. London, Allen and Unwin, 1934; New York, Knopf, 1934.

Egolin, A. M. *Osvoboditelnye i patrioticheskie idei russkoy literatury XIX veka* (*The Ideas of Liberation and Patriotism in Nineteenth Century Russian Literature*). [Leningrad], Sovetsky Pisatel, 1946.

————. *Za vysokuyu ideynost sovetskoy literatury* (*For the High Ideological Content of Soviet Literature*). Moscow, Pravda, 1946. In English: *The Ideological Content of Soviet Literature*, tr. by Mary Kriger. Washington, Public Affairs Press, [1948].

Engelhardt, B. *Formalny metod v istorii literatury* (*The Formal Method in the History of Literature*). Leningrad, Academia, 1927.

Fadeyev, A. *Stolbovaya doroga proletarskoy literatury* (*The Highway of Proletarian Literature*). Leningrad, LAPP-Priboy, 1929.

————. *Literatura i zhizn* (*Literature and Life*). [Moscow], Sovetsky Pisatel, 1939.

Fedin, K. *Gorky sredi nas: dvadtsatye gody* (*Gorky in Our Midst: The 1920's*). [Moscow], OGIZ, 1943.

Gorbachov, G. *Ocherki sovremennoy russkoy literatury* (*Studies of Contemporary Russian Literature*). Second enlarged edition. Leningrad, Gosizdat, 1925.

————. *Sovremennaya russkaya literatura* (*Contemporary Russian Literature*). Second edition, revised and enlarged. [Leningrad], Priboy, 1929.

Gorky, M. *O literature. Statyi i rechi 1928–1936* (*About Literature. Articles and Addresses 1928–1936*). Moscow, 1937. In English (partially): *Literature and Life: A Selection from the Writings of Maxim Gorki*. Tr. by Edith Bone. London and New York, Hutchinson International Authors, 1946.

Kaun, Alexander. *Soviet Poets and Poetry*. Berkeley and Los Angeles, University of California Press, 1943.

Konovalov, S. (ed.). *Bonfire: Stories Out of Soviet Russia*. London, Benn, 1932.

Lelevich, G. *Tvorcheskie puti proletarskoy literatury* (*The Creative Paths of Proletarian Literature*). Leningrad, Priboy, 1925.

Lezhnev, A. *Voprosy literatury i kritiki* (*Problems of Literature and Criticism*). Moscow-Leningrad, Krug, [1924–25?].

————. *Sovremenniki. Literaturno-kriticheskie ocherki* (*Contemporaries: Literary-Critical Studies*). [Moscow], Krug, 1927.

————. *Literaturnye budni* (*Literary Weekdays*). Moscow, Federatsiya, 1929.

————. *Ob iskusstve* (*About Art*). Moscow, Gos. izd. "Khudozhestvennaya literatura," 1935.

———— and D. Gorbov. *Literatura revolyutsionnogo desyatiletiya* (*Literature of the Revolutionary Decade*). Kharkov, 1929.

Lezhnev, I. *Mikhail Sholokhov*. [Leningrad], Sovetsky Pisatel, 1948.

Lidin, Vl. (ed.). *Pisateli. Avtobiografii i portrety sovremennykh russkikh prozaikov* (*Writers: Autobiographies and Portraits of Contemporary Russian Prose-Fiction Authors*). Second edition, enlarged and revised. Moscow, Kn-vo "Sovremennye Problemy" N. A. Stoll-yar, 1928.

Literaturnye otkliki (Literary Echoes). Moscow, Kn-vo pisateley, [1923].

Littlepage, John, and Demaree Bess. *In Search of Soviet Gold*. New York, Harcourt Brace, 1938.

[Mayakovsky, V.]. *Smert Vladimira Mayakovskogo (The Death of Vladimir Mayakovsky)*. Berlin, Petropolis, 1931.

Maynard, Sir John. *Russia in Flux*. Edited and abridged by S. Haden Guest, from "Russia in Flux" and "The Russian Peasants and Other Studies." New York, Macmillan, 1948.

Mirsky, D. S. *Contemporary Russian Literature: 1881–1925*. New York, Knopf, 1926; London, Routledge, 1926.

———. *A History of Russian Literature*. Edited by Francis J. Whitfield. New York, Knopf, 1949; London, Routledge, 1950.

Mosely, Philip E. (ed.). *The Soviet Union Since World War II*. Special issue of *The Annals of the American Academy of Political and Social Sciences,* Vol. CCLXIII (May, 1949).

Nusinov, I. *Pushkin i mirovaya literatura (Pushkin and World Literature)*. Moscow, Sovetsky Pisatel, 1941.

Oksyonov, I. (ed.). *Sovremennaya russkaya kritika: 1918–1924 (Contemporary Russian Criticism: 1918–1924)*. Leningrad, Gosizdat, 1925.

Pankratova, A. M. (ed.). *Istoriya SSSR (A History of the U. S. S. R.)*. 3 vols. Moscow, Gosudarstvennoye uchebno-pedagogicheskoye izdatelstvo, 1946–48. In English: *A History of the U. S. S. R.* Moscow, Foreign Languages Publishing House, 1947–48.

Patrick, G. Z. *Popular Poetry in Soviet Russia*. Berkeley and Los Angeles, University of California Press, 1929.

Pisateli ob iskusstve i o sebe. Sbornik statey No. 1 (Writers About Art and About Themselves. Collection of Essays No. 1). Moscow-Leningrad, Krug, 1924.

Pozner, Vladimir. *Panorama de la littérature russe contemporaine*. Paris, Kra, 1929.

Proletariat i literatura (Proletariat and Literature). Leningrad, Gosizdat, 1925.

Radek, K. *Sovremennaya mirovaya literatura i zadachi proletarskogo iskusstva (Contemporary World Literature and the Tasks of Proletarian Art)*. Moscow, Gos. Izd. "Khudozhestvennaya literatura," 1934. In English: in Scott, H. G. (ed.). *Problems of Soviet Literature*.

Reavey, George. *Soviet Literature To-Day*. London, Lindsay Drummond, 1946; New Haven, Yale University Press, 1947.

Scott, H. G. (ed.). *Problems of Soviet Literature. Reports and Speeches at the First Writers' Congress.* London, Lawrence, 1935.

Serebryansky, M. *Sovetsky istorichesky roman (The Soviet Historical Novel).* Moscow, Gos. Izd. "Khudozhestvennaya literatura," 1936.

Stalin, I. *O velikoy Otechestvennoy Voyne Sovetskogo Soyuza (About the Great War for the Fatherland Waged by the Soviet Union).* Moscow, Gos. Izd. politicheskoy literatury, 1944.

Tarasenkov, An. *Idei i obrazy sovetskoy literatury (Ideas and Images in Soviet Literature).* Moscow, 1949.

Tarsis, V. *Sovremennye russkie pisateli (Contemporary Russian Writers).* Edited by Inn. Oksyonov. Leningrad, Izdatelstvo pisateley, 1930.

Tolstoy, A. N. *Chetvert veka sovetskoy literatury. Doklad na yubileynoy sessii Akademii Nauk SSSR 18 noyabrya 1942 goda (A Quarter of a Century of Soviet Literature. Report read at the Jubilee Session of the Academy of Sciences of the U. S. S. R. on November 18, 1942).* Moscow, Sovetsky Pisatel, 1943.

Tomashevsky, B. *Teoriya literatury. Poetika (Theory of Literature: Poetics).* Third revised edition. Moscow-Leningrad, Gosizdat, 1927.

Trotsky, L. *Literature and Revolution.* Tr. by Rose Strunsky. New York, International Publishers, 1925; London, Allen and Unwin, 1925.

Veksler, I. *Alexey Nikolayevich Tolstoy. Zhiznenny i tvorchesky put (A. N. Tolstoy: His Life and Work).* Moscow, Goz. Izd. "Khudozhestvennaya literatura," 1947.

Vladislavlev, I. *Russkie pisateli (Russian Writers).* Moscow-Leningrad, Gosizdat, 1924.

Voronsky, A. *Literaturnye portrety (Literary Portraits).* 2 vols. Moscow, Federatsiya, 1928–29.

Weidlé, Wladimir. *La Russie absente et présente.* Paris, Gallimard, 1949.

Zaidel, R., and M. Zwieback. *Klassovy vrag na istoricheskom fronte: Tarle i Platonov i ikh shkoly (The Class Enemy on the History Front: Tarle and Platonov and Their Schools).* Moscow-Leningrad, OGIZ, 1931.

Zhdanov, A. *Sovetskaya literatura—samaya ideynaya, samaya peredovaya literatura v mire (Soviet Literature—the Richest in Ideas, the Most Progressive Literature in the World).* Moscow, Gos. Izd. "Khudozhestvennaya literatura," 1934. In English: in Scott, H. G. (ed.). *Problems of Soviet Literature.*

Soviet Russian Literature

Section II. *Bibliographical and bio-bibliographical reference works*

a. *In Russian*

Balukhaty, S. *Teoriya literatury. Annotirovannaya bibliografiya.* i. *Obshchie voprosy* (*Theory of Literature: An Annotated Bibliography.* i. *General Problems*). Leningrad, Priboy, 1929.

Kozmin, B. (ed.). *Pisateli sovremennoy epokhi. Bio-bibliografichesky slovar russkikh pisateley XX veka* (*Writers of the Contemporary Period. A Bio-Bibliographical Dictionary of Russian Writers of the Twentieth Century*). Vol. 1 (no more were published). Moscow, GAKhN, 1928.

"Letopis sovetskoy literatury 1917–1932" ("Chronicle of Soviet Literature 1917–1932"), *Literaturny kritik,* Nos. 7–12 (1937), No. 1 (1938).

Lidin, Vl. (ed.). *Literaturnaya Rossiya* (*Literary Russia*). Moscow, Novye Vekhi, 1924.

——— (ed.). *Pisateli. Avtobiografii i portrety* (*Writers: Autobiographies and Portraits*). See Section I.

Matsuyev, N. *Khudozhestvennaya literatura, russkaya i perevodnaya. Ukazatel statey i retsenziy* (*Imaginative Literature, Russian and Translated: A Guide to Articles and Book Reviews*). 4 vols. Moscow, 1926–40.

———. *Tri goda sovetskoy literatury* (*Three Years of Soviet Literature*). Moscow, Sovetskaya Literatura, 1934.

Muratova, K. *Periodika po literature i iskusstvu za gody Revolyutsii: 1917–1932* (*Periodical Literature about Literature and Art during The Years of the Revolution: 1917–1932*). Edited by S. D. Balukhaty. Leningrad, Izd-vo Akademii Nauk SSSR, 1933.

Nikitina, E. *Russkaya literatura ot simvolizma do nashikh dney. Literaturno-sotsiologichesky seminary* (*Russian Literature from Symbolism to Our Days: A Literary-Sociological Seminar*). Moscow, Nikitinskie Subbotniki, 1926.

Rozanov, I. N. *Putevoditel po sovremennoy russkoy literature* (*A Guide to Contemporary Russian Literature*). Moscow, Rabochee Prosveshchenie, 1929.

Tarsis, V. *Sovremennye russkie pisateli* (*Contemporary Russian Writers*). See Section I.

Vitman, A. M., N. D. Pokrovskaya, and M. E. Ettinger. *Vosem let russkoy khudozhestvennoy literatury* (*1917–1925*). *Bibliografichesky spravochnik* (*Eight Years of Russian Imaginative Literature: 1917–1925. A Bibliographical Reference Guide*). Moscow, GIZ, 1926.

Vladislavlev, I. *Literatura velikogo desyatiletiya, 1917–1927* (*Litera-*

ture of the Great Decade, 1917–1927). Vol 1. Moscow-Leningrad, Gosizdat, 1928.

———. *Russkie pisateli (Russian Writers)*. See Section 1.

b. *In English and other languages*

Boutchik, V. *Bibliographie des oeuvres littéraires russes traduites en français*. Paris, Orobitg, 1935; 2e fascicule, 1936; supplément, 1938; 2e supplément, 1941; 3e supplément, 1943.

———. *La Littérature russe en France*. Paris, Champion, 1947.

Dana, H. W. L. *Handbook on Soviet Drama: Lists of Theatres, Plays, Operas, Ballets, Films and Books and Articles about Them*. New York, American-Russian Institute, 1938.

Ettlinger, A., and J. Gladstone. *Russian Literature, Theatre and Art: A Bibliography of Works in English Published 1900–1945*. London, Hutchinson, 1947.

Grierson, Philip. *Books on Soviet Russia:1917–1942: A Bibliography and a Guide to Reading*. London, Methuen, 1943. For a continuation of this bibliography see "Books and Pamphlets on Russia," in *The Slavonic and East European Review*, Vol. XXIV (1946), 133–47; Vol. XXV (1947), 508–17; Vol. XXVI (1948), 512–18; Vol. XXVII (1949), 556–62; and Vol. XXVIII (1950), 486–92.

Kerner, Robert J. *Slavic Europe: A Selected Bibliography in the Western European Languages. Comprising History, Languages and Literature*. Cambridge, Harvard University Press; London, Humphrey Milford, 1918.

Martianov, N. *Books Available in English by Russians and on Russia, Published in the United States*. Fourth edition. New York, privately printed, 1950.

Mehnert, Klaus (ed.). *Die Sovet Union, 1917–1932. Systematische, mit Kommentaren versehene Bibliographie der 1917–1932 in deutscher Sprache ausserhalb der Sovet-Union veröffentlichten 1900 wichtigsten Bücher und Aufsätze über den Bolschewismus und die Sovet-Union*. Königsberg Pr. und Berlin, Ost-Europa Verlag, 1933.

Messina, Giuseppe L. "Le traduzioni dal russo nel 1920–1943," *Belfagor*, Vol. IV, No. 6 (1949), 693–703.

Mohrenschildt, D. S. von. "Books in English on Russian Literature, 1917–42," *Russian Review*, Vol. II, No. 1 (Autumn, 1942), 122–28.

Victorof-Toporoff, V. *Rossica et Sovietica: Bibliographie des ouvrages parus en français de 1917 à 1930 inclus relatifs à la Russie et à l'URSS*. Saint-Cloud, Editions documentaires et bibliographiques, 1930.

Section III. *General background works in English about Russia and the Soviet Union*

Backer, G. *The Deadly Parallel: Stalin and Ivan the Terrible.* New York, Random House, 1950.

Barghoorn, Frederick C. *The Soviet Image of the United States: A Study in Distortion.* New York, Harcourt, Brace, 1950.

Baring, M. *The Russian People.* London, Methuen, 1911.

――――. *Landmarks in Russian Literature.* London, Methuen, 1916.

Basily, N. de. *Russia under Soviet Rule: Twenty Years of Bolshevik Experiment.* London, Allen and Unwin, 1938.

Beloff, M. *The Foreign Policy of Soviet Russia.* 2 vols. London and New York, Oxford University Press, 1947–49.

Borkenau, F. *The Communist International.* London, Faber and Faber, 1938.

Carr, E. H. *The Soviet Impact on the Western World.* London, Macmillan, 1946; New York, Macmillan, 1947.

――――. *A History of Soviet Russia: Vol. I. The Bolshevik Revolution 1917–1923.* London, Macmillan, 1950.

Chamberlin, W. H. *Russia's Iron Age.* Boston, Little Brown and Co., 1934; London, Duckworth, 1935.

――――. *The Russian Revolution.* New York, Macmillan, 1935; London, Duckworth, 1935.

――――. *The Russian Enigma.* New York, Scribners, 1944.

――――. *World Order or Chaos?* London, Duckworth, 1946. American edition: *The European Cockpit.* New York, Macmillan, 1947.

Chesterton, Mrs. Cecil. *Sickle or Swastika?* London, Stanley Paul, 1938.

Counts, George S., and Nucia Lodge. *The Country of the Blind: The Soviet System of Mind Control.* Boston, Houghton Mifflin, 1949.

Crossman, R. H. S. (ed.). *The God That Failed* [essays by Arthur Koestler, Ignazio Silone, and others]. New York, Harper, 1949; London, Hamish Hamilton, 1950.

Dallin, David. *The Real Soviet Russia.* Revised edition. New Haven, Yale University Press, 1947.

―――― and Boris Nicolaevsky. *Forced Labor in Soviet Russia.* New Haven, Yale University Press, 1947.

Deane, J. R. *Strange Alliance: The Story of our Efforts at Wartime Cooperation with Russia.* New York, The Viking Press, 1947.

Fischer, Louis. *Machines and Men in Russia.* New York, Harrison Smith, 1932; London, Cape, 1932.

Fülöp-Müller, R., and J. Gregor. *Mind and Face of Bolshevism: An Examination of Cultural Life in Soviet Russia.* Tr. by F. S. Flint and D. F. Tait. London, Putnam, 1927.

Bibliography

Griffith, H. (ed.). *Playtime in Russia*. London, Methuen, 1935.

Hill, Christopher. *Lenin and the Russian Revolution*. London, Hodder and Stoughton for the English Universities Press, 1947.

Hunt, R. N. Carew. *The Theory and Practice of Communism*. London and New York, Macmillan, 1950.

Inkeles, Alex. *Public Opinion in Soviet Russia*. Cambridge, Harvard University Press, 1950.

Koestler, Arthur. *The Yogi and the Commissar and Other Essays*. London and New York, Macmillan, 1946.

Kolarz, W. *Myths and Realities in Eastern Europe*. London, Lindsay Drummond, 1946.

Koriakov, M. *I'll Never Go Back: A Red Officer Talks*. Tr. by N. Wreden. London and New York, Harrap, 1949.

Kravchenko, V. *I Chose Freedom*. New York, Scribners, 1946.

Langdon-Davies, John. *Russia Puts the Clock Back: A Study of Soviet Science and Some British Scientists*. London, Gollancz, 1949.

Lawrence, John. *Life in Russia*. London, Allen, 1947.

Lovell, M. *The Soviet Way of Life: An Examination*. London, Methuen, 1948.

Lyons, Eugene. *Modern Moscow*. London, Hurst and Blackett, 1935. American edition: *Moscow Carrousel*. New York, Knopf, 1935.

———. *Assignment in Utopia*. New York, Harcourt Brace, 1937; London, Harrap, 1938.

Masaryk, Thomas G. *The Spirit of Russia*. Tr. by E. and C. Paul. 2 vols. London, Allen and Unwin, 1919; New York, Macmillan, 1919.

Maynard, Sir John. *Russia in Flux Before October*. London, Gollancz, 1941.

———. *Russian Peasant and Other Studies*. London, Gollancz, 1942.

———. *Russia in Flux*. New York, Macmillan, 1948. (A combined and condensed edition of the two preceding books. See also under Section I).

Meyendorff, Baron A. *The Background of the Russian Revolution*. New York, Henry Holt, 1929.

Miliukov, Paul N. *Outlines of Russian Culture*. 3 vols. Edited by Michael Karpovich. Tr. by Valentine Ughet and Eleanor Davis. Philadelphia, University of Pennsylvania Press, 1943.

Mirsky, D. S. *A History of Russian Literature*. Edited by Francis J. Whitfield. New York, Knopf, 1949.

Moore, Barrington, Jr. *Soviet Politics—The Dilemma of Power*. Cambridge, Harvard University Press, 1950.

Muggeridge, Malcolm. *Winter in Moscow*. London, Eyre and Spottiswoode, 1934; Boston, Little Brown and Co., 1934.

Pares, Sir Bernard. *Russia*. London, Penguin Books, 1941; Washington and New York, Penguin Books, 1944.
———. *Russia and the Peace*. New York, Macmillan, 1944.
———. *A History of Russia*. Fourth edition. New York, Knopf, 1946; London, Cape, 1946.
Schlesinger, Rudolf. *Spirit of Post-War Russia: Soviet Ideology, 1917–1946*. New York, Universal Distributors, 1947.
———. (ed.). *Changing Attitudes in Soviet Russia: The Family in the U. S. S. R. Documents and Readings*. London, Routledge and Kegan Paul, 1949.
Serge, Victor. *From Lenin to Stalin*. Tr. by Ralph Manheim. New York, Pioneer Publications, 1937.
Shub, D. *Lenin: A Biography*. Garden City, Doubleday, 1948.
Simmons, Ernest J. (ed.). *U. S. S. R.: A Concise Handbook*. Ithaca, Cornell University Press, 1947.
Smith, Walter Bedell. *My Three Years in Moscow*. Philadelphia, Lippincott, 1949.
Souvarine, B. *Stalin: A Critical Survey of Bolshevism*. Tr. by C. L. R. James. London, Secker and Warburg, 1939; New York, Longmans Green, 1939.
Soviet Comes of Age. By 28 of the foremost citizens of the U. S. S. R. Foreword by S. and B. Webb. London, Hodge, 1938.
Soviet Foreign Policy during the Patriotic War. Documents and Materials. Tr. by A. Rothstein. London, Hutchinson, 1946.
Soviet Union Year Book, 1930. Edited by A. A. Santalov and L. Segal. London, Allen and Unwin, 1930. (Contains "Who's Who in Literature.")
[Stalin]. *Joseph Stalin*. New York, International Publishers, 1950.
Stalin. *War Speeches, Orders of the Day, and Interviews to Foreign Correspondents during the Great Patriotic War, July 3, 1941–June 22, 1945*. London, Hutchinson, 1946.
Steinberg, Julian (ed.). *Verdict of Three Decades*. New York, Duell, Sloan and Pearce, 1950.
Stevens, Edmund. *This Is Russia Uncensored: Everyday Life under the Soviet Regime*. New York, Didier, 1950.
Sumner, B. H. *Survey of Russian History*. Second edition. London, Duckworth, 1948. American edition: *A Short History of Russia*. New York, Reynal and Hitchcock, 1943.
Tchernavin, V. V. *I Speak for the Silent Prisoners of the Soviets*. Tr. by N. Oushakoff. Boston and New York, Hale, Cushman and Flint, 1935.
Terrell, R. *Soviet Understanding*. London, Heinemann, 1937.
Timasheff, N. *Religion in Soviet Russia: 1917–1942*. New York, Sheed and Ward, 1942.

Bibliography

———. *The Great Retreat: The Growth and Decline of Communism in Russia.* New York, Dutton, 1946.

Trotsky, L. *The History of the Russian Revolution.* Tr. by Max Eastman. 3 vols. New York, Simon and Schuster, 1932.

———. *The Revolution Betrayed.* Tr. by Max Eastman. London, Secker and Warburg, 1937; New York, Doubleday, 1937.

———. *Stalin: An Appraisal of the Man and His Influence.* Tr. by C. Malamuth. New York and London, Harper and Brothers, 1941.

U. S. S. R. Handbook. London, Gollancz, 1936. (Contains a chapter on literature and Who's Who.)

Utley, Freda. *Lost Illusion.* Philadelphia, Fireside Press, 1948; London, Allen and Unwin, 1949.

Vernadsky, G. *A History of Russia.* New Haven, Yale University Press, 1944.

Voigt, F. A. *Unto Caesar.* London, Constable, 1938.

Webb, Sidney and Beatrice. *Soviet Communism: A New Civilization.* 2 vols. London, New York, Longmans Green, 1935.

Werth, A. *Musical Uproar in Moscow.* London, Turnstile Press, 1949.

Williams, A. R. *The Soviets.* New York, Harcourt Brace, 1937. (Contains a valuable bibliography.)

———. *The Russians: The Land, the People and Why They Fight.* London, Harrap, 1943.

Williams, Harold W. *Russia of the Russians.* London, Pitman, 1914.

Wolfe, Bertram D. *Three Who Made a Revolution: A Biographical History.* New York, The Dial Press, 1948.

Section IV. Works about Soviet literature

a. *In Russian*

Averbakh, L. *Za proletarskuyu literaturu (For Proletarian Literature).* Leningrad, Priboy, 1926.

———. *Kulturnaya revolyutsiya i problemy sovremennoy literatury (Cultural Revolution and Problems of Contemporary Literature).* Moscow, Gosizdat, 1928.

———. *Na putyakh kulturnoy revolyutsii (Along the Roads of Cultural Revolution).* Third edition. Moscow, Moskovsky Rabochy, 1929.

Egolin, A. M. *Tridtsat let sovetskoy literatury (Thirty Years of Soviet Literature).* Moscow, "Pravda," 1948.

——— and others. *Protiv bezideynosti v literature. Sbornik statey zhurnala "Zvezda" (Against Lack of Ideas in Literature: A Collection of Articles from the Zvezda Magazine).* Edited by V. Druzin. [Leningrad], Sovetsky Pisatel, 1947.

Gorbachov, G. *Polemika* (*Polemics*). Leningrad-Moscow, Goz. Izd. khudozhestvennoy literatury, 1931. (Mostly polemics with Pereverzev).

Gorky, M. *O literature. Statyi i rechi 1928–1936* (*About Literature: Articles and Addresses 1928–1936*). Third edition. Edited by N. F. Belchikov. Moscow, Sovetsky Pisatel, 1937.

Grinberg, I., and others. *Obraz bolshevika. Sbornik kriticheskikh statey* (*The Image of a Bolshevik: A Collection of Critical Articles*). Leningrad, Gos. Izd. "Khudozhestvennaya literatura," 1938.

Gurvich, A. *V poiskakh geroya. Literaturno-kriticheskie statyi* (*In Search of a Hero: Literary-Critical Essays*). Moscow-Leningrad, Gos. Izd. "Iskusstvo," 1938.

Kirpotin, V. *Sovetskaya dramaturgiya* (*Soviet Dramaturgy*). Moscow, Gos. Izd. "Khudozhestvennaya literatura," 1934.

———. *Proza, dramaturgiya i teatr* (*Prose Fiction, Dramaturgy and the Theater*). Moscow, Gos. Izd. "Khudozhestvennaya literatura," 1935.

——— and L. Subotsky. *Literatura na novom etape* (*Literature in a New Phase*). Moscow-Leningrad, Gos. Izd. khudozhestvennoy literatury, 1933.

Kirshon, V. *Za sotsialistichesky realizm v dramaturgii* (*For Socialist Realism in Dramaturgy*). Moscow, Gos. Izd. "Khudozhestvennaya literatura," 1934.

Kogan, P. *Literatura velikogo desyatiletiya* (*Literature of the Great Decade*). Moscow-Leningrad, Moskovsky Rabochy, 1927.

Lelevich, G. *Na literaturnom postu. Statyi i zametki* (*On Literary Guard: Articles and Notes*). Moscow, Partizdat "Oktyabr," 1924.

Lunacharsky, A. *Lenin i literaturovedenie* (*Lenin and the Study of Literature*). Moscow, Sovetskaya literatura, 1934.

———. *Russkaya literatura. Izbrannye statyi* (*Russian Literature: Selected Articles*). Edited by N. F. Belchikov. Moscow, Gos. Izd. khudozhestvennoy literatury, 1947.

Lvov-Rogachevsky, V. *Ocherki proletarskoy literatury* (*Studies in Proletarian Literature*). Moscow-Leningrad, Mosk. Akts. Izdatelskoye Obshchestvo, 1927.

Nikitina, E. *V masterskoy sovremennoy khudozhestvennoy prozy* (*In the Workshop of Contemporary Prose Fiction*). 2 vols. Moscow, Nikitinskie Subbotniki, 1931.

——— and S. V. Shuvalov. *Belletristy-sovremenniki* (*Contemporary Prose Fiction Writers*). 4 vols. Moscow, Nikitinskie Subbotniki, 1927–31.

Pertsov, V. *Literatura zavtrashnego dnya* (*Literature of Tomorrow*). Moscow, Federatsiya, 1929.

———. *Podvig i geroy. Etyudy o sovetskoy literature* (*The Feat and the Hero: Studies of Soviet Literature*). Moscow, Sovetsky Pisatel, 1946.

Polonsky, V. *Na literaturnye temy. Statyi kriticheskie i polemicheskie* (*On Literary Themes: Critical and Polemical Articles*). Moscow, Krug, 1927.

———. *O sovremennoy literature* (*About Contemporary Literature*). Moscow-Leningrad, Gosizdat, 1928.

———. *Ocherki literaturnogo dvizheniya revolyutsionnoy epokhi* (*Studies in the Literary Movement of the Revolutionary Period*). Second edition. Moscow-Leningrad, Gosizdat, 1929.

———. *Ocherki sovremennoy literatury* (*Studies in Contemporary Literature*). Moscow, 1930.

Polyansky, V. (P. I. Lebedev). *Voprosy sovremennoy kritiki* (*Problems of Contemporary Criticism*). Moscow-Leningrad, Gosizdat, 1927.

Rosental, M. (ed.). *O sovetskoy literature. Kriticheskie statyi* (*About Soviet Literature: Critical Articles*). Moscow, Gos. Izd. "Khudozhestvennaya literatura," 1936.

Selivanovsky, A. *Ocherki po istorii russkoy sovetskoy poezii* (*Studies in the History of Soviet Russian Poetry*). Moscow, 1930.

Slonim, M. *Portrety sovetskikh pisateley* (*Portraits of Soviet Writers*). Paris, Parabola, 1932.

Trotsky, L. *Literatura i Revolyutsiya* (*Literature and Revolution*). Moscow, Krasnaya Nov, 1923.

Usievich, E. *Sovetskaya literatura na novom etape* (*Soviet Literature in a New Phase*). Moscow-Leningrad, Gos. Izd. khudozhestvennoy literatury, 1934.

———. *Pisateli i deystvitelnost* (*Writers and Reality*). Moscow, Gos. Izd. "Khudozhestvennaya literatura." 1936.

———. *Puti khudozhestvennoy literatury* (*The Paths of Imaginative Literature.*) Moscow, Sovetsky Pisatel, 1939.

———. *Cherty geroya nashego vremeni. Kriticheskie statyi* (*Characteristics of the Hero of Our Times: Critical Essays*). Moscow, Sovetsky Pisatel, 1941.

Voronsky, A. *Literaturnye tipy* (*Literary Types*). Moscow, Federatsiya, 1927.

Yudin, P. *Ob ustave Soyuza sovetskikh pisateley* (*About the Statute of the Union of Soviet Writers*). Moscow, Gos. Izd. "Khudozhestvennaya literatura," 1934.

See also Section I under Brodsky, Bukharin, Byalik, Chuzhak, Fadeyev, Fedin, Gorbachov, Lelevich, Lezhnev, *Literaturnye otkliki,* Oksyonov, *Pisateli ob iskusstve i o sebe, Proletariat i literatura,* Radek, Serebryansky, Tarasenkov, Tolstoy, Voronsky, and Zhdanov.

Much interesting and valuable material will also be found in the

Soviet Literary Encyclopaedia: *Literaturnaya Entsiklopediya,* Moscow, Izdatelstvo Kommunisticheskoy Akademii, 1929 ff. (eleven volumes were published before the war, covering the greater part of the alphabet). The Encyclopaedia was withdrawn from circulation, for among its editors and principal contributors were numerous Trotskyites and other "oppositionists." A reprint of it was recently issued in the United States by the American Council of Learned Societies.

The following principal Soviet periodicals are also invaluable for the study of Soviet literature: *Kniga i Revolyutsiya* (1920–23) *Krasnaya Niva* (1923–?), *Krasnaya Nov* (1921–40), *Leningrad* (1930–46), *LEF* (1923–25), *Literatura i Marksizm* (1928–31), *Literaturnaya Gazeta* (since 1929; still published), *Literaturnoye Obozrenie* (1936–41), *Literaturny Kritik* (1933–41), *Literaturny Sovremennik* (1933–41), *Novaya Rossiya* (1922; continued as *Rossiya,* 1922–25; and as *Novaya Rossiya,* 1926), *Novy LEF* (1927–28), *Novy Mir* (since 1925; still published), *Oktyabr* (since 1924; still published), *Pechat i Revolyutsiya* (1921–30; continued as *Literatura i Iskusstvo,* 1930–31; continued as *Marksistsko-leninskoye iskusstvoznanie,* 1932–?), *Russky Sovremennik* (1924), *30 Dney* (1925–41), *Znamya* (since 1935; still published), and *Zvezda* (since 1926; still published). For the earlier period *Russkaya Kniga* (Berlin, 1921–23) is of considerable interest.

b. *In English and other languages*

Apletin, M. (ed.). *Literature of the Peoples of the USSR.* Moscow, VOKS, 1934.

Arseniew, N. von. *Die russische Literatur der Neuzeit und Gegenwart in ihren geistigen Zusammenhängen.* Mainz, Dioskuren-Verlag, 1929.

Bonnard, André. *Vers un Humanisme nouveau: Refléxions sur la littérature soviétique (1917–1947).* Lausanne, Association Suisse-URSS, 1948.

Borland, Harriet. *Soviet Literary Theory and Practice during the First Five-Year Plan.* New York, King's Crown Press, 1950.

Carter, H. *The New Spirit in the Russian Theatre, 1917–1928.* New York, Brentano's, 1929; London, Shaylor, 1929.

Dana, H. W. L. *Drama in Wartime Russia.* New York, National Council of American-Soviet Friendship, 1943.

Dickinson, T. H., and others. *The Theatre in a Changing Europe.* New York, Henry Holt, 1937; London, Putnam, 1938. (Articles on Russian theater by G. Gregor and H. W. L. Dana.)

Eastman, Max. *Artists in Uniform: A Study of Literature and Bureaucratism.* London, Allen and Unwin, 1934; New York, Knopf, 1934.

Bibliography

Egolin, A. M. *The Ideological Content of Soviet Literature.* Tr. by Mary Kriger. Washington, D. C., Public Affairs Press, 1948.

Fadeyev, A. "The Tasks of Literary Criticism," (tr. by Zina Voynow), *The American Review on the Soviet Union,* Vol. IX, No. 1 (March, 1948), 30–59.

Flores, A. (ed.). *Literature and Marxism: A Controversy by Soviet Critics.* New York, Critics Group, 1938.

Freeman, J., J. Kunitz, and L. Lozowick. *Voices of October: Art and Literature in Soviet Russia.* New York, The Vanguard Press, 1930.

Ginzburg, L. *Scrittori russi.* Torino, 1948.

Goriély, B. *La nouvelle poésie en U. S. S. R.* Bruxelles, Ed. du Canard Sauvage, 1928.

———. *Les Poètes dans la révolution russe.* Paris, Gallimard, 1934.

———. *Science des lettres soviétiques.* Paris, Ed. des Portes de France, 1947.

Gourfinkel, N. *Le Théâtre russe contemporain.* Paris, 1931.

Grindea, M. (ed.). *Soviet Literature, Art, Music.* London, Practical Press, 1942.

Gyseghem, A. van. *Theatre in Soviet Russia.* London, Faber, 1943.

Hare, R. *Russian Literature from Pushkin to the Present Day.* London, Methuen, 1947.

Houghton, Norris. *Moscow Rehearsals: An Account of Methods of Production in the Soviet Theatre.* New York, Harcourt Brace, 1936; London, Allen and Unwin, 1938.

Kaun, Alexander. *Soviet Poets and Poetry.* Berkeley and Los Angeles, University of California Press, 1943.

Lavrin, Janko. *An Introduction to the Russian Novel.* London, Methuen, 1942; New York, Whittlesey House, McGraw-Hill Book Co., 1947.

———. *From Pushkin to Mayakovsky: A Study in the Evolution of a Literature.* London, Sylvan Press, 1948.

Lo Gatto, Ettore. *La Letteratura sovietista.* Roma, 1929.

———. *Dall' epica alla cronaca nella Russia soviettista.* Roma, 1929.

——— (ed.). *Russia.* Roma, 1945.

London, Kurt. *The Seven Soviet Arts.* London, Faber and Faber, 1937; New Haven, Yale University Press, 1938.

Markov, P. A. *The Soviet Theatre.* London, Gollancz, 1934.

McLeod, Joseph. *The Actors Cross the Volga: A Study of the 19th Century Russian Theatre and of Soviet Theatres in War.* London, Allen and Unwin, 1946.

———. *The New Soviet Theatre.* London, Allen and Unwin, 1943.

Messina, Giuseppe L. *La letteratura sovietica.* Firenze, Le Monnier, 1950.

Miliukov, Paul. *Outlines of Russian Culture.* Edited by Michael Karpovich. Tr. by V. Ughet and E. Davis. Philadelphia, University of Pennsylvania Press, 1943. (Part II: Literature.)

Mirsky, D. S. *Contemporary Russian Literature.* London, Routledge, 1926; New York, Knopf, 1926.

Nilsson, Nils Åke. *Sovjetrysk Litteratur 1917–1947.* Stockholm, Forum, 1948.

Patrick, G. Z. *Popular Poetry in Soviet Russia.* Berkeley and Los Angeles, University of California Press, 1929.

Poggioli, Renato. *Politica letteraria sovietica: Bilancio d'un ventennio.* Roma, 1937.

———. *Pietre di paragone.* Firenze, 1939. (Essays on Gorky, Zamyatin, Mandelstam, Esenin, and Mayakovsky.)

Pozner, Vladimir. *Panorama de la littérature contemporaine russe.* Paris, Kra, 1929.

Reavey, George. *Soviet Literature To-Day.* London, Lindsay Drummond, 1946; New Haven, Yale University Press, 1947.

Scott, H. G. (ed.). *Problems of Soviet Literature: Reports and Speeches at the First Writers' Congress.* London, Lawrence, 1935. (Reports and speeches by Zhdanov, Gorky, Bukharin, Radek, and Stetsky.)

Sayler, O. M. *Russian Theatre under the Revolution.* New York and London, Brentano's, 1922.

———. *Inside the Moscow Art Theatre.* New York, Brentano's, 1925; London, Brentano's, 1928.

Soviet Writers' Reply to English Writers' Questions. Foreword by J. B. Priestley. London, Society for Cultural Relations, 1948.

Stanislavsky, Constantin. *Building a Character.* Tr. by E. Hapgood. London, Reinhardt and Evans, 1950; New York, Theatre Art Books, 1950.

———. *Stanislavsky on the Art of the Stage.* London, Faber and Faber, 1950.

Struve, Gleb. *Soviet Russian Literature.* London, Routledge, 1935.

———. *25 Years of Soviet Russian Literature.* London, Routledge, 1944.

———. *Histoire de la littérature soviétique.* Paris, Editions du Chêne, 1946.

———. "Anti-Westernism in Recent Soviet Literature," *The Yale Review,* Vol. XXXIX, No. 2 (Winter, 1950), 209–24.

The Theatre in the U.S.S.R. Moscow, VOKS, 1934.

Thorgevsky, I. *De Gorki à nos jours: la nouvelle littérature russe.* Paris, La Renaissance, 1945.

Timofejew, L. *Sowjetische Literatur.* Leipzig, 1949.

Tolstoy, A. N. "Trends in Soviet Literature," *Science and Society,* Vol. VII, No. 3 (Summer, 1943), 233–50.

Trotsky, L. *Literature and Revolution.* Tr. by Rose Strunsky. New York, International Publishers, 1925.

Walpole, H. (ed.). *Tendencies of the Modern Novel.* London, Allen and Unwin, 1934. (D. S. Mirsky on "Soviet Russian Novel.")

Wilczkowski, C. *Ecrivains soviétiques.* Paris, Ed. de la Revue des Jeunes, 1949.

Zhdanov, A. A. *Essays on Literature, Philosophy and Music.* New York, International Publishers, 1950.

Numerous articles on Soviet literature and translations of Soviet works, including some major novels, will be found in the English-language Moscow monthly *International Literature* (1933–45; thereafter continued as *Soviet Literature*).

Section v. Soviet literature in English translations

a. *Anthologies and collections*

Blake, Ben (ed.). *Four Soviet Plays.* Tr. by A. Wixley, H. G. Scott, and R. S. Carr. London, Lawrence and Wishart, 1937; New York, International Publishers, 1937. (Gorky, Vishnevsky, Pogodin, and Kocherga.)

Bowra, C. M. (ed.). *A Second Book of Russian Verse.* London, Macmillan, 1948.

Cournos, John (compiler and translator). *Short Stories out of Soviet Russia.* London, Dent, 1929; New York, Dutton, 1929.

——— (ed.). *A Treasury of Russian Life and Humor.* New York, Coward-McCann, 1943.

Deutsch, Babette, and Avrahm Yarmolinsky. *Russian Poetry: An Anthology.* New and revised edition. New York, International Publishers, 1930.

Fineberg, J. (ed.). *Heroic Leningrad: Documents, Sketches and Stories.* Moscow, Foreign Languages Publishing House, 1945. (Tikhonov, Fadeyev, Vishnevsky, Bergholz, and others.)

Four Soviet War Plays. London, Hutchinson, 1943. (Korneychuk, Leonov, and Simonov.)

Flying Osip. Stories of New Russia. Tr. by L. S. Friedland and J. R. Piroshnikoff. London, Fisher Unwin, 1925.

Graham, Stephen (ed.). *Russian Great Short Stories.* London, Benn, 1929.

Guerney, Bernard G. (ed.). *Portable Russian Reader.* New York, The Viking Press, 1947. (Gorky, A. Tolstoy, Ilf and Petrov, Babel, Ehrenburg, Katayev, and Zoshchenko.)

———— (ed.). *A Treasury of Russian Literature*. New York, Vanguard Press, 1947; London, Bodley Head, 1948.

Konovalov, S. (ed.). *Bonfire: Stories out of Soviet Russia*. London, Benn, 1932.

Kunitz, J. (ed.). *Azure Cities: Stories of New Russia*. Tr. by J. J. Robbins. New York, International Publishers, 1929; London, Modern Books, 1929.

————. (ed.). *Russian Literature Since the Revolution*. New York, Boni and Gaer, 1948.

Laughlin, J. (ed.). *New Directions in Prose and Poetry, 1941*. Norfolk, Conn., New Directions, 1941.

Lavrin, Janko (ed.). *Russian Humorous Stories*. London, Sylvan Press, 1946.

Lyons, Eugene (ed.). *Six Soviet Plays*. Boston and New York, Houghton Mifflin, 1934; London, Gollancz, 1935.

Modern Poets from Russia. Tr. by Gerard Shelley. London, Allen and Unwin, 1942.

Modern Russian Stories. Selected and translated by Elisaveta Fen. London, Methuen, 1943.

Montagu, I., and H. Marshall (ed.). *Soviet Short Stories, 1942*. London, The Pilot Press, 1942.

————. (ed.). *Soviet Short Stories, 1942–43*. London, The Pilot Press, 1943.

————. (ed.). *Soviet Short Stories, 1944*. London, The Pilot Press, 1944.

Noyes, George R. *Masterpieces of the Russian Drama*. New York and London, Appleton, 1933. (Mayakovsky's "Mystery-Bouffe.")

Reavey, George, and Marc Slonim. *Soviet Literature: An Anthology*. London, Wishart, 1933; New York, Covici-Friede, 1934.

Road to the West. Sixty Soviet War Poems. Chosen and translated by A. M. Williams and V. de Sola Pinto. London, Frederick Muller, 1945.

Road to Victory. Twelve Tales of the Red Army. London, Hutchinson, [1945].

Rodker, John (ed.). *Soviet Anthology*. Tr. by A. Brown, S. Garry, and others. London, Cape, 1943.

Russian Short Stories. London, Faber and Faber, [1943?].

Soviet Scene. Six Plays of Russian Life. Tr. by A. Bakshy. New Haven, Yale University Press, 1946.

Soviet Short Stories. Moscow, Foreign Languages Publishing House, 1947.

Soviet Stories of the Last Decade. Selected and translated by Elisaveta Fen. London, Methuen, 1945.

Soviet War Stories. London, Hutchinson, 1943.

Bibliography

We Carry On: Tales of the War. Moscow, Foreign Languages Publishing House, 1942.

Yarmolinsky, Avrahm (ed.). *A Treasury of Russian Verse.* New York, Macmillan, 1949.

b. *Individual authors*

Afinogenov, A. *Distant Point.* Translated and adapted by H. Griffith. London, The Pushkin Press, 1941. (Translation of the play *Dalyokoye.*)

———. *Fear.* Tr. by C. Malamuth. In Lyons, *Six Soviet Plays.* See under Section v–a. Also: tr. by N. Strelsky, D. B. Colman, and A. Greene. Poughkeepsie, New York, 1934.

———. *Listen, Professor!* American acting version by Peggy Phillips. New York and Los Angeles, French, 1944. (Adaptation of *Mashenka.*)

Arseniev, V. K. *Dersu, the Trapper: A Hunter's Life in Ussuria.* Tr. by M. Burr. London, Secker and Warburg, 1939; New York, Dutton, 1941.

Avdeyenko, A. *I Love.* Tr. by A. Wixley. London, Lawrence, 1935; New York, International Publishers, 1935.

Averbakh, L. (ed.). *Belomor: An Account of the Construction of the New Canal between the White Sea and the Baltic Sea.* New York, Smith and Haas, 1935.

Babel, I. *Red Cavalry.* Tr. by N. Helstein. New York and London, Knopf, 1929.

———. *Benia Krik: A Film Novel.* Tr. by I. Montagu and S. Nalbandov. London, Collet's, 1935.

———. *Benya Krik, the Gangster, and Other Stories.* Edited by A. Yarmolinsky. New York, Schocken Books, 1948.

Bazhov, P. *The Malachite Casket: Tales from the Urals.* Tr. by A. M. Williams. London and New York, Hutchinson, 1944.

Beck, A. *On the Forward Fringe. A Novel of General Panfilov's Division.* London, Hutchinson, 1945.

Bill-Belotserkovsky, V. *Life Is Calling. A play in four acts.* Tr. by A. Wixley. London, Lawrence and Wishart, 1938; New York, International Publishers, 1938.

Blok, A. *The Twelve.* Tr. by C. E. Bechhofer. London, Chatto and Windus, 1920. Also: tr. by B. Deutsch and A. Yarmolinsky. New York, Rudge, 1931.

———. *The Spirit of Music.* Tr. by I. Freiman. London, Lindsay Drummond, 1947. (Includes several of Blok's post-Revolutionary essays.)

Bulgakov, M. *Days of the Turbins.* Tr. by E. Lyons. In Lyons, *Six Soviet Plays.* See under v–a.

Chapygin, A. *Stepan Razin.* Tr. by C. Paul. London and New York, Hutchinson, 1946.

Chukovsky, K. *Crocodile.* Tr. by B. Deutsch. New York, Lippincott, 1931; London, Mathews, 1932.

Chumandrin, M. *White Star.* London, Lawrence, 1933.

Efremov, I. *A Meeting Over Tuscarora, and Other Adventures.* Tr. by M. and N. Nichols. London, Hutchinson, 1946.

Ehrenburg. I. *The Love of Jeanne Nev.* Tr. by H. Chrouschoff Matheson. London, Peter Davies, 1929.

————. *The Extraordinary Adventures of Julio Jurenito and His Disciples.* Tr. by U. Vanzler. New York, Covici-Friede, 1930.

————. *A Street in Moscow.* Tr. by S. Volochova. New York, Covici-Friede, 1932; London, Grayson and Grayson, 1933. (Translation of *In Protochny Lane.*)

————. *A Soviet Writer Looks at Vienna.* Tr. by I. Montagu. London, Lawerence, 1934.

————. *Out of Chaos.* Tr. by A. Bakshy. New York, Henry Holt, 1934. (Translation of *The Second Day.*)

————. *Russia at War.* Tr. by G. Shelley. Introduction by J. B. Priestley. London, Hutchinson, 1943.

————. *The Fall of Paris,* Tr. by G. Shelley. London, Hutchinson, 1942; New York, Knopf, 1943.

————. *European Crossroad: A Soviet Journalist in the Balkans.* Tr. by A. Markov. New York, Knopf, 1947. (Translation of *Roads of Europe.*)

————. *The Storm.* Tr. by E. Hartley and T. Shebunina. London and New York, Hutchinson, 1949.

Emelyanova, Nina. *The Surgeon.* Tr. by J. Fineberg. London, Hutchinson, 1945.

Fadeyev, A. *The Nineteen.* Tr. by R. D. Charques. London, Lawrence, 1929; New York, International Publishers, 1929. (Translation of *The Rout.*)

————. *Leningrad in the Days of the Blockade.* Tr. by R. D. Charques. London, 1946.

Furmanov, D. *Chapayev.* London, Lawrence, 1935; New York, International Publishers, 1935.

Gaydar, A. *Timur and His Comrades.* Tr. by R. Renbourn. London, The Pilot Press, 1942. American edition: *Timur and His Gang,* New York, Scribner's, 1943.

Gladkov, F. *Cement.* Tr. by A. S. Arthur and C. A. Ashleigh. London, Lawrence, 1929; New York, International Publishers, 1929.

Glebov, A. *Inga. A play in four acts.* Tr. by C. Malamuth. In Lyons, *Six Soviet Plays.* See under Section v–a.

Gorky, Maxim. *Reminiscences of My Youth.* Tr. by V. Dewey. London, Heinemann, 1924.

―――. *The Judge. A Play in Four Acts.* Tr. by M. Zakrevsky and B. H. Clark. New York, McBride and Co., 1924.

―――. *The Story of the Novel and Other Stories.* Tr. by M. Zakrevsky. New York, The Dial Press, 1925.

―――. *Decadence.* Tr. by V. Dewey. New York, McBride, 1927; London, Cassell, 1927. (Translation of *The Artamonov Business.*)

―――. *Bystander.* Tr. by B. G. Guerney. New York, Cape and Smith, 1930; London, Cape, 1930. (First volume of *The Life of Klim Samgin.*)

―――. *On Guard for the Soviet Union.* London, Lawrence, 1931; New York, International Publishers, 1933.

―――. *The Magnet.* Tr. by A. Bakshy. New York, Cape and Smith, 1931; London, Cape, 1931. (Second volume of *Klim Samgin.*)

―――. *Reminiscences of Leonid Andreyev.* Tr. by Katherine Mansfield and S. S. Koteliansky. London, Heinemann, 1931.

―――. *To American Intellectuals.* New York, International Pamphlets, 1932.

―――. *Days with Lenin.* London, Lawrence, 1933.

―――. *Other Fires.* Tr. by A. Bakshy. New York and London, Appleton, 1933. (Third volume of *Klim Samgin.*)

―――. *The Last Plays.* Adapted by Gibson-Cowan. London, Lawrence and Wishart, 1937. (*Egor Bulychev and Others* and *Dostigayev and Others.*)

―――. *The Specter.* Tr. by A. Bakshy. New York and London, D. Appleton-Century Co., 1938. (Fourth volume of *Klim Samgin.*)

―――. *Best Short Stories.* Edited by A. Yarmolinsky and Moura Budberg. London, Cape, 1939; New York, Grayson, 1939.

―――. *Culture and the People.* London, Lawrence and Wishart, 1939.

―――. *Seven Plays by Maxim Gorky.* Tr. by A. Bakshy. New Haven, Yale University Press, 1945.

―――. *Literature and Life.* Tr. by E. Bone. London, Hutchinson, 1946.

―――. *Orphan Paul.* Tr. by Lily Turner and Mark Strever. New York, Boni and Gaer, 1946. (also: "How I Became a Writer.")

―――. (ed.). *History of the Civil War in the U.S.S.R.* Vol. 2: *The Great Proletarian Revolution, October-November, 1917.* Tr. by J. Fineberg. London, Lawrence, 1947.

―――. *The Artamonov Business.* Tr. by Alec Brown. London, Hamilton, 1948; New York, Pantheon Books, 1948.

―――. *Reminiscences of Tolstoy, Chekov and Andreyev.* Tr. by Katherine Mansfield, S. S. Koteliansky, and Leonard Woolf. New edition. London, Hogarth Press, 1949.

———. *Unrequited Love and Other Stories.* Tr. by Moura Budberg. London, Weidenfeld and Nicolson, 1949.

Grossman, V. *Stalingrad Hits Back.* Tr. by A. Fineberg and D. Fromberg. Moscow, Foreign Languages Publishing House, 1942.

———. *The People Immortal.* Tr. by E. Donnelly. Moscow, Foreign Languages Publishing House, 1943.

———. *No Beautiful Nights.* New York, Julian Messner, 1944. (Another version of *The People Immortal.*)

———. *The Years of War (1941–1945).* Tr. by E. Donnelly and R. Prokofiev. Moscow, Foreign Languages Publishing House, 1946.

Herman, Yuri. *Antonina.* Tr. by Stephen Garry. London, Routledge, 1937. American edition: *Tonia.* New York, Knopf, 1938. (Translation of *Our Friends.*)

———. *Alexei the Gangster.* Tr. by Stephen Garry. London, Routledge, 1940. (Translation of "Alexey Zhmakin" and "Lapshin.")

Ignatov, P. K. *Partisans of the Kuban.* Tr. by J. Fineberg. London, Hutchinson, 1945.

Ilf, I. and E. Petrov. *Diamonds to Sit On.* Tr. by Elizabeth Hill and Doris Mudie. London, Methuen, 1930. (Translation of *Twelve Chairs.*)

———. *The Little Golden Calf. A Satiric Novel.* Tr. by Charles Malamuth. London, Grayson and Grayson, 1932; New York, Farrar and Rinehart, 1932.

———. *The Little Golden America: Two Famous Soviet Humorists Survey These United States.* New York, Farrar and Rinehart, 1937.

Ilyenkov, V. *Driving Axle. A Novel of Socialist Reconstruction.* London, Lawrence, 1933; New York, International Publishers, 1933.

———. *The Square of Flowers.* In *Soviet Scene.* See under Section v–a.

Ivanov, Vsevolod. *Armoured Train 14–69.* Tr. by Gibson-Cowan and A. T. K. Grant. London, Lawrence, 1933.

———. *The Adventures of a Fakir.* New York, The Vanguard Press, n. d. Also under the titles: *Patched Breeches.* Toronto, Macmillan, [1936]. And: *I Live A Queer Life: An Extraordinary Biography.* London, Lovat Dickson, 1936.

Kalinin, A. *In the South.* Tr. by S. Garry. London, Hutchinson, 1946.

Kallinikov, I. *Women and Monks.* Tr. by P. Kirwin. London, Secker, 1930; New York, Harcourt Brace, 1930.

———. *Land of Bondage.* Tr. by P. Kirwin. London, Grayson, 1931.

Kassil, L. *Land of Shvambrania: A Novel with Maps, A Coat of Arms and a Flag.* Tr. by S. Glass and N. Guterman. New York, The Viking Press, 1935.

———. *The Story of Alesha-Ryazan and Uncle White-Sea.* London, Lawrence, 1935; New York, Co-operative Publishing Society, 1935.

Bibliography

Katayev, V. *The Embezzlers.* Tr. by L. Zarine. London, Benn, 1929; New York, The Dial Press, 1929.

——. *Time, Forward!* Tr. by C. Malamuth. New York, Farrar and Rinehart, 1933. British edition: *Forward, Oh Time!* London, Gollancz, 1934.

——. *Squaring the Circle.* Tr. by N. Goold-Verschoyle. London, Wishart, 1934. Also: a revised edition by A. Dukes. New York, 1935. Also: a translation by E. Lyons and C. Malamuth. In Lyons, *Six Soviet Plays.* See under Section v–a.

——. *Lonely White Sail, or Peace Is Where the Tempests Blow.* Tr. by C. Malamuth. London, Allen and Unwin, 1937; New York, Farrar and Rinehart, 1937.

——. *The Wife.* London, Hutchinson, 1946.

Kaverin, V. *The Larger View.* Tr. by E. Swan. New York, Stackpole Sons, 1938; London, Collins, 1938. (Translation of *Fulfillment of Desires.*)

——. *Two Captains.* Tr. by E. Swan. London, Cassell, 1938; New York, Modern Age, 1942.

——. *The Unknown Artist.* Tr. by P. Ross. London, Westhouse, 1947.

Kirshon, V. *Bread. A play in five acts.* Tr. by S. Volochova. In Lyons, *Six Soviet Plays.* See under Section v.–a.

—— and A. V. Uspensky. *Red Rust.* Tr. by V. and F. Vernon. New York, Brentano's, 1930.

Kocherga, I. *Masters of Time. A play in four acts.* Tr. by A. Wixley. In Blake, *Four Soviet Plays.* See under Section v–a. (Translation of *The Watchmaker and the Hen.*)

Kollontay, A. *Red Love.* New York, Seven Arts Publishing Co., 1927. Also as: *Great Love.* Tr. by L. Lore. New York, The Vanguard Press, 1929. Also as: *Free Love.* Tr. by C. J. Hogarth. London, Dent, 1934. (All translations of *The Love of Toiling Bees.*)

Korneychuk, A. *The Front.* In *Four Soviet War Plays.* See under Section v–a.

——. *Guerrillas in the Ukrainian Steppes.* In *Four Soviet War Plays.* See under Section v–a.

Larry, Ya. *The Extraordinary Adventures of Karik and Valda.* Tr. by J. P. Mandeville. London, Hutchinson, 1945.

Leonov, L. *Sot.* Tr. by I. Montagu and S. Nalbandov. London and New York, Putnam, 1931. (American edition under the title *Soviet River.*)

——. *The Thief.* Tr. by H. Butler. London, Secker, 1931; New York, The Dial Press, 1931.

——. *Tuatamur.* Tr. by I. Montagu and S. Nalbandov. London, Collet's, 1935.

———. *Skutarevsky.* Tr. by Alec Brown. London, Lovat Dickson, 1936; New York, Harcourt Brace, 1936.

———. *Road to the Ocean.* Tr. by N. Guterman. New York, Fischer, 1944.

———. *The Badgers.* London, Hutchinson, 1946.

———. *Chariot of Wrath.* Tr. by N. Guterman. New York, Fischer, 1946. (Translation of *The Taking of Velikoshumsk.*)

———. *The Invasion.* In *Four Soviet War Plays.* See under Section v–a.

Libedinsky, Yu. *A Week.* London, Allen and Unwin, 1923; New York, Huebsch, 1923.

Lidin, V. *The Apostate.* Tr. by H. Chrouschoff Matheson. London, Cape, 1931. American edition: *The Price of Life.* New York, Harper and Brothers, 1932.

Lunacharsky, A. *Three Plays* (*Faust and the City, Vasilisa the Wise, The Magi*). Tr. by L. A. Magnus and K. Walter. London, Routledge, 1923.

———. *The Bear's Wedding.* Tr. by L. Zamkovsky and N. Borudin. London, 1926.

Luntz, L. *The City of Truth. A play in three acts.* Tr. by J. Silver. London, 1929.

Makarenko, A. *Road to Life.* Tr. by S. Garry. London, Nott, 1936. (Translation of *Educational Epic.*)

Marienhoff, A. *Cynics.* Tr. by V. D. Bell and L. Coleman. New York, Boni, 1930.

Matveyev, V. *Bitter Draught.* Tr. by D. Flower. London, Collins, 1935.

———. *Commissar of the Gold Express, An Episode in the Civil War.* London, Lawrence, 1933; New York, International Publishers, 1933. (Translation of *The Golden Train.*)

[Mayakovsky, V.] *Mayakovsky and His Poetry.* Compiled by H. Marshall. London, The Pilot Press, 1942; revised edition, 1945.

Mayakovsky, V. *Mystery-Bouffe.* Tr. by G. R. Noyes and A. Kaun. In Noyes, *Masterpieces of the Russian Drama.* See under Section v–a.

Neverov, A. *Tashkent.* Tr. by Reginald Merton and W. G. Walton. London, Gollancz, 1930. (Translation of *Tashkent, City of Bread.*)

———. *City of Bread.* New York, Doran, 1927. (An anonymous version of *Tashkent, City of Bread.*)

Nizovoy, P. *The Ocean.* Tr. by John Cournos. New York and London, Harper and Brothers, 1936.

Novikov-Proboy, A. *Tsushima.* Tr. by E. and C. Paul. London, Allen and Unwin, 1936.

———. *The Captain.* London, Hutchinson, 1946.

Ognyov, N. *The Diary of a Communist Schoolboy.* Tr. by A. Werth. London, Gollancz, 1928; New York, Payson and Clarke, 1928.

——. *The Diary of a Communist Undergraduate.* Tr. by A. Werth. London, Gollancz, 1929; New York, Payson and Clarke, 1929.

Olesha, Yu. *Envy.* Tr. by A. Wolfe. London, Hogarth Press, 1936. Also: tr. by P. Ross. London, Westhouse, 1947.

Panfyorov, E. *Brusski: A Story of Peasant Life in Soviet Russia.* Tr. by Z. Mitrov and J. Tabrisky. New York, International Publishers, 1930; London, Lawrence, [1930].

——. *And Then The Harvest.* Tr. by S. Garry. London, Putnam, 1939. (The third and fourth volumes of *Bruski.*)

Pasternak, B. *Childhood.* Tr. by R. Payne. Singapore, Straits Times Press, 1941.

——. *The Collected Prose Works.* Tr. by R. Payne and B. Scott. London, Lindsay Drummond, 1945. (*The Safe Conduct* and four short stories.)

——. *Selected Poems.* Tr. by J. M. Cohen. London, Lindsay Drummond, 1947.

——. *Selected Writings.* Norfolk, Conn., New Directions, 1949. (*The Safe Conduct,* four stories, and selected poems.)

Paustovsky, K. *The Black Gulf. Stories.* Tr. by E. Schimanskaya. London, Hutchinson, 1946.

Pavlenko, P. *Red Planes Fly East.* Tr. by S. Garry. London, Routledge, 1938. (Translation of *In the East.*)

——. *Flames of Vengeance.* Moscow, Foreign Languages Publishing House, 1942. (Translation of *A Russian Tale.*)

Perventsev, A. *Cossack Commander.* Tr. by S. Garry. London, Routledge, 1939. (Translation of *Kochubey.*)

——. *The Ordeal.* New York and London, Harper and Brothers, 1944. British edition: *The Test.*

Pilnyak, B. *Tales of the Wilderness.* Tr. by F. O'Dempsey. New York, Knopf, 1925.

——. *The Naked Year.* Tr. by Alec Brown. New York, Payson and Clarke, 1928; London, Putnam, 1928.

——. *The Volga Flows to the Caspian Sea.* Tr. by C. Malamuth. New York, Farrar and Rinehart, 1931; London, Davies, 1932.

——. *Ivan Moscow.* Tr. by A. S. Schwartzmann. New York, Christopher, 1935.

Pogodin, N. *Aristocrats. A comedy in four acts.* Tr. by A. Wixley and R. S. Carr. In Blake, *Four Soviet Plays.* See under Section v–a. Also: action edition. London, Lawrence, 1937.

——. *Tempo.* Tr. by I. D. W. Talmadge. In Lyons, *Six Soviet Plays.* See under Section v–a.

Polevoy, B. *To the Last Breath.* London, Hutchinson, 1945.

———. *A Russian Looks at Reborn Europe.* London, "Soviet News," 1946.

Polvakov, A. *Russians Don't Surrender.* Tr. by N. Guterman. New York, Dutton, 1942.

———. *White Mammoths. The Dramatic Story of Russian Tanks.* Tr. by N. Guterman. New York, Dutton, 1943. British edition: *Westbound Tanks.* London, Hutchinson, 1943.

———. *With a Soviet Unit Through the Nazi Lines.* London, Hutchinson, 1944.

Prishvin, M. *Jen Sheng: The Root of Life.* Tr. by G. Walton and P. Gibbons. London, Melrose, 1936.

Romanov, P. *Without Cherry Blossom.* Tr. by L. Zarine. London, Benn, 1930.

———. *On the Volga and Other Stories.* Tr. by Ann Gretton. New York, Scribners, 1931; London, Benn, 1931.

———. *Three Pairs of Silk Stockings.* Tr. by L. Zarine. New York, Scribners, 1931; London, Benn, 1931. (Translation of *Comrade Kislyakov.*)

———. *The New Commandment.* Tr. by Valentine Snow. New York, Scribners, 1933; London, Benn, 1933.

———. *Diary of a Soviet Marriage.* Tr. by J. Furnivall and R. Parmenter. London, Nutt, 1936.

Ryss, E. *Before the Shadows Fell.* London, Hutchinson, 1946.

Serafimovich, A. *The Iron Flood.* London, Lawrence, 1935.

Sergeyev-Tsensky, S. *Transfiguration.* Tr. by Marie Budberg. Edited with an Introduction by Maxim Gorky. New York, McBride, 1926. (Translation of *Valya.*)

Shiryaev, P. *Taglioni's Grandson: The Story of a Russian Horse.* Tr. by A. Fremantle. London, Putnam, 1937. American edition: *Flattery's Foal.* New York, Knopf, 1938.

Shishkov, V. *Children of Darkness.* London, Gollancz, 1931.

Shkvarkin, V. *Father Unknown.* (Translation of *Another Man's Child.*) In *Soviet Scene.* See under Section v–a.

Sholokhov, M. *And Quiet Flows the Don.* Tr. by Stephen Garry. London, Putnam, 1934; New York, Knopf, 1935. (The first two volumes of *The Quiet Don.*)

———. *The Don Flows Home to the Sea.* Tr. by S. Garry. London, Putnam, 1940; New York, Knopf, 1941. (Continuation of the preceding.)

———. *Virgin Soil Upturned.* Tr. by S. Garry. London, Putnam, 1935, American edition: *Seeds of Tomorrow.* New York, Knopf, 1942.

Simonov, K. *Days and Nights.* Tr. by Joseph Barnes. New York, Simon and Schuster, 1945. Also: Tr. by J. Fineberg. London, Hutchinson, 1945.

————. *The Russians.* In *Four Soviet War Plays.* See under Section v–a.

Smirnov, V. *Sons.* Tr. by Naomi Y. Yohel. New York, Doubleday, 1947.

Smirnova, N. *Marfa: A Siberian Novel.* Tr. by M. Burr. London, Boriswood, 1932.

Sobol, A. *Freak Show.* Tr. by J. Cowan. New York and London, Kendall, 1930.

Sobolev, L. *Storm Warning.* Tr. by A. Fremantle. London, 1935. American edition: *Romanoff.* New York, Longmans Green, 1935. (Abridged version of *Capital Refitting.*)

————. *Soul of the Sea.* Tr. by N. Orloff. Philadelphia and New York, Lippincott, 1946.

Tarasov-Rodionov, A. *February 1917.* Tr. by W. A. Drake. New York, Covici-Friede, 1931.

————. *Chocolate.* Tr. by C. Malamuth. New York, Doubleday Doran, 1932; London, Heinemann, 1933.

Teleshov, N. *A Writer Remembers.* Tr. by L. Britton. London, Hutchinson, 1946.

Tolstoy, A. N. *The Road to Calvary.* Tr. by Mrs. R. S. Townsend. New York, Boni and Liveright, 1923. (The first part of *The Way Through Hell.*)

————. *Imperial Majesty.* Tr. by H. Chrouschoff Matheson. London, Mathews and Marrot, 1932. American edition: *Peter the Great.* New York, Covici-Friede, 1932. (First volume of *Peter the First.*)

————. *Darkness and Dawn.* Tr. by E. Bone and E. Burns. London, Gollancz, 1935; New York, Longmans Green, 1936. (The first two parts of *The Way Through Hell.*)

————. *The Death Box.* Tr. by B. G. Guerney. London, Methuen, 1936.

————. *Peter the Great.* Tr. by E. Bone and E. Burns. London, Gollancz, 1936. (First two volumes of *Peter the First.*)

————. *Bread.* Tr. by S. Garry. London, Gollancz, 1937.

————. *Daredevils and Other Stories.* Tr. by D. Fromberg. Moscow, Foreign Languages Publishing House, 1942.

————. *Road to Calvary.* Tr. by E. Bone. New York, Knopf, 1946. (Complete version of *The Way Through Hell.*)

————. *Nikita's Childhood.* Tr. by V. Lansbury-Dutt. London, Hutchinson, n. d.

Trenyov, K. *Lyubov Yarovaya.* In *Soviet Scene.* See under Section v–a.

Tretyakov, S. *Roar, China!* Tr. by E. Polianovska and B. Nixon. London, Lawrence, 1931.

————. *Chinese Testament: The Autobiography of Tan-Shih-hua as Told to Tretyakov.* London, Gollancz, 1934.

Tynyanov, Yu. *Death and Diplomacy in Persia.* Tr. by A. Brown. London, Boriswood, 1938. (Translation of *The Death of Wazir-Muchtar.*)

Veresayev, V. *The Deadlock.* Tr. by N. Vissotsky and C. Coventry. London, Faber and Gwyer, 1927. (Translation of *In a Blind Alley.*)

———. *The Sisters.* Tr. by J. Soskice. London, Hutchinson, 1934.

Vinogradov, A. *The Black Consul.* Tr. by E. Burns. London, Gollancz, 1935; New York, The Viking Press, 1935.

———. *The Condemnation of Paganini.* Tr. by S. Garry. London, Hutchinson, 1946.

———. *Three Colours of Time.* London, Hutchinson, 1946.

Vishnevsky, V. *An Optimistic Tragedy. A play in three acts.* Tr. by H. G. Scott and R. S. Carr. In Blake, *Four Soviet Plays.* See under Section v–a.

Voronsky, A. *Waters of Life and Death.* Tr. by L. Zarine. London, Allen and Unwin, 1936. (Voronsky's novelized autobiography.)

Voynova, A. *Semi-Precious Stones.* Tr. by V. Snow. New York, Cape and Smith, 1931. British edition: *Glittering Stones.* London, Heinemann, 1933.

Voytekhov, B. *Last Days of Sevastopol.* Tr. by R. Parker and V. M. Genne. New York, Knopf, 1943; London, Cassell, 1943.

Yugov, A. *Immortality.* Tr. by D. Magarshchack. London, Hutchinson, 1946.

Zamyatin, E. *We.* Tr. by G. Zilboorg. New York, Dutton, 1924.

Zoshchenko, M. *Russia Laughs.* Tr. by H. Clayton. Boston, Lothrop Lee and Shepard, 1935.

———. *The Woman Who Could Not Read, and Other Tales.* Tr. by E. Fen. London, Methuen, 1940.

———. *The Wonderful Dog, and Other Tales.* Tr. by E. Fen. London, Methuen, 1942.

Index

Note on transliteration: The system of transliteration of Russian names adopted in this book is the one used in the *Slavonic and East European Review* (London) and based on that of the British Academy, with a few minor modifications of which the principal is the rendering of the Russian *ë* by *yo* in most cases and by *o* after *ch, sh, shch* and *zh* (e.g., Gorbachov or Shchogolev). For most of the Russian names of non-Russian origin the original spelling has been retained (e.g., Ehrenburg, Eichenbaum, or Meyerhold—in preference to Erenburg, Eikhenbaum, or Meyerkhold). Some of the first names that are common to Russian and other languages are given in their English form (e.g., Alexander or Victor), though the author must admit to some inconsistency in this respect.

The tonic stress is indicated throughout the index to help students of Russian literature with the pronunciation of Russian names; it is, however, omitted in first names when these are given in their English form.

Index

Index

Index

Index